International Conference on e-Learning 2019

Held at the Multi-Conference on Computer Science and Information Systems (MCCSIS 2019)

Porto, Portugal
16-19 July 2019

Editors:

Miguel Baptista
Pedro Isaías
Piet Kommers
Luís Rodrigues

ISBN: 978-1-5108-9240-8

Printed from e-media with permission by:

Curran Associates, Inc.
57 Morehouse Lane
Red Hook, NY 12571

Some format issues inherent in the e-media version may also appear in this print version.

Printed by Curran Associates, Inc. (2019)

For permission requests, please contact International Association for Development of the Information Society (IADIS) at the address below.

International Association for Development of the Information Society (IADIS)
Rua Sao Sebastiao Da Pedreira
No. 100, 30, 1050-209
Lisbon, Portugal

Phone: 351 21 3151373
Fax: 351 21 3151244

secretariat@iadis.org

Additional copies of this publication are available from:

Curran Associates, Inc.
57 Morehouse Lane
Red Hook, NY 12571 USA
Phone: 845-758-0400
Fax: 845-758-2633
Email: curran@proceedings.com
Web: www.proceedings.com

MULTI CONFERENCE ON COMPUTER SCIENCE AND INFORMATION SYSTEMS

MCCSIS 2019

16-19 JULY PORTO, PORTUGAL

Proceedings of the International Conference

e-Learning 2019

Edited by
Miguel Baptista Nunes
Pedro Isaias

iadis
international association for development of the information society

Volume Editors:
Miguel Baptista Nunes and Pedro Isaias

Computer Science and Information Systems Series Editors:
Piet Kommers and Pedro Isaias

Associate Editor: Luís Rodrigues

PROCEEDINGS OF THE INTERNATIONAL CONFERENCE

E-LEARNING 2019

Porto, Portugal
JULY 17 - 19, 2019

Organised by

iadis
international association for development of the information society

Co-Organised by

isep Instituto Superior de Engenharia do Porto

INTERNATIONAL CONFERENCE

E-LEARNING 2019

part of the

MULTI CONFERENCE ON COMPUTER SCIENCE

AND INFORMATION SYSTEMS 2019

TABLE OF CONTENTS

SHORT PAPERS

REFLECTION PAPERS

POSTERS

DOCTORAL CONSORTIA

FOREWORD

These proceedings contain the papers of the International Conference e-Learning 2019, which was organised by the International Association for Development of the Information Society and co-organised by ISEP – Instituto Superior de Engenharia do Porto, 17 - 19 July, 2019. This conference is part of the Multi Conference on Computer Science and Information Systems 2019, 16 - 19 July, which had a total of 926 submissions.

The e-Learning (EL) 2019 conference aims to address the main issues of concern within e-Learning. This conference covers both technical as well as the non-technical aspects of e-Learning.

The conference accepted submissions in the following seven main areas: Organisational Strategy and Management Issues; Technological Issues; e-Learning Curriculum Development Issues; Instructional Design Issues; e-Learning Delivery Issues; e-Learning Research Methods and Approaches; e-Skills and Information Literacy for Learning.

The above referred main submission areas are detailed:

Organisational Strategy and Management Issues
- Higher and Further Education
- Primary and Secondary Education
- Workplace Learning
- Vocational Training
- Home Schooling
- Distance Learning
- Blended Learning
- Change Management
- Educational Management
- Continuous Professional Development (CPD) for Educational and Training Staff
- Return on e-Learning Investments (ROI)

Technological Issues
- Learning Management Systems (LMS)
- Managed Learning Environments (MLEs)
- Virtual Learning Environments (VLEs)
- Computer-Mediated Communication (CMC) Tools
- Social Support Software
- Architecture of Educational Information Systems Infrastructure
- Security and Data Protection
- Learning Objects
- XML Schemas and the Semantic Web
- Web 2.0 Applications

e-Learning Curriculum Development Issues
- Philosophies and Epistemologies for e-learning
- Learning Theories and Approaches for e-learning
- e-Learning Models
- Conceptual Representations
- Pedagogical Models
- e-Learning Pedagogical Strategies
- e-Learning Tactics
- Developing e-Learning for Specific Subject Domains

Instructional Design Issues
- Designing e-Learning Settings
- Developing e-Learning Pilots and Prototypes
- Creating e-Learning Courses
    - Collaborative learning
    - Problem-based learning
    - Inquiry-based learning
    - Blended Learning
    - Distance Learning
- Designing e-Learning Tasks
    - E-learning activities
    - Online Groupwork
    - Experiential Learning
    - Simulations and Modelling
    - Gaming and Edutainment
    - Creativity and Design Activities
    - Exploratory Programming

e-Learning Delivery Issues
- e-Delivery in different contexts
    - Higher and Further Education
    - Primary and Secondary Schools
    - Workplace Learning
    - Vocational Training
    - Distance Learning
- Online Assessment
- Innovations in e-Assessment
- e-Moderating
- e-Tutoring
- e-Facilitating
- Leadership in e-Learning Delivery
- Networked Information and Communication Literacy Skills
- Participation and Motivation in e-Learning

e-Learning Research Methods and Approaches
- Action Research
- Design Research
- Course and Programme Evaluations
- Systematic Literature Reviews
- Historical Analysis
- Case Studies
- Meta-analysis of Case Studies
- Effectiveness and Impact Studies
- Evaluation of e-Learning Technologies
- Evaluation of Student and Tutor Satisfaction
- Learning and Cognitive Styles
- Ethical Issues in e-Learning

e-Skills and Information Literacy for Learning
- Teaching Information Literacy
- Electronic Library and Information Search Skills
- ICT Skills Education
  - in schools and colleges
  - for business, industry and the public sector
  - in adult, community, home and prison education
  - informal methods (peer groups, family)
- Education for Computer-mediated Communication Skills
  - Netiquette
  - Online safety for children and vulnerable users
  - Cybercrime awareness and personal prevention
- Student Production of Online Media
  - Web design
  - Digital storytelling
  - Web 2.0 tools
  - etc.
- Digital Media Studies

The e-Learning 2019 conference received 187 submissions from more than 40 countries. Each submission has been anonymously reviewed by an average of four independent reviewers, to ensure that accepted submissions were of a high standard. Consequently, only 30 full papers were approved, which meant an acceptance rate of 16 %. A few more papers were accepted as short papers, reflection papers, posters and doctoral consortia. An extended version of the best papers will be selected for publishing in the Interactive Technology and Smart Education (ITSE) journal (ISSN:1741-5659) and also in the IADIS International Journal on WWW/Internet (ISSN: 1645-7641). Other outlets may also receive extended versions of the best papers, including journals from Inderscience.

Besides the presentation of full, short and reflection papers, posters and doctoral consortia, the conference also included one keynote presentation from an internationally distinguished researcher. We would therefore like to express our gratitude to Prof. Jaime Villate, Faculty of Engineering, University of Porto, Portugal, for being the e-Learning

2019 keynote speaker. Furthermore, the conference featured a workshop entitled "Learning as a Verb: Promoting Active Learning in Higher Education through Effective Design Strategies and Measurement" by Prof. Pedro Isaías, The University of Queensland, Brisbane, Australia and Prof. Paula Miranda, Sustain.RD center, School of Technology, Polytechnic Institute of Setubal, Portugal.

A successful conference requires the effort of many individuals. We would like to thank the members of the Program Committee for their hard work in reviewing and selecting the papers that appear in this book. We are especially grateful to the authors who submitted their papers to this conference and to the presenters who provided the substance of the meeting. We wish to thank all members of our organizing committee.

Last but not the least, we hope that everybody will have a good time in Porto, and we invite all participants for the next years´ edition of this conference.

Miguel Baptista Nunes, School of Information Management, Sun Yat-Sen University, Guangzhou, China
Pedro Isaias, The University of Queensland, Australia
e-Learning 2019 Conference Program Co-Chairs

Piet Kommers, University of Twente, The Netherlands
Pedro Isaias, The University of Queensland, Australia
MCCSIS 2019 General Conference Co-Chairs

Bertil Marques, ISEP, Portugal
MCCSIS 2019 Local Organising Chair

Porto, Portugal
July 2019

PROGRAM COMMITTEE

E-LEARNING CONFERENCE PROGRAM CO-CHAIRS

Miguel Baptista Nunes, School of Information Management, Sun Yat-Sen University, Guangzhou, China
Pedro Isaias, The University of Queensland, Australia

MCCSIS GENERAL CONFERENCE CO-CHAIRS

Piet Kommers, University of Twente, The Netherlands
Pedro Isaias, The University of Queensland, Australia

MCCSIS LOCAL ORGANISING CHAIR

Bertil Marques, ISEP, Portugal

E-LEARNING CONFERENCE COMMITTEE MEMBERS

Adamantios Koumpis, Universität Passau Fakultät für Informatik und Mathematik, Germany
Airina Volungevičienė, Vytautas Magnus University, Lithuania
Alexandru Vulpe, University Politehnica of Bucharest, Romania
Ana Barata, ISEP-GILT, Portugal
Andreas Bollin, Klagenfurt University, Austria
Andreas Papasalouros, University of The Aegean, Greece
Andreja Pucihar, University of Maribor, Slovenia
Andrew Lian, Suranaree University of Technology, Thailand
Ania Lian, Australian Catholic University, Australia
Antoanela Naaji, Vasile Goldis West University of Arad, Romania
Antonio Hervás-Jorge, Universidad Politécnica de Valencia, Spain
Antonio Navarro, Universidad Complutense de Madrid, Spain
Apostolos Gkamas, University Ecclesiastical Academy of Vella of Ioannina, Greece
Ben Chang, National Central University, Taiwan
Bertil Marques, Polytechnic Institute of Porto, Portugal
Charalampos Karagiannidis, University of Thessaly, Greece
Christina Gloerfeld, Fernuniversität in Hagen, Germany
Christos Bouras, University of Patras, Greece
Christos Troussas, University of Piraeus, Greece
Claudia Steinberger, Klagenfurt University, Austria
David Guralnick, Kaleidoscope Learning, USA
Dessislava Vassileva, Sofia University “st. Kliment Ohridski”, Bulgaria
Dimitra Pappa, National Centre of Scientific Research "Demokritos", Greece
Egle Butkeviciene, Kaunas University of Technology, Lithuania
Eliza Stefanova, Sofia University, Bulgaria
Elvis Mazzoni, University of Bologna, Italy
Emma Briend, Mary Immaculate College, Ireland
Erick Araya, University Austral of Chile, Chile
Essaid Elbachari, Cadi Ayyad University, Morocco

KEYNOTE LECTURE

HOW TO USE E-LEARNING FOR TESTING AND ASSESSING LARGE CLASSES

Professor Jaime Villate
Faculty of Engineering, University of Porto, Portugal

ABSTRACT

On-line quizzes provide many advantages for students and teachers. The student doesn't have to be in the same place as the examiner, results and feedback can be given to the student immediately, and the student might be able to keep a copy of the quiz in digital form. However, exams given simultaneously to a large class are usually conducted in the traditional written form, because an on-line approach would pose many issues hard to solve. Students might have to wait several days before getting the results and feedback. We report on a hybrid method we have been using with over 200 students enrolled in Engineering Physics courses. Traditional written exams are used, but the results and feedback are published in an e-learning site, as if the exam had been taken on-line. The e-learning platform is also used to help students prepare for the exams.

WORKSHOP

LEARNING AS A VERB: PROMOTING ACTIVE LEARNING IN HIGHER EDUCATION THROUGH EFFECTIVE DESIGN STRATEGIES AND MEASUREMENT

Professor Pedro Isaías, The University of Queensland, Brisbane, Australia
and
Professor Paula Miranda, Sustain.RD center, School of Technology, Polytechnic Institute of Setubal, Portugal

ABSTRACT

Higher education research is abundant on evidence about the importance of fostering active learning in the classroom, nonetheless, some teachers seem to remain reticent to its implementation. This reticence can have many origins, but in some cases it derives from the teachers' uncertainty as to how to implement active learning and how to assess if it is a truly effective method with clear advantages to student learning. This workshop focuses on specific design strategies to maximise the effectiveness of active learning initiatives in higher education and on the methods that can be used to evaluate them. It proposes a framework to guide implementation and assist teachers with the most common barriers of the development of active learning approaches. At the same time, it will explore a comprehensive range of methods that can be employed during and after the active learning experience in order to determine its effectiveness. This interactive workshop aims to provide attendees with the tools that they require to more confidently and more meaningful transform their courses into effective active learning experiences.

Full Papers

THREE-DIMENSIONAL COLLABORATIVE VIRTUAL ENVIRONMENTS TO ENHANCE LEARNING MATHEMATICS

Rosa Maria Reis
GILT- Graphics, Interaction and Learning Technologies
Instituto Superior de Engenharia do Porto (ISEP)
Rua Dr. Bernardino de Almeida, 431, 4200-072 Porto-Portugal

ABSTRACT

Web2.0 platforms are allowed to implement worlds completely virtual through technological devices, where the user has the ability to be anywhere anytime and can do almost anything you can imagine. These worlds allow to rediscover the senses through the use of technology. The virtual space can be used to bring students and teachers to this space because they promote new concepts, new approaches and new strategies, that in the educational field have been changing the paradigm of teaching and learning. This study aims to investigate how the students react to the three-dimensional collaborative virtual environments and to what extent does it affect their learning behavior patterns.
OpenSim, an immersive virtual environment, was selected as a platform to develop one collaborative virtual environment that presented instructional materials to support a math class for students of the 5th year of basic education. The results suggested that the three-dimensional collaborative virtual environments can contribute to the involvement of the students in the resolution of the activities motivating the spirit of help among students.

KEYWORDS

3D Virtual Environments, Immersive, Collaborative learning, OpenSim

1. INTRODUCTION

Nowadays the education increasingly must resort to new forms of learning, emphasizing the new environments called the three-dimensional virtual environments because the new generation of students are attracted by technologies that make the articulation between communication and social networks. (Ayres,2009).

A growing number of studies have explored affordances of three-dimensional virtual environments (3DVEs) in education. The 3DVEs allow learners to create and manipulate virtual objects, explore novel environments, have embodied experience and interact with others through avatars (Dalgarno & Lee, 2010). 3DVEs provide "an electronic surrogate for face-to-face interaction and allow the creation of simulated environments and experiences that otherwise not possible due to high cost and physical or logistics constraints. By providing a platform that closely resembles physical interaction, 3DVEs permit interaction with a computing environment and the work of other users, while creating the perception that one exists within the environment "(Arya, et al, 2011). 3DVES have peculiar characteristics, such as, synthetic, immersive, presence, interactive, realistic and three-dimensional space, that allow giving support for innovative pedagogical paradigms enabling teachers exploring effective educational formats (Reis, R. et al, 2011). 3DVEs can being used in the learning process where we can create spaces which provide set of services.

Despite the potential of 3DVEs we must have attention that these environments by itself are not the solution to increasing student learning. The 3DVEs must be combined with teaching method to influence the way in which a way in which a student receives, processes, learns, applies, and reflects on the content. "*Educators and technical advisors not only seek to teach students about the content; they also explore ways to engage students in the learning process. Educators must be lifelong learners willing to understand the ever-evolving teaching practice*". (Hodge and Collins, 2010).

To obtain a comprehensible view of this trend, this paper analyzes "How do students react to the availability of an environment developed based on our criteria and to what extent does it affect their learning behavior patterns?"

In this sense paper is organized as follows: section 2 introduces the 3CVE whose main objective is to support the teaching/learning process in mathematics; in the section 3 whole the process of developed is described, whose main objective is explained how we idealized this application; in section 4 is demonstrated the analysis and results obtained and finally some the conclusions will draw.

2. SPECIFICATION OF 3CVE

This project consisted in the development of a prototype of an educational virtual collaborative environment to support a Mathematics class for students in the 5th year of the second cycle of basic education. The subject to be addressed is part of the programmatic content of this curricular unit - Geometric Solids.

The syllabus of this subject, are based on the proposal of the Ministry of Education, whose general learning objectives should allow:

- to describe geometric solids and identify their elements;
- to understand the properties of geometric solids and classify them;
- to identify the elements of a polygon, understand its properties and classify polygons;
- to relate the number of faces, edges and vertices of a pyramid and a prism with the polygon of the base;
- consolidate previously completed learning;
- to identify solids through representations in the plane and vice versa;
- to Identify I, validate and design solid planning and build models from these planning;
- to have tasks that provide opportunities to observe, analyze, relate and construct geometric figures and operate with them. Thus, we have a dynamic learning of geometric concepts and the deepening of their understanding;
- the students should be able to solve problems, communicate and to think mathematically in situations involving geometric contexts.

Based on the previous assumptions, our environment was developed to provide knowledge on the subject - Geometric Solids, using interactive activities where students can test the acquired knowledge and intuitively. Also, we wanted to encourage students to immerse themselves in a three-dimensional virtual environment, so that objects were to invade the real space of the user and this in turn, represented by an avatar, interacted with the objects in the same space.

The environment was implemented in the OpenSim virtual world. The choice was based on the following criteria:

- is an open source platform and has the current SL APIs;
- is compatible with Linux and Windows operating systems;
- is a platform where the creation of static content of users is simple;
- It allows the creation of content in real time, using its own tools that allow the sharing of text, images and video;
- Interactivity is achieved through the coding of scripts;
- the users interact with each other through avatars and they communicate through tools that exists in other virtual worlds, example, chat, voice, and asynchronous messages;
- allows to access to Moodle.

In this first phase, the proposed environment aims to support the classroom teaching and it is suggested as a means of communication. At a later stage, we suggest using as a form of interaction outside of classes, where students can exchange information, clarify of doubts and problem solving.

3. ENVIRONMENT MODELATION

The modelling of 3DCVE began after the identification of the requirements. Initially, an environment proposal was defined that would be useful for the classroom and would allow:

- as tool, bring the world to class – it is possible access to multiples information sources and online communities, from classroom;
- support the activities in the classroom for the possibility of evaluations and the realization of innovative activities;
- open the class to the world for easy access to information, viewing and contact with others.

Also, we tried to identify the essential needs for the development of the system, type of tasks according to the learning objectives and expected interactions that allow obtaining a suitable environment for target audience.

After this phase, the virtual environment was implemented iteratively passing through different phases of development, that we describe.

Analysis phase - begins by focusing on the functionalities, in terms of operations and conditions of the system leaving aside the details of the platform on which the environment will develop. From the information collected in the initial phase, we decided to divide the space into three main areas: space for discussion, information and activities, as we can see in figure 1.

Figure 1. Scenarios of the different spaces of environment

The aim of the discussion area is to allow teachers to clarify some concepts to the students and / or to propose something that is related to the subject, leading the students to reflect, debate and draw conclusions.

The information area presents all the didactic contents to be addressed. It has a set of panels that present the concepts related to the theme and some solids in 3D, where the student with a simple click can access the specific information of the solid in question. Finally, the area of activities has as main objective to present a set of activities that allow students to consolidate the concepts learned. Some of the activities can be accessed by links to collaboration tools found on the Web, such as Scribblar.

Throughout the area of activities students will be able to find indication of some problems to be realized. The activities are directed to be carried out in groups. Groups were defined by the teacher in the classroom. Each group chooses a representative to solve the problem. All members of the group should go to the panel that corresponds to the problem under analysis. The group leader should develop the problem under the guidance of others. all group members can help, through chatting, or other element of the group solves problem.

Typical examples of problems are crosswords and the jigsaw. The jigsaw is presented to students in the discussion space by the teacher (represented by their avatar). Each group is responsible for studying a component of the problem. The information and activities for each component should be found in the environment. After a certain time, the students return to the discussion space and discuss each component, among all (students and teacher).

When the group cannot resolve the activities in a given time, they receive penalties. These penalties interfere in the final test result, which each group member will resolve. This test must do when all students have been finished all activities. The test is intended to assess whether all elements of the group have learned the basics of geometric solid.

Design phase – the aim is to determine how we can facilitate interaction between the user and the environment. The activities were developed based on the personal intrinsic factors, such are curiosity, control, fantasy, and the challenge. "Assessing the factors deemed to support individual student intrinsic motivation may assist in enhancing intrinsically motivated behavior in technology-supported learning environments" (Shroff 2009). The figure 2 show some those activities. It was necessary to detail the interaction techniques associated with the learning activities.

Figure 2. Scenario of some activities to be carried out by the users

In order to understand the decisions, we made, we decided to proceed with the creation of the first prototype of the environment. This environment was evaluated through a set of evaluation requirements, already pre-defined in the initial phase of the project with the aim to analyze whether requirements were being met.

Figure 3 shows the entire development process for the Geometric Solids application.

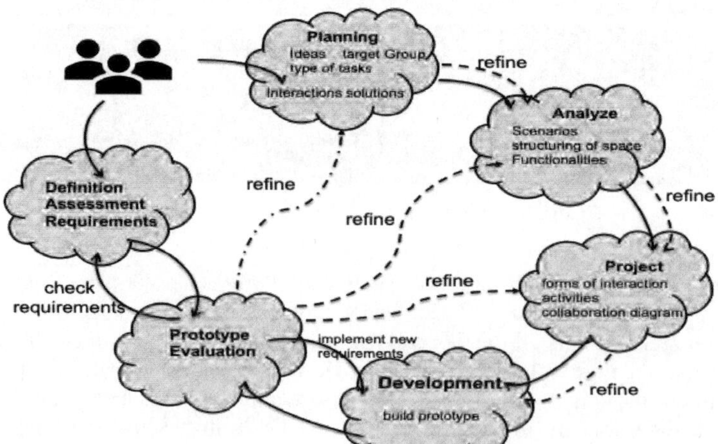

Figure 3. Development process of the Geometric Solid Environment

After completing the assessment requirements, we decided to make the environment available to students in the 5th grade of basic education in order to answer on the following question:

"How do students react to the availability of an environment developed based on our criteria and to what extent does it affect their learning behavior patterns?"

The environment was made available to a group of 20 students, aged between 10 and 11 years. Participants were asked to do a series of tasks involving research, and individual and collaborative activities.

Finally, the students were invited to completed one questionnaire. Here the students answered questions about the use of the system, especially about the usability, usefulness of the environment, satisfaction and motivation. For ethical reasons we had to require the authorization of the institution where the investigation was carried out, taking care to safeguard the interests and rights of all those involved in the study. We inform the students and request their collaboration and authorization to collect all the data.

This questionnaire was structured and oriented to the analysis of the degree of satisfaction of the student / environment because we wanted to collect data that would allow us to analyze rigorously the students' reaction to the environment, degree of satisfaction and degree of knowledge acquisition. This led to the design of a questionnaire consisting of a set of questions that were selected by the development team and the math teacher from the school where the test was held. Each question has a scale that allow a quantitative evaluation.

The collected data were structured in an organized way, allowing a triangulation of the information, which facilitated the confirmation of the assumptions initially established, and later were stored in spreadsheets designed according to the objectives outlined.

4. ANALYSIS OF EXPERIMENTAL RESULTS

To analyze the data, we established a formula to determine a percentage result for each scale of the questionnaire. This was necessary because we judged that a percentage result per scale, in addition to partial percentage values per question, would give a better view of the usefulness of the environment.

The data analysis about the use of the environment, it allowed us to draw some conclusions about usability, navigability, activities and know the general opinion of the students.

As noted throughout the session, most students easily used the virtual learning environment. Few students asked for help in gaining access to different areas of the environment. Most knew where to find what was needed to help solve the activities.

In fact, the data collected through the questionnaire confirm that most of the students considered it easy to navigate the environment (87%) and find the activities (100%). The remaining 13% had some difficulties, which were overcome with the help of the teachers present at the session. (figure 4).

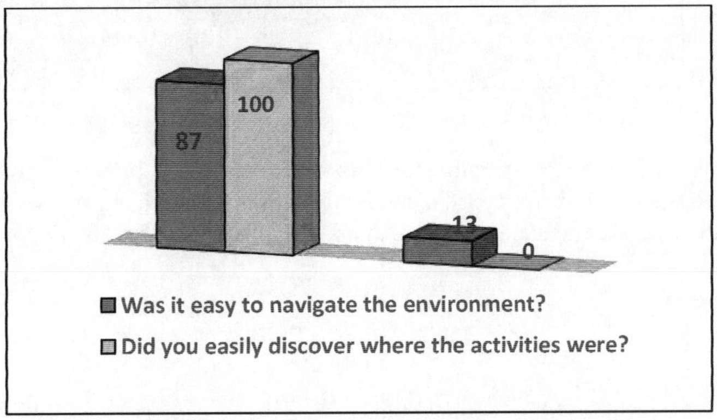

Figure 4. Aspect of use in terms of usability and navigability

Analyzing this data, the students throughout the session commented that liked the graphic aspect: It was simple, appealing and accessible; and, the text presented was quite clear.

When asked about what they liked most when they navigated throughout the environment, was verified that 70% liked to solve the activities and 30% liked watching the video (see figure 5).

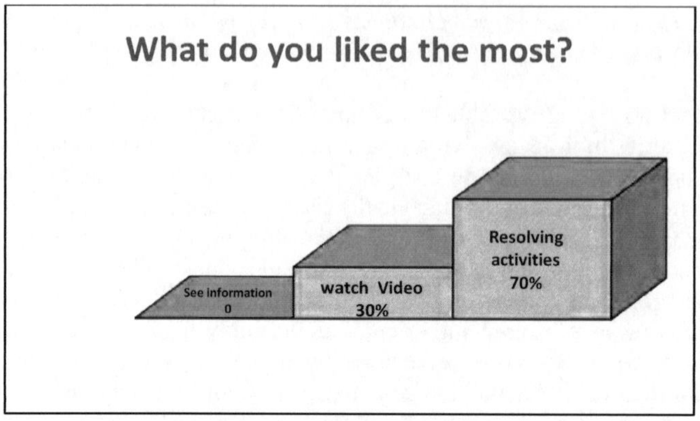

Figure 5. What they liked most in the 3DCVE

Indeed, these data allowing to assert that the computer generates a great interest to the students, because gives the opportunity to keep all students motivated and helps in to carry out the activities. In virtual environments, the student interacts through a set of resources, which make possible the development of learning, and these resources vary from environment to environment.

Regarding the accomplishment of the activities, the majority (87%) of the students did not experience difficulties in their resolution (figure 6). Only 13% felt difficulty in solving the exercises. It was because they did not follow the initial instructions to access the contents of the geometric solids.

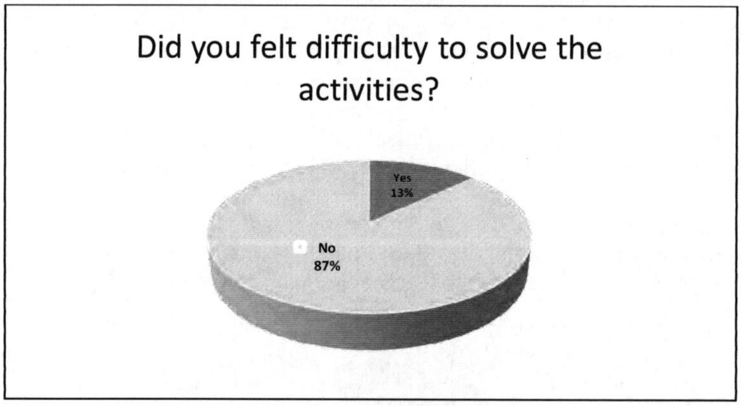

Figure 6. Opinion about the activities in 3DCVE

Finally, with regard to the presentation of data on the general opinion component of the prototype, the opinions registered were somewhat consensual: They said that they liked to use this environment more often and to use them in different curricular units, such as we can see in figure 7.

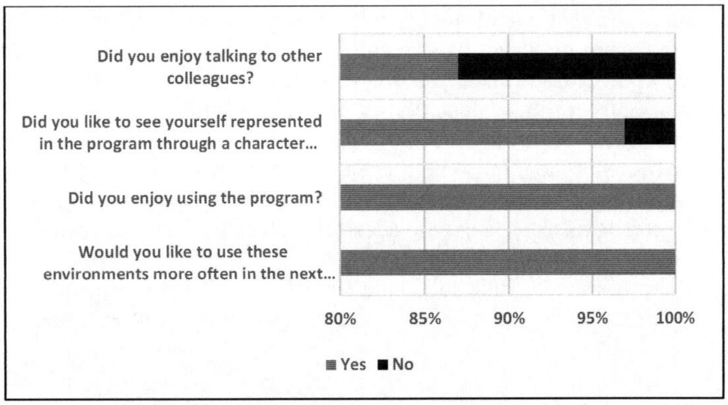

Figure 7. Opinion about the 3DCVE

After the students answered a questionnaire, they took part in a debriefing interview with the teachers. The interview was aims to know the opinion of students about learning activities conducted in environment. This allowed extract the information bellow:

- Most of the students evaluated their collaboration in the environment as very interesting and they liked teacher's presence in virtual environment because helps the clarification of doubts;
- The students expressed their desire to use the environment at any time in order to able to repeat the learning activities;
- Most of the students found voice chat more useful that text chat form communication.Thus, they have their hands free to for navigation and object manipulation.

In Summary

From what we observed regarding students' attitudes and opinions, regarding the use of the environment we can conclude that the majority felt motivated during the session period. This motivation was reinforced when several students expressed their willingness to continue using the environment after the end of the study.

From what was exposed, and although the indicators are quite positive regarding the adoption of virtual collaborative environments as a complement to face-to-face teaching, we are aware that more tests should be performed, since these data are not statistically relevant. However, this study allowed us to obtain some relevant qualitative data regarding the use and satisfaction with collaborative virtual environments for education.

From the analysis of the data extracted from the teachers' registers throughout the session, we have checked that all students collaborated with each other and engaged in the search for resources to achieve the proposed objectives and in the accomplishment of the tasks.

These conclusions allowed reinforce the idea that through virtual education, it is possible to achieve a better relationship with young people who will surely be grateful for a sign of desire to understand their modes of communication as transformation of traditional learning environments (Zorica, M. et al, 2009).

5. CONCLUSION

The main objective of this study was to verify if 3D collaborative virtual environments when used in a classroom context can help students to build their knowledge and modify their approach by increasing their ability to participate in the reality in which they are inserted (Ayres, 2009).

With this study we believe that the 3CVE can contribute for a significant improvement in the acquisition of skills and allow that students actively take part in the classroom activities, helping other students in study related subjects. Active participation is very essential for having clear understanding of the theories discussed in the classroom. We believe that satisfactory, engaging and effective collaborative learning activities can be realized in 3DCVE. Even though, 3DCVEs developed under platforms, such Second life, OpenSim, may never replace traditional labs and classrooms, they provide powerful and flexible alternatives that do not have the temporal and spatial restraints of the former, making more learning opportunities available (Vrellis et al. 2010).

However, we are aware that one of the limitations of the study is in the population sample. Only a small number of participants were involved, having chosen to sample consisting of students easily accessible, for reasons of proximity and because it is a less time-consuming process. Further studies are needed to validate whether the 3DVEs actually fulfills expectations. For example, more experiments should be performed for the results to be more accurate.

Also, further experiments should also be carried out with larger and diverse user groups, because with the use of a small sample of users only basic statistics can be applied. This can lead to inaccurate results. Large-scale experience allows us to use more accurate statistics techniques, which are better suited to handle large datasets.

We intend as future work to include some non-verbal communication capacities through real time motion capture in order to increase social presence and the quality of collaboration among the participants.

REFERENCES

Arya, A., et al. (2011). Virtual space as a learning environment: Two case studies. Paper presented at the International Education Technology Conference, Istanbul, Turkey.

Ayres, D. (2009). Software Educativo: Uma reflexão sobre a avaliação e utilização no ambiente escolar. Accessed in 20 the august 2012, http://www.redem.org/boletin/boletin310709f.php .

Dalgarno, B. & Lee, M. (2010). What are the learning affordances of 3-D virtual environments? British Journal of Educational Technology, 41(1), 10-32.

Hodge, E. and Collins. S. (2010). Collaborative Efforts: Teaching and Learning in Virtual Worlds. EDUCAUSEreview. http://creativecommons.org/licenses/by-sa/3.0

Reis, R. et al. (2011). Three-Dimensional Educational Virtual Environments: Guidelines for Learning Spaces Design. Proceedings NHIBE 7th International conference on "New Horizons in Industry, Business and Education. Chios, Greece.

Shroff, R. H., Vogel, D. R. (2009). Assessing the factors deemed to support individual student intrinsic motivation in technology supported online and face-to-face discussions. Retrieved from http://jite.org/documents/Vol8/JITEv8p059-085Shroff416.pdd.

Vrellis I., Nikiforos M., Bellow J., Avouris N., Mikropoulos T., (2010). Designing a Collaborative Learning Activity in Second Life - An Exploratory Study in Physics. ICALT 2010: 210-214

Zorica B., Lujanac A, (2009). Education in virtual environment. Digital Re-sources and Knowledge Sharing, pp. 557-564 -http://bib.irb.hr/datoteka/458632.6-06_Banek_Zorica_Lujanac_Education_in_Virtual_Environment.pdf

DO STUDENT RESPONSES DECREASE IF TEACHERS KEEP ASKING QUESTIONS THROUGH STUDENT RESPONSE SYSTEMS: A QUANTITATIVE RESEARCH

Paul Lam, Carmen K. M. Lau, Kevin Wong and Chi Him Chan
The Chinese University of Hong Kong, Hong Kong

ABSTRACT

Student Response System (SRS) allows all students to have a chance to participate in the classroom with their own devices. While it is an effective tool for promoting active participation and classroom interaction, previous studies argue that overuse and over-dependence of the technology can pose a problem of student disengagement. This paper reports on a quantitative research about the relationship between the number of questions and the number of student responses, drawing data from a self-invented student response system that has been used campus-wide between 2012 and 2015 at The Chinese University of Hong Kong. Our results show that in general student responses are stable with virtually no significant drop at the end of the lessons regardless of how many questions are asked. To conclude, we refute the hypothesis that excess use of the technology would lower student participation.

KEYWORDS

Student Response System, Student Engagement

1. INTRODUCTION

Student Response System (SRS), also known as "Classroom Response System" or "Audience Response System", is a variety of sets of hardware and software that allows teachers to pose different kinds of questions to students in class, and students can submit their answer to the questions using handheld devices or even their own mobile devices or laptop computers through wireless network simultaneously. Teachers can collect and analyze all student responses instantly and convert them into different statistics (Kay and LeSage, 2009). Before the introduction of SRS, question-and-answering activities in the classroom are usually characterized by the teacher calling upon one student at a time to respond. In this setting, only a small number of students answer questions consistently, and the rest of the class is neglected and is subjected to passive listening (Fitch, 2004; Narayan et al., 1990). This technological innovation revolutionizes the question-and-answering activities in the classroom by providing opportunities for all students to respond to teachers in class.

The advantages of the SRS include stimulating students' participation, enhancing students' engagement, and refreshing students' attention span. Filer (2010) explains that SRS requires students to engage in the classroom, process information independently and commit to an answer, so it promotes active participation in class. Moreover, SRS enables anonymity that protects students from the embarrassment of making incorrect responses (Filer, 2010; Florenthal, 2018) and motivates introverted or anxious students to participate in more classroom activities (Stowell and Nelson, 2007; Stowell et al, 2010; Florenthal, 2018). Research also suggests that students' attention decreases dramatically after 20 minutes in the lecture, however, the use of SRS and the question-and-answering activities can serve as a break to students and refresh their attention span (Kay and Lesage, 2009). Hunsu et al. (2016) examine empirical studies on the use of SRS and confirms the positive effects SRS has on students' engagement and participation, attendance, and self-efficacy across different subjects.

Despite these advantages, teachers are warned against the potential danger of overusing the new technology. For example, Robertson (2000) believes that students' enthusiasm will fade away if they are presented with questions after questions, and Martyn (2007) also advises against asking too many questions. Regarding the number of questions, Premkumar (2009) suggests that 3 to 4 questions in a 60-minute lecture would be adequate. Carnaghan (2011) prefers no more than 4 questions per hour of class. These warnings suggest that the overuse of SRS may diminish the benefits of the technology.

The current study investigates whether students' participation in class will decrease if teachers keep asking questions through SRS. This idea can be formulated into a research hypothesis: if the number of questions teachers ask increases, the number of student responses will decrease. A quantitative research on the data set of a self-invented SRS in The Chinese University of Hong Kong is undertaken. The research examines the quantity of questions teachers posed per session and the number of student responses. The research result disproves the research hypothesis, showing that there is no significant decrease in student responses as teachers ask more questions. That means students' participation can be sustained throughout the class with the help of SRS.

2. METHODOLOGY

2.1 Data Collection

Research data of this study comes from a self-invented, web-based SRS that has been in use campus-wide since 2012 at The Chinese University of Hong Kong. This SRS, uReply, is a cloud-based classroom communication system. Teachers can ask a question by simply typing the question on the spot or picking a ready-made question item from his/her personal question bank. Students can input their answers via their Internet-connected mobile devices or laptop computers. uReply supports multiple-choice questions, text questions without word limits, Likert scale, fill-in-the-blanks, and direct messages. Student responses are by default anonymous unless the teacher requires students to enter their name or student ID when they submit their response. The system also automatically records all activities for future use. At the time of writing this paper, the system consistently recorded more than 2500 student-visits per week during teaching days.

The researchers retrieved the raw usage data from the system recorded over a 3-year period from May 2012 to May 2015. The raw usage data contains 5370 sessions. One session stands for one activity that can last for a whole lecture, which is around two to three hours. A teacher can ask as many questions as they like in one session and they normally would close the session when their lecture ends. A total of 606 teacher users from all 8 faculties of The Chinese University of Hong Kong has contributed to these data.

2.2 Data Refinement

Among these 5370 sessions, two types of sessions are to be excluded from our research: the sessions that are not real classroom usage, and the sessions that contain data invalid for our research. The former type of sessions includes 1, sessions created by our development team when they built and tested the system; 2, teachers' trial usage sessions; 3, sessions without accurate information about the course, the teachers, and the students. The latter type of sessions includes 4, sessions that were used across multiple lectures; and 5, sessions that contain only one question and session groups that contain too few sessions for valid analysis. The refinement process of the dataset is divided into five stages as listed below:

In the first stage, sessions from non-teacher accounts, including team project users and developers were deleted. A total of 89 user accounts and 1911 sessions were deleted in this stage.

In the second stage, sessions with incorrect information regarding teacher users, course codes, and student IDs were deleted. These sessions were deleted because they could not be proven to be actual classroom usage. A total of 338 sessions were deleted in this stage.

In the third stage, we identified and deleted sessions of trial usage. Trial usage sessions were identified by the number of respondents in each session. Because the teachers would not create too many respondents in their trial usage sessions, these sessions should contain a fewer number of respondents. Therefore, we focused on five groups of sessions that had 2 to 6 respondents respectively. We randomly selected 30 sessions from each of these five groups as samples. All the questions and answers in these total 150 sessions were examined to judge whether they were trial usage or not. Some sessions were still unable to be classified because there was no clear evidence.

After that, we calculated the rate of real cases (TRUE session / (No. of sessions – undefined sessions) of each of the five groups. Table 1 shows the results of this analysis. It shows that in groups of sessions that had 5 or more respondents, more than 90% of the sessions are identifiable real classroom usages. We determined that 90% could be the acceptable margin for our study to balance off data quality and data quantity. Therefore, we deleted all the sessions that had fewer than 5 respondents. In this stage, 686 sessions were deleted.

Table 1. Analysis of identifiable real classroom usage for sessions containing 2-6 respondents

No. of Respondents	2	3	4	5	6
No. of Sessions	30	30	30	30	30
Real-usage Sessions	13	18	22	24	27
Trial-usage Sessions	12	5	3	2	2
*Undefined Sessions**	*5*	*7*	*5*	*4*	*1*
Rate of Real Cases (%)	52.00%	78.26%	88.00%	**92.31%**	**93.10%**

In the fourth stage, sessions that were used across multiple lectures were deleted. uReply allows users to reuse the session they created. But when a session is reused in another lecture, the number of respondents and questions differ from the previous use. Therefore, the data of reused sessions is not valid for analysis, so we also deleted these sessions. In this stage, 571 sessions were deleted.

Finally, the remaining 1864 sessions were grouped according to the number of questions asked in each session. The group of sessions that contain only one question was excluded because sessions containing only one question do not have any change in student response rate. Moreover, groups that contain too few sessions for a valid study were also excluded. These groups are mainly the sessions that contain over 20 questions. In this stage, 852 sessions were excluded. The remaining 1012 sessions are eligible for our analysis.

Table 2. The data refinement process

	Sessions excluded	Sessions remained
Total number of sessions		5370
Sessions from non-teaching accounts	1911	3459
Sessions with incorrect information	338	3121
Sessions with fewer than 5 respondents	686	2435
Sessions used across multiple lectures	571	1864
Sessions containing only 1 question and over 20 questions	852	1012
Total number of sessions for analysis		1012

3. RESULTS

In order to find out whether there are statistically significant differences in student responses between the beginning and the end of a session, it would be necessary to first define the “beginning” and the “end” portions for sessions containing various numbers of questions. As shown in table 3, the sessions in this study have numbers of questions ranged from as few as 2 questions to as many as 20 questions. Because the response of a single question may rise or fall drastically due to various reasons (as seen in Figure 3-5), this research avoids using solely the first and the last item for measurement except for the group of sessions containing 2 to 4 questions. This research defines the “beginning” and the “end” portion as roughly one-third to one-fourth of the whole session. For example, in sessions containing 7 questions, the beginning portion is the first 2 questions, and the end portion is the last 2 questions. In table 3, the columns on the left illustrate the number of responses received in the beginning portions, including the minimum value, the maximum value, and the mean; the columns on the right illustrate the number of responses received at the end of the course, including the minimum value, maximum value, and the mean. The result shows that the numbers of responses collected in the beginning and at the end of the class are quite close, indicating that students keep responding to the teacher while the number of questions increase. For example, in sessions that contain 7 questions, a mean of 1406 responses for each question are collected in the beginning portion (the first 2 questions) comparing to around 1360 at the end portion (the last 2 questions).

Table 3. Comparison of the number of student responses between the beginning and the end portions

No. of Questions in a Session	No. of Sessions	Question(s) in portion	Beginning portion				End portion			
			Min	Max	Mean	SD	Min	Max	Mean	SD
2	283	1	-	-	9121	-	-	-	9043	-
3	198	1	-	-	5585	-	-	-	5404	-
4	145	1	-	-	4039	-	-	-	4045	-
5	115	2	3082	3181	3131.5	70.0	3013	3035	3024	15.6
6	53	2	1286	1367	1326.5	57.3	1380	1454	1417	52.3
7	56	2	1366	1446	1406	56.6	1329	1392	1360.5	44.5
8	44	2	1752	1892	1822	99.0	1493	1563	1528	49.5
9	28	3	545	571	558	13	519	541	531	11.1
10	39	3	1373	1503	1438.7	65.0	1388	1408	1400.7	11.0
11	11	3	378	421	392.7	24.5	352	386	366.3	17.6
12	4	3	160	177	168.7	8.5	174	201	183.3	15.3
13	5	4	207	250	228	19.9	193	214	206	9.8
14	8	4	263	283	270.8	9.0	212	235	223.8	12.4
15	4	4	159	168	163.8	3.8	148	158	152	4.5
16	12	4	656	690	679.8	16.0	658	691	673.3	13.6
17	3	5	125	145	138.8	8.0	124	142	134.4	7.4
20	4	5	199	218	208.6	6.9	131	220	198.8	38.0
	1012									

From the first two columns of table 3, it can also be observed that teachers tend to ask fewer than 10 questions in a single session. Figure 1 below shows the distribution of groups of sessions according to the number of questions. Twenty-eight percent of the sessions contain only 2 questions, and sessions with 2 to 5 questions account for 73% of all sessions. For sessions containing 6 to 10 questions, they occupy another 22%. These sessions occupy a total of 95% of all sessions. Because of the small number of sessions containing more than 10 questions, the average number of responses for each question in these sessions rise and fall sharply, as shown in Figure 4 and 5. However, a significant trend of decrease between the beginning and the end portion is not notable in most of these sessions. Rather, the number of student responses varies between questions, suggesting that there are other factors affecting the number of student responses.

Table 4 below shows the result of t-tests to each pair of the beginning and the end portion for groups that consist of more than 20 sessions. As shown in table 4, most beginning and end portions of the sessions do not show statistically significant differences (set at .05) in terms of the number of responses collected, except the group of sessions containing 8 questions. It can be further observed from Figure 3 that the average number of student responses for the group of sessions containing 8 questions reach its peak on the 2nd question and starts to decrease from the 3rd question to the 5th question, afterward it remains stable. A similar phenomenon of sudden decrease immediately after the beginning portion of the sessions can also be observed in the group of sessions containing 13 questions.

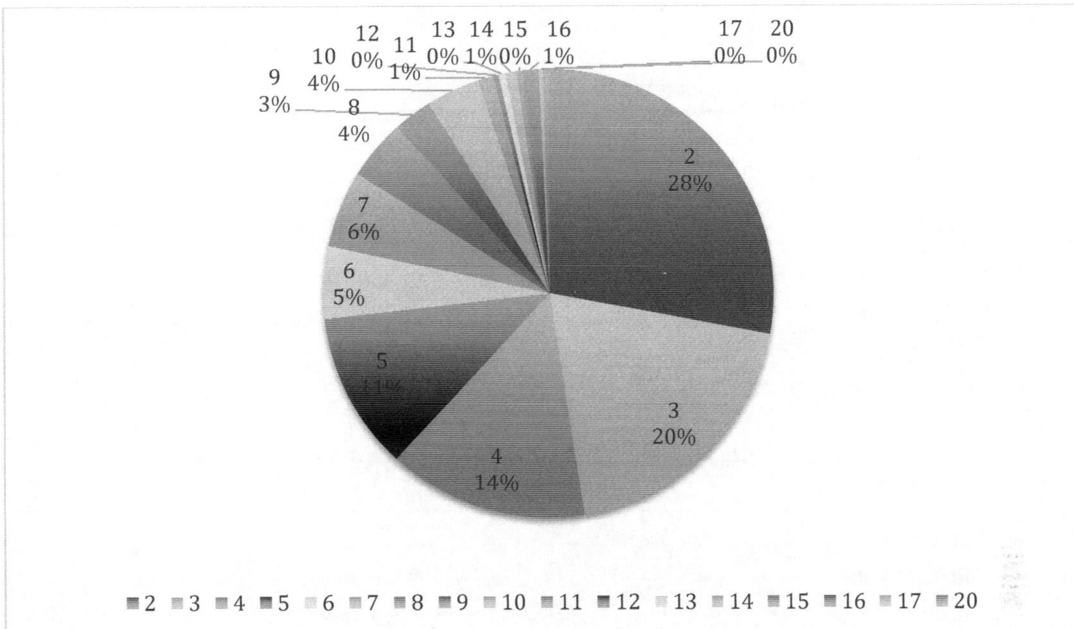

Figure 1. Distribution of sessions according to the number of questions

Table 4. T-test analysis to pairs of the beginning and the end portions for each group

No. of Questions in Sessions	No. of Sessions	T-Test Result	Range (Total Response)	Mean±SD
2	283	0.677	9043 – 9121	9082±55.2
3	198	0.397	5404 – 5670	5627.5 ±135.9
4	145	0.970	4039 – 4251	4146.3±120.4
5	115	0.195	3013 – 3181	3082.6 ±65.5
6	53	0.102	1286 – 1462	1382.3 ±66.9
7	56	0.375	1329 – 1467	1389.9±52.1
8	44	**0.032**	1493 – 1892	1654±149.5
9	28	0.235	519 – 571	545.2±16.4
10	39	0.437	1373 – 1503	1424.7 ±38.8
*11**	11	--	329 – 421	370.3±24.3
*12**	4	--	160 – 201	172.7±10.4
*13**	5	--	193 – 250	214.8±14.8
*14**	8	--	205 – 283	250.0±25.4
*15**	4	--	147 – 168	159.5±7.2
*16**	12	--	634 – 710	673.5±21.5
*17**	3	--	124 – 147	139.1±6.9
*20**	4	--	131 – 223	211±19.8

Figures 2-5 below show the average number of responses in each question for each group in graphs. Figure 2 plots the sessions with 2 to 5 questions; figure 3 plots the sessions with 6 to 10 questions; figure 4 plots the sessions with 11 to 15 questions; and figure 5 plots the sessions with 16, 17 and 20 questions.

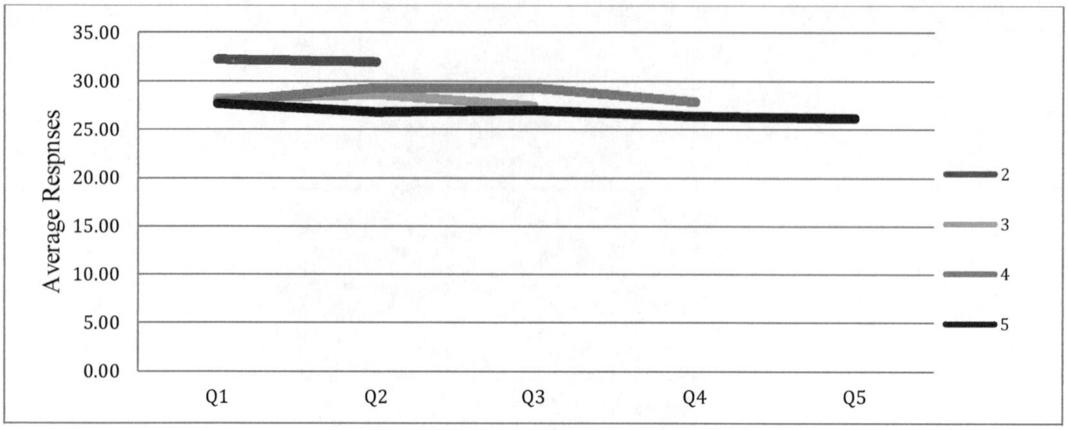

Figure 2. Average responses of each question for sessions with 2 to 5 questions

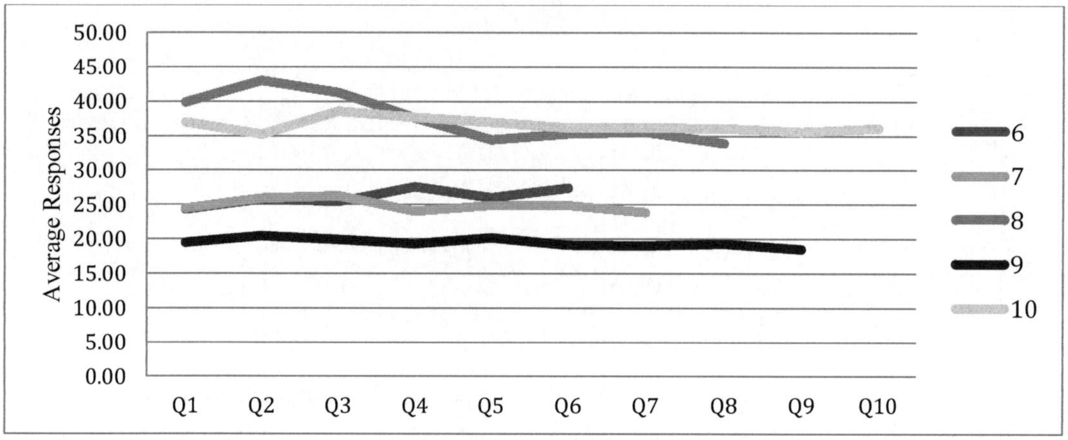

Figure 3. Average responses of each question for sessions with 6 to 10 questions

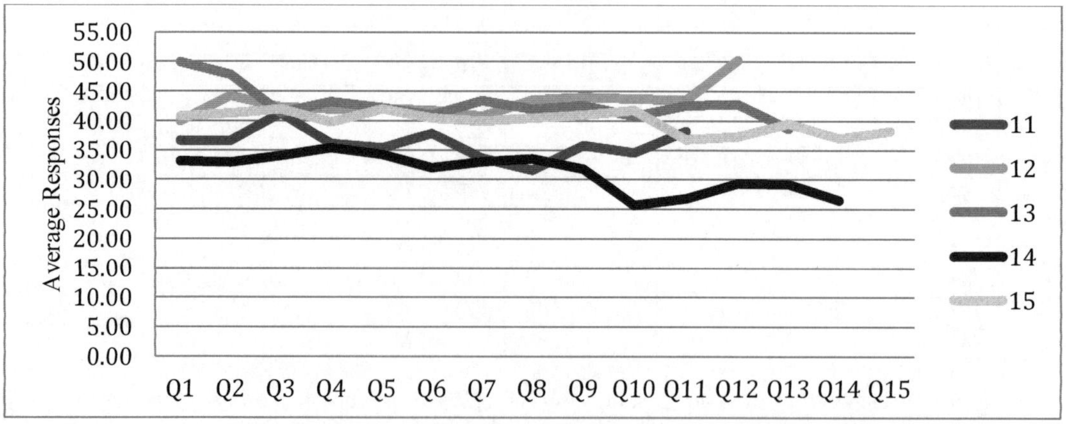

Figure 4. Average responses of each question for sessions with 11 to 15 questions

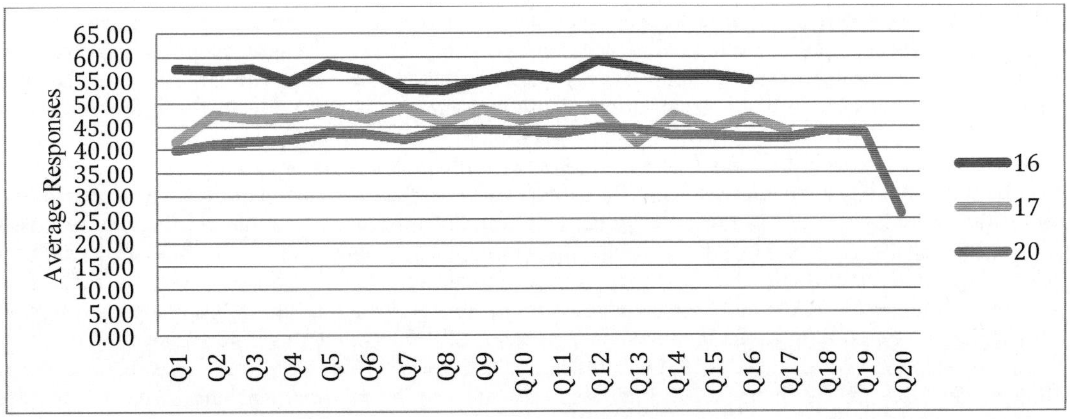

Figure 5. Average responses of each question for sessions with 16, 17 and 20 questions

It should be noted that there is a sudden drop of average responses for the last question in the group of sessions containing 20 questions. It is because there are only 4 sessions in this group. A significant drop of responses in a single session affects the whole statistic. The sudden drop of responses occurred only in session no. 1522. In this session, the first nineteen questions are multiple-choices question, but the last question requires students to respond in text form. The multiple-choice questions are easier for students because they allow some test-wise strategies, such as response elimination strategy. On the contrary, the constructive response questions that require students to produce text would generate test anxiety to students (Martinez, 1999). Therefore, the change of the question format is probably the cause for the decrease in the number of student responses.

4. DISCUSSION

The main discovery of our research is that there is no significant drop in the student responses with the increasing number of questions. This refutes the hypothesis that constant use of the technology will reduce students' participation. Our statistic disproves the hypothesis that "if the number of questions teachers asked increases, the number of student responses will decrease". Instead, it shows that the student responses rate for SRS is more sustaining than expected. For teachers concerned that keep asking questions may drive students away, the result of this research is a relief. It may encourage the teachers to use SRS more boldly and venture on different use of this technology. Another discovery is that teachers often favor a session containing questions ranging from 2 to 5. Figure 2 shows that the number of student responses remains stable in these sessions, which occupy 73% of all sessions. Figure 3 shows that the groups of sessions containing 8 and 10 questions experience a greater change in the average number of responses at the beginning of the sessions, which might due to issues related to time management. A detailed investigation of the time for each question being asked may reveal more on this change. Nevertheless, since 95% of sessions contain fewer than 10 questions, and the response rates for these questions are stable, we can conclude that the issue of losing students' participation and engagement is minimal for most of the sessions.

5. LIMITATION AND FUTURE WORK

There are a few limitations regarding this research. First, since the total number of students in each session is unknown, it is hard to estimate student engagement rate because the total response rate cannot be calculated. Due to this limitation, this research can only show that students who participated at the beginning of the session will continue to respond to teacher throughout the whole session. Second, the study cannot exclude the possibility that student responses are compulsory in class. It is reported that some teachers may use SRS to take attendance (Kay and LeSage, 2009; Hunsu et al., 2016). There is a function in uReply for teachers to collect registered students response. Under this function, students have to provide their name or student IDs along with their answers. Because teachers may use these responses as evidence of students' attendance, students may feel compulsory to respond. Further research that separates the anonymous and registered student responses and focus only on anonymous data may exclude such a possibility. Third, the current study uses the data from the early stage of implementation of this system, hence the data sample is limited to a single university. With the use of uReply extending to other universities in Hong Kong, future studies on the uReply dataset may include samples from different universities through co-operation efforts.

The current study also observes that different factors may affect the quantity of student response. As seen from the example above, regarding the forms and types of questions, multiple choice may receive more responses than text questions (Martinez, 1999; Wong et al., 2018). Previous researches also speculate that other elements such as the difficulty level of the questions (Carnaghan, 2007), the time allowed for students to pose response (Wang et al., 2018), and the type of activities in the classroom may also affect students' response rate. Regarding the types of activities in the classroom, using SRS for competition and games may receive more positive reception (Wang et al., 2018; Newland and Black, 2019). Therefore, future research that focuses on how teachers design the sessions with high response rate may reveal what teaching practice with SRS can increase students' participation and engagement.

REFERENCES

Carnaghan, C and Webb, A. 2007. Investigating the Effects of Group Response Systems on Student Satisfaction, Learning and Engagement in Accounting Education. *Issues in Accounting Education*, *22*(3), 391-409.

Carnaghan, C. et al. 2011. Using Student Response Systems in the Accounting Classroom: Strengths, Strategies and Limitation. *Journal of Accounting Education*, *29*(4), 265-283.

Filer, D. 2010. Everyone's Answering: Using Technology to Increase Classroom Participation. *Nurse Education Perspective*, *31*(4), 247-250.

Fitch, J. 2004. Student Feedback in the College Classroom: A Technology Solution. *Educational Technology Research and Development*, *52*(1), 71-77.

Florenthal, B. 2018. Students' Motivation to Participate via Mobile Technology in the Classroom: A Uses and Gratification Approach. *Journal of Marketing Education*.

Hunsu, N. et al. 2016. A meta-analysis of the effects of audience response systems (clicker-based technologies) on cognition and affect. *Computers & Education*, *94*, 102-119.

Kay, R. H. and Lesage, A. 2009. Examining the Benefits and Challenges of Using Audience Response Systems: A Review of the Literature. *Computers & Education*, *53*, 819-827.

Martinez, M. E. 1999. Cognition and the Question of Test Item Format. *Educational Psychologist*, *34*(4), 207-218.

Martyn, M. 2007. Clickers in the Classroom: An Active Learning Approach. *EDUCAUSE Quarterly, 30*(2), 71-74.

Narayan, J. et al. 1990. Using Response Cards to Increase Student Participation in an Elementary Classroom. *Journal of Applied Behavior Analysis*, *23*(4), 483-490.

Newland, S. and Black, B. 2019. More than multiple choice: a toolbox for incorporating clickers into political science courses. *Journal of Political Science Education*. doi: 10.1080/15512169.2018.1544906

Premkumar, K. 2009. Rules of Engagement – 12 Tips for Successful Use of "Clickers" in the Classroom. *Medical Teacher*, *30*(2), 146-149.

Robertson, L. J. 2000. Twelve Tips for Using a Computerised Interactive Audience Response System. *Medical Teacher*, *22*(3), 237-239.

Stowell, J. R. and Nelson, J. M. 2007. Benefits of Electronic Audience Response Systems on Student Participation, Learning, and Emotion. *Teaching of Psychology*, *34*(4), 253-258.

Stowell, J. R. et al. 2010. Using Student Response Systems ("Clickers") to Combat Conformity and Shyness. *Teaching of Psychology*, *37*(2), 135-140.

Trees, A. R. and Jackson, M. H. 2007. The Learning Environment in Clicker Classrooms: Student Processes of Learning and Involvement in Large University-level Courses Using Student Response Systems. *Learning, Media and Technology*, *32*(1), 21-40.

Wang, W. et al. 2018. Student Perceptions of Classic and Game-Based Online Student Response Systems. *Nurse Educator*. doi: 10.1097/NNE.0000000000000591

Wong, A. et al. 2018. Student perceptions on the use of student response system in higher education in Hong Kong. *Proceedings of the 5th Teaching & Education Conference*, Amsterdam, Netherlands, pp. 118-135.

A SEQUENTIAL ANALYSIS OF TEACHING BEHAVIORS TOWARD THE USE OF BLACKBOARD LEARNING MANAGEMENT SYSTEM

Yu-Hang Li, Chien-Yuan Su and Yue Hu
Department of Curriculum and Learning Science, Zhejiang University
Hangzhou, China

ABSTRACT

In the era of online learning, Learning Management Systems (LMSs) such as Blackboard and Moodle offer a great variety of functions to facilitate teaching and learning and are widely used in the context of higher education. Most previous studies using data mining have focused on exploring student behavior patterns toward using LMSs, but seldom address the behavior patterns of teachers. The main purpose of this study is to utilize frequency and sequential analyses to investigate the behavioral patterns of university teachers toward using Blackboard. The operational behaviors of 268 teachers at Zhejiang University were extracted from the Blackboard platform for the period from August 2018 to January 2019 and further classified into five types: (1) *course and content*; (2) *assignment*; (3) *communication and collaboration*; (4) *assessment*; and (5) *administration*, according to the study from Dabbagh (2005). Frequency analysis results indicated that the most frequently observed teacher operational behavior was *course and content*, followed by *assessment* and then *administration*. In addition, sequential analysis results showed that most teachers are willing to use *communication and collaboration* and *assignment* after using *course and content*. We further compared these two sets of data and found that *communication and collaboration* were the most frequently used functions besides *course and content*. Almost all of the teachers only expressed the individual *assessment* behavior without combining other behaviors despite *assessment* appearing at a higher usage frequency. In contrast, *communication and collaboration* and *assignment* showed a lower frequency of usage, but there was a higher frequency of use either before or after using *course and content*. Results from this study have practical implications for educators and researchers in order to clearly understand university teacher behavior regarding the use of Blackboard.

KEYWORDS

Teacher Behavior, Learning Management System, Sequential Analysis

1. INTRODUCTION

Learning management systems (LMSs) as web-based instructional infrastructures, such as Blackboard or Moodle, have been widely adopted to support teaching and learning via built-in platform tools to carry out the delivery of teaching content, assessing student outcomes, tracking learning processes, and providing interactions with others (Mohd Kasim and Khalid, 2016; Watson et al., 2007). When teachers or students participated in these online teaching and learning activities or tasks through LMSs, such as downloading notes, accessing grades, performing tests or quizzes and participating in online discussions, their operational behaviors were recorded at that time into the specific format set from the database of LMS platforms. A number of prior research studies have examined user behavior regarding the use of LMSs. For instance, Cerezo et al. (2016) used an educational data mining (EDM) approach to explore students' learning patterns through focusing on learning effort, time spent working and procrastination by analyzing Moodle logs. Munoz-Organero et al. (2010) analyzed the behavioral patterns of 180 students from six different universities through the interactions of each particular student with the content and services of a learning management system (LMS). Tempelaar et al. (2017) incorporated dispositional dimensions (such as self-regulation and emotion) into conventional learning analysis models to explore the behavior of students using LMSs. Li and Tsai (2017) used cluster analysis to investigate students' LMS behavioral patterns and found these different behavioral patterns were associated with their motivation and learning performance. De Smet et al. (2012)

attempted to investigate instructional use and the technology acceptance of LMSs by examining the usage behaviors of 505 secondary school teachers regarding the functions of LMSs such as document publishing, announcements, uploading or publishing exercises, among others. Hou (2013) used sequential analysis to explore learner's interactive behaviors and behavioral patterns in using an educational game and explored the behavioral differences between students of different genders, plus those with high/low prior knowledge and high/low learning performance. Most of these studies were conducted to investigate the behavior of students. However, few studies have been done on the teachers, in particular those working at the university level.

The major purpose of this study was to investigate the behaviors of university teachers toward the use of Blackboard by utilizing both frequency and sequential analysis. Frequency analysis is a descriptive statistical analysis that can show frequency and times of access to determine usage patterns (Peled and Rashty, 1999). In addition, sequential analysis can be used to explore behavioral patterns via calculating the frequency of each behavioral category immediately following another behavioral category (Chiang et al., 2014; Hou, 2013; Hou et al., 2010; Sun et al., 2017). To achieve the purpose of this study, the two specific questions to be addressed are as follows:

(1) What are the frequency and distribution of teachers' behaviors using Blackboard?

(2) Behind the behavioral distributions, what are the displayed patterns of teacher sequential behaviors toward the use of Blackboard?

2. METHODOLOGY

2.1 Data Acquisition and Extraction

This study extracted teacher usage logs from the Blackboard platform operating at Zhejiang University during the period from August 2018 to January 2019. The preliminary examination found that 689 teachers used BB; after deducting the less-used sample of teachers, there remained 268 teachers who more actively used Blackboard to serve as an analysis sample in our study. Through data cleaning and pre-processing, a total of 34561 behaviors were marked.

2.2 Data Coding and Analysis

In this study, 34561 teacher operational records of using Blackboard were identified; in turn, these were divided into five different usage types according to the LMS tool categories identified by Dabbagh and Kitsantas (2005): *Course and Content* (T1); *Assignment* (T2); *Communication and Collaboration* (T3); *Assessment* (T4); and *Administration* (T5) (see Table 1). To test the reliability of the data coding, all coded records were double checked by two graduate students of educational technology who received the same coding training. The Cohan's Kappa reliability was 0.989 ($p < .001$), demonstrating the scheme coding to be reasonable and credible.

Table 1. The coding scheme of teacher LMS behaviors

Code	Tool category of Blackboard	Example
T1	Course and Content	Creating course content, announcements, syllabus, introductions, videos, etc.
T2	Assignment	Creating tests, quizzes, surveys, questions, assignments, tasks, homework, etc.
T3	Communication and Collaboration	Using Ding talk, email, logs, discussion forums, blogs, Wikis, groups, etc.
T4	Assessment	Using grades, grade indicator boards, grade centers, self-evaluations, mutual-evaluations, etc.
T5	Administration	Using class management, data management, contacts, teaching calendars, course reports, etc.

In order to gain a richer insight into the way teachers behave toward the use of Blackboard, we first conducted frequency analysis to estimate the frequency (monthly) and distribution of five different usage behavioral types regarding Blackboard. Afterward, a lag-two sequential analysis approach was used to explore the overall sequential behavioral patterns displayed by teachers. The behavioral codes are used to simplify the sequential characterizations according to chronological order, and formed a series of sequential analysis matrix calculations to discover the behavioral transitions among two different behavioral types (for example, T1→T2 means using *assignment* after using *course and content*) (Bakeman and Gottman, 1997; Hou, 2012). It should be noted that continuous or repeated operational behaviors for each behavioral type were ignored (such as T1→T1 signifying the repetitive use of *course and content*).

3. RESULTS

3.1 Frequency Analysis

To answer the first research question, 34561 LMS records involving 268 teachers were coded into five different behavioral types; as such, the overall distribution of the behavioral frequencies is presented in Table 2.

Table 2. Distribution of the quantitative frequency analysis of codes within the five behavioral types

Code	Tool category of Blackboard	Frequency	%
T1	Course and Content	15200	43.98
T2	Assignment	2811	8.13
T3	Communication and Collaboration	3873	11.21
T4	Assessment	7821	22.63
T5	Administration	4856	14.05
	Total	**34561**	**100.00**

Table 2 indicates that the highest frequency of teacher behavior is focused on *course and content* (T1, 43.98%) and is followed by *assessment* (T4, 22.63%). The frequency of the other three behaviors (*administration*, *communication and collaboration*, *assignment*) is less than 15%, with the difference in frequency among each of these only 3%. The distribution trend diagram of the frequency regarding teachers' LMS usage behaviors is shown in Figure 1. Four types of frequency trend change (T1, T2, T3, and T5) decremented over time, yet the frequency of T4 increased with time.

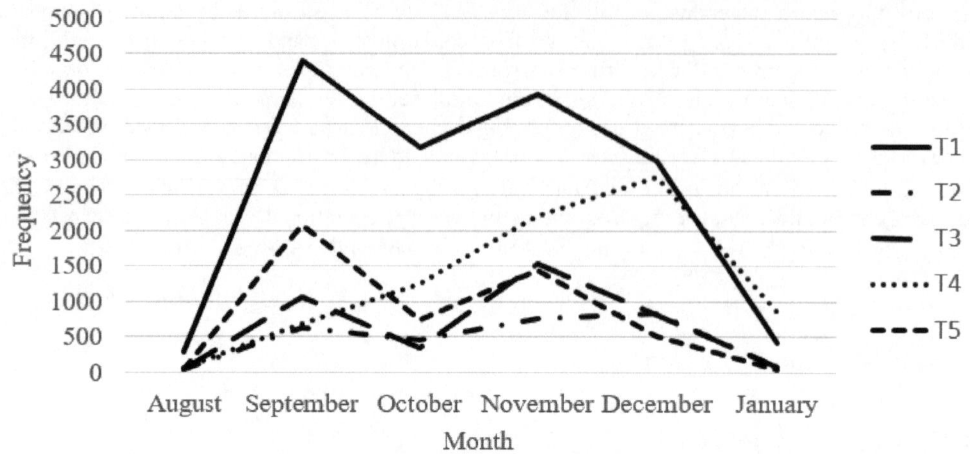

Figure 1. The frequency diagram of teachers' LMS behaviors

3.2 Sequential Analysis

To answer the second research question, the result of lag-two sequential analyses is shown in Table 3, where the rows represent the former teacher behaviors and the columns represent the latter ones. The values of the adjusted residuals (Z-score) between the two behavioral types are estimated, and the z-score higher than 1.96 indicates the behavioral transition (such as T1→T2, 12.49 in Table 3) is reaching significance (Bakeman and Gottman, 1997).

Table 3. The adjusted residual table for all teacher behaviors toward the use of Blackboard

Z	T1	T2	T3	T4	T5
T1	-11.71	**12.49***	**16.41***	1.01	**11.33***
T2	**21.65***	-11.71	-5.04	-7.26	-6.28
T3	**23.88***	-5.39	-11.71	-5.84	-3.97
T4	**4.57***	-5.21	-4.06	-11.71	-8.77
T5	**20.32***	-5.39	**3.06***	1.01	-11.71

* $p < 0.05$

In order to clearly demonstrate the sequential transition of teacher behavioral types. Figure 2 showed the entire range of teachers' sequential behaviors regarding the use Blackboard; the node size represents the frequency strength of the teacher behavioral types, arrows represent the order of the operation, while line thickness represents the amount of the operation frequency of occurrence from one behavioral type to another.

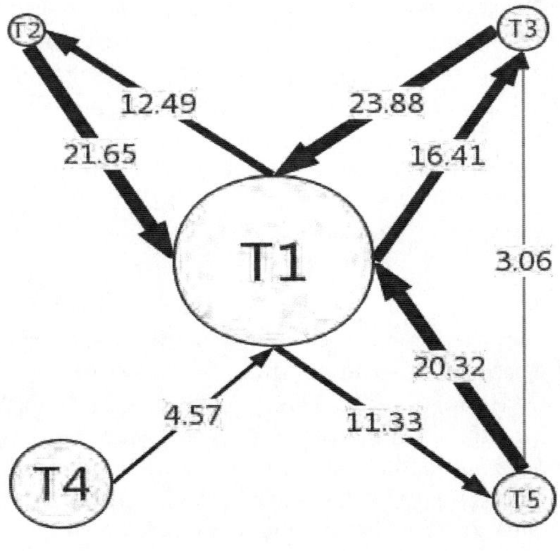

Figure 2. The behavioral pattern diagram of all teachers

When observing the results of Table 2 and Figure 2, there is obvious behavioral transition between T1 and T3 (T1→T3, 16.41; T3→T1, 23.88), followed by behavioral transition between T1 and T2 (T1→T2, 12.49; T2→T1, 21.65), meaning that teachers are more likely to use *communication and collaboration* and *assignment* after using *course and content*, and vice versa. Most of the operational behavior revolves around *course and content* (T1). No matter what kind of behavior changes, the behavior is transformed into other behavior types through *course and content*. To analyze the line direction and line thickness in Figure 2, we observed that the last behavior of most teachers on the platform was *course and content*. Unexpectedly, there is no obvious behavioral transition from *course and content* (T1) to *assessment* (T4), although *assessment* showed a high frequency of usage. Another interesting finding is the transition from *administration* to *communication and collaboration*—there are fewer connections between these two functions according to our coding scheme.

4. DISCUSSION

According to the results of frequency analysis exploring teachers' usage of the Blackboard platform, it found that the frequency of using courses and content is the highest, while using *assignment* is the lowest. The above results reveal that the LMS usage behavior of teachers was primarily confined to creating or uploading instructional materials or course content for students to download or access. This is consistent with other LMS utilization studies reporting that tools for content distribution are used more often than other tools (Garrote Jurado et al., 2014; Phillips, 2006). Macfadyen and Dawson (2012) also pointed out that teachers usually have relatively higher usage of LMS tools such as content and announcements because they require less effort, time and technical skill to implement. Moreover, according to the time chart of frequency analysis, the *assessment* behavior has a tendency to increase in frequency with time. The cause may be due to its proximity to the semester's final exam, which increases the number of times teachers use *assessment*.

On the other hand, some interesting analysis results regarding teacher behaviors are presented via lag sequential analysis. For example, to compare teacher behavioral transitions in multiple directions, two significant behavioral transitions appeared between both *course and content* and *communication and collaboration* (T1↔T3) and between *course and content* and *assignment* (T1↔T2). The high rate of behavioral transitions between *course and content* and *administration* (T1↔T5) indicated that teachers were more likely to deal with online content of teaching materials and teaching management when they used the Blackboard platform. There is also a significant behavioral transition phenomenon from *administration* to *communication and collaboration* (T5→T3). It is considered that teachers often manage class data and contacts, and then use group or communication functions to interact/communicate with their students.

Moreover, the frequency of teacher *assessment* (T4) behavior appeared to be quite high, but only showed significant one-way behavioral transition (*assessment* to *course and content* (T4→T1)). In addition, we found a behavioral phenomenon in which some teachers repeatedly undertook the same action behavior in some insignificant function modules. This may imply that teachers may not have been quite familiar with how to use Blackboard when they performed some teaching tasks. This result is consistent with Chow et al. (2018), which indicated that trained teachers presented more behaviors in operating various LMS functions than did untrained teachers.

5. CONCLUSION

This study explored teacher behavioral patterns toward the use of Blackboard by using frequency and sequential analysis. The results showed that a majority of teacher behaviors focused on *course and content*, as well as there being a higher behavioral transition that occurs between *course and content* and *assignment* or *course and content* and *communication and collaboration*. In addition, teachers typically use only the *assessment* functions to conduct *assessment* tasks and seldom carry out other teaching tasks when they use LMSs. One limitation of this study is not taking continuous operating behaviors into account when conducting the sequential analysis. Future research might add other analytical methods, such as cluster analysis, to explore other different teacher groups according to behavioral characteristics. Furthermore, some individual characteristics of teachers could be considered to explore their impact on teacher behavior toward the use of Blackboard, such as gender, age, beliefs, and ICT competency. In summary, this study presents a behavioral frequency distribution and sequential behavioral patterns for university teachers toward the use of Blackboard, delivering a deeper and broader understanding of the LMS usage behavior of university teachers in a higher education context.

ACKNOWLEDGEMENT

This research was supported by the Philosophy and Social Sciences Planning Project of Zhejiang Province, China (P. R. C.) under Grant No. 18NDJC026Z, and the teaching and scientific research project for liberal arts teachers in Zhejiang University.

REFERENCES

Bakeman, R. and Gottman, J., 1997. *Observing interaction: An introduction to sequential analysis*. 2nd ed. Cambridge University Press, Cambridge, UK.

Cerezo, R. et al, 2016. Students' LMS interaction patterns and their relationship with achievement: A case study in higher education, *Computers & Education*, 96, pp. 42–54.

Chiang, T. H. C. et al, 2014. Students' online interactive patterns in augmented reality-based inquiry activities, *Computers & Education*, 78, pp. 97–108.

Chow, J. et al, 2018. Comparing trained and untrained teachers on their use of LMS tools using the Rasch analysis, *Computers & Education*, 123, pp. 124–137.

Dabbagh, N. and Kitsantas, A, 2005. Using Web-based Pedagogical Tools as Scaffolds for Self-regulated Learning, *Instructional Science*, 33(5–6), pp. 513–540.

De Smet, C. et al, 2012. Researching instructional use and the technology acceptation of learning management systems by secondary school teachers, *Computers & Education*, 58(2), pp. 688–696.

Garrote Jurado, R. et al, 2014. Classification of the features in learning management systems, *Proceedings of XVII Scientific Convention on Engineering and Architecture*, Havana, Cuba, pp.1-12.

Hou, H.-T., 2012. Exploring the behavioral patterns of learners in an educational massively multiple online role-playing game (MMORPG), *Computers & Education*, 58(4), pp. 1225–1233.

Hou, H.-T., 2013. Analyzing the behavioral differences between students of different genders, prior knowledge and learning performance with an educational MMORPG: A longitudinal case study in an elementary school, *British Journal of Educational Technology*, 44(3), pp. E85–E89.

Hou, H.-T. et al, 2010. Applying lag sequential analysis to detect visual behavioural patterns of online learning activities, *British Journal of Educational Technology*, 41(2), pp. E25–E27.

Li, L.-Y. and Tsai, C.-C., 2017. Accessing online learning material: Quantitative behavior patterns and their effects on motivation and learning performance, *Computers & Education*, 114(300), pp. 286–297.

Macfadyen, L. P. and Dawson, S., 2012. Numbers are not enough. Why e-learning analytics failed to inform an institutional strategic plan, *Journal of Educational Technology & Society*, 15(3), pp. 149–163.

Mohd Kasim, N. N. and Khalid, F., 2016. Choosing the Right Learning Management System (LMS) for the Higher Education Institution Context: A Systematic Review, *International Journal of Emerging Technologies in Learning*, 11(6), p. 55.

Munoz-Organero, M. et al, 2010. Student Behavior and Interaction Patterns With an LMS as Motivation Predictors in E-Learning Settings, *IEEE Transactions on Education*, 53(3), pp. 463–470.

Peled, A. and Rashty, D., 1999. Logging for success: Advancing the use of WWW logs to improve computer mediated distance learning, *Journal of Educational Computing Research*, 21(4), pp. 413–431.

Phillips, R., 2006. Tools used in Learning Management Systems: analysis of WebCT usage logs, *Proceedings of the 23rd annual ascilite conference: Who's learning? Whose technology?*, Sydney, Australia, pp. 663–673.

Sun, J. C. Y. et al, 2017. Exploring learners' sequential behavioral patterns, flow experience, and learning performance in an anti-phishing educational game, *Educational Technology and Society*, 20(1), pp. 45–60.

Tempelaar, D. T. et al, 2017. Towards Actionable Learning Analytics Using Dispositions, *IEEE Transactions on Learning Technologies*, 10(1), pp. 6–16.

Watson, W. R. et al, 2007. An Argument for Clarity: What are Learning Management Systems, What are They Not, and What Should They Become?, *TechTrends*, 51(2), pp. 28–34.

THE IMPACT OF E-LEARNING ON LEARNER KNOWLEDGE SHARING QUALITY

Sameh M. Reyad[1], Anjum Razzaque[1], Sherine Badawi[1], Allam Hamdan[1], Reem Khamis[2] and Abdalmuttaleb Al-Sartawi[1]

[1]*Ahlia University, Manama, Bahrain*

[2]*Brunel University. London, United Kingdom*

ABSTRACT

E-learning is an emerging approach in universities where self- directed students and motivated learning increases the utilization and integration of knowledge sharing in e-learning. The learning virtual community is a domain where inquiries, interest or needs, are shared. Such circumstances lead to interactions that allows virtual participants to learn from each other. This study examines the impact of e-learning on learner knowledge sharing quality. To fulfill the requirement, a quantitative approach was used to measure the e-learning approach developed in Ahlia University in Bahrain, and whether it directs the students to the required knowledge sharing quality. A constructed questionnaire has been developed and a sample of 376 Ahlia University respondents generalizable over College of Business and Finance's. The study concluded that there's an impact of e-learning on learner knowledge sharing quality and this is due to the e-learning environments at Ahlia University are composed of those technologies that aid in the teaching and learning; such as Moodle, where students log-on to attain blended e-learning experiences. This study and its conclusion overcome the gap exists in which students expressed an influential role of self-directed and motivation for learning and knowledge sharing in e-learning environments.

KEYWORDS

E-Learning, Online Platforms, Knowledge Sharing Quality, Ahlia University Students

1. INTRODUCTION

In today modern education, e-learning is considered as an emerging approach that supports teaching and learning process (Khan, 2001). The use of e-learning as a teaching and learning tool is now rapidly expanding into education. Its major driving forces are: 1-The emergence of a worldwide communication network, with computer technologies leading to a revolution in education, 2-The perception of e-learning as a solution to the cost and quality problems of universities (Selim, 2007).

E-learning or (online education) has become a quotidian practice in many educational institutes as a way to deliver knowledge and information to students (Allen and Seaman, 2013) which in turn increased the learners' autonomy and independence in the learning process. Moreover, e-learning provides flexible learning materials and consistent information, with ease of use which in turn motivates universities to invest their resources in developing online practices (Wenchieh, Lan-Yin, 2010). As e-learning refers to the use of electronic devices for learning, including the delivery of content through electronic media such as internet, audio, or video (ASTD, 2001), universities are placing increased emphasis on improving the quality of their educational services (Kuo and Ye, 2009).

Nowadays, with the development of internet communication technologies, a large number of virtual communities emerged (Yao et al., 2015). They are networks wherein members may exchange information, knowledge, and resources and have repeated interaction through electronics means including online forums and platforms (Asvanund et al., 2004). Virtual communities sites provide a platform for participants to generate value, information and knowledge and to share them among members (Kuo, 2003) as knowledge is utilized through knowledge sharing (Sousa &Pinto, 2013). In this context, learners' self -control; self- directed and motivated learning, has been cited as a major determinant of e-learning (Sorgenfrei and Smolnik, 2016). The increasing use of e-learning is changing the traditional understanding of educational activities (Martinez-Caro et. al,2015).

Many previous studies have been evaluating the effectiveness of e-learning system, however, some of them focused on the technology-based components (Islas et al., 2007) and the others focused on human factor of e-learning system (Liaw, 2007). Therefore, the study contributes in examining the impact of e-learning with its determinants; Self- directed students and motivated learning by the use of online platforms on the knowledge sharing quality in higher educational institutions.

2. LITERATURE REVIEW

Since decade, with the advent of information and communication Technologies (ICT), learning environments (e.g., web 2.0 e-learning tools: Moodle, email, instant messaging, wiki blogs, social networks, video conferencing) and changing practices, there is an increasing tendency for student-centered and virtual community-based learning (Yilmaz, 2016; Kunthi, Wahyuni, Al-Hafidz, & Sensuse, 2018). In this scenario, the learning virtual community is a domain where inquiries, interest or needs, are shared. Such circumstances lead to interactions that allows virtual participants to learn from each other. A learning community environment is responsible for fostering its own learning and managing of knowledge to develop competencies. Here, such communities, allow the transfer of knowledge between learners; enabling participating learners in such communities to learn from each another, as well as, foster new knowledge creation within the social capital of resources of such a learning community. Here interactions help learning, problem-solving, new knowledge creation and motivation for learning during the moderation of ICT, when one thinks of virtual learning communities. In such situations, knowledge societies are part of knowledge dependent operations-based knowledge economies that transition into strategies and policies-matured learning environments. Every society holds a diverse group of people's skills and experiences, where knowledge is a commodity in the form of the social capital of the society's resources, that when subsidized empowers the knowledge economy of a society. Unfortunately, there are no strategies or policies assisting a society to become knowledge intensive economies. Knowledge increases as a society globalizes. Knowledge assets become goods, which increase with time, and get utilized, unlike tangible goods`. A knowledge society is constructed upon four pillars being infrastructure, governance, human capital and culture (Karolak & Razzaque, 2013; (Moylan & Razzaque, NYIT Education Survey, 2014) (Moylan & Razzaque, 2014)). There has been a reported a growth in virtual classrooms for academic teaching and learning, and for workplace training. While 70% of the teaching and learning is classroom based, such teaching and learning is a blend between e-learning using online learning platforms and traditional in-class teaching and learning, with an increase adaption of cell phone for m-learning. When learners enroll in an online course, interactions occur via text, audio and video messages across time and space. Hence, e-learning is a blend of asynchronous and synchronous communications where synchronous live teaching and learning in chat rooms with continuous conversation but asynchronous learning is across breaks in interaction within virtual discussions (Baehr, 2012). With tools like instant messaging, e-mails, forums, blog, social platforms and virtual conferencing; virtual learning has become an alternative channel to support learning in and outside classrooms. Hence, social media is especially applied as virtual learning environments to engage learning through interactions in social environment as learners participate. Through the construction of new knowledge in the minds of these learners, learn can also occur through observations of discussions on a discussed issue, which his being shared within a community of learners. This indicates that using the virtual environment, even social platforms like Facebook, could prove useful in ensure knowledge exchange and diffusion within no time, as well as an environment that harvests cooperation and interaction between learners. In such learning environments knowledge is shared as the main motion, which encourages community participants to share more knowledge, increasing motivation to learn and participate through their behavior of knowledge sharing, as well as, frequently share knowledge. Knowledge sharing is also the main challenge encountered within the learning process in online learning environments (Yilmaz, 2016). Knowledge enrichens and becomes deeper during knowledge sharing while e-learning in groupware, chat-room, and forums. Knowledge sharing in e-learning is vital for enriching the social capital of knowledge; or else e-learning will discontinue. Social media platforms like Facebook, WhatsApp or Line are vital and popular tools for virtual learning interactions, far better than plan e-learning environments like Moodle. The application of social media as virtual communities reinforces the ease in the use and acceptance is virtual learning platform to interact and, therefore, learn (Kunthi, Wahyuni, Al-Hafidz, & Sensuse, 2018). E-learning is also a buzz word within the commercial sector of the globe. "Learning organization" is a term that arouses conceptualization reflecting a structure where, knowledge is utilized through knowledge sharing, acquisition and diffusion, a participating behavior to improve competition. Such a process to build learning organization is fundament as an underpinning infrastructure to formulate an organizational memory. With the development of the ICT that promotes virtual conditions to increase organizational memory; e-learning tool forms the stepping stone for a fundamental environment for systems interoperations and knowledge communications. The adoption of the E-learning as a knowledge communication tool is so to allow organizations to access others' experiences from which they could develop unique knowledge. Such available knowledge allows organizations to learn in competitive environments thus, to pursue sustainability from learning and innovation (Sousa & Pinto, 2013). Blended e-learning is mixing online and traditional teachings and learning modes; a combination of both, or by the use of variances in media types, technologies, and communication modes. Hence, developing effective virtual teaching and learning environments requires a complex understanding of how technology is integrated with users such that learner participants can interact to share knowledge in order to learn. Such challenges are further complex for the instructors who have limited experience in teaching methods, in addition to virtual teaching and learning experiences. Such e-learning environment requires higher digital literacy from the instructor and learning point of view. E-learning environments that are mediated by ICT help learners create a social learning environment where knowledge gets shared for cooperative learning, and online the sharing of knowledge formulates an appropriate learning culture, whether in a traditional classroom or an e-learning mode of teaching and learning; where learners should take a more active role in knowledge exchange, particularly in online training (Baehr, 2012; Caspersen, Frølich, & Muller, 2017; Honey & Mumford, 1992).

3. SAMPLE DESIGN AND DEMOGRAPHIC ANALYSIS

This study initiated with a critique of a literature review to understand gaps in research focused on e-learning. After this phase was the pinpointing of the research question and research objectives followed by the formulation of a conceptual framework, and the relative hypothesis. To test the hypothesis; data were collected from 376 Ahlia University respondents generalizable over College of Business and Finance's 700 students (i.e. close to approximate) population. Collected data were analyzed using descriptive and advanced descriptive analysis followed by correlation analysis and explained in the data analysis section. This a deductive research approach seeks confirmation on its hypothesis and its cross-sectional data collection on 376 responses were based on completely filled online survey forms. The survey instrument was adapted from two sources: learning readiness and learner knowledge sharing quality. The needs for assessing this study's hypothesis is literature driven; s past scholars have not assessed this role in the higher education sector; hence a novel assessment of this study.

Table 1. Demographic distribution

Sample Characteristics		Frequency	Percent
Gender	Male	212	56%
	Female	164	44%
	Total	**376**	**100%**
Age	12 - 17 years old	16	4%
	18 - 24 years old	312	83%
	25 - 34 years old	48	13%
	Total	**376**	**100%**
Student Status	GCC student	250	66%
	Non-GCC student	126	34%
	Total	**376**	**100%**

Table (1) indicates that in terms of gender, the respondents who participated in the survey were mostly Males with 56%, while the females represent 44%. In terms of age, most of the respondents (83%) were between ages of 18 & 24, 13% of the respondents were between the ages of 25 & 34, while 4% of the respondents were between the ages of 12 & 17. Regarding the status it can be seen that in terms of nationality, majority of the respondents (250) were those the GCC students representing 66%, while Non-GCC student (126) represent 34%.

4. FINDINGS AND DISCUSSION

4.1 Descriptive Analysis

Table (2) shows the mean of all respondents' opinions about learner knowledge sharing quality. The highest mean of learner knowledge sharing quality was 3.915 related to "The knowledge shared between instructor and students in Moodle is easy to understand" with general percent 78%, followed by" The knowledge shared between instructor and students in Moodle is relevant" with mean equals to (3.883). On the other hand the analysis also determined that "The knowledge shared between instructor and students in Moodle is timely" had the lowest mean which was 3.617 with general percent 72%.

Table 2. Learner knowledge sharing quality

Learner Knowledge sharing quality	The Answers%							
	Strongly disagree	Disagree	Neither	Agree	Strongly agree	Mean	SD	General Percent
The knowledge shared between instructor and students in Moodle is easy to understand.	9.574	1.064	4.255	58.511	26.596	3.915	1.099	78%
The knowledge shared between instructor and students in Moodle is relevant.	5.319	6.383	6.383	58.511	23.404	3.883	1.010	78%
The knowledge shared between instructor and students in Moodle is easy to understand.	7.447	3.191	11.702	54.255	23.404	3.830	1.060	77%
The knowledge shared between instructor and students in Moodle is accurate.	7.447	3.191	17.021	50.000	22.340	3.766	1.068	75%
The knowledge shared between instructor and students in Moodle is complete.	6.383	4.255	17.021	46.809	25.532	3.809	1.066	76%
The knowledge shared between instructor and students in Moodle is reliable.	6.383	6.383	7.447	54.255	25.532	3.862	1.069	77%
The knowledge shared between instructor and students in Moodle is timely.	9.574	5.319	15.957	52.128	17.021	3.617	1.123	72%

Table (3) shows the mean of all respondents' opinions about Self-Directed Learning, the highest mean of Self-Directed Learning was 3.85 related to "I have higher expectations for my learning performance" with general percent 77%, followed by" *I carry out my own study plan*" with mean equals to 3.75. On the other hand, the analysis also determined that "*I manage time well*" had the lowest mean which was 3.54 with general percent 71%.

Table 3. Self-Directed Learning

Self-Directed Learning	The Answers%							
	Strongly disagree	Disagree	Neither	Agree	Strongly agree	Mean	SD	General Percent
I carry out my own study plan.	8.3	7.5	17.4	34.4	32.4	3.75	1.22	75%
I seek assistance when facing learning problems.	7.5	14.2	14.2	40.3	23.7	3.58	1.207	72%
I manage time well.	10.7	9.1	20.2	35.6	24.5	3.54	1.252	71%
I set up my learning goals	7.9	7.1	17.8	42.3	24.9	3.69	1.155	74%
I have higher expectations for my learning performance.	5.5	7.5	15.8	39.1	32	3.85	1.122	77%

Table (4) shows the mean of all respondents' opinions about Motivated Learning, the highest mean of Motivate Learning was 3.78 related to "*Have motivation to learn*" & "*improve from my mistakes*" with general percent 76%, followed by "*I am open to new ideas*" with mean equals to 3.77. On the other hand, the analysis also determined that "*I like to share my ideas with others*" had the lowest mean which was 3.68 with general percent 74%.

Table 4. Motivate Learning

Motivate Learning	The Answers%							
	Strongly disagree	Disagree	Neither	Agree	Strongly agree	Mean	SD	General Percent
I am open to new ideas.	6.7	8.7	17.8	34.8	32	3.77	1.184	75%
Have motivation to learn.	6.3	8.7	15.8	39.1	30	3.78	1.154	76%
improve from my mistakes.	6.3	9.5	11.9	44.7	27.7	3.78	1.14	76%
I like to share my ideas with others.	7.1	9.9	16.2	41.1	25.7	3.68	1.166	74%

4.2 Path Analysis

The researchers made advanced analysis to study the relation between gender and knowledge sharing, also the overall sample was divided male and female according to the median after that the researchers calculated the mean for gender and tested the differences according to the parametric test (T test), in addition they studied the correlation between gender and knowledge sharing according to the parametric test (Pearson). For the relation between gender and knowledge sharing (table 5), the study revealed that male had sharing knowledge more than female in most of the variables because the mean of male was higher than female also the differences between both but statistically not significant, in addition there was a negative relation in most of the variables and statistically not significant between gender and knowledge sharing according to Pearson test.

Table 5. Path analysis for the relationship between gender and knowledge sharing

Learner Knowledge sharing quality		Mean	Std. Deviation	Correlation		Paired Samples Test	
				p	Sig.	t-test	Sig.
The knowledge shared between instructor and students in Moodle is easy to understand.	Male	3.980	1.159	-0.069	0.184	1.330	0.185
	Female	3.830	0.988				
The knowledge shared between instructor and students in Moodle is relevant	Male	3.980	1.024	-0.111	0.032	2.106	0.037
	Female	3.760	0.960				
The knowledge shared between instructor and students in Moodle is easy to understand.	Male	3.790	1.105	0.060	0.243	-0.976	0.330
	Female	3.900	0.986				
The knowledge shared between instructor and students in Moodle is accurate.	Male	3.800	1.081	-0.028	0.585	0.589	0.556
	Female	3.730	1.040				
The knowledge shared between instructor and students in Moodle is complete.	Male	3.810	1.111	-0.003	0.954	0.051	0.959
	Female	3.800	0.996				
The knowledge shared between instructor and students in Moodle is reliable.	Male	3.870	1.120	-0.007	0.898	0.161	0.873
	Female	3.850	0.980				
The knowledge shared between instructor and students in Moodle is timely.	Male	3.590	1.242	0.013	0.795	-0.353	0.725
	Female	3.630	0.959				

5. CONCLUSION

The aim of this study was to assess the role of learner's self-directed and motivated learning on the quality of their shared knowledge behavior, while they conduct teaching and learning with their instructors, and particularly their peers during e-learning. Considering that this study occurs with the target population of Ahlia University students, from the College of Business and Finance's 700 enrolled undergrad students; the empirical findings are not surprising to the authors of this study. It is important to take note here that e-learning environments at Ahlia University are composed of those technologies that aid in the teaching and learning; such as Moodle, where students log-on to attain blended e-learning experiences, smart board technologies, used during face-to-face traditional classroom teachings; but not limited to only such ICTs. This is since students also indulge in in-class participations while using their cell-phones in order to participate to instructors' teaching inquiries; like for instance when an instructor may ask students to check the definition of a term, since the best learning is from self-inquiring. Students at Ahlia University prefer using Google to do such searches, in order to participate to learn. However, other forms of ICTs are also used for e-learning but those technologies are more in association with social media (such as WhatsApp for out-of-class student-instructor communications, etc.) and m-commerce, or m-learning (Moodle thru cell-phones, etc.). It is no wonder why students expressed an influential role of self-directed and motivation for learning and knowledge sharing in e-learning environments, since such students are tech-savvy, as this is an observed phenomenon by the authors of this student, not only for the students of Ahlia University, or the citizens of Bahrain but in general for those who reside in the Gulf Corporation Council (GCC) region.

The empirical evidences in this study shed new knowledge on how further research is inevitably evident to further understand the key issues that pertain to e-learning in this part of the developing world. However, it does without saying that this study has few limitations. First, an online survey was hosted on Google Forms and it was cross-sectional data collection; whereas future research could assess this study's model with further details when assessing this instrument longitudinally. Second, the timeline given to conduct this research project was only one semester, while other issues remain under the pending list, e.g., using such a phenomenon using social media or thru m-learning means, should, and will be, assessed in future research. Also, considering that internet action is a trendy, but more importantly a serious research subject of concern, should also be assessed from the prism of e-learning, considering that students constantly are online, with lack of empirical evidence actually informing parents, to what extend such platforms are used for sharing knowledge versus wasting time establishing friendship ties.

Furthermore, this study has implications to theory and practice. From the point of view of theory, the model is viable for improving curriculum design, such that students' learning readiness and knowledge sharing should spear head a stronger drive for Ahlia University to use e-learning more comprehensively, though still with caution. Practically speaking, findings of this study set a benchmark for assuring quality in teaching and learning; with the emphasis on future research to also example to what extent students are motivated to share knowledge, so that such knowledge drives their imagination, creativity, hence innovation.

ACKNOWLEDGEMENT

The authors wish to thank the Ahlia University for all the support given to the research group, and special thanks to the founder Prof. Abdulla Yusuf Al Hawaj and the president Prof. Mansoor Ahmed Alaali.

REFERENCES

Allen, I. E., Seaman, J. (2013). Changing course: Ten years of tracking online education in the United States. *Babson Survey Research group and Quahog Research group,* LLC. Massachusettes, USA

American Society of Training and Development(ASTD), (2001). A vision of e-learning for America's workforce: *Report of the commission on technology and adult learning,* ED455432, Alexandria, VA.

Asvanund, A., Clay, K., Khrishnan, R.,Smith, M.D.(2004). An empirical analysis of network externalitiesin peer-to-peer music sharing networks. *Information Systems Ressearch,* Vol. 15, 155-174.

Baehr, C. (2012). Incorporating User Appropriation, Media Richness, and Collaborative Knowledge Sharing into Blended E-Learning Training. IEEE Transactions on Professional Commnuications, 55(2), 175-184.

Caspersen, J., Frølich, N., & Muller, J. (2017). Higher education learning outcomes – Ambiguity and change in higher education. *European Journal of Education*, 52(1), 8-19.

Chen-Yen, Y., Chin-Chung, T., Yen-Chiang, F. (2015). Understanding social capital, Team learning, members e-loyalty and knowledge sharing in virtual communities, *Total Quality Management*, Vol. 26 No.6, 619-631.

Clark, R. C. Mayer, R. E. (2011). E-learning and the science of instruction: Proven guidelines for consumers and designers of multimedia learning. san Francisco, CA: Jossey-Bass.

De Rouin, R. E., Fritsche, B., Salas, E. (2005). E-learning in organizations. Journal of Management, Vol. 31. No. 6, 920-940.

Honey, P., & Mumford, A. (1992). The Manual of Learning Styles. London: Peter Honey.

Islas, E., Perez, M., Rodriguez, G., Parades, I., Avila, I., Mendoza, M.(2007).E-learning tools evaluation and roadmap development for an electrical utility, *Journal of Theoritical and Applied Electronic Commerce Research*, Vol. 2, No.1, 63-75.

Karolak, M., & Razzaque, A. (2013). Virtual Communities: New Perspectives on Collaboration. *Studia Sociologica* UP, 5(1), 29-40.

Kunthi, R., Wahyuni, R., Al-Hafidz, M. U., & Sensuse, D. I. (2018). Exploring antecedent factors toward knowledge sharing intention in E-learning. 2018 IEEE Symposium on Computer Applications & Industrial Electronics (ISCAIE) (pp. 108-113). Penang, Malaysia: IEEE Xplore.

Kuo, Y., Ye, K. (2009). The causal relationship between service quality, corporate image and adults' learning satisfaction and loyalty: A study of preofessional training programmes in a Taiwanese vocational institute. *Total quality Management and Business Excellence*, Vol. 20, No.7, 749-762.

Kuo,Y. F. (2003).A study on service quality of virtual community websites, *Total Quality Management and Business Excellence*, Vol. 14, No.4, 461-473.

Liaw, S. S., Huang, H. M., Chen, G. D. (2007). Surveying instructor and learner attitudes toward e-learning, *Computer Education*, Vol. 49, No.4, 1066-1080.

Martinez-Caro, E., Cegarra-Navarro,J., Cepeda- Carrion,G.(2015). An application of the performance-evaluation model for e-learning quality in higher education. *Total Quality Management,* Vol. 26, No. 6, 632-647.

Moylan, C., & Razzaque, A. (2014). NYIT Education Survey. Retrieved June 28, 2017, from NYIT Education Survey: https://docs.google.com/forms/d/e/1FAIpQLSfpyS4KcpwsQJYvPKkwIoYY1Jk4ZUSTwUgLV5oGh2rlwEelBg/viewform

Moylan, C., & Razzaque, A. (2014). The Importance of students' National Culture on their Innovative Capacity: A Literature Review. IERG 9th International Conference 2014 - July 2 - 4, 2014. Vancouver, British Columbia, Canada: OGPR - Office of Graduate Programs and Research.

Selim, H. M. (2007). Critical success factors for e-learning acceptance: Confirmatory factor models. *Computers and Education*, Vol. 49, 396-413.

Sorgenfrei, C., Smolnik,S. (2016). The Effectiveness of E-Learning Systems: A Review of the Empirical Literature on Learner Control, *Decision Sciences Journal of Innovative Education*, Vol. 14, No. 2, 154-184.

Sousa, J. L., & Pinto, A. S. (2013). The integration of Information Systems Shared Services Center with E-Learning for Sharing Knowledge Capabilities. *Procedia Technology*, 9, 480 – 488.

Yilmaz, R. (2016). Knowledge sharing behaviors in e-learning community: Exploring the role of academic self-efficacy and sense of community. *Computers in Human Behavior*, 63, 373-382

ASSESSING OPEN-BOOK-OPEN-WEB EXAM IN HIGH SCHOOLS: THE CASE OF A DEVELOPING COUNTRY

Mary Ann Barbour El Rassi
Saint Jospeh University, Beyrouth

ABSTRACT

It has long been debated whether the Open-Book-Open-Web exam was useful and efficient as the traditional closed book exams. Some scholars and practitioners have doubted the efficiency and the possibility of cheating in the OBOW as it is not directly monitored. This paper tends to investigate the effectiveness of OBOW exams by comparing them with the traditional closed book exams to reject or confirm the possibility of cheating and efficiency. Two different exams were conducted in three high schools and in a developing country, whereas 307 students participated in it. The first exam was done during the midterm with closed books and well monitored. Then the second exam was done at the end of semester by adopting the OBOW method. Each exam was done in two phases. Phase one consisted of multiple choice questions and phase two consisted of a mini case analysis. The results obtained were compared with each other. Furthermore, a focus group chosen from the teachers and students were done in order to support the findings in addition to questionnaire that was sent by email. The results had showed that there is no difference when it comes to cheating but on the contrary, there is a difference in the quality of the learning outcome. This paper provides contribution to improving knowledge of e-learning for educational institutions developing countries.

KEYWORDS

Open Book Open Web Exams, Closed Book Exams, Traditional Exams, E-Learning, Developing Countries

1. INTRODUCTION

In a world where globalization is considered as a multidimensional phenomenon, e-leaning appears to be one of the emerging trends and is increasingly weighing not only in developed economies but also in developing economies (Broadfoot, 2016; Guàrdia, Crisp & Alsina, 2017). It is an innovative tool, mainly for subjects that necessitate multimedia and collaboration. As a result, the student profile has changed economically, culturally and socially as new online teaching techniques have emerged, encouraging students from all over the globe to enroll in e-distance learning (Joi, Camille & Krista, 2011). This has resulted in an impressive change in the educational technology. A transformation that has been of a major interest to scholars and journals recently which have lead to the creation of a stream of literature that examined this topic from different angles such as blended learning techniques and wholly online techniques among others (Sims,2004). Despite this new revolution, one facet of the academic life has hardly changed at all, which is the traditional exam model for conducting exams that still dominates. Given the fact, that most of the modern academic institutions use the internet platform to communicate with their students, exchange information such as lessons and homework's, they still fear conducting online exams and prefer to rely on a physical examination that is physically monitored. We cannot deny the fact that most of this new generation is an internet savvy and depend largely on the use of the net very often and easily in their daily activities. Therefore, this paper is centered on the following questions: Could Open-Book-Open-Web (OBOW) exams methods encourage cheating? Are there any advantages or disadvantages for the OBOW model that could be interesting to our era? Finding a suitable model in theory is not simple, especially that the objective of this research doesn't follow a mainstream management or have enough relevance in the literature in developing countries (El Rassi,2018, El Rassi & Harfouche, 2016). Most of the cases and research that were previously done were done in developed countries. Whereas developing countries differ from developed countries in terms of culture and ICT infrastructure. Our major objective in this research is to better understand the difference between a traditional examination compared to an OBOW in an era where it appears that there is a gap in literature when it comes to assessing and comparing those two methods in a developing country. For the purpose of this study, several dimensions were recognized and most important were two subjects: the possibility of cheating and the learning outcome. To accomplish the study's objectives outlined in this paper, we proceed by presenting a literature review concerning the employment of e-learning in the education system, the OBOW. Then we present the methodology employed, the results and the outcome that might result from this analysis.

2. LITERATURE REVIEW

2.1 E- Learning

E-learning has recently become more crucial for educational institutions especially in a world where the fierce competition has become global. The introduction and adoption of new methods and tools in educational institutions, such as delivery and support systems had a great effect on their performance (Broadfoot, 2016; Guàrdia, Crisp & Alsina, 2017). Before proceeding further, we aim at briefly defining e-learning. E-learning could be related to any mean that is enabled electronically or empowered by the use of digital technologies. Other scholars have defined it as a concept that refers to the use of applications, learning methodologies or processes. Thus, it is not easy to agree on a definition that could be adopted but we may summarize it as the employment of online technologies to facilitate the access to educational materials such as online courses or online exams. Several schools and higher educational institutions have realized what e-learning could bring to them in terms of added value as it could shape people's knowledge and enhance their skills. E-learning could take different shapes and types and could also be employed with different techniques. For example, three different models of e-learning could be implemented in an educational institution: adjunct, blended e-Learning and holly (Algahtani, 2011; Zeitouni & Milstein,2017). The "adjunct e-Learning" model refers to the e-learning that is adopted by educational institutions and considered as a supportive tool to the traditional old way. This could be used as a link between the staff, faculty, students and parents as well. In the "blended e-Learning" model, e-learning is blended with the traditional way of teaching. Which means delivering the course material explanation either in class or online and sometimes both (Algahtani, 2011; Zeitouni & Milstein,2017). The "wholly online" model refers to the course materials and explanations exchanged online between the instructor and students. It is a total virtual system. Regardless of the quite significant transformation in the education system, one feature has hardly changed at all and more precisely the exams methods. Indeed, final exams are still the standard that are conducted in a traditional way and that is by using a pen and a paper. This is a relic by itself, and most significantly, is considered as a measurement tool and the most frequently used in educational institutional nowadays. Nevertheless, several authors believe that the "open-book-open-web" (OBOW) examination could be considered as an interesting alternative to be used in assessing students' performance (Lam, Williams & Chua, 2007).

2.2 Traditional Examination versus OBOW

The traditional closed book examination methods are able to investigate the student's knowledge based on their learning (Broadfoot, 2016; Guàrdia, Crisp & Alsina, 2017). These methods are entirely based on the student's memory and is considered as an assessment instrument more likely to foster cramming/ data dumping, or deep learning (Macdonald, 2004). Thus, sometimes, these methods are not very efficient in assessing the students' knowledge and have been questioned by many scholars. Some scholars have argued that the closed books exam method does not always assess the deep understanding of the questioned concept because it allows, or perhaps requires, the student to retain all the required data and pump them in on the exam paper with "little knowledge retention" afterwards (Williams, 2004). In some cases, the students could answer the exam questions very efficiently under pressure but without being able to reference their information and may end up memorizing the concept rather than understanding it (Steve, Ferrante & Heppard,2016). It is also found that traditional exams sometimes result in higher scores but those same students might fail to pass the competitive recruitment exams when required because they lack the freedom of analyzing (Steve et al,2016). In order to overcome this issue, some scholars have encouraged educators to reassess their traditional format by proposing an Open –Book-Open –Web exam among other options (Lam et al,2007; Steve et al, 2016). Thus, a new trend had emerged where some universities for example have started to accommodate grades from traditional examination to OBOW to award program degrees. This new pattern called OBOW allows students to use electronic devices during their exam assessment. It reflects a major change and difference from the traditional format as it allows the student to take full advantage of all the available resources through the Web (Williams, 2004). This new pattern also prepares the students to acquire a new experience in answering the questions, which is reflective and enhances their future skills that could be required in a professional environment. Another interesting outcome of the OBOW examination is that questions represent "real world problems" which requires general knowledge and research and this minimizes the chance of copying or cheating by students (Williams, 2004; Steve et al,2016). Even though this looks quite easy to be done by cheating or copying, a submission procedure such as plagiarism software could be used to detect any academic fraud (Williams, 2004). The major idea in the OBOW model is to urge the students to think in a conceptual way to analyze and solve a given problem or mini-case and that is by employing their knowledge and expertise that they have acquired during their course of studies (Herrington & Herrington, 1998). In addition to the use of plagiarism software, and the time constraints that the student faces when conducting his exam (2 or 3 hours), it would be impossible for them to outsource or buy the solution as the accomplice should be first familiar with the subject which makes it more difficult for them to cheat. Therefore, may authors have considered that the OBOW exams represent an efficient way to engage students whether they are monitored for cheating as in the traditional exams or not (Williams, 2004; Steve et al,2016). For the purpose of our study, we have ttempted to carry out two different exams for high school students, OBOW and traditional exam that could help us better understand the differences between the two streams and detect if there is any difference in the results that could hint some cheating.

3. METHODOLOGY

The research was conducted in a high school that has adopted the web as a support to its teaching methods. Students can connect with their teachers, consult their lessons and grades as well through an application called "pronote". In addition to that, the school has initiated many electronic initiatives and had merged them into their learning processes for their students' access and use. OBOW was one of the concepts that were adopted by this school. Nevertheless, the tradition learning model is still valid. This paper is based on a comparison between the traditional method examination and the OBOW. Two methods that were conducted during the same year and for the same courses, in addition to a focus group that was selected from the students who had experienced both methods that are stated in our paper. The traditional exam was obviously conducted at school and monitored by instructors, while the OBOW exam was made outside the school on a day off and the due time limit was fixed on that day from 9 am to 12 noon. This had allowed the students to take the test at their convenience, fear free, and from any place they may chose to be comfortable with. And as the school is an international French school that usually have 3 different campuses in the same city, the students were divided into 3 different groups sharing in common the same educational level (senior high school year) and course offerings. The total number of students that participated in this exam was 307 students and their age range was expected to be 17-18. We have also considered that students who usually score a high GPA (higher than 16/20) are considered "excellent students". Those who score between 14 and 16 are considered" "Good students". Those who score between 10 and 14 are considered "average students". Those who score less than 10 are considered as "below average". This is based on the French system grading that is usually different than the English system where "excellent" for example could be equal to an "A" student. All three groups have taken the same exam, at the same time without knowing each other or without even knowing that the others have had a similar case. Then we compared the grades of OBOW exams of the students by the same group of students from the traditional closed books exams. As we have targeted three different campuses for the same school and the same courses taken, we have divided our groups into 3 main groups depending on their grades as mentioned before. Having three different locations have helped us a lot because students aren't supposed to be familiar with each other which could decrease the possibility of cheating when doing the first and second phase of the exam. Both exams consisted of two phases: the first phase consisted of 30 multiple choice questions and was estimated to be finished within 45 minutes, and students were given 60 minutes. While the second part consisted of a mini case where the students should be able to illustrate and analyze based on their personal knowledge. Once they start, they cannot keep it on hold or save and return to it later. While the second phase consisted of a mini-case analysis that was well-researched, well thought-out scripts along with a reflection that represents the value of this approach for the improvement of students' learning outcome. The second phase couldn't be copied as it was automatically passed through the plagiarism software and was based on a personal writing skill. After finishing the two exams, we then interviewed 3 focus groups to evaluate their experience and assessment of this new experience and compare the differences, if found, in the two adopted models in addition to their instructors. Each focus group was chosen from the three campuses based on their academic level. Then we carried on our study by sending a questionnaire by email to the same students. In an attempt to detect any possible cheating or difficulties encountered in part I of the OBOW exam, we have estimated that when a student took more than 5 minutes to answer a question, he could possibly be looking to find another alternative with other peers. Considering that 30 multiple choice questions needed between 45 to 60 minutes to be completed and there is no penalty in answering any question falsely, therefore we expected the student to pick any answer if he doesn't know it within a time frame of 2 minutes' maximum. A previous sample test was done online and in campus with the students to avoid any technical mistakes they might encounter.

4. RESULTS

In this section we will start by presenting the results of the exams conducted in both models and their grade scores. When the idea of OBOW was presented to the students at first, they showed some skepticism, confusion and surprise (James, Nonacs & Hayes, 2017). Not being used to conduct an exam online and without being monitored was a challenge for them. Then we proceed by choosing a focus group that equally represents all three schools.

Starting with the first phase of the exam, we have conducted two exams for the same course. One midterm that was done through traditional means, with a pen and paper, while the second was done during the final exam using the OBOW method.

Table 1 explains in details the results of the first phase that consisted of a "Multiple Choice Question" (MCQ) exam. It included 30 questions that equally varied between difficult, medium and easy. In the traditional method, pen and paper, students were monitored in class and the supervisors were able to detect any technical or cheating problems directly on the spot. In the OBOW method, the answers were chosen randomly for each student which means that cheating is not an easy task for them to do due to the time constraints unless they waste their time and efforts to make it happen. The below table explains the differences between the two methods and as follows: Instructors participated in screening the degree of cheating during the examination period. Cheating was evaluated based on the time the students took to finish their exam whether phase one or phase two.

Table 1. QCM exam results comparison

Phase 1 : Multiple choice questions (MCQ) - 30 questions- 60 mn							
	Type of exam	Grp1-execllent >16/20	Grp2-good From 14/20 to 16 /20	Grp3-average from 10/20 to 14/20	Grp4-below average < 10/20	Invalid	Numbers of students
School I	OBOW	32	40	24	6	0	102
	Traditional	38	47	16	1	1*	
School II	OBOW	44	33	17	3	1*	98
	Traditional	45	30	20	2	1*	
School III	OBOW	50	37	14	4	2*	107
	Traditional	53	29	22	3	0	
Total number of students	OBOW	126 (41%)	110 (35.8%)	55 (18%)	13 (6%)	3	307
	Traditional	136 (44.22%)	106 (34.5%)	58 (18.9%)	5(2%)	2	

*Cheating

In the first and second groups, the OBOW exam performance reached 41% for Group1 compared to 44.22% for the traditional model and 35.8% for the OBOW in group 2 compared with 34.5% in for the traditional model. Summing them together, 76.8% of the grades in OBW were slightly lower than 78.7% in the traditional model. This means that both methods were at the same level of efficiency in the MCQ exam. Cheating in the OBOW was less significant than in the traditional model as it was detected that they took more time (between 7 and 10 minutes) for answering some of the questions. This difference could be considered insignificant (3 for OBOW and 2 for the traditional model).

Table 2. Mini-case exam results comparison

Phase 2 : Mini case assessment- 90 minutes							
	Type of exam	Grp1-execllent (above 16/20)	Grp2-good\ (between 14/20 and 16 /20	Grp3-average between 10 and 14/20	Grp4-below average less than 10/20	Invalid cheating	Numbers of students
School I	OBOW	35	34	31	1	1*	102
	Traditional	28	33	37	4	0	
School II	OBOW	46	32	18	2	0	98
	Traditional	44	30	20	2	2*	
School III	OBOW	41	39	22	5	0	107
	Traditional	29	32	39	6	1*	
Total number of students	OBOW	122 (40%)	105(34.2%)	71 (23.1%)	8 (2.6%)	1	307
	Traditional	101 (33%)	95(31%)	96 (31.2%)	12(4%)	3	

*Cheating

In the second phase, the students were offered a mini case and were expected to have a personal contribution. Unless the student didn't attend the previous seminars, he cannot fulfill the requirements and analyze the case study. For the same reasons as in phase I, a student that has been detected to be wasting time or encountering some technical difficulties is considered either cheating or having technical problems. The OBOW exam performance reached 40% for group1 compared to 33% for the traditional model and 34.2% in OBOW for group 2 compared to 31% for the traditional model. Summing them together, 74.2 of the grades in OBW were scattered between group 1 and group 2 which is higher than the sum of those two groups in the traditional model (64%). While cheating in the OBOW was less significant than in the traditional model (1 student in the OBOW took more than 10 minutes in answering 2 questions). And a higher number of failing students that scored below the average were identified in the traditional exam.

We proceeded our investigating by choosing a focus group of 9 students and three teachers. Three students and one teacher from each institution in order to evaluate their experience and perspectives regarding the pros and cons of this OBOW exam and to note their objections, if any. The results of those focus groups had helped us to better frame several factors. We have identified those factors and organized them in a questionnaire that we had randomly sent to a group of students from the same sample (sample of 307 students). They were solicited by emails, and a set of 12 questions were asked and the students were expected to answer on a likert scale from 1 to 5 such as 1= strongly disagree and 5 =strongly agree (see table 3).

Table 3. Traditional closed book exam versus OBOW exams: a gap analysis n=66)

	Traditional model	OBOW	Diff
Fear of misuse (facing technical problems etc...)	3.6	3.9	0.3
Intellectually challenging and quality outcome	3.15	4.25	1.1
Timing and location convenience	3.3	4.51	1.21
Matched with student's learning style (positive outcome)	2.88	4.8	1.92
Exam content engaging	3.1	4.87	1.77
Cheating opportunity	2.7	2.85	0.15

While the students were well informed ahead of time about the OBOW exam that will be taken by the end of the semester, they expressed some fears and concerns at the beginning especially that the exam was supposed to be conducted individually and off campus. Their major concern was that in case they encounter any technical problem, they will be all by themselves and could not complete the task on time. Despite these concerns, some others welcomed the idea and considered it as an opportunity and a new challenge to accomplish the required tasks (for a reason or another) and thought that it would be easier than the traditional method. The difference in questions concerning "fear of misuse" resulted in a difference of (+ 0.3) which could be considered as insignificant (see table 3).

"I felt relaxed and stress free in doing it at home and at my convenience, even though I thought it would be complicated. On the contrary, it wasn't at all" (Student fro group 1-school 1)

"I felt more comfortable doing the exam at home. I thought it would be more difficult when it is an OBOW exam, but it was ok" Student from (student from group 2- school 2)

"This is very innovative and different from what we usually see. I find it interesting even though I have encountered some difficulties at the beginning and the timing was short for me" (Student from group 3- school 3).

The majority of students in the focus groups expressed their enthusiasm for completing the first part of the exam online and have described it as a challenging and relaxing experience beside the quality of the exam. This could lead us to conclude that the OBOW exam approach seems to be quite interesting in such cases (Guardia, Crisp & Alsina, 2017). When students were given part II of the final exam online, which requires them to conduct a personal analysis based on their class lectures during the semester, they were given the choice to do it in a group of two people or personally. Most of the students worked on it solely, ninety percent of the students worked individually and only 30 students presented their work in common. So we ended up having 30 students who worked as pairs. This was quite interesting for us as we expected them all to work in groups as this will give them an opportunity to depend on the other peer in their group in case they do not want to make an effort and be serious about it. They literally said that they felt that this had given them the opportunity to do an individual reflection and a peer-based approach. They were impressed with the outcome of this new experience as it gave them more flexibility and an opportunity to be more creative in their analysis by showing their skills and competences and that is by going out of the traditional box which they considered as "intellectually challenging" (+1.1). (see table 3).

"Being able to search the web when needed gave us the chance to relate our acquaintance and skills to real challenges whilst bringing in merits. This is different than memorizing and dictating what we have memorized. We feel more self dependent and gained more credit by adding our personal touch" (Student from group 1- school 1)

"It was an excellent experience because it was a learning-oriented concept that encourages a personal critical thinking"(student from group 3- school 2)

"It is a good idea. This gave me more space to think, write and express my personal opinion to a subject that could be broadly and endlessly discussed" (student from group 2- school 3).

"it is a summative assessment that allowed me to draw on all that I have learnt and relate what was relevant". (Student from group 2- school 2).

While intellectually challenging and quality outcome emerged as an important indicator, another factor emerged to be very important and in favor of OBOW: "timing and location convenience" (+1.21), as most of the participants appreciated the fact that, with an OBOW, they can easily manage their exams timetable to better fit their schedule:

"Giving me the opportunity to do the exam at my convenience and in a stress free environment is awesome and very helpful". (Student from group 2- school 2).

In addition, when asked about the outcome of this new method and how possibly could be an added value and consistent with their learning style, most of them expressed a positive outcome (+1.92) and an exam content engaging (+1.77).

The last topic that was discussed with them was the possibility of cheating. And because we have anticipated the fact that they might not be very open in this subject, we have questioned their professors as they are usually monitoring and correcting exams. When doing so, we have noticed a sense of appreciation. Even though students ranked higher in the traditional exam in part I, the resulted outcome of part II was quite impressive for them and the results in table 3 show an insignificant difference of (+0.15).

"I expected them to work together as groups as it would facilitate their tasks and minimize their efforts. I am impressed that most of them chose to do it individually" (instructor from school 1).

"They have done an excellent job. I can feel their enthusiasm. The outcome is a great relief for me as I see excellent results in phase II compared to a traditional exam. Which means, working home and at their convenience could help them to give more in a fear free environment" (instructor from school 3).

"We used to think that we have to invigilate assessment because it's the only way we know for sure that they aren't cheating". (instructor from school 2).

5. DISCUSSION

Our main concern when examining the students results in high school and comparing the two models was to investigate further the credibility of the OBOW versus the traditional model. Evidently, we were neither after harassing them nor filtering them. The progress in the teaching methods that appeared recently had driven many scholars to identify the best way to examine students and the OBOW was one of those methods (Fluck, 2009). When observing the performance of the models (Tables 1 and 2), it is observed that there isn't much difference in the results. As for the cheating, we have suspected 4 cases in the OBOW based on the software results and tracking system compared to 5 cases in the traditional exam that were detected by the instructors. Comparing the results together, we cannot point out that cheating was more evident in any of the models nor in any of the two phases. The results in the second phase show an evident improvement with the OBOW model where the students had all the resources available in an exam that required a personal effort and was made at their convenience in a stress free environment. Based on the above stated results, we observe that the OBOW method is efficient if not more than the traditional method at least the same. We noticed that cheating has been almost at the same level, the results in the QCM were almost the same while the mini case study gave better results and better reflection from the students (Williams, 2004). This opposes what has been stated by scholars and doubted by practitioners that the information technology could be considered as canalization for cheating or dishonest behavior (McMurtry, 2001) and that it could be a source of confusion for the participants. On the contrary, such method can pave the way for students to get ready for the real-world problems by giving them more motivation and confidence in a stress free environment and helping them in get engaged with multi-media and depth in learning as four important factors had proven to be as of importance for the OBOW exams: Intellectually challenging and quality outcome, timing and location convenience, matched with student's learning style (positive outcome) and exam content engaging.

6. CONCLUSION

As the traditional closed-books exams still dominate most of the educational institutions, it I sometimes necessary to look in a different angle as the business world need for a knowledge economy opens the probability for new proposed models such e-learning and more specifically OBOW. OBOW is more compatible with constructive learning that smoothes the progress of a different type of examination that can harness the offered multimedia today to engage the students in a better experience. This can improve the results and the depth of the students' experience and learning. While there will always be a number of students who will tend to cheat, whether in a closed or OBOW model, the OBOW is a manageable model that could be managed on campus or off campus and could provide a more convenient and an efficient way to improve the learning quality. Therefore, cheating is not a barrier for adopting OBOW and could be a better mean for assessing the student's capacities to comprehend the topic and replicate it. Like any other research, this study has some limitations. The current study could be carried out on larger sample to take into consideration different cases and analyzed with a quantitative method to have a more solid result. Furthermore, a comparison between females and males' attitude would be interesting as several studies have that in the online world, females' attitude might differ from male attitudes (Lian & Yen, 2014).

REFERENCES

Algahtani, A,2011. Evaluating the Effectiveness of the e-Learning Experience in Some Universities in Saudi Arabia from Male Students' Perceptions. *Diss. Durham University.*

Broadfoot, P., 2016. Assessment for Twenty-First-Century Learning: The Challenges Ahead. *Learning, Design, and Technology, Springer*, pp. 1-23.

El Rassi, M, 2018. Firm's Size Effect in the e-Service Industry: The Case of a Developing Country. *AIS electronic library (AISeL).*https://aisel.aisnet.org/cgi/viewcontent.cgi?article=1013&context=ecis2018_rp

El Rassi, M. A. B., & Harfouche, A., 2016. E-Business Assimilation Levels in Lebanon. In Information and Communication Technologies in Organizations and Society. *Springer, Cham.* pp. 141-160.

Herrington ,J. and Herrington, A.,1998.Authentic assessment and multimedia: how university students respond to a model of authentic assessment", *Higher Education Research and Development,* vol.no.17, 3, pp.305–322.

James, C. K., Nonacs, P., and. Hayes, D.,2017. Evaluating an Open-Exam Approach to Engaging Students in Evolutionary Paradoxes: Cheating to Learn. *The American Biology Teacher*, vol. 79 .2, pp. 144-148.

Joi, L. M., Camille, D. D.& Krista, G, 2011. E-Learning, Online Learning and Distance Learning Environments: Are they the Same? *Internet High Educ*, Vol, no.14, pp. 129-135.

Lam, W, Williams, J.B. and Chua, A.Y.K, 2004. Exams: Harnessing the Power of ICTs to Enhance Authenticity. *Educational Technology & Society*, vol. no10, 3, pp. 209-221.

Lian, J. W. and Yen, D. D.,2014. Online Shopping Drivers and Barriers for Older Adults: Age and Gender Differences". *Computers in Human Behavior*, vol.no.37, pp. 133-143.

Macdonald, J. ,2004. Developing Competent e-Learners: The Role of Assessment. *Assessment & Evaluation in Higher Education* vol.no.29.2, pp.215-226

McMurtry, K., 2001. E-Cheating: Combating a 21st Century Challenge. *The Journal Technological Horizons In Education,* vol. o .29.4 .

Sims, R., 2004. Trends, Fads and Futures: 21 Years of Educational Multimedia: Where Have We Got to, and Where Should We Go?. *Proceedings of World Conference on Educational Multimedia, Hypermedia and Telecommunications. Chesapeake*, VA: AACE, pp.3755-3766.

Steve, G., Ferrante, C. J., and Heppard, K.A.,2016. Using Open-Book Exams to Enhance Student Learning, Performance, and Motivation.

Williams, J. B., 2004. Creating Authentic Assessments: A Method for the Authoring of Open Book Open Web Examinations. In R. *Atkinson, C. McBeath, D. Jonas-Dwyer & R. Phillips (Eds), Beyond the comfort zone: proceedings of the 21st ASCILITE Conference*, pp. 934-937.

Zeitouni, N. and Milstein, I., 2017. The Role of Social Support in Teachers' Intention to Use ICT Tools in Their Classrooms. *Management of Engineering and Technology.*

CRISS: A CLOUD BASED PLATFORM FOR GUIDED ACQUISITION, EVALUATION AND CERTIFICATION OF DIGITAL COMPETENCE

Igor Balaban, Danijel Filipovic and Marko Peras
University of Zagreb, Faculty of Organization and Informatics
Pavlinska 2, 42000 Varazdin, Croatia

ABSTRACT

This paper deals with a problem of digital competence acquisition and certification. In order to overcome the problem of still inadequate number of digitally competent students and the tools that merely focus on skills acquisition, this paper proposes the CRISS platform which is a unique cloud-based digital learning solution, based on the most advanced pedagogical methodologies and technological solutions Its purpose is to allow guided acquisition, evaluation and certification of digital competence in primary and secondary schools in Europe. The platform is based on the CRISS Digital Competence (DC) Framework created as an adaptation of a well-established European digital competence framework, DigComp. The platform's architecture includes seven different modules that support the CRISS DC Framework and employ advanced techniques such as learning analytics, intelligent tutoring and certification. The platform will enable teachers to track the work of their students acquiring the digital competence with a detail insight into their learning paths. CRISS platform is piloted in around 90 schools, with 600 teachers and 3400 students during the school year 2018/2019.

KEYWORDS

Digital Competence, Certification, e-Learning Platform, Learning Analytics, Intelligent Tutoring

1. INTRODUCTION

Digital competence is one of the eight key competences for lifelong learning identified by the European Parliament and Council of the European Union (2006). It is a transversal key competence, which, as such, enables the acquisition of other key competences (e.g. mathematics, communication in mother tongue and foreign languages, cultural awareness, etc.). Also, according to Ferrari (2012) and Calvani et al. (2008) digital competence is a "set of knowledge, skills and attitudes (including abilities, strategies, values & awareness) that are required when using ICT and digital media to perform tasks; solve problems; communicate; manage information; etc." There is a need to support citizens in the acquisition and development of digital competence, as well as schools, teachers, learners, parents and educational actors with a series of tools that could facilitate the implementation of media and digital competence courses and interventions.

European Commission (2013) reports that only 30% of students in the EU can be considered as digitally competent. To address this problem and create a common language between the worlds of education and labour market, the European Commission developed and published in 2013 the European Digital Competence Framework for Citizens (hereafter DigComp) (Ferrari, 2013). However, DigComp is by all means a generic framework that needs adaptation for different levels of education and for different national context (Ferrari, 2013).

With that respect, an EU funded research project CRISS has been established in order to develop a standard methodological framework and the online platform for digital competence acquisition, evaluation and certification for students of primary and secondary school.

This paper describes the model and implementation of a CRISS platform which is a flexible, scalable and cost-effective cloud-based digital learning ecosystem that delivers a user-driven and adaptive technological solution to allow the guided acquisition, evaluation and certification of digital competence in primary and secondary education, and scalable to other educational levels.

2. CRISS DIGITAL COMPETENCE FRAMEWORK

As indicated in Kluzer (2015), DigComp framework is widely used across Europe as a reference framework for digital competence. It was inspired by three existing frameworks: The Common European Framework of Reference for Languages (CEFR), the European Qualification Framework (EQF) and the e-Competence framework for ICT professionals, from which four of DigComp's five framework areas were taken (Kluzer, 2015).

In order to adapt DigComp to enable digital competence acquisition, evaluation and certification for students of primary and secondary school, an innovative CRISS Digital Competence framework (hereafter CRISS DC Framework) was developed (Guardia et al, 2017). It follows the "integration pedagogy" concept introduced by Roegiers (2010) as a valid approach to developing competence assessment. The pedagogy of integration focuses on learning (mastering) competences, as opposed to the simple juxtaposition of skills (Roegiers, 2000). The CRISS DC Framework is aligned with DigComp and decomposes digital competence into 5 Areas and 12 sub-competences. Each sub-competence is composed of a set of performance criteria (PC) that translate the sub-competences into more specific elements of what a student should be able to demonstrate. Each performance criterion is composed of a set of indicators that provide measurements or conditions required to interpret the evidence in terms of performance criteria and competence attainment.

CRISS DC Framework proposes the development of Competence Assessment Scenarios (CAS) (see Figure 1) with activities and tasks enabling the assessment of one or more performance criteria. Teachers are responsible to plan the learning, to provide feedback and to evaluate activities and tasks. The activities and tasks are retrieved by the CRISS repository and teachers can apply or adapt them in their curricula. The students should realize the activities by performing one or more tasks and generate products (the evidences) as a result of a task that can be used to prove the acquisition of a specific competence.

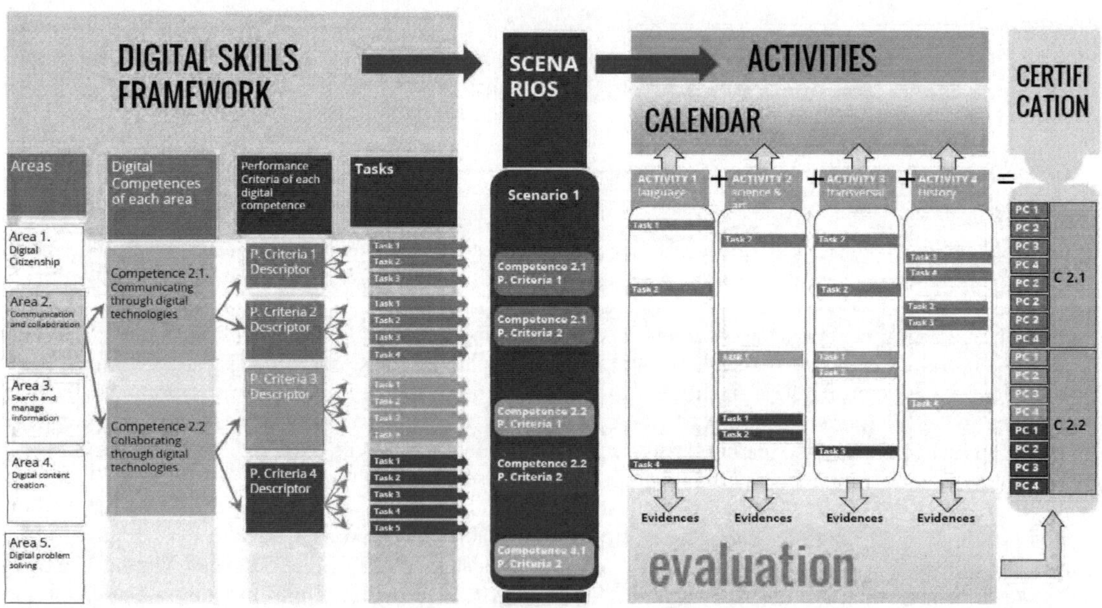

Figure 1. Overview of the CRISS certification process

The assessment of digital competence is performed through two types of interventions: human and technological. Human interventions are carried out by teachers and students using tools like Rubrics, Check Lists, Scales, etc., that will be automatically generated by the CRISS platform and customised by teachers. All these tools are created to be easily used for teacher, self and/or peer evaluation. The technological intervention is executed by the CRISS platform which is set to track the students while working in their assigned activities and collect relevant information i.e. the indicators of the evaluation of the evidences.

3. RESEARCH BACKGROUND

In order to design a cloud-based learning infrastructure for acquisition, evaluation and certification of digital competence based on the current CRISS DC framework we approached the literature review to reveal any existing implementations of similar platforms that deal with competence acquisition, evaluation and/or certification. The most relevant electronic journal databases were selected and searched to provide a comprehensive bibliography of research papers on digital competence assessment. The selected sources include IEEE Xplore Digital Library, ScienceDirect, Web of Science, Springer Link, Taylor & Francis, and Wiley Online Library.

To search the sources, we used phrases "digital competence", "competence certification", "competence assessment", "competence acquisition" and "competency measurement". In sources that offer advanced search, we used these phrases with operator OR. Additional filters were used to limit results to area related to computer science, education or both. Finally, through the application of inclusion and exclusion criteria, 136 related papers, published between 2001 and 2018, were selected.

Review of these papers showed that while many of them focus on theoretic models of digital competence assessment, very few of them deal with practical ICT implementations of digital competence assessment, let alone certification of digital competence. We describe some of them very briefly.

The first example is Ikanos project by the Basque Government who uses the DigComp framework to deploy their Digital Agenda (Kluzer, 2015). This includes a free online testing tool for self-assessment based on DigComp's five areas of digital competence grouped in 3 thematic blocks. The test addresses these blocks by asking about 30 questions of different type (yes/no, single or multiple choice, scoring etc.). Depending on the respondent's answers, additional information about local resources and initiatives related to specific questions may be given. The test produces a personalized "Digital profile report" in 4 sections: (1) Overall assessment score (basic, intermediate, advanced with a related visualization) and a short explanation about its meaning; (2) Visualization of the results according to DigComp's 3-level scale; (3) Aggregate result for each of the DigComp's 5 areas of competence, with a visualization and a description of each competence area content; and (4) Results for each one of DigComp's 21 digital competences.

The second example (Kluzer, 2015) is Skillage which is an online tool for ICT skills assessment. It contains about 100 questions grouped into five competence areas. Questions were originally identified according to Skillage's employability orientation and aligned to DigComp. Since 2012, about 10,000 tests have been gathered each year, mostly during the Get Online Week organized by Telecentre Europe and now part of the eSkills for Jobs campaign of the European Commission.

ACTIC - *Acreditación de Competencias en TIC* (ICT competences accreditation) is the digital competence certification system for citizens 16 years old and above, developed by regional government of Catalunya. Currently, it contains eight competences and provides three certification levels (basic, intermediate, advanced). ACTIC certification is delivered by Catalan telecentres network of Punt TICs, member of Telecentre Europe. ACTIC was one of the cases studied in DigComp's preparation process (Kluzer, 2015).

Some other examples involve the e-Schools project by Croatian Academic and Research Network to support the professional development of teachers, the ECDL certification which is focused on tools and applications which cover competences defined in DigComp framework and the French platform PIX that provides all citizens with opportunity to evaluate and certify their digital competence.

Another example is from Florian-Gaviria et al (2013) who propose an adaptive evaluation engine architecture implemented in their AEEA software. This approach is aligned with the European Qualification Framework (EQF). For each competence, this framework provides a set of capabilities that need to be proven for each level. This framework enables learning providers to adapt their offers toward achieving these capabilities in learners and certify learning outcomes accordingly. The arrangement of learning activities represents a scenario for moderating and guiding students learning process. This scenario can be visualized as a matrix of learning activities and competences. Each entry in this matrix represents an expected competence level for an activity. A row of this matrix defines the steps from the initial qualification level (prerequisite) to the final expected qualification level (learning outcome) through one or more assessment activities. (Florian-Gaviria et al, 2010).

The above described examples were thoroughly analysed and will present a backbone for the design of a novel CRISS platform for digital competence acquisition, evaluation and certification.

4. CRISS PLATFORM

When designing the CRISS platform the main aim was to implement requirements from the CRISS DC Framework and to employ innovative pedagogical elements, guidance for users and gamification.

CRISS platform follows a modular design with two main parts: the CRISS Core and the CRISS Certification and Learning Analytics (Figure 2). The different modules, sub-modules, components and elements can be plugged in and unplugged from the CRISS Core. Such approach also allows a more flexible approach to the market, as the different components can be used separately, depending on the specific needs of a potential client.

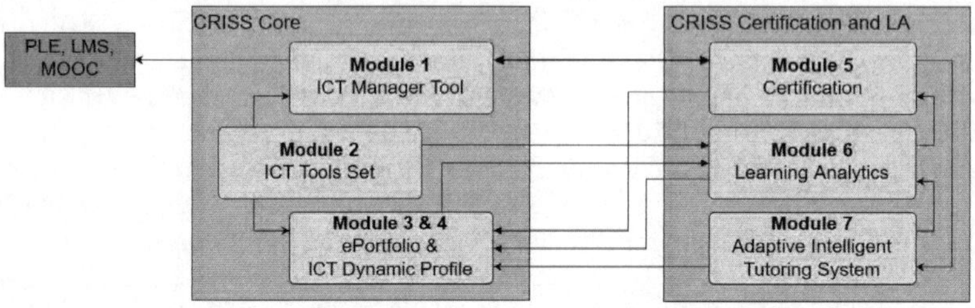

Figure 2. High-level overview of the CRISS platform

CRISS core comprises of four modules which allow teachers and students to work and perform their tasks: (1) ICT Manager Tool (module 1) allows the user management, activities planning and assessment (together with the ePortfolio and the Certification Module, submodule A); (2) EPortfolio (module 3) showcases the students' progress and assessments; (3) ICT dynamic profile of each student (module 4); and (4)ICT tools set (module 2) allows the users to create unique content.

Within Certification and Learning Analytics we distinguish among: (1) Certification of Digital Competence (module 5); (2) Learning Analytics (module 6) which provides insights useful for the certification and personalization of the learning process and (3) Adaptive Intelligent Tutoring System (module 7) which infers adequate actions meant to fill learning gaps during students' ICT lifecycle.

In the next sections we describe the CRISS platform modules in detail.

4.1 Module 1: ICT Manager Tool

On the one hand, this module allows to perform general functions such as registration and user management, permission management, etc., and on the other, it offers specific modules for managing activities related to acquisition, curriculum planning, evaluation and certification of digital competence and sub-competences.

It includes the following submodules:

1. Administration - designed for user creation, management of roles and permissions, credentials etc. It is composed by several submodules: User Manager Module; Data Connector Module; Authentication System and SSO; User API.
2. ICT Planning - designed for teachers to create, individually or in teams, their lesson plans (calendar, dates of assessments, in order to provide the students with the necessary Scenarios, activities and tasks to acquire the Digital Competence).
3. Scenarios Creation - allows CRISS partners and teachers to create the scenarios, activities and tasks for the acquisition of digital competence. It is connected to the Certification Module in order to allow teachers to align their scenarios with the criteria established in the CRISS DC Framework. There is a set of predefined scenarios available, each including a set of activities and the relevant evaluation tools. Each scenario covers a certain level of DC acquisition which is depicted to a "Certification Weight", according to the number and type of included activities and tasks. The user is able to search for specific scenarios based on specific criteria i.e. by subject, area, level of difficulty etc.
4. Evaluation and Assessment - provides all the necessary features and tools for the assessment and evaluation of Scenarios, tasks and activities, and, through this, for the assessment and certification of Digital Competence.

4.2 Module 2: ICT Tools Set

This module offers a set of ICT Tools that enable users to enhance their experience and achieve their pedagogical objectives by using different ICT tools. It allows teachers to include different tools in their courses and lessons as is or to use them to create educational experiences. Students will use them for their individual or collaborative productions related to the tasks assigned by their teachers.

These ICT tools include: (1) Social Network, where students and teachers participate in groups, post comments, express preferences or create circles of relationships; (2) Magellan, a visual programming environment enabling an author to quickly create any type of interactive applications including 3D, VR, AR, from serious gaming to Location Based Experiences; (3) Portabily, a tool for the creation of custom-made multimedia content in multiple formats; and (4) a selection of External ICT tools such as mind maps, timelines, etc.

4.3 Module 3: EPortfolio

This module allows students to recollect and show the evidences of their learning through their entire educational life (Lorenzo & Ittelson, 2005), and to become reflective learners (Stefani et al., 2007). It is the place where all student activities converge: work, evaluation communication with peers and teachers, behaviour, collaborations, interests, etc. In addition, it collects and shows the certificates and badges. The students' portfolios follow them throughout their academic lives and beyond.

On the other hand, for a teacher, this is a place where they can access and follow their students' work and follow progress, organize and share their contents and educational materials.

4.4 Module 4: ICT Dynamic Profile

The enrichment of the student's ePortfolio with the ICT dynamic profile provides a 360 degrees picture of the students daily learning activity, considering among this activity not only the results of tasks, exams or group work but also the students' behavior, interests and social attitudes. This dynamic and continuously evolving picture allows teacher and students for themselves to know their strengths and weaknesses based on the objective measurements, to detect opportunities, to improve and progress, to understand and recommend training actions, to enhance such evolution and to understand different topics.

The ICT Dynamic profile offers the teachers and students the visualization of the data related to the results of evaluation and assessments, the level of acquisition of digital competence, and the certification of digital competence, including sub-competences.

4.5 Module 5: Certification

The Certification module is a core module for CRISS as it implements the criteria and indicators determined in the CRISS DC Framework for evaluation and certification of digital competence. It enables the teachers to evaluate the student's performance throughout the learning procedure based on the aforementioned criteria and indicators and provides the ICT Manager Tool with the criteria and feedback to create scenarios, activities, tasks and evaluations according to the CRISS DC Framework.

The certification module is based on CRISS DC Framework and follows example from Vuorikari et al. (2016). Also, the works by Hickey (2012) and Sullivan (2013) were used as basis for implementing Open Badges into the system as part of the certification of sub-competences and areas of CRISS DC Framework.

4.6 Module 6: Learning Analytics (LA)

The Learning Analytics module (LA) constantly gauges students' assessment data and provides teachers with a comprehensive tool to monitor student progress, lesson plan delivery and assessment records and various other data in real time allowing them to navigate seamlessly through comprehensive key metrics to help them get insights, draw conclusions and take appropriate actions. Teachers will be able to design and improve the learning activities for a specific student by taking into consideration personalized insights delivered by the LA.

The works of Williams (2014) and Redecker & Johannessen (2013) were used, which cover the use of learning analytics and data mining for assessment and accreditation in educational context, as a basis for implementing this module.

4.7 Module 7: Adaptive Intelligent Tutoring System (AITS)

The Adaptive Intelligent Tutoring System module provides feedback to students and teachers (alerts, notifications, suggestions) on how to adjust the learning path of each individual student to improve their learning experiences and outcomes. It provides individualized gap analysis between student's achievement to date and the progressive/final certification threshold. It also enables teachers to proactively identify students at risk and spot their areas of improvements. For students, it will enable automatic matching of their required academic assistance and personal coaching need with the tutors' profiles.

This module follows examples from Adaptive Hypermedia Systems such as InterBook (Brusilovsky et al, 1998) and INSPIRE (Papanikolaou et al, 2003); Adaptive Information Filtering systems like MLTutor (Smith and Blandford, 2003); and Intelligent Tutoring Systems like German Tutor (Heift, 2000).

5. TESTING THE CRISS PLATFORM

The CRISS platform is piloted in around 90 primary and secondary schools during the school year 2018/2019, with 600 teachers and 3400 students in Italy, Spain, Croatia, Greece, Sweden, and Romania. The main objective of the pilot is to test the effectiveness and acceptance of the CRISS platform.

The piloting activities require teachers to apply or to adapt Competence Assessment Scenarios (CAS) within their curricula (i.e. Mathematics, Geography, etc.). A CAS is a set of activities and tasks that correspond to performance criteria established in the DC Framework (see Fig. 1) stored in the CRISS platform. Teachers are responsible to assign tasks to their students based on CAS within their subjects and to plan their learning, to provide feedback and to evaluate activities and tasks. In such way, digital competence acquisition is horizontally integrated into curriculum across number of different subjects. The students are allowed to use any ICT tool they find appropriate to realize the task and generate and upload content (the evidences) into the CRISS platform as a result of a task that can be used to prove the acquisition of a specific competence.

The completion of a set of tasks within a CAS is automatically mapped by the CRISS platform to a completion of an accompanied performance criteria (PC) that leads towards the acquisition of a sub-competence. On the other hand, teachers are notified by the Intelligent Tutoring System in case a student is about to fail his/her tasks. The platform can suggest teacher to replace tasks if possible.

The CRISS platform is also designed to automatically generate a Certificate of completion if a student has acquired a complete DC, or a Certificate of progress in case student has acquired at least one sub-competence.

At the end of the pilot, in June 2019, once the participants will be using the CRISS platform for a reasonable number of months, the platform will be tested for usability and sustainability by employing and adapting the Expectation Confirmation Model originally developed by Bhattacherjee (2001). Besides taking into account the number of certificates issued, a series of qualitative and quantitative tests will be performed to measure the success of its implementation and to explain the impact of such approach on both, students and teachers, by adapting the well-known DeLone&McLean Model for assessing a successful implementation of an information system (DeLone and McLean, 2016).

6. DISCUSSION

From the research literature, we found that skills or competence assessment platforms are very rare and are mostly based on self-assessments. Furthermore, none of the platforms introduced digital competence to primary or secondary schools, nor they imply advanced learning technologies such as intelligent systems, digital badges or learning analytics.

However, a similarity between CRISS platform and other platforms for digital competence certification is evident. CRISS also follows the idea of a variety of self-assessments and teacher assessments as introduced in Kluzer (2015). Certification elements are similar to those on other platforms. The adaptation and scenarios' similarities can be found with AEEA software introduced by Florian-Gaviria et al (2013).

Despite similarities, there are also some differences that reflect the novelty of CRISS approach:

1. CRISS platform implements CRISS DC Framework developed for primary and secondary schools.
2. It follows the integration pedagogy concept as introduced by Roegiers (2010).
3. Process of digital competence assessment, evaluation and certification is fully integrated in the school's curriculum. It involves teachers, students and CRISS platform.
4. EPortfolio allows students to collect evidence and showcase their work and to become active learners.
5. Learning analytics is employed for comprehensive monitoring of students by their teachers, and also to give students a full insight into their current progress across 5 areas and 12 sub-competences.
6. Gamification elements are introduced with Open badges, so students are awarded with a badge for each sub-competence they achieve.
7. The CRISS platform introduces guidance concept by utilizing an Intelligent Tutoring System for both students and teachers. Both students and teachers receive alerts, notifications and suggestions from the system in respect to current students' progress and their learning path. That way students can be self-guided but also monitored and guided by their teachers.

7. CONCLUSION

This paper describes the original approach related to the modelling and implementation of a platform for guided acquisition, evaluation and certification of digital competence in primary and secondary schools. CRISS platform offers a new and innovative approach that covers the need of a complete model and ecosystem for the development, evaluation and accreditation of the digital competence (understood as a wider approach than just to evaluate digital skills as most of other existing models are providing).

It facilitates user-driven innovation by allowing teachers and students to become the core focus of the knowledge generation process. Moreover, teachers are able to create new assets to be used in the tools or to embrace novel approaches to utilize existing educational content and learning tools. At the same time, harnessing student's experience analytics enriches the entire process of deploying, analysing, learning, and adapting based on the actual student performance indicators, thus allowing them to co-create the next generations of educational approaches and learning frameworks.

In technological sense, the platform is modular which in return enables it to be flexible and scalable by adding modules as necessary to the CRISS Core. Its first part, CRISS core solution is composed of a set of services and new learning experiences in the context of digital competence and digital curriculum portfolio, that enable acquisition and evaluation of digital competence. CRISS Certification and Learning analytics is a support component to offer real-time assessment, analysis and tutoring based on a cutting-edge technology such as Big data and data analytics.

Given the pioneering nature of the proposed CRISS platform, it is necessary to perform additional research to confirm the efficiency of the proposed CRISS platform along with the underlying CRISS DC Framework and to identify needs and possibilities for its further improvements.

ACKNOWLEDGEMENT

This study was carried out as a part of "Demonstration of a scalable and cost-effective cloud-based digital learning infrastructure through the Certification of digital competence in primary and secondary schools" (CRISS) project funded by European Union's Horizon 2020 research and innovation program under Grant Agreement No 732489.

Each of the CRISS platform module was developed by the following CRISS project partners:

- Modules 1, 3 and 4 - MyDocumenta (Spain)
- Module 2 - EXUS (United Kingdom, Greece)
- Module 5 - Education4Sight (Germany, Tunisia) and MyDocumenta (Spain)
- Modules 6 and 7 - Education4Sight (Germany, Tunisia).

REFERENCES

Bhattacherjee, A., 2001. Understanding Information Systems Continuance: An Expectation Confirmation Model. *MIS Quarterly*, Vol. 25, No. 3, pp. 351–370.

Brusilovsky, P., Eklund, J., Schwarz, E., 1998. Web based education for all: a tool for development adaptive courseware. *Computer Networks and ISDN Systems*, Vol. 30, No. 1-7, pp. 291-300.

DeLone, W. H., McLean E. R., 2016. Information Systems Success Measurement. *Foundations and Trends® in Information Systems*, Vol. 2, No. 1, pp. 1–116.

Calvani A., Cartelli A., Fini A., Ranieri M., 2008. Models and instruments for assessing digital competence at school. *Journal of E-Learning and Knowledge Society*, Vol. 4, No. 3, pp. 183–193.

European Commission, 2013. *Communication from the Commission to the European Parliament, the Council, the European Economic and Social Committee and the Committee of the Regions Opening up Education: Innovative teaching and learning for all through new Technologies and Open Educational Resources*, accessed 24 February 2019, https://eur-lex.europa.eu/legal-content/EN/TXT/?uri=CELEX:52013DC0654

European Parliament, Council of the European Union, 2006. Recommendation of the European Parliament and of the Council of 18 December 2006 on key competences for lifelong learning. *Official Journal of the European Union*, Vol. 49, pp. 10-18.

Ferrari, A., 2012. *Digital Competence in Practice: An Analysis of Frameworks*. Publications Office of the European Union, Luxembourg.

Ferrari, A., 2013. *DIGCOMP: A Framework for Developing and Understanding Digital Competence in Europe*. Publications Office of the European Union, Luxembourg.

Florian-Gaviria B., Glahn C., Fabregat Gesa R., 2013. A Software Suite for Efficient Use of the European Qualifications Framework in Online and Blended Courses. *IEEE Transactions on Learning Technologies*, Vol. 6, No. 3, pp. 283-296.

Florian-Gaviria, B., Baldiris, S., Fabregat, R., 2010. A new competency-based e-assessment data model: Implementing the AEEA proposal. *2010 IEEE Education Engineering Conference (EDUCON 2010)*, pp. 473-480.

Guardia, L., Maina, M., Julia, A., 2017. Digital Competence Assessment System: Supporting Teachers with the CRISS platform. *2017 Central European Conference on Information and Intelligent Systems (CECIIS 2017)*, Faculty of Organization and Informatics, Varazdin, Croatia.

Heift, T., 2000. *An Interactive Intelligent Language Tutor Over the Internet*, accessed 26 February 2019, https://www.researchgate.net/publication/2484103_An_Interactive_Intelligent_Language_Tutor_Over_The_Internet

Hickey, D., (2012) *Digital Badges as "Transformative Assessment"*, accessed 26 February 2019, http://remediatingassessment.blogspot.com/2012/06/digital-badges-as-transformative.html

Kluzer S., 2015., *Guidelines on the adoption of DigComp*, accessed 26 February 2019, https://all-digital.org/wp-content/uploads/2015/12/TE-Guidelines-on-the-adoption-of-DIGCOMP_Dec2015.pdf

Lorenzo G, Ittelson J., 2005. *Demonstrating and Assessing Student Learning With e-Portfolios*, accessed 29 February 2019, https://library.educause.edu/-/media/files/library/2005/1/eli3003-pdf.pdf

Papanikolaou K.A., Grigoriadou M., Kornilakis H., Magoulas G.D., 2002. INSPIRE: An INtelligent System for Personalized Instruction in a Remote Environment. In Reich S., Tzagarakis M.M., De Bra P.M.E. (eds.) *Hypermedia: Openness, Structural Awareness, and Adaptivity*. Springer, Germany, pp. 215-225.

Redecker, C., Johannessen, Ø., 2013. Changing Assessment - Towards a New Assessment Paradigm Using ICT. *European Journal of Education*, Vol. 48, pp. 79-96.

Roegiers, X., 2000. *Une Pédagogie de L'intégration*. De Boeck University, Bruxelles.

Roegiers, X., 2010. *Pedagogy of Integration: Education and training systems at the heart of our societies*. De Boeck University, Bruxelles.

Smith, S., Blandford, A., 2003. ML Tutor: An Application of Machine Learning Algorithms for an Adaptive Web-based Information System. *I. J. Artificial Intelligence in Education*, Vol. 13, pp 235-261.

Stefani L, Mason R, Pegler C., 2007. *The educational potential of e-Portfolios*. Routledge T&F Group, London, England.

Sullivan, F. M., 2013. *New and Alternative Assessments, Digital Badges, and Civics: An Overview of Emerging Themes and Promising Directions*, accessed 26 February 2019, http://www.civicyouth.org/wp-content/uploads /2013/03/WP_77_Sullivan_Final.pdf

Vuorikari, R., Punie, Y., Carretero Gomez S., Van den Brande, G. (2016). *DigComp 2.0: The Digital Competence Framework for Citizens. Update Phase 1: The Conceptual Reference Model*. Publication Office of the European Union, Luxembourg.

Williams, P., (2014). Squaring the circle: A new alternative to alternative-assessment. *Teaching in Higher Education*, Vol. 19, No. 5, pp. 565-577.

LEARNING READINESS WHEN SHARING KNOWLEDGE WHILE E-LEARNING

Anjum Razzaque[1], Allam M. Hamdan[2], Mukhtar Al-Hashimi[3] and Esra S. Aldahean[4]
Ahlia University, Bahrain
[1]Assistant Professor, MIS Dept. Chairperson, College of Business & Finance
[2]Associate Professor, Dean of College of Business & Finance
[3]Professor, Vice President of Academic Affairs
[4]Assistant Professor, Director of Centre for Accreditation & Quality Assurance

ABSTRACT

Past research indicates the importance of assessing the role of higher education (HE) students' Learning Readiness's (LR's (Self-Directed Learning - SDL and Motivation for Learning - MFL) on learning behaviors (Knowledge Sharing Quality -KSQ) during e-learning in developing countries. This article is a critique of a literature review led to a conceptual framework which in turn was empirically investigated (correlation analysis, using Pearson and Spearman correlation) shed new knowledge. This deductive cross-sectional research confirms this role via an adopted survey, n = 253 Ahlia University undergraduate e-learners, hence confirming positively significance between SDL → KSQ and, MFL → KSQ: new knowledge contributions.

KEYWORDS

Knowledge Sharing, Learner Readiness, E-Learning, Moodle, Higher Education.

1. INTRODUCTION

The teaching and learning domain incorporates e-learning with regular face-to-face teaching to harness online work collaboration. The question is whether students are ready for this. Therefore, assessing learner readiness using a survey instrument, for e-learning, is essential. Such a quantitative instrument has been used, been improved and re-used again by scholars, particularly in the educational sector. Initially learning readiness (LR) was based on learning self-management of e-learning. (Hung, et al., 2010). LR is an inquiry driven interest. It is, therefore, a driving force behind the behavior of sharing quality knowledge (Rotgans and Schmidt, 2017). Rotgans and Schmidt assessed such a statement as a hypothesis, and reported two types of interests, individual and situational, where individual interest is personal interest and situational interest is a temporary event encountered by a learner. Individual interest encounters ample engagement and as a result experiences an inspiration for deeper learning through deeper processing of reading materials encountered through personal interest upon a topic of research. Therefore being interested determines how much can be achieved from a learning outcome (LO) (Rotgans and Schmidt, 2017).

In education research scholars have contributed instruments pertaining to e-LR and mobile- learning readiness. They made empirical evidenced conclusions based on investigations done at regional and country-level. Scholars performed micro-level investigations, in which learners and instructors were the target populations. At the micro-level, individual attitudes, skills and knowledge become the key aspects of the investigation. Unfortunately, such conceptual frameworks fall short since they tend to adapt inconsistent unidimensional understandings of LR (Blayone, et al., 2018). Hao (2016) targeted undergrad Education majors and attained 84 responses when they wanted to assess the role of LR on flipped learning (FL). FL is highly important in higher education (HE) learning environments. This student-centered form of learning evidences successful during its LO achievements in the HE environments and in a FL approach student are required to learn facets of knowledge before arriving to their class. This way during class sessions, an instructor can direct learners through personalized and individually oriented instructions, i.e. through assignments, problem-solving session for personalized in-class learning. Unfortunately, on the one hand some scholars report students outperform in FL vs. traditional classroom while some other scholars express lack of LR towards FL. This is due to limited empirical evidence. Additional research is necessary to furnish more empirical confirmation for FL LR to appreciate what learners truly want from FL; considering that FL cannot satisfy needs of all students (Hao, 2016).

As per the gap and since LR drives acquisition of knowledge, driver of knowledge sharing (KS) (Rotgans and Schmidt, 2017), one can investigate the role of LR on KS quality (KSQ): un-chartered territory as a need to assess the role of e-LR for effective utilization of KS for better learning support. In such networks teaching-learning quality is enhanced, yet research is needed for assessing LR →KSQ during e-learning: a need for future research in developing countries. Past scholars assessed LR scales, to explore knowledge and skills for e-learning by testing technical skills and teacher/learner achieved behaviors when preparing for LR. However past scales identified problem areas without a solution to correcting any short-coming (Gay, 2016).

The role of LR for KS in e-learning environments like Moodle, a platform used at Ahlia University (i.e. Case University for this research context in the Kingdom of Bahrain - a Middle Eastern developing country) is an important area of research. Furthermore, learners' KS behavior is important in the e-learning context when learners share knowledge to learning experiences on platforms like Facebook. KSQ becomes an effective measure of perceived learning effectiveness because SDL occurs virtually during KS, which further strengthens their knowledge (Li, et al., 2016). When KS occurs within virtual environments, such a behavior transforms traditional learning environments to an e-learning environment where participation within virtual contexts and KS can be between learners and their instructors. E.g. KS can be learners attaining feedback from their instructors in virtual e-learning environments (Li, et al., 2016). Last but not least, the KS behavior gained little focus from scholars when it comes to investigating the unclear episodic nature of KS: particularly when it comes to KS being a citizen behavior; as this is one of the two types of KS behaviors with the other being the rewarded behavior. The citizen behavior implies that supervisor (i.e. instructor in the case of the HE) and coworkers (i.e. learners as the case of higher education) perceive usefulness of KS, thus indulge in this behavior. However, it is unclear if such KS is a reward behavior and if so then it is due to indulging in such a behavior (Zhang and Jiang, 2015). Similar is the dilemma within the education sector and this is the reason for the following conceptual framework of this study.

2. CONCEPTUAL FRAMEWORK

This study assesses the role of LR (independent variable) on their KSQ (dependent variable). LR's SDL and motivation for learning (ML) (independent variables). Hence proposing 2 hypotheses: (1) learners' SLD is positively signifies with KSQ and ML positively signifies withr KSQ.

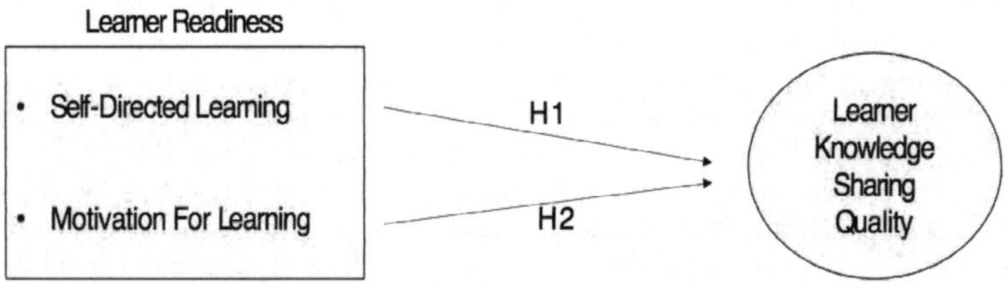

Figure 1. Conceptual Framework

3. LITERATURE REVIEW

Technical skills and learner control significantly define learning readiness: a concept originated from Australia since 1998. The first LR instrument was developed and tested in 2000. LR shapes online attitudes and behaviors making students more active learners and instructors no longer central in virtual environments. Learner control makes learner responsible of self-learning. The two dimensions of LR are SDL, which inspires learners for self-learning and ML, which sets the learner's attitude and behavior such that ML affects learning performance (Hung, et al., 2010). Hung, et al. empirically assessed LR instrument on a five-point-Likert-Scale on 1,051 students from 3 Taiwan universities. A model was confirmed valid and reliable. With reference to learner readiness, 121 studies, from 1965 to 1992, empirically confirmed a correlation between interest and academic achievement; making future scholars gain interest on LR as the independent and knowledge outcomes as the dependent variable in empirical assessments. Still, the confusion is whether it is LR that causes learners to gain knowledge since it is possible that increase of knowledge of a topic inspires interest in that topic (Rotgans and Schmidt, 2017). Rotgans and Schmidt ventures forth to establish the right empirically evidenced direction between interest and knowledge. The confusion is that while some scholars support the notion that knowledge inspires interest, other scholars assessing the role of attitudes on learning, state that not knowledge alone, but achievement, predict an attitude to inspire an interest for learning especially in female learners. Two studies tested these three hypotheses; i.e. (1) cross-lagging of panel analysis on 186 primary science students to a problem oriented learning activity where interest and knowledge were separately studies at two different times. To further validate the empirical findings (2) two quasi-experiments were carried out via 68 secondary 14 year old students to assess the nature of the relation between interest and knowledge. In another study, 84 undergraduate students, from two courses, participated by first watching YouTube videos, Audios via Moodle, textbook readings and other information-lookups on the Internet before class: as per norms of FL strategy. Students were given an e-quiz assessing their academic performance via their own devices, like smart phones, tablets, etc. Group discussion were instructor-led and tasks involved website-evaluations and end-of-class discussions. Students participated in a survey providing feedback on FL strategy. Empirical findings indicate 60% respondents recognized merits of FL. Those learners who did not prepare before classes still appreciate FL. While students appreciated FL they were not responsible due to low ML (Hao, 2016).

SDL has existed for forty years in tertiary education and has inspired student in self-learning. It requires self-determination: dependable on aptitude and self-assertiveness. Such characteristics are investigated and empirically indicate that instructor can inspire SDL in learners and prove that SDL influences KS (Alshaikh, et.al, 2017). So, an instructor's positive behavior inspires learners to gain knowledge. SDL is an objective of HE institutions with growing acknowledgement for implementation, especially with rising challenges in GCC HE institutions for quality assurance requirements (Costandi, et.al, 2018). SDL proves vital since such is a human powering learner characteristic for sustaining knowledge society via metacognition, thinking and self-recognition (Toit-Brits and Zyl, 2017). Research is lacking on students with disabilities due to limited HE resources. In this scenario SDL proves most effective since it is a cost effect means of learning, especially for students with disabilities (Garderen, et al., 2017). Such a learning technique is encouraged in graduate medical schools. To assess SDL, medical and post-grad students were exposed to simulation based in-lab training sessions and requested to practice laparoscopic skills. Subsequently a survey was conducted addressed learners habits and obtain learners feedback for curriculum improvements. Empirical evidence suggested that participants improved in their practical skills and reported SDL during their individual endeavors to improve practical skills (Aho, et al., 2015). Since technology is widely used in education it should be integrated with teaching and learning (TaL). Impact of technological on TaL is still unclear in research, i.e., to what extent technology enhances academic performance via e-learning. Research in the past two-decades evidenced positives and negatives of integrating technology in e-learning. While research probed technology's role on e-learning other studies examined SDL's role in education. Current literature suggests integrating these two research themes. Even though scholars explore these themes, there is still lacking empirical evidence to holistically assess technology's role, student engagement, SDL and academic performance (Rashid and Asghar, 2016). It is evident how positively SDL affects academic performance. Also, accumulative assessment encourages learners to work harder: the issue being that not all students are responsive towards SDL. Current research expresses the importance of assessing learner behavior to improve their responsiveness (Tio, et al., 2016).

The motivation of informal learning is not institutional sponsored but originates with the learner who seeks knowledge and skills by reading or by peer KS for feedback. Such ML aids a learner to stay abreast with the dynamics of updating one's self of new knowledge and such collective knowledge proves sustainable versus the knowledge gained through an instructor. Informal form of learning, i.e. ML, has gained scholarly interest in recent literature. This is especially considering that past research has been paying a lot of attention on factors like self-efficacy and learning motivation (van Rijn, et al., 2013). The ML research area is investigated before the e-learning ear in schools but less in HE though such need exists. E.g. five students were targets of a case study investigating their ability to tackle math problems of a particular discipline. Empirical evidence confirmed that challenging students in problem-solving improves ML in math. Since math is hard problem-solving via rigid algorithms. Scarce research assesses ML in mathematics for Arab student with disabilities. Future research could investigate this matter (Bishara, 2016). In another study 7th grade Cyprus students' ML in Biology was examined when these target students' tests were used as indicators to measure level of understanding of a material, following survey distribution to assess ML in this subject. Findings indicated the contribution of gender, prior knowledge and ML moderate learning in Biology via inquiry: an important finding since past scholars indicated lack of understanding regarding gender, knowledge or ML (Hadjichambis, et al., 2016).

4. RESEARCH METHODOLOGY

This study's critiqued literature to understand the research gap in e-learning research. The review phase led to research questions and objectives and a conceptual framework with two hypotheses, tested thru collected data from 253 of 700 Ahlia University College of Business and Finance students. Data analysis via descriptive and advanced descriptive analysis occurred by correlation analysis (next section). This deductive research approach cross-sectionally confirms two hypotheses via an adopted survey instrument from: LR adapted from (Hung, et al., 2010) and KSQ adapted from (Chiuet al., 2006). Though this instrument is adapted; past research has not assessed the role of KSQ in a HE sectors.

5. DATA ANALYSIS

The following section portrays the analyzed data expressed through the six tables depicted below. Table 1 depicts the respondents' profiles as data, using an adapted and integrated survey was used. 253 respondents participated and as per Table 1, gender wise the same has 133 males and 120 females in multicultural classrooms. This evidences that there is a normal distribution in this study's sample. Student level wise the data is normally distributed considering that freshmen, sophomore, junior and seniors were around 25% mark of responding participants. Student status wise; majority of target student population at Ahlia University's College of Business and Finance is Gulf Corporation Council (GCC) students. College of Business and Finance program wise: there seems to be a normal distribution considering the total number of students in their respective programs versus the total number to students in the College of Business and Finance.

Table 1. Profile of respondents

Sample Characteristics		Frequency	Percent
Gender	Male	133	53%
	Female	120	47%
	Total	253	100%
Student Level	Freshman	65	26%
	Sophomore	64	25%
	Junior	64	25%
	Senior	60	24%
	Total	253	100%
Student Status	GCC student	185	73%
	Non-GCC student	68	27%
	Total	253	100%
Program Enrolled in	BSMIS	40	16%
	BSAF	94	37%
	BSMM	53	21%
	BSBF	44	17%
	BSEF	22	9%
	Total	253	100%

As per KSQ (Table 2) 64% agree and 31% strongly agree, with mean = 3.8, i.e. > 3 with SD = 1.5, indicating that the general % = 78%, i.e. 78% of sample agree that e-learning aids KSQ. Quite similar were analysis of remaining KSQ items; with highest general % for KS1 and lowest for KS6. Similarly, learners' SDL (Table 3), and learners' ML (Table 4) express all items satisfactory mean (3.54 to 3.78) i.e. > 3 and general % (71% to 77%). Path analysis of 3 variables, SDL. ML and KSQ, (Table 5), based on gender, student level and College of Business and Finance program; the authors of this article divided sample in two parts as per sample characteristic. E.g. gender, male and female, compared with 3 variables indicates KSQ for males reflected similar with females: no difference significance > 5% for t and z-test. Gender difference would be reflected if the significance was < 5.

Table 2. Learners' Knowledges sharing quality

Learners' KSQ	Strongly disagree	Disagree	Neither	Agree	Strongly agree	Mean	SD	General Percent
KS1: The knowledge shared between instructor and students in Moodle is easy to understand.	6.7	6.7	8.7	46.6	31.2	3.89	1.125	78%
KS2: The knowledge shared between instructor and students in Moodle is relevant	5.5	7.5	10.3	47.4	29.2	3.87	1.087	77%
KS3: The knowledge shared between instructor and students in Moodle is accurate.	5.9	4.3	17	50.2	22.5	3.79	1.031	76%
KS4: The knowledge shared between instructor and students in Moodle is complete.	7.9	6.7	16.2	40.3	28.9	3.75	1.173	75%
KS5: The knowledge shared between instructor and students in Moodle is reliable.	5.1	7.1	13.4	49	25.3	3.82	1.052	76%
KS6: The knowledge shared between instructor and students in Moodle is timely.	6.7	6.3	18.2	47.8	20.9	3.7	1.079	74%

For student level; this study's sample was divided to four levels: freshman, sophomore, junior and senior: to be compared with three variables; thus resulting into three variables similarly distributed amongst four student levels: i.e. there is no empirically difference in the three variables and students' level as significance is > 5% for the t and z-test. The three variables were compared with College of Business and Finance's programs: (1) BSMIS – B.Sc. Management Information Systems, (2) BSAF –Accounting and Finance, (3) BSMM –Management and Marketing, (4) BSBF - Banking and Finance and (5) BSEF – B.Sc. Economic and Finance. There is no difference between programs with reference to three variables: BSMIS was highest (mean = 4.114) following BSEF (4.000), BSMM (3.814), BSAF (3.432) and BSBF (1.023): i.e. sig. < 5%: expressing difference in College of Business and Finance programs. Table 6 describe, Correlation Matrix, and considering that the independent variable in Figure 1 is learner readiness's two dimension, SDL and ML (independent variables) and learners' KSQ (dependent variable); empirical findings are based on the correlations using parametric test, i.e. Pearson correlation and non-parametric test, i.e. spearman test. This is to confirm this study's empirical results, which therefore. Indicate a positively significant correlation (sig < 0.01%) between learner learners' SDL → learners' KSQ, i.e. based on 62.5% positive correlation. Furthermore, there is positive correlation between learners' ML → learners' KSQ.

Table 3. Learners' SDL

(SDL	Strongly disagree	Disagree	Neither	Agree	Strongly agree	Mean	SD	General Percent
SDL1: I carry out my own study plan.	8.3	7.5	17.4	34.4	32.4	3.75	1.22	75%
SDL2: I seek assistance when facing learnin; problems.	7.5	14.2	14.2	40.3	23.7	3.58	1.207	72%
SDL3: I manage time well.	10.7	9.1	20.2	35.6	24.5	3.54	1.252	71%
SDL4: I set up my learning goals	7.9	7.1	17.8	42.3	24.9	3.69	1.155	74%
SDL5: I have higher expectations for my learning performance.	5.5	7.5	15.8	39.1	32	3.85	1.122	77%

Table 4. Learners' ML

ML	Strongly disagre	Disagree	Neither	Agree	Strongly agree	Mean	SD	General Percen
ML1: I am open to new ideas.	6.7	8.7	17.8	34.8	32	3.77	1.184	75%
ML2: I have motivation to learn.	6.3	8.7	15.8	39.1	30	3.78	1.154	76%
ML3: I improve from my mistakes.	6.3	9.5	11.9	44.7	27.7	3.78	1.14	76%
ML4: I like to share my ideas with others.	7.1	9.9	16.2	41.1	25.7	3.68	1.166	74%

Table 5. Path analysis for study variables

Characteristics		Number	KSQ	SDL	Motivate Learning
Gender	Male	133	3.800	3.683	3.752
	Female	120	3.800	3.703	3.765
Difference tests	t-test		-0.158	-0.162	-0.100
	Sig.		(0.874)	(0.871)	(0.920)
	z-test		-0.533	-0.011	-0.946
	Sig.		(0.594)	(0.991)	(0.344)
Student Level	Freshman	22	3.932	3.713	3.598
	Sophomore	174	3.826	3.698	3.794
	Junior	51	3.711	3.635	3.667
	Senior	6	3.571	3.450	3.875
Difference tests	F-test		0.450	0.128	0.411
	Sig.		(0.717)	(0.943)	(0.746)
	Chi-square		5.122	1.219	0.717
	Sig.		(0.163)	(0.748)	(0.869)

Program	BSMIS	40	3.864	3.723	4.114
	BSAF	94	3.814	3.632	3.432
	BSMM	53	3.914	3.838	3.814
	BSBF	44	3.584	3.441	1.023
	BSEF	22	3.883	3.945	4.000
Difference tests	F-test		0.933	1.403	2.903
	Sig.		(0.446)	(0.233)	(0.022**)
	Chi-square		2.705	2.577	8.248
	Sig.		(0.608)	(0.631)	(0.083*)

Note: Significance at: *10%; **5% and ***1% levels. Significance value are marked within (brackets),

Table 6. Correlations Matrix

	KSQ	SDL	Motivate Learning
Learner KSQ		0.625***	0.564***
Sig.		0.000	0.000
SDL	0.670***		0.716***
Sig.	0.000		0.000
ML	0.691***	0.796***	
Sig.	0.000	0.000	

Notes: Above Spearman correlation, and below Pearson correlation. Significance at: *10%; **5% and ***1% levels.

6. DISCUSSION & CONCLUSION

Gaps were described in this section and can be utilized for future research through this section. Furthermore, a constructive critique of structured literature review led to identify opportunities to narrow the research gap portrayed in these just-mentioned sections. As a result, two hypotheses were empirically testing, as depicted in Figure 1 of this article, using correlation analysis, followed by basic and advance descriptive analysis. Unfortunately, lack of time was encountered due to which the authors express part of this study's continuing study. However, the empirical results bare theoretical and practical implications. Form the theory point of view this study identified the research gap, and therefore its conceptual model and empirical evidenced the need of SDL and ML for learners to engage in KSQ. Future research can assess how this plays a broader significant role of learners' academic performance, in addition to how technology use expresses its importance within the context of Ahlia University's other programs outside College of Business and Finance. Practical implications this model could be adapted by HE for improvement. In addition, expanding this study's model and re-assess it to better understand what new technologies can better facilitate Ahlia University's e-learning agendas.

REFERENCES

Aho, J. M. et al., 2015. Mentor-Guided Self-Directed Learning Affects Resident Practice. *Journal of Surgical Education,* 72(4), pp. 674-679.

Alshaikh, I. Y., Razzaque, A. & Alalawi, M., 2017. *Positive Emotion and Social Capital affect Knowledge Sharing: Case of the Public Sector of the Kingdom of Bahrain.* Coimbra, Portugal, Springer Lecture Notes in Business Information Processing volume.

Bishara, S., 2016. Creativity in unique problem-solving in mathematics and its influence on motivation for learning. *Bishara, Cogent Education,* Volume 3, pp. 1-14.

Blayone, T. J. B., Mykhailenko, O., vanOostveen, R. & Barber, W., 2018. Ready for digital learning? A mixed-methods exploration of surveyed technology competencies and authentic performance activity. *Education and Information Technologies,* Volume 23, p. 1377–1402.

Bondevik, G. T. et al., 2015. Interprofessional Workplace Learning in Primary Care: Students from Different Health Professions Work in Teams in Real-Life Settings. *International Journal of Teaching and Learning in Higher Education,* 27(2), pp. 175-182.

Çakıroğlu, Ü., Kokoç, M., Kol, E. & Turan, E., 2016. Exploring Teaching Programming Online through Web Conferencing System: The Lens of Activity Theory. *Educational Technology & Society,* 19(4), p. 126–139.

Chiu, C.-M., Hsu, M.-H. & Wang, E. T., 2006. Understanding knowledge sharing in virtual communities: An integration of social capital and social cognitive theories. *Decision Support Systems,* 42(3), p. 1872–1888.

Costandi, , S., Hamdan, , A., Alareeni, , B. & Hassan, , A., 2018. Educational governance and challenges to universities in Arabian Gulf Region. *Educational philosophy and theory.*

Garderen, D. v. et al., 2017. Self-Directed Learning to Improve Science Content Knowledge for Teachers. *Intervention in School and Clinic,* 52(4), p. 236–242.

Gay, G. H. E., 2016. An assessment of online instructor e-learning readiness before, during, and after course delivery. *Journal of Computer and Higher Education,* Volume 28, p. 199–220.

Hadjichambis, A. C. et al., 2016. Investigating the Effectiveness of an Inquiry-Based Intervention on Human Reproduction in Relation to Students' Gender, Prior Knowledge and Motivation for Learning in Biology. *Journal of Biological Education,* 50(3), pp. 261-274.

Hao, Y., 2016. Exploring undergraduates' perspectives and flipped learning readiness in their flipped classrooms. *Computers in Human Behavior,* Volume 59, p. 82e92.

Hung, M.-L., Chou, C., Chen, C.-H. & Own, Z.-Y., 2010. Learner readiness for online learning: Scale development and student perceptions. *Computers & Education,* Volume 55, p. 1080–1090.

Lin, H.-H., Lin, S., Yeh, C.-H. & Wang, Y.-S., 2016. Measuring mobile learning readiness: scale development and validation. *Internet Research,* 26(1), pp. 265-287.

Li, T. M. H. et al., 2016. Design and evaluation of a Facebook game for self-directed e-learning. *Knowledge Management & E-Learning,* 8(3), p. 464–480.

Rashid, T. & Asghar, H. M., 2016. Technology use, self-directed learning, student engagement and academic performance: Examining the interrelations. *Computers in Human Behavior,* Volume 63, pp. 604-612.

Rotgans, J. I. & Schmidt, H. G., 2017. The relation between individual interest and knowledge acquisition. *British Educational Research Journal,* 43(2), p. 350–371.

Tio, R. A. et al., 2016. Weak self-directed learning skills hamper performance in cumulative assessment. *Medical Teacher,* Volume 38, pp. 421-423.

Toit-Brits, C. d. & Zyl, C.-M. v., 2017. Self-directed learning characteristics: making learning personal, empowering and successful. *Africa Education Review,* 14(3-4), pp. 122-141.

van Rijn, M. B., Yang, H. & Sanders, K., 2013. Understanding employees' informal workplace learning: The joint influence of career motivation and self-construal. *Career Development International,* 18(6), pp. 610-628.

Zhang, X. & Jiang, J. Y., 2015. With whom shall I share my knowledge? A recipient perspective of knowledge sharing. *Journal of Knowledge Management,* 19(2), pp. 277-295.

LEARNING RELATED DEVICE USAGE OF GERMAN AND INDIAN STUDENTS

Joachim Griesbaum[1], Tessy Thadathil[2] and Sophie März[1]
[1]University of Hildesheim, Universitätsplatz 1, 31141 Hildesheim, Germany
[2]Symbiosis College of Arts & Commerce, Senapati Bapat Road, Pune, India

ABSTRACT

This paper investigates learning related device usage of German and Indian students. For that purpose, an exploratory survey of students at the University of Hildesheim and the Symbiosis College of Arts and Commerce in Pune is executed. The aim of the research is to uncover basic patterns of overall device usage, studying behavior, employment of learning tools and assessment of e-learning. Collected data deliver a broad picture on students' needs with regard to e-learning support. Results show, students from Pune are engaged in e-learning more frequently than students from Hildesheim. For students from India, smartphones are the most important learning devices. For German students, laptops are more important. Although both groups are experienced in e-learning, the Indian students employ a wider range of resources. In addition, Indian students communicate more often with their peers and instructors via computer mediated communication channels than the Germans. Whereas German students talk about content related and organizational aspects of learning, Indians focus on content related topics when communicating with peers and instructors.

KEYWORDS

e-Learning, Online Survey, Studying Behavior, Device Usage

1. INTRODUCTION

According to Velayo (2012), in an increasingly interconnected world, there is a need to prepare students to become more knowledgeable of different cultures and global matters. One way to foster the internationalization of higher education is to employ information and communication technology to build up joint (cross-national) e-learning infrastructures. And there is a chance to do that as technology is no longer at the periphery of education, but increasingly influences teaching (Bates & Bates 2015). At part, learning has already become global as MOOCs (Massive Open Online Courses) offer a magnitude of location-independent learning opportunities for everyone interested (Zawacki-Richter et al. 2018). Still, research on cross-national learning infrastructures and learning cultures is not that common (Kasunic et al. 2015).

This is the starting point and motivation of our work. Our investigation generates data-based insights into learning related habits of students of two institutions of higher education in different countries. This information can then serve as a base to build joint learning infrastructures that consider the different needs and patterns of users in the two locations. In order to achieve this, user acceptance should be ensured beforehand.

The paper is structured as follows. First, we provide a short sketch of literature in the field. Following that, we lay out our research design. After that, the data is presented. The paper closes with an estimation of the results.

2. REVIEW OF LITERATURE

As a preliminary remark, it is important to state that writing a state of the art with regard to learning related device usage of students in different countries is no easy task. There are many studies on students' needs and technology employment that focus on local samples (e.g. Maifarth et al. 2013, Sharma, & Madhusudhan

2017). However, investigations that collect data on learning related device usage in different locations are rather scarce. In the following, we present the works of Kukulksa-Hulme et al. (2011), Viberg and Gronlund (2013), Khaddage and Knezek (2014), Ko et al. (2014), Arpaci (2015), and Shuter et al. (2016) to get an impression on learning related device usage from a transnational perspective.

Kukulksa-Hulme et al. (2011) surveyed 270 master and doctoral students in Australia, Hong Kong, Portugal, Sweden, and the United Kingdom. They collected data concerned with learners' usage of mobile technologies in the domains of learning, work, social interaction and entertainment. Data indicate a wide spectrum of mobile device usage. With regard to learning, the most frequent uses were communication, information access, consumption of learning material and organizing. Convenience of information access and the ability to contact others immediately were seen as the main advantages of mobile devices.

Viberg and Gronlund (2013) conducted an analysis of Swedish and Chinese students' attitude towards the use of mobile devices for second and foreign language learning in higher education. In their survey of 139 language students from Sweden and 206 learners from China, they find positive attitudes toward mobile learning. Students assess it as fostering personalization, collaboration, and the authenticity of learning processes. Concerning the impact of cultural dimensions (according to Hofstede 2001), the authors only found very weak correlations with students' attitude on mobile-assisted language learning. Thus, they argue that cultural background (nationality) has no significant influence.

In an online survey of 261 students from China, Lebanon, the United Arab Emirates and the United States, Khaddage and Knezek (2014) captured attitudes towards the integration of mobile technologies in education. Data indicates that students in all countries were receptive to the idea of using mobile devices in formal and informal learning. Nevertheless, differences between the four nations could be observed. Students from Lebanon reached the highest scores and students from the United Arab Emirates the lowest.

Ko et al. (2015) surveyed the usage of mobile devices for learning purposes of 267 Library and Information Science students from Hong Kong, Japan, and Taiwan. Results indicate that students from all regions employ mobile devices and tools for learning related purposes. The study could not detect substantial differences in mobile learning usage between the three regions with one exception. Students from Hong Kong access learning management platforms more frequently than students from Japan and Taiwan.

Arpaci (2015) investigated cultural differences on the adoption of mobile learning with the help of an online survey that collected data from 190 students in Turkey and 163 students in Canada with regard to cultural aspects and adoption behavior. Arpaci argues a connection between national culture and adoption behavior. Data indicates a higher adoption rate in Canada (a more individualistic and low uncertainty avoidance-based culture) than in Turkey (a more collectivistic and high uncertainty avoidance culture).

Shuter et al. (2016) examined the influence of cultural values and social context on the digital behavior of students from the United States and Denmark. Data from a survey with 534 students from two US universities and 361 students from one college in Denmark show that both groups differ in their device usage. Danish students use their laptops and tablets in class more often whereas American students employ their mobile phones more often than their Danish counterparts. This is true for teaching sessions as well as outside the classroom. These results are consistent with economic trends as U.S. cell phone services and equipment are cheaper than Danish ones. As a result, mobile devices exhibit a higher diffusion and usage rate in the United States. In addition, it seems that cultural values with regard to authority may influence preferred policies of digital media usage in the classroom. More students from Denmark believe there should be no policy for in-class use of digital media. This corresponds to Danish and United States citizen authority value differences with the Danish valuing equalitarianism more whereas the Americans being more hierarchical.

What have we learned from the literature presented? First, we gained insights into research approaches and methods. It is evident that online surveys are the dominant data collection method. The transnational participants can mostly be categorized as a kind of convenience samples. They often represent the population of specific learning institutions, but are not necessarily representative for wider learner populations. In addition, the collected data are of a rather self-declarative character and not objective. Furthermore, we see the focus of research mostly on the micro level of the individuum. Questions are often concerned with individual adoption and usage behavior. At times, meso- or even macro levels are also implied, e.g. when the students are asked on their assessment of classroom policies or when economic data on the macro-level is included into the argumentation. But it seems, there is no systematic research on meso and macro-levels. We also did not find investigations covering cross-national learning infrastructures. Currently such infrastructures might be rather scarce. In sum, seen from a methodological perspective research is not that comprehensive but rather limited. Basically, findings should be assessed as explorative.

Second, with regard to the findings of the research presented, we see a clear trend but overall there is no clear picture. On the one hand, one can easily recognize a great willingness of students to apply information and communication devices in learning contexts and for learning purposes. Indeed, it seems that such devices are already employed widely in learning contexts, at least as tools for information and communication management. On the other hand, with regard to the impact of individual, cultural, and socio-economic factors on learning related device usage and attitudes on e-learning, findings are not so clear-cut and even partly inconsistent. Some investigations argue culture as an important factor, whereas others do not. Such deviations are not surprising when considering the broad spectrum of the different research scenarios. Still, we have to take into account that we cannot rely on generalizable findings. It is important to consider the specific context of every scenario under investigation. This is also and especially true in a context that aims to design learning environments. As the cross-national learning space is still widely untapped territory, additional research should be welcomed.

3. RESEARCH DESIGN

The goal of this research is to get insights into learning related device usage of German and Indian students. For that purpose, we aim to find basic patterns of overall device and learning tool usage, studying behavior and estimations of e-learning. Specifically, we cover three research questions.

RQ1: What devices do students employ and what are the connected learning activities? This first research question is concerned with the types of devices used, usage frequency and types of learning activities.

RQ2: What are the basic characteristics of e-learning in both groups? The second research question explores which online learning resources are employed. It also investigates students' assessment of e-learning.

RQ3: How do students use technology to communicate with peers and instructors? The last research question's focus is on communication patterns.

The study was conducted with the help of an online survey. Table 1 shows the structure of the questionnaire and mentions literature consulted for item construction.

Table 1. Structure of the questionnaire and conducted literature for the item construction

Survey Topic	Items	Reference
Device usage	**Device Usage intensity**	Sharma & Madhusudan 2017
	Learning activities per device	Maifarth et al. 2013
Studying behavior	**Online learning resource access and purpose**	Kukulska et al. 2011, Martin & Bolliger 2018, Sandoval-Lucero et al. 2012, Sharma & Madhusudan 2017
Communication patterns	**Estimation of e-learning**	Biesenbach-Lucas 2005, Deng & Tavares 2015, Kukulska et al. 2011, Madge et al. 2009, Martin & Bolliger 2018, Trenkov 2014
	With fellows	Calvo et al. 2013, Deng & Tavares 2015, Goodwin et al. 2010, Kukulska et al. 2011, Martin & Bolliger 2018, Madge et al. 2009
	With instructors	Sandoval-Lucero et al. 2012, Sharma & Madhusudan 2017

The survey was designed in an iterative process in which one of the authors prepared a draft (a). After that, the other authors checked the draft and made suggestions for improvement (b). Finally, all authors discussed the current state in a video-conference (c). Overall, the survey was prepared in three cycles that included the stages a-c. During the process, pre-tests with German and Indian students were executed and improvements were integrated into the final survey design. The questionnaire was provided from the 25th of May to the 8th of September 2018. Participants were primarily recruited from the study programs on International Information Management in Hildesheim and Bachelor of Commerce in Pune. Recruiting was executed via mailing-lists, blogs, Facebook, WhatsApp and courses at both universities.

4. ANALYSIS

Overall, 172 students took part in the study and completed the online survey. Data from one participant had to be eliminated as this specific student was neither from Hildesheim nor from Pune. On the average, it took students 16 minutes to fill out the questionnaire. In the following, we first give an overview on the two samples. Then, the analysis is structured according to the research questions.

4.1 Overview of the Samples

Table 2 gives an overview of the participants that took part in the study.

Table 2. Overview of participants (*indicates a significant difference with p <=0.05 according to the Chi-square test #indicates a significant difference with p <=0.05 according to the Mann-Whitney U test)

Attribute	University of Hildesheim	Symbiosis College of Arts and Commerce in Pune
Number of participants	66	105
Gender*	27% male, 73% female	43% male, 56% female
Age in years#	below 25: 74%, above 25: 26%	below 25: 100%, above 25: 0%
Program: bachelor or master*	70% bachelor, 30% master	87% bachelor,3% master, 10% other
Internet experience* (scale: 1="no experience", 5="expert")	MW=4.15 (SD=0.63)	MW=3.81 (SD=0.65)
Intensity of online learning (scale: 1= "never", 7="several times a day")	MW=3.85 (SD=1.84)	MW=4.61 (SD=1,73)
University attendance in days per week	MW=3.80 (SD=1.09)	MW=5.22 (SD=1.14)

One can easily see that the German and Indian samples are different with regard to all important attributes listed. Whereas in the German sample are mainly women, the Indian sample is more balanced with regard to gender. The Indian students are younger, think of themselves as less internet experienced and exhibit a higher grade of online learning intensity and attendance at the university than the Germans do.

Naturally, a comparison of students from Hildesheim and Pune would seem to be easier, if both groups would be more similar. Nevertheless, these deviations are probably typical for groups with a different cultural and socio-economic background. Additionally, as the aim of this research is not primarily to "detect" such differences. It is to gain knowledge that can serve as a common ground when the aim is to build up joint learning structures. The analysis is therefore not handicapped by the fact, that both groups are very different.

4.2 Device Usage

The first research interest is on learning related device usage. What devices do students employ and what are the connected learning activities? Table 3 gives an overview on the types of devices used.

Table 3. Device usage for university purposes
(* indicates a significant difference with p <=0.05 according to the Mann-Whitney U test)

Attribute	University of Hildesheim	Symbiosis College of Arts and Commerce in Pune
Smartphone	92%	95%
Tablet*	27%	8%
Laptop	91%	67%

Table 3 indicates that nearly every student in both locations employs a smartphone for university purposes. With regard to larger devices, penetration is higher at the University of Hildesheim. The next question is, what the devices are used for? If we investigate the use cases according to Maifarth et al. (2013), we get the following picture as stated in Figure 1. Overall, we see a higher rate of multiple device usage by German students. With the exception of information gathering, they employ more device types to accomplish the learning related activities listed. Furthermore, data shows that different devices are preferred for different activities.

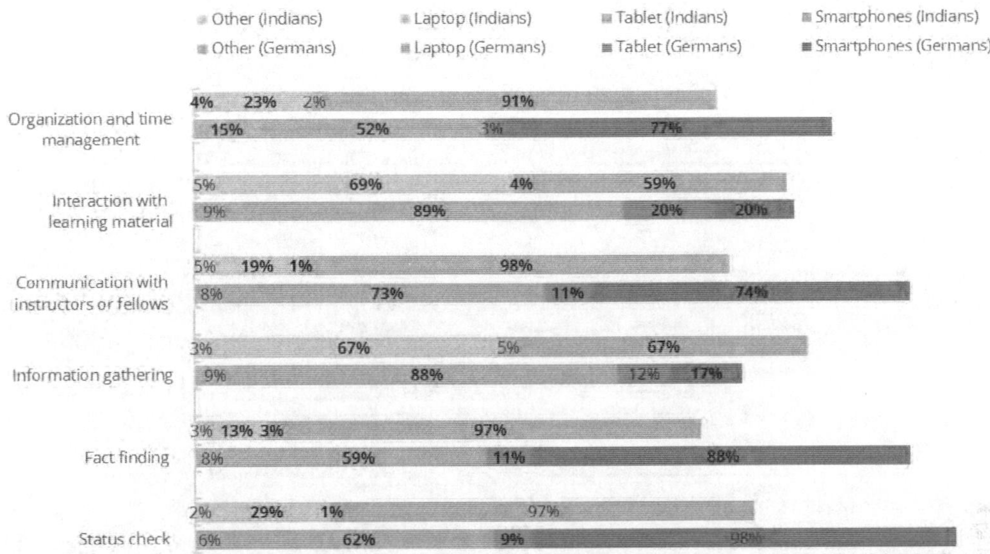

Figure 1. Device usage patterns. patterns (German students, n=66, Indian students, n=105, numbers marked bold indicate a significant difference with p <=0.05 according to the Mann-Whitney U test)

While tablets and other devices are used only marginally by the Indian sample, such devices nearly reach 30% usage fraction in the use case *interaction with learning material* for the students from Germany. For both groups, it seems that the more complex the use case the more often devices with larger screens are used. For *information gathering* and *interaction with learning material,* smartphones are used by only a small fraction of the German learners (17% and 20%). For the Indian students these two use cases are those with the most intense employment of large screen devices. Still, a majority of the Indian students uses smartphones to accomplish these tasks.

4.3 Basic Characteristics of e-Learning

How do students learn and how do they allocate their time to use different online learning resources? First of all, if we look at the expenditure of study-time, we see no significant differences between German and Indian students, neither with regard to weekly study time for lectures, seminars, etc. nor concerning the time allocated for self-study (*preparing lectures, presentations, term papers, exam preparation* etc.). Most of the students are spending either 11-20 hours or 21-30 hours attending lectures etc. And the majority allocates up to 20 hours for self-studying purposes. Most of the time, both student groups prefer to self-study alone rather than in groups. This means that although there are differences with regard to the intensity of online learning and the attendance at university between both groups, their overall learning effort is rather similar.

With regard to learning resource usage, both groups behave differently as all tests for significance are positive (according to the Mann-Whitney U test, p<=0.05). This can be seen in Figure 2. Videos are learning resources used most often for both groups followed by E-Books and E-Papers. MOOCs and special e-learning applications are less popular. Overall, we see a kind of similar ranking for both groups but a much more intense resource usage on part of the Indian students. This resembles the results from Table 1. Overall, we see that e-learning is an important part of learning especially for students from Pune. Acceptance rate is quite high as 88% of the German students and 96% of the Indian students declare that they like e-learning. Asked for reasons why they like it, most answers fall into a convenient information access category, providing easy and flexible information access. In addition to that, some of the students also mention factors directly related to learning, e.g. the possibility of clarifying questions and to deepen and widen the knowledge beyond what is provided in class.

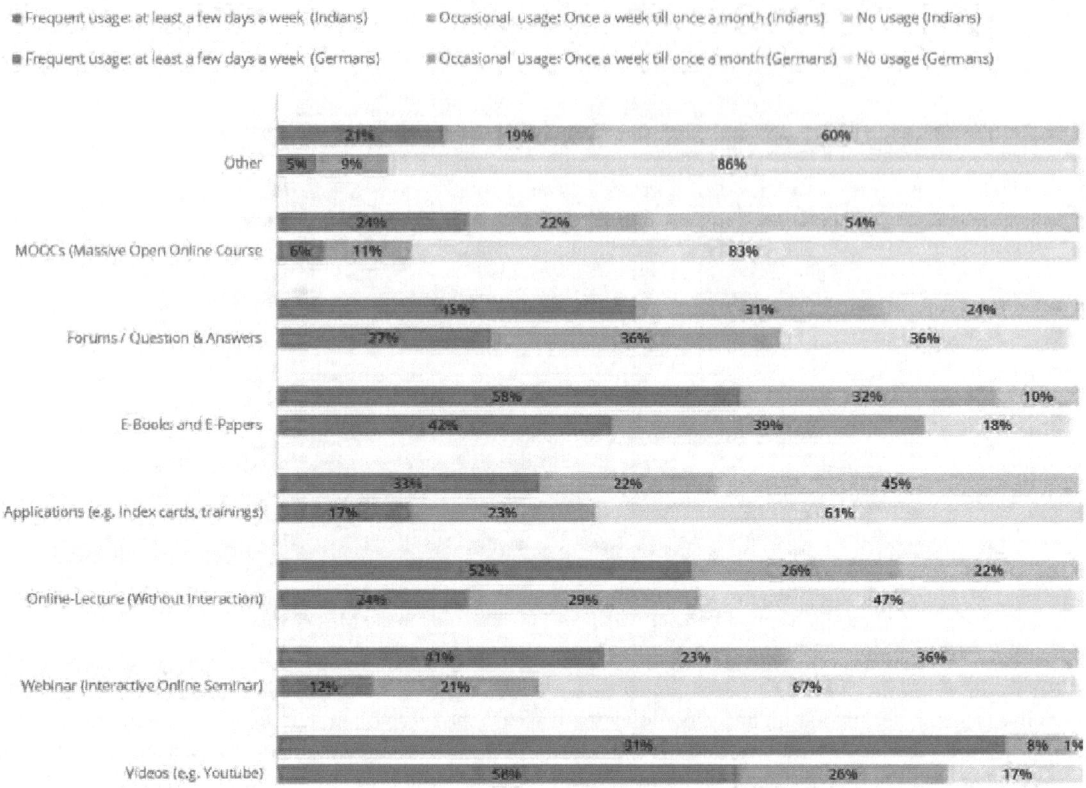

Figure 2. Usage of learning resources (German students, n=66, Indian students, n=105, all group comparisons significant according to the Mann-Whitney U test)

4.4 Communication related Technology Employment

The last research question is concerned with technology usage for communication purposes. With regard to student-to-student communication, the questions were related to communication purposes, frequency and tools used. Data shows, Indian students (90%) communicate daily more frequently with their peers (Mann-Whitney U test, p=0,01) than Germans do (68%). In addition, both groups are distinct with regard to learning related communication purposes. Germans have a stronger impetus to use communication technology as a tool to organize learning. Indians, on the other hand, use these tools for content related discussions more often e.g. 61% of Germans use technology to make appointments whereas only 16% of the Indian students are employing technology for this purpose. Asking for the tools they employ, we see that WhatsApp is very popular among students of both groups. In addition, E-mail and Facebook are also frequently used. While the majority of students in Germany employs a platform provided by the university for communication purposes, only a minority of students from India also behave this way.

Finally, the investigation also aims at insights concerning student-instructor communication. To start, we see a strong difference with regard to the overall frequency of student-instructor communication (Mann-Whitney U test, p=0,00). 30% of the Indian students communicate every day and another 30% a few days a week with the instructor. This is the case for only 2% and 8% of the German students. The majority of these communicate on a weekly (42%) or monthly (27%) basis with the instructor. With regard to the purpose of communication, again, we see that in contrast to the students from Germany the students from India are rather not used to make appointments (Chi-square test, p=0,00) with the instructor via computer mediated communication but are more prone to ask learning related questions (Chi-square test, p=0,00).

5. RESULTS AND DISCUSSION

What have we learned in this study? How can we estimate this research and in which ways can we use it?

To start, the goal of this investigation was to uncover learning related patterns of device usage in two distinct locations to get a picture of students needs with regard to e-learning support. In the literature section it was shown that research on transnational learning infrastructures and learning cultures is not that common. The investigations presented imply that students all over the world show a great willingness to apply digital devices for learning purposes. Still, findings relating to individual, cultural, and socio-economic factors on learning related device usage and attitudes on e-learning, are not so clear-cut and even partly inconsistent. Thus, in the context of our investigation, prefabricated notions should be avoided.

In this investigation, we focused on actual behavior and assessments of the participants as provided by participants' self-declaration. Items used in the survey were adopted from a collection of literature that investigates e-learning related behavior and patterns. The aim was to provide answers to three research questions. The first covers device usages and types of learning activities (RQ1), the second investigates the usage of learning related online resources and assessments of e-learning (RQ2), and the third concentrates on device usage and behavior in student-to-student and student-to-instructor communication (RQ3).

What are the main results of our investigation? First and foremost, the participants resemble two rather deviant samples. They differ with regard to all important attributes listed, not only on socio-demographic factors but also in relation to attendance at the university and intensity of online learning. The students from Pune are more often engaged in e-learning activities than the students from Hildesheim.

Concerning RQ1 (devices and learning activities), we see that both groups differ with regard to their equipment. They also show different devices usage patterns. For the German students, laptops are the primary learning devices. For the Indian students, smartphones are the most important ones. Although there is a tendency to use larger screens for more complex tasks, Indian students still use smartphones frequently. Thus, when one thinks about joint learning infrastructures, we can reason that all communication platforms and all of learning material provided needs be accessible and usable with smartphones.

With regard to RQ2 (use of learning resources, assessment of e-learning), we can hypothesize that students will have no problem to accept transnational e-learning as both groups like e-learning. Furthermore, the vast majority of students is already experienced in e-learning. Nevertheless, when one designs and executes a concrete conjoint learning scenario, one has to be aware that both groups exhibit different patterns of online resource usage. Whereas learning videos are a popular learning resource for most of the students from both groups, nearly half of the German students have no experience with online-lectures, learning applications, webinars, or MOOCs. Thus, one cannot assume that every learning resource is already known and ready to be employed immediately. In contrast, there probably is a need to introduce and train students about online resources, that they are not familiar with. In our case, the Indian students could operate as tutors for the German students. This could also help students to get familiar with each other and to build some basic trust.

In relation to RQ3 (communication behavior), we see substantial differences between both groups. The Indian students communicate much more frequently and use different tools than the Germans. The latter is especially obvious with regard to student-instructor communication. It seems that WhatsApp is the tool of choice for both groups for student-to-student related communication. This is also the case with regard to student-instructor communication for the Indians but not for the Germans. In Germany this tool is used scarcely for student-instructor communication. This can not only be connected to behavioral preferences but also to legal conditions as WhatsApp usage is not in concordance with the General Data Protection Regulation. In addition, the pragmatics of communication seems to be different too. German students communicate about content related and organizational aspects of learning. Indian students focus primarily on content related topics when communicating with peers and instructors. It is probably not going too far to assume that such differences in behavior could lead to some serious misunderstandings in common learning environments. Therefore, it seems to be a sensible approach to inform the students (and instructors) about these differences at the start of such a common learning endeavors.

In sum, although only of an explorative character, we can clearly see the knowledge value of this investigation. Besides delivering additional knowledge in a still largely unexplored field, this work provides directly applicable clues on how to build joint learning infrastructures.

REFERENCES

Arpaci, I., 2015. A comparative study of the effects of cultural differences on the adoption of mobile learning. *British Journal of Educational Technology,* Vol. 46, No.4, pp. 699-712.

Bates, A.W. and Bates, A.W., 2015. *Teaching in a digital age. Guidelines for designing teaching and learning.* Tony Bates Associates Ltd, https://opentextbc.ca/teachinginadigitalage/

Biesenbach-Lucas, S., 2005. Communication topics and strategies in e-mail consultation: Comparison between American and international university students. *Language Learning & Technology*, Vol. 9, No.2, pp. 24-46.

Calvo, R., Arbiol, A., and Iglesias, A., 2014. Are all chats suitable for learning purposes? A study of the required characteristics. *Procedia Computer Science*, Vol. 27, pp. 251-260.

Deng, L., and Tavares, N. J., 2015. Exploring university students' use of technologies beyond the formal learning context: A tale of two online platforms. *Australasian Journal of Educational Technology*, Vol. 31, No. 3, pp. 313-327.

Goodwin, K., Kennedy, G., and Vetere, F., 2010. Getting together out-of-class: Using technologies for informal interaction and learning. *Curriculum, technology & transformation for an unknown future*. Sydney, pp. 387-392.

Hofstede, G., 2001. *Culture's consequences: Comparing values, behaviors, institutions and organizations across nations.* Sage publications, Thousand Oaks, CA.

Kasunic, A., Hammer, J., and Ogan, A., 2015. Cultural relevance in MOOCs: Asking about socioeconomic context. *Proceedings of the Second (2015) ACM Conference on Learning@ Scale.* Vancouver, pp. 389-392.

Khaddage, F., and Knezek, G., 2014. A comparison of mobile learning attitudes among university students in four nations. *Advanced Learning Technologies (ICALT)* of the *2014 IEEE 14th International Conference.* Washington, pp. 141-142.

Ko, E. H., Chiu, D. K., Lo, P., and Ho, K. K., 2015. Comparative study on m-learning usage among LIS students from Hong Kong, Japan and Taiwan. *The Journal of Academic Librarianship*, Vol. 41, No. 5, pp. 567-577.

Krull, G., & Duart, J. M. (2017). Research Trends in Mobile Learning in Higher Education: A Systematic Review of Articles (2011–2015). *International Review of Research in Open and Distributed Learning*, Vol. 18, No. 7.

Kukulska-Hulme, A., Pettit, J., Bradley, L., Carvalho, A. A., Herrington, A., Kennedy, D. M., and Walker, A., 2011. Mature Students Using Mobile Devices in Life and Learning. *International Journal of Mobile and Blended Learning (IJMBL)*, Vol. 3, No.1, pp. 18-52.

Madge, C., Meek, J., Wellens, J., and Hooley, T., 2009. Facebook, social integration and informal learning at university: 'It is more for socialising and talking to friends about work than for actually doing work'. *Learning, media and technology*, Vol. 34, No. 2, pp. 141-155.

Maifarth, M., Griesbaum, J. and Kölle, R., 2013. Mobile device usage in higher education. In Bremer, C. & Krömker, D., E-Learning zwischen Vision und Alltag. Zum Stand der Dinge. Münster, pp.332-337.

Martin, F., and Bolliger, D. U., 2018. Engagement Matters: Student Perceptions on the Importance of Engagement Strategies in the Online Learning Environment, *Online Learning,* Vol. 22, No.1, pp. 205-222.

Sandoval-Lucero, E., Blasius, E., Klingsmith, L., and Waite, C., 2012. Student-Initiated Study Groups for STEM Classes in Community College Settings. *Higher Education Studies*, Vol. 2, No. 2, pp. 31-39.

Sharma, R., and Madhusudhan, M., 2017. Use of Mobile Devices by Library and Information Science Students in Central Universities of Uttar Pradesh. *DESIDOC Journal of Library & Information Technology*, Vol. 37, No. 4, pp. 287–296.

Shuter, R., Cheong, P., and Chen, Y., 2016. The influence of cultural values on US and Danish students' digital behavior: Exploring culture, new media, and social context. *Journal of International and Intercultural Communication*, Vol. 9, No. 2, pp. 161-178.

Trenkov, L., 2014. Managing teacher-student interaction via WhatsApp platform. *EDULEARN14 Proceedings*. Barcelona, pp. 6596-6600.

Zawacki-Richter, O., Bozkurt, A., Alturki, U., & Aldraiweesh, A., 2018. What Research Says About MOOCs–An Explorative Content Analysis. *The International Review of Research in Open and Distributed Learning*, Vol. 19, No. 1.

Velayo, R.S., 2012. Internationalizing the curriculum. Handbook of college and university teaching: A global perspective, pp.268-278.

Viberg, O., & Gronlund, A. (2013). Cross-cultural analysis of users' attitudes toward the use of mobile devices in second and foreign language learning in higher education: A case from Sweden and China. *Computers & Education*, Vol. 69, pp. 169-180.

5G TECHNOLOGY AND ITS APPLICATIONS TO MUSIC EDUCATION

Adriano Baratè, Goffredo Haus, Luca A. Ludovico, Elena Pagani and Nello Scarabottolo
Department of Computer Science "Giovanni Degli Antoni"
Via G. Celoria, 18 – 20133 Milano (Italy)

ABSTRACT

The goal of this paper is to discuss and provide some practical examples of how the emerging 5G technology can change current e-learning approaches. Thanks to the main characteristics of 5G networks, and specifically improved bandwidth, reliability, and density of devices in an area, it is possible to conceive and implement new educational services rich in multimedia content, supporting multimodal interaction, and highly customizable depending on users' requirements and special needs. In order to show the didactic efficacy, we will discuss an application to the field of music education that could benefit from this novel approach.

KEYWORDS

Education, e-Learning, Interactive Media System, Music Teaching, 5G

1. INTRODUCTION

Even if technological innovation in education is source of debates and controversies among scholars and experts, an aspect on which most of them agree is that technology-based didactic innovation should not be an end in itself, but, rather, a way to drastically improve the educational experience and to better meet the needs of teachers and learners.

A technology that, in the near future, is likely to change our lives is the latest generation of cellular mobile communications known as 5G, from "5th Generation". As discussed below, 5G introduces significant improvements with respect to current network technologies in terms of a larger bandwidth, a more reliable service, and a higher density of devices.

Narrowing the field to music education, the research questions we want to address in this paper are: Can 5G be profitably applied to such an educational context? What didactic services, currently hard or impossible to implement, will become potentially available to music learners? Finally, how will 5G affect the way we learn music and practice an instrument?

In order to answer these questions, the paper will provide details about the technical specifications and the expected performances of 5G networks (Section 2), will shed some light on brand new or enhanced educational services (Section 3), and, finally, will present some music-related scenarios where 5G is expected to show its potential (Section 4). Section 5 concludes the work.

2. KEY FEATURES OF 5G TECHNOLOGY

The standard document for 5G technology (3GPP 2019) has been published in March 2018 by 3GPP and officially approved in the Plenary Meeting in June 2018. 5G technology promises to be able to support a number of both traditional and novel applications, such as device-to-device communication and Internet of Things (IoT).

For the goals of this paper, we are interested in investigating 5G functionalities and performances that may facilitate the implementation of advanced e-learning services. Since in this paper we focus on music education, we analyze in particular the support 5G may give to audio and video data exchange, and on its capabilities of facilitating data sharing through the formation of extemporary classrooms anywhere using just users' devices. To this purpose, we carried out an analysis of existing – mainly European – 5G trials in order to assess the feasibility of e-learning platforms leveraging this technology.

Let us start from an analysis of the typical requirements of multimedia applications, regardless of 5G networks. Table 1 summarizes the bandwidth, latency, and reliability requested by different applications and data traffics. As far as latency is concerned, while streaming applications tolerate delays of a few seconds, two-way conferencing applications have a more stringent requirement in the order of around 100 ms in order to supply high Quality of Experience (QoE) to the users (Cisco 2017). 4G cellular telephony still meets the characteristics of high quality (4K) video streaming such as that supplied by some media-service providers (Gonzales 2018). By contrast, applications involving Augmented Reality (AR) and Virtual Reality (VR) significantly push forward these requirements (Mangiante, et al. 2017; Qualcomm Technologies Inc. 2018; Mushroom Networks 2017): in order to supply a realistic and immersive experience to users, ultra-low latencies of less than 10 ms are needed; for retina-experience video, the requested bandwidth may increase up to some Gbps.

Table 1. Summary of needed network performance for multimedia applications

Application	Bandwidth	Latency	Reliability
standard A/V streaming	$\leq$ 3 Mbps	4-5 s	$\geq$ 95%
HD video streaming	4-8 Mbps	4-5 s	$\geq$ 95%
3D HD video streaming	9 Mbps	4-5 s	$\geq$ 95%
4K video streaming	25 Mbps	4-5 s	$\geq$ 95%
interactive real-time conferencing	$\geq$ 2 Mbps	~ 100 ms	99.0% - 99.5%
AR	100 Mbps - 5 Gbps	1 ms	99.0% - 99.5%
VR (interactive)	100 Mbps - 2.35 Gbps	10-30 ms	99.0% - 99.5%

Considering how recent the standardization of 5G is, it is not easy to determine to what extent 5G will be able to fulfill the requirements in Table 1. In the following, we summarize and discuss the characteristics of 5G services and of deployed 5G trials with respect to the expected needs of e-learning platforms.

As far as services are concerned, 5G includes both an ultra-reliable low-latency communications (URLLC) service, and an enhanced mobile broadband (eMBB) service (3GPP 2019). Deliverable D1.1 of the 5G-EVE consortium (5G EVE 2018) published in Oct. 2018 defines the characteristics of these services. URLLC aims at providing latencies no greater than 50 msec. and reliability of more than 99.9% (Li, et al. 2018); it is intended for use mainly with industrial and vehicular applications in order to guarantee prompt delivery of emergency notifications. Under these points of view, it also fits the requirements of AR and VR applications; though, it will be able to provide a data rate of up to 10 Mbps. By contrast, eMBB aims at providing ultra-high throughput so as to address the needs of users accessing multimedia content, ranging from real-time video streaming to online gaming with 3D 4K video; in particular, it should provide a peak data rate of up to 20 Gbps for the base station, with a minimum guaranteed to users of 100 Mbps. This service seems best suitable for e-learning applications. In the same document, the goal for Media & Entertainment applications is TV service for mobile users with throughput of 100-200 Mbps (with peaks of up to 250 Mbps in downlink) and latency lower than 100 msec. An aspect that is still under investigation is how the different services will coexist; their combination seems impossible since different mechanisms are adopted to implement each of them (Ji, et al. 2017). Coexistence of URLLC and eMBB might delay network access for eMBB traffic, thus affecting its performance; this will depend on the mix of different traffics in real infrastructures.

An interesting characteristic of 5G is its multi-RAT (multi-Radio Access Technology) nature. This means that 5G will be able to cooperate with different technologies such as 4G cellular telephony, but also with Bluetooth or WiFi. Both Bluetooth and WiFi are license-free technologies, which however might provide limited bandwidths: Bluetooth 5 supplies a bitrate around 2 Mbps, while WiFi – in version 802.11ac – can reach, in real deployments, up to ~200 Mbps. An alternative incoming possibility is that of using LTE Direct: it is an addition to 4G LTE technology, standardized on March 2015 in 3GPP Release 12 (3GPP 2015), that allows to offload base stations by supporting direct device-to-device communications between devices in the same cell. In 2015, Deutsche Telekom deployed a first trial of LTE Direct, validating the feasibility of the technology (Qualcomm Technologies Inc. 2015). LTE Direct supplies a higher radio range than WiFi also in urban areas, it supports quite high mobility (up to 30 Km/h), but provides throughputs of the order of 3.5 Mbps uplink and 13 Mbps downlink.

With these premises, a number of scenarios currently not implementable will be achievable in the future, through an accurate combination of radio technologies and services. Figure 1 outlines some possible applications, by arranging them along the axes that link the peculiar features of 5G systems: capacity enhancement, ultra-high reliability & low latency, and a third type of service, namely, the ability of connecting an ultra-high number of devices.

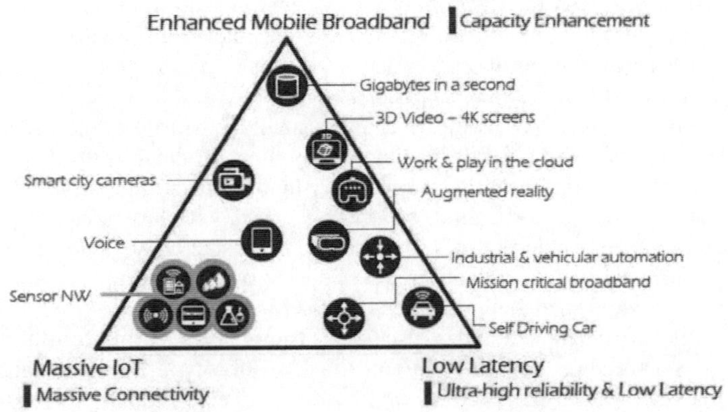

Figure 1. The triangle of 5G applications (source: ETRI graphic, from ITU-R IMT 2020 requirements)

In (Fallgren & Timus, 2013) these scenarios are described as follows:

- *Amazingly fast* – Users can obtain very high data rates with instantaneous connectivity and low latency. This is crucial for multi-layer applications based on multiple high-quality media streams;
- *Great service in a crowd* – Currently, connectivity is limited when many users share the same area (e.g., stadiums, concert halls, etc.), but in the future also crowded places will permit a satisfactory experience;
- *Ubiquitous things communicating* – The mix of IoT and human-centric communications tends to have different needs, and the 5G technology will efficiently handle these new requirements;
- *Best experience follows you* – Even when users are on the move (e.g., traveling by car or commuting), a high quality of service will be guaranteed;
- *Super real-time and reliable connections* – Future wireless systems will support new applications that take full advantage of very high reliability and low latency, thus allowing real-time fruition (e.g., augmented/virtual reality) as well as control (e.g., self-driving vehicles and industrial automation).

2.1 5G State-of-the-Art and Trials

In order to assess the characteristics of 5G networks in real or realistic environments, a number of experiments are ongoing. On December 2018, the Italian Inter-University Consortium for Telecommunications (CNIT) promoted a conference involving information technology companies, telecommunication companies and representatives of the European Commission (CNIT, 5G Italy Global Meeting website 2018). The talk by Enrico Salvatori of Qualcomm supplied a measure of bandwidth of 1.4 Gbps in a testbed in San Francisco. According to Peter Stuckmann of the European Commission, the 26 GHz frequency band will be reserved for fixed wireless access with a throughput of up to 10 Gbps, while the 3.6 GHz frequency band will be used for urban mobile access guaranteeing users a data rate of 1-3 Gbps.

For the Bari-Matera installation in Italy, the 5G-PPP consortium (The 5G Infrastructure Public Private Partnership 2018) reports an obtained throughput of around 3 Gbps with a latency of about 2 ms (Fastweb 2018). In this case – as mentioned above – 5G is mixed with the LTE technology (Tim, Fastweb and Huawei 2018); the migration towards pure 5G is scheduled for mid-2019. A laboratory testbed in Turin achieved a peak rate of 23 Gbps; however, this experiment does not seem to mimic realistic situations.

The 5G-EVE consortium (5G-EVE 2018) was founded in June 2018 with the goal of coordinating and tracing the experiences conducted in European trials. According to Deliverable 3.1 published in December 2018, two trials are planned for Media & Entertainment applications: the former in Spain with the goal of achieving 200 Mbps throughput with around 100 msec. of latency; the latter in France with comparable latency and a lower throughput of 80-200 Mbps.

The European 5G Observatory (European 5G Observatory 2018) provides data from around 180 trials and experiments. Data are contradictory, as noticed in the site, with bandwidths variable between 1.7 Gbps and 25 Gbps; this likely depends on whether measurements are taken in a real urban infrastructure, or rather are conducted in a laboratory. From the data analysis, it seems that the most realistic measures have achieved 700 Mbps to 1 Gbps data rate in download; this test was conducted in Finland in urban area, hence possibly with a reasonable user density. Over all experiments, peak data rates have been achieved between 250 Mbps and 70 Gbps, with an average of 1 to 4.5 Gbps for user devices, and latencies < 5 msec. It is worth noticing, however, that the peak data rates have been obtained in small testbeds (e.g., involving just a small number of users and one antenna) possibly in laboratory, and their applicability is thus limited.

Summarizing the above considerations, we may say that the existing realistic trials are able to provide a 700 Mbps to 1 Gbps (or more) of throughput on user's devices, with low latencies, also of the order of a few milliseconds. According to Table 1, this performance satisfactorily supports the requirements of all applications including AR/VR, thus making 5G the elective technology to support the deployment of innovative e-learning services such as those discussed later in this paper.

However, a couple of remarks must be discussed. The analyzed trials results have been obtained with currently existing infrastructures, which represent the first prototype implementations of the 5G standard, possibly built from existing 4G infrastructures of providers that are gradually trying to commute to 5G; better results will be likely obtained in future years with the improvement of both the hardware and software components. Moreover, the performance really observed by users will strongly depend on the mix of traffics (asking different services) that will be injected into the networks, and on how they will compete for the network resources.

3. 5G-BASED APPLICATIONS FOR EDUCATION

After analyzing the technical features of 5G networks and the state of the art about trials in real or artificial environments, we can try to answer the research questions raised in the introduction, concerning new educational services based on 5G technology and their implications on teaching and learning.

First, network features introduced by 5G – as reported in Section 2 – may support the simulation of in-presence learning (*remote synchronous*), wherever learners actually are, thanks to high-bandwidth and low-latency services. As far as network applications are concerned, *remote synchronous* learning is one of the hardest in terms of quality of service (QoS). A strict requirement is seamless interactivity in distant education, which implies little bidirectional delay. Even if time constraints are not as strict as for self-driving cars or other critical real-time applications, the interaction should be perceived as fluid, so the suffered delay should be in the order of 100 ms or less. Learners can experience a didactic session in a private as well as in a public and crowded place, thanks to the support of a high number of devices in a small area. In this sense, a very specific application could be the real-time replication of a lesson in another classroom. This situation is already common in case of, e.g., crowded university courses, but, differently from "on-site" students, "distant" colleagues are forced to watch the same big screen or projection, with no possibility to interact with the professor (e.g., if blackboard notes are too small) or customize the experience (e.g., focusing on the professor's face or on his/her multimedia presentation). Such an example can be easily extended to non-institutional places, such as a park, a bus, or a stadium. In this sense, for students there is also the possibility to attend live lessons in mobility, within an interactive and customizable learning environment, and this novel modality can represent a paradigm shift for non-attending and off-site students.

Student groups can be formed dynamically using participants' devices, in a BYOD (*bring your own device*) context, exploiting massive connectivity support. Thanks to the 5G multi-RAT feature, it is possible to constitute impromptu ad hoc groups formed by the devices of both teachers and learners, wherever they are. This is for instance possible by using the LTE Direct technology. In case no fixed infrastructure exists, users may leverage the ad-hoc networking capabilities of WiFi and Bluetooth. Another practical issue, especially in case of high transfer rates and consistent data volumes, could be the cost of data traffic for students. Once again, the expected features of 5G could solve the problem. In fact, through the use of free radio channels such as Bluetooth and WiFi, the educational experience could require no fees and imply no usage of Gb per month. Since an impromptu classroom is expected to cover a small geographical area, latencies should not be an issue.

As far as *remote asynchronous* learning is concerned: the 5G architecture assumes to involve cloud or fog computing. Students may take tests and exercises offline and then upload their results on the cloud, where statistical processing of their data may either bring into evidence topics that are unclear to a majority of students (and must thus be discussed in more depth during lessons) or highlight students with a significantly low rate of success in assessment (thus needing special tutoring).

Finally, let us remark that 5G networks foster educational applications with highly-demanding transfer rates, such as the virtualization of lab experiences through virtual reality (VR). In this sense, an educational application can take benefit of high bitrates through ultrahigh-definition video streams (4K is not very defined when applied to a spherical video), and exploit low latency coupled with cloud/fog/edge computing for the real time calculation in response to user actions, gestures and movements.

4. CASE STUDY: MULTI LAYER MUSIC EDUCATION

In this section, we will propose a case study covering heterogeneous educational goals and investigating different aspects of 5G technologies. Specifically, we will discuss the possibility to deliver simultaneous and synchronized high-quality data streams in applications for music education.

A demanding application in terms of bandwidth is multi-layer teaching. With the locution *multi-layer* we denote an approach to the description of an information entity from multiple points of view, possibly making their heterogeneous relationships emerge.

In this sense, a relevant application field is music education, where the single music piece can represent the object to be described in a multi-layer framework. Let us consider a typical music lesson for young learners: a music tune can be studied in terms of music notation (actually, multiple forms of notation can be employed), gestures and movements used to play the musical instrument (or instruments), already available performances, etc. A publicly available example is represented by a web-based interface realized by the Laboratory of Music Informatics, University of Milan for an educational book by Pearson, whose interface is shown in Figure 2 (Ludovico and Mangione 2014). Such a multi-layer approach embraces different kinds of representation: a logic description of music events, one or many graphical representations for notation, one or many audio/video tracks of human or computer-based performances, a structural description for analytical considerations, etc.

The first educational advantage of a multi-layer approach is the possibility to offer a more articulated set of organized information to students. A young learner, for example, can take benefit from an audio track corresponding to the score to study and showing the expected result, in particular if a computer-based application is able to support synchronized experience of graphical notation and an already available human performance. Another advantage is user-tailored customization, which implies, in our example:

- the possibility to choose alternative forms of notation (e.g., colored notation for children affected by dyslexia or Braille notation for blind people);
- the most suitable types of video content (e.g., a timed animation of the keys to play or a close-up footage over the hands of an experienced pianist);
- the comparison of already-available performances to improve expressiveness;
- the use of learning aids, e.g., the possibility to reduce the beats per minutes during playback, which requires materials with a high sampling rate.

Unfortunately, this approach presents a drawback: the need to send a number of simultaneous high-quality materials over the network.

In order to evaluate requirements, let us consider the bandwidth requested by digital media formats commonly in use, focusing on audio and video. Audio streams for Red Book audio CDs are two-channel signed 16-bit Linear PCM sampled at 44100 Hz, whose bit rate is 1411.2 kbps, or 176400 bytes per second. The DVD-Audio format presents a maximum permissible total bit rate of 9.6 Mbps. Concerning compressed audio, files typically present highly variable bit rates, depending on the encoding format, the expected quality, and the characteristics of media content. FLAC files usually have a bit rate that ranges from 220 to 1184 kbps, whereas for MP3 files acceptable values for music applications usually span from 128 to 320 kbps. Also for video formats there are many standards and settings. At the moment of writing, YouTube adopts an MP4 container with AAC-LC as the audio codec and H.264 as the video codec. Audio playback bitrate is not related to video resolution. Recommended bitrates for audio are: 128 kbps for mono, 384 kbps for stereo, and 512 kbps for 5.1; values for video are shown in Table 2.

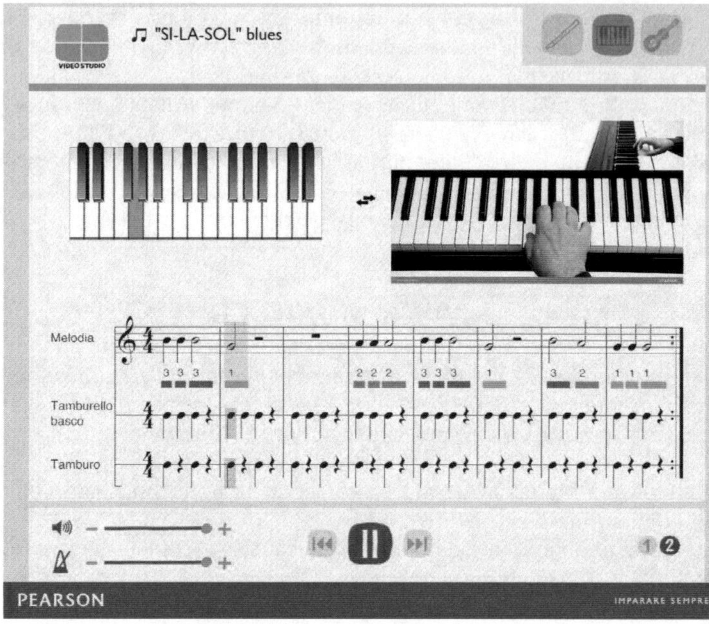

Figure 2. An example of multi-layer application for music education

Table 2. Video bitrates recommended by YouTube for standard-dynamic-range (SDR) uploads. Values for high-dynamic-range (HDR) videos are similar

Type	Video Bit Rate Standard Frame Rate (24, 25, 30)	Video Bit Rate High Frame Rate (48, 50, 60)
2160p (4K)	35-45 Mbps	53-68 Mbps
1440p (2K)	16 Mpbs	24 Mpbs
1080p	8 Mpbs	12 Mpbs
720p	5 Mpbs	7.5 Mpbs
480p	2.5 Mpbs	4 Mpbs
360p	1 Mpbs	1.5 Mpbs

Let us consider some cases of multi-layer applications dealing with music performances, particularly rich in multimedia materials and based on simultaneous delivery of audio and video streams. An example could be an educational product conceived to let learners practice their instrument alone or in group, playing over a previously recorded symphonic orchestra. Besides providing score following features, such an application should offer the possibility to suppress 1 to *n* audio tracks in a multi-track recording and choose one of many available video angles. Score events should be synchronized with multiple audio/video streams and mapped onto one or more scores (e.g., the full score and single parts). This kind of approach implies a high number of audio tracks, one per instrumental group and soloists, and as many different cameras as possible. Commercially available examples are Music Minus One music productions, meant to be accompanied by the listener on whichever instrument (or voice type) by excluding it from the recording. The technique is the same as the later development of karaoke for the voice. A computer-based generalization of the approach, allowing to subtract *n* sound sources, has been discussed in (Baratè, Haus and Ludovico 2018), and its graphical interface is shown in Figure 3. The latter case study, very close to the educational goals described in Section 4, could not be easily implemented as a web application with current network technologies.

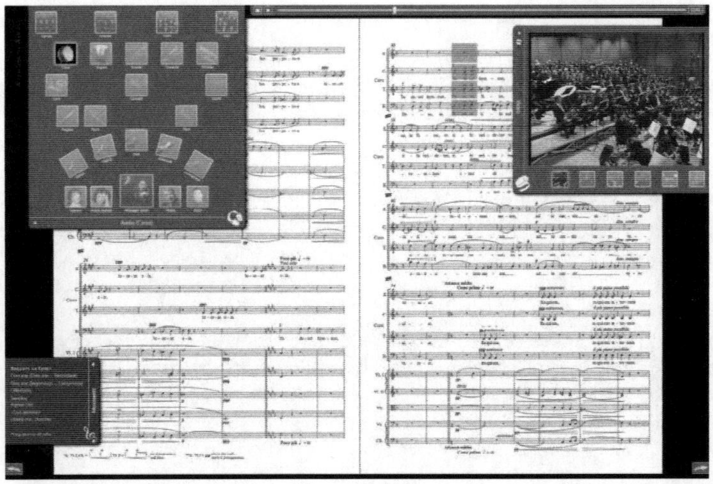

Figure 3. An application presenting multi-track audio and multi-angle video

5G technology fosters this kind of applications, first providing the user with an improved bandwidth and guaranteeing a high QoS. Moreover, 5G networks present a very low latency, so the client-server request to send a new stream can occur on the fly, with no significant delay perceived in multimedia experience. In other words, it is no more necessary for the client to have a number of media streams simultaneously available and ready to be switched in real time, and the band available to single users can be exploited in better ways, e.g. delivering on demand an 8K HDR 60FPS (FUHD) spherical video that requires 100 Mbps approximatively.

The possibilities offered to music education by such a massive delivering of high-definition media streams are countless, ranging from a customizable multi-angle fruition of ad hoc materials for instrumental practice to the realistic virtualization of the experience occurring in a real performing context, such as a rehearsal room or an opera house.

5. CONCLUSIONS

This paper focused on the applicability of 5G technology to novel educational scenarios, proposing a number of advanced didactic services and applications in the field of music. Due to the tight connections with multimedia and to low-latency requirements, music education is a good testbed to design demanding environments and stress their performances.

Among other advantages, it is worth citing the possibility to organize synchronous interactive sessions with a student population mainly constituted by already employed people, having difficulties in connecting through a PC during working hours. In this context, the availability of 5G technology can offer an interesting option for overcoming the above limit, allowing students to interact with teachers/tutors with full access to visual materials.

In conclusion, 5G technology can open innovative e-learning scenarios, like the one dealing with music education described in this paper, also in the context of augmented/virtual reality (Baratè et al. 2019b). Besides, 5G can significantly improve already available e-learning initiatives, such as on-line versions of university degrees (Baratè et al. 2019a).

In the near future, we can expect that the mentioned experiences will constitute a testbed for advanced learning services, providing scholars and researchers from different domains with the possibility to assess 5G applicability and impact on students' performances in a real-world scenario.

REFERENCES

3GPP. «Overview of 3GPP Release 12 V0.2.0.» September 2015. http://www.3gpp.org/specifications/releases/68-release-12 (last accessed on February 28, 2019).

3GPP. «Release 15, TR 21.915 v0.6.0.» February 2019. http://www.3gpp.org/release-15 (last accessed on February 28, 2019).

5G EVE. *5G European Validation platform for Extensive trials.* 2018. https://www.5g-eve.eu/ (last accessed on February 28, 2019).

Baratè, Adriano, Goffredo Haus, and Luca Andrea Ludovico. «Advanced Experience of Music through 5G Technology.» *Florence Heri-Tech - The Future of Heritage Science and Technologies, 16–18 May 2018, Florence, Italy.* IOP Conference Series, 2018. 012021.1-012021.13.

Baratè, Adriano, Goffredo Haus, Luca Andrea Ludovico, Elena Pagani, and Nello Scarabottolo. «5G Technology and Its Application to E-Learning.» *Proceedings of the 11th annual International Conference on Education and New Learning Technologies*. 2019a. In press.

—. «5G Technology for Augmented and Virtual Reality in Education.» *Proceedings of the International Conference on Education and New Developments 2019 (END 2019)*. 2019b. In press.

Cisco. «Video Quality of Service (QOS) Tutorial.» September 2017. https://www.cisco.com/c/en/us/support/docs/quality-of-service-qos/qos-video/212134-Video-Quality-of-Service-QOS-Tutorial.html (last accessed on February 28, 2019).

CNIT. *5G Italy Global Meeting website.* 2018. https://www.5gitaly.eu/en/home2/ (last accessed on February 28, 2019).

European 5G Observatory. *Major European 5G trials and pilots.* 2018. http://5gobservatory.eu/5g-trial/major-european-5g-trials-and-pilots/ (last accessed on February 28, 2019).

Fallgren, Mikael, and Bogdan Timus. *Scenarios, requirements and KPIs for 5G mobile and wireless system.* Mobile and wireless communications Enablers for the Twenty-twenty Information Society (METIS), 2013.

Fastweb. *Rete 5G a Matera, accesa la prima antenna del progetto Bari-Matera 5G.* 5 March 2018. https://www.fastweb.it/internet/5g-matera-fastweb/ (last accessed on February 28, 2019).

Gonzales, Barb. «Internet Speed Requirements for Video Streaming.» *Lifewire.* October 2018. https://www.lifewire.com/internet-speed-requirements-for-movie-viewing-1847401 (last accessed on February 28, 2019).

Ji, Hyoungju, Sunho Park, Jeongho Yeo, Younsun Kim, Juho Lee, and Byonghyo Shim. «Introduction to ultra reliable and low latency communications in 5G.» *ArXiv*, 2017.

Li, Zexian, Mikko A. Uusitalo, Hamidreza Shariatmadari, and Bikramjit Singh. «5G URLLC: Design Challenges and System Concepts.» *Proc. 15th International Symposium on Wireless Communication Systems (ISWCS).* 2018. 1-6.

Ludovico, Luca Andrea, and Giuseppina Rita Mangione. «An Active E-book to Foster Self-regulation in Music Education.» *Interactive Technology and Smart Education 11.4*, 2014: 254-269.

Mangiante, Simone, Guenter Klas, Amit Navon, Zhuang GuanHua, Ju Ran, and Marco Dias Silva. «VR is on the Edge: How to Deliver 360° Videos in Mobile Networks.» *Proc. ACM Workshop on Virtual Reality and Augmented Reality Network (VR/AR Network).* 2017. 30-35.

Mushroom Networks. «Bandwidth requirements for Virtual Reality (VR) and Augmented Reality (AR).» 2017. https://www.mushroomnetworks.com/infographics/bandwidth-requirements-for-virtual-reality-vr-and-augmented-reality-ar-infographic/ (last accessed on February 28, 2019).

Qualcomm Technologies Inc. «LTE Direct trial - White Paper.» February 2015. https://www.qualcomm.com/media/documents/files/lte-direct-trial-whitepaper.pdf (last accessed on February 28, 2019).

—. «VR and AR pushing connectivity limits.» October 2018. https://www.qualcomm.com/media/documents/files/vr-and-ar-pushing-connectivity-limits.pdf (last accessed on February 28, 2019).

The 5G Infrastructure Public Private Partnership. *European 5G trials.* 2018. https://5g-ppp.eu/5g-trials-2/ (last accessed on February 28, 2019).

Tim, Fastweb, and Huawei. *Bari Matera 5G web site.* 2018. http://www.barimatera5g.it/ (last accessed on February 28, 2019).

TEACHER ATTITUDES REGARDING THE USE OF GAME-BASED PROGRAMMING TOOLS IN K-12 EDUCATION

Chien-Yuan Su, Yue Hu and Yu-Hang Li
Department of Curriculum and Learning Science, Zhejiang University
Hangzhou, China

ABSTRACT

In recent years, game-based programming tools (GBPTs) such as Code.org, Lightbot, and Cargo-Bot have been developed to help children worldwide better understand programming concepts through an interesting, enjoyable and visualizable programming learning experience. However, in-service teachers' perceptions regarding the use of these game-based programming tools in K-12 instruction have received little attention. To understand the perceptions of teachers, this study integrated perceived enjoyment into the Technology Acceptance Model (TAM) to explore the factors that influence the intentions of K-12 in-service teachers to use game-based programming tools in their instructional tasks. Thirty Chinese teachers in elementary and secondary schools were invited to finish at least one hour of code tutorial at the code.org site, and then undertake a paper-and-pencil questionnaire. We applied the partial least squares structural equation modeling technique to analyze the extended TAM model. Results demonstrated that teachers' behavioral intention was determined by their attitudes toward using GBPTs. Perceived usefulness and perceived ease of use had a significant and positive influence on teachers' attitude. In addition, the results also indicated that perceived enjoyment has a significant influence on perceived usefulness and perceived ease of use, but no significant effect on the attitude of teachers regarding the use of GBPTs.

KEYWORDS

Game-based Programming Tools, Technology Acceptance Model, Perceived Enjoyment, K-12 Teachers

1. INTRODUCTION

There is sufficient evidence to show that "learning to program" could benefit children's development of skills in general planning, problem-solving, creativity and cooperation, as well as skills of computational thinking in other settings (Ching et al. 2018; Topalli and Cagiltay, 2018; Wing, 2006). Nowadays, some emerging game-based programming tools (e.g., Code.org, Lightbot, and Cargo-Bot) have been designed to provide an easy-to-use, interactive, challenging and enjoyable learning environment to engage children and motivate them to learn programming. For example, Kalelioglu (2015) used Code.org (https://code.org/) to teach 32 fourth-grade primary school students programming concepts and found that students developed a positive attitude toward programming and improved their programming, mathematical and geometrical knowledge. Lopez et al. (2016) applied an educational programming game called Lightbot (https://lightbot.com/flash.html) to teach university students programming concepts. They observed that students seemed to enjoy learning with Lightbot and attained a better understanding of programming concepts. Similarly, Tessler et al. (2013) examined the effects of teaching programming concepts on high school students by playing Cargo-Bot (http://twolivesleft.com/CargoBot). They discovered that playing Cargo-Bot is indeed an enjoyable and effective way to learn programming.

These GBPTs can make programming learning more enjoyable and may facilitate programming instruction applications in existing K-12 education strategies (Rajeev et al., 2018). While some attention has been paid in the past to researching issues related to GBPTs, little is known about in-service teachers' perceptions of using GBPTs in K-12 education. This study presents an empirical investigation using TAM as a framework to explore K-12 in-service teachers' perceptions of utilizing GBPTs to reinforce their instruction. The technology acceptance model (TAM) (Davis et al., 1989) has been broadly applied to explore users' perceptions in the application of a particular learning system and its tools. However, the existing constructs of TAM are not adequate enough to fully reflect the enjoyment of the user experience when operating these game-based programming tools. Therefore, one determinant variable—perceived enjoyment—was added to enhance the understanding of perceptions of teachers with regard to utilizing GBPTs.

2. THEORETICAL BACKGROUND

2.1 Technology Acceptance Model

The technology acceptance model (TAM) (Davis, 1989) is a well-recognized framework developed to explore user attitudes and behavioral intentions toward the use of different technology systems/tools. TAM was proposed by Davis in 1989, emphasizing that perceived usefulness and perceived ease of use are important for users who are deciding whether to accept or reject specific information technologies. Perceived usefulness is considered to be "the degree to which a person believes that using a particular system would enhance his or her job performance," and perceived ease of use is defined as "the degree to which a person believes that using a particular system would be free from effort" (Davis, 1989; Davis et al., 1989). Specifically, behavioral intention is determined by user attitudes toward, a particular technology system or tool, which in turn is determined by its perceived usefulness and perceived ease of use. In addition, perceived ease of use has a direct and significant influence on perceived usefulness.

TAM has been widely applied and modified to explore attitudes and intentions of teachers to utilize different e-learning systems/tools. For example, Chiu (2017) used TAM to investigate external factors such as anxiety, computer self-efficacy, voluntariness, and institutional support to determine how these factors affected in-service secondary school teachers' adoption of electronic textbooks. Liu et al. (2017) revised TAM by adding the pedagogical beliefs of teachers to investigate the acceptance of information and communication technology (ICT) for university teachers of English as a Foreign Language (EFL) in China. Su et al. (2018) extended TAM by additionally considering external factors such as management support, computer anxiety, intrinsic motivation, and job relevance to explore in-service teachers' attitudes and behavioral intentions to use ICT in primary and secondary school education in China. However, little attention has been focused on the attitudes and behavioral intentions of teachers with respect to the usage of GBPTs in K-12 education.

2.2 Perceived Enjoyment

Perceived enjoyment is at the core of the media entertainment experience (Vorderer et al., 2004), and is defined as "the extent to which the activity of using technology is perceived to be enjoyable in its own right, apart from any performance consequences that may be anticipated" (Davis et al., 1989). Some studies emphasized that perceived enjoyment plays an important role, and as such have incorporated it to explain certain phenomena regarding teachers' perceptions of using an e-learning system/tool (Abdullah and Ward, 2016; Sun and Zhang, 2008). For example, Teo and Noyes (2011) incorporated perceived enjoyment into a TAM framework to explore pre-service teachers' intentions to use technology and found that perceived enjoyment had a significant impact on teachers' attitudes and intentions for computer usage. Elkaseh et al. (2015) extended TAM by incorporating perceived enjoyment and social influence to explore students' and university teachers' perceptions of e-learning tools for teaching and learning. This study showed that perceived enjoyment significantly affects perceived usefulness and perceived ease of use. Park and Kwon (2016) employed TAM, examining two external factors—perceived enjoyment and service quality—to forecast teachers' intentions in using teaching assistant robots. They demonstrated that perceived enjoyment and service quality were extremely significant influencing factors in which perceived enjoyment had a positive effect on perceived usefulness and perceived ease of use. Adukaite et al. (2017) conducted an empirical study to investigate South African tourism teachers' perceptions regarding acceptance of a gamified application in tourism instruction, and demonstrated that perceived enjoyment was one important determinant affecting teachers' behavioral intentions to use gamified applications for tourism education.

According to the relevant literature, perceived enjoyment seems to be a key influencing factor for teachers that may affect their perceived usefulness, perceived ease of use and attitude toward utilizing GBPTs in K-12 education.

3. RESEARCH MODEL AND HYPOTHESES

Based on the previous literature review, an extended technology acceptance model (TAM) was applied and integrated with perceived enjoyment to better investigate in-service teachers' perceptions regarding the use of game-based programming tools in K-12 instruction. Figure 1 shows the research model for this study.

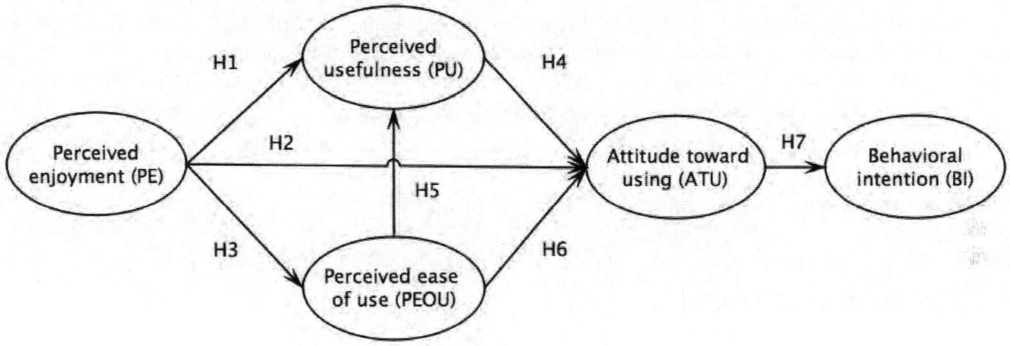

Figure 1. The hypothesis model

Specifically, this study attempts to answer the following research hypotheses:

H1. Perceived enjoyment will have a direct positive influence on K-12 in-service teachers' perceived usefulness.

H2. Perceived enjoyment will have a direct positive influence on K-12 in-service teachers' attitude toward using GBPTs.

H3. Perceived enjoyment will have a direct positive influence on K-12 in-service teachers' perceived ease of use.

H4. Perceived usefulness will have a direct positive influence on K-12 in-service teachers' attitude toward using GBPTs.

H5. Perceived ease of use will have a direct positive influence on K-12 in-service teachers' perceived usefulness.

H6. Perceived ease of use will have a direct positive influence on K-12 in-service teachers' attitude toward using GBPTs.

H7. Attitude toward using GBPTs will have a direct positive influence on K-12 in-service teachers' behavioral intention.

4. METHOD

4.1 Participants

A convenience sampling method was used, with 30 in-service teachers participating in this study hailing from elementary and secondary schools in Zhejiang Province, China. The participants totaled 28 females and 2 males, aged 26 to 40.

4.2 Instrument

A specific questionnaire containing 15 items was developed from the published items of previous studies (Rubio et al., 2015; Balog and Pribeanu, 2010; Ahn et al., 2004; Venkatesh, 2000; Davis, 1989; Taylor and Todd, 1995). Each item was measured on a 5-point Likert scale, with values ranging from 1 (strongly disagree) to 5 (strongly agree). To ensure the clarity and validity of the aforementioned items, the contents of the questionnaire were reviewed and revised several times by two educational technology experts.

4.3 Procedure and Data Analysis

The paper-and-pencil questionnaire was administered once the K-12 teachers completed at least one hour of code tutorial from code.org. Partial Least Squares Structural Equation Modeling (PLS-SEM) was used to test our hypothesis model, as this approach has greater power for small sample sizes (Chin, 1998). SmartPLS 3.0 was adopted to present the PLS-SEM approach and to assess the measurements (reliability and validity) and structural model (all hypotheses in the research model) for this study.

5. RESULTS

5.1 Measurement Model

The measurement model was used for assessment in terms of factor loading, Cronbach's alpha (CA), composite reliability (CR), average extracted variance (AVE), and discriminant validity. As shown in Table 1, factor loadings for the corresponding constructs are greater than the threshold value of 0.70 (Chin and Newsted, 1999), while the AVE values ranged from 0.792 to 0.893—exceeding the standard minimum level of 0.5, and as a consequence demonstrating adequate convergent validity (Hair et al., 2006). The reliability of the measures was acceptable, due to the values of CR and Cronbach's alpha being higher than 0.7 and 0.6, respectively (Hair et al., 2006). The discriminant validity was assessed by the square root of AVE and latent variable correlations. Table 2 demonstrates that the results delivered by the measurement model were significant and acceptable, with all values meeting the required standards (Fornell and Larcker, 1981).

Table 1. The measurement model

Construct	Item	Factor Loading	Cronbach's alpha	Composite reliability	Average extracted variance
Perceived usefulness			0.896	0.919	0.792
	PU1	0.888			
	PU2	0.871			
	PU3	0.911			
Perceived ease of use			0.940	0.961	0.893
	PEOU1	0.938			
	PEOU2	0.934			
	PEOU3	0.962			
Perceived enjoyment			0.915	0.947	0.855
	PE1	0.886			
	PE2	0.955			
	PE3	0.932			
Attitude toward using			0.872	0.922	0.797
	ATU1	0.856			
	ATU2	0.878			
	ATU3	0.943			
Behavioral intention			0.907	0.941	0.842
	BI1	0.919			
	BI2	0.935			
	BI3	0.899			

Table 2. Discriminant validity

Construct	1	2	3	4	5
1. Perceived usefulness	0.890				
2. Perceived ease of use	0.546	0.945			
3. Perceived enjoyment	0.600	0.546	0.925		
4. Attitude toward using	0.676	0.871	0.511	0.893	
5. Behavioral intention	0.665	0.736	0.400	0.827	0.918

5.2 Structural Model

The structural model was examined through assessing the path coefficients and R2 values; the former was used as the indicator for the statistical significance of these hypotheses, and the latter was used to assess the model's ability in explaining the variance in the dependent variables (Chin and Newsted, 1999). Figure 2 shows the path coefficients, path significance and variance explained for each dependent variable. It implies that the hypothesis model explained 43.1% of the variance in perceived usefulness, 29.9% of the variance in perceived ease of use, 82.1% of the variance in teachers' attitude, and 68.4% of the variance in behavioral intention. Figure 2 also illustrates the seven path coefficients among the variables of the model. It was also found that the perceived enjoyment had a direct positive and significant impact on perceived usefulness ($\beta = 0.430$, $p < 0.05$) and perceived ease of use ($\beta = 0.546$, $p < 0.001$), supporting H1 and H3. For the attitude, perceived usefulness ($\beta = 0.286$, $p < 0.05$) and perceived ease of use ($\beta = 0.715$, $p < 0.001$) were direct positive and significant factors, supporting H4 and H6. Attitude ($\beta = 0.821$, $p < 0.001$) had a direct positive and significant effect on behavioral intention, supporting H7. However, perceived enjoyment had no significant effect on attitude, and perceived ease of use also had no significant effect on perceived usefulness. Thus, results showed that all hypotheses were supported with the exceptions of H2 and H5.

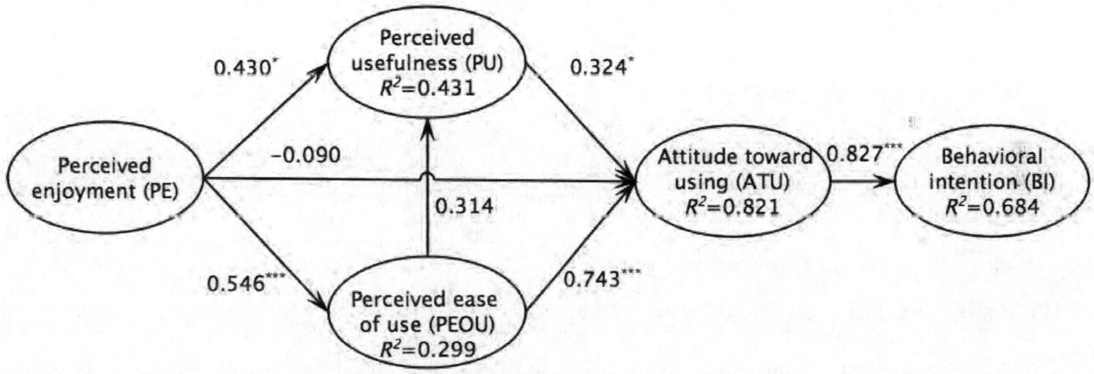

$^{*}p < 0.05$; $^{**}p < 0.01$; $^{***}p < 0.001$.

Figure 2. Path coefficients of the research model

6. DISCUSSION

This study attempted to investigate perceptions of in-service teachers with regard to using GBPTs in elementary and secondary schools by implementing an extended TAM integrated with perceived enjoyment as its theoretical base. All hypotheses, except two, were supported. The results demonstrated that the behavioral intention of teachers is determined by their attitudes toward using GBPTs in K-12 education, which in turn is determined by perceived usefulness and perceived ease of use. These findings are in line with the results of some previous studies (Chiu, 2017; Liu et al., 2017). However, this study found that perceived ease of use does not posit a significant impact on perceived usefulness, which is in agreement with the results by Su et al. (2018), but not in agreement with the findings by Chiu (2017) and Liu et al. (2017).

Moreover, this study showed that perceived enjoyment is positively associated with the core constructs of TAM—perceived usefulness (β=0.430) and perceived ease of use (β=0.546)—suggesting that an enjoyable learning experience is increasing the utility and ease of use of GBPTs. This study confirms that perceived enjoyment has a positive influence on perceived usefulness and perceived ease of use, which is consistent with previous studies (Park and Kwon, 2016; Elkaseh et al., 2015; Teo and Noyes, 2011). If in-service teachers feel the GBPTs to be enjoyable, they are more likely to perceive them as purposeful and easy to use. Surprisingly, perceived enjoyment is not found to posit a significant effect on teachers' attitudes toward using GBPTs. The results are not consistent with the findings by Cabada et al. (2018), which had previously found that perceived enjoyment does not influence students' attitudes toward using GBPTs. One possible explanation for this effect is that perceived enjoyment may affect attitude toward using only if the teachers themselves perceive GBPTs to be useful and easy to implement.

7. CONCLUSION

Our study provided several managerial implications of K-12 teachers' perceptions regarding the use of game-based programming tools in the classroom. These implications may serve to support academics, and assist academics, instructors and the general public in reaching a deeper understanding. Nevertheless, several limitations to this empirical study need to be acknowledged. First, this study did not perform a long-term investigation into teachers' use of GBPTs, nor did it consider individual differences such as gender (Venkatesh and Davis, 2000). Future research could examine other influencing factors/moderators on teachers' perceptions having previously used GBPTs in the classroom. Second, the study carried out a convenience sampling method in which just thirty Chinese K-12 teachers participated. The results may not be generalizable to the broader teacher population. Future studies could undertake multi-stage sampling to increase the sample size, or consider different user groups to examine and compare their perceptions regarding the use of game-based programming tools (GBPTs).

ACKNOWLEDGEMENT

This study was supported by the Philosophy and Social Sciences Planning Project of Zhejiang Province, China (P.R.C.) under grant number 18NDJC026Z. This research was also supported by the Teaching and Scientific Research Project for Liberal Arts Teachers in Zhejiang University.

REFERENCES

Abdullah, F. and Ward, R., 2016. Developing a General Extended Technology Acceptance Model for E-Learning (GETAMEL) by Analysing Commonly Used External Factors. *Computers in Human Behavior*, Vol. 56, pp 238-256.

Adukaite, A. et al, 2017. Teacher Perceptions on the Use of Digital Gamified Learning in Tourism Education : The Case of South African Secondary Schools. *Computers and Education*, Vol. 111, pp 172-190.

Ahn, T. et al, 2004. The Impact of the Online and Offline Features on the User Acceptance of Internet Shopping Malls. *Electronic Commerce Research and Applications*, Vol. 3, No. 4, pp 405-420.

Balog, A. and Pribeanu, C., 2010. The Role of Perceived Enjoyment in the Students' Acceptance of an Augmented Reality Teaching Platform: A Structural Equation Modelling Approach. *Studies in Informatics and Control*, Vol. 19, No. 3, pp 319-330.

Cabada, R. Z. et al, 2018. An Affective and Web 3.0-Based Learning Environment for a Programming Language. Telematics and Informatics, Vol. 35, No. 3, pp 611-628.

Chin, W. W., 1998. The Partial Least Squares Approach to Structural Equation Modelling. In G. A. Marcoulides (Ed.), Modern Methods for Business Research. Lawrence Erlbaum Associates, Mahwah, NJ, USA, pp. 295-336.

Chin, W. W. and Newsted, P. R. 1999. Structural Equation Modeling Analysis with Small Samples Using Partial Least Squares. In R. H. Hoyle (Ed.), Statistical Strategies for Small Sample Research. Sage Publications, Thousand Oaks, CA, USA, pp. 307–341.

Ching, Y. H. et al, 2018. Developing Computational Thinking with Educational Technologies for Young Learners. *TechTrends*, Vol. 62, pp 563-573.

Chiu, T. K. F. 2017. Introducing Eectronic Textbooks as Daily-Use Technology in Schools : A Top-Down Adoption Process. *British Journal of Educational Technology*, Vol. 48, No. 2, pp 524-537.

Davis, F. D. 1989. Perceived Usefulness, Perceived Ease of Use, and User Acceptance of Information Technology. *MIS Quarterly*, Vol. 13, No. 3, pp 319-340.

Davis, F. D. et al, 1989. User Acceptance of Computer Technology: A Comparison of Two Theoretical Models. *Management Science*, Vol. 35, No. 8, pp 982-1003.

Elkaseh, A. M. et al, 2015. The Acceptance of E-Learning as a Tool for Teaching and Learning in Libyan Higher Education. *International Journal of Information Technology*, Vol. 3, No. 4, pp 1-11.

Fornell, C. and Larcker, D. F. 1981. Evaluating Structural Equation Models with Unobservable Variables and Measurement Error. *Journal of Marketing Research*, Vol. 18, No. 1, pp 39-50.

Hair, J. F. et al, 2006. *Multivariate Data Analysis* (6th Ed.). Prentice Hall, New Jersey, USA.

Kalelioglu, F., 2015. A New Way of Teaching Programming Skills to K-12 Students: Code.org. *Computers in Human Behavior*, Vol. 52, pp 200-210.

Liu, H. et al, 2017. Pedagogical Beliefs and Attitudes Toward Information and Communication Technology : A Survey of Teachers of English as a Foreign Language in China. *Computer Assisted Language Learning*, Vol. 30, No. 8, pp 745-765.

Lopez, M. A. et al, 2016. Teaching Abstraction, Function and Reuse in the First Class of CS1: A Lightbot Experience. *Proceedings of the 2016 ACM Conference on Innovation and Technology in Computer Science Education (ITiCSE '16)*. Arequipa, Peru, pp. 256-257.

Park, E. and Kwon, S. J., 2016. The Adoption of Teaching Assistant Robots : A Technology Acceptance Model Approach. *Program*, Vol. 50, No. 4, pp 354-366.

Rajeev, S. et al, 2018. Educational Game-Theme Based Instructional Module for Teaching. *IECON 2018 - 44th Annual Conference of the IEEE Industrial Electronics Society*. Washington, DC, USA, pp. 3039-3044.

Rubio, M. A. et al, 2015. Closing the Gender Gap in an Introductory Programming Course. *Computers and Education*, Vol. 82, pp 409-420.

Su, C. Y. et al, 2018. A Path Analysis of In-Service Teachers' Intentions to Use ICT in Primary and Secondary Curricula: Applying and Extending the Technology Acceptance Model. *Proceedings of the 12th International Technology, Education and Development Conference (INTED 2018)*. Valencia, Spain, pp. 4433-4437.

Sun, H. and Zhang, P., 2008. An Exploration of Affect Factors and Their Role in User Technology Acceptance : Mediation and Causality. *Journal of American Society for Information Science and Technology*, Vol. 59, No. 8, pp 1252-1263.

Taylor, S. and Todd, P. A., 1995. Understanding Information Technology Usage: A Test of Competing Models. *Information Systems Research*, Vol. 6, No. 2, pp 144-176.

Teo, T. and Noyes, J., 2011. An Assessment of the Influence of Perceived Enjoyment and Attitude on the Intention to Use Technology among Pre-Service Teachers: A Structural Equation Modeling Approach. *Computers and Education*, Vol. 57, No. 2, pp 1645-1653.

Tessler, J. et al, 2013. Using Cargo-Bot to Provide Contextualized Learning of Recursion. *Proceedings of the 9th Annual International ACM Conference on International Computing Education Research (ICER '13)*. La Jolla, CA, USA, pp. 161-168.

Topalli, D. and Cagiltay, N. E., 2018. Improving Programming Skills in Engineering Education through Problem-Based Game Projects with Scratch. *Computers and Education*, Vol. 120, pp 64-74.

Venkatesh, V., 2000. Determinants of Perceived Ease of Use : Integrating Control, Intrinsic Motivation, Acceptance Model. *Information System Research*, Vol. 11, No. 4, pp 344-365.

Venkatesh, V. and Davis, F. D., 2000. A Theoretical Extension of the Technology Acceptance Model : Four Longitudinal Field Studies. *Management Science*, Vol. 46, No. 2, pp 186-204.

Vorderer, P. et al, 2004. Enjoyment : At the Heart of Media. *Communication Theory*, Vol. 14, No. 4, pp 388-408.

Wing, J. M., 2006. Computational Thinking. *Communications of the ACM*, Vol. 49, No. 3, pp 32-35.

THE DYNAMICS OF SUCCESSFUL TEAMS IN A MASSIVE OPEN ONLINE COURSE

Majd Alomar
Department of Education Technology, College of Education, Qassim University
Buraydah, Saudi Arabia

ABSTRACT

This paper explores the dynamics of teamwork in a team-based Massive Open Online Course. The purpose of the study is to discover patterns and characteristics of the students in teams that completed the course. Many studies have revealed that a very small percentage of students complete Massive Open Online Courses. The percentage is even smaller in MOOCs that involve peer-assessment. This study aims to give conscious advice for future MOOC students on how to complete a team-based peer-assessed MOOC by studying the dynamics of successful teams. A qualitative research method was utilized in the study. Data were collected from observing the MOOC platform and conducting interviews with successful team members and team leaders.

KEYWORDS

MOOC, Massive Open Online Course, Online learning, Team based learning, Collaborative learning, Qualitative Method

1. INTRODUCTION

Massive Open Online Courseware is an online phenomenon; which has been gaining popularity in recent years. MOOCs accommodate the connectivity of social networking, the facilitation of an acknowledged expert in a certain field of study, and a collection of free accessible online resources. The number of participants on a MOOC range from several hundred to thousand students who self-organize their engagement and participation by their learning goals, prior knowledge and participation and common interests (McAuley, Stewart, Siemens & Cormier, 2010).

MOOCs share some aspects of traditional courses such as predefined timeline and weekly topics and are facilitated by a knowledgeable expert (McAuley, Stewart, Siemens & Cormier, 2010). However, MOOCs in general, are free for everyone and only require Internet access to enroll. Moreover, they do not carry formal accreditation, although experts are expecting MOOCs to be provided for university credit in the near future (Pappano, 2012).

A survey was conducted on a MOOC provided by Dr. Agarwal from MIT; revealed interesting results. It discovered that 63 percent of students who completed Dr. Agarwal's course as well as a similar course on campus found that the MOOC was better comparatively, 36 percent found them comparable, and only 1 percent found it worse (Pappano, 2012). The U.S. Department of Education have expressed their opinion on this, in a recent study they concluded that students learning online performed, on average, better than those learning the same material through traditional face-to-face settings (Means, Toyama, Murphy, Bakia, & Jones, 2010).

1.1 Literature Review

Students engaging in MOOCs sometimes continue to use their central social platform to participate or they may use social media sites such as Facebook and Twitter to develop their discussions. Some create their own blogs and develop and maintain ties through these courses. What makes MOOCs so successful is the social aspect of it. Students negotiate with their peers, work on collaborative projects, and meet others who share their interests and skills. According to (McAuley et. al, 2010) "the network negotiated is just as important as the topic covered, if not more so. Participation in a MOOC is emergent, fragmented, diffuse, and diverse." In the time of rising education costs and decreasing budgets and government funding, MOOCs have the potential to generate changes in both higher education and online education. Advanced online platforms such as Coursera, edX, and Udacity are already attracting millions of students from all around the world.

1.1.1 Team-based Learning

Team-based learning is an instructional strategy that encourages students to collaborate and work in groups to achieve the same goals (Brindley, Walti, & Blaschke, 2009). In a collaborative learning environment; students work together to construct their knowledge by incorporating new information and skills into a learning community. Collaboration is described as a "process of shared creation: two or more individuals with complementary skills interacting to create a shared understanding that none had previously processed or could have come to on their own. Collaboration creates a shared meaning about a process, a product, or event" (Schrage, 1990).

Team-based Learning is thought to enhance student's skills on problem solving, social interaction and communication, as well as, positive attitude toward learning, and critical thinking (Law, 2011).

1.1.2 Project-based Learning

Problem Based Learning or PBL is a model that is related to inquiry based learning and was developed by Piaget and Vygotsky respectively. PBL is a combination of cognitive and social constructivist theories and focuses on collaborative learning. It teaches students 'soft skills' as well as specific content and subject skills. Generally, PBL teaches students five skills: Solving real-life problems, efficient problem solving, independent learning, self-monitoring, and teamwork. It encourages life-long learning and does not test the skill; rather it assists in developing the skill.

1.2 Purpose of this Study

Students who enroll in MOOCs are often very diverse. They come from all around the world with different languages, backgrounds, age differences and levels of education. Hundreds to thousands of students enroll on these courses. The completion rate for MOOCs in general is usually less than 7 percent, as for MOOCs that involve peer assessment (which is the main method of assessment in the MOOC regarded in this study) it is estimated to be 4.8 percent, which is a far less completion rate than the automatic graded MOOCs (Parr, 2013). Due to the high percentage of dropouts, it is essential for students to understand how to build and maintain successful teams. This study will discover how successful groups are formed and what strategies are used to ensure successful completion of a MOOC that is taken for professional development.

The following research question guided the study: What are the strategies, characteristics and dynamics of a successful team on a Massive Open Online Course?

2. RESEARCH METHODS

The researcher performed the study on a MOOC platform offered by Stanford University. Dr. Amin Saberi and his PhD student Farnaz Ronaghi created a project called Venture Lab to offer Stanford courses for free to the public. Venture Lab has officially re-branded and re-launched as NovoEd. The platform offers many MOOC for free and focuses on collaboration and project-based and team-based learning. The platform offers many courses to the general public as well as some private courses available only to Stanford students. The NovoEd platform in general is the focus of this study. 'Technology Entrepreneurship' a course that is available to the public, is observed in more detail.

The 37,000 students (from 150 countries) initially enrolled in this course offered some information about themselves: their country, language, background, skills, etc. The platform provides information about the students and teams on the course, including assignment submissions, latest activity, team name, team rank, team members and endorsements, which are testimonials from other students that have collaborated on a project on the platform. Using this information I searched for highly achieving teams that worked together to complete the course.

The participants were four teams that have completed the 'Technology Entrepreneurship' course. Five students from these teams were interviewed. Four of them were team leaders and one student was a team member. They were all highly achieving students that have completed the online course and some have participated in other successful teams on other MOOCs. Table 1 provides more information about the participants in this study.

Table 1. Participants' Information

Team #	Psudonym	Job Title	Role in team	Gender	Major	Country	Participated in Interview
Team 1	Bob	Lecturer	Team leader	Male	Marketing	Pakistan	Yes
Team 1	Clare	IT Student	Active member	Female	Information Technology	India	Yes
Team 2	Kyle	Entrepreneur	Team leader	Male	Computer Science	United States	Yes
Team 2	Jack	Web Designer	Active member	Male	Computer Science	United States	No
Team 3	Mark	Software Engineer	Team leader	Male	Computer Science	Pakistan	Yes
Team 3	Mary	Teenager	Active member	Female	High School	China	No
Team 4	Joseph	Graduate Student	Team leader	Male	Mechatronics Engineering	Pakistan	Yes

The students were contacted through the platform messaging service as well as email. Some students were contacted on Facebook and LinkedIn and requested to participate in the study. The interviews were semi-structured. Three of the interviews were conducted virtually via Zoom, one was by email and one interview was done using the Skype chatting service. The Zoom interviews lasted approximately one hour and were all video recorded. The Skype interview also lasted approximately one hour and included many follow up questions.

The interview questions were as follows:

Q1: How did you find out about this course?

Q2: What were your reasons or incentives for taking the course?

Q3: How did you choose your team members? What was your strategy?

Q4: There are many teams that drop out, but your teams are successful what are the tips or advice that you can give other teams to be successful?

Q5: How many people were in your team at the start? and how many finished?

Q6: How many MOOCs have you taken? How many have you finished? How many MOOCs have you taken that involve teamwork and how many of them have you finished?

Q8: What was positive or negative about the course?

Q9: What was positive or negative about your team?

Q10: What are some things that you wish the team would have done better?

A qualitative research method was utilized in this study. Qualitative data are "detailed descriptions of situations, events, people, interactions, and observed behaviors; direct quotations from people about their experiences, attitudes, beliefs, and thoughts; and excerpts or entire passages from documents, correspondence, records, and case histories" (Merriam & Simpson, 1995). It focuses on the 'significance, meaning, impact, individual or collective interpretation of events' (Wragg, 2012). To obtain a better understanding of the events and happenings on the course and to give a more accurate description, two different qualitative data collection methods were used for this study including: observation and interviews.

The research question was answered by; systematically searching and organizing the interview transcripts, observation fieldnotes, and other materials gathered. A thematic analysis was conducted to code and analyze the data. The purpose of this analytical method was to synthesize data as a whole and to decide how much data supported emerging themes (Bogdan and Biklen, 2007).

3. FINDINGS

All participants' responses to interviews and field notes gathered to study their behavior were categorized into three characteristics and included competence, experience and skill, determination and intrinsic motivation. All of the interview participants demonstrated their passion for knowledge, their high ambition, and set high standards for themselves and their teams. None of the students was taking the course for credit.

There was an emerging pattern with Bob, Mark and Joseph, which was not apparent amongst the others in the study. Firstly, they were all team leaders and all from Pakistan. They all displayed a unique passion for collaborative learning and an immense interest in MOOCs. Their purpose for signing up for 'Technology Entrepreneurship' was purely due to curiosity and interest; as well as a desire to work and learn in a collaborative environment. They all finished more than 6 MOOCs with Bob and Joseph mentoring 2 MOOCs on NovoEd. Interestingly, they were very driven by the social aspects of this course. Mark states, "I like to work with people I don't like to work on my own". They all collaborated with a very diverse range of team members on the course.

Both Bob and Mark expressed that when they started taking MOOCs, they led their teams. However after their first couple courses they started to join other teams and contributed as team members instead of taking charge and managing the team. All of these team leaders expressed their appreciation for the diversity on the course. Mark states, "It's like living in a global village". These MOOC students seemed to really enjoy the social aspects of the MOOC, which seems to motivate them to take more courses. Mark explained that he signed up for many Coursera courses but he did not complete any of them "I didn't like them because I felt like I'm on my own taking lectures", "I don't like that way of learning".

Kyle, the team leader in Team 2 signed up for the course because he was aspiring to expand his IT consultancy business. This course gave him the knowledge in Business and Entrepreneurship that he believed would help him succeed in his career. He met his team member Jack on the platform and they both contributed greatly to the project. In their team they started with six students and four finished. Kyle, the team leader states "I sent an email to my team members after the first set of no-show meetings and lack of cooperation and got a follow up email from every member stating that they were in and on the team for the long haul and they would be present at the next meeting but two of them did not show" "One of them was auditing the course" Kyle said. When asked when this happened he said "about halfway through the course". Those two members were then dropped from the team due to their lack of cooperation. Kyle has contributed the most to the course projects and was satisfied with Jack's contribution. " I knew there was at least one other person with me on this course. He was as he said he was in it for the long haul". He was not pleased however with the other students' commitment to the course.

In team 3, 15 people were on the team at the beginning and only 8 finished the course together. Starting with a large team as Mark explains is a clever plan to decrease the workload for the students on the team, and his plan appears to work as many members on his team complete the MOOC. However, Mark expressed, that having a team that is too large is not always recommended because it makes it very difficult to come up with a good time for meetings. The difference in time zones makes it nearly impossible for everyone to attend a meeting. His team decided to record their virtual meetings for the members that could not attend so they could watch them later. The students that were not able to attend still contributed to the projects.

3.1 Strategies for choosing Team Members

Kyle's strategy for choosing members was to make a list of active students that have the skillset that he was looking for and invite them to join the team. He looked for students that live in the United States and not abroad. The reason for this is to manage the time zones, as he explains "I did not want to have someone waking up at the middle of the night to attend a meeting".

Bob, Mark and Joseph's strategy was to make the team as diverse as possible. "I had five different countries on my team" Mark explained, "The international exposure of working with these people was very beneficial" "Also we get different points of views when we're working with people from different countries".

3.2 Implications for K-12 Education

Another important factor in choosing team members according to Mark and Bob is age. Interestingly, they have contrasting views as to the right age of the participants on the team. Bob expressed that most of the students that drop out are young people. He clarifies that 'senior members' or members that are older in age are more likely to succeed and complete the course. Mark's experience was very different. The student that contributed the most to his projects was Mary, a high school student in her mid teens. He explained, "She had video editing skills that nobody else had. She had done some work on animation and did some animation work for us. She had a lot of time on her hands so she was very active in the course". Mark collaborated with her on many projects on other MOOCs. He reveals that there were many teenagers on the courses that he had taken.

MOOCs seem to be making a difference in the amount and quality of education that the younger generation will gain. It is already happening. The opportunities that MOOCs provide for high school students are highlighted by Mary's experience on NovoEd. Mark describes this experience:

> "For example 'Mary' participated in Crack it, a competition organized by an advertising society in Pakistan. So I know 'Mary' from NovoEd and I asked her are you interested in participating in this competition and she participated with me in Crack it. I was here in Karachi and she was working with me in her home in Hong Kong."

Even if they do not win in the competition, the amount of knowledge and information that this high school student is exposed to and the opportunities that are opened up for her are truly empowering. Mark discusses another project that the two of them were working on together:

> "She was working with me on a business plan for a mobile app. The only way that she could contribute to the business plan was because of the other courses that she took on NovoEd 'Decision Thinking' and 'Crash Course on Creativity'. These courses prepared her to contribute to the business plan and participate in these competitions where most of the people who were participating were graduates. Some of these teenagers are taking MOOCs very seriously and they are adding a lot to it."

3.3 Mentors

The only team that had mentors for their team was team 3. Mark reveals that they have contributed very little to their work because mentors themselves are very busy people. He explains his impression of mentors and students contribution "From my observation everyone is active on the first week of the course. You can't judge how good your team is from the first week. But once the first week has passed once you submit your first assignment. Afterwards people start becoming inactive and after the third week you're on your own."

3.4 Certification

Many people enroll on MOOCs for the certification. The certificate for 'Crash Course on Creativity' another Stanford MOOC was observed and the following was imprinted on it:

> "Please note: Some online courses may draw on material from courses taught on campus but they are not equivalent to on-campus courses. This statement does not affirm that this student was enrolled as a student at Stanford University in any way. It does not confer a Stanford University grade, course credit, or degree; and it does not verify the identity of the student".

The participants were asked about their views about this Mark responded, "when you have a certificate that states that it is from the teacher and not from the university and that they have not confirmed your identity. This certificate is null and void". Mark recommends taking these classes to learn something new but not for the certification.

4. DISCUSSION

Most of the students that participated in the interview seemed to enjoy their experience with team-based MOOCs. Kyle seemed frustrated with the lack of contribution from some of his team members, however he expressed a determination to complete as many MOOCs as he needs to achieve his purpose.

All of the team leaders in this study had a systematic plan in place for dealing with inactive team members. Their strategy for dealing with inactive team members was surprisingly similar. They all recommended removing inactive team members if they did not cooperate or respond to emails. Mark recommends starting with a large team, around 8 or 9 members, so if the team loses 3-4 members, the workload would still be manageable as there would be at least four active members.

The way in which the course is designed replicates a real life experience, which requires collaboration, teamwork, submitting projects in a timely manner and communicating effectively with a very diverse range of people. One of the things that became instantly apparent while observing the course was the professionalism of the team leaders in the teams that finished the MOOC. The team members' dedication and commitment to the course was also evident. They all appeared to be highly motivated students that were following personal interests and driven by intrinsic motivation. Their management and collaboration skills are exceptional and replicate what is needed to manage a successful project in real life.

Some of the students were working professionals who were interested in a career change and saw this as an opportunity to search for their interest. Many others had graduate degrees in Engineering, Business, Economics and so forth. There was also an interesting trend of serial MOOC takers. Some students enrolled on every free MOOC available on NovoEd. These courses are equivalent to senior and graduate level Stanford courses. Although they are not accredited as such, they still require as much work and effort as many campus university level courses.

4.1 Strategies and Recommendations

Based on the experiences of successful MOOC students, the following guidelines have been accumulated. These guidelines are constructed from the observations and interviews of successful team members' experiences.

1- Leading a team involves much more work and effort in the project. If a student does not have enough time to dedicate to a MOOC, then join a team as a member instead of starting a new team.
2- Search for the teams that are open and ensure that you know the limit on the team size. This is so as not to waste time on contacting teams that have reached the limit and are not able to add any more students.
3- Search the journals. Usually if a team has many recent journal entries and there are multiple members contributing to the journals then they are likely to be an active team.
4- Contact three or four teams, it is more likely to get an answer.
5- Make sure the workload is manageable. Do not take too many courses and then end up not finishing any of them.
6- Be prepared for every kind of person. Keep in mind that the platform is open and free and although most people are serious and have good intentions, some do not.
7- The courses are relevant if the student's purpose is to learn something new or meet new people with diverse skills. However, the courses are not accredited and the certification is useless.

5. CONCLUSION

MOOCs have enabled people to follow their interests and learn from the best universities in the world. The subjects are as diverse as playing music, telling stories, entrepreneurship, mathematics, computer science and languages. The diversity of its students and the social aspects of these courses as well as the quality of education provided have intrigued academics and researchers.

This study followed four successful MOOC teams and studied their characteristics, dynamics and strategies for successfully completing a Massive Open Online Course. The researcher performed the study on a MOOC platform offered by Stanford University. The researcher conducted observations and interviews with successful team members and team leaders. The findings of this study revealed that all of the members in successful teams showed signs of competence, experience and skill, determination and intrinsic motivation. All of the interview participants demonstrated their passion for knowledge, their high ambition, and set high standards for themselves and their teams. None of the students was taking MOOCs for credit. Participants reported that the certificates were useless to them but they appreciated the knowledge they accumulated from these courses.

ACKNOWLEDGEMENT

The researcher would like to acknowledge the participants who cooperated and participated in this study.

REFERENCES

Bogdan, R. C., & Biklen, S. K. (2007). Qualitative research for education: An introduction to theory and methods (5 ed.) Boston: Pearson.

Brindley, J. E., Walti, C., & Blaschke, L. M. (2009). Creating effective collaborative learning groups in an online environment. *The International Review of Research in Open and Distance Learning*, 10(3), 1–18.

Law, Y. (2011). The effects of cooperative learning on enhancing Hong Kong fifth graders' achievement goals, autonomous motivation and reading proficiency. *Journal of Research in Reading*, 34(4), 402–425.

McAuley, A., Stewart, B., Siemens, G., & Cormier, D. (2010). The MOOC model for digital practice.

Means, B., Toyama, Y., Murphy, R., Bakia, M., & Jones, K. (2010). Evaluation of evidence based practices in online learning: A meta-analysis and review of online learning studies.

Merriam, S. B., & Simpson, E. L. (1995). A guide to research for educators and trainers of adults (2nd ed.). Malabar, FL: Krieger.

Pappano, L. (2012). The Year of the MOOC. The New York Times, 4.

Parr, C. (2013). Not Staying the Course. Times Higher Education.

Schrage, M. (1990). Shared minds: The new technologies of collaboration. New York: Random House.

Wragg, E. C. (2012). An introduction to classroom observation. New York, NY: Routledge.

MODELS, PROCESS AND TOOL TO ASSIST COOPERATIVE SCENARIZATION OF DISTANT LEARNING MODULES

Christophe Marquesuzaà[1], Patrick Etcheverry[1], Pantxika Dagorret[1],
Philippe Lopistéguy[1], Thierry Nodenot[1] and Marta Toribio Fontenla[2]
[1]*Univ Pau & Pays ADOUR/ E2S UPPA,*
Laboratoire D'informatique de L'universite de Pau et des Pays Del'adour, EA3000
2, allée du Parc Montaury, 64600 Anglet, France
[2]*IUT de Bayonne et du Pays Basque, service TICE, 2, allée du Parc Montaury, 64600 anglet, France*

ABSTRACT

This paper deals with cooperative pedagogical scenarization. It presents a work carried out after an experience aiming at creating online training courses for an university degree. In the experience, lecturers had no experience in designing full online courses, and needed the support of pedagogical engineers to adapt their courses to suit online learner's requirements. The paper presents several models allowing pedagogical engineers to specify scenarios and also the process to be carried out in order to design these scenarios with lecturers.

These models have been integrated in an online platform allowing pedagogical engineers to assist lecturers all along the design process to export the produced scenarios on the Moodle platform.

KEYWORDS

Pedagogical Scenarization, Scenario Models, Scenarization Platform, Moodle

1. INTRODUCTION

Digital competences are becoming increasingly important, whether in the daily lives of the general public, in companies or in the educational field from elementary school to University.

For example, the private french Orange telecommunications company aims to train 50% of its 100 000 employees by using MOOC platforms.On March 5, 2018, Muriel Pénicaud, the French Minister of Labour, unveiled the outline of her professional training reform project to facilitate access to any kind of training programs. In this reform, the use of MOOC platforms is promoted and become eligible by employees as part of their Training Personal Account (CPF in French). The designers of these MOOCs would have to provide high-quality educational pathways that would be assessed by a National Agency.

Within the university sector, lecturers have recognized skills and long-standing experience in creating face-to-face courses. Many educational institutions now offer online workspaces allowing at least access to digital resources in the course of traditional classroom (teaching/learning sessions). These resources can be used before classes, for example in the context of "flipped classrooms", during the class to access non-photocopied documents or after the class, for revision. The hybrid form (face-to-face + online support) aims at making people work better together in order to smooth the training time, not to contract it. Generally, these pedagogical resources have strong dependences with the classroom teaching/learning session in which they are used and they often lose their relevance when one tries to exploit them on learning platforms such as MOOCs where classroom teaching/learning sessions disappear.

If lecturers have no difficulties in elaborating educational pathways for classroom teaching/learning session, their experience is currently quite limited when it is about designing courses that are fully online and not including any classroom session. In this context, they need the support of pedagogical engineers to see to what extent existing or new courses can be adapted to suit e-learner's requirements.

While (Bakki, A. *et al*, 2017) proposes a model to assist pedagogical scenario building process for MOOCs in a connectivist approach, in this paper we propose a methodology and an associated online platform allowing pedagogical engineers to assist lecturers all along the process aiming at designing online learning modules in a constructivist approach.

The expected spinoffs are numerous. From the learner's point of view, it means improving the learning modes and their arrangement and enhancing their motivation by diversifying available teaching methods. As regards lecturers, the aim is to expand their teaching practice by diversifying the ways to share their knowledge. As to the educational institutions, the main interest is to be equipped with a methodological framework facilitating the development of online courses and also to participate actively in the process of raising the level of knowledge and skills of all the actors involved, from the design to the implementation of an education offer.

This paper is structured as follows. In section 2, we present a feedback on a scenarization process used to set up an online degree course. Considering this experience, in section 3 we present related works dealing with pedagogical scenarios modelling but also design processes aiming at elaborating pedagogical scenarios. Section 4 presents several models to deal with both (1) educational scenarios, (2) scenarization methodologies. In section 5, we describe an online environment implementing the previous models. This platform allows lecturers and pedagogical engineers to design, remotely and cooperatively, online learning modules. Finally, we conclude this paper by presenting several ideas concerning potential future work.

2. FEEDBACK CONCERNING THE IMPLEMENTATION OF A REAL DESIGN PROCESS

We conducted a design work aiming at creating a university degree that can be obtained through an online degree course. This university degree, called DU ASR in French, focuses on systems and network administration. The target audience consists of adult learners living in Latin America and wishing to acquire knowledge and skills related to networking and operating systems in order to work as high-level technicians.

Trainers involved in the design of the pedagogical modules forming this university degree come from various higher education institutions from France (IUT de Bayonne et du Pays Basque), Spain (Universidad del País Vasco / Euskal Herriko Unibertsitatea UPV/EHU), Argentina (ITU Mendoza), Chile (CEDUC Universidad Católica del Norte) and Colombia (Universidad Tecnológica de Pereira).

The design process carried out to elaborate all these online modules has been developed by a pedagogical engineer who worked in cooperation with 18 trainers. Each elaborated modules corresponding to 30 or 60 hours of learning/training that learners can follow remotely and in total autonomy.

For each pedagogical module, the scenarization process is composed of three main steps:

1. Contacting concerned trainers in order to identify the objective of the module
2. Establishing a synthetic description of the chapters composing the module
3. Designing the scenario describing accurately the contents of each chapter.

The first step takes the form of a questionnaire composed of 50 questions to the course author. The aim of this questionnaire is to help the pedagogical engineer get acquainted with the author and identify some of his/her pedagogical practices. This questionnaire also allows the pedagogical engineer to identify the level of the trainer's skills and personal practice related to e-teaching/learning.

The second step deals with the general structure of the course. The pedagogical engineer provides the trainer with a commented and illustrated form aiming at formalizing a full specification of the module to bring online. This form allows the trainer to specify the target audiences, the necessary prerequisites, knowledge and skills to be acquired, equipment and software needed, the planned assessment method and a first list of pedagogical sequences (chapters).

Basing on this list of pedagogical sequences, the third step of the design process details the pedagogical scenario of the course. It consists of:

- Dividing each chapter into activities while checking that each activity objective contributes to the general objective of the chapter;
- Defining the pedagogical resources which must be mediatized for each activity;
- Defining when and how each resource must be produced.

An extract of the documents produced at each step can be obtained at the following URL: https://goo.gl/nYnzay.

This scenarization task takes the form of an iterative specification process resulting in several exchanges in which the pedagogical engineer brings his/her expertise and his/her recommendations in order to assist lecturers elaborating a qualitative pedagogical scenario adapted to distance learning to be implemented on the Moodle platform. This platform has been chosen for two main reasons:

- it supports a social constructivism design approach which favours rich interactions between pedagogical engineers and lecturers ;
- it provides adaptivity to address users requirements when designing e-education courses (Despotovic-Zrakic, M. *et al*, 2012) ;
- it is based on open source code and may be easily customized.

The scenarization process carried out to elaborate the DU ASR learning modules presents undeniable qualities which allowed the pedagogical engineer to remotely design each module with lecturers located in several countries and with different practices. The first learning modules were put online in September 2015 and since March 2017, the 11 modules composing the whole diploma course are available online (https://elearn.univ-pau.fr/course/index.php?categoryid=6).

Despite these satisfactory results, the work carried out to design this online degree course has allowed us to characterize several improvable points:

- The forms currently used at each design stage (Word and Excel files sent by e-mail) are ill-adapted to a cooperative scenarization task which requires several exchanges between lecturers and pedagogical engineers but also sometimes between lecturers themselves when several lecturers are involved in a same learning module). All these exchanges imply to manage the different versions of each document and it is sometimes tiresome to produce a document satisfying at the same time the pedagogical engineers and all the lecturers implied in the design process.
- The scenarization design process is currently formalized through document models which offer little flexibility when it becomes necessary to adapt some stages/questions to take into account the specific features of some modules or the profile and/or language of lecturers implied in the scenarization process.
- The online publication of a new learning module is tiresome and time-consuming because it is carried out manually and it implies to gather and to take into account all pedagogical elements specified in the documents describing the scenario.

From these observations, we have elaborated models and a platform support:

- allowing pedagogical engineers to create, adapt and make scenarization processes evolve;
- facilitating cooperative work between pedagogical engineers and lecturers;
- automating the export of a pedagogical scenario towards the Moodle LMS (Learning System Management) to facilitate the publication of the corresponding course.

These different contributions are presented in the following sections

3. RELATED WORK

As defined in (Schneider, D. K. *et al*, 2003) and (Peter, Y. *et al*, 2008) a pedagogical scenario is an ordered set of learning activities implying actors who use and produce resources (or "learning objects"). A pedagogical scenario can take several forms (text, audio or narrative video) and aims at describing the sequences, and sometimes the objectives, the actors, the stages, even the instructions, the tools and documents used or to be produced. These concepts are also described in (Alario-Hoyos, C. and Muñoz Cristóbal, J., 2012) and (Martel, C. *et al*, 2006).

There are two standards to describe a scenario where each scenario is a pedagogical "design" which can be recorded into an XML file:

- The SCORM (Sharable Content Object Reference Model) standard (http://www. scorm.fr) is a compromise between several proposals aiming at standardizing the contents aggregation and data exchanges between a course and a compatible LMS. However, this standard presents various drawbacks concerning learner tracking or the choice of the teaching methods (mono-actor, simple sequencing)
- The IMS-LD (Instructional Management Systems Learning Design) (www. imsglobal.org/learningdesign) is a generalization of SCORM with a multiactor model. This model is more flexible and supports an

approach which focuses on activities and collaborations rather than on a succession of contents. However, this standard is relatively technical and also has some limitations concerning the management of actors and their production, informal definition of learning goals or prerequisites). So, the most complete models are not necessarily the best and they must be customized to pedagogical practices and needs while making them accessible to the users.

These pedagogical scenario models are integrated into scenarization tools like SCENARI - OPALE (Crozat, S., 2011), LAMS (Dalziel, J. and Cameron, L., 2014) or G-MOT/TELOS (http://lice.licef.ca/) but also into an LMS such as Moodle.

As part of the experiment conducted for the DU ASR, and because the diploma had to be available on a Moodle platform, the pedagogical engineer scripted the pedagogical scenario of each learning module on the base of his/her own knowledge of the underlying scenario of Moodle (Loiseau, E. *et al*, 2014). Moodle's built in scenario model operationalizes a scenario with entities like courses, composed of sections in which learners will find resources (files, directories...) and tools (ambiguously referred to as "activities") such as MCQs, forums, wikis, etc.

From a methodological point of view, the pedagogical engineer elaborated each learning module of the DU ASR degree in five steps, according to the ADDIE model (Analysis, Design, Development, Implementation and Evaluation).

ADDIE model has provided the basis for many methods of pedagogical design (Gagne, R.M., 1992), because it identifies the life cycle phases of a learning system according to a classic approach used in software design methods (Serhat, K., 2017). ADDIE model leads to a directive design approach. It differs to SAM, the Successive Approximation Models (Allen, M. *et al*, 2012), which proposes an iterative design approach close to agile methods and relying on three stages: Evaluation, Design and Development, with a set of iterations on the whole process. Iterations can lead to the reconsideration of each result and may lead to carry out the evaluation step at each milestone.

The particular context of DU ASR project (various institutions and interlocutors, different native languages, different pedagogical approaches) led the pedagogical engineer to choose ADDIE model and its structuring character where each step can be repeated as often as necessary to improve the obtained result but necessarily ends with a validation before taking the next step.

Based on the experience gained on the DU ASR degree, our goal is to design models for developing educational scenarios garanteeing the operationalization of these scenarios on Moodle. We distinguish two types of approaches to tackle this problem:

- Design approaches with ad hoc tools allowing pedagogical engineers to elaborate pedagogical scenarios whose specification must, afterwards, be matched with data expected by Moodle (Alario-Hoyos, C. and Muñoz Cristóbal, J., 2012), (Gagne, R.M., 1992). Considering the important dissimilarity between the scenarization language and the data model of the LMS, these approaches often entail modifications and semantic losses during the mapping process.
- Design approaches based on IDM to transform a given scenario according to a given model towards a specification compliant with the Moodle model. However, these transformations are complex and often induce a manual intervention and semantic losses.

To avoid these semantic losses, we decided as in (Loiseau, E. *et al*, 2014), to take Moodle's scenario model directly as a basis and to offer pedagogical engineers facilities to elaborate tailor-made design processes aiming at specifying scenarios in accordance with this model.

The pedagogical scenario is led by the teachers' intentions and in accordance with their values (Emin, V. and Pernin, J.P., 2009). It is therefore important to be able to adapt the scenarisation approach in order to take into account teachers pedagogical requirements. To this end, we propose a design approach model that is flexible and can be adapted by the pedagogical engineer according to the needs of the teachers with whom he/she cooperates.

We expect that the elaborated design processes be both rigorous and structuring like ADDIE but also flexible like SAM to allow pedagogical engineers to adapt their manner to assist lecturers during the design process as suggested in (Peter, Y. *et al*, 2008). With this purpose, we propose a design process model allowing pedagogical engineers to elaborate design processes producing pedagogical scenario descriptions compliant with the scenario model integrated in Moodle.

4. PEDAGOGICAL SCENARIZATION MODELS

The scenarization models we propose include two aspects: modelling the description of a pedagogical scenario in terms of components, and modelling the scenarization approach, it means the steps followed by the pedagogical engineer when building a new course.

4.1 A Scenario Model

The definition of the elements making up a pedagogical scenario has been achieved in tight cooperation with the pedagogical engineer, who settled a vocabulary derived from the experience she acquired during the DU ASR project and her knowledge of the Moodle platform where the scenario had to be implemented.

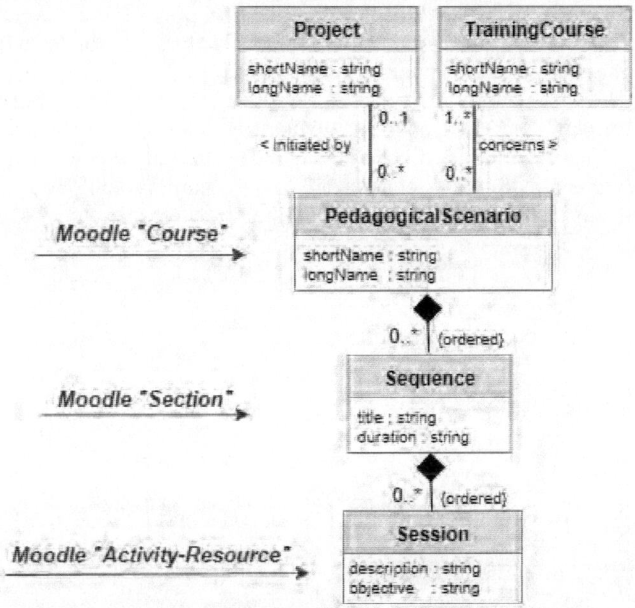

Figure 1. Scenario model

The model includes the following terminology (Figure 1): a pedagogical scenario (or course module) is composed of a set of chapters (or sections / pedagogical sequences). Each chapter may be composed of sessions where learners use resources (PDF files, videos, MCQs, forums, chats…) to carry out a given activity.

Then, in order to allow the exportation of all scenarios items defined by the pedagogical engineer and lecturers to a Moodle platform, we built a correlation table between this terminology and the concepts which are specific to the Moodle platform (Table 1).

Table 1. Matching pedagogical items with Moodle artefacts

Pedagogical engineer vocabulary	Corresponding Moodle concepts
Module – Pedagogical Scenario	Course
Chapter – Pedagogical Sequence	Section
Session	Activity - Resource

4.2 A Scenarization Approach Model

In order to facilitate the capitalization and reuse of the formerly described pedagogical engineer's scenarization approach, we first formalized it. Then, we generalized the concept of scenarization approach to allow the pedagogical engineers to customize their scenarization approach, or to develop their own new approach(es).

According to our point of view, a scenarization approach has to be developed by a pedagogical engineer. The application of an approach is cooperatively implemented between one or more lecturers and one or more pedagogical engineers assisting them in the scenario specification task. The experiment conducted as part of the definition of the modules on the DU ASR showed that it was important to appoint a lecturer as a supervisor when several lecturers participate in the scenarization of a same module. As a supervisor, this person is the privileged interlocutor of the pedagogical engineer for the synchronisation and coordination of the specification task led by the teaching staff.

Hence, the term "pedagogical engineer", as used hereafter may refer to a single or more person coordinating the specification task. Similarly, the word "lecturer" may refer to a unique lecturer or the lecturer responsible for the coordination of a teaching staff.

Our scenarization approach model is presented in the right hand of Figure 2. In this model, a scenarization approach is composed of a set of ordered steps, each intented to specify part of a scenario. The specification objective of each step is defined by the pedagogical engineer. He/She also, depending on the step of the scripting work, defines whether this step is currently accessible or not to the lecturer. As suggested in ADDIE, this property allows the pedagogical engineer to manage the progress of the specification task by giving access to a new step only if the specification work of the previous one is considered satisfactory and completed.

A scenarization step is composed of a set of questions whose content and order are defined by the pedagogical engineer. These questions will be asked to the lecturer in order to let him/her specify the properties of his/her pedagogical scenario. Since we considered that a scenario (module) was composed of chapters which are composed of sessions (Table 1), the questions defined by the pedagogical engineer will have to lead the lecturer to specify these items.

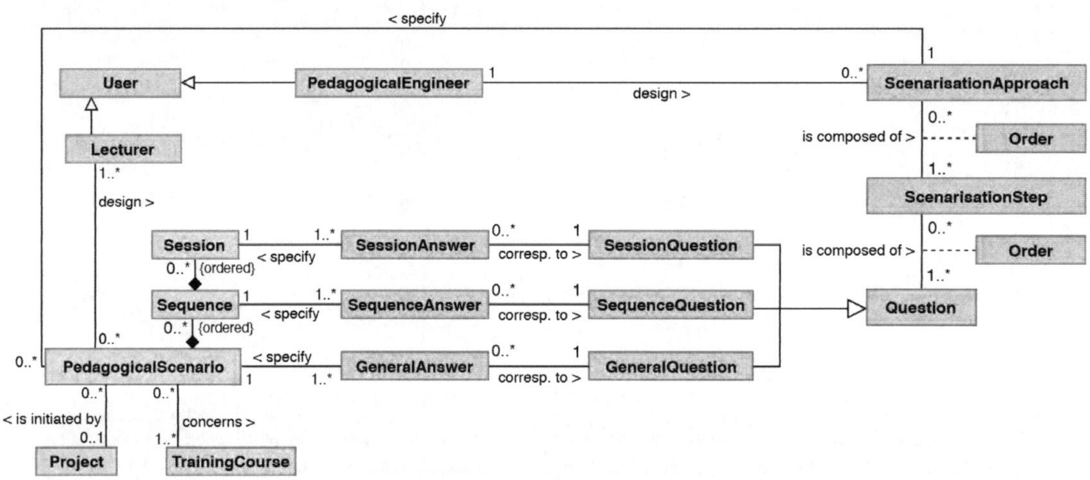

Figure 2. General model

Our model distinguishes three types of questions:

- General questions are not directly related to the scenario (module) to develop. These may be questions that allow the pedagogical engineer to better understand the lecturer with whom he/she is working (scenarization abilities, ICTE skills…) or questions that will prepare the lecturer for the identification of chapters and sessions composing his/her scenario (module);
- Sequence-type questions aim at precisely specifying the chapters composing his/her scenario (module);
- Session-type questions aim at defining the sessions composing each chapter.

As shown in Figure 2, the answers given to sequence-type and session-type questions match the specifications of chapters and sessions of the scenario (module) which will later be implemented on the educational platform.

Our study's final model gathers the two former models and some additional classes, like Lecturer and PedagogicalEngineer, and relationships between them. The lecturer is responsible for coordinating the proposals of his/her colleagues when the module is designed by several lecturers. It is he/she who is in direct relationship with the pedagogical engineer.

5. A PLATFORM FOR COOPERATIVE DESIGN OF DISTANCE OR MIXED LEARNING MODULES

To evaluate the interest and relevance of our approach, we have integrated our models into a cooperative scenarization platform in order to determine their relevance during the design of new modules. The platform allows pedagogical engineers to design their own scenarization approach and implement it while cooperating with lecturers. The design of scenarization approaches is flexible and may be led according to different ways:

- Top-down: firstly defining the goals of the approach, next producing the steps composing the approach and lastly specifying the questions to be asked to the lecturers at each step;
- Bottom-up: firstly defining the relevant questions to specify a scenario (module), next sharing these questions according to each step;
- Mixed: creating for example a first step and then defining the associated questions, next creating a second step and its associated questions, and so forth.

To support this flexible designing approach, the scenarization platform allows the pedagogical engineers to define in any order:

- The questions to add to a bank of questions and which can later be associated with a step.
- The steps to add to a bank of steps and which can later be used to design a specific approach step.

If the scenarization approach is top-down, then the pedagogical engineer will:

1. Give a name to the approach to be created;
2. Integrate in his/her approach the necessary steps while selecting them from the bank of steps or creating them on the fly (in the latter case, the design approach is mixed);
3. Define for each step the questions to answer while choosing them in the bank of questions or creating them on the fly (mixed approach).

If the scenarization approach is bottom-up, then the pedagogical engineer will:

1. Define the questions to be used in his/her approach;
2. Create (name) the steps composing his/her approach;
3. Associate the questions with each created step;
4. Merge and order the previously created steps to complete his/her approach.

This flexible design approach has been used to create new learning modules dedicated to ICT for business (https://www.iutbayonne.univ-pau. fr/espace-entreprises/modules-formation.html).

6. CONCLUSION AND FUTURE WORK

The design models implemented on our scenarization platform are currently being evaluated. The evaluation focuses on the relevance (and the limitations) of the models allowing to design new scenarization approaches or to customize existing approaches.

The above scenario model and the scenarization approaches model are both a first stage allowing pedagogical engineers and lecturers to design the frame of a scenario/module (sessions and chapters) and to export it to the educational platform. The proposed models do not currently allow to specify/create the educational resources involved in each learning module. These resources are therefore currently defined directly on Moodle and not on the scenarization platform. Future works therefore aim at extending the scenario model to support the specification of the educational resources involved in each educational activity. This also implies to extend the scenarization approaches model in order to specify this dimension of the scenario.

In order to cover a wider range of educational practices and to streamline the progression of the activities to be conducted to create the learning modules, the general model should be extended to also take into account the pedagogical roles which are commonly identified in the literature. We may here cite for example the roles identified in (Peter, Y and Vantroys, T., 2005): module manager, module author, scriptwriter, media creator, tutor, administrative manager…

More broadly, it is necessary to define more precisely the type of scenarization approaches that can be designed with our models to identify the teaching practices that are not covered and make our models evolve accordingly.

REFERENCES

Allen, M. *et al*, 2012. Leaving ADDIE for SAM: An Agile Model for Developing the Best Learning Experiences. *American Society for Training & Development.*

Alario-Hoyos, C. and Muñoz Cristóbal, J., 2012. GLUE! - GLUE!-PS: An approach to deploy non-trivial collaborative learning situations that require the integration of external tools in VLEs. *In 1st Moodle Research Conference*, pp. 77–85.

Bakki, A. *et al*, 2017. A Model to Assist Pedagogical Scenario Building Process in cMOOCs. *IEEE 17th International Conference on AdvancedLearning Technologies (ICALT)*, Timisouara, Romania. hal-01646823

Crozat, S., 2011. *Scenari - La chaîne éditoriale libre : Structurer et publier textes, images et son*. Accès libre. Eyrolles.

Dalziel, J. and Cameron, L., 2014. *Proceedings of the 9th International LAMS and Learning Design Conference*, Nanyang Technological University, Singapore.

Despotovic-Zrakic, M. *et al*, 2012. Providing adaptivity in moodle lms courses. *Educational Technology & Society,* 15(1), pp. 326–338.

Emin, V. and Pernin, J.P., 2009. Model and tool to clarify intentions and strategies in learning scenarios design. In Learning in the Synergy of Multiple Disciplines, *4th European Conference on Technology Enhanced Learning (EC-TEL)*, Nice, France, pp. 462–476.

Gagne, R.M., 1992. *Principles of Instructional Design.* Wadsworth Publishing, fourth edition.

Katsamani, M. *et al*, 2012. Designing a Moodle course with the CADMOS learning design tool. *Educational Media International,* 49(4): pp. 317–331.

(http://lice.licef.ca/) LICÉ – Laboratoire en ingénierie cognitive et éducative, Centre de recherche LICEF, Université TELUQ

Koper, R. and Olivier, B., 2004. Representing the learning design of units of learning. *Journal of Educational Technology & Society,* 7(3): pp. 97–111.

Loiseau, E. *et al*, 2014. Abstraction of learning management systems instructional design semantics: A meta-modeling approach applied to the moodle case-study. *In Open Learning and Teaching in Educational Communities - 9th European Conference on Technology Enhanced Learning, (EC-TEL)*, Graz, Austria, pp. 249–262.

Martel, C. *et al*, 2006. Modeling collaborative learning activities on e-learning platforms. *In IEEE International Conference on Advanced Learning Technologies (ICALT)*, Kerkrade, Netherlands, pp. 707–709.

Peter, Y and Vantroys, T., 2005. Platform support for pedagogical scenarios. *Educational Technology & Society,* 8(3): pp. 122–137.

Peter, Y. *et al*, 2008. *Pedagogical scenario modelling, deployment, execution and evolution.* In Architecture Solutions for E-Learning Systems, IGI Global, pp. 283–305.

Schneider, D. K. *et al*, 2003. Conception and implementation of rich pedagogical scenarios through collaborative portal sites: clear focus and fuzzy edges. *In International Conference on Open Online Learning (ICOOL)*, pp. 243–268.

Serhat, K., 2017. *ADDIE Model: Instructional Design*, web site, https://educationaltechnology.net/the-addie-model-instructional-design/

O TEU MESTRE- A DISTANCE LEARNING PLATFORM (RESULTS)

Daniel Azevedo[1] and Paula Morais[2]
[1]*Polytechnic Institute of Viseu, Portugal*
[2]*Portucalense University, Portugal*

ABSTRACT

We live in an age of change regarding mentalities and a consequent time of change in the learning processes. In this sense, it is necessary to create new methodologies and alternative practices to learn, teach and, more importantly, to learn how to learn. In recent years there has been a widespread commitment to use Information and Communication Technologies as a tool to support teaching. It is in this context that this work is inserted. The aim is to validate a digital educational resource of school that will be able to contribute to the aid of students of traditional education and also of those hospitalized and/or prevented from being present in the classroom. The proposed model was validated through a case study developed during the second and third periods of the 2014/2015 school year, involving special education students, in a hospital context, students of Mathematics A of the 12th grade of a Porto school and high school mathematics teachers.

KEYWORDS

Digital Educational Resources, Educational Platform

1. INTRODUCTION

The main objective of school is to prepare the student for life, in all its aspects. To achieve this difficult goal, school in parallel with the rest of society, has been adapted and has undergone through several technological changes. As early as 2002 Joly stated: "The technology that impacts today's society in a scary way has become a major school challenge" (p.1). With the recent technological upgrading of schools, this challenge has become easier to achieve, but there is still a long and controversial way to go, especially regarding to the use these new technologies.

Prensky (2007) is of the opinion that, although a major technological investment has been made in education in recent years, change has fallen short of expectations.

Gil (2014) points out that in the current situation, education has a favorable context since the nowaday students are digital natives, who have been born and live with digital devices and tools, demanding their use at school so it can be a space where they like to be and not out of step with the reality of their daily lives.

The main objective of this work is to validate a model of a DER (Digital Educational Resources) to enhance the learning of mathematics of students of traditional teaching and students hospitalized and/or prevented from being present in the classroom. In the specific case of mathematics, a recurrent problem of relatively low national test averages is observed in 2013 (8.2 points) and in 2014 (7.7 points).

If we consider the students hospitalized and / or prevented from being present in the classroom, these difficulties are even more evident. Correia (1997) considers these pupils with special educational needs to be special, as they exhibit certain specific conditions and may require support and special education services during all or part of their school career, in order to facilitate their academic, personal, social and emotional development. Most of these students are hospitalized for long periods of time and are faced with an unknown environment, with the aggravation of being away from their familiar, social and schoolar environment.

Over the last few years, there has been a growing concern in supporting these students, especially those with cancer disease. In this sense, the XVII Portuguese Constitutional Government created Law No. 71/2009, which establishes a special regime for the protection of children and young people with cancer.

Although this legislation has been published, school support for these students is confronted with numerous difficulties

In this context, the OERs (Digital Educational Resources) can be seen as a means to battle the difficulties of teaching traditional students and, in particular, students who are hospitalized and / or prevented from attending classes, opposing isolation and linking them to the school community, providing new ways of learning.

2. METHODOLOGY

As mentioned previously, the main objective of this research is to propose a model of a DER to enhance the learning of mathematics to traditional students and to students hospitalized and/or prevented from being present in the classroom.

In this study qualitative and quantitative approaches will be used. We will also use a case study that was developed with a mixed approach, that allows evaluating the educational platform and collecting information to correct some aspects and improve it in the future. It should be noted, however, that like most case studies, it will not allow generalization on the model.

This case study was divided into 4 phases which can be summarized in:

1. The prototype of the platform "O Teu Mestre";
2. Presentation and formation of the platform;
3. Monitoring students' use of the platform;
4. Analysis of the results of the surveys completed by the interveners.

The participants in this study were:

A 12th grade class consisting of **17 public school students**, many attending Mathematics A, from Fontes Pereira de Melo School in Porto; **Four students** signaled by the Acreditar Association (Association of Parents and Friends of Children with Cancer); These students are hospitalized and / or unable to be present in the classroom. Although there is legislation that provides for school support, in most cases this support does not materialize or is not adequate to their needs.Thus, due to a protocol established between the author and Acreditar, we considered in this study 4 students suffering from oncological disease and that alternated between hospital and outpatient regimens. **Five mathematical teachers** with more than five years of experience used the educational platform. Four of these teachers that used this platform are from the district of Viseu.

The teacher of the Fontes Pereira de Melo School used this platform as an educational resource in the classroom.

The collection of data was done through different methods and techniques that complement each other, namely: the logbook and a questionnaire survey. The logbook was one of the instruments of the case study, since it was necessary to record all the follow-up done to the students through the educational platform. This registration began at the beginning of the second school term of 2014/2015, when students signaled by Acreditar and Fontes Pereira de Melo were able to use the platform. Therefore, there was a monitoring of all the steps, which allowed to evaluate, redo and evaluate again, repeating this process countless times, in order to improve the service provided. In general, this register made possible to observe the students' difficulties at the pedagogical and technological levels. In this study we opted for 3 questionnaires, one directed to the students of the 12th grade group of the Fontes Pereira de Melo Schools Association, a second to the students signaled by Acreditar, and the last one to the teachers who had contact with the platform.

The objective of these questionnaires consisted in evaluating the prototype of the educational platform to which they had access. The design of the three questionnaires was based on the criteria of the Learning Object Review Instrument (LORI) table that analyzes the items: content quality, learning objective, adaptation and feedback, motivation, presentation and design, usability, accessibility, reuse, norm compliances. These items were addressed in the three questionnaires through questions distributed by 9 parts. The first 7 are closed questions, with simple indications about the purposes of each one, in order to try to obtain the desired information about the LORI criteria. The last two have open questions in order to gather opinions about the advantages or disadvantages of the platform and suggestions for it.

The differences between the questionnaire given to the students of the Fontes Pereira de Melo School and the one given to the students signaled by Acreditar resides in the adequacy of the first question in the content item. The first questionnaire intends to analyze if the contents available meet the themes addressed in the refered School and, in the case of students signaled by Acreditar, if the contents made available meet their needs and difficulties. In the accessibility topic, a question was added: "Do you consider that the use of this platform is accessible in different electronic media (such as portable devices) and therefore an advantage in a hospital environment?". This question is intended to gather the opinion on whether accessibility in different electronic media is an advantage in the hospital environment.

In the questionnaire addressed to teachers, the questions were adjusted taking into account the professional aspect, ie, based on the criteria of LORI, what is the teachers' opinion regarding the evaluation of the platform, as a digital educational resource in use in classroom or as a complement to teaching.

We have also taken into account in the preparation of the questionnaires, ethical issues such as informed consent, anonymity and confidentiality of the data.

3. DIGITAL EDUCATIONAL RESOURCES EVALUATION

The increase in the quantity of pedagogical materials in computer support leads to the need to reflect on the technical and pedagogical quality of these materials, as well as their conditions of use; according to Lévy (2000) the diversity and multiplicity of available information is not a guarantee of any quality.

Ramos (2010) states that the evaluation of OERs is a concern in different countries and Portugal followed this concern and in 2004, the Portuguese Ministry of Education created a team of specialists and teachers with the objective of developing a collection system , dissemination, evaluation and certification of educational products in digital media (Costa, Peralta & Viseu, 2007), which was designated by the SACAUSEF project (System for Evaluation, Certification and Support to the Use of Software for Education and Training). This project proposed the existence of three phases (Costa, Peralta & Viseu, 2007): i) the submission of resources; ii) evaluation of resources in an educational context; iii) publication of the evaluation process in a portal, with the main objective of promoting the quality of the existing offer.

Belikov and Bodily (2016) consider a barrier to OER adoption is the amount of time that it takes to evaluate these new resources, some of which have not yet been through a review process. According to Hylen (2012) the idea is that it is not possible to guarantee the quality of such a high abundance of resources and materials that are made freely available on the web. In addition, the concept of quality is not peaceful, so in the next point we will approach the concept of quality in particular in a OER.

3.1 The Quality Concept

Quality can be defined as "an appropriate meeting between objectives of the interested parts and the needs as a result of a transparent participatory negotiation process in an organization" (Pawlowski, 2007, p 1).

According to Pinto (2007), the quality of information in a OER is determined by its ability to meet the expectations and needs of information and training of teachers and students who use them.

These definitions imply that quality assessment depends not only on the resource but on various context factors.

In order to guarantee the quality of a OER it is necessary to evaluate it. For Shaughnessy (2002) this evaluation process implies in itself the use of a set of tools and methods, such as the use of checklists designed by experts, use of surveys and observation, supervision and control of published information at the evaluation level. Some of these criteria will be discussed in the following section. In the particular case of the evaluation criteria of distance learning, there are numerous tables of evaluation criteria, we can refer to the table of LORI, Allen & Mugisa and Pinheiro. These tables have the particularity of being able to evaluate a wider range of digital educational resources, from a simple presentation to the most complex structure of distance education.

3.2 LORI Evaluation

In 2003, the Learning Object Review Instrument (LORI) was created by John Nesbit, Karen Belfer and Tracey Leacock, and has been one of the most widely used tools for evaluating OERs (Belfer, Nesbit, & Leacock, 2002). In 2008 it is improved by the team consisting of Akpinar, Leacock and Nesbit (Akpinar, 2008).

The LORI is not only a simple tool, but also an infrastructure for evaluating digital educational resources that allows evaluators to evaluate and comment on OER (Leacock & Nesbit, 2007). This evaluation is done using a five-point Likert scale [from low (1) to high (5)].

Fortunato, Marcelino e Souza (2018) considers that LORI's assessment is a simple tool to evaluate the variety and quantity of the existing OERs.

The LORI consists of nine items: Quality of content; Learning Objective; Adaptation and Feedback; Motivation; Presentation and Design; Usability and interaction; Accessibility; Reuse and Compliance Standards.

These points will then be considered in the light of the first wording of 2003 and also the changes made in 2008.

• Content Quality - This refers to veracity, accuracy, balanced presentation of ideas, and the level of detail if it is appropriate for the target audience. Content should be free of errors.

• Learning Objective - Learning objectives are indicated. The resource presents an adjustment between learning objectives, activities, assessments, and student characteristics. Learning activities such as content and assessments should be tailored to previously defined objectives.

• Adaptation and Feedback - Content should be tailored to different students or to a student model. The resource should give feedback to different students or to student models.

• Motivation -The resource should have the capacity to motivate and arouse interest in a student population. It should be relevant to the personal goals and interests of the students for whom it is intended.

• Presentation and Design - You should present simple visual and auditory information for better learning and efficient mental processing. The resource should enable students to learn effectively. Feature presentations should minimize visual search, for example: text and graphics presentations should be clear, concise, and error-free. In addition, the components of the screen do not interfere with the learning objectives in question.

• Usability and interaction - The feature is easy to navigate and there is predictability at the user interface. The UI design implicitly informs students about how to interact with the NET. Navigating through OER is simple. The behavior of the user interface is consistent and predictable.

• Accessibility - The design of OER buttons should have presentation formats that are accessible to students with special educational needs or who are mobile and do not have access to the traditional school. The resource shall be accessible through different electronic means including portable devices.

• Reuse - Can be used in various tasks, in various contexts and in students from different school paths. The resource should be independent of others and easily transferable to other learning and other contexts.

• Standards Compliance - Comply with relevant international standards and specifications. It should have a metadata identification that allows the user to easily identify the resource.

We considered that the LORI table presents the most balanced criteria, without being very specific or very comprehensive, unlike other tables analyzed, which focus on very particular aspects. In addition, the LORI table shows an evolution over the years and has been improved to meet current requirements.

4. RESULTS ANALYSIS

This particular chapter presents a detailed analysis of the results obtained from the responses to the evaluation surveys of the "O Teu Mestre" platform model. The questionnaires were sent by email to all participants.

A questionnaire was sent to the 17 students in the 12th grade, another to the 4 students signaled by Acreditar and a third to 5 high school teachers who teach mathematics, including Professor Maria José Losada. All respondents responded to the survey, which corresponds to a 100% rate of return.

As for the gender distribution, 47% of the students of the Fontes Pereira de Melo School are female and 53% are male. The students signaled by Acreditar are 3 (75%) female and 1 male (25%).

The average age of students is 18 years, according to the year of school attendance.

As for teachers, 1 is male (20%) and 4 are female (80%), in relation to the average age of teachers is 43, reflecting a reasonable professional experience.

The results presented are related to the LORI evaluation criteria.

A) Content

Regarding the content, the students of Fontes Pereira de Melo school, in relation to the first question "Do you think that the contents made available meet the topics addressed in the School?", 59% of the students considered them useful and 41% very useful. Concerning question number 2 "Do you think that the information is presented in a language that you understand easily and in a logical way?", It is worth noting that 53% of the students assigned it level 4.

Regarding the students signaled by Acreditar, the following questions were presented: "Do you think that the contents made available meet your needs and difficulties?" and "Do you think that information is presented in a language that you understand easily and in a logical way?". All the students assigned them level 4 (very useful) thus expressing their degree of satisfaction with the contents of the platform.

In this criterion, teachers answered a first question "Do you consider the information made available on the platform accurate and appropriate to the subject?", 20% of the respondents considered it useful and 80% very useful. Regarding the 2nd question "How do you rate the information presented regarding the level of detail and organization?" It was considered useful by 40% of the respondents and very useful by 60%.

The third question was common to all (students and teachers) with the following text: "How satisfied are you with the following content - essential theoretical, quizzes, exams and intermediate tests and service have a doubt?"

It was verified that 82% of the students of Fontes Pereira de Melo school, regarding the last question of this group considered the item "theoretical essential" and 18% very useful, which demonstrates the relevance of a theoretical support in solving problems, as a synthesis / summary of the subject matter. 65% of the students attributed the rating of useful to the item quizzes and 35% of very useful. 71% of the students evaluated as useful access to the resolution of "exams and intermediate tests" and 29% very useful. 71% of the students surveyed were very satisfied with the "Tens uma dúvida" (Do you have a question?) item, which demonstrates the importance of clarifying doubts as they arise.

Graphically we can observe it in graph 1.

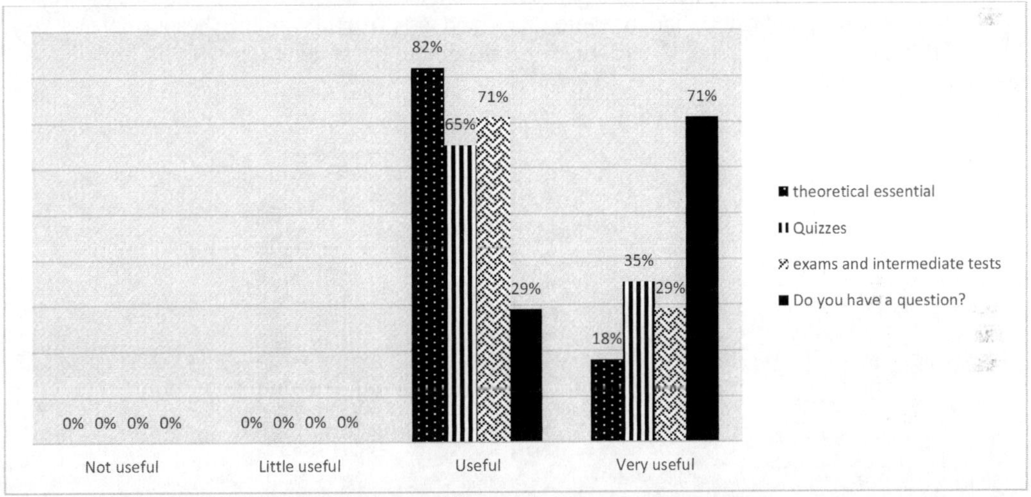

Figure 1. Level of satisfaction of FPM students in content

According the students indicated by "Acreditar" the items "theoretical essentials" and "intermediate exams and tests" were useful (75%) and very useful (25%).

The quizzes item was considered useful by 50% of the students and very useful by the other 50%.

All students were very satisfied with the service "Tens uma Dúvida?" since they, unable to attend classes regularly and contact directly with the teacher of the discipline, find in this service timely answers to their questions and difficulties.

There were no students assigning levels 1 and 2 to the presented items, which shows the good acceptance of the contents available. We can see in graph 2 these results.

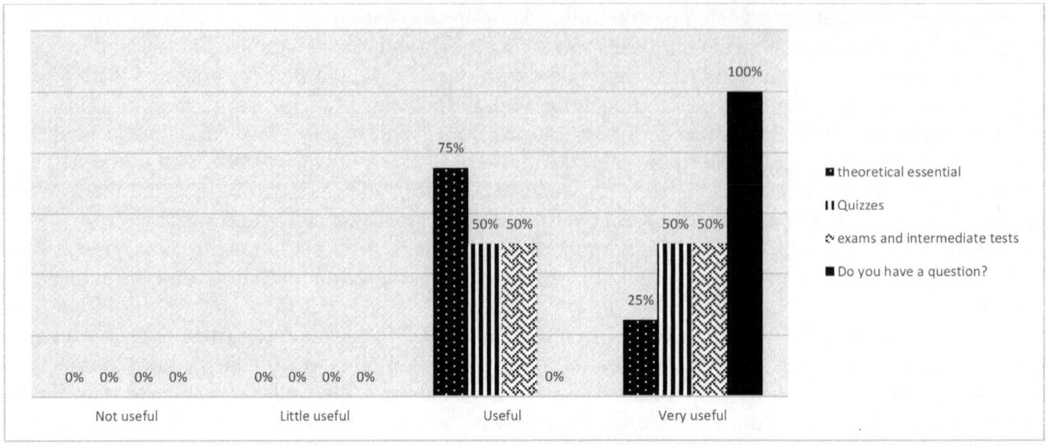

Figure 2. Acreditar students' level of satisfaction with content

With regard to teachers,

- 60% of the respondents considered the item "theoretical essential" useful and 40% very useful.
- 80% assigned level 4 to item quizzes and 20% considered it useful.
- 80% considered the item "intermediate exams and tests" useful, while 20% considered it very useful.
- 100% of teachers surveyed attributed the maximum score to the service item "Do you have a question?"

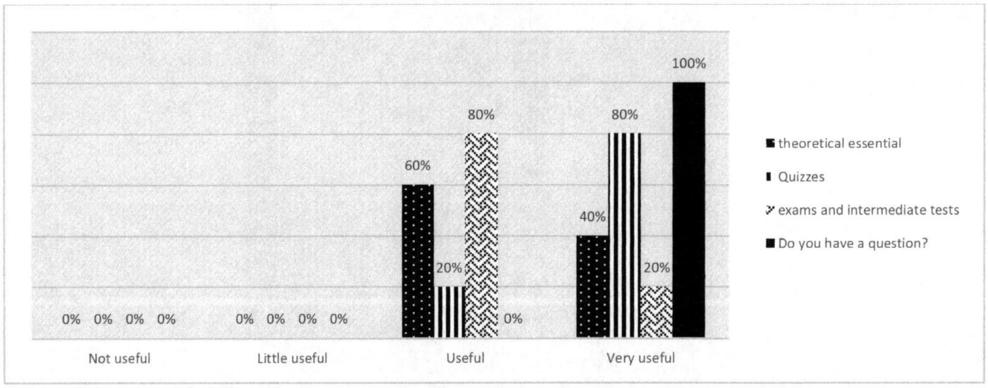

Figure 3. Level of teacher satisfaction with content

B) Objectives

In this item to the students of the Fontes Pereira de Melo school, two questions were posed: "Does the information provided on the platform meet your learning needs and doubts?"

It was found that 88% of the group of students considered the information useful and very useful, with only 12% who classified it as level 2 and therefore not very useful.

The questions addressed to the students identified by Acreditar, were "How do you classify the use of the platform with regard to the school attendance?" and "In case you are deprived of ongoing school support, do you believe that this platform can function as an important substitute for this even support? "

From the analysis of the results it is concluded that:

- Regarding the ease of school monitoring, using the platform, 75% consider it useful and 25% very useful.
- 75% consider that the platform is a very useful support for students who are deprived of ongoing school support, acting as a substitute for this same support.

These figures confirm the need for these types of educational platform for students who, due to long-term illness, cannot attend the classroom or benefit from more individualized teaching.

Regarding the issues addressed to teachers:

"Do you consider the platform made available as a means to facilitate the teaching of the discipline?" It should be noted that all the teachers who completed the survey considered the platform available as a facilitator of teaching the subject.

Also in this item, the question "Do you think it can work as an important complement in teaching the discipline?" was directed to all involved (students and teachers).

Regarding the students of Fontes Pereira de Melo school, it was evaluated positively by 94% of the them, being considered useful by 59% and very useful by 49%. Only one student considered it to be of little value, which corresponds to 6% of respondents.

All the students signaled by Acreditar considered that the platform is a very useful complement in the teaching of the subject.

Regarding teachers, 60% considered the platform useful, constituting an important complement in the teaching-learning process of the student. 40% of the respondents attributed the maximum score, considering it very useful.

C) Motivation

The answer to the question "Do you think that the use of the platform motivates you to study the discipline?", shows that most of the students at Fontes Pereira de Melo are more motivated (level 3 and 4 answer) with use of the platform (71%).

As for the students signaled by Acreditar, the answer to the question shows that 50% of the respondents considered this tool very useful as a motivating element for the study of the discipline.

The question for teachers has been rephrased with the text "Do you think using the platform motivates students to study the discipline?"

In this item it was verified that 80% of the teachers considered the platform very useful, functioning as a motivating agent in the teaching-learning process of the discipline.

D) Graphic

In this item, the students of Fontes Pereira de Melo were asked to answer the following question: "The text, graphics and images presented are: (1. not 2. yes 3. excellent) easy, clear, nice to see. "

The vast majority of respondents considered it excellent as to the ease and clarity in reading the text, graphics and images presented. 76% of the respondents attributed excellent to the visual aspect of the platform.

Regarding the item graphics (text, graphics and images), they was considered excellent by all the respondents of Acreditar, which demonstrates that they appreciate the visual aspect, the clarity and ease of reading the information available.

All the teachers considered excellent the simplicity with which the platform presents the auditory and visual information. 80% of the respondents thought the information was presented in a clear way and 20% considered it to be excellent.

As for the graphic aspect, 80% of the teachers considered the platform very attractive.

E) Usability interaction and accessibility

In relation to this item the following questions were posed:

1- "How difficult is it to navigate the various fields of the platform?"

Regarding this first question, it was verified that all the students signaled by Acreditar considered easy to navigate on the platform, which shows the functionality and clarity of the associated tools.

Regarding the teachers, 40% considered it easy to navigate the various fields of the platform, while 60% considered this task very easy.

Relatively to the question "Do you think the platform is easy to interact with and that desktop icons are simple to use and intuitive?"

The majority of the students and teachers emphasized the ease of interaction with the platform, appreciating the intuitive and elucidative character of the iconography used.

The third question "Do you think information can be easily accessed and that it is simple to find the answers to your doubts?"

We can conclude that, in a general way, the students were able to easily access the information provided. In fact, 65% of the respondents (students of Fontes Pereira de Melo school) considered access to the platform easy and 35% very easy.

As for of the students signaled by Acreditar, 75% consider that access to the platform is very easy and 25% easy.

Concerning the question addressed only to teachers "How does the platform consider the level of accessibility?", all teachers agreed that it was easy to access the platform.

The last question in this item was only directed to the students signaled by Acreditar: "Do you consider that the use of this platform is accessible in different electronic means (such as portable devices) and therefore an advantage in a hospital environment? (Yes / No response) "

With regard to this qestion, it is worth mentioning that all the students answered affirmatively to the possibility of using the platform in different electronic means, which represents a great advantage in a hospital environment.

F) Reuse

In this item students and teachers were asked to answer the following question: "How do you classify the platform with regard to: the possibility of storing the information, possibility of reuse and the possibility of printing content or sending by email."

88% of respondents (Fontes Pereira de Melo school) appreciated the possibility of storing the information, of reusing it as well as of printing it or sending it by email.

All the students signaled by Acreditar understood that it was easy to save the information, reuse it and be able to print it or send it by email.

40% of teachers indicated being easy to keep information, while 60% understood it to be very easy.

Regarding the possibility of reusing, printing or sending by email, 80% of teachers understood it to be very easy.

G) Interest

In general, the students of Escola Fontes Pereira de Melo considered this platform of great interest, since 88% attributed to it the classification of very useful and 12% of useful.

Worthy of note are the same results regarding the platform's capacity for innovation.

All the students signaled by Acreditar considered this platform of great interest, attributing level 4 to it. The same results with respect to the platform's capacity for innovation.

All the teachers also pointed out the interest of the platform, being classified as very useful by 60% of them. It should be noted that all teachers have considered this platform to be very innovative.

H) Advantages and disadvantages of the platform fpm

Regarding this issue of opinion placed at the end of this group we can observe the following advantages:

For the students of Escola Fontes Pereira de Melo the platform presents a diversified set that meets the needs of the student; simplicity of navigation and ease of access to the platform; intuitive and user-friendly design; easy contact and flexible hours with a teacher through the "Tens uma dúvida?" service; possibility of assistance for students with reduced mobility or residing in places far from school.

The students signaled by Acreditar considered as advantages: the possibility and speed of access in different electronic media namely tablet and smartphone; flexibility of schedules for educational monitoring; easy navigation.

Teachers referred as advantages: allow review of content through interactive games; easy contact and flexible hours for a teacher through the "Tens uma Dúvida?" service; possibility of assistance for students with reduced mobility or residing in places far from school.

As disadvantages, the students of Escola Fontes Pereira de Melo highlighted: the lack of integration of the videoconference tool in the platform; 24-hour deadline to answer students' questions when requested by video; reduced number of queries in the "Tens uma Dúvida?" service.

The AC students pointed out the following: the impossibility of continuous monitoring; reduced number of queries in the "Tens uma dúvida?" service.

Regarding teachers, the disadvantages mentioned were: not having an area to put content; not allowing the creation of virtual groups and the management of the evaluation; lack of integration of the videoconferencing tool in the platform.

I) Suggestions

The main suggestions indicated were: extension of service to other disciplines; online classes and the possibility of networking among students.

5. CONCLUSION

In this section the main conclusions of this research work are presented, whose main objective is to propose a model of a OER to promote the learning of mathematics for students of traditional teaching and for students hospitalized and / or prevented from being present in the classroom.

By analyzing the theoretical basis and results achieved, we can affirm that we reached the guiding objective of this research, that is, the creation of a model of a OER, the educational platform "O Teu Mestre", which enhances students' mathematics learning of traditional teaching and of students hospitalized and / or prevented from being present in the classroom.

In fact, we can conclude that this model of educational platform contributes to the success in the mathematics discipline, functioning as an important complement and motivating agent of the teaching-learning process, inside and outside the classroom, as evidenced by the answers to the questions of the quiz:

"Do you think that the platform can work as an important complement in the teaching of the discipline?" (All students in hospital context, 94% of those attending regular school and 60% of teachers answered affirmatively);

"Do you consider that the use of this platform can act as a motivating agent for the teaching and learning of the discipline?" (71% of regular students, 50% of those in a hospital setting and 80% of teachers said yes).

In general, respondents were satisfied with the usability and interaction content, navigation, accessibility, graphic aspect and information.

We can conclude that the participants in this process realize that this platform, by allowing great flexibility in terms of space, time and learning pace, allows to rationalize resources, respect the needs and preferences of each one, facilitating the teaching- learning.

In the particular case of hospitalized students, it is notorious that the OER model presented here allows to support these students without the need of human resources with exclusive dedication to these students. It also allows content to be organized in counterpoint to the lack of autonomy of the school that involuntarily contributes to a disorganized teaching and not adequate to the needs and current reality of the student. In addition, the platform does not need a great training of the actors since it is intuitive, as we can verify in the results of the questionnaires.

As for the gigantism of information, this platform simplifies the contents by summarizing them, always based on the national curriculum.

The analysis of the obtained results allowed to conclude that this model of OER contributes to the success in the mathematics subject, functioning as an important complement and motivating agent of the teaching-learning process in the classroom and also outside it, as an instrument of fundamental support to pupils who, for reasons of health, are prevented from attending school regularly.

5.1 Main Study Limitations

The first limitation: the period of time in which this work was developed presents itself as a limitation to the scope of the study, to the technological aspects related to the creation of the platform and to the changes made during the study to improve it. On the other hand, the pedagogical aspect implied a rigorous work in what refers to the selection of programmatic contents of the discipline of mathematics of the 12th grade, the accomplishment of works of synthesis / summary of the matter, the placement in the platform of exercises and its resolution and the creation of videos.

The second limitation: the small number of students in the study questionnaire, especially in the hospital context, is related to logistic issues, namely the lack of a pedagogical team available to ensure a continuous and adequate response to all the requests of the students that use the platform.

ACKNOWLEDGEMENT

This research was supported by Acreditar Association and Fontes Pereira de Melo School from Oporto.

REFERENCES

Akpinar, Y. (2008). *Validation of a Learning Object Review Instrument: Relationship between Ratings of Learning Objects and Actual Learning Outcomes.* Interdisciplinary Journal of E-Learning and Learning Objects, 4, 291–302.

Belfer, K., Nesbit, J., & Leacock, T. (2002) *LORI Manual.* http://edutechwiki.unige.ch/en/Learning_Object_Review_Instrument

Belikov, O. & Brigham, R. (2016). *Incentives and barriers to OER adoption: A qualitative analysis of faculty perceptions.* Open Praxis, 235–246.

Correia, L. M. (1997). *Alunos com Necessidades Educativas Especiais na Classe Regular.* Porto Editora.

Costa, F. A., & Peralta, M. H. (2007). *Primary Teachers' Competence and Confidence Level Regarding the Use of ICT.* In Proceedings of World Conference on Educational Multimedia, Hypermedia and Telecommunications (pp. 46–52). Orlando: E Pearson & P Bohman.

Gil, H. (2014). *A passagem da Web 1.0 para a Web 2.0 e... Web 3.0: potenciais consequências para uma «humanização» em contexto educativo.* Tese de Doutoramento. Universidade do Minho.

Joly, M. (2002). *A Tecnologia no Ensino: Implicações para Aprendizagem.* São Paulo: Casa Do Psicólogo. Recuperado de http://www.scielo.br/pdf/pee/v6n2/v6n2a10.pdf

Leacock, T. L., & Nesbit, J. C. (2007). *A Framework for Evaluating the Quality of Multimedia Learning Resources.* Educational Technology & Society, 10(2), 44–59.

Pawlowski, J. M. (2007). *The Quality Adaptation Model: Adaptation and Adoption of the Quality Standard ISO/IEC 19796-1 for Learning, Education, and Training.* Educational Technology & Society, 10(2), 3–16.

Pinto, M. (2007). *Evaluación de la cálida de recursos electrónicos educativos para el aprendizage significativo.* Sacausef 2, 25–43. http://www.crie.min- edu.pt/files/@crie/1225103966_03_CADERNOII_p25_43_MPpdf.pdf

Prenksy, M. (2007). *How to teach with technology: Keeping both teachers and students comfortable in an era of exponential change. In Emerging Technologies for Learning* (Vol. 2, pp. 39-47).

Ramos, J. L. (coord.), Teodoro, V. D., Fernandes, J. P. S., Ferreira, M. F., & Chagas, I. (2010). *Portal das Escolas: Recursos Educativos Digitais para Portugal. Estudo Estratégico.* Lisboa: GEPE. http://www.gepe.min-edu.pt/np4/364.html

República, D. da. (2009). Lei nº 71/2009. Lisboa, Portugal: Governo de Portugal.

Shaugnessy, M. (2002). *Educational Software Evaluation. A contextual approach.* Ph. d. dissertation Cincinnaty Unniversity.

Souza, M., Marcelino, R., Fortunato, I. (2018). *LORI como método de avaliação de objetos de aprendizagem: estudo de revisão.* Revista de estudos aplicados em Educação.

Torres, P. (2007). *Laboratório On-line de aprendizagem: Uma experiência de aprendizagem colaborativa por meios de ambiente virtual de aprendizagem EUREK@KIDS.* http://www.scielo.br/pdf/ccedes/v27n73/06.pdf

COMPARING THREE INPUT DEVICES FOR SKETCHING ASSIGNMENTS IN E-EXAMS IN COMPUTER SCIENCE

Suhas Govind Joshi and Live Årmot Brastad
Department of Informatics, Faculty of Mathematics and Natural Sciences, University of Oslo, Norway

ABSTRACT

E-exams used in higher education can accommodate a range of assignment types that have traditionally been conducted with pen-and-paper. However, one issue that remains a challenge is proper support of sketching in larger, generic e-exams systems. Different types of sketching assignment demand input devices suited to the specific type of problem-solving. Adopting an e-exam system may involve compromises in terms of restricted opportunities to use sketching assignments as part of the e-exam that affect the students' performance or their experience of the e-exam. This paper presents a comparison of 77 students' performance and preferences with three different input devices (a mouse, a graphical tablet, and a touchpad) when solving sketching assignments from three different computer science courses. The study focused on capturing the students' perspective, and the findings include identified benefits and challenges associated with using the three different input devices during sketching.

KEYWORDS

Sketching, e-Exam, Graphical Tablet, Touchpad

1. INTRODUCTION

The increasing presence of e-exams in higher education has brought forward new opportunities to organize exams in ways that were not possible with traditional pen-and-paper exams. Sketching has always been a part of how students are tested in different courses within higher education. Visual communication is an important part of how students attain and convey their knowledge in many learning situations, including e-exam situations. However, shifting sketching assignments that have traditionally been conducted with pen-and-paper over to larger, generic e-exam systems remains a challenge. While e-exams have opened up new possibilities that may replace old sketching assignments with other pedagogical alternatives, technical restrictions or inefficiencies should not prevent sketching assignments from appearing in exam situations.

This paper reports from a study on how students experience sketching assignments as part of e-exams. We have conducted a comparison of performance and preference when students use three different input devices, namely a mouse, a graphical tablet, and a touchpad, to solve representative sketching assignments from computer science courses using an e-exam software. 77 students participated in testing these three input devices in three different undergraduate courses within computer science that build of different traditions and represent different types of sketching assignments.

The study aimed to investigate differences in performance and preference within each course rather than make an overarching cross-course comparison where the sketching assignments were normalized in complexity and degree of freedom. Our underlying assumption was that the different courses would yield different performances with the three input devices due to the variation in complexity and degree of freedom between the representative sketching assignments from each course. We argue that normalizing these assignments would compromise on important details in each course and no longer be representative of how the students experience them during real e-exam situations. As such, the study was a bottom-up comparison where the performance time and preferences with each input device were mainly considered within each course. However, we also studied how the rank and order within each course compared across the three courses to answer the overarching two-folded research question. The two objectives that the research question aimed to answer were: (1) does one input device perform unanimously better in completion time and preference for sketching assignments across the three courses, and (2) what are the main benefits and challenges associated with the three input devices when used in sketching assignments? Throughout the study, our focus remained on answering these questions from the students' perspective exclusively rather than attempt to include other important end-users of the e-exams systems such as the teachers (Osang, 2012).

To answer our overarching research question, we collected both quantitative and qualitative data to analyze performance and preference. The quantitative data was gathered by measuring the completion time in a randomized experiment and analyzed using a two-way factorial ANOVA. The analysis was complemented with qualitative data from post-test interviews with all participants. Based on the analysis, we present an overview of main benefits and challenges associated with each of the three input devices. The discussion aligns our findings with the literature on students' perspective on e-exams and e-exams including sketching assignments.

2. RELATED WORK

There is a multitude of studies concerning the use of e-examination and e-assessment. The shift to e-exams has been motivated by a range of underlying practical and economic concerns, e.g., streamlining of academic assessment to avoid paper-based work (Ibrahim et al., 2015, p. 48), reducing time spent on the assessment (Kuikka et al., 2014, p. 4; Wibowo et al., 2016), preventing cheating, environmental concerns (Wibowo et al., 2016, p. 18), and for security and authentication reasons (Abdel Karim and Shukur, 2016). Even digital learning technologies with student-focused overarching goals or innovative approaches to exploration with new interaction techniques and tools have yielded varying results (Drake et al., 2015, pp. 125–126).

Most studies on e-exams emphasize the students' view, and many such studies advocate the importance of localizing to support local cultures in teaching specific topics (Lazem, 2016). Examples of strategies for localization within the context of e-exams include building on existing practice in teaching (Oviatt et al., 2006, p. 1), incorporating learning modalities from early childhood to stimulate familiarity (Rante et al., 2018, p. 2), or bringing in familiar technologies to increase the overall learning potential (Romero et al., 2009, p. 445; Wibowo et al., 2016, p. 8). While our study is limited to the perspective of the students, the issue of considering all end-users have been emphasized by multiple studies. For instance, adapting the design of the learning technologies to include concerns at individual, social, and cultural level is an important part of addressing higher-order issues such as inclusion and accessibility (Drake et al., 2015, p. 133). Other examples of relevant considerations include *"aspects of flexibility, clarity, security, and convenience"* (Wibowo et al., 2016, p. 26) and the usability concerns of the teachers during the introduction of a digital system (Kuikka et al., 2014, pp. 5–6).

Prior work of particular interest to our research are those studies concerned with either how students perceive the digital input devices as part the digitalization of exams, or that examine the use of drawing or sketching as the part of the e-examination or a larger learning environment.

2.1 Digital Input Devices and Sketching

Learning systems that incorporate various digital input devices have also been studied in the past. Several studies have examined the role of alternative input devices in learning situations to enhance learning, e.g., studies applying tablets or touch- or pen-based interfaces, (Barreto et al., 2016; Koile and Rubin, 2016; Lara-Garduno et al., 2016; Polsley et al., 2016; Wang et al., 2016; Williford et al., 2016). These studies have reported on various aspects of sketching such as benefits of shifting from paper-and-pencil tests to digital alternatives (Barreto et al., 2016, p. 143; Lara-Garduno et al., 2016, p. 166), automation of interpretation of freehand sketching (Williford et al., 2016, p. 117), performance and behavior in problem solving (Polsley et al., 2016, p. 110), and how digitalizing teaching with tablet-based technology may affect conceptual understanding (Koile and Rubin, 2016, p. 72). Studies have also been done where different input devices have been compared (Oviatt et al., 2006; Thompson et al., 2016).

Sketching as a part of learning and teaching is not something new, and the idea of digitalizing sketching was discussed already two decades ago (Landay and Myers, 2001). For the longest time, sketching has been a natural part of examinations, which were mainly conducted on pen-and-paper that did not introduce any technical challenges. Studies have discussed the importance of sketching within different traditions adopted or embraced by computer science courses, e.g., engineering (Williford et al., 2016; Yang and Cham, 2006), mechanics (Polsley et al., 2016), and mathematics (Oviatt et al., 2006). One of the arguments of replacing paper exams with e-exams is the support of multimedia content (Wibowo et al., 2016, p. 6). While not being specifically limited to sketching-based exams, studies of performance in digital assessments versus pen-and-paper assessment have been mixed, and in certain exam formats, yielded small differences that were not practically significant (Walker and Handley, 2016, p. 2). In studies of preference rather than performance, similar equally divided results have been reported (Wibowo et al., 2016, p. 16). Comparisons between different input devices have also suggested that the performance of stylus and touch did not vary to any statistically significant degree (Thompson et al., 2016, p. 67). Nevertheless, the challenge of retaining the benefits of paper while digitalizing the interaction has motivated many relevant studies on the use of novel digital interfaces, e.g., with the use of graphical tablets or digital stylus (Lee et al., 2017; Oviatt et al., 2006; Rante et al., 2018; Thompson et al., 2016; Williford et al., 2016). Other examples of state-of-the-art concepts building on experiences with paper include thin-film display technologies (Klamka and Dachselt, 2017) or augmented paper interfaces (Tsandilas et al., 2015).

2.2 Defining Sketching

In the midst of digitalization, sketching remains a tacit skill that enables visual communication during exams. There are many definitions of sketching, and it carries different meanings in different contexts (Lewis et al., 2019, p. 2). The literature also contains ambiguities (Lane 2017, p. 5). Sketching serves multiple roles in a learning situation, and different problems involve sketching in different capacities. Exam systems with tools that support any form of drawing are usually well received, e.g., as seen in (Wibowo et al., 2016, p. 22). However, the understanding of what such tools need to do to support sketching varies greatly from one context to another. The call for automatic correction of multimedia content in e-exam systems has been reported (Kuikka et al., 2014, p. 10), but such content usually refer to videos and pictures. From our perspective, tools offering simplistic self-composed graphic from a predefined array of elements or supporting drawing of a simple line would only constitute as *"drawing with a pen"* (Do, 2002, p. 151), rather than actually support sketching. For instance, we consider freedom and flexibility to remain an important characteristic of sketching (Landay and Myers, 2001, p. 56). The understanding of sketching in our study aligns with how Lane defines sketching as a *"fundamental skill that supports higher-order cognitive processes such as creative problem-solving and innovative critical-thinking"* (2017, p. 2) and that can also serve as a thinking tool for both spatial and visual reasoning. During an exam situation, sketching serves as a part of the reflection of the cognitive activities of the student and is valuable for communicating ideas (Yang and Cham, 2006, p. 476). The sketching assignments included in our study suit the definition of *"study sketches"* and the definition of freehand sketching as a *"reflexive process in which externalizations are communicated"* (Lane, 2017, p. 7) aligns well with how the students answer them.

3. RESEARCH METHOD

This study included 77 students who participated in solving sketching assignments from three different courses where performance times were measured and then followed up by a post-test interview. As our overarching goal was to conduct a bottom-up study where each course was considered individually, we were not interested in the absolute values of the performance, but rather the relative differences between the three input devices observed in the three courses included. The comparison between the three courses was only made to assess the relative rank and order in performance time and preference rather than attempt to make independent comparisons of absolute values.

3.1 Courses and Sketching Assignments

We included representative sketching tasks from three different entry-level courses at the undergraduate program. The courses were selected based on their representation of different branches of computer science that build on different traditions, namely electronics and electrical engineering, design and art, and programming and software modeling. We refer to the courses by their overarching topics, but the sketching assignments were not necessarily representative of the whole course curriculum and were mainly included as examples of different sketching assignments traditionally found within computer science. Table 1 presents an overview of the three courses and examples of assignments.

Table 1. Overview of the courses and sketching assignments

Course topic	Extracts from the curriculum	Examples of specific models
Electronics	Sketching simple digital logic circuits	Circuit diagrams, logic gates (e.g., full adder)
Interaction design	Sketching complex models and freehand sketches	Customer journey maps, storyboards, lifecycle models
Database and software modeling	Sketching relational models and diagrams	Object-role modeling, UML diagrams (e.g., sequence diagram)

As mentioned in the introduction, we did not normalize the assignments from the three courses to avoid any important details of each course disappearing while attempting to align the complexity and degree of freedom. One such example is the freehand assignments in the interaction design course where we wanted to capture underlying issues, e.g., multi-gestures with the graphical tablet used to perform complicated tasks that have previously been discussed as a source of confusion (Rante et al., 2018, p. 5).

3.2 Performance Testing and Post-Test Interview

The performance testing was conducted at the university premises and included testing stations with separate test setups for each of the input device to allow parallel testing. See Figure 1 for examples of the testing stations. Each of the 77 participants solved assignments with the three input devices for one specific course. The test was conducted in this manner due to the participants having different backgrounds and familiarity with the different courses. Recruiting participants who were equally proficient in the three subjects would have proved challenging as the course combination is not representative of courses typically taken in combination during an undergraduate degree at this university. This decision had a positive impact on the learning effects on using the three input devices as each participant only used each device once during the test. The 77 students were recruited sequentially to reach an equal distribution between the three courses and ended with 25, 24, and 28 participants in the three courses.

Figure 1. Setup of two testing stations

To ensure familiarity with the exam format and assignments, and to avoid bias in the method (Walker and Handley, 2016, p. 5), we utilized a nation-wide adopted online e-exam software in this study. 69 of the 77 participating students (89.6 %) had prior experience with digital exams using this specific e-exam software. All participants reported having experience with both a mouse and a touchpad while 36 of the 77 participants (46.8 %) had tried a graphical tablet before. These 36 participants were distributed evenly across the three courses.

Each participant was observed while solving the assignment, and then later questioned in a post-test interview. Screenshots were taken of each sketch. While visual analyses of the sketches were not a part of this study, it could be subject to a complementing follow-up study similar to (Taele and Hammond, 2016).

Interesting observations made during the performance tests were included in the post-test interviews to corroborate any suspicions of underlying issues.

The order of the three input devices and the assignment order were both randomized at the participant level to minimize learning bias. The participants solved different assignments within each course, and we used time-to-complete as the metric. A similar approach has been adopted by Oviatt et al. (2006, p. 5) when comparing different input devices, and Landay and Myers (2001, p. 62) also argue that task completion can be used as a measure for efficiency in such contexts.

4. RESULTS AND FINDINGS

4.1 Statistical Analysis

The performance tests resulted in three data points on performance time for each of the 77 students, separated into the three courses. We ran a two-way factorial ANOVA to determine the effects of the two independent variables *course* (electronics, interaction design, database) and *input device* (mouse, graphical tablet, touchpad) on the dependent variable completion time. All effects were statistically significant at the 0.05 level. The main effect of the course on the completion time, $F(2, 222) = 31.06$, $p < .05$, $\eta_p^2 = .219$, confirmed our initial suspicion that our sample size and research design would not support any cross-course comparisons of the three input devices due to variation in the courses, i.e., the assignments given and the complexity involved. This observation was further supported by the effect size of course ($\eta_p^2 = .219$) being larger than the effect size for the input device ($\eta_p^2 = .154$). However, our study continued with the outlined emphasis on the variation observed within each course based on the input device. The main effects of course and input device were qualified by a statistically significant interaction effect on completion time, $F(4, 222) = 4.43$, $p < .05$, $\eta_p^2 = .074$. To understand the exact nature of the interaction, we continued with a Bonferroni-adjusted test of simple effects. The comparisons indicated the course had a nonsignificant impact on performance when using the mouse as input device, $F(2, 222) = 3.56$, $p = .31$, while the course did impact the performance for both graphical tablet ($F(2, 222) = 7.70$, $p < .05$) and touchpad ($F(2, 222) = 28.66$, $p < .05$) users. Figure 2 (left) illustrates how the marginal means in performance time (seconds) within each course differed with an almost similar pattern, i.e., the touchpad yielding the highest time within each course and being statistically different from the homogenous subset of mouse and graphical tablet. The heat map in Figure 2 (right) visualizes a corresponding pattern with emphasis on the distribution of mean performance time.

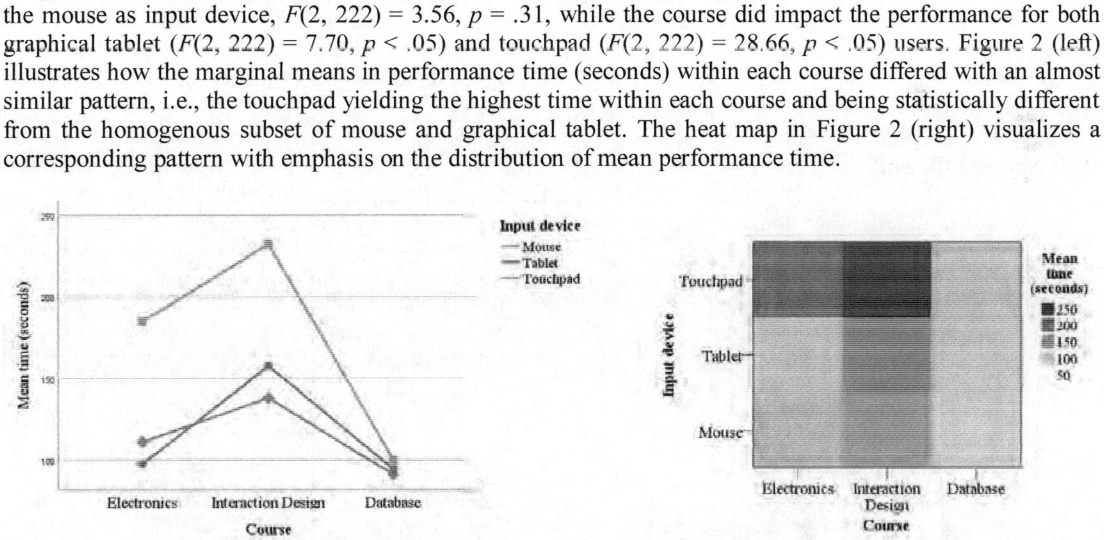

Figure 2. The mean performance time (left) and the distribution (right) for each input device across the three courses

4.2 Post-Test Interviews

While not evident from the statistical analysis alone, the qualitative data from the post-test interviews with the participants revealed further insight into the results (referred to as P1-P77). For instance, the participants explained the coinciding performance time observed as a direct result of using the mouse. The explanations were almost unanimously reported as caused by two overarching factors, namely familiarity and forced simplicity. Familiarity in this context refers to the general experience the participants had when using a mouse for general purposes, which yielded knowledge of its interaction mechanisms and ranges of use. This experience was highly transferrable to the e-exam situation (P31, P70). Forced simplicity reflects the general knowledge people had gained using a mouse in the past performing similar tasks, which automatically balanced the complexity of the sketch according to prior experience with how a mouse performs during such tasks. As an example of forced simplicity, we observed very few instances of overcomplicating sketches for the mouse compared to the two other input devices.

An important observation made was that many students chose to enhance or comment their sketching by using built-in auxiliary elements not intended for sketching purposes, e.g., text boxes and arrows, to compensate for missing or hidden functions they were familiar with from software used in the past. Making these actions were reported as both quicker and easier in use when interacting with a mouse rather than either the graphical tablet or the touchpad. Students were also quick to make comparisons with other, more familiar alternatives and argue that specialized and adapted software would enhance the overall sketching experience. This was a recurring feedback in all courses: "*this would be best with Logisim*" (P7 on sketching of digital logic circuits in the electronics course), *"If things were like Sketch, I would have spent only half the time"* (P32 sketching a customer journey map in the interaction design course), and *"draw.io would be both faster and more intuitive"* (P53 on sketching of database and class models in the database course). This pattern was also reflected in several comments during the post-test interviews directed at the input devices' ability to interact with specific software components rather than addressing the input device itself as a sketching tool.

The details from the statistical analysis concerning each individual course suggest that the mouse and the graphical tablet performed quite equally on average. They were only matched by the touchpad in the database course where the three mean performance times were quite similar with only nonsignificant differences. The participants reported that the assignments typical for that course did not require any smaller details nor any high level of precision to convey the message behind the sketch. The general feedback for the touchpad was that it was unsuitable for most types of sketches associated with the three courses in this study. Multiple participants (P10, P12, P14, P43) went as far as to state that the touchpad was practically impossible to use for several of the assignments: *"I would rather write how it would look than handing in this sketch"* (P43). Another recurring issue most prominent in the case of the electronics and interaction design course was the interaction mechanisms of the touchpad. The limited physical size of the touchpad and the inaccuracy of the fingertip compared to a mouse prevented students from making either longer movements and gesture or precise movements needed for detailed sketches (P12, P31).

The main positive comment mentioned about the touchpad was its proximity to the keyboard and the increased efficiency for smaller, simple sketches with text elements (P29, P50). The simplistic and minimal solutions to sketching assignments in the electronic course were mainly responsible for the huge difference in performance time when comparing the electronic course versus the interaction design and database course (illustrated in Figure 3). The feedback from the students indicated that the smaller, more detailed sketching such as circuit sketches required fewer or no large movements in the physical space while simultaneously occupying a smaller portion of the screen.

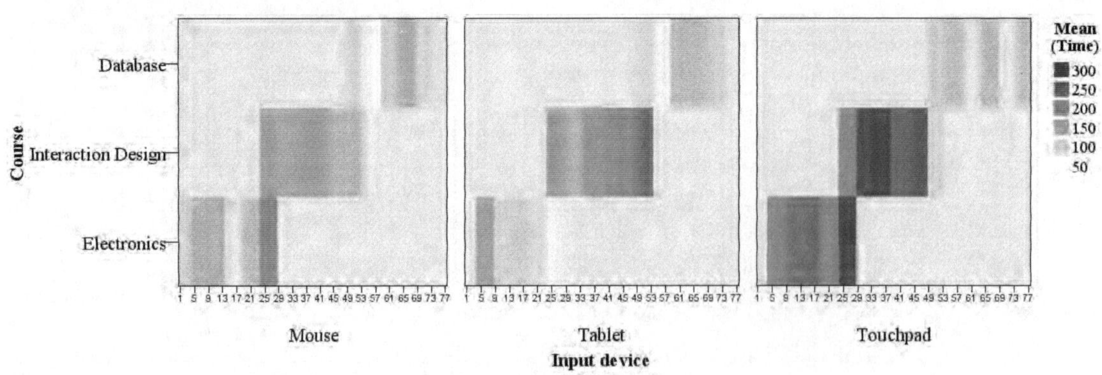

Figure 3. Distribution of mean time for each input device across the three courses

The performance using the graphical tablet yielded results similar to using the mouse in all three courses. The participants reported their experience with using the graphical tablet with mixed results. Most people preferred the graphical tablet to the two alternatives for more complex sketches, predominantly in the interaction design course, where there were less formal structures and elements involved. Regardless of the overall performance, the participants seemed pleased with the graphical tablet, and several participants even reported it as the most favorable alternative, despite not being the fastest (P8, P61, P63). Even though almost half the participants (46.8 %) had used a graphical tablet before, and a recurring feedback was that it was considered the best alternative, it still required practice within the e-exam situation with both the hardware and software available. This was especially the case for those without prior experience, as highlighted by one participant: *"I do believe that the graphical tablet would be better than a mouse, but I have not used it before. I use the mouse every day, so I have a certain level of control, but it is still a hopeless tool for sketching"* (P12).

With experience, students would be less prone to time spent on understanding how the hardware and software harmonized, and use gestures that are more advanced as part of the sketch. The lack of experience with graphical tablets is the main explanation for the spike in performance time for the interaction design course (Figure 2, left). However, experience with the graphical tablet alone would not solve all issues. The participants who had used graphical tablets in the past, especially those considering themselves proficient users, experienced dissonance between expectation and behavior. Most advanced features of a generic tablet, e.g., multi-touch gestures, pressure sensitivity, and tilt support, are not readily available in generic browser-based exam software, which limited their use also in our study. Multiple participants explained their performance with a lack of support for expected gestures and time spent trying to find interface-specific alternatives (P40, P71).

4.3 Findings

The two sets of data allowed us to study patterns of mean performance times within each course and qualify any statistically significant results with feedback received during the post-test interviews. The specific benefits and challenges of each input device themselves are not the main point of this paper, but rather how they fulfill different roles and functions in the different types of sketching assignments. As such, the absolute values of performance are of less interest than their relative value.

Both the statistical analysis and the post-test interviews suggest that one input device cannot be considered unanimously better than its alternatives, and that remains the overarching answer to our initial research question. While the performance score of the mouse was the most consistent in all three courses, the preferences of the participants suggested that the graphical tablet was the most preferred input device for several types of sketches. The touchpad rated lowest in both performance and preference except for a scope of specific types of smaller, simple sketches. However, the data also revealed specific benefits and challenges with all three input devices that can suggest opportunities and limitations relevant to other studies. Table 2 outlines the main benefits and main challenges identified for each input device.

Table 2. Overview of the main benefits and challenges for each input device

Input device	Main benefits	Main challenges
Mouse	▪ The most consistent performance for sketching assignments across the three courses ▪ Gave the best balance between expectations and attempted complexity in the sketching ▪ No significant difference in performance times for the three courses	▪ Demanded a larger physical space when sketching bigger figures that involve longer dragging movements with the mouse ▪ Preferences of the users required adjustment of sensitivity for more complex and detailed sketches

Input device	Main benefits	Main challenges
Graphical Tablet	▪ The most preferred option for larger and complex sketches ▪ Suitable for sketches involving both technical, precise elements and freehand, conceptual elements ▪ The input device perceived as most similar to classic pen-and-paper sketches	▪ Usually more time-consuming, even for proficient users with experience ▪ Less familiar as an input device in an e-exam situation for many students ▪ Heavily dependent on a software-hardware symbiosis to maximize its potential
Touchpad	▪ Can be used with students' own laptops without the need for additional devices ▪ Considered the most efficient option for smaller, simple sketches in combination with text elements	▪ Unsuitable for most situations involving both detailed, precise sketches and larger, complex sketches ▪ The small physical surface prevents long gestures which may preclude certain types of sketches ▪ Consistently the most time-consuming and frustrating input device

5. DISCUSSION

Our answer to the initial research question was that all input devices for e-exams within computer science courses that include sketching assignments involve compromises, either in terms of efficiency or in terms of the perceived experience from the students' point of view. In line with previous studies, our research design revolved around emphasizing the perspective of the student, and we have scoped our study to very specific issues rather than attempting to address the broadness of challenges associated with e-exam, as seen in, e.g., (Wibowo et al., 2016). As a result, our discussion aligns the findings with existing literature on similar studies, specifically targeting e-exams or sketching assignments.

The generic nature of the e-exam tool generated both frustrating and unfamiliar responses due to the deviation in behavior from other specialized software that the students had previously used in their studies. Building on existing practice in teaching through customized interfaces may minimize the unnecessary complexity and help the students keep their attention directed towards the actual problem-solving (Oviatt et al., 2006, p. 2). However, the strong variation in the sketch complexity and degree of freedom seen in our study would suggest that the teachers' sense of ownership and control (Motschnig et al., 2016) should be extended to include shaping or adjusting of the exam interface. A similar argument has been raised by Lazem who calls for the *"adaptation and appropriation of the methods to the local culture"* (2016, p. 8) when discussing a course with a similar curriculum as the interaction design course. However, accommodating to teachers' needs may prove challenging as teachers may require equally simplified interfaces to support their workload and work practice (Kuikka et al., 2014), especially considering teachers have reported to be evaluated in their production of learning outcomes when using online assessment against assessment based on traditional methodologies (Crisp, 2011, p. 12). This is of increased importance for sketching assignments as the teacher's ability to shape the assignments is also dependent on the physical setup of the e-exam. In our study, the physical surface area of the touchpad yielded high variation in the average mean performance time across the three courses. For certain exam setups, e.g., BYOD approaches (Walker and Handley, 2016, p. 2), using self-brought laptop with different touchpads may be of such importance to the students' performance that it may end up restricting the teacher's freedom in designing exam assignments involving sketches.

During the post-test interviews, we also discovered that several participants suggested that they suspected their own performance to be greatly increased with just minimal time to familiarize themselves with the mechanisms of the graphical tablet. The graphical tablet scored best on preference despite not being the fastest option, and participants claimed to be willing to invest time into practice if it had been a real alternative. This is an interesting contrast to similar studies in mathematics, where the graphical tablet was disliked (Oviatt et al., 2006, p. 9). Nevertheless, the argument of motivating through and with familiarity has been previously discussed, e.g., by (Rante et al., 2018) who discuss building on learning modalities from childhood, or through the use of already familiar technologies such as mobile phones to prolong learning (Romero et al., 2009). As such, it would be interesting to follow up with additional studies where participants were allowed more training ahead of the assessment to increase their familiarity with the interface. For shorter assignments, Polsley et al. have argued that increasing time spent on problems from just one to two minutes can increase the completion rates significantly (2016, p. 109).

Another important everlasting issue of digitalized versions of traditionally analog tasks is the struggle to convey enough familiarity, safety, and security to embrace all relevant end-users. In our case, the post-test interviews revealed that 28 % of the participants still preferred pen-and-paper after testing with the three input devices. As such, our results are not as equally divided in performance and preference as for instance (Walker and Handley, 2016; Wibowo et al., 2016). While the students who participated in this study are particularly familiar with computers and arguably less prone to computer-related unease, the experience of facing unfamiliar systems, especially in the context of an exam, may still provoke or reinforce computer aversion or anxiety (Walker and Handley, 2016, p. 8). Studies have pointed to unfamiliarity and inefficiency as contributors to why some students still prefer paper-based exams over e-exams (Wibowo et al., 2016, p. 19). Our participants did not express any issues with anxiety or stress, but this was probably due to the lack of an actual exam situation. Nevertheless, the participants vividly expressed their frustration over unnecessary inefficiency. This was the case, in particular, for the touchpad. These experiences were an important contributing factor to a large number of participants that reported that they still preferred pen-and-paper during the post-test interviews. Another relevant factor that emerged in the post-test interviews was the fact that the digitalization of pen-and-paper depended on a screen, which disturbed the hand-eye coordination, a concern that several participants claimed was of utmost importance in sketching assignments. Rante et al. point to similar results where the separation of eye and hand while looking at a screen and simultaneously making moves on a tablet out of the visual range may complicate the interaction (2018, p. 4), and believe that stylus against a screen may better the results. As such, it remains to be seen whether the digitalization mimicking a pen-gesture in its common form have intrinsic challenges that may never make it a full worthy replacement for pen-and-paper in an e-exam context, at least not without becoming an entirely different experience. However, recent studies have experimented with novel interfaces, e.g., enabling augmentation of paper interfaces (Tsandilas et al., 2015) and illuminated, interactive paper (Klamka and Dachselt, 2017), and such approaches may be able to overcome the challenge experienced with all three input devices included in our study.

A final point worth mentioning concerns the challenges experienced by the participants of our study that were directly linked to the lack of coordination between the input devices and the exam tool. Issues were reported on both the software behavior and the mechanisms of the interface, but the e-exam software was not adapted to support the full range of gestures and features of the mouse, touchpad, and graphical tablet. This was notably the case for the graphical tablet as it supported the broadest range of features. Participants new to such an interface struggled with unfamiliarity due to inexperience, while proficient users of graphical tablets encountered challenges due to a mismatch between expected and actual behavior. As such, returning to the point of familiarity, we argue that a good exam tool should have a strong cohesion between how the teacher expects the students to answer assignments as well as the coordination between the hardware and software involved to support the students while doing so. Having systems for e-exams that are adaptable to different input modalities at both a hardware and software level may also overcome some of the challenges related to achieving proper inclusion and accessibility (Drake et al., 2015, p. 133).

It might be unlikely or even impossible to shape the e-exam in a manner that accommodates the preferences of all students (Walker and Handley, 2016, p. 11). However, supporting the perspective of the students through familiarity may contribute to shifting the students' perspective on e-exam tools as merely a measurement tool to something that can stimulate learning (Walters et al., 2017, p. 1163).

6. CONCLUSION

Our findings point to benefits and challenges observed and experienced with the three input devices and serve as indicators of opportunities and limitations on when and how the respective input devices could be utilized in an e-exam context. Our study only investigated sketching assignments from the field of computer science, yet the differences in both the performance and preference were significant. As such, we argue that e-exam systems intending to support sketching assignments should avoid the one generic solution and rather support a multitude of input devices. However, the input device alone is not the only source of challenges when solving sketching assignments. Issues such as familiarity, expectations, and the hardware-software harmony were among the related concerns that have been discussed to shed light on the complexity of the matter.

REFERENCES

Abdel Karim, N., Shukur, Z., 2016. Using preferences as user identification in the online examination. Int. J. Adv. Sci. Eng. Inf. Technol. 6, 1026–1032.

Barreto, L., Taele, P., Hammond, T., 2016. A Stylus-Driven Intelligent Tutoring System for Music Education Instruction, in: Hammond, T., Valentine, S., Adler, A. (Eds.), Revolutionizing Education with Digital Ink: The Impact of Pen and Touch Technology on Education, Human–Computer Interaction Series. Springer International Publishing, Cham, pp. 141–161. https://doi.org/10.1007/978-3-319-31193-7_10

Crisp, G., 2011. Teacher's Handbook on e-Assessment. Transform. Assess.- ALTC Fellowsh. Act. 18.

Do, E.Y.-L., 2002. Drawing marks, acts, and reacts: Toward a computational sketching interface for architectural design. AI EDAM 16, 149–171.

Drake, J.R., O'Hara, M., Seeman, E., 2015. Five principles for MOOC design: With a case study. J. Inf. Technol. Educ. Innov. Pract. 14, 125–143.

Ibrahim, W., Atif, Y., Shuaib, K., Sampson, D., 2015. A web-based course assessment tool with direct mapping to student outcomes. Educ. Technol. Soc. 18, 46–59.

Klamka, K., Dachselt, R., 2017. IllumiPaper: Illuminated interactive paper, in: Proceedings of the 2017 CHI Conference on Human Factors in Computing Systems. ACM, pp. 5605–5618.

Koile, K., Rubin, A., 2016. Tablet-Based Technology to Support Students' Understanding of Division, in: Hammond, T., Valentine, S., Adler, A. (Eds.), Revolutionizing Education with Digital Ink: The Impact of Pen and Touch Technology on Education, Human–Computer Interaction Series. Springer International Publishing, Cham, pp. 71–89. https://doi.org/10.1007/978-3-319-31193-7_5

Kuikka, M., Kitola, M., Laakso, M.-J., 2014. Challenges when introducing electronic exam. Res. Learn. Technol. 22.

Landay, J.A., Myers, B.A., 2001. Sketching interfaces: Toward more human interface design. Computer 34, 56–64.

Lane, D., 2017. Drawing and Sketching: Understanding the Complexity of Paper-Pencil Interactions within Technology Education. Handb. Technol. Educ. 1–18.

Lara-Garduno, R., Leslie, N., Hammond, T., 2016. SmartStrokes: Digitizing Paper-Based Neuropsychological Tests, in: Hammond, T., Valentine, S., Adler, A. (Eds.), Revolutionizing Education with Digital Ink: The Impact of Pen and Touch Technology on Education, Human–Computer Interaction Series. Springer International Publishing, Cham, pp. 163–175. https://doi.org/10.1007/978-3-319-31193-7_11

Lazem, S., 2016. A case study for sensitising Egyptian engineering students to user-experience in technology design, in: Proceedings of the 7th Annual Symposium on Computing for Development. ACM, p. 12.

Lee, T.-H., Wu, F.-G., Chen, H.-T., 2017. Innovation & evaluation of tangible direct manipulation digital drawing pens for children. Appl. Ergon. 60, 207–219.

Lewis, M., Sturdee, M., Marquardt, N., 2019. Sketching in HCI: Hands-on Course of Sketching Techniques, in: Extended Abstracts of the 2019 CHI Conference on Human Factors in Computing Systems, CHI EA '19. ACM, New York, NY, USA, p. C04:1–C04:5. https://doi.org/10.1145/3290607.3298805

Motschnig, R., Sedlmair, M., Schröder, S., Möller, T., 2016. A team-approach to putting learner-centered principles to practice in a large course on Human-Computer Interaction, in: 2016 IEEE Frontiers in Education Conference (FIE). IEEE, pp. 1–9.

Osang, F., 2012. Electronic examination in Nigeria, academic staff perspective—Case study: National Open University of Nigeria (NOUN). Int. J. Inf. Educ. Technol. 2, 304–307.

Oviatt, S., Arthur, A., Cohen, J., 2006. Quiet interfaces that help students think, in: Proceedings of the 19th Annual ACM Symposium on User Interface Software and Technology. ACM, pp. 191–200.

Polsley, S., Ray, J., Nelligan, T., Helms, M., Linsey, J., Hammond, T., 2016. Leveraging Trends in Student Interaction to Enhance the Effectiveness of Sketch-Based Educational Software, in: Hammond, T., Valentine, S., Adler, A. (Eds.), Revolutionizing Education with Digital Ink: The Impact of Pen and Touch Technology on Education, Human–Computer Interaction Series. Springer International Publishing, Cham, pp. 103–114. https://doi.org/10.1007/978-3-319-31193-7_7

Rante, H., Lund, M., Caliz, D., 2018. The Role of Tangible Interfaces in Enhancing Children's Engagement in Learning, in: MATEC Web of Conferences. EDP Sciences, p. 01013.

Romero, C., Ventura, S., De Bra, P., 2009. Using mobile and web-based computerized tests to evaluate university students. Comput. Appl. Eng. Educ. 17, 435–447.

Taele, P., Hammond, T., 2016. An Intelligent Sketch-Based Educational Interface for Learning Complex Written East Asian Phonetic Symbols, in: Hammond, T., Valentine, S., Adler, A. (Eds.), Revolutionizing Education with Digital Ink: The Impact of Pen and Touch Technology on Education, Human–Computer Interaction Series. Springer International Publishing, Cham, pp. 129–140. https://doi.org/10.1007/978-3-319-31193-7_9

Thompson, R., Tanimoto, S., Berninger, V., Nagy, W., 2016. Design Studies for Stylus and Finger-Based Interaction in Writing Instruction on Tablets, in: Revolutionizing Education with Digital Ink. Springer, pp. 51–69.

Tsandilas, T., Grammatikou, M., Huot, S., 2015. Bricosketch: Mixing paper and computer drawing tools in professional illustration. Presented at the Proceedings of the 2015 International Conference on Interactive Tabletops & Surfaces, ACM, pp. 127–136.

Walker, R., Handley, Z., 2016. Designing for learner engagement with computer-based testing. Res. Learn. Technol. 24.

Walters, S.R., Raposo Ferreira da Silva, P.L., Nikolai, J., 2017. Teaching, learning, and assessment: insights into students' motivation to learn.

Wang, G., Bowditch, N., Zeleznik, R., Kwon, M., LaViola, J.J., 2016. A Tablet-Based Math Tutor for Beginning Algebra, in: Hammond, T., Valentine, S., Adler, A. (Eds.), Revolutionizing Education with Digital Ink: The Impact of Pen and Touch Technology on Education, Human–Computer Interaction Series. Springer International Publishing, Cham, pp. 91–102. https://doi.org/10.1007/978-3-319-31193-7_6

Wibowo, S., Grandhi, S., Chugh, R., Sawir, E., 2016. A pilot study of an electronic exam system at an Australian University. J. Educ. Technol. Syst. 45, 5–33.

Williford, B., Taele, P., Nelligan, T., Li, W., Linsey, J., Hammond, T., 2016. Persketchtivity: an intelligent pen-based educational application for design sketching instruction, in: Revolutionizing Education with Digital Ink. Springer, pp. 115–127.

Yang, M.C., Cham, J.G., 2006. An Analysis of Sketching Skill and Its Role in Early Stage Engineering Design. J. Mech. Des. 129, 476–482. https://doi.org/10.1115/1.2712214

STUDENTS' TEAM-LEARNING INSPIRES CREATIVITY

Sayed Jawwad, Mukhtar AL-Hashimi, Anjum Razzaque and Allam Hamdan
College of Business and Finance, Ahlia University, Manama, Bahrain

ABSTRACT

Research catalyzes positive change for the economic development of a country which will lead to investments and job opportunities, consequently leading to a high Gross National Product. In recent year's higher education bodies has been emphasizing on embedding research activities within the undergraduate teaching activities leading to better students employability. Current education system transforms its teaching and learning quality using e-learning strategies. Also, past research assessed role of social capital on knowledge sharing behavior in virtual environment; scant research assessed the moderation of positive emotions and gender for (1) higher education sector and (2) developing countries. And, the success of such a statement has not been properly documented in the past research. As the result, the aim of this study is to empirically assess the role of Social Capital Theory on Knowledge sharing, when moderated by positive emotions. This deductive research's literature review identified research gaps; to form research questions and a model with three hypotheses. Multi-correlation analysis was performed using SPSS to test hypotheses thru, data collected from 334 participants: a sample size above required threshold, to generalize population of higher education undergraduate business students of a private university in Bahrain. Findings supported all hypotheses, indicating positive moderation between social capital and knowledge sharing, when students e-learn on Moodle.

KEYWORDS

Social Capital Theory, Knowledge Sharing, Positive Emotions, e-Learning, Higher Education

1. INTRODUCTION

Regarding the significant factors that can affect the learning outcomes successfully, motivation and positive emotions are now being recognized for their impact on learning, especially in higher education degrees (Ainley, 2008; Beard, Clegg, & Smith,2007; Pekrun & Stephens, 2010). Despite these outcomes, few studies have investigated the students' sensitiveness of positive emotions in relation with knowledge sharing and social capital theory. In addition, the Self-directed learning is "*a process in which individuals take the initiative with or without the help of others in diagnosing their learning needs, formulating goals, identifying human and material resources, selecting appropriate learning strategies and evaluating learning outcomes*" (Rager, 2013). When it comes to positive emotions in leaning, studies of the role of positive emotions in learning goals achievement show that pride, joy and hope positively correlate with students' academic self-efficacy, academic interest, and overall achievement. Therefore, this research aims to study how factors such as positive emotions affect social capital theory and knowledge sharing.

The objectives of this research is to examine: (1) is it important that students experience positive emotions during learning; (2) Is positive emotions affecting knowledge sharing; (3) Is positive emotions affecting social capital theory. This study used quantitative method whereby a questionnaire was spread amongst university students across Bahrain such as, Ahlia University, Royal University for Women, AMA University and University of Bahrain. Literature review on the relationship between the variables used in this research is presented in the next chapter. Chapter 3 and 4 consists of the research methodology and the data analysis including hypotheses. The findings, discussion and conclusion will be presented in chapter 5.

2. LITERATURE REVIEW

2.1 The Role of Positive Emotions on Student Success

Currently emotions are playing a big role in learning especially for higher education students. By joining emotions with growing recognition of the impact of emotional well-being on student's academic success will help in introducing new ways of teaching which will lead to a successful change in learning theory and practices (Rowe, 2013). In addition, according to Williams (2013): All the studies of positive emotions show that whenever a student is positive this will lead him to glorious achievements and it also shows that the emotions of the student affects his concentration and the way he receives knowledge and how much focus he gives to the tutor. Positive emotions and emotional intelligence play in experiential learning. Students' field practicum journals were analysed using the Linguistic Inquiry and Word Count Program (LIWC) and a measure of emotional intelligence was obtained using the Mayer–Salovey–Caruso Emotional Intelligence Test (MSCEIT) (Abe, 2011). Moreover, Research on multimedia learning has begun to consider the influence of affective processes, such as emotions based on the established fact that emotions influence cognitive learning processes (Park, 2015). On the other hand, Emotional intelligence describes and operationalizes adaptive emotional functioning Perception, understanding, and managing emotions effectively in the self and others are described as core competencies in most operationalization's of emotional intelligence, Higher levels of emotional intelligence are associated with a variety of general positive intrapersonal outcomes (Schutte, 2014). According to Vulpe (2011) "*Concerning the relationship between positive emotions and creative thinking, it was found that people who were positively manipulated showed higher performances in terms of general creative thinking and its three dimensions: fluency, flexibility and originality, than did the neutral group. It was also found that there were no differences concerning the performances with regard to creative thinking*." Another emotions concept is discussed in an article by Rahimi et al. (2014). It mentions the Broaden-and-Build theory, one of the primary focuses in the field of English language teaching is on interventions, either at the level of material development or teaching strategies and learning tasks, aimed at not only fostering positive emotions in language learners and but also preventing or minimizing negative emotions. On the other hand, Bondarenko (2017) explains that some studies of the role of positive emotions in learning goals achievement show that pride, joy and hope positively correlate with students' academic self-efficacy, academic interest, and overall achievement. Another explanation to this indirect relationship between positive emotion and academic achievement can be provided through activation. Bondarenko also explains that Pekrun's cognitive-motivational model proposes to differentiate between emotions of enjoyment of learning, hope for success or pride, which are considered positive emotions, and emotions of relief, relaxation after success and contentment, which are positive deactivating emotions.

In his article "*The effect of experiential learning on subsidiary knowledge and performance*", Bhatti, (2016) mentioned, "*For subsidiary growth to exist, firms must store, transfer, and manage knowledge, and learn and share that knowledge through socialization. A growing interest exists in the process of acquisition of knowledge, but this topic lacks an in depth investigation regarding the internationalization of firms*". Chang (2016) mentioned that investment in Human Resources is basic to the improvement of human capitals. To encourage better learning and training activities, the use of online resources have been blended successfully with education. Rovai (2002) explained in his article that the purpose of this study was to explore the factors that influence students' community experiences, to develop and field-test the Classroom Community Scale and to determine its validity and reliability for use with postsecondary students taking online courses. When educational researchers are armed with an effective tool to measure community in a learning environment, they will be better be equipped to conduct research on how to design and deliver instruction at a distance in order to promote community. Additionally, by implication, to promote satisfaction and instructors, and other learners, but without the requirement to be online at the same time. Seeking into (Putnam, 1995, p. 67). Social support can also be recognized as a form of social capital in the workplace. The term of Social capital is defined as ''features of social organization such as networks, norms, and social trust that facilitate coordination and cooperation for mutual benefit.

2.2 Emotional Exhaustion

A brief introduction to what emotional exhaustion is defined. It is defined as being overstretched and exhausted, and this has a huge mental impact on students while they are learning. Students who work while attending college may face time limitations and other added stressors, which may ultimately lead to emotional exhaustion. Additionally, an increasing number of non-traditional and re-entry students are attending college. These individuals may be required to juggle work, school, and family life (King & Bannon, 2002).

2.3 Instructor Attributes

Research has found that the desired characteristics of effective teachers have been consistent during the past three decades. For example, communication and understanding skills are essential characters that characterize effective teachers (Kelley, Conant, & Smart, 1991; Smart, Kelley, & Conant, 2003). Going through in order for a teacher to have a good attribute among his students he need to be fair and equal towards his students (Grunenwald & Ackerman, 1986). Having a good time throughout the lesson and not sticking into teaching only, and is the main reason of students getting bored, during the lesson and having some entertaining time makes it more interesting for students. (Dana, Brown, & Dodd, 2001) creating more than one teaching technique to keep then enthusiastic towards the course they are studying (Badrinarayanan & Madhavaram, 2008; Paraskevas & Sigala, 2003). Furthermore, the more the teacher interacts and makes the student interested in the course, this will cause positive emotions towards not only one student but the whole class. Creating such positive environments inside a classroom are more likely to make students ready and motivated and this should lead to greater intellectual involvement. Therefore, the roles of the instructors have a huge impact and a big way to test how positive emotions can affect the way of teaching the students and keeping the environment of the class positive like it should be and this may lead to success.

3. SAMPLING AND DATA COLLECTION

This research focuses on undergraduate university students in Bahrain. The questionnaire was distributed amongst undergrad students at Ahlia University, and the focus was particularly to gain feedback from those students who had indulged in face-to-face and e-learning education using Moodle, as well as, have experienced positive emotions during their course of study. The males concluded to be 166 which is 53.2% and females concluded to be 146 which is 46.8%, which brings the total to 312 participants, as shown in Table 1.

Table 1. Gender

Gender	Frequency	Percent
Male	166	53.2
Female	146	46.8
Total	312	100

4. DATA ANALYSIS

The total number of participants was 312, SPSS 23.0 was used for data analysis. Before the analysis was carried out, however, the data was filtered to meet the research needs of students who have experience with positive emotions during the course of their studies. All variables referred to in Table 2 are used for testing hypotheses.

4.1 Hypothesis Testing

4.1.1 Correlation Analysis

Table 2 shows that if significant levels fell below 0.05, the variables would be statistically correlated. A significant positive correlation exists between social capital theory and sharing of knowledge, $r^2=0.291$, $p<0.05$. In addition, there is a positive correlation between social capital theory knowledge sharing moderated by positive emotions $r^2=0.319$, $p<0.05$. As shown in the table, gender moderation has a significant impact on the relationship between SCT and KSQ, with gender (male) representing 29.1 percent and increasing to 32.2 percent, particularly when male gender has been introduced as a moderator. This is not the case for women since r^2 fell from 29.1 percent to 25.6 percent and therefore the gender as a whole (male and female): r^2 fell from 29.1 to 2.5 percent. This therefore demonstrates support for the hypothesis 4 that males moderate to make it easier for social capital to share knowledge while experiencing positive emotions.

4.1.2 Regression Analysis

To test the hypothesis, multiple regression tests were performed as shown in Table 2. Hypothesis 1, 2 and 4 are significantly accepted and hypothesis 3 and 5 are rejected. There is a positive relationship between the theory of social capital and the sharing of knowledge, B= 0.540, $p < 0.05$. In addition, since there is a positive relationship between the theory of social capital and the sharing of knowledge, the addition of positive emotions as a moderating variable enhanced the relationship, which shows that they all have a strong effect on each other, B=0.565, $p<0.05$. However, adding gender as a moderator significantly reduces all values from B=0.540 to B=0.159, $p<0.05$. To further investigate why gender has a negative impact on the relationship, each gender has been separated and interpreted to discover the root of the problem. When the female gender was introduced as a moderator, however, it showed a negative relationship with SCT and KSQ, B=0.506, $p<0.05$. Respectively, when male gender was introduced as a moderator, it showed a positive relationship with SCT and KSQ as the beta increased to B=0.568, $p<0.05$. Which shows the problem lies with the female gender findings.

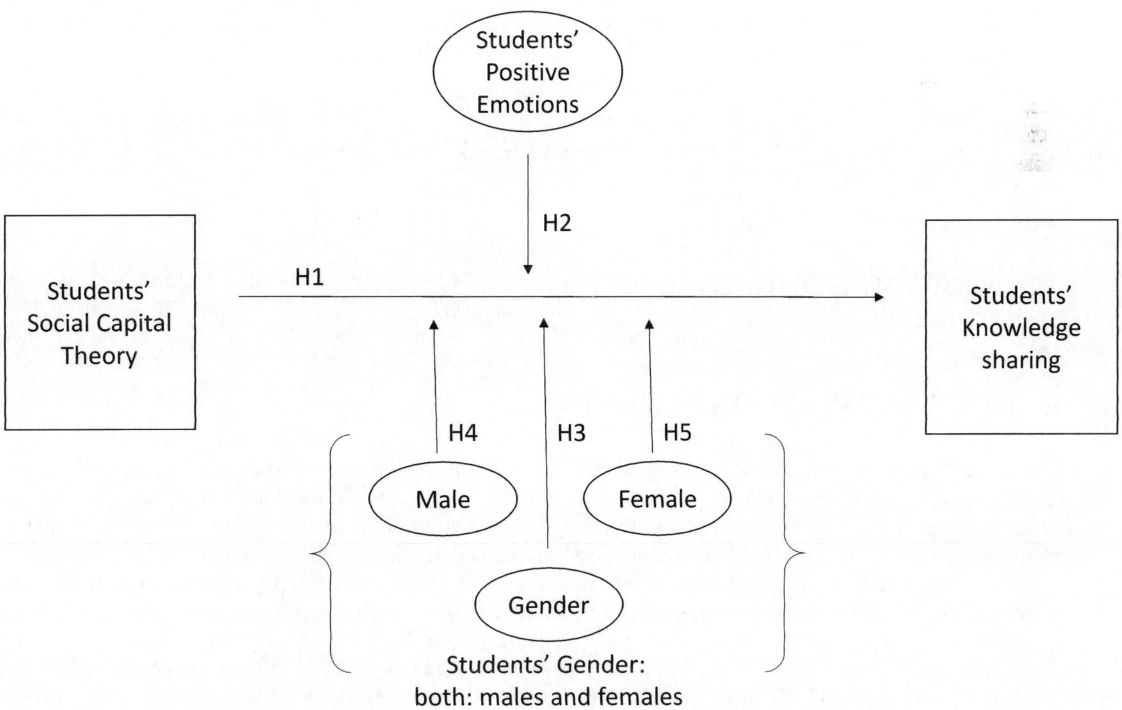

Figure 1. Concept Model

Table 2. Regression results

Model	Relationship between variables	F	t	R^2	B
M1	Social Capital theory → Knowledge Sharing	127.431 Sig 0.00	11.289 Sig 0.00	29.1%	0.540
M2	Positive emotions * Social Capital theory → Knowledge Sharing	145.478 Sig 0.00	12.061 Sig 0.00	31.9%	0.565
M3	Gender * Social Capital theory → Knowledge Sharing	8.060 Sig 0.005[b]	2.839 Sig 0.005[b]	2.5%	0.159
M4	MaleGender * Social Capital theory → Knowledge Sharing	77.936 Sig 0.00	8.828 Sig 0.00	32.2%	0.568
M5	FemaleGender * Social Capital theory → Knowledge Sharing	49.564 Sig 0.00	7.040 Sig 0.00	25.6%	0.506

H 1: *There is a positive relationship between social capital theory and knowledge sharing.*

H 2: *There is a positive relationship between social capital theory and knowledge sharing with the assist of positive emotion.*

H 3: *There is a positive relationship between social capital theory and knowledge sharing whilst moderated by both genders.*

H 4: *There is a positive relationship between social capital theory and knowledge sharing whilst moderated by only the male gender.*

H 5: *There is a positive relationship between social capital theory and knowledge sharing whilst moderated by only the female gender.*

4.2 Advance Discerption Analysis

Male counts are 166 and female counts are 146, bringing the total to 312. As shown in Table 3, there is a slight difference between men and women, as the male findings precede the female, but nothing that would have a major impact on the study. Both genders have nearly the same results.

Table 3. Difference between genders

Variable:	Gender	Mean	Standard Deviation
Positive emotion	Male	4.0206	0.74205
	Female	4.0049	0.64353
Social capital theory	Male	4.0608	0.59613
	Female	4.0138	0.62180
Knowledge Sharing	Male	4.2740	0.66328
	Female	4..2089	0.61520

5. DISCUSSION & CONCLUSION

This research is a study of the effect of positive emotions in university institutes such as Ahlia University, AMA University and University of Bahrain. A correlation of the quality structure can be seen in this paper, which is the theory of social capital and the sharing of knowledge. Four other moderating variables that have been tested to see the impact on the theory of social capital and the sharing of knowledge are positive emotions, gender as whole and constructing women and men apart. This paper will focus on positive emotional effects on Social Capital Theory and Knowledge Sharing. Firstly, a positive relationship exists between Social Capital Theory and Knowledge Sharing, as evident in the analysis of data, $B= 0.540$, $p < 0.05$. This makes social capital a valuable mechanism through which universities can share knowledge. For this reason, universities are suggested to increase confidence, networks and standards between lectures in order to facilitate knowledge sharing. The process of knowledge sharing could be accelerated through such a strong relationship (Harjanti, 2017). This outline stresses the importance of the contextual point of view in information and the sharing of knowledge. In particular, the dimensions of social capital mean the roles of structures and relationships that differ according to context (Widen, Gunilla, 2011). The second quality of construct is the outcome of positive emotions on Social Capital Theory and Knowledge Sharing. Which likewise presented a positive relationship between them. As shown by Pearson (2016), almost 78 percent of lecturers admit that digital education has benefited their students in their classrooms, encouraging them to integrate e - learning into their daily classes.

The third construction quality is the impact of both genders on Social Capital Theory and Knowledge Sharing. This structure showed a negative connection. The Beta for Social Capital Theory and Knowledge Sharing was B= 0.540 which fell to B=0.159 when both genders were commenced. To broaden our understanding as to why it happened, Genders were divided into their own constructs. Either the two genders have a negative relationship between the first construction or one of them. When the male gender was tested, a positive relationship existed between it and Social Capital Theory and Knowledge Sharing, B= 0.568, $p < 0.05$. On the other hand, When the female gender was tested, a negative relationship existed between it and Social Capital Theory and Knowledge Sharing, B= 0.506, $p < 0.05$. This concludes that the main problem lies with the findings of the female gender. This could indicate that women do not accept the theory of social capital and the sharing of knowledge as men.

This research is a study of the effect of positive emotions in university institutes. As an outcome of the data analysis, three hypotheses (H1, H2 and H4) are accepted and (H3 and H5) are rejected. The findings of this research encourage the relationship of Social Capital Theory and Knowledge Sharing. And it showed how sharing knowledge has to do with academic performance. Similarly, positive emotions presented positive relationship between Social Capital Theory and Knowledge Sharing, which shows that Social Capital Theory and Knowledge Sharing foster positive emotions. On the other hand, when gender was presented to analyze the result on Social Capital Theory and Knowledge Sharing, it displayed a negative relationship. When further tested, it showed that men do not accept the theory of social capital and the sharing of knowledge.

REFERENCES

Abachi (2014). The impact of m-learning technology on students and educators, *Computers in Human Behavior*.

Abe, (2011). Positive emotions, emotional intelligence, and successful experiential learning. *Personality and Individual Differences Journal*.

Abu-Al-Aish, (2012), Mathematics Students' Readiness for Mobile Learning, *International Journal of Mobile and Blended Learning*.

Alshaikh, I. Y., Razzaque, A., & Alalawi, M. (2017). Positive Emotion and Social Capital affect Knowledge Sharing: Case of the Public Sector of the Kingdom of Bahrain. European, Mediterranean and Middle Eastern Conference on Information Systems (EMCIS 2017 - Sept 7-9, 2017). Coimbra, Portugal: Springer Lecture Notes in Business Information Processing volume.

Baehr (2013), Incorporating User Appropriation, Media Richness, and Collaborative Knowledge Sharing into Blended E-Learning Training Tutorial. Ieee Transactions On Professional Communication

Basak (2018). E-learning, M-learning and D-learning: Conceptual definition and comparative analysis. E-Learning and Digital Media Journal

Bhatti, (2016). The effect of experiential learning on subsidiary knowledge and performance. *Journal of Business Research*

Bondarenko (2017). The role of positive emotions and type of feedback in self-regulation

Chang (2016). Review and discussion: E-learning for academia and industry. *International Journal of Information Management*

Chiu, C.-M., Hsu, M.-H., & Wang, E. T. (2006). Understanding knowledge sharing in virtual communities: An integration of social capital and social cognitive theories. *Decision Support Systems*, 42(3), 1872–1888.

Conklin (2014).Toward More Joyful Learning: Integrating Play into Frameworks of Middle Grades Teaching. *American Educational Research Journal*

Hwang, (2016). Understanding social influence theory and personal goals in e-learning. *Information Development*

Islam (2016), E-learning system use and its outcomes: Moderating role of perceived compatibility. Telematics and Informatics

Kunthi, (2018). Exploring antecedent factors toward knowledge sharing intention in E-learning. HIBAH PITTA Language Learning. Procedia - Social and Behavioral Sciences

Lee (2007), Effects of Shared Leadership on Team Creativity through Knowledge-sharing in an e-Learning Environment, Sungkyunkwan University

Lee (2014), Students' perceptions of self-directed learning and collaborative learning with and without technology. Journal of Computer Assisted Learning

Motivation? Society for Personality and Social Psychology

Navimipour, (2015), A model for assessing the impact of e-learning systems on employees'

Nedungadi, (2012), A new approach to personalization: integrating e-learning and m-learning, Association for Educational Communications and Technology of learning goals achievement: experimental research. Procedia - Social and Behavioral Sciences

Park, (2015). Emotional design and positive emotions in multimedia learning: An eye tracking study on the use of anthropomorphisms. *Computers & Education Journal*

Rager, (2013), I Feel, Therefore, I Learn: The Role of Emotion in Self-Directed Learning, New Horizons in Adult Education

Rahimi et al. (2014). The Broaden-and-Build Theory of Positive Emotions in Second

Rovai (2002). Development of an instrument to measure classroom community. Internet and Higher Education

Rowe, (2013). University student and lecturer perceptions of positive emotions in learning. *International Journal of Qualitative Studies in Education* Satisfaction. Computers in Human Behavior

Razzaque, A., Eldabi, T., & Jalal-Karim, A. (2012). An Integrated Framework to Classify Healthcare Virtual Communities. European, Mediterranean & Middle Eastern Conference on Information Systems (EMCIS 2012). Munich, Germany.

Razzaque, A., Eldabi, T., & Jalal-Karim, A. (2013). Physician Virtual Community and Medical Decision-Making: Mediating Role of Knowledge Sharing. Journal of Enterprise Information Management, 26(1).

Schutte, (2014). Connections between emotional intelligence and workplace flourishing. Personality and Individual Differences.

Sousa, (2013). The integration of Information Systems Shared Services Center with E-Learning for Sharing Knowledge Capabilities. Procedia Technology.

Septianto, F., & Chiew, T. M. (2018). The effects of different, discrete positive emotions on electronic word-of mouth. *Journal of Retailing and Consumer Services*, 44, 1-10.

Vasquez, (2007). Seeing Future Success: Does Imagery Perspective Influence Achievement

Vulpe (2011). Positive emotions' influence on attitude toward change, creative thinking and their relationship with irrational thinking in Romanian adolescents. Procedia - Social and Behavioral Sciences

Williams (2013). Stimulating and Enhancing Student Learning Through Positive Emotions. Journal of Teaching in Travel & Tourism.

Yilmaz (2017). Exploring the role of e-learning readiness on student satisfaction and motivation in flipped classroom. Computers in Human Behavior

Yilmaz (2017). Knowledge sharing behaviors in e-learning community: Exploring the role of academic self-efficacy and sense of community. Computers in Human Behavior.

Sergis (2018). Investigating the impact of Flipped Classroom on students' learning experiences: A Self-Determination Theory approach. Computers in Human Behavior

Harjanti, Dhyah & Noerchoidah, Noerchoidah. (2017). The Effect of Social Capital and Knowledge Sharing on Innovation Capability. Jurnal Manajemen dan Kewirausahaan. 19. 10.9744/jmk.19.2.72-78.

Widen, Gunilla. (2011). Social Capital and Knowledge Sharing – Lessons Learned. IFIP Advances in Information and Communication Technology. 362. 48-57. 10.1007/978-3-642-23330-2_6.

Pearson (2016) Digital appetite vs. whats on the table: student attitudes toward digital course material in 2016https://www.pearson.com/us/0/digital-appetite-report-infographic.html

FLIPPED CLASSROOM ASSESSMENT: A LEARNING PROCESS APPROACH

Paul Lam, Carmen K. M. Lau and Chi Him Chan
The Chinese University of Hong Kong, Hong Kong

ABSTRACT

A successful flipped classroom relies heavily on student engagement in pre-class learning and their active participation in classroom activities. However, much to students' disappointment, their efforts in the learning process often go unnoticed in traditional assessment approaches (such as term papers and final examinations) that are more product-oriented. As one of the important goals of the flipped classroom approach is to improve students' learning behaviors and attitudes, we argue that more attention should be shifted to assessing the learning process in order to align with such goal. In this paper, we advocate the use of learning analytics as one of the assessment components in flipped classrooms. We show how this change in assessment can be beneficial to both student learning and teacher reflection. We also indicate some limitations on current learning management systems (LMS) in providing the learning analytics for assessment purposes and suggest several revisions on LMS for better facilitating implementation of the flipped classroom approach.

KEYWORDS

Flipped Classroom, Assessment, Learning Process, Learning Analytics

1. INTRODUCTION

A typical flipped classroom model moves lectures out of the classroom (usually in the form of multimedia) and allocates more class time for students to actively engage in higher-order tasks such as problem-solving and debates (Bergmann et al., 2012). The pedagogy is believed to be able to meet the recent higher education standards which place emphasis on the value of student-centered learning environments and active learning strategies. The learning activities introduced into the flipped classroom not only invite students' engagement and thinking but also provide opportunities for students to construct their own knowledge by exploring learning materials themselves. These agree with the active learning principle (Gannod et al., 2008). Moreover, these learning activities are often designed according to students' ability, learning style, and learning pace. In this student-centered learning environment, teachers can have more interaction with students, and it would be easier for teachers to discover and pay attention to weaker students.

Previous studies show that students achieve better learning outcomes in the flipped classroom. In the research of Davies et al. (2013) and Mason et al. (2013), statistical evidence shows that students in a flipped classroom perform better and show greater satisfaction than their traditional classroom counterparts. Three factors may contribute to the enhancement of students' performance. First, the flipped classroom allows teachers to use class time more effectively, so they can cover more topics (Bhagat et al., 2016; Gannod et al., 2008). Second, engaging learning activities in the flipped classroom motivate students to learn. Third, the performance of low achievers improves because the learning environment allows teachers to pay more attention to them (Bhagat et al., 2016).

The advantages of the flipped classroom pedagogy are not limited to improving students' achievement on the learning outcomes. In a flipped classroom, learning materials are distributed in the form of multimedia outside the classroom, so students can access anytime whenever they need (Gannod et al., 2008). On the one hand, it provides the flexibility for students to work at their own pace (Fautch, 2015). On the other hand, it cultivates their responsibility for and self-regulation in learning (Baker, 2000). The learning activities that introduced into the classroom also increase students' engagement (Khanova et al., 2015). In short, it can be said that the benefits of the flipped classroom approach also encompass students' learning process.

Besides the learning outcomes and the learning process, assessment is also an important component in an instructional process. In such a process, "learning outcomes" describes the desired result. These outcomes include disciplinary knowledge and skills. "Learning process" contains activities that are the means to help students attain these outcomes. "Assessment" provides information that helps teachers decide how well students are progressing or attaining the outcomes (Russell and Airasian, 2014). The three components must be closely connected for a successful instructional process. The learning outcomes guide the planning of the learning process so that the learning process can assist students to attain the learning outcomes. The learning outcomes define the standard and criteria for the assessment so that the assessment allows students to demonstrate how well they have attained the learning outcomes. The learning process hence becomes a preparation for the assessment. On the other hand, the assessment also assesses the effectiveness of the learning process (Russell and Airasian, 2014). This relationship can be conceptualized as figure 1. It is believed that students' achievement in the learning outcomes is derived from the learning process, so the effectiveness of the learning process can be assessed solely by assessing students' achievement in the learning outcomes. However, some researchers point out that alignment of test content to learning outcomes are not enough; test content should also align with the learning process in order to enhance students' motivation, attitude and classroom climate (Bonner, 2013; Nitko, 1989). In the past, however, without ways to assess the learning process, it was difficult to align the assessment with the learning process.

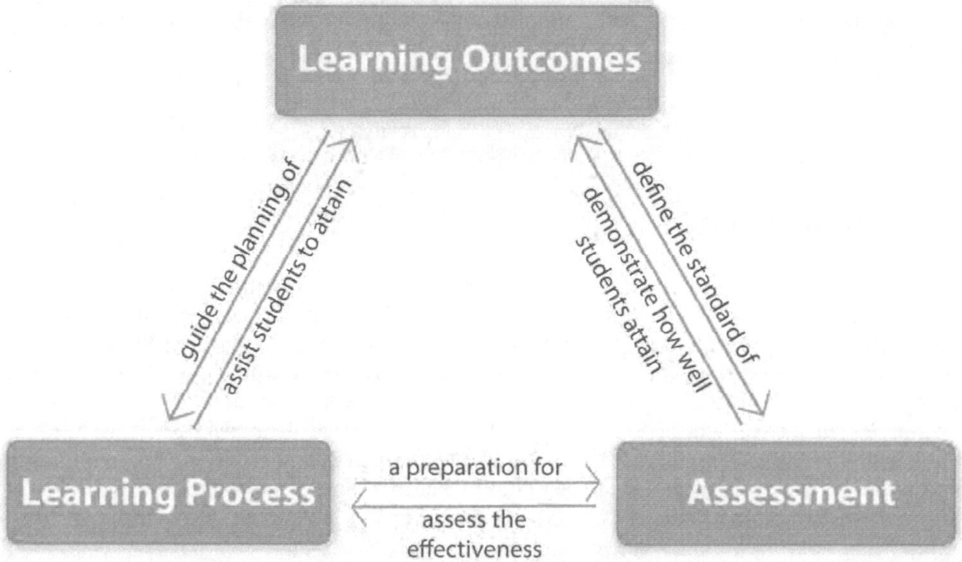

Figure 1. A successful instructional process

This article demonstrates how assessment approaches in the traditional, non-flipped class fail to align with the flipped classroom pedagogy and advocates an assessment that focuses on the learning process. The next part of this article explores this misalignment in detail. The third part of this article introduces an assessment that focuses on students' learning process through the use of learning analytics. In addition to assessing students' learning process, this assessment can also provide feedback for students' improvement and offer data for teachers' reflection. Because this assessment approach is highly dependent on learning analytics, some improvement to the existing LMS and some functions that can enhance this assessment are suggested.

2. THE PROBLEMS OF TRADITIONAL ASSESSMENT IN FLIPPED CLASSROOMS

2.1 Assessment Approaches in a Traditional Classroom: Outcome Assessment

In implementing the flipped classroom, retaining assessment approaches in a traditional, non-flipped classroom will have a potential danger of misalignment. Previous research warns that these "traditional assessment approaches" might not be able to adequately assess the benefits of the flipped classroom, especially those on students' skills, learning attitudes and behaviors, which can only be observed through the learning process (O'Flaherty and Phillips, 2015; Gillette et al., 2018; Persky and McLaughlin, 2017; Chen et al., 2018; White et al., 2017). The "traditional assessment approaches" that previous researchers mentioned includes pen and paper examinations (Persky and McLaughlin, 2017), assessment that focuses on students' performance, including examinations on theoretical knowledge and practice (Cheng et al., 2017; White et al., 2017), essay writing (Cheng et al., 2017), and projects (Persky and McLaughlin, 2017). These approaches can be summarized as the "outcome assessment" (Chen et al., 2018). Other forms of outcome assessment include the form of a quiz, end-of-chapter test, midterm or final examination, completing homework or worksheet, producing essay or term paper, or finishing project (Russell and Airasian, 2014). These outcome assessment approaches fail to align with the flipped classroom because they cannot assess the learning process of the flipped classroom.

The aim of the outcome assessment is to summarize students' achievement in terms of the learning outcomes (Russell and Airasian, 2014). Therefore, these assessment approaches only assess students' final achievement in order to assign grades to them. To summarize, the outcome assessment has the following weaknesses, making it ineffective in assessing students' learning process.

2.1.1 Product-oriented

In practice, the outcome assessment often requires students to produce tangible outcomes or products to demonstrate what they have learned in the whole instructional process. These products include not only projects, essays, and performances, but also includes tests and exams. Teachers will only assess students' products to judge whether students have achieved the desired outcomes or not (Russell and Airasian, 2014). Students know that only their attainment of the learning outcomes as demonstrated in their final products will be subjected to assessment. Their participation in the learning process is not being considered, hence they lack the incentive to participate in the learning process, and the benefits of participation in the learning process cannot be assessed.

2.1.2 Lack of Frequency

For the sake of efficiency, the outcome assessment often only takes place at the end of the learning process (Russell and Airasian, 2014). It is because the focus of the assessment is on the result of the learning process instead of the process itself, and the criteria of the assessment are the attainment of the desired outcomes at the end of the learning process. The outcome assessment thus becomes only a mechanism to indicate students' success. However, assessment in the flipped classroom should also serve as a mechanism to provide feedback about student learning (Persky and McLaughlin, 2017). This feedback can both evaluate and enhance students' learning process (Nitko, 1989). Frequent assessment of students' learning process thus can monitor and enhance students' learning process. Therefore, outcome assessment that only takes place at the end of the learning process fails to assess the learning process, and thus fails to align with the flipped classroom.

2.2 The Flipped Classroom Approach: An Emphasis on the Learning Process

In essence, the flipped classroom requires students to gain first exposure to the learning material before class. Different kinds of activities that promote deeper learning are introduced into the class, and students are required to participate in these activities with the help of the teachers (Brame, 2013). Therefore, preparation for class and participation in class are keys to the flipped classroom. The flipped classroom approach also requires students to be self-disciplined, responsible learners and to engage in the learning process.

Because students' active participation in the learning process is essential in the flipped classroom, students' limited preparation before class becomes one of the frequent challenges in the pedagogy (Akçayır and Akçayır, 2018). Both preparation and participation in the flipped classroom require students to pay more effort than conventional lecture-based classes (Al-Zahrani, 2015). Students sometimes do not prepare for their class, especially when there are no proper ways to check their preparation (Fautch, 2015). Regarding this challenge, Brame (2013) suggests that assessment tasks can be set to assess students' preparation, and the completion of these tasks can serve as evidence of students' preparation and part of the motivation for students to prepare for the class. In short, in the flipped classroom, assessment should also monitor students' learning process.

In conclusion, assessment approaches in traditional classroom focus only on students' learning outcomes, thus ignoring students' learning process. On the contrary, the assessment in the flipped classroom approach should assess students' learning process in terms of their participation and preparation in addition to their learning outcome. Traditional assessment approaches cannot fulfill the requirement of flipped classroom assessment, so it fails to align with the flipped classroom. Previous researchers propose some measures of assessment that focus on the learning process for the flipped classroom. In holding students accountable for pre-class learning, Persky and McLaughlin (2017) believe that frequent low-stakes assessment instead of high-stakes summative assessment at the end of the term would be more efficient. O'Flaherty and Philips (2015) also call our attention to the need for assessing students' engagement in flipped classes in addition to examination scores. The benefits of the flipped classroom can be better measured by an assessment that focuses on the learning process (Chen et al., 2018).

3. ASSESSING THE LEARNING PROCESS WITH THE LEARNING ANALYTICS

With the advancement in technology, students' learning process can now be observed and evaluated more accurately. This part introduces the use of learning analytics in assessing students' learning process. Through mining and analyzing the LMS data, students' participation in class and engagement with the learning materials outside the classroom can be assessed.

3.1 Learning Analytics: The Key to Assessing the Learning Process

Previously, observation of students' learning process has limitations in terms of the scope and the authenticity of the data. Teachers can only observe activities in the classroom, and such observation is subjective (Russell and Airasian, 2014). Students' engagement with learning material out of class is highly dependent on their self-report, which is limited due to issues on sampling and the size of data (Greller and Draschler, 2012).

The advancement in technology and the widespread use of the learning management system (LMS) provides us a way to directly observe students' learning process. The LMS can automatically track behind the screen all online activities of students when they access the system. It captures all digital footprints by all users, so it contains all data relating to students' learning process. Every click, every post, every social interaction, and every view-count of every page are recorded in the LMS. This corpus of learner-produced data can provide us valuable insight into students' learning process. The measurement, collection, analysis, and reporting of this data are termed "learning analytics" (Long and Siemens, 2011).

Researchers have already employed learning analytics to observe students' learning process. Their attempts prove that it is a reliable source for observation and can provide feedbacks to students, predict students' performance, detect students' behavior, group students, and analyze students' social network. (Romero and Ventura, 2010). By detecting students' behavior and analyzing students' social network, students' learning process can be assessed.

Since 2011, all the major LMS has included at least rudimentary analytics "dashboards" (Shum and Ferguson, 2012), providing some basic statistics of learning analytics. However, even for Moodle, one of the widely used LMS, reports of data and the function of data visualization are limited. Currently, plugins are required in Moodle to generate specific reports on the learning analytics and visualize them (Gaftandzhieva et al., 2018; Triantafyllou et al., 2018) and some researchers would transfer the LMS data to other statistic software for detailed analysis instead of using the LMS statistic module (Ravat and Dwivedi, 2019; Cantabella et al., 2019). In order to use learning analytics for assessment, some improvement of the current LMS is needed. These will be discussed in the discussion and conclusion.

3.2 An Assessment that makes use of the Learning Analytics

The learning analytics can provide various kinds of data for assessing students' learning behavior. For example, students' completion rate of different tasks and their behaviors in asynchronous discussion forums can be good indicators of their learning engagement and participation. In addition to assessing students, this assessment can provide feedback to teachers and students whenever they need because the learning analytics can be accessed anytime during the semester. Therefore, this assessment can serve three functions: it can assess students' learning process in the flipped classroom, it can provide feedback to students for their improvement, and it can offer data for teachers' reflection.

3.2.1 Assessing Students' Learning Process

The LMS contains data on students' access and completion of different tasks. Digital footprints would be left in the LMS when students access the LMS, download any learning materials, or finish any required tasks. Moreover, students' participation in the discussion forum can be revealed by mining the learning analytics. These data can show their engagement in the course.

Students' completion rate on tasks and assignments can be assessed on the LMS. Teachers can require their students to submit assignments on the LMS, and the LMS can show whether students' submission is on-time, late or not received. Moreover, learning analytics contains the data on students' number of downloads of learning materials (Cantabella et al., 2019), their number of different pages browsed, and total time for their browsing (Henrie et al., 2018). These sets of data can demonstrate how much time students spend on their learning. By visualizing these sets of data into simple statistic graphs, teachers can have a clear picture of their students' participation in the learning process.

Students' activity on asynchronous discussion forums may reflect their engagement level (Macfadyen and Dawson, 2010; Slattery, 2018). It is believed that engaging students tend to have more participation in discussion and have communicative connections with more peers. On the contrary, students with low engagement have communicative connections to a relatively small number of peers (Macfadyen and Dawson, 2010). Students' engagement can be measured by the number of posts, the number of replies, and the total number of words they posted (Slattery, 2018), and then, a network analysis on students' engagement in terms of how many other students they connected can serve as supplementary information.

Students' completion rate of tasks, access rate of materials, and their activity on discussion forums can help teacher evaluate their participation in a course, thus these sets of data can serve as an assessment. However, in some cases, "simply spending more time or having more activity on an assignment does not necessarily mean positive student engagement (Henrie et al., 2018: 359)", especially when students know that their learning process will be assessed. Students can pretend to be a self-regulated learner and engage in discussion forums without really paying attention to the learning content. Due to this limitation, it is not recommended that teachers assigning grades to students directly based on this assessment, although this assessment can still serve as a reference for teachers. On the other hand, teachers can use the result of this assessment to provide feedback for students' improvement in their learning process.

3.2.2 Providing Feedback for Students' Improvement

With accurate data on students' participation and engagement in their learning process, teachers can provide feedback regarding students' learning process. Since this assessment is carried out during the instruction period instead of assessing students at the end of the semester, teachers can provide feedback anytime in the whole semester. Students can use the feedback teachers provided to improve their learning behaviors and attitudes. It can be said that this assessment is a formative assessment (Russell and Airasian, 2014).

Assessment on the learning process is a continuous process. The LMS keeps tracking students' digital footprints. Teachers can access the learning analytics anytime to assess their students and provide feedback to students anytime they needed. Previous studies already show that teachers, with the help of learning analytics, can identify "slowing-down" students and provide assistance for them to catch up with the rest (Rosmanyah et al., 2017). Teachers can easily discover students with a very low number of accesses, assignments, and completion of quizzes by a simple statistic (Romero et al., 2008). Timely assistance can be provided to these students.

An early warning system that can identify at-risk students basing on learning analytics is demonstrated in Macfadyen and Dawson (2010). Their system used the number of forums posting, mail message sent, and assessment completed as variables. Students with low numbers in these variables were identified as disengaged students. The system would then automatically flag these at-risk students and remind the teacher to provide early intervention (Macfadyen and Dawson, 2010).

The flipped classroom can employ a similar system together with the assessment advocated above. The assessment on the learning process can evaluate students' access rate of the learning materials, completion rate of tasks and assignment, and their engagement rate by posts on discussion forums. These sets of data can be used as the variables for an early warning system. The system can highlight at-risk students and send warning messages to them. It can also remind teachers to assist them. These measures can prevent students from dropping out and motivate their engagement in the learning process.

3.2.3 Offering Data for Teachers' Reflection

The assessment can also offer data for teachers' reflection. Students' participation rate, completion of tasks and access rate of each of and all the learning materials can help teachers reflect upon their course design and teaching style (Greller and Drachsler, 2012), so they can improve their instructional design and manage classroom activities (Persky and McLaughlin, 2017). Students' access rate, participation rate and feedback, including the duration of students viewing and the view-count of each piece of material, can indicate which part of their course receives less student attention, and which part of their course is viewed by most students. Teachers can examine whether the form and style of delivery are ineffective in leading to student participation. In addition, by co-relating the access rate of each piece of learning materials to students' examination performance, teachers can also observe whether students' use of any particular learning material(s) have any positive or negative impact on their grade (Romero and Ventura, 2010). Thus, teachers can evaluate the effectiveness of their teaching through this assessment.

4. DISCUSSION AND CONCLUSION: A CUSTOMIZED LEARNING MANAGEMENT SYSTEM FOR FLIPPED CLASSROOMS

The flipped classroom pedagogy improves both the learning outcomes and the learning process, but assessment approaches in a traditional, non-flipped classroom usually focus only on the learning outcomes and fail to assess the learning process. In order to align with the flipped classroom, this article advocates an assessment that focuses on the learning process of the flipped classroom. This assessment assesses students by mining the dataset provided by the LMS. The data mining process, the "learning analytics", can demonstrate students' online learning process in a comprehensive way, thus making the assessment of the learning process possible. Such an assessment can assess students' participation and engagement in class. In addition, this assessment can also improve students' performance by identifying at-risk students during the semester, so that teachers can provide adequate help to them. Furthermore, it can provide data for teachers' reflection.

Because such an assessment is highly dependent on an LMS, the data provided must be accurate to ensure the fairness of the assessment. Previous research identifies some issues on the accuracy of the learning analytics. First, inaccurate data are recorded because of different technical issues. For example, the data on the duration of viewing may be inaccurate if the LMS allows students to keep logging in and opening another browser for other tasks (Koh et al., 2018). Second, the LMS should be able to identify and prevent students' abuse of the system, such as gaming and cheating behavior (Koh et al., 2018). Current LMS requires improvement in software design regarding the above issues in order to maintain the assessment to be fair.

To enhance the assessment for the flipped classrooms advocated by this article, some development on the LMS should be made. First, it is reported that the function of calendar builder, including course calendar, schedule, and due date management system is not commonly provided by most of the LMS (Shannon and Rice, 2017). Since monitoring students' learning process is key to the assessment approaches in flipped classrooms, the LMS should be improved by implementing a clear course schedule and be available to set deadlines for every task. This function can automatically highlight students' late submission of work, late completion of tasks, and late access to materials. It can also allow teachers to assess students' learning process more efficiently. Second, a clear indication or separation on pre-class, in-class, and post-class activities by, for example, displayed in different colors, can serve as a checklist for assessment. This design can help teachers assess students' completion of different types of task and give feedback to students. Third, in order to fulfill different needs of providing feedback to students and to offer data for teachers' reflection, as stated above, the LMS should improve their function on analyzing and visualizing the learning analytics (Macfadyen and Dawson, 2010). Different statistic modules shall be implemented into the LMS so that teachers can obtain specific reports on students' access rate, completion rate, performance, and engagements (Romero et al., 2008). Finally, the LMS can be improved by connecting with students' mobile device. Gaftandzhieva et al. (2018) have designed a mobile learning analytics application which has the function of sending alerts on low participation rate and assessment events to students' mobile device. The early warning system would be more effective if it can employ a similar function of sending mobile push notifications to students' mobile device. The push notification can include warning messages regarding their at-risk behaviors and reminders to completing the tasks. This function would help students improve their learning process.

ACKNOWLEDGEMENT

The authors would like to thank for Miss Li, Ji Hazel of the Chinese University of Hong Kong for producing Figure 1.

REFERENCES

Akçayır, G. and Akçayır, M. 2018. The Flipped Classroom: A Review of its Advantages and Challenges. *Computers & Education*, *126*, 334-345.

Al-Zahrani, A. M. 2015. From Passive to Active: The Impact of the Flipped Classroom through Social Learning Platforms on Higher Education Students' Creative Thinking. *British Journal of Educational Technology*, *46*(6), 1133-1148.

Baker, J. W. 2000. The "Classroom Flip": Using Web Course Management Tools to Become the Guide on the Side. Chambers, J. ed. *Selected Papers from the 11th International Conference on College Teaching and Learning*. Jacksonville: Center for the Advancement of Teaching and Learning, Florida Community College, pp. 9-17.

Bergmann, J. et al. 2012. The Flipped Class: Myth vs. Reality (1 of 3). The Daily Riff-Be Smarter. About Education. Retrieved [23 Jan. 19] from http://www.thedailyriff.com/articles/the-flipped-class-conversation-689.php

Bhagat, K. K. et al. 2016. The Impact of the Flipped Classroom on Mathematics Concept Learning in High School. *Educational Technology & Society*, *19*(3), 134-142.

Bonner, S. M. 2013. Validity in Classroom Assessment: Purpose, Properties, and Principle. McMillan, J. H. ed. *SAGE Handbook of Research on Classroom Assessment*. Thousand Oaks: SAGE Publication Inc., pp. 87-106.

Brame, C. 2013. "Flipping the Classroom". Retrieved [7 Nov. 18] from http://cft.vanderbilt.edu/guides-sub-pages/flipping-the-classroom/.

Cantabella, M. et al. 2019. Analysis of Student Behavior in Learning Management Systems through a Big Data Framework. *Future Generation Computer System*, *90*, 262-272.

Chen, K.-S. et al. 2018. Academic Outcomes of Flipped Classroom Learning: A Meta-analysis. *Medical Education*, *52*(9), 910-924.

Cheng, X. et al. 2017. The "Flipped Classroom" Approach: Stimulating Positive Learning Attitudes and Improving Mastery of Histology among Medical Students. *Anatomical Science Education*, *10*(4), 317-327.

Davies, R. S. et al. 2013. Flipping the Classroom and Instructional Technology Integration in a College-level Information Systems Spreadsheet Course. *Educational Technology Research and Development*, *61*(4), 563-580.

Fautch, J. M. 2015. The Flipped Classroom for Teaching Organic Chemistry in Small Classes: Is it Effective? *Chemistry Education: Research and Practice*, *16*(1), 179-186.

Gaftandzhieva, S. et al. 2018. Mobile Learning Analytics Application: Using Students' Big Data to Improve Student Success. *International Journal on Information Technologies & Security*, *10*(3), 53-64.

Gannod, G. C. et al. 2008. Using the Inverted Classroom to Teach Software Engineering. In *ICSE '08: Proceedings of the 30th International Conference on Software Engineering*. NY: Association for Computer Machinery, pp. 777-786.

Gillette, C. et al. 2018. A Meta-Analysis of Outcomes Comparing Flipped Classroom and Lecture. *American Journal of Pharmaceutical Education*, *82*(5), 433-440.

Greller, W. and Drachsler, H. 2012. Translating Learning into Numbers: A Generic Framework for Learning Analytics. *Educational Technology & Society*, *15*(3), 42-57.

Henrie, C. R. et al. 2018. Exploring the Potential of LMS Log Data as a Proxy Measure of Student Engagement. *Journal of Computing in Higher Education*, *30*(2), 344-362.

Khanova, J. et al. 2015. Student Experiences Across Multiple Flipped Courses in a Single Curriculum. *Medical Education*, *49*(10), 1038-1048.

Koh, K. H. et al. 2018. Experience: Learner Analytics Data Quality for an eTextbook System. *ACM Journal of Data and Information Quality*, *9*(2), 10:1-10:10.

Long, P. and Siemens, G. 2011. Penetrating the Fog: Analytics in Learning and Education. *EDUCAUSE Review*, *46*(5), 30-40.

Macfadyen, L. P. and Dawson, S. 2010. Mining LMS Data to Develop an "Early Warning System" for Educators: A Proof of Concept. *Computers & Education*, *54*, 588-599.

Mason et. al. 2013. Comparing the Effectiveness of an Inverted Classroom to a Traditional Classroom in an Upper-Division Engineering Course. *IEEE Transactions on Education*, *56*(4), 430-435.

Nitko, A. J. 1989. Designing Tests that are Integrated with Instruction. Linn, R. L. ed. *Educational Measurement*. 3rd ed. New York: Macmillan, pp. 447-474.

O'Flaherty, J. and Phillips, C. 2015. The Use of Flipped Classrooms in Higher Education: A Scoping Review. *The Internet and Higher Education*, *25*, 85-95.

Persky, A. M. and McLaughlin, J. E. 2017. The Flipped Classroom – From Theory to Practice in Health Professional Education. *American Journal of Pharmaceutical Education*, *81*(6), 1-11.

Ravat, B. and Dwivedi, S. K. 2019. Discovering Learners' Characteristics Through Cluster Analysis for Recommendation of Courses in E-Learning Environment. *International Journal of Information and Communication Technology Education*, *15*(1), 42-66.

Romero, C. et al. 2008. Data Mining in Course Management Systems: Moodle Case Study and Tutorial. *Computers & Education*, *51*, 368-384.

Romero, C. and Ventura, S. 2010. Educational Data Mining: A Review of the State of the Art. *IEEE Transactions on Systems, Man and Cybernetics*, *40*(6), 601-618.

Rosmansyah, Y. et al. 2017. A Learning Analytics Tool for Monitoring and Improving Students' Learning Process. *Proceedings of the 2017 6th International Conference on Electrical Engineering and Informatics*, Langkawi, Malaysia, pp. 1-5.

Russell, M. K. and Airasian, P. W. 2014. *Classroom Assessment: Concepts and Applications*. NY.: McGraw Hill.

Shannon, L. J. Y. and Rice, M. 2017. Scoring the Open Source Learning Management Systems. *International Journal of Information and Education Technology*, *7*(6), 432-436.

Shum, S. B. and Ferguson. R. 2012. Social Learning Analytics. *Journal of Educational Technology & Society*, *15*(3), 3-26.

Slattery, D. M. 2018. Learning Analytics as a Tool for Evaluating Engagement in Technical Communication Discussion Forums. *Proceedings of the 2018 IEEE International Professional Communication Conference (ProComm)*, Toronto, ON, pp. 215-218.

Triantafyllou, E. et al. 2018. Employing Learning Analytics for Monitoring Student Learning Pathways during Problem-Based Learning Group Work: A Novel Approach. Wang, S. et al. eds. *7th International Research Symposium on PBL: Innovation, PBL and Competence in Engineering Education*. Beijing, China, pp. 542-551.

White, P. J. et al. 2017. Student Engagement with a Flipped Classroom Teaching Design Affects Pharmacology Examination Performance in a Manner Dependent on Question Type. *American Journal of Pharmaceutical Education*, *81*(9), 10-23.

OPEN PROFESSIONAL DEVELOPMENT OF MATH TEACHERS THROUGH AN ONLINE COURSE

Anna Brancaccio[1], Massimo Esposito[1], Marina Marchisio[2], Matteo Sacchet[2] and Claudio Pardini[3]
[1]*Direzione generale per gli ordinamenti scolastici e la valutazione del sistema nazionale di istruzione, MIUR Viale Trastevere 76/A, Roma, Italy*
[2]*Department of Mathematics "G. Peano", Università degli Studi di Torino, Via Carlo Alberto, 10, 10124 Torino, Italy*
[3]*Istituto Statale Superiore Carlo Anti, Via Magenta 7, Villafranca di Verona (VR), Italy*

ABSTRACT

The professional development of teachers is a task recognized by the European parliament and pursued by many institutions, both national and international ones. The support to teachers in STEM disciplines was one of the aims of the Erasmus+ SMART (Science and Mathematics Advanced Research for good Teaching) project, born in a European context, which developed as its main intellectual output two open online courses called Mathematical Modelling and Observing, Measuring and Modelling in Science, in order to help teachers in their continuous professional development. Both courses contain interactive problem-based materials ready to be downloaded, modified, used in the classroom and redistributed to the community. This paper gives an overview of the structure of the course Mathematical Modelling and analyzes its instructional quality, taking into account some measurables obtained in two years of operativity.

KEYWORDS

Continuous Professional Development, Digital Education, E-learning, Mathematical Modelling, Problem Solving, Teacher Training

1. INTRODUCTION

The training of teachers, especially in disciplines such as Science, Technology, Engineering and Mathematics (STEM), is essential for the development of society in Europe. In this respect, in 2006, the EU member states developed the "key competences for all" as part of their learning strategies and "Key competences for Lifelong Learning – A European Reference Framework" was approved as Recommendation of the European Parliament and the Council (European Parliament and Council, 2006). These policies, shared by the community, spread in all European countries. These guidelines were taken into account in Italy through a national action, born in 2012, involving secondary school teachers of STEM disciplines, called the "Problem Posing and Solving" project (Brancaccio et al., 2015b, 2014; Demartini et al., 2015, 2013). In this context, the European Erasmus + SMART Project was born. SMART, which stands for "Science and Mathematics Advanced Research for good Teaching", was coordinated by the "Carlo Anti" Italian high school in cooperation with an international partnership composed of other vocational schools, universities and corporate representatives of the countries: Italy, Germany, Hungary, the Netherlands and Sweden. This large partnership aims at developing initiatives addressing different fields of education and training and at promoting innovation, the exchange of experiences and know-how between different types of organizations. (Brancaccio et al., 2015a, 2016).

This project has many different aims: the first one is to improve professional competences of teachers and to support innovation in teacher training system. Secondly, another objective is to develop skills which can be used in order to contribute to a cohesive society, in particular to increase opportunities for learning mobility and strengthening cooperation between the world of education and training and the world of work, formulating and solving complex problems autonomously, consciously and constructively. Finally, yet importantly, one last task is to provide teachers with an online environment where to find teaching materials that are validated and ready for use in the classroom.

The project operated in these directions through pedagogical solutions and innovative practices based on the new computer and multimedia technologies in order to provide tools and methodologies to facilitate the acquisition of STEM skills - mathematical competence and basic competences in Science and Technology. All those involved took advantage of discussion and sharing with European partners, and of the introduction of advanced technological tools in the teaching of Mathematics and Science to support learning.

The expected results arising from this experience are the definition of common educational models, the development of a European database on training needs, the development of a European database containing Best Practices, the implementation of a dedicated international website report on the results of the experimentation of laboratory modules, the delivery of two open online courses for teachers: one called "Mathematical Modelling" for teachers of Mathematics, and one called "Observing, Measuring and Modelling in Science" for teachers of Physics and Science.

This paper analyzes and discusses the open online course Mathematical Modelling both from the perspective of structure, of organization of resources, instructional quality, and from the point of view of measurables obtained in two years of operativity. Section 2 explains the state of the art of teacher training and instructional design in different contexts, especially the online ones. Section 3 presents the methodology adopted for the analysis of the open online course Mathematical Modelling. Section 4 and 5 present the results and the discussion of the outcomes of the analysis.

2. STATE OF THE ART

Teacher training play a very important role in the development of good practices in schools and in many other contexts of contemporary society. It is clear that teachers need a follow-up during their first years of work. That is why Murray and Male (Murray and Male, 2005) analyzed the path of 28 new teacher educators for their first three years. The study shows that, despite the previous successful teaching careers. It took them between two and three years to adapt to their new professional profile.

Teacher training is usually given in person, even though online contexts seem to be the most suitable according to the condition of teachers, who work fulltime at school and find it hard to attend scheduled meetings (Barana et al., 2018a). With a blended modality, teachers can follow synchronous online meetings and interact with the tutors in an asynchronous way, sharing materials in a virtual community, which is peer supported and facilitates the building of new professional competences and knowledge.

The online components become essential when teacher work in very distant or rural areas, not easy to reach (Eaton et al., 2015): with this approach teachers are motivated in using technology in the classroom, with a positive effect on students, too. It is thus very important to take care of all the needs of students and teachers with careful planning. In (West and Jones, 2007), the authors prepared a framework to assist people who want to integrate technology and teacher training programs. Among the many tools available for online support, Fry (Fry, n.d.) found a discussion board and compressed video sessions to be effective in their supportive role. Beyond these basics, for STEM disciplines there is plenty in the literature about the use of an Advanced Computing Environment (ACE) (Marchisio et al., 2017). One tool which is known to be very effective and well-integrated with other tools is the Maple suite, which, besides the powerful computer engine, allows us to use an interactive online worksheet player and integrates with the Automatic Assessment System (AAS) Möbius (Barana et al., 2018b). Apart from teacher training, this environment has been proved to be effective with students, because of its interactive components and its graphics in two and three dimensions (Barana and Marchisio, 2016).

It is important then to consider Massive Open Online Courses (MOOCs) to be delivered for teacher training, which is one of the outcomes of the SMART project. The University of Torino has a long history of e-learning about e-learning with many online projects. The basis for the development of SMART mainly follows two experiences. The already mentioned "Problem Posing and Solving" project, which deals with Mathematics and Italian teachers in high school, involved in a community of practice with online meetings and asynchronous support provided by tutors and "Orient@mente" (Barana et al., 2016, 2017a), which provides open online courses for university guidance and realignment courses, created to support students in the transition from high school to university, in particular to fill the knowledge gaps in the STEM disciplines.

The design of an online course has several factors to take into considerations. In the last few years a discipline that is valid for traditional teaching as well has been associated more and more to online materials: Instructional Design (ID). According to the current situations, many MOOCs are well-packed, but they have poor instructional quality: in (Margaryan et al., 2015) the author analyzed many online courses hosted in the most famous platform, taking into account instructional parameters.

3. METHODOLOGY

The methodology of analysis of the MOOC "Mathematical Modelling" passes through several steps:

- exploring the structure and the number of users who subscribed to the course;
- observing the measurables of the course: how many problems and materials have been posted, how big the repository of question is;
- studying the materials from the Instructional Design point of view.

We decided to use the method adopted in (Margaryan et al., 2015), called CourseScan, in order to detect the presence or the absence of the main principles of effective learning: problem-centeredness, activation, demonstration, application, integration, interactivity and other further properties, like collective knowledge, collaboration, differentiation, authenticity, feedback. Moreover, teachers attending "Mathematical Modelling" were frequently asked to fill in a questionnaire about their previous experience, the expectations and their improvements: this helped to scan the usability of the course.

4. RESULTS

4.1 Structure

The course is available at https://opensmart.miurprogettopps.unito.it, whose homepage is depicted in Figure 1.

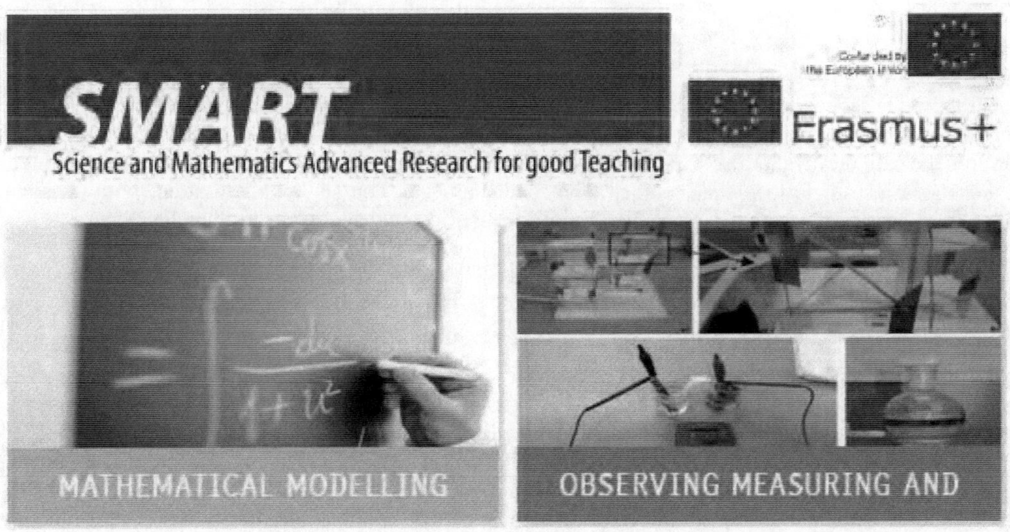

Figure1. Two captures from the platform homepage

It is an instance dedicated to the project of a Moodle platform (https://moodle.org) and it is entirely in English, managed by the University of Turin. The platform is integrated with various tools useful for learning STEM disciplines, in particular the Advanced Computing Environment Maple (https://www.maplesoft.com/) and the Automatic Assessment System Moebius Assessment (https://www.digitaled.com). The University of Turin has a great experience in the development and use of the Moodle platform for teaching (Barana et al.,

2017b, 2017c). The open online course is designed for teachers of Mathematics, but access is free through any social media, so all interested people can access it.

The course is divided into 11 sections. The first module contains one section and this part is the introduction to the course. The second module contains one section about the methodology adopted by the course, namely problem posing and problem solving, including a reflection on what these competences are and how to activate them in the students. The three following modules are devoted to self-training in: Virtual Learning Environment, Advanced Computing Environment, and Automatic Assessment System, three tools considered important for teaching and learning mathematics. Then there are an explanatory and four Topic modules, which contain ready-to-use learning materials, about the four main areas of Mathematics: Quantity, Space and shape, Change and relation, Uncertainty (see Figure 2).

Uncertainty

Topic Uncertainty:

- Production of data (valid methods for measuring certain features; statistic survey)
- Data analysis, their visualization and graphic representation; concept of mean and median
- Probability

Problem	Assignment	Required in advance	Contents	Abilities	Competences	Key ideas
Who is right?	☑	basics of statistics	Bivariate statistics	Conducting a statistic survey, organising data and representing it in tables, computing frequence and contingence indexes	Distinguishng and organising collected data, choosing a strategy for the analysis and drawing conclusion from the results	data analysis, production of data
The birthday paradox	☑	Elementar probability	Conditional probability, decomposition formula, Bayes' theorem	Applying formulas of probability theory	Understanding the dependence between events, individuating the laws of probability to apply, formalising a real situation	Probability

Figure 2. A glance on the topic Uncertainty

Finally, the last part is a course evaluation module. The user can freely decide which sections to follow. Perhaps a conceptual map may facilitate a better understanding of the possible prerequisites and guide the users towards the path they wish to take. Probably a presentation of the 11 sections through Moodle grid mode would make it easier to follow the course. The open on-line course is all written with Easy Reading (http://www.easyreading.it/en/), a certified font for dyslexics, which ensures high inclusiveness.

4.2 Measurables

Up to the 21st January, 253 users have self-enrolled to the course, most of them from Italy. The number of users at the moment is not particularly high, but probably many secondary school teachers in European countries have not heard about the existence of the course through official channels. In Italy the general manager of the Direzione generale per gli ordinamenti scolastici e la valutazione del sistema nazionale di istruzione [1] has issued a note on the opening of online courses to all managers of secondary Italian schools. Probably for this reason, the number of Italian users is higher. Certainly, a further presentation of the courses could be carried out in order to reach the professors of the STEM disciplines on a nationwide basis. The course is composed by 111 activities and interactive resources, 37 of which are assessment activities of two different types. Those of the first type are formative assessment activities that the teacher can use with their students related to the interactive materials of the four areas of High School Mathematics: Quantity, Space and shape, Change and relations, Uncertainty. They are prepared with Moebius assessment because it allows immediate and interactive feedback. The tests contain algorithmic questions of different types (multiple choice, true or false, insert a

[1] The Italian Ministry of Education

formula, numerical, matching ...). Some of them are adaptive for a personalized teaching. The Maple mathematical engine behind Moebius Assessment allows recognizing the accuracy of a mathematical formula independently of the formulation chosen by the student among the infinite possibilities (Figure 3).

SOLAR PANELS

▼ Problem

We want to instal a squared solar panel in a terrace of Rome; its side is *3 m* long.
The manufacturer recommended to install the panel so that it forms with the horizontal floor an angle of 10° lower than the latitude of the place; we recall that Rome is located at a latitude of 41°.
Referring to the image, which will be the room occupied by the panel?
That is, we want to find out:
- Which is the vertical height reached by the panel;
- Which is the horizontal space occupied by the panel;

Figure 3. A problem-based approach with Maple

The evaluation activities of the second type are 10 questionnaires, which allow the user to receive feedback on the course. The course also contains videos, but it does not contain animations. The files prepared with Maple contain completely solved contextual problems, discussed through interactive components, which can be used both to develop precise mathematical skills and problem-solving skills (Figure 4).

The winery

Question 5

1 point

A local company produces in a day up to **700** craft beers.
The daily fixed cost that the company encounters is **450** €,while for each bottle of beer produced there is an addition of a variable cost equal to **3.50** €.
Knowing that each beer is sold at the price of **7** € and according to the following diagram of profitability determine the point of equilibrium and the maximum profit.

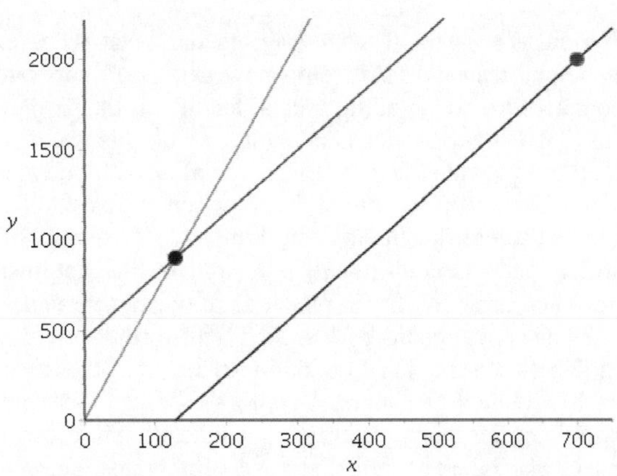

Note that the functions of cost, revenue and profit are respectively shown in the graph in red, green and blue, while the equilibrium point and maximum profit are respectively represented by the colors blue and red.

Figure 4. A problem-based approach with Möbius

For each problem, the prerequisites are declared as well as the knowledge, skills and competences that are to be developed. The variety of resources present in the course ensures a high level of effectiveness and usability. The materials were created under the Creative commons license.

From the teacher's point of view, only 18 users completed the entire course. Many users only attended a part of the course, only accessing activities deemed useful and interesting for their teaching. The completely open character of this course allows you to move in a targeted way. From the questionnaires, it emerged that 52% of teachers particularly appreciated the Problem Posing and Solving methodology proposed. They said that it was effective when applied in class, because it improved student motivation, as well as because of visualization of concepts and its connection to real life. 44% of teachers used learning materials from the course, mainly problems, with good evaluation of the materials both from the teacher's and from students' side. The teachers of the schools participating in the project with their students have tested the proposed materials. This has certainly increased the teaching effectiveness of the materials.

4.3 Instructional Point of View

The course is explained and organized quite well. It is clearly described that the main target of the course are secondary school teachers, even if anyone can attend the course. There is a first section, called "Getting started" that states which the main objectives are. There is also a complete outline of the course, which does not have a fixed but just a recommended structure. It is also specified how to get badges and certificates, and which license the materials hold. About the problem-centered approach, one has to be very precise because it is a course in problem solving and certainly there are many real-life problems, but these are related to the contents that students will face, while a problem-centered approach for teachers would be, for example, how to present a specific topic to the class or which technique to use with respect to the students. It would have been useful to study some successful and unsuccessful cases, what to do and what not to do. It must be recognized that all resource can be re-used in the work place of users and the activities plunge the teacher directly into the knowledge and skill they need for every day's life in the classroom. There are no collaboration activities, due to the nature of the course, which is completely open, and any user can attend lessons at their own pace anytime in the day. All the traits that have been considered delineate a phase of instructional design prior to the implementation of the course. The sections dedicated to learning how to use the Virtual Learning Environment Moodle, the Advanced Computing Environment Maple and the Automatic Assessment System Moebius should be accessible without prerequisites because in this way it is possible to make use of parts aimed to deepen the knowledge without forcing those who are already familiar with those tools to complete the entire required path.

5. DISCUSSION

The presence of an online course for teacher training has been recognized to be useful by its users. The self-training modules helped teachers to develop new skills and competences, from didactics to the use of technology in classroom activities. One of the special features is the permanent availability of online resources. The literature confirms that this experience is in some way unique, since many experiences in teacher training mediated by technology are provided in a blended modality or by means of a MOOC that set the pace and therefore teachers are not always able to attend them for school and family commitments.

It is still to be noted that some adjustments could improve the quality of the course. The navigation through the course in some of its parts is conditional, mediated by the completion of questionnaires, making the navigation more tiring. There is a significant presence of hyper-references to activities, which is beneficial to a nonlinear navigation. The course could be enriched with further interdisciplinary characterization activities to facilitate the dialogue between the STEM disciplines and the other disciplines. In order to make the online course known to more Mathematics teachers, it could be useful to make it available on platforms like Merlot (www.merlot.org) which contains many different open educational resources. In Italy, the course can be a valid tool for implementing CLIL - Content and Language Integrated Learning - which includes teaching some content in a foreign language.

6. CONCLUSION

During the last year, the University of Turin has developed a great experience in open online designing courses in several areas. For example, 20 full online university modules were prepared with the project start@unito (Bruschi et al., 2018). This competence could be used to improve the Mathematical Modelling course to further increase its effectiveness. Mathematical Modelling could also foster the development of a similar course of continuous training for professors in Mathematics and more generally in STEM disciplines at the university, to professors that teach to students enrolled in degree courses other than Mathematics. The latter are often to be motivated and are more interested in applications than theory.

ACKNOWLEDGEMENT

The author would like to thank all the people involved in the SMART project at different levels, especially the ones involved in the design of the MOOCs, as well as the teachers that tested all the materials with their students during the preparation of the open online course, and the users, who provided useful feedback.

REFERENCES

Barana, A., Bogino, A., Fioravera, M., Marchisio, M., Rabellino, S., 2017a. Open Platform of self-paced MOOCs for the continual improvement of Academic Guidance and Knowledge Strengthening in Tertiary Education. J. E-Learn. Knowl. Soc. Vol 13 No 3 2017 EMEMITALIA Conf. 2016 109–119. https://doi.org/10.20368/1971-8829/1383

Barana, A., Bogino, A., Fioravera, M., Marchisio, M., Rabellino, S., 2016. Digital Support for University Guidance and Improvement of Study Results. Procedia - Soc. Behav. Sci. 228, 547–552. https://doi.org/10.1016/j.sbspro.2016.07.084

Barana, A., Brancaccio, A., Esposito, M., Fioravera, M., Fissore, C., Marchisio, M., Pardini, C., Rabellino, S., 2018a. Online Asynchronous Collaboration for Enhancing Teacher Professional Knowledges and Competences. 14th Int. Sci. Conf. ELearning Softw. Educ. https://doi.org/10.12753/2066-026x-18-023

Barana, A., Conte, A., Fioravera, M., Marchisio, M., Rabellino, S., 2018b. A Model of Formative Automatic Assessment and Interactive Feedback for STEM, in: Proceedings of 2018 IEEE 42nd Annual Computer Software and Applications Conference (COMPSAC). Presented at the 2018 IEEE 42nd Annual Computer Software and Applications Conference (COMPSAC), IEEE, Tokyo, Japan, pp. 1016–1025. https://doi.org/10.1109/COMPSAC.2018.00178

Barana, A., Fioravera, M., Marchisio, M., Rabellino, S., 2017b. Adaptive Teaching Supported by ICTs to Reduce the School Failure in the Project "Scuola Dei Compiti," in: Proceedings of 2017 IEEE 41st Annual Computer Software and Applications Conference (COMPSAC). Presented at the 2017 IEEE 41st Annual Computer Software and Applications Conference (COMPSAC), IEEE, pp. 432–437. https://doi.org/10.1109/COMPSAC.2017.44

Barana, A., Marchisio, M., 2016. Dall'esperienza di Digital Mate Training all'attività di Alternanza Scuola Lavoro. MONDO Digit. 15, 10.

Barana, A., Marchisio, M., Bogino, A., Operti, L., Fioravera, M., Rabellino, S., Floris, F., 2017c. Self-Paced Approach in Synergistic Model for Supporting and Testing Students, in: Proceedings of 2017 IEEE 41st Annual Computer Software and Applications Conference (COMPSAC). Presented at the 2017 IEEE 41st Annual Computer Software and Applications Conference (COMPSAC), IEEE, Turin, pp. 407–412. https://doi.org/10.1109/COMPSAC.2017.211

Brancaccio, A., Demartini, C.G., Marchisio, M., Pardini, C., Patrucco, A., 2014. The PP&S computer science project in school. Mondo Digit. 13, 565–574.

Brancaccio, A., Esposito, M., Marchisio, M., Pardini, C., 2016. L'efficacia dell'apprendimento in rete degli immigrati digitali. L'esperienza SMART per le discipline scientifiche. MONDO Digit. 15, 10.

Brancaccio, A., Marchisio, M., Meneghini, C., Pardini, C., 2015a. Matematica e Scienze più SMART per l'Insegnamento e l'Apprendimento. MONDO Digit. 14, 8.

Brancaccio, A., Marchisio, M., Palumbo, C., Pardini, C., Patrucco, A., Zich, R., 2015b. Problem Posing and Solving: Strategic Italian Key Action to Enhance Teaching and Learning Mathematics and Informatics in the High School, in: Proceedings of 2015 IEEE 39th Annual Computer Software and Applications Conference. Presented at the 2015 IEEE 39th Annual Computer Software and Applications Conference (COMPSAC), IEEE, Taichung, Taiwan, pp. 845–850. https://doi.org/10.1109/COMPSAC.2015.126

Bruschi, B., Cantino, V., Cavallo Perin, R., Culasso, F., Giors, B., Marchisio, M., Marello, C., Milani, M., Operti, L., Parola, A., Rabellino, S., Sacchet, M., Scomparin, L., 2018. Start@unito: a Supporting Model for High School Students Enrolling to University. Presented at the IADIS International Conference Cognition and Exploratory Learning in Digital Age 2018, pp. 307–312.

Demartini, C.G., Bizzarri, G., Cabrini, M., Di Luca, M., Franza, G., Maggi, P., Marchisio, M., Morello, L., Tani, C., 2015. Problem posing (& solving) in the second grade higher secondary school. Mondo Digit. 14, 418–422.

Demartini, C.G., Marchisio, M., Mezzalama, M., Pardini, C., Patrucco, A., 2013. The PP&S100 Project: Process Control as an Information System Instance. 50 Congr. Naz. Aica 2013 Front. Digit. Dal Digit. Divide Alla Smart Soc. Congr. Naz. Aica 2013 Front. Digit. Dal Digit. Divide Alla Smart Soc. 10.

In DigitalEd | Online Courseware and Assessment Platform for STEM Courses. Retrieved from https://www.digitaled.com

In EasyReading. Retrieved from http://www.easyreading.it/en/

In Maplesof – Software for Mathematics, Online Learning, Engineering https://www.maplesoft.com/

In MERLOT. Retireved from https://www.merlot.org/merlot/index.htm

In Moodle - Open-source learning platform | Moodle.org. Retrieved from https://moodle.org/

Eaton, S.E., Dressler, R., Gereluk, D., Becker, S., 2015. A Review of the Literature on Rural and Remote Pre-Service Teacher Preparation With a Focus on Blended and E-Learning Models. http://dx.doi.org/10.11575/PRISM/31625

European Parliament and Council, 2006. Recommendation of the European Parliament and the Council of 18 December 2006 on key competences for lifelong learning.

Fry, S.W., 2006. A Technology Supported Induction Network for Rural Student Teachers 10.

Marchisio, M., Rabellino, S., Spinello, E., Torbidone, G., 2017. Advanced e-learning for IT-Army officers through Virtual Learning Eenvironments. J. E-Learn. Knowl. Soc. Vol 13, 59–70. https://doi.org/10.20368/1971-8829/1382

Margaryan, A., Bianco, M., Littlejohn, A., 2015. Instructional quality of Massive Open Online Courses (MOOCs). Comput. Educ. 80, 77–83. https://doi.org/10.1016/j.compedu.2014.08.005

Murray, J., Male, T., 2005. Becoming a teacher educator: evidence from the field. Teach. Teach. Educ. 21, 125–142. https://doi.org/10.1016/j.tate.2004.12.006

West, E., Jones, P., 2007. A Framework for Planning Technology Used in Teacher Education Programs that Serve Rural Communities. Rural Spec. Educ. Q. 26, 3–15. https://doi.org/10.1177/875687050702600402

THE MODERATING ROLE OF M-LEARNING ACTIVITIES IN THE RELATIONSHIP BETWEEN STUDENTS' SOCIAL CAPITAL AND KNOWLEDGE SHARING

Marya Ali Al-Ansari, Allam Hamdan, Anjum Razzaque, Sameh Reyad
and Abdalmuttaleb Al-Sartawi
Ahlia University, Manama, Bahrain

ABSTRACT

Purpose: Current education system is transforming from e-learning to m-learning. The benefit of m-learning is particularly important when it comes to motivating one to self-direct his/her learnings online. Though past research has assessed what role social capital theory plays on knowledge sharing quality, in virtual environment, scant research has assessed the moderation of positive emotions an m-learning support tools, particularly for (1) higher education sector students as well as (2) developing countries. However, the success of such a statement has not been properly documented in the past research. As the result, the aim of this study is to empirically assess the role of Social Capital Theory on Knowledge sharing, when moderated by m-learning.
Research Design: This study is a deductive research approach that initiated with a literature review. Upon identifying a gap in research, research questions were designed. Based on the research questions a conceptual model was proposed and hence this model proposed three hypotheses. This conceptual model was tested using multi-correlation analysis using SPSS, after data was collected from 334 participants, a sample size above the required threshold, to generalize over the population of higher education undergraduate business students of a private university from the Kingdom of Bahrain.
Findings: The results of the empirical findings supported all hypotheses, indicating that m-learning moderate between the role of social capital theory and knowledge sharing quality, when students indulge in e-learning activities using platforms like Moodle. Also, there are implications to theory and practice portrayed in this paper.

KEYWORDS

Social Capital Theory, Knowledge Sharing Quality, Positive Emotions, m-Learning, Higher Education

1. INTRODUCTION

Mobility devices has invaded our world nowadays and we can see that most of the children in school are using mobile telephones. When looking at the devices that we can use to access the World Wide Web we will notice that most of the devices can be used to access the Web and there was a very big change in devices the last few years (Prema, 2012,173a). Furthermore, M-learning has brought many benefits to education because it makes resources easily accessible for the students and gives them the ability to self-study; m-learning also gives the student the advantage of exchanging information while they are not in the university (Abu-Al-Aish, 2012). To encourage better learning and training activities, the use of online resources has been blended successfully with education. It can save operational costs including costs for accommodation, travel and booking of physical classrooms that require every one of the representatives to go to physically (Chang, 2016). This research aims to study how factors such as M-learning affect social capital theory and knowledge sharing. The objectives of this research are to examine: (1) is it important that students use m-learning; (2) Is m-learning affecting knowledge sharing; (3) Is m-learning affecting social capital theory. This study used quantitative method whereby a questionnaire was spread amongst university students across Bahrain such as, Ahlia University, Royal University for Women, AMA University and University of Bahrain. Literature review on the relationship between the variables used in this research is presented in the next part. part 3 and 4 consists of the research methodology and the data analysis including hypotheses. The findings, discussion and conclusion will be presented in part 5.

2. LITERATURE REVIEW

These days, technology is becoming a vital part of our life and it demands professionals, educators, and learners to change their way of thinking and how they use technology for the re-design or re-engineering of education and training system (Basak, 2018). Seeking into (Kothamasu, 2010) argued that five basic parameters are used in m-learning, namely, portable, social interaction, sensitive to the context, connectivity, and customized. In the case of portable, it is easy to carry such as PDA along with users everywhere, including a restroom and this can help learners to get information very quick and rapid. Looking at it in social interaction way, it helps to interact with friends to send messages. Furthermore, it also helps in exchanging data with other people which is also considered as knowledge. In the case of sensitive to the context, it helps in collecting (real data and tested data) something rare to the time environment and current location. In the case of connectivity, it helps to get a strong network where a learner can connect to mobile phones, data collection devices, and to a common network. Finally, in the case of customized, it is very unique because it can help learners to customize learning information. A study was conducted by Sobri and Fatimah (2012) in Malaysian students' on the awareness and requirements of mobile learning services in higher education and the results of the study revealed that students have enough knowledge and awareness to incorporate m-learning in their education environment. Another study conducted by Mao (2014) at the southwest university on 300 undergraduate learners and the study revealed that 76% of the learners were satisfied to use m-learning. In addition, 84% of the respondents also indicated that they will use m-learning as a future learning. Furthermore, the study also revealed that the majority of the learners was immensely benefited from the m-learning because it helped them to solve problems very quickly that they were encountered in the learning. In a study by Lee (2014) stated that it may be advisable for teachers to develop students' learning processes in the face-to-face context without technology before engaging them in technology-supported learning. Consisted of three phases: the development of the survey, the finalization of the survey, and the investigation of the relationship between students' perceptions of CL and SDL without technology and those with technology. Few studies have investigated student and academic perceptions of m-learning and learning. Perceptions are important because they influence students' and teachers' approaches to learning and teaching, which in turn affect learning outcomes Further, they can be used to identify the range of people's experience, as well as their subjective experience of the m-learning (Rowe, 2013). M-learning is one of the ways that enterprises to improve the processes of information flow for knowledge sharing, improvement and achievement. Its web-based system nature removes the users or learners time restrictions or geographic limitations. Moreover, availability and flexibility are often presented advantages when comparing with traditional face-to-face. However, too many projects have high failure costs or user's difficult adoption. Furthermore, M-learning overcomes the limitations of time and space of traditional teaching; it allows learners to learn independently (Navimipour, 2015).

Using m-learning, learning setting is changing frequently because of the mobility of learners, learning technology, and learning content. According to Chen and Kotz (2000), there are four categories of mobile context, namely, computing context, user context, physical context, and the time context. The context of computing mainly focuses about the internet connection, communication bandwidth, and the used resources. Meanwhile, the context of the user focuses about the learner profile and his. Looking through the physical context it focuses about noise, lighting, traffic conditions, the temperature of the learner's physical location. Finally, in the case of time context, it is all about the specific time of learning. Similarly, Zhao and Zhu (2010) and Li and Qiu (2011) have stated that there are three factors that should be held under consideration when you deal with the m-learning systems and having considered, those three factors can provide the desired level of quality. Prior those three factors are, learner's style, mobile, mobile device or applications, Basak et al. 203 and the learning content. Furthermore, the advanced hardware of mobile devices such as camera, accelerometer, and different software such as Apps provides more capability to manipulate, organize, and to generate the formation for teaching and learning (Chen et al., 2008; Keskin and Metcalf, 2011). Knowledge sharing in m-learning play important role to keep the flow of knowledge and make the knowledge richer and deeper, if knowledge sharing in m-learning discontinued the knowledge will stuck and couldn't optimally distribute to learner community (Kunthi, 2018). A study by (Ziad Hunaiti, 2012) indicates that the majority of students own smart phones, a few students have tablet PCs or PDAs and the remaining students have ordinary mobile phones. Students do access the internet via their mobile devices inside and outside the campus regularly and their thoughts about the price of accessing the internet suggest that they did not think that the price was too expensive for accessing these types of services.

3. SAMPLING AND DATA COLLECTION

This research targets undergraduate university students in Bahrain. The questionnaire was distributed amongst university institutions all around Bahrain such as, Ahlia University, Royal University for Women, AMA University and University of Bahrain. Thus, the questionnaire was answered by students whom are knowledgeable of the use of m-learning during their course of study. 312 students took part in this study with Males computing to 166 which is 53.2% and Females compute to 146 which is 46.8%.

4. DATA ANALYSIS

4.1 Descriptive Analysis

Tables 1 show the five-point Likert Scale in detail, mean and standard deviation of social capital theory.

Table 1. The mean and standard deviation of Social Capital Theory

Social Capital Theory	Strongly Agree	Agree	Neither	Disagree	Strongly Disagree	Mean	Standard Deviation
1-I maintain close relationships with some members in my online communities	139 44.6%	123 39.4%	38 12.2%	10 3.2%	2 0.6%	4.24 84.8%	0.835
2-I spend a lot of time interacting with some members on a personal level in my online communities	112 35.9%	137 43.9%	47 15.1%	12 3.8%	4 1.3%	4.09 81.8%	0.879
3-I know some members in my online communities	119 38.1%	132 42.3%	48 15.4%	10 3.2%	3 1%	4.13 82.6%	0.857
4-I have frequent communication with some members in my online communities	101 32.4%	141 45.2%	48 15.4%	16 5.1%	6 1.9%	4.01 80.2%	0.927
5-Members in my online communities will not take advantage of others even when the opportunity arises	107 34.3%	124 39.7%	64 20.5%	13 4.2%	4 1.3%	4.02 80.4%	0.912
6-Members in my online communities would not knowingly do anything to disrupt the conversation	104 33.3%	127 40.7%	62 19.9%	11 3.5%	8 2.6%	3.99 79.8%	0.925
7-Members in my online communities behave in a consistent manner	103 33%	122 39.1%	71 22.8%	9 2.9%	7 2.2%	3.98 79.6%	0.937

8-Members in my online communities are truthful in dealing with one another	102 32.7%	142 45.5%	51 16.3%	14 4.5%	3 1%	4.04 80.8%	0.870
9-I know that other members in my online communities will help me, so it's only fair to help other members	111 35.6%	134 42.9%	54 17.3%	10 3.2%	3 1%	4.09 81.8%	0.859
10-I believe that members in my online communities would help me if I need it	106 34%	136 43.6%	49 15.7%	17 5.4%	4 1.3%	4.04 80.8%	0.912
11-I feel a sense of belonging towards the members of my online communities	118 37.8%	126 40.4%	46 14.7%	17 5.4%	5 1.6%	4.07 81.4%	0.941
12-I have the feeling of togetherness or closeness with members of my online communities	101 32.4%	136 43.6%	54 17.3%	16 5.1%	5 1.6%	4.00 80%	0.921
13-I have a strong positive feeling towards members of my online communities	100 32.1%	147 47.1%	52 16.7%	9 2.9%	4 1.3%	4.06 81.2%	0.847
14-I am proud to be a member of my online communities	101 32.4%	145 46.5%	45 14.4%	19 6.1%	2 0.6%	4.04 80.8%	0.878
15-Members in my online communities will always keep the promise they make to one another	89 28.5%	148 47.4%	56 17.9%	18 5.8%	1 0.3%	3.98 79.6%	0.852
16-Members in my online communities would not knowingly do anything to disrupt the conversation	89 28.5%	149 47.8%	54 17.3%	17 5.4%	3 1%	3.97 79.4%	0.874
17-Members in my online communities behave in a consistent manner	97 31.1%	135 43.3%	52 16.7%	24 7.7%	4 1.3%	3.95 79%	0.949
18-Members in my online communities are truthful in dealing with one another	99 31.7%	141 45.2%	54 17.3%	15 4.8%	3 1%	4.02 80.4%	0.878

19-Members in my online communities use common terms or jargons	99 31.7%	134 42.9%	60 19.2%	15 4.8%	4 1.3%	3.99 79.8%	0.905
20-Members in my online communities use understandable communication pattern during the discussion	111 35.6%	135 43.3%	46 14.7%	14 4.5%	6 1.9%	4.06 81.2%	0.925
21-Members in my online communities use understandable narrative forms of post messages or articles	109 34.9%	136 43.6%	52 16.7%	11 3.5%	4 1.3%	4.07 81.4%	0.877
22-Members in my online communities share the vision of helping others solve their professional problems	96 30.8%	145 46.5%	53 17%	16 5.1%	2 0.6%	4.02 80.4%	0.862
23-Members in my online communities share the same goal of learning from each other	107 34.3%	146 46.8%	44 14.1%	12 3.8%	3 1%	4.10 82%	0.847
24-Members in my online communities share the same value that helping others is pleasant	106 34%	140 44.9%	45 14.4%	14 4.5%	7 2.2%	4.04 80.8%	0.931

4.2 Hypothesis Testing

4.2.1 Correlation Analysis

Table 2 shows the variables would be statistically correlated to each other if significant levels fall beneath 0.05. There is a significant positive correlation between social capital theory and knowledge sharing, $r^2= 0.291$, $p < 0.05$. Moreover, there is a positive correlation between social capital theory and knowledge sharing that is moderated by m-learning, $r^2= 0.373$, $p < 0.05$. As depicted in the table, the moderation of gender significantly impacts the relation between SCT and KSQ, such that presenting gender (male) the R^2 was 29.1% and increased to 32.2%; particularly when male gender was introduced as a moderator. This is not the case of females since R^2 dropped from 29.1% to 25.6% and therefore the gender as a whole (male and female): R^2 dropping from 29.1% to 2.5%. Hence, this evidences the support for hypothesis 4 such that males moderate to facilitate the banking of social capital to improve sharing of knowledge behaviour while e-learning.

4.2.2 Regression Analysis

Multiple regression testing was done to test the hypothesis as shown in Table 2. Hypothesis 1, 2 and 4 are significantly accepted and hypothesis 3 and 5 are rejected. There is a positive relationship between social capital theory and knowledge sharing, $B= 0.540$, $p < 0.05$. Also, as there is a positive relationship between social capital theory and knowledge sharing, adding m-learning as a moderating variable enhanced the relation, which shows they all have a strong effect on each other, $B=0.611$, $p < 0.05$. However, adding gender as a moderator decreases all values significantly from $B= 0.540$ it dropped to $B= 0.159$, $p < 0.05$. To investigate further as to why gender has a negative impact on the relationship, each gender got separated and interpreted to discover the root of the issue. When male gender was introduced as moderator it showed positive relationship to SCT and KSQ as the Beta increased to B= 0.568, $p < 0.05$. On the other hand, when the female gender was introduced as a moderator it showed a negative relationship to SCT and KSQ, B= 0.506, $p < 0.05$. Which shows the issue resides with the findings of the female gender.

Table 2. Regression analysis

Model	Relationship between variables	F	t	R^2	B
M1	Social Capital theory => Knowledge Sharing	127.431 Sig 0.00	11.289 Sig 0.00	29.1%	0.540
M2	M-Learning * Social Capital theory => Knowledge Sharing	184.545 Sig 0.00	13.585 Sig 0.00	37.3%	0.611
M3	Gender * Social Capital theory => Knowledge Sharing	8.060 Sig 0.005^b	2.839 Sig 0.005^b	2.5%	0.159
M4	Male Gender * Social Capital theory => Knowledge Sharing	77.936 Sig 0.00	8.828 Sig 0.00	32.2%	0.568
M5	Female Gender * Social Capital theory => Knowledge Sharing	49.564 Sig 0.00	7.040 Sig 0.00	25.6%	0.506

Hypothesis 1: *There is a positive relationship between social capital theory and knowledge sharing.*
Hypothesis 2: *There is a positive relationship between social capital theory and knowledge sharing with the use of m-learning.*
Hypothesis 3: *There is a positive relationship between social capital theory and knowledge sharing whilst moderated by both genders.*
Hypothesis 4: *There is a positive relationship between social capital theory and knowledge sharing whilst moderated by only the male gender.*
Hypothesis 5: *There is a positive relationship between social capital theory and knowledge sharing whilst moderated by only the female gender.*

5. CONCLUSION

This research is a study of the acceptance of m-learning services in university institutes such as Ahlia University, AMA University and University of Bahrain. One correlation of quality construct can be observed in this paper and they are Social Capital Theory and Knowledge Sharing. Four other moderating variables can be observed that were tested to see the effect on Social Capital Theory and Knowledge Sharing are m-learning, gender as a whole and female and male construct apart. This paper will focus on the effect of m-learning on Social Capital Theory and Knowledge Sharing. Firstly, there is a positive relationship between Social Capital Theory and Knowledge Sharing, as evident in the data analysis, B= 0.540, $p < 0.05$. Which means that Social capital is becoming a valuable mechanism by which universities can share knowledge. For this reason, it is suggested that universities increase confidence, networks and standards among lectures to facilitate the sharing of knowledge. Through such a strong relationship, the process knowledge sharing could be accelerated (Harjanti, 2017). This outline underlines the importance of the contextual standpoint in information and knowledge sharing. The dimensions of social capital signify in particular the roles of structures and relations that are indorsed differently depending on the context (Widen, Gunilla, 2011). The second quality of construct is the effect of m-learning on Social Capital Theory and Knowledge Sharing. Which also showed a positive relationship between them. As shown by Pearson (2016), almost 78% of lecturers admit having digital education in their classroom has shown benefits for their students, which encouraged them to incorporate e-learning into their daily classes. The third quality of construct is the effect of both genders on Social Capital Theory and Knowledge Sharing. This construct showed a negative relationship. The Beta for Social Capital Theory and Knowledge Sharing was B= 0.540 which dropped to B=0.159 when both genders were introduced. To further investigate as to why it happened, the genders were separated into constructs of their own. Either both genders will show negative relationship between the first construct or one of them. When the male gender was tested it showed a positive relationship between it and Social Capital Theory and Knowledge Sharing, B=0.568, $p < 0.05$. On the other hand, when the female gender was tested it showed a negative relationship between it and Social Capital Theory and Knowledge Sharing, B= 0.506, $p < 0.05$. Which concludes that the main issue resides with the female gender's findings. Which could indicate that the women are not as accepting of Social Capital Theory and Knowledge Sharing as men are.

This research is a study of the acceptance of m-learning services in university institutes. As a result of the data analysis, three hypotheses (H1,H2 and H4) are accepted and (H3 and H5) are rejected. The findings of this research support the relationship of Social Capital Theory and Knowledge Sharing, and it showed how knowledge sharing relates to academic performance. Similarly, m-learning showed positive relationship between Social Capital Theory and Knowledge Sharing, which shows incorporating m-learning into university classroom would show a positive reaction. On the other hand, when gender was introduced to test the effect on Social Capital Theory and Knowledge Sharing, it showed a negative relationship. When further tested it showed that men accept Social Capital Theory and Knowledge Sharing, and women do not.

REFERENCES

Abachi (2014), The impact of m-learning technology on students and educators, Computers in Human Behavior.

Abe, (2011). Positive emotions, emotional intelligence, and successful experiential learning. Personality and Individual Differences Journal.

Abu-Al-Aish, (2012), Mathematics Students' Readiness for Mobile Learning, International Journal of Mobile and Blended Learning.

Baehr (2013), Incorporating User Appropriation, Media Richness, and Collaborative Knowledge Sharing into Blended E-Learning Training Tutorial. Ieee Transactions On Professional Communication

Basak (2018). E-learning, M-learning and D-learning: Conceptual definition and comparative analysis. E-Learning and Digital Media Journal

Bhatti, (2016). The effect of experiential learning on subsidiary knowledge and performance. Journal of Business Research

Bondarenko (2017). The role of positive emotions and type of feedback in self-regulation

Chang (2016). Review and discussion: E-learning for academia and industry. International Journal of Information Management

Conklin (2014). Toward More Joyful Learning:Integrating Play Into Frameworks of Middle Grades Teaching. American Educational Research Journal

Harjanti, Dhyah&Noerchoidah, Noerchoidah. (2017). THE EFFECT OF SOCIAL CAPITAL AND KNOWLEDGE SHARING ON INNOVATION CAPABILITY. JurnalManajemendanKewirausahaan. 19. 10.9744/jmk.19.2.72-78.

Hwang, (2016). Understanding social influence theory and personal goals in e-learning.Information Development

Islam (2016), E-learning system use and its outcomes: Moderating role of perceived compatibility. Telematics and Informatics

Kunthi, (2018), Exploring antecedent factors toward knowledge sharing intention in E-learning. HIBAH PITTA

Language Learning. Procedia - Social and Behavioral Sciences

Lee (2007), Effects of Shared Leadership on Team Creativity through Knowledge-sharing in an e-Learning Environment, Sungkyunkwan University

Lee (2014), Students' perceptions of self-directed learning and collaborative learning with and without technology. Journal of Computer Assisted Learning

Motivation? Society for Personality and Social Psychology

Navimipour, (2015), A model for assessing the impact of e-learning systems on employees'

Nedungadi, (2012), A new approach to personalization: integrating e-learning and m-learning, Association for Educational Communications and Technology of learning goals achievement: experimental research. Procedia - Social and Behavioral Sciences

Park, (2015). Emotional design and positive emotions in multimedia learning: An eyetracking study on the use of anthropomorphisms. Computers & Education Journal

Pearson (2016) Digital appetite vs. whats on the table: student attitudes toward digital course material in 2016https://www.pearson.com/us/0/digital-appetite-report-infographic.html

Rager, (2013), I Feel, Therefore, I Learn: The Role of Emotion in Self-Directed Learning, New Horizons in Adult Education

Rahimi et al. (2014). The Broaden-and-Build Theory of Positive Emotions in Second

Rovai (2002). Development of an instrument to measure classroom community. Internet and Higher Education

Rowe, (2013). University student and lecturer perceptions of positive emotions in learning.International Journal of Qualitative Studies in Education

Satisfaction. Computers in Human Behavior

Schutte, (2014). Connections between emotional intelligence and workplace flourishing. Personality and Individual Differences.

Sergis (2018). Investigating the impact of Flipped Classroom on students' learningexperiences: A Self-Determination Theory approach.Computers in Human Behavior

Sousa, (2013). The integration of Information Systems Shared Services Center with E-Learning for Sharing Knowledge Capabilities. Procedia Technology.

Vasquez, (2007), Seeing Future Success: Does Imagery Perspective Influence Achievement

Vulpe (2011). Positive emotions' influence on attitude toward change, creative thinking and their relationship with irrational thinking in Romanian adolescents. Procedia - Social and Behavioral Sciences

Widen, Gunilla. (2011). Social Capital and Knowledge Sharing – Lessons Learned. IFIP Advances in Information and Communication Technology. 362. 48-57. 10.1007/978-3-642-23330-2_6.

Williams (2013). Stimulating and Enhancing Student Learning Through Positive Emotions. Journal of Teaching in Travel & Tourism.

Yilmaz (2017), Exploring the role of e-learning readiness on student satisfaction and motivation in flipped classroom. Computers in Human Behavior

Yilmaz (2017), Knowledge sharing behaviors in e-learning community: Exploring the role of academic self-efficacy and sense of community. Computers in Human Behavior.

E-LEARNING MODEL FOR TRAINING OF DRIVERS IN TRAFFIC BASED ON FREQUENT MISTAKES ON THE PRACTICAL EXAM

Goran Jovanov[1], Jovica Vasiljevic[2], Nemanja Jovanov[3], Dejan Antic[4] and Djordje Vranjes[5]
[1]University of Criminal Investigation and Police Studies-Republic of Serbia, Cara Dusana 196, Zemun-Belgrade, Serbia
[2]Secretariat for Public Transport-City Administration of Belgrade-Republic of Serbia, 27 Marta 43-45-Belgrade, Serbia
[3]"Union - Nikola Tesla" University Faculty of Business and Law-Belgrad-Serbia, Knez Mihaila 71-Belgrade, Serbia
[4]Road Traffic Safety Agency Republic of Serbia, Bulevar Mihaila Pupina 2-Belgrade, Serbia
[5]National Institute of Serbia, Vinca-Belgrade, Serbia

ABSTRACT

This paper presents the previous experience in the licensing process of the examiners at the driving test in the Republic of Serbia, with an analysis of the way in which the examiners assess the polygonal actions. The analysis covers the most common mistakes that have been registered with the examiners as well as in the candidates in the training. The main groups of application of this model are only candidates for the training for passing a driving test. The material is a practical part of taking the driver's exam. Based on the database of errors in the work of the examiners and the candidates themselves, a database of electronic knowledge is modeled - (video material with comments) based on which the training model of the training candidate will be formed, based on frequent and observed errors. Further analysis of the database will be updated continuously in everyday work. Forming a database of errors is the first step in the model. At the same time, the selection of candidates with observed errors in the practical part of the training is formed. The formed target group independently examines the video material (as well as the examiner) evaluates its and the practical content of other candidates. A comparative analysis compares the observed errors of examiners and candidates. The collected data is analyzed and interpreted with the aim of identifying frequent errors both in training and in the practical exam itself. E content of the new training in the second cycle is enriched by documenting (video material with comments on past mistakes). After a short cycle of do-training with the application of the model, the newly acquired knowledge is checked by assessing the knowledge test based on the review of the simulated video with errors. The aim of this paper is to create a model of e-learning based on mistakes, which will annoy the creation of mistakes that a candidate creates in taking the practical part of the driving test.
We believe that the application of this model in constant work would create conditions for improving the quality of training, as well as easier learning model with the candidate. The result would be excellent quality training and a quality driver in traffic.

KEYWORDS

Database, Errors, Practical training, E-learning Model

1. INTRODUCTION

Having in the mind that the most important resource at the market today is information, there are more and more jobs which deal with collecting, creating, processing, distribution and warehousing the information. New technologies change our attitude toward life in short time intervals. New jobs are created, the old one are modified, the knowledge is more and more looked for and valued, intellectual jobs are overwhelming over the manual ones. Expert predictions talk about future demand of mostly the jobs requiring IT skills. In order to adequately respond to the requests of new jobs, the adequate education is required, because the IT knowledge and skills are not inborn, these are acquired by work and learning. The concept of today's school, according to many authors, is old fashioned and it needs to be changes, which is not surprising since it was created back in the 17th century by great European pedagogue, John Amos Comenius. At that time the school responded to the requests of informatics revolution and the needs of contemporary life. Pedagogues and educational theorists try to find a new model which would satisfy todays' and future needs of young population. With the development of technology, it is necessary to change also educational methods which will use new technology and teach on how to use it. On the way to success, it is normal that the errors occur. Either they are big or small, we consider these to be bad or, even worse, we feel unsuccessful about them. The fact we do not know is that we actually learn based on the principle of efforts and errors – this is how our mind functions. Our attitude toward the errors is important, because they can be excellent tool for creativity and inspiration. Because of the mistakes, we have been criticized from our childhood, and if there had not been for them, we would not learn and develop ourselves. By studying complex systems, we can find surprising connection between those which are successful. Their success has been built in the manner of trying and making mistakes. It is very hard and extremely unpleasant to admit own mistakes. The world has become too unpredictable and complex for today's challenges and it is dangerous to be led by tested and ready solutions, as well as expert opinions. The mistakes should be accepted and appreciated. Based on them we will find out how to do something new. Let the mistakes be our journey to the success. The time in which we live and jobs we do every day demand from us flexibility, quick learning and adapting to situation. The jobs in which, once gained knowledge is applied in the same manner, are more and more rare.

In the Republic of Serbia, in the area of training candidates for drivers, the effectiveness of the Law, as well as by-laws which closely regulate this area, has brought significant changes as compared to current practice. Some of the most important ones are certainly the introduction of obligatory theoretical training and passing theoretical exam of candidates for a driver prior to the practical training, as well as licensing of personnel for training of candidates for drivers. The jobs of licensing of personnel for candidates training for drivers – which include driving instructors, theoretical training trainers and examiners – are by the Law trsuted to the Agency. In the focus of Agency jobs in 2014, and especially during the first half of the year, certainly were the jobs of licensing the examiners at the driving tests, because form July 1st, 2014, the obligation has become effective by which all of the examiners who want to practice these jobs must have the license for examiner issued by the Agency (Alimpić, Z., Bogićević, S., Dragutinović-J., N., (2013)).

In this work current experiences have been represented, in regards to the process of licensing the examiners in the Republic of Serbia, with the analysis of the manner in which the examiners evaluate acting on polygon. The analysis include the most common mistakes, differences in the manner of evaluation between the examiners, as well as the reconciliation with the predefined manner of evaluation in accordance with the relevant by-laws, for three polygon operations. The training is vital request in professional world and life at all. Driving schools and organizations spend significant amount of time and money in candidates/drivers training, in order to behave in accordance with the Law and regulations by their knowledge and attitude. Quality training helps in improving, reliability and safety of the traffic participants. Thru quality training and criteria, weakness and disadvantages can be identified so that additional improvements can be added too and the frequency of mistakes can be minimized. Practical part of the exam for the examiner is passed in the following manner: candidates for examiners watch on computers recorded driving of "candidate for a driver". As it has been very hard to provide and record the driving of real candidate for a driver, from organizational, time and technical aspect, the Agency videotaped experienced driving instructor and examiner who simulated the driving of candidate for a driver in a vehicle provid by the Agency and which is not the vehicle of any legal entity which trains the candidate for driving. Recorded driving practice include the driving at polygon and driving in traffic at public road, and detailed description of passing practical part of the exam for examiner is provided below. While evaluating, the examiner himself makes mistakes. On practical part of the exam, the task of a candidate for an examiner is to, during the period of 2 hours, watching video material on a computer, evaluate simulated driving of a candidate for driver who operates a vehicle of "B" category, using the rating list and evaluation form, in accordance with the Rulebook. **We are of the opinion that these mistakes are useful and the model of e-learning can be created based on mistakes.**

2. METHODOLOGY

Numerous researches have shown that a student better memorizes contents if these are shown as multimedia. The percentage of memorizing increases if the following are added to the transfer of information by reading: live word and motion picture, and 90% of successful rate happens if the motion is included, i.e. motoric activity which follows audio-visual perception (Mayer, R. E. & Anderson, R. B. (1992).).

Video material on practical part of an exam consists of 6 video clips of polygon operations and a video clip of traffic on public road, at total duration of not more than 25 minutes. A candidate for examiner watches video clips with the task to record, rate and write down the noticed mistakes in the rating list, write down total number of negative points and evaluate simulated driving of a candidate for examiner. Together with filling in rating list, a candidate must fill in evaluation form, also, which represents the explanation of their rating list. This means that each mistake recorded in the rating list has to be included in the evaluation form with detailed description, i.e. the comment which refer to a mistake made by a candidate for driver.

The evaluation of polygon operations in the exam form is made by a candidate for an examiner in the following manner:

1) by ***circling*** one of provided answers for each polygon operation;
2) in the filed ***Comment*** detailed description of mistake is provided, based on which a candidate has been evaluated;
3) in a part ***NNP*** the number of negative points is filled in, and the rating "not passed" ***NP*** is circled if such a rating is predicted for done mistake.

Figure 1. Screen shot of video clip for polygon operations (from the Agency gallery)

After polygon operations, a candidate for an examiner watches and evaluates recorded driving simulation of a candidate for a driver in traffic on public road, for which a screen shot of video material and content of exam form have specially been adapted. Video clip of traffic on public road is separated into five sectors, and each sector lasts for several minutes. A candidate for examiner evaluates the driving of a candidate for a driver in traffic on public road by writing down all found mistakes from the video clip in the exam form in each sector, together with recording the mistakes in rating list. The applied evaluation methodology provides us with the possibility to record noticed mistakes and, this way, to create mistakes/errors database. At the same time we will make the selection of examiners who have not passed the exam and thus we create targeted group of candidates for the application of new model of e-learning. Also, those candidates who have passed the exam and have had minimum number of errors should not be put aside. Those errors are also recorded. By comparative analysis of mistakes we come to frequent mistakes. They direct us to the causes that lead to the creation of mistakes, i.e. gaps in the training.

Material with mistakes, i.e. formed database represents the basis for e-platform. We approach to the creation of new video material with noticed mistakes. Simulated video material represents the correction in the form of additional training in a new cycle of knowledge creation.

Additional training with the presentation of material in virtual classroom, where candidates can see and record the errors. After new presentation with the accent on recorded errors, a candidate-examiner repeats the exam reviewing video material of practical part of the exam.

2.1 Methodology and Analysis of Polygon Operations Evaluation Manner

In this work the method of evaluation of three polygon operations has been analyzed at the sample of 178 candidates for examiner, who passed a practical part of the exam for examiner. Also, it is very important to point out that the analysis includes only those candidates for examiners who have taken a practical part of the exam for the first time. Analyzed period has been chosen because this manner of passing the exam has been applied in the licensing process for the first time, so the candidates for examiners have had minimal knowledge and experience on the manner and type of passing practical part of the exam, which enabled to the Agency to consider their real knowledge from the area of evaluation of the candidates for drivers at practical exam. The analysis has been done on percentage of candidates for examiners (using chosen sample) who correctly evaluated three polygon operations, two polygon operations and only one polygon operation, and correctly evaluated each polygon operation – individually.

Also, for all candidate for examiners who have not correctly evaluated some of the polygon operations (in accordance with the described manner of passing practical part of the exam for examiners and the manner of evaluation of polygon operations (Point 3), the 3 variables have been analyzed:

- If a candidate for examiner knows how to recognize the mistake (by circling one of the offered responses);
- If a candidate for examiner knows how to describe a mistake made by a candidate for a driver from video clip, i.e. if they know to explain what was wrong during operating on a polygon and
- If a candidate for examiner knows how to rate a candidate for driver correctly in accordance with the Rulebook.

Analyzed polygon operations are:

1) Driving forward with the change of gear and backward with the change of traffic line (Polygon operation 1)
2) Parking the vehicle horizontally, by driving reverse (Polygon operation 2)
3) Parking the vehicle under right angle, driving backwards (Polygon operation 3)

Performing each polygon operation has been defined by the Article 16 of the Rulebook, in the following manner:

Polygon operation 1 is performed in accordance with the situation from the Figure 2. A candidate for a driver from the starting field „I", speeds up a vehicle with the change of shift of gear and stops in stopping field „II", while horizontal projection of horizontal most elongated of front of the vehicle on the surface has to be in that field. From that position the vehicle moves backwards with the change of traffic line, passing thru the passing field.

„III" and by repeated change of traffic line is returned to the starting field „I", while whole vehicle stops in that field. While moving of the vehicle backwards, a candidate for driver uses driving mirrors, i.e. looks over shoulders/ while moving backwards from the stopping field „II" to the starting field „I" the vehicle can stop not more than 2 times and make one step of correction (one step of correction is vehicle moving opposite to given direction).

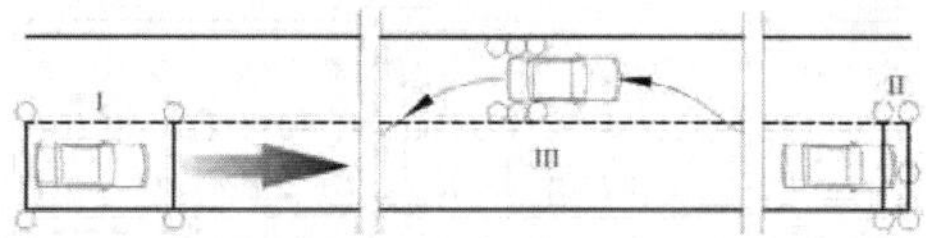

Figure 2. Polygon Operation 1 (Rulebook, 2012)

Polygon operation 2, is performed in accordance with the situation as shown in the figure 3. A candidate for driver starts by vehicle from the position „1" and moves moving forward in a straight line to the position „2", from where by one step backwards and not more than one step forward, stops the vehicle on a parking spot, while whole vehicle has to be in the field of parking spot.

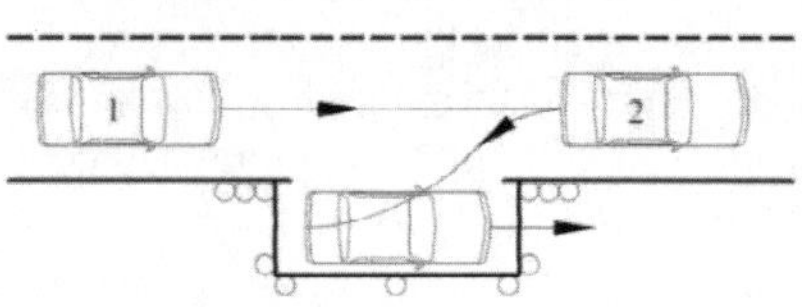

Figure 3. Polygon Operation 2 (Rulebook, 2012)

Polygon operation 3, is performed in accordance with the situation as shown in the figure 4. A candidate for driver moves by vehicle from the position „1" moving forward to the position „2", and occupies it in the manner that enables it to stop the vehicle at parking spot by moving backwards, while whole vehicle has to be in the field of parking spot.

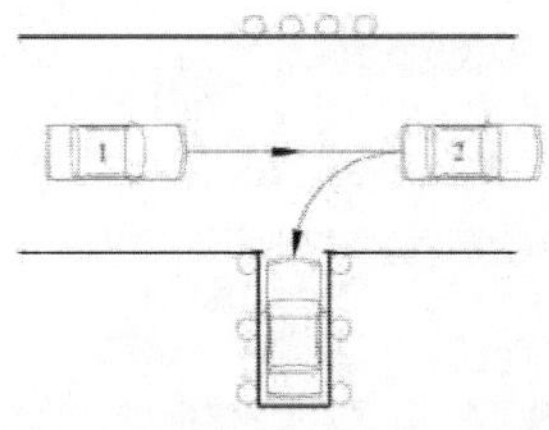

Figure 4. Polygon Operation 3 (Rulebook, 2012)

Also, the Rulebook defines that Polygon Operations 1 a candidate for driver performs in one attempt, while Polygon Operations 2 and 3 can be performed in not more than two attempts.

2.2 Theoretical Model of E-Learning based on Errors/Mistakes

In order for us to understand how technology, such as multimedia, can improve learning, we have to think of 5 principles of multimedia design of teaching instructions (Mayer, R. E. (1997), as follows:

1. Principle of multiple representation: it is better to represent the explanation in words and pictures than only words.
2. Principle of union: when providing multimedia explanation, it is better to represent relevant words and picture together, than separately.
3. Principle of divided attention: when providing multimedia explanation it is better to represent words as sound narration than only visually, as text on screen.
4. Principle of individual differentiations: mentioned principles are more important for students with less knowledge, as well as for students who orientate themselves better in the space.
5. Principle of coherency: when providing multimedia explanation it is better to use less, than a lot of unnecessary and redundant words and pictures. Wising to influence the examiners and their cognitive processes, these principles are applied in the preparation of the material for seminar aimed for the targeted group.

Former training model has been based on theoretical basis which have been supported by different rulebooks on passing the exams for examiners. Individual evaluation of canidate represents the essence which each candidate will recognize in themsleves, and these are the errors themselves know they make. The model will simply show to a candidate almost all errors created by this targeted error.

At the same time, the erros will show the weakness of training.

The model is based on strong database of noticed and frequent mistakes, made both by the examiners during evaluations and candidates themselves. .

The model in the structure represents the following steps which will be shown by an algorithm :

1. Candidate training
2. Exam – video clips review ta the practical part of exam.
3. Recording the mistakes/errors, both at candidates and examiners
4. Mistakes database
5. Comparative analysis of mistakes
6. Candidate selection
7. Creating simulated video material with showing mistakes in the operation/process
8. Virtual classroom with new simulated video material
9. Discussion / analysis of noticed mistakes by candidates – participants of virtual classroom
10. Repeating the exam from the Point 2.
11. Analysis of success

The Figure No.5. shows the algorithm of a model of e-learning based on mistakes.

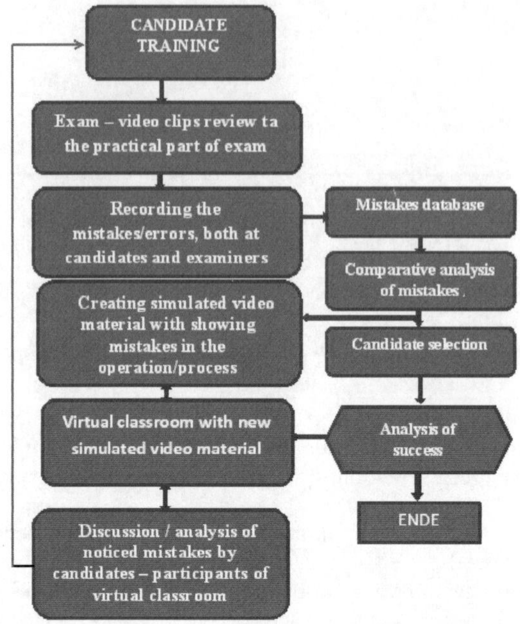

Figure 5. Algorithm of a model of e-learning based on mistakes

3. RESULT AND DISCUSSION

Out of 178 candidates for examiners, 6% (11 candidates) has not correctly evaluated any of analyzed polygon operations, while 84% of them correctly evaluated one, i.e. two polygon operations. All three polygon operations have correctly been evaluated by only 10% of candidates for examiners.

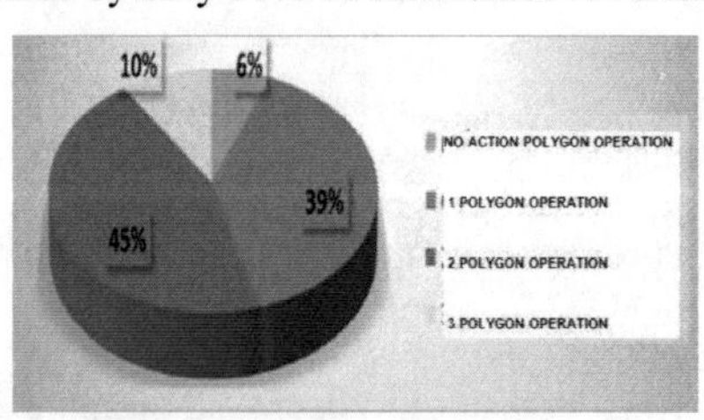

Figure 6. Percentage of No of Candidates for Examiners Who Correctly Evaluated Analyzed Polygon Operations

Polygon Operation 1 has been correctly, i.e. incorrectly, evaluated by almost equal number of candidates for examiners, and at the evaluation of Polygon Operation 2 and Polygon Operation 3 the percentage is significantly different. To be more precise, the largest number of candidates for examiners (87%) has correctly evaluated Polygon Operation 2, whole only 20% of candidates for examiners correctly evaluated Polygon Operation 3, i.e. 80% of candidates for examiners incorrectly evaluated this polygon operation.

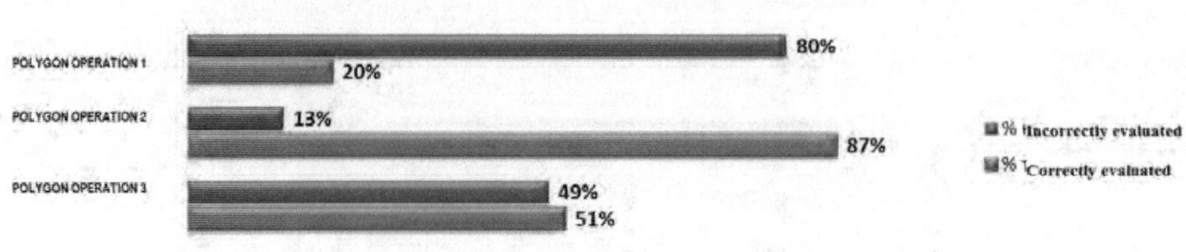

Figure 7. Percentage of Results of Evaluation of Polygon Operations

Polygon Operation 1

Out of 87 candidates for examiner who incorrectly evaluated Polygon Operation 1, the highest percentage of them (44%) knew to recognize the mistake made by a candidate for driver on video clip and knew how to correctly evaluate, but they provided bad explanation, i.e. did not know to precisely explain what kind of mistake a candidate for driver made. This can have as a consequence that the candidates for drivers may get from the examiners at their first real practical exam not so precise explanation of the mistake they have made.

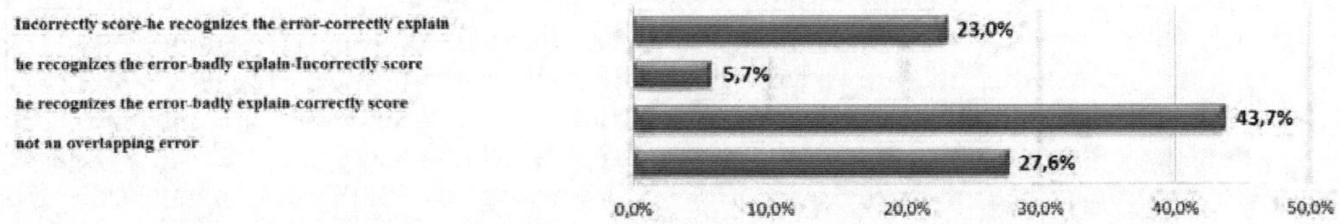

Figure 8. Graph Showing Analyzed Mistakes after Evaluation of Polygon Operation 1

Almost one quarter of candidates for examiners who incorrectly evaluated this polygon operation do not know how to correctly rate recognized and well explained mistake. To be more precise, 23% of candidates for examiners does not know that the step of correction when performing the Polygon Operation 1 is allowed and that for it a candidate for driver does not get negative points. This can also directly influence to the result of practical exam of a candidate for driver, i.e. candidates can be damaged, because it is not rae that they get from the examiners negative point for allowed step of correction. The fact a candidate for driver at video clip made polygon operation 1 correctly with one step of correction was not recognized by 28% of candidates for examiners, i.e. the responses have been that the candidate performed the operation incorrectly in some case without, and in some cases with the step of correction.

Polygon Operation 2

Out of 23 candidates for examiners who incorrectly evaluated Polygon Operation 2, the highest percentage of them (875) did not know that a candidate for driver performed this polygon operation correctly from the first attempt. The situation some of the candidates for examiners think of as the mistake and negatively rate it is the one in which a candidate for driver, while vehicle is moving backwards and by wheel it "steps" broken center line on the polygon and after entering in the marked field of parking spot, moves the vehicle by moving forward (which is allowed by the Rulebook), after which the vehicle is stopped inside the marked field of parking spot.By this evaluation, a candidate for driver on practical part of the exam can be damaged because they can get negative point for correctly performed polygon operation.

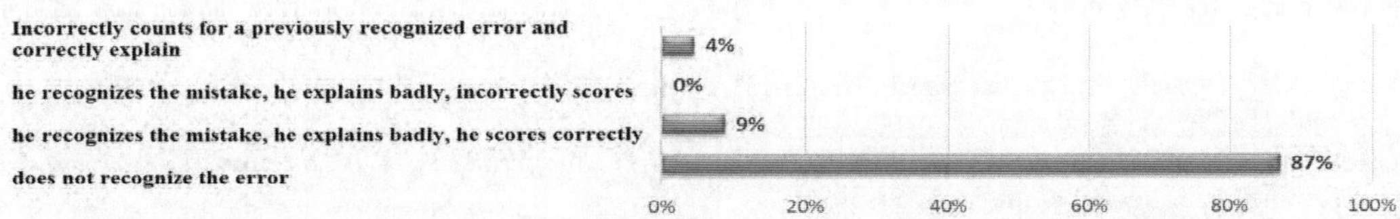

Figure 9. Graph Showing Analyzed Mistakes in Evaluation of Polygon Operation 2

Polygon Operation 3

Out of 143 candidates for examiner who incorrectly evaluated Polygon Operation 3, only two candidates for examiner knew to recognize that the candidate for driver on video clip incorrectly made this polygon operation. To be more precise, 141 candidate for examiner (99%) could not recognize that the candidate for driver at their first attempt used not-allowed step of correction while performing this polygon operation and that there was no another second attempt. The response provided by them was that the candidate for driver performed Polygon Operation 3 correctly from the second attempt, i.e. not-allowed step of correction they considered to be the second attempt. A candidate for driver did not go back to the starting position when performing this operation (Figure 9 - position „1"), and tried the second time, but they performed not-allowed step of correction. When they saw that from the first attempt the vehicle could not be parked under right angle from the first attempt in the field of marked parking spot, i.e. that they will hit the cones which were marking a parking spot, a candidate has, by moving forward, moved the vehicle only to the position which enabled them to try again by moving vehicle backwards and park the vehicle in the field of marked parking spot.

4. CONCLUSION

By the application of this model the examiner will understand in which manner they will recognize and explain a mistake made by a candidate. Created database of recognized, frequent mistakes leads to perfect knowledge of examiner. The application of this model on the candidate themselves is of great importance. The continuity of updating of mistakes and updating video material in the application will result in minimal conditions for errors/mistakes creation. With the help of all of the above mentioned, we enable to a candidate to virtually recognize the mistakes that emerge in traffic situation. The analysis and discussion of participant of virtual classroom will make the concept of examiners' self-confidence stronger. The model has been shown in this work as the concept, both graphically and descriptively. The innovative approach of represented model mirrors in unique form of several steps which gradually make the participant of the course being independent in their mastering over presented knowledge and skills. Key point in the application of model have the development of learning material, the activities which encourage explorative approach, the motivation, monitoring participants work and progress and the communication between participants and moderator. The materials for learning should gradually be transferred from complete information to starting information demanding further exploring. The testing of knowledge should be continued thru the application of knowledge in practice. It is necessary to elaborate proposed experimental research model by theoretical and practical applications from the aspect of knowledge management. This system uses a model for misconception detection and identification (MDI) and an inference system for the dynamic delivery of the learning objects tailored to learners' needs.More specifically, the MDI mechanism incorporates the Fuzzy String Searching and The String Interpreting Resemblance algorithms in order to reason between possible learners' misconceptions. Furthermore, the inference system utilizes the knowledge inference relationship between the learning objects and creates a personalized learning environment for each student (Troussas C.,Chrysafiadi K., Virvou M., (2019). Tools for learning analytics are becoming essential features of Learning Management Systems (LMS) and various course delivery platforms. These tools collect data from online learning platforms, analyze the collected data, and present the extracted information in a visually appealing manner. Representing the design-level concerns of such tools is one of the significant challenges faced by software developers. One way of overcoming this challenge is to adopt architectural perspectives which is a mechanism used by software architects to capture high-level design concerns (Arvind W. Kiwelekar, (2019).

REFERENCES

Alimpić, Z., Bogićević, S., Dragutinović-J., N., (2013). *Licensing of personnel for training candidates for drivers in the Republic of Serbia.* Road Traffic Safety Agency, Republic of Serbia

Kiwelekar A., LaddhaLaxman M., NetakSanil Gandhi (2009). *An Architectural Perspective of Learning Analytics,* Machine Learning Paradigms pp 115-130

Law on Road Traffic Safety (2009), *Official Gazette of the Republic of Serbia*, no. 41/09, 53/10, 101/11.

Mayer, R. E. (1997). Multimedia learning: Are we asking the right questions. Educational Psychologist, 32, 1-19.

Mayer, R. E. & Anderson, R. B. (1992). *The instructive animation: Helping students build connections between words and pictures in multimedia learning.* Journal of Educational Psychology, 84, 444-452.

Ordinance on the organization, implementation and manner of taking the driver's exam, keeping and the deadlines for keeping records of the driving test and the conditions to be met by the vehicle in which the driving test is conducted (2012), Official Gazette of the Republic of Serbia, no. 53/12, 93/13, 116/13 and 108/14.

Rules on the program for taking the exam for the examiner, the program and deadlines for the seminar, the manner of taking the professional exam and the examination of the knowledge test and the appearance and content of the license form for the examiner (2012), Official Gazette of the Republic of Serbia no. 21/12.

Rulebook on conducting exams, organizing seminars for improving knowledge and keeping a registry of issued permits (licenses) for examiners (2012), Official Gazette of the Republic of Serbia no. 53/12.

Troussas C., Chrysafiadi K., Virvou M., (2019, *An intelligent adaptive fuzzy-based inference system for computer-assisted language learning,* Expert Systems with Applications, vol 127, pp.85-96

E-LEARNING - EVOLUTION, TRENDS, METHODS, EXAMPLES, EXPERIENCE

Eugenia Smyrnova-Trybulska
University of Silesia in Katowice, Bankowa 12, 40-007 Katowice, Poland
Faculty of Ethnology and Sciences of Education
Bielska 62, 43-400 Cieszyn

ABSTRACT

The article focuses on an overview of evolution, trends, methods, examples and analyses of the experience of e-learning. The author presents theoretical and practical aspects of the use of e-learning in higher education, based on her own long-time experience. The paper comprises a description of stages of e-learning evolution and discusses such aspects as current and future trends (in addition to the LMS system / Next-Generation LMS also Augmented and virtual reality, Artificial intelligence, Natural User Interface, Videos, Podcasts); methods (Problem–based learning; Project–based learning; Inquiry–based learning; Flipped Classroom; Digital Storytelling; Gamification; App-based learning, Video-based learning); examples of experience (projects (earlier, current, and future (UPGOW, IRNet, Faculty Distance learning platform, MOOCs, teacher training in the area of innovative technologies and methods)), analysis of E-learning and universities' electronic environment.

KEYWORDS

e-Learning, Evolution, Trends, Methods, Technologies, Experience

1. INTRODUCTION

"E-Learning is a new educational paradigm in the age of information technology. These days, most universities worldwide consider e-learning as a strategic asset to make education accessible to everyone." (Sohrabi, Vanani, Iraj, 2019)

The conceptual basis for the creation and functioning of modern systems of teaching and learning in remote mode and e-learning includes: the theory of the constructivism (Bruner, 1960, 1974, Piaget, 1977, 1985, 1995, 1996, Papert, 1991, 1992, 1996, Vygocki, 1982, 1991), behavioral learning concept (Skinner, 1968, 1976, 1986, Thorndike, 1927, 1990, Watson, 1990), humanistic pedagogy (Dewey, 1910, Maslow, 1969, Strahan, Rogers, 2012), cognitive basics of learning (Bruner, 1960 , 1974, Piaget, 1977, 1985, 1995, 1996, Vygockij, 1982, 1991, Smith, 2007, Hayes, 1978), functional theory (Davydov, 1986, Gal'perin, 1976, Talyzina, 1969, 1975; Vygocki, 1982, 1991; Krygowska, 1977), the theory of developing teaching (Davydov, 1986, Leontev, 1997, Elkonin, 1984), sociocultural theory, built on the notions of intersubjectivity and its immediate development zone (Vygockij, 1982, 1991), theory of connectivism (Downes, 2012; Levy , 1994, 1997, Siemens, 2005, 2013, 2014), theory of problem-oriented learning (Group "Awareness and Technologies" Vanderbilt University, Cognition and Technology Group at Vanderbilt University, 1990, 1994), theory of cognitive flexibility (Spiro, Coulson, Feltovich, Anderson, 1988; Feltovich, 1992), reflexive teaching (Schoenfeld, 1987, 1992, Woronowicz, 1997), situational models of cognition processes (Brown, Collins, Duguid, 1989), the model of "shared cognition" (Oshima, 1995, 1996; Bereiter, Scardamalia, 1994, 1995, 1996), the teaching and learning model of "master-student" and many others (Smyrnova-Trybulska, 2018), research concerning designing an Integrated Web-based Personal Learning Environment conducted by Amberg, Reinhardt, Haushahn, Hofmann (2009), new methods of e-learning focuses in research areas Malach Kostolányová, Chmura M., Prextová (2016).

Simultaneously, we could observe that the technologies are developing faster than methods and faster than users become prepared to use them. It is a great problem, a challenge and a contradiction. This article is devoted to an analysis of certain aspects and solutions to this issue.

2. EVOLUTION OF E-LEARNING

"The technological evolution during the last 7 decades could bring down one "room computer" (Mark I, 1943) weighting several tons into a small tiny laptop, weighting just a few grams and a thousand times more powerful than his "grandfather". (Reis, 2010: p.13)

E-learning is unrelated to the technological progress, scientific development, development of computer hardware and means of communication. The history of the computer dates back to 1940's. The mechanical computing machine - 600 years, basic tools to perform calculations - 3000 years.

"This technological revolution was followed by an enormous change in methodologies and didactic tools where adjusted in a view to their implementation." (Reis, 2010: p.13).

In his own research A.D.Reis (2010) analysed the evolution of e-learning and stages, conditions, in particular he noted that one of the important educational as well as technological event in this subject area was: "Skinner introduced in 1954, CAI (Computer Assisted Instruction) in his classic article ("The science of learning and the art of teaching") and summarized the basics about "The teaching machine". The teaching machine and the programmed texts are the previous format of CBI (computer based instruction) turned into reality later with the PCs."

During the last decades the concept of e-learning has changed and evolved. It can be typified in *five* different phases. What distinguishes the different phases is: the presence of interactivity or not; the existence or not of *multimedia contents; and the existence of synchronous and asynchronous online support, elements of augmented reality and virtual reality, artificial intelligence and learning assistance*. The evolution of technology, pedagogic methodology and teacher skills allow us today to use all the above mentioned approaches. (Reis, 2007)

I. First distance learning stage (-» 1970): course contents were totally delivered by regular mail (Reis A. (2010). s.15)
II. Second stage (1970 -1980): Open Universities
III. Third stage (1980 - 1990): Video cassettes and TV
IV. Forth stage (1990 - 2000): Computers, multimedia, interactivity, e-Learning
V. Online Learning Environment (Reis, 2010, p.15)

According to other research (Lamandini 2009), there were "limits of e-learning 1.0. Although in recent years there has been a steady increase in the number of e-learning projects with the extensive use of technology platforms (LMS Learning Management System or Virtual Learning Environment VLE), in fact few of them have caused significant changes in terms of stability and the quality of learning. The reasons are:

- excessive focus on technological aspects,
- lack of effectiveness of adopted teaching strategies,
- poor skills in the field of design and management and greater emphasis on the economy than on the use of technology for innovation, improvement and strengthening of the learning process."

The next generation of e-learning according to (Lamandini 2009) is Web 2.0 and e-learning 2.0. "In Web 2.0 (Tim O'Reilly) the network is more interactive and dynamic, and users, more than technology, add value to the services offered by the network. Thanks to the participative architecture provided by new applications, each person can become an actor and author of content (content generated by the user or UGC), exchange and share (social networks), in accordance with participative methods and cooperation with the rest of the "community". The network becomes a place collective intelligence (P. Lévy), dispersed everywhere and constantly improved and the place of collective intelligence (D. De Kerckhove), which, privileged by connections, is activated in order to solve specific problems practically, multiplying knowledge and skills."

"New technologies facilitate communication and joint construction of new knowledge in communities and between different communities. This transformation of new ways of learning is characterized by innovative models of e-learning and the learning environment, which leads to the definition of e-learning 2.0 (Stephen Downes, 2004). It aims to regain the potential associated with spontaneous, informal (Bonaiuti, 2006) ways of using the network, both through individual learning and through building a network of experts, communities of interest that spontaneously aggregate to solve specific problems. The network becomes a training environment for the integration between formal and informal learning and is implemented by developing the concept of the *Personal Learning Environment or PLE* (Tosh and Wermuller, 2004, Wilson, 2005)." (Lamandini 2009).

Among contemporary trends and direction of development of e-learning the following can be distinguished: *Augmented and virtual reality, Artificial intelligence and learning assistance.*

- *Augmented Reality (AR):* Overlay of content (video, photo, sound, GPS data, etc.) onto the real world. Real world and overlaid content cannot interact with each other. (Dirksen, J., DiTommaso D., Plunkett, C. 2019.).
- *Virtual Reality (VR):* Simulates a world (real or imagined) and allows the user to interact in that world. (Dirksen, J., DiTommaso D., Plunkett, C. 2019.)
- *Artificial intelligence and learning assistance.* Timeline (figure 1) shows the evolution of the development of e-learning trend in the last decade.

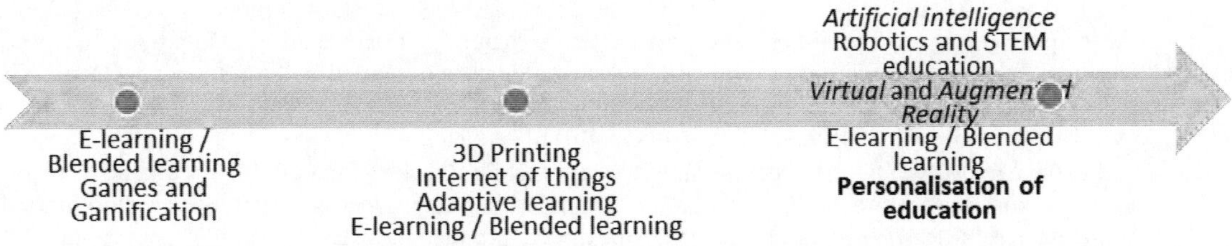

Figure 1. Timeline of the evolution of the development of the e-learning trend in the last decade

The final sentence of a Contemporary education is constantly innovating and adapting to new generations of students and to the fluctuating demands of the job market. Independent, collaborative and lifelong learning, self–regulation and high–order thinking skills are some of the dominant keywords for academic and professional achievement of the 21st century. The development of such competences requires an educational system that moves beyond the traditional delivery of content through the conventional lecture format. While active learning is far from being a novel concept in education, it is progressively being cited as a valuable method for the promotion of the abovementioned skills. It fosters student engagement, self–directed learning and student collaboration by requiring the students to take action in the classroom. Active learning can assume a variety of shapes and is, therefore, a method that can be interpreted by lecturers according to a wide range of definitions (Isaias, 2019, p. xiv).

3. ACTIVE TEACHING / LEARNING METHODS

J. Dewey and K.D. Ushinsky substantiated, from the point of view of psychology, the most important didactic principles of teaching education: visibility, systematic and consistent, thoroughness and strength of assimilation by students of educational material, a variety of methods of teaching, in particular active methods teaching and learning. In the conditions of global implementation and use of digital technologies, in particular in education, the conditions and possibilities of using teaching methods and didactics principles change.

Definitions of these contemporary active teaching / learning methods, which are more adequate and effective in conditions of digital tools support, include in particular:

- *Adaptive learning* - supported by confidence-based assessments and strong analytics and measurement of training effectiveness, is taking learning to the next level. LMSs are slowly gearing up to compete with platforms that are offering adaptive learning. (Kumar 2018). Aimed at individualisation and, to a certain degree, personalisation of learning, the so-called Intelligent Adaptive Learning (IAL) has been on the rise since the beginning of the 21st century. (Malach, Kostolányová, Chmura, Nagyová, Prextová, 2016: p. 29)
- *Microlearning* – It is a good method of implementing learning in small chunks that are objective-driven and can be easily and quickly deployed within organizations. Learners benefit too as they get through the modules quickly and can repeat the learning many times as well. Retention is better, and they are less fussy about going through a boring hour-long module. Microlearning can be implemented as videos, small games, quizzes, and infographics. The great advantage of microlearning is that it can be implemented on any device. (Kumar 2018).

– *Video- and Podcasts-based learning* - Videos are one of the hottest modes of training right now. The popularity of video-based sites like YouTube has forced organizations to adopt more videos into their training. Be it Instructor-Led Training that is interspersed with anecdotal or contextual videos, or eLearning where videos play an integral part in disseminating information, videos are here to stay. The focus is on decreasing the load time and the size of videos using various tools. Video-based learning will continue to grow and will be an important trend to watch out for in the year 2019 and beyond (Own research based on Key Elearning Trends for 2019. Origin Learning (Nov 6, 2018) and https://elearningindustry.com/elearning-trends-for-2019-8-top).
– *Problem–based learning* – is a teaching method in which complex real–world problems are used as a vehicle to promote student learning of concepts and principles as opposed to direct presentation of facts and concepts. In addition to course content, PBL can promote the development of critical thinking skills, problem–solving abilities, and communication skills. It can also provide opportunities for working in groups, finding and evaluating research materials, and life–long learning (Duch, Groh, Allen, 2001). In PBL, the teacher acts as a facilitator and mentor, rather than a source of "solutions." (Morze, Smyrnova–Trybulska, Gladun, 2018, p. 367)
– *Project–based learning* – has been defined as "a systematic teaching method that engages students in learning knowledge and skills through an extended inquiry process structured around complex, authentic (real–life) questions and carefully designed products and tasks" (English, Kitsantas, 2013: p.130). Similarly, problem based learning has been defined as an instructional method in which students learn through facilitated problem solving that centers on a complex problem that does not have a single correct answer (Hmelo–Silver, 2004; English, Kitsantas, 2013, p. 130).
– *App-based learning* – In particular, Mobile learning applications are quickly gaining momentum.
– *Digital Storytelling* – is the practice of combining narrative with digital content, included images, sound, and video, to create a short movie, typically with a strong emotional component (Educause, 2007). Digital storytelling is a good way to engage students in both traditional and innovative ways of telling a story. The students learn how to combine some basic multimedia tools such as graphics, animation, with skills such as research, writing, presentation, technology, interview, interpersonal, problem–solving, and assessment skills (Robin, 2005; Barrett, 2005; Signes 2010).
– *Flipped Classroom* – was born in the USA and functions there under the name flipped learning or flipped classroom. The originators of this way of learning were: Salman Khan (Khan Academy) and teachers: Jon Bergman and Aaron Sams, who set the main goal for students to be more active during classes at school. In contrast to the classic lesson during which the teacher's lecture dominates, while the students take notes, the FL method "flips" the lecture to students, thus reversing the time and manner of work (Kozik 2015: p.1). In Poland, this method was studied by K. Grzędowska, M. Rostkowska, among others, and implemented by A. Bogdańska, J.P. Sawiński (Smyrnova–Trybulska, 2018: p. 153–154).
– *Gamification and Game-Based Learning; Gamification* – Gamification is the process of using game elements, game mechanics, and game thinking to engage people, motivate action, promote learning, or solve problems. "Though commonly found in marketing strategies, it is now being implemented in educational programs as well to help educators to find the balance between achieving their objectives and catering to evolving student needs" (Dichev, Dicheva, Angelova, Agre, 2014, p.81). The problem is rooted in the traditional educational system that encourages extrinsic motivation. "Most people, although probably not completely aware of it, have experienced some type of gamification. People earn loyalty points for participating in the shopping program or a frequent flyer program. It is possible to download a fitness app for smartphone and been encouraged to create goals and track progress against those goals. People can try to improve their memory by participating in game like exercises on a regular basis. Elements of games outside of a traditional game environment motivate people to action. One way to understand gamification is to break down a familiar game into its components and elements, and mechanics, to see how these individual pieces can be applied outside of the game space" (Vygotsky, 1978).
– *Inquiry–based learning* - The term IBL is defined in several ways in the literature. First, it means the study of learning participants' interest in a topic in which they participated in social interaction for a common understanding [11; 15]. De Jong and W. Van Joolingen (1998) defined it as an educational strategy based on the discovery of knowledge that promotes active participation and responsibility of

the student. Pedaste and Sarapuu (2006) called IBL an approach by which students solve problems using their research skills. (Morze, Smyrnova–Trybulska, Gladun, 2018, p. 368)

And others such as Bite-sized learning, Blended learning; Case–based learning.

– Blended learning - Among modern teaching methods, combined learning or mixed (or blended learning) is a leader. According to the Sloan Consortium definition, education is considered mixed if between 20% and 80% of the classes are taught remotely. In this form, the educational process combines a focused process of developing knowledge and skills through the integration of academic and extracurricular activities and the educational process using traditional teaching-learning methods, using electronic technology and remote and mobile, ensuring student self-control regardless of time, place, method and pace of learning. (Smyrnova-Trybulska, 2018, p. 252)
– Collaborative learning - Collaborative learning is meant to benefit agents of education due to the fact that it could sharpen skills in collaboration (remote collaboration) as a process of cooperation to accomplish objectives by combining mutual efforts in the dialogue and interaction to eventually obtain results for all the participants of the process. Therefore, it is important to implement collaborative techniques for classroom (virtual classroom) instruction. Quality education is supposed to be promoted and facilitated by effective collaborative communication.(Morze, Pavlova, Makhahchashvili R., Smyrnova-Trybulska E., 2016: p. 195)

4. SOME EXAMPLES AND EXPERIENCE

The distance learning platform of The Faculty of Ethnology and Sciences of Education (WEiNoE) University of Silesia, which is coordinated and administered by the author of this article, is based on the LMS MOODLE system and serves, among other things, to:

– provide support for teaching programme courses, run in the full-time and part-time mode (hybrid learning),
– prepare future teachers to take advantage of distance learning – to use e-learning in their own profession and to perform the role of a tutor,
– provide assistance with academic research and pedagogical experiments carried out by department staff, graduate students as well as post-graduate students,
– provide access to educational materials for students, the local community and all other people interested, also for the disabled, people with financial limitations, residents from small and remote towns and other users in order to give all citizens the equal chance to have access to the knowledge, as one of the main priority aims of the European Community,
– ensure the implementation of the educational, scientific projects, strengthening of international cooperation

In 2009-2010 an international project “E-learning as a road to communicating in multicultural environments” was successful implemented with cooperation with Ostrava University (Czech Republic), Matej Bel University (Slovak Republic), co-financed by IVF (No 10920089). The international project “E-learning - as a Road to Communication in a Multicultural Environment” has successfully served the following purposes:

Popularization of E-learning in academic environments and among students through the organization of a 2-day conference (19-20.10.2009) entitled: "Theoretical and Practical Aspects of Distance Learning” with 97 participants (academic staff, teachers, students and others) and a workshop "Distance Course Design Using CLMS MOODLE” (20.10.2009) with 35 participants (as above). The participants of these activities were from all the above mentioned countries (Smyrnova-Trybulska, 2010: p. 162).

The major EU funded project pursued at the University of Silesia is called UPGOW (University as a Partner of Knowledge Economy). The project includes more than 40 reviewed open e-courses on various topics in different fields of study (http://el.us.edu.pl/upgow) with participation more then 35000 students. The author of the article contributed as a co-author and methodological consultant in preparing 11 distance learning courses, in which more than 7600 students took part from the University of Silesia and from outside organisations (Smyrnova-Trybulska, 2018: p. 361).

IRNet - *International Research Network for study and development of new tools and methods for advanced pedagogical science in the field of ICT instruments, e-learning and intercultural competences.* This project was financed by the European Commission under the 7th Framework Programme, within the Marie Curie Actions International Research Staff Exchange Scheme. Grant Agreement No: PIRSES-GA-2013-612536 Duration of the project: 48 months1/01/2014 – 31/12/2017. www.irnet.us.edu.pl . The coordinator is the University of Silesia, and author of the article. The IRNet project aims to establish a thematic multidisciplinary joint exchange programme dedicated to the development of new tools for advanced pedagogical science in the field of ICT instruments, distance learning and intercultural competences in the EU, Australia, Ukraine and Russia. The programme will strengthen existing collaboration between EU partners, and 3 third country institutions of higher education through mutual secondments of researchers. The concept of the project in more detail is described in the Project application and on the project web-site (www.irnet.us.edu.pl). One of the results of the project is MOOC "ICT tools for e-learning" which was successfully developed (http://el.us.edu.pl/irnet). The structure of the course includes:

1. E-learning in higher education
2. ICT-tools for presentation of content and Tools for making didactic video
3. Tools for adaptive learning. Learning Styles
4. Tools for mind maps and infographics knowledge
5. Gamification in education
6. Tools for communication and collaboration
7. Tools for formative assessment and control
8. Digital Storytelling
9. ICT-tools for developing Intercultural competences in e-learning
10. Social Presence and online tutoring

During the last 2 years more than 110 users have participated in this course. Soon a version in the Edex system will be prepared. This will help the project course to reach wider audiences.

4.1 E-Learning and University's Electronic Environment

The functioning of the university's electronic environment is considered at three levels: at the *micro* level (achievement of educational goals at the level of the discipline, e-course); *meso* (solution of scientific and educational problems in the corporate environment of the university - interdisciplinary communication, cooperation, exchange of experience, macro (achievement of scientific and educational goals by inclusion in the external scientific and educational environment.).

University strategies in the field of e-learning and ICT at various levels are signalled by:

• electronic scientific and educational resources;

• network communications in the scientific and educational environment;

• framework regulations and management of scientific and educational activities in the information and educational environment of universities. At the level of the micro- and university-level educational environment, personal competences are very important in choosing an effective learning strategy. The educational strategy in some cases determines educational environmental parameters. The student's approach to learning depends on the perception of the learning environment, which is defined as the characteristics of the environment (educational activities, resources, interactions) and personal characteristics (personal educational strategies) and learning styles (Kozielska, 2011; Kostolányová, 2013; Kostolányová, Šarmanová, Takács, 2011). In the study (Parra, Blanca, 2016) on the strategy of learning and styles as the basis for building personal learning environments (PLE), the authors formulated the conclusion that each person learns differently; their learning style strategies are influenced by the environment and resources in their possession. As a result, educational institutions can identify and share technological and pedagogical tools and strategies necessary to strengthen and build PLEs, which are more assertive and better adapted to the needs and interests of students (Parra, Blanca, 2016). (Smyrnova–Trybulska, 2018).

The concept of a Smart University in the context of global e-learning implementation includes several components:

- *Technologies* (e.g.: cloud computing technology, 3D visualization technology, Augmented Reality, Virtual Reality, Artificial intelligence and learning assistance);

– *Software systems* (e.g. Web-lecturing systems, Systems for seamless collaborative learning; *University system of study services (USOS)*);

– *Hardware/Equipment/devices* (e.g., Panoramic video cameras, SMART boards and/or interactive white boards, etc.)

– *Smart curricula* (e.g. Adaptive programs of study, Adaptive courses (with various types of teaching form: face-to-face, blended, online)

– *Students, lecturers, administration* (competent members of e-learning environment, advanced users, e.g.: Blended or fully Online, Life-long learners (retirees) in open education);

– *Smart pedagogy* (e.g. Collaborative teaching-learning, Learning-by-doing, Adaptive teaching-learning, Flipped classroom, Gamification, Problem-Based Learning, Project-Based Learning, Inquiry- Based Learning,);

– *Smart Classroom* (e.g. Smart classrooms with corresponding technologies. Software hardware systems. Smart pedagogy for smart education); (Smyrnova-Trybulska, 2018)

– *Open Source publication (*e.g., Repository (https://rebus.us.edu.pl), digital Library (www.ciniba.us.edu.pl), Bibliography of the work of the employee of the University of Silesia (http://biblio.bg.us.edu.pl/cgi-bin/wspd_cgi.sh/wo2_search.p?ID1=KIIMIPMINQBJHGQNBIHGEDCBR IN&ln=pl)

The University of Silesia e-learning platforms provide students with more than 8,000 hours of effective work (http://el.us.edu.pl), The Faculty has developed a distance learning platform for training and educational activities (http://el.us.edu.pl/weinoe). *Distance Learning Center* of the University of Silesia provides technical support, course administration and training for teaching staff and students.

5. CONCLUSION

We have already witnessed web 3.0 as the third phase of e-learning and network evolution, characterized by a semantic approach, personalized learning, use of artificial intelligence whereby applications will be able to respond to complex requests to obtain more meaning out of the current network of connections. To respond to complex demands, an evolutionary path to *artificial intelligence* is required that will lead the user to interact with the network in an *almost human* way. The contemporary educational institutions should be open and prepared for such challenges, comprehensive changes and evolution all components of informational and educational environment.

REFERENCES

Amberg, M., Reinhardt, M., Haushahn, M., & Hofmann, P., 2009. Designing an Integrated Web-based Personal Learning Environment based on the Crucial Success Factors of Social Networks. Research, Reflections and Innovations in Integrating ICT in Education, 1, 1075–1080.

Barrett, H. 2005. Storytelling in higher education: A theory of reflection on practice to support deep learning. Technology and Teacher Education Annual 2005. Charlottesville, VA: Association for the Advancement of Computing in Education, pp. 1878–1883. online: http://electronicportfolios.com/portfolios/ Kean.pdf

Bates, T. 2011. Understanding Web 2.0 and its Implications for E-Learning. Web 2.0-Based E- Learning: Applying Social Informatics for Tertiary Teaching, 21-42.

Benson, P. 2007. Autonomy and its role in learning. International Handbook of English Language Teaching pp. 733–745. Springer.

Dichev C., Dicheva D., Angelova G, Agre G., 2014 From Gamification to Gameful Design and Gameful Experience in Learning. Cybernetics and Information Technologies. Volume 14, No 4

Dirksen, J., DiTommaso D., Plunkett, C. 2019. *Augmented and Virtual Reality for Behavior Change* The eLearning Guild https://www.researchgate.net/publication/332763727_Augmented_and_Virtual_ Reality_for_ Behavior_Change

Downes, S. 2005. E-Learning 2.0. eLearn Magazine. Retrieved from http://www.elearnmag.org/ subpage.cfm?section=articles&article=29-1

Duch, B.J., Groh, S.E., Allen, D.E. 2001. Why Problem–Based Learning? A Case Study of Institutional Change in Undergraduate Education. In B. Duch, S. Groh, & D. Allen (Eds.). The Power of Problem–Based Learning pp.3–11. Sterling, VA: Stylus.

English, M. C., & Kitsantas, A. 2013. Supporting Student Self–Regulated Learning in Problem– and Project–Based Learning. Interdisciplinary Journal of Problem–Based Learning, 7(2). Available at: https://doi.org/10.7771/1541–5015.1339 https://docs.lib.purdue.edu/ijpbl/vol7/iss2/6/

Gregori Signes C. 2010 Practical uses of digital storytelling ResearchGate On–line: https://www.researchgate.net/publication/253907387_practical_uses_of_digital_storytelling

Hmelo–Silver, C. E. 2004. Problem based learning: What and how do students learn? Educational Psychology Review, 16(3), 235–266. http://dx.doi.org/10.1023/B: EDPR.0000034022.16470.f3

https://www.teachthought.com/pedagogy/a-primer-in-heutagogy-and-self-directed-learning/

Isaias P. 2019. Active learning in higher education: definition, design and evaluation In E–Society. Conference Proceedings, 17th International Conference e–Society, 11–13 April 2019, Utrecht, IADIS, p. xiv

Key Elearning Trends for 2019. Origin Learning (Nov 6, 2018) on-line https://medium.com/@Origin_Learning/key-elearning-trends-for-2019-541fdfbfa91a

Kozik B. 2015. Nauczyciel w świecie TIK. Cz. 5: Nauczanie odwrócone – Flipped Learning (FL). http://www.pbwnowysacz.pl/edc_user_data/ dat_files/cz.5_ nauczanie_odwrocone.pdf

Kumar S. DN, October 16, 2018. 8 Top eLearning Trends For 2019 https://elearningindustry.com/elearning-trends-for-2019-8-top

Lamandini A., 2009. L'evoluzione dell'e-learning ed e-learning in evoluzione. *Ricerche di Pedagogia e Didattica,* 4 (2009) – *Didattica e Nuove Tecnologie,* pp.1-15

Li, KC (Li, Kam Cheong), 2018. The evolution of open learning: A review of the transition from pre-e-learning to the era of e-learning. KNOWLEDGE MANAGEMENT & E-LEARNING-AN INTERNATIONAL JOURNAL. Volume: 10, Issue: 4, Pages: 408-425

Malach J., Kostolányová K., Chmura M., Nagyová I., Prextová T. 2016. Objectives and Content of E-module "Tools for Adaptive Learning. Learning Styles" within the MOOC Course "ICT Tools for E-learning" *International Journal of Research in E-learning* Vol. 2(1) 2016, pp. 28-40

Morze N., Smyrnova–Trybulska E., Gladun M., 2018. Selected Aspects of IBL in STEM–Education. In E.Smyrnova–Trybulska (ed.). E–learning and Smart Learning Environment for the Preparation of New Generation Specialists Vol. 10 (2018) Katowice–Cieszyn: Studio Noa for University of Silesia, pp. 361–379

Morze N., Pavlova H., Makhahchashvili R., Smyrnova-Trybulska E., 2016. Teacher-student collaboration: challenges and opportunities. In E. Smyrnova-Trybulska (ed.), *E-learning methodology - implementation and evaluation* (pp. 195-208). Katowice: Studio Noa for University of Silesia in Katowice

Raja Maznah, R. H. 2004. eLearning in Higher Education Institutions in Malaysia. E-mentor, 5(7), 72-75.

Reis A. 2007. Media Knowledge and Education, University of Innsbruck, INSB 978-3-902571-67-0

Reis A. 2010. E-Learning - the E-Volution In E.Smyrnova-Trybulska (ed.) *Use of E-learning in the Training of Professionals in the Knowledge Society*, Cieszyn: Studio Noa for University of Silesia, 2010, pp. 13-31

Reis, A. 2013. *How should we teach in the school of the future?* In E. Smyrnova-Trybulska (Ed.), E-learning & Lifelong Learning (pp. 13–38). Katowice–Cieszyn: Studio Noa for University of Silesia.

Robin, B. R. 2005. Online http://www.coe.uh.edu/digital–storytelling /introductiontroduction.htm

Smyrnova–Trybulska E., 2010. The International Educational Project "E-learning – as a Road to the Communication in a Multicultural Environment". In: J. Kapounova (Ed.) *ICTE 2010*, Conference Proceedings. 14–16 September 2010 (pp. 161–164). University of Ostrava, Rožnov pod Radhoštěm

Smyrnova–Trybulska E., 2018. Technologie informacyjno–komunikacyjne i e–learning we współczesnej edukacji. Katowice: Wydawnictwo Uniwersytetu Śląskiego w Katowicach

Sohrabi, B.; Vanani, Iraj. H., 2019. The evolution of e-learning practices at the University of Tehran: A case study, *Knowledge Management & E-Learning - an International Journal* Volume: 11, Issue: 1, Pages: 20-37

IMPACT OF EDUCATIONAL TECHNOLOGY ON STUDENTS' PERFORMANCE

Maryam Murad[1], Anjum Razzaque[2], Allam Hamdan[2] and Anji Benhamed[2]
[1]*Ministry of Education, Manama, Bahrain*
[2]*Ahlia University, Manama, Bahrain*

ABSTRACT

The current study is focused on the impact of educational technology on students' performance in the secondary stage. Selection of this stage is attributed to fact that it is impossible to focus on all the stages as there are about 130 thousand students in all stages which is a very big population. Also, students of universities who are about 31 can provide clearer and more accurate data. The sample was selected randomly with the electronic sample calculator showing that the minimum number is 380 individuals. The questionnaire was circulated electronically via university administration in the four governorates. The received responses were 342 indicating that the return rate is 90%. The researchers made use of the descriptive statistical analysis to answer the research questions. The data analysis processes guided the researchers to find out that universities effectively apply technology-based education both in terms of perceived ease of use and perceived usefulness as indicated by the mean scores. It was found out that there is a significant impact of technology-based education on students' performance. Further to that it was found out that technology-based education in terms of ease of use and in terms of perceived usefulness significantly impact students' performance in the Ahlia University.

KEYWORDS

Educational Technology, Students' Performance, Bahrain

1. BACKGROUND

There is an agreement that there is a significant increase in technology investments in the educational sector all over the entire world in the past two decades. The major assumption upon which the vast majority of these investments were made was that "technology-mediated learning environments positively contribute to create endless opportunities for learners to search, analyze, work out problematic issues, communicate other and work in teams" (Lim, et al., 2013). They are then equipped with a multiple competency that make themes much competitive as possible in the twenty first century marketplace. Nevertheless, it is perceived from the history of implementing technology in education that educators tend to abandon any type of technology that is not complaint with the social organization of schooling (Cuban, 2005). The recognized benefits of implementing technology in education created significant interest not only for researchers but governments and agencies responsible for funding as well. Great amounts of money were spent; particularly in Europe and the USA, hoping that integrating computers in the learning process can enable students improve their learning as well as minimizing the workload on instructors. It was found through research that several advancements were reached especially in intelligent tutoring, simulations, advanced learning management systems, automatic assessment systems and adaptive systems (Lim, et al., 2013). It was also found out that dependence on new technologies in education has significant effects on the educational outputs, especially in the field of student schooling. Since multimedia plays a powerful role as a vehicle for expanding learning in the process of educational training, it is being used widely to fulfill the education process in an easy and interesting way (Alroaini, 2012). Technology plays an important role in education. When it is applied properly, it can be a determining factor in influencing students' knowledge and learning (Lister, 2015). Some of the benefits of implementing technology in basic education include making learning more interactive and less boring. It improves students' attitudes towards knowledge and their interest in learning. In addition, technology provides opportunities for learning control as well as it can help students investigate and answer complex questions, develop new thinking skills, and access, evaluate, and synthesize information (Hanus & Fox, 2015). Furthermore, technology can help students set goals, form and test hypotheses. Technology also offers tools to share knowledge and learn in teams rather than individually. Moreover, education technologies make students more efficient and organized in their way of learning (Delgado, et al., 2015). Thanks to advances witnessed in the information technology, there is now what is known as M-learning (Mobile learning) in which the internet and smart phones are integrated in education. One way through which the internet and smart phones technology impact education and learning is through enabling instructors to enhance their formative assessment abilities (Higgins & Xiao, 2013). instructors grow more likely to assess their students' competencies and knowledge the instructional process. There are various programs and applications that enable instructors to immediate feedback during the formative assessment process, with the aim of improving students' performance (Elmahdi, et al., 2018). Given the uncertainties surrounding any change, education professionals always tend not to breach the status quo.

Thus, we are able to build the study hypotheses as follows:

Hypothesis 1. *There is a significant impact of users' perceived usefulness of technology-based education in Ahlia University on students' performance in the kingdom of Bahrain.*

Hypothesis 2. *There is a significant impact of ease of use of the technology-based education in Ahlia University on students' performance in the kingdom of Bahrain.*

In accordance to the literature review carried out by the researcher in this chapter, the following theoretical framework is suggested for the study. This theoretical model is suggested in light of the Technology Acceptance Model (TAM). It is a fact that several models occurred to interpret and enable researchers identify the basis of which users of any technological system accept it and how impacts those users. This included explaining user's acceptance of the new technologies introduced by the computer and the internet in the different fields of life such as: communication, marketing; e-learning; e-commerce and e-shopping. Technology Acceptance Model (TAM) has proved to be one of the most efficient models in that area.

It is assumed that Technology Acceptance Model (TAM) constitutes one of the most widely implemented models through which users of any system attitudes to accept or reject technology can be investigated. As matter of fact, such research presented verified empirical evidence for the effects of perceived ease-of-use and perceived usefulness and they both significant contribute to explain the online adaption intention (Majid, et al., 2016). TAM was initially introduced by Davis (1989) so that the computer usage behavior becomes an understandable thing. The model assumes that perceived usefulness and perceived ease-of-use do actually have influences on the acceptance attitudes of the individuals towards technology. It was indicated that such attitudes of technology users and intentions are influenced by perceived usefulness and perceived ease-of-use (Khatibi, et al., 2002).

2. STUDY SAMPLE

The population of the present research includes all the students of the secondary school's stage in the government schools in the four governorates of the kingdom of Bahrain. In accordance to the statistics of the ministry of education in Bahrain, there are 35 secondary schools including 31,519 students. The calculated sample size was 380 according to Roasoft electronic sample size calculator. Thus, 380 students were targeted in the secondary stage schools in the four governorates (Manama, Muharraq, the Southern, and the Northern). The questionnaires were sent to the students by what's app on their mobile phones by the school's administrations. The returned questionnaire responses to the researcher's Google account were 342. This means that the rate of the returned questionnaires is 90%.

3. IMPACT OF EDUCATIONAL TECHNOLOGY

This part is made up of two sub-sections where there are 24 items. The first section casts light on the status of technology-based education in terms of ease of use and includes 12 items while the second section casts light on technology-based education in terms of users' perceived usefulness and includes 12 items. Mean scores and standard deviations are used.

3.1 Impact of Educational Technology in Terms of ease of use

From the descriptive statistical analysis (see table 1) for the twelve items representing the status of technology-based education in terms of the perceived ease of use, it is evident that there are educational means applied in facilitating the educational processes in the secondary school stage in the kingdom of Bahrain. This is because the average mean score of is 3.08. Students perceive that they can use technology-based education by 61.6%. This is the relative weight of 3.08. And the average standard deviation is 1.30. The item that comes in the first rank is the 10th. Since its mean score is 3.86, this means that there is an agreement that "Applications and programs used in our classes are easily downloaded and are for free". The item that can be ranked in the 2nd place is the 12th since its mean score is 3.62. This means that there is an agreement that "All our courses, sample exams, and previous exam questions are all available for us online to train". The 1st item whose mean score is 3.58 comes in the 3rd rank. There is an agreement that "Classes are equipped with technological equipment as overhead projectors". The third item comes in the 4th rank as its mean score is 3.54. There is an agreement that "instructors prepare material that is presented on smart boards". Item seven comes in the 5th rank since its mean score is 3.40 indicating that there is an agreement that "We have easy access to moodle". The item that comes in rank 6 is the 11th since its mean score is 3.01. This means that the respondents are neutral towards the content stating "There are training sessions for making use of electronic facilities for better educational experiences". Items four whose mean score is 2.95 comes in rank 7 indicating that the respondents are neutral about the content stating that "Different educational programs and applications are easily used in classroom". The 9th item comes in the 8th rank as its mean score is 2.80. This also shows that the respondents are neutral about the content indicating "We are given the required assistance to make use of the available technologies to fulfil our tasks". The 8th item whose mean score is 2.74 comes in the 9th rank indicating the respondents are neutral about the content stating "instructors communicate us via moodle to inform us about projects, assignments, grades, and observation about our performance". The 5th item is the one that comes in the tenth rank as its mean score is 2.62 indicating the respondents are neutral about the content stating "We are given the opportunity to prepare presentations and projects online at university and at home". Item two comes in the 11th rank as its mean score is 2.49. This means that the respondents disagree that "Internet accessible is available at university". The items with the lowest mean score 2.39 is the 6th. This shows that the respondents disagree on the content showing that "Sometimes our homework assignments are placed on our pages on moodle".

Table 1. Impact of educational technology in terms of ease of use

	N	Mean	Std.	Interpretation	Rank
Classes are equipped with technological equipment as overhead projectors.	342	3.58	1.22	Agree	3
Internet accessible is available at university.	342	2.49	1.33	Disagree	11
instructors prepare material that is presented on smart boards.	342	3.54	1.31	Agree	4
Different educational programs and applications are easily used in classroom.	342	2.95	1.33	Neutral	7
We are given the opportunity to prepare presentations and projects online at university and at home.	342	2.62	1.23	Neutral	10
Sometimes our homework assignments are placed on our pages on moodle.	342	2.39	1.30	Disagree	12
We have easy access to moodle.	342	3.40	1.29	Agree	5
instructors communicate us via moodle to inform us about projects, assignments, grades, and observation about our performance.	342	2.74	1.28	Neutral	9
We are given the required assistance to make use of the available technologies to fulfil our tasks.	342	2.80	1.29	Neutral	8
Applications and programs used in our classes are easily downloaded and are for free.	342	3.86	1.35	Agree	1
There are training sessions for making use of electronic facilities for better educational experiences.	342	3.01	1.37	Neutral	6
All our courses, sample exams, and previous exam questions are all available for us online to train.	342	3.62	1.25	Agree	2

3.2 Impact of Educational Technology in Terms of Perceived Usefulness

Table 2. Impact of educational technology in terms of perceived usefulness

	N	Mean	Std.	Interpretation	Rank
Using education technology facility is an enjoyable thing.	342	2.93	1.456	Neutral	11
Lessons presented by smart board and PowerPoint presentations are more exciting than traditional lessons.	342	4.04	.932	Agree	4
There is a chance for gamification in our lessons which increase our attention for the lessons.	342	3.66	1.028	Agree	8
We finding participating in such technological activities is a useful thing.	342	3.18	1.138	Neutral	10
Doing our assignments online is more interactive.	342	3.50	1.092	Agree	9
Being assessed by applications as Kahoot and Flickers provides instant feedback about our understanding of the taught material.	342	3.99	.938	Agree	5
Being assessed online is a fantasy for us.	342	3.84	1.122	Agree	6
Participating in online games in class is more motivating.	342	2.56	1.309	Neutral	12
We feel enthusiastic and real challenge when we compete to win electronic games in the class.	342	3.74	1.019	Agree	7
Our instructors are available online when we are at home doing our assignments and provide us with remarks.	342	4.08	.935	Agree	2
We are allowed to create and innovate when we use technological facilities in our lessons.	342	4.15	.927	Agree	1
We are granted opportunities to think critically and reached creative solutions through electronic lessons.	342	4.07	1.051	Agree	3

From the descriptive statistical analysis (see table 2) for the twelve items representing the status of technology-based education in terms of the perceived usefulness, it is evident that students as users of the technology-educational means feel these technologies are useful for them. This is because the average mean score of is 3.62. Students perceive that technology-based education is useful by 72.4%. This is the relative weight of 3.62. And the average standard deviation is 1.07. The item that comes in the first rank is the 23rd item. Since its mean score is 4.15, this means that there is an agreement that "We are allowed to create and innovate when we use technological facilities in our lessons.". The item that can be ranked in the 2nd place is the 22nd since its mean score is 4.08. This means that there is an agreement that "Our instructors are available online when we are at home doing our assignments and provide us with remarks." The 24th item whose mean score is 4.07 comes in the 3rd rank. There is an agreement that "We are granted opportunities to think critically and reached creative solutions through electronic lessons". The 14th item comes in the 4th rank as its mean score is 4.04. There is an agreement that "Lessons presented by smart board and PowerPoint presentations are more exciting than traditional lessons". Item 18 comes in the 5th rank since its mean score is 3.99 indicating that there is an agreement that "Being assessed by applications as Kahoot and Flickers provides instant feedback about our understanding of the taught material". The item that comes in rank 6 is the 19th since its mean score is 3.84. This means that the respondents agree on the content stating "Being assessed online is a fantasy for us". Items 21 whose mean score is 3.74 comes in rank 7 indicating that the respondents agree on the content stating that "We feel enthusiastic and real challenge when we compete to win electronic games in the class.". The 15th item comes in the 8th rank as its mean score is 3.66. This shows that the respondents agree on the content indicating "There is a chance for gamification in our lessons which increase our attention for the lessons". The 17th item whose mean score is 3.50 comes in the 9th rank indicating the respondents agree on the content stating "Doing our assignments online is more interactive". The 16th item is the one that comes in the tenth rank as its mean score is 3.18 indicating the respondents are neutral about the content stating "We finding participating in such technological activities is a useful thing". Item 13 comes in the 11 thrank as its mean score is 2.93. This means that the respondents are neutral that "education technology facility is an enjoyable thing". The items with the lowest mean score 2.56 is the 20th. This shows that the respondents are neutral on the content showing that "Participating in online games in class is more motivating".

3.3 Descriptive Statistics for Impact of Students' Performance

This part is made up of three sub-sections where there are 17 items. The first section casts light on the status of students' performance in terms of participation and includes 7 items, the second section casts light on students' performance in terms of oral representations and includes 6 items, and the third section casts light on students' performance in terms of written work. Mean scores and standard deviations are used.

3.3.1 Descriptive Statistics for Impact of Students' Performance in Terms of Participation

Identifying the status of students' performance in the Ahlia University in Bahrain (table 3) shows that students are neutral about their performance level in terms of participation. Thus, it can be concluded that their level of performance in terms of participation is average as the percentage is 63.4%. The item with the highest mean amongst all the seven of this sub-section is the 25th since its mean score is 3.95. This shows that there is an agreement that "We contribute effectively in classroom tasks". The 29th item comes in the 2nd rank as its mean score is 3.50. Thus, there is an agreement that "We demonstrate knowledge gained from the presented material". Item 28 comes in the 3rd rank since its mean score is 3.47. Thus, there is an agreement that "We provide creative solutions for questions". The 26th item comes in the 4th rank as its mean score is 3.20 showing the respondents are neutral about the content stating "We prepare material to be presented in class". The 31st item comes in the 5th rank as its mean score is 2.80. Thus, the respondents are neutral about the content stating "We remain focused throughout the class time". The 30th item comes in the 7th rank as its mean score is 2.74 indicating the respondents are neutral about "We are able to communicate with our classmates or instructors effectively whether we work in groups, pairs, or individually". The item with the lowest mean score 2.58 is the 27th as its mean score is 2.58 indicating that the respondents are neutral about the content stating that "We work in groups effectively where everyone has a specific mission".

Table 3. Impact of Students' Performance in Terms of Participation

	N	Mean	Std.	Interpretation	Rank
We contribute effectively in classroom tasks.	342	3.95	1.049	Agree	1
We prepare material to be presented in class.	342	3.20	1.186	Neutral	4
We work in groups effectively where everyone has a specific mission.	342	2.58	1.341		7
We provide creative solutions for questions.	342	3.47	1.280	Agree	3
We demonstrate knowledge gained from the presented material.	342	3.50	1.069	Agree	2
We are able to communicate with our classmates or instructors effectively whether we work in groups, pairs, or individually	342	2.74	1.287	Neutral	6
We remain focused throughout the class time.	342	2.80	1.295	Neutral	5

3.3.2 Hypotheses Testing and Discussion

In accordance to the outcomes of the Pearson's correlation test (table 4) between technology-based education in terms of the perceived ease of use and perceived usefulness (independent variable) and students' performance (dependent variable), it is found out that the Pearson correlation value between technology-based education in terms of perceived ease of use is 0.707 which is a high and significant correlation value indicating that technology-based education in terms of perceived ease is correlated with students' performance at the level 0.01 as the sig. is 0.00 ≥0.01 where both of them impact each other negatively and positively. likewise, the Pearson correlation value between technology-based education in terms of perceived usefulness is 0.582 ** which is a high and significant correlation value indicating that technology-based education in terms of perceived usefulness is correlated with students' performance at the level 0.01 as the sig. is 0.00 ≥0.01 where both of them impact each other negatively and positively.

Table 4. Pearson's Correlation test

		Perceived ease of use	Perceived usefulness	Students' performance
Perceived ease	Pearson Correlation	1		
of use.	Sig.			
Perceived	Pearson Correlation	.413**	1	
usefulness.	Sig.	.000		
Students'	Pearson Correlation	.707**	.582**	1
performance	Sig.	.000	.000	

**. Correlation is significant at the 0.01 level (2-tailed).

As a result of the data analysis process that has just been carried out through this chapter, the researcher was able to reach a number of findings that are worth given due attention and being discussed for the purpose of more clarity for the audience of the study. The data analysis shows that technology-based education is given attention in the Ahlia University in the kingdom of Bahrain. Employing technology is the domain of teaching and learning is being adopted in terms of the devices being used and the applications and programs that are applied by the instructors. In accordance to the findings, Ahlia University equips classes and university with different types of technological sets such as overhead projectors, smartboards, and instructors use their own laptops and or the university. Making use of smartboards and overhead projectors create more fund within the class and motivates students to pay too much attention. instructors present their lessons in a virtual manner where there are sound effects, visual effects, and other technological effects that bring students to be part of the lesson. Some funny videos may add more excitement and enthusiasm to students (Al–Ammary, 2012). One of the most important, and accessible programs in Ahlia University in Bahrain depend on moodle through which students are linked with their instructors at university and at home. The students assured that all their courses, sample exams, and previous exam questions are available for them online on moodle in order to follow and train. Instructors place assignments, project requirements, grades, notices, etc. for the students on moodle. instructors play the most important role in facilitating students' usage of the technological aspects in the teaching and learning process (Majid, et al., 2016). For example, they are committed to prepare material that is presented on smart boards. They train students on making use of technology in learning. They are also committed to encouraging students to use moodle. Thus, it is concluded that students of the Ahlia University in Bahrain perceive that there is a good level of ease of use of technology in education in Bahrain. These findings go along with the outcomes of the study of (Razzaque, 2016). Making use of technology in learning and teaching in the Ahlia University in Bahrain has been proved to be of perceived usefulness. This is attributed to a number of factors. The first of which is that students are allowed to create and innovate when they use technological facilities in their lessons. The contribution of technology to innovation and creativity is something assured through prior research. Students are given opportunities to innovate and create when they prepare materials to be presented in class especially in subjects as science and math. This is proved to be compliant with the outcomes of the study of (Xu, et al., 2011). Another thing is that when instructors and students are connected through internet applications as moodle of the Ahlia University in Bahrain, instructors are available online when the students are at home doing our assignments and provide them with remarks. This is consistent with the findings of (Backåberg, 2016). One of the most perceived fruits harvested from the implementation of technology in education is that student are granted opportunities to think critically and reached creative solutions through electronic lessons. Further to that, technology-based education where instructors present their lessons via smart board and PowerPoint are more exciting than traditional lessons. Moreover, incorporating technology in education helped instructors to integrate more tools for the assessment process (Bates & Martin, 2013). One method is the usage of internet applications as Kahoot and Flickers and Socrative where the students are provided with instant feedback about their understanding of the taught material. Making use of internet-based formative assessment is currently one of the most enjoyable means that eliminated fear from being assessed and brought more fun to the assessment process students can be assessed individually, in pairs, or in groups. The students assure that being assessed online is a fantasy for them. They feel enthusiastic and real challenge when they compete to win electronic games in the class. There is a chance for gamification in their lessons which increases their attention for the lessons. Gamification is a recent issue whose positive impacts are well perceived on the processes of teaching and learning (Hanus & Fox, 2015). Interactivity is very significant thing that is too much assured through the usage of technology in education these days. Students assure that doing their assignments online is more interactive. When students interact with each other and with their pairs at university and even at home when doing assignments on moodle they learn better and get highly motivated (Graham, 2012). Performance is actually one of the most ambiguous concepts especially when it is related to performance in relation to teaching and learning. Prior research assured that performance can be measured in different manners. When students are meant, it is better to measure it in terms of their participation in the class, their oral representation, and their written work. For one thing, students' performance in the Ahlia University in Bahrain is found to be effective in terms of students' classroom participation. They assure that they contribute effectively in their classroom tasks. They grow more likely to demonstrate knowledge gained from the presented material. When technology is applied in class, students' opportunities to gain knowledge increase as they can easily search the internet, their tables, etc to gain knowledge. When they are equipped with the essential tools, their ability to provide creative solutions for questions is maximized. This is compliant with the findings of (Al–Ammary, 2012). Students are allowed to prepare material to be presented in class. This is an evidence that when technology is applied, they are given opportunities to increase their self-dependence. This may be opposed to what was concluded by (Stakkestad & Størdal , 2017). Inconsequence the students remain focused throughout the class time. In addition, they are able to communicate with their classmates or instructors effectively whether they work in groups, pairs, or individually. The students work in groups effectively where everyone has a specific mission. Participation is a very important indicator for student's attentiveness and positive existence within the class. This is actually achieved in a more effective manner when technological means are applied in the class as the students find the class a more enjoyable area. When it comes to students' performance in terms of oral representation, their performance level is good they have opportunities to play roles and present everyday life situations clearly. This of course can take place via recorded videos. Sometimes instructors ask students to act videos representing some lessons or some of their classroom situations. In addition, students can make use of audio-visual aids presented in class to enhance their oral presentation abilities. This directly supports their abilities to analyze situations and provide recommendations. Using the internet maximizes their ability to do thorough research and respond when particular answers are required. Their ability to express their points of view clearly is enhanced. This is compliant with the findings of the research presented by (Bates & Martin, 2013). Students' performance in terms of written work is found to be effective. The students participate on online games to assess their performance in a written manner. They are more likely to produce lengthy essays about specific topics.

4. CONCLUSION

It can be concluding that technology has become an additional common feature of education globally, over the past twenty years, and Bahrain is not an exception. Indeed, the kingdom has turned more and more towards the implementation of technology-based education. The results of testing the study hypothesis of the study show that there is a significant positive relationship between Educational Technology and students' performance. The results also show that there is Ahlia University that predominantly working with emerging technologies. However, instructors, classrooms, etc. are improvised although there is a quality or quantity of resources. In Bahrain, Educational technology has evolved as a teaching tool, then as a learning aid, and finally as a systems approach. instructors are responsible and committed to find innovative ways to generate improved learning situations for the students. The findings of the study can be used as a basis for future research about the relationship e-learning and effective educational outcomes.

REFERENCES

Acaps, 2012. Qualitative and Quantitative Research Techniques for Humanitarian Needs Assessment an Introductory Brief, s.l.: ACAPS.

Al–Ammary, J., 2012. Educational Technology: A Way to Enhance Student Achievement at The University Of Bahrain. The Online Journal of New Horizons in Education, 3(3), pp. 45-54.

AlNoaimi, H., 2018. The Impact of Person-Organization Fit on Employee Retention: The Case of Ministry of Education in Bahrain A dissertation in partial fulfilment of the requirements for the degree of master of business administration, Manama: cAhlia University, college of business and finance.

Alroaini, S., 2012. The impact of using multimedia on students' academic achievement in the College of Education at King Saud University. Journal of King Saud University - Languages and Translation, 24(2), pp. 75-82.

Arukaroon, B. & Krairti, D., 2017. Impact of ICT usage in primary -schoosl students: learning in the case of Thailand. International Journal of web-based learning and tecahing technologies, 12(2), pp. 21-42.

Backåberg, S., 2016. Video-supported Interactive Learning for Movement Awareness – a learning model for the individual development of movement performance among nursing students, s.l.: s.n.

Baran, E., 2014. A Review of Research on Mobile Learning in Teacher Education. Educational Technology & Society, 17(4), pp. 17-3.

Bates, C. & Martin, A., 2013. Using mobile technology to support literacy coaching practices. Journal of Digital Learning in Teacher Education, 30(2), p. 60–66.

Brains, C., Willnat, L., Manheim, J. & Rich, R., 2011. Empirical Political Analysis 8th edition. Boston, MA: Longman.

Bryman, A. & Bell, E., 2015. Business Research Methods. 4th ed. Oxford: Oxford University Press.

Bryman, A. & Bell, E., 2015. Business Research Methods" 4th edition, s.l.: Oxford University Press.

Buisness Dictionary, 2017. Definition of Performance. [Online]

Business Dictionay, 2015. Definition of Independnet Variable. [Online]

Cochrane, T., 2012. Critical success factors for transforming pedagogy with mobile Web 2.0. British Journal of Educational Technology, 45(1), p. 65–82.

Cohen, J. et al., 2013. Listening to an educational podcast while walking or jogging: Can students really multitask. International Journal of Mobile and Blended Learning, 3(3), pp. 23-33.

Creswell, J., 2012. Educational research: Planning, conducting, and evaluating quantitative and qualitative research. Upper Saddle River, NJ: Prentice Hall.

Cronbach, L., 1990. Essentials of psychological testing. New York.: Harper & Row.

Cuban, L., 2005. The blackboard and the bottom line: Why schools can't be businesses. Cambridge, MA: Harvard University Press.

Dahmani, M., 2013. The Impact of ICT on Student Performance in Higher Education: Direct Effects, Indirect Effects and. RUSC, s.l.: Revista de Universidad y Sociedad del Conocimiento.

Delgado, A. J., Wardlow, L., McKnight, K. & O'Malley, K., 2015. Educational technology: A review of the integration, resources, and effectiveness of technology in K -12 classrooms. Journal of Information Technology Education: Research, Volume 14, pp. 397 -416.

DJS Research, 2014. What is Causal Research?. Market Research World: s.n.

Dugger, J., William, E. & Naik, N., 2001. Clarifying Misconceptions between Technology Education and Educational Technology. Technology Teacher, 61(1), p. 31–35.

Education & training Quality Authority, 2018. Schools Review Reports, Manama: ETQA.

Elmahdi, I., Al-Hattami, A. & Fawzia, H., 2018. Using Technology for Formative Assessment to Improve Students' Learning. Turkish Online Journal of Educational Technology, 17(2), pp. 182-188.

Flanagan, A., 2008. Technology: The Positive and Negative Effects on Student Achievement, New York: The College at Brockport: State University of New York.

Freedman, D., 2009. Statistical Models: Theory and Practice. s.l.: Cambridge University Press.

DESIGN AND IMPLEMENTATION OF AN ENGLISH LESSON BASED ON HANDWRITING RECOGNITION AND AUGMENTED REALITY IN PRIMARY SCHOOL

Junyan Xu, Sining He, Haozhe Jiang, Yang Yang and Su Cai
Beijing Normal University
No. 19, XinJieKouWai St., HaiDian District, Beijing 100875, P. R. China

ABSTRACT

In recent years, the development of mobile technology and devices makes Artificial Intelligence (AI) and Augmented Reality (AR) available tools in classroom teaching and learning. AI and AR are used to improve the learning effect as well as motivate the students' learning enthusiasm. In English as a second language (ESL) learning, several previous studies show the potential advantages of the usage of AI and AR. In this study, an English learning lesson with a mobile based handwriting recognition and AR application was designed and implemented in primary school lower grade. A series of class activities using the application as teaching tool are developed. The aim of this research is to find out the effect of the possible effect of AR application in practical English class and the influence of it on the pupils. Pre-post test and face-to-face interview are made and they show that there are some advantages the usage of the application has led to both teacher and students. Handwriting recognition-based AR application in ESL could motivate the students to pay more attention to the class and improve their learning enthusiasm.

KEYWORDS

Artificial Intelligence, Augmented Reality, English as Second Language, ESL

1. INTRODUCTION

The 21st century is a global century. With the development of Transportation Technology and communication technology, international cultural exchanges are deepening, and the international flow of talents is becoming more frequent. To make our education responsive to the needs of such an era of globalization, learning English has gradually become a compulsory part of the basic education , which has become the most widely used language in the world and an international communication tool.

However, in the filed of English teaching and learning in primary school, especially vocabulary teaching, still has many common problems. According to a questionnaire survey conducted by Shandong Normal University's Liu Youai, there are many common problems in the field of English teaching in primary schools, such as the teaching methods demand more diversity, the content of the textbooks go against the students' developing process, the lack of guidance of students' independent learning, and the low utilization of the existing teaching equipment, especially the high-tech teaching equipment. From the students' point of view, the problems in teachers' teaching lead to the students' poor autonomous learning ability and lack of interest in word learning.

In recent years, augmented reality (AR) and artificial intelligence (AI) have been widely used in education, and more and more courses and teaching have been designed based on AR and AI technology. In May 2019, the UNESCO organized the International Conference on Artificial Intelligence and Education to study emerging artificial intelligence technologies and innovative practices in the application of artificial intelligence (AI) in education. It shows that the application of AI in education has become a common topic of reflection and practice in the global education. He, Ren, Zhu, Cai and Chen (2014) have designed the "happy words" software based on mobile smart platforms such as smart phones and tablets. The software scans the word cards with the camera, and when it does, it displays a 3D model of the words on the screen and plays back the speech. The results show that this augmented reality-based approach can increase learners' interest in learning English spelling and reading aloud, and improve their learning effectiveness. Cai in the "augmented reality (Ar) in the teaching of the application of case review" in which a summary of the existing courses based on augmented reality technology design, this paper empirically found, there was a positive correlation between students' learning attitude and the use of AR Teaching(Cai et al.,2017).

Many studies and projects have proved that using AR in education could improve students' English learning and teachers' teaching. So, to deal with the common problems in the field of English learning in the primary schools in China, we plan to design and implement a mobile-base handwriting recognition AR application, which can motivate students in ESL lesson learning and integrate technology with classroom teaching deeply.

2. RELATED WORKS

2.1 AR in Education

In recent years, Augmented Reality (also known as AR) has gradually entered people's daily life and caused widespread concern. As the smart phones becoming more and more capable for AR operation and AR devices becoming more and more affordable, mobile-based AR has been applied in many fields. Since the very beginning of AR, many teachers and scholars have paid great attention to this emerging technology especially with its further application in education(Akçayır & Akçayır, 2017). AR has great potential for learning activities because of its rich visual presentations and various user interaction(Cai, Chiang, Sun, Lin, & Lee, 2017), and teachers show their interests and willingness in using AR. Evidences show that AR has the ability to work on students' practical skills and conceptual understanding, as well as be able to support inquiry activities(Cheng & Tsai, 2013). Primary school students would have better performance in motivation, confidence and related dimension by using of AR in learning activities(Chiang, Yang, & Hwang, 2014; Han, Jo, Hyun, & So, 2015; Lu & Liu, 2015). So that AR has been regarded as a revolutionary solution of some teaching difficulties, like teaching of abstract concepts(Crandall et al., 2015).

In recent years, several AR projects were mainly used to teach the meaning and pronunciation of words. For instance, an AR application, named Leihoa, help pre-school children to remember some basic vocabulary when they take exploration activities. Study shows that children would be enthusiasm when extra audios presented with AR. There were also some researchers taking notice of promoting learners to interact with special labels or the AR system. AR would present vivid 3D model for learners to have deeper memories when studying the same word in different language through MOW, learners needed to match word card and national flag card or meaning card accurately. Almost of these studies also showed AR's effects on improve students' motivation, satisfaction or attention.

Further researches later confirmed AR's effectiveness in teaching children and attempted to use AR in higher education to improve learners' language skills. An experimental research study scrutinized the effectiveness of using augmented reality applications as a teaching and learning tool when instructing kindergarten children in the English alphabet in the State of Kuwait(Safar, Al-Jafar, & Al-Yousefi, 2017). In a study Richardson (Richardson, 2016) used location-based mobile AR games creatively and proved that AR could be used to arrange tasks for advanced level language learners to improve their motivation and learning performance. In Yang and Mei's research(S. Yang & Mei, 2018) shows that afforded by the AR programming learners could had positive perception and attitude towards the immersive language learning experience.

In summary, previous studies have proved that AR used in EFL learning was able to ensure better attitude and performance through more interesting activities or immersive experiences. Therefore, we hope in our study, we could use our AR application as an efficient learning and teaching tool, to forward prove the previous researches' results, and to help improving the second language acquisition in the school's formal lessons.

2.2 AI in Education

Artificial Intelligence including pattern recognition, deep learning, machine learning, data mining and intelligent algorithm, etc. In our project, the main application of artificial intelligence is using Optical character recognition or optical character reader, often abbreviated as OCR to scan and recognize the words on the card. We want to use handwriting recognition AR in English as a foreign/second language (also known as ESL) learning field of China.

With many studies proving that AR could help with the teaching of Mathematics or physics courses, we believe that AR has potential in ESL learning especially when combined with AI text recognition. Christos Troussas and others present a fully operating and evaluated adaptive and intelligent e-learning system for second language acquisition. This system uses a hybrid model for misconception detection and identification (MDI) and an inference system for the dynamic delivery of the learning and the results of the study are very encouraging and promising since they reveal that the hybrid model for misconception detection and identification and the inference system operate collaboratively and enhance the adaptivity of the students' needs and preferences objects tailored to learners' needs. (Troussas et al., 2019)

And Yang in his paper gives us a good conclusion of the application of the AI in the ESL field. He summarizes that with a wide variety of meaningful and interesting AI, giving learners easier access to the tools can help them develop their language skills. This AI technology can provide learners with more opportunities for interaction beyond the restriction from time and locations. It is hoped that language learning can be more fun and more efficient(S.-h. Yang, 2007).

In summary, previous studies have proved that AI could be apply to the education field, especially in the second language acquisition to make the language learning more interesting and efficient. In this study, we are going to use the handwriting recognition to develop a mobile-based application as a teaching and learning tool to make the English class more efficient in primary school.

3. DESIGN

The core goal of this study is to design and implement a mobile-base handwriting recognition AR application, which can motivate students in ESL lesson learning and integrate technology with classroom teaching deeply.

We designed a 40-minute class with handwriting recognition AR application which played as an exploring tool role in the class for lower-grade pupils in the primary school in China. We collected multi-dimensional data including the effect of the application and the attitude toward it, from teacher and students' point of view.

3.1 Instructional Design

In this study, several learning activities with the mobile-base handwriting recognition AR application were designed for the lesson named "Can you tell me the way to...?". In this lesson, every group students had two tablets, so they could cooperate to learn with the handwriting recognition AR application.

The basic goal of this lesson is to memorize the words about position and distinguish direction in English. Beside that, reading and speaking activities were devised to make students to communicate with partners practicing the words and sentences they learnt. Based on the basic space imagination, facts about buildings were also mentioned to help students understand the function and structure of buildings.

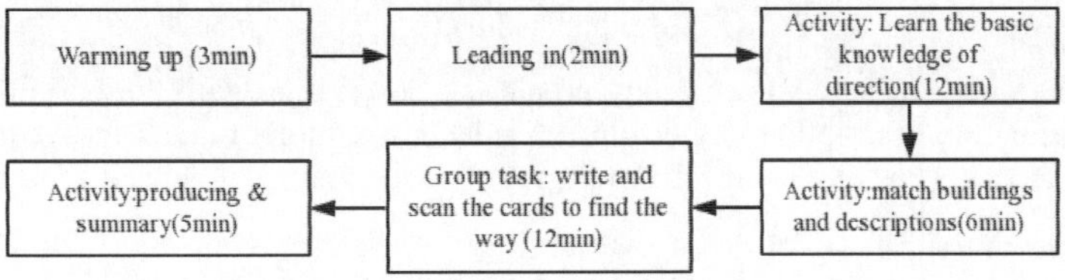

Figure 1. Structure of lesson

Figure 1 presents the basic structure. Warming up and leading in occupied the first 5 minutes of the lesson. The instructor drew out the topic through a short introduction and a flash animation.

Next the students learnt the basic knowledge of direction. In this section, several mini games involving teacher and students were designed. Under the teacher's instructions, the students work together to find the right locations in the classroom.

Then the route scope extended. Students were asked to place several buildings to their corresponding places on the map. First, the students needed to be familiar with the buildings. They were asked to match the buildings with their functions on the tablet which displayed the fundamental knowledge about the buildings. After that, they began to explore and find the way to different buildings. Due to the difficulty of this task, students would cooperate with their group mates. One student named A wrote and arranged the cards while his or her partner named B taking the tablet's camera to capture them. Student B could see the route to the corresponding building and he or she needed to retell student A what he or she have read. According to student B's guidance, student A placed the buildings to their appropriate places on the map. After 10 minutes, the instructor led the class to find the right locations together while the students could check whether their match was right and corrected their own mistakes.

In the last part of this lesson, the instructor summarize the key points and help students to review the basic descriptions about the buildings and fundamental knowledge of direction by interactive games.

3.2 Augmented Reality Application Design

There are two main features in this mobile-based handwriting recognition AR application Way to the Buildings. It could run on both iOS and Android devices with good portability. To provide assistant for the different parts of the lesson, Way to the Building contains two separate features: (1) Buildings and descriptions matching and (2) Finding the way. These features are designed and implemented to make the activities in instructional design more vivid and interactive. The new way of presenting and examining knowledge were used to develop the student's learning enthusiasm.

This application was developed based on the Unity 3D engine. To realizing the function of Artificial Intelligence text recognition and building the Augmented Reality scenes, Vuforia SDK was used.

3.2.1 Buildings and Descriptions Matching

In this feature, students were asked to match the specific building with the description of each of them. For instance, the students should pair the description: "You can go here to buy medicine and you can also buy some food and drinks here." with the model of drugstore. In this part, students were asked to pair all the nine buildings with their description by dragging the models to the correct place.

Figure 2. Matching buildings and descriptions

As shown in Figure 2, if students correctly match the description with the building model, the building would be fixed below the description in the frame. Students would get the instant feedback during the whole tasks completing process. Positive feedback would appear once they completed all the nine pairing tasks.

3.2.2 Finding the Way

In this stage of learning activities, the application and physical teaching tools (paper map, word cards etc.) are used synergistically. By scanning the word cards by tablet, students could get the position information of each building. For example, when scanning the card "hospital", the corresponding location information will be displayed on the screen: " Please walk on, and then turn right at the first corner. It's on your right." Combining with the paper map which showed the start points, students could infer the location of the buildings and attach the word card to the paper map. Applying the handwriting recognition technology, no special card which is necessary for traditional AR application is needed. All the word cards provided for the students can be print in nearly any typeface even hand-writing. Students can also write the word themselves at any time.

In this feature, students can also interact with the building model. By gesture on the screen, the building models can be rotated and zoomed. After scanning the word card, the application will provide the word pronunciation for the students automatically. Moreover, by simple touch at the model, students could listen to the pronunciation again if they want.

3.3 Participants and Research Design

Students of two parallel classes in the 4th Grade took part in this study, 35 of them divided into the experimental group and 32 into the control group. The experimental group cooperated to learn with handwriting recognition AR application as shown in Figure 3, while the control group learning by analyzing the materials and discussing with the group instead.

Figure 3. Cooperating in groups

For those students, English is their second language. They began to learn English in 1st grade in common. In the primary school level, the main goal of learning English is to enlarge the vocabulary and exalt the communication ability. This study paid attention to not only the learning of English but also the ability in communication in second language and cooperating.

A pretest- posttest control group study design was utilized for data collection to infer the learning performance with and without handwriting recognition AR. And after this lesson, both interviews and questionnaire surveys were conducted with the teacher and students to learn their view towards teaching and learning with handwriting recognition AR. Then a statistical analysis was made of the results.

4. RESULT

4.1 Performance Through Test Analysis

First, we examined the effectiveness of the performance test to ensure whether students could benefit from this learning approach. The inter-rater reliability of the ratings given by the two teachers was 0.745, showing high consistency. The full mark of the test is 12 points.

A paired sample t test was conducted first to compare scores of the experimental group. Table 1 shows the result. The posttest scores ($M = 7.23$, $SD = 3.19$) were higher than the pretest scores ($M = 5.26$, $SD = 3.00$), and the p-value(two-tailed) is of the mean is close to zero($t = -4.87$, $p < .01$). When the significance level is 0.01, we can draw to the result that students' scores with handwriting recognition AR application are significantly higher than those attained before the learning activity. As a conclusion, application has a statistically significant improvement in English learning and students' averages scores increased by 1.97 points.

Table 1. Paired t-test for pre-test and post-test score variables.

	Paired differences			t	df	Sig (2-tailed)
	Mean	Std. deviation	Std. error mean			
Post-test score –pre-test score	-1.971	2.395	.405	-4.870	34	.000

In addition, the posttest data collected from two groups were analyzed with independent samples t test. The descriptive statistics obtained are shown in Table 2. In the table, we can observe that the mean score of the experimental group(M = 7.23, SD = 3.19) is higher than that of the control group (M = 6.03, SD = 2.80), though the two groups do not have significant differences. According to the data, we conclude that with other unobserved variables controlled, the handwriting recognition AR learning tool has an improvement on the score of the performance test, and the difference is1.20 points.

Table 2. Independent t-test for the experimental group and the control group

		Levene's Test for Equality of Variances		t-test for Equality of Means				
		F	Sig.	t	df	df Sig. (2-tailed)	Mean Difference	Std. Error Difference
score	Equal variances assumed	1.307	.257	1.090	65	.280	1.426	1.308
	Equal variances not assumed			1.093	64.963	.278	1.426	1.304

4.2 Attitude Through Questionnaire Analysis

We calculated the score of each construct by averaging all of the corresponding items within each construct through analyzing the questionnaire. Table 3 shows the result. The value of the "Learning Attitude with handwriting recognition AR application" construct(M = 14.77, SD = 3.57) is significantly higher than that of the "Learning Attitude"(M = 11.57, SD =2.71; t = -7.52, p < .01), which suggests that the application could attract and intrigue the students.

Table 3. Paired t-test for attitude

	Paired differences			t	df	Sig (2-tailed)
	Mean	Std. deviation	Std. error mean			
without app-with app	-3.200	2.518	.426	-7.518	34	.000

Furthermore, the descriptive statistics of each item in "Learning Attitude with handwriting recognition AR application" construct are as fellowing. The statement "I like learning English with handwriting recognition AR- based learning tool " has the highest value, which equals to the full mark, suggesting the application can enhance the students' interest and enthusiasm of English learning greatly. "I like reciting the English words using handwriting recognition AR." and "I think English class is interesting with handwriting recognition AR-based learning tools." both have a score of 4.89 , which is very close to full mark, indicating that most students consider the application is a good tool to recite words and makes the English class more enjoyable.

4.3 Attitude through Interview Analysis

After the class, we took both paper based post-test and face-to-face interviews with teacher and several students. All the feedback and data could help us to ensure the usability and acceptance of this handwriting recognition AR application, from both knowledge skills and emotional attitudes.

4.3.1 Interview with the Teacher

In the interview with the teacher who acts as the instructor of the English lesson, our question mainly focus on the role AI and AR playing in the class and the advantages and flaws of them when applied to real class learning situation. The teacher took part in the design and improvement process when developing the application. The basic features in the application are designed for the activities in the lesson.

The first question of the interview is "Do you think this kind of application is helpful for the teaching process?". The teacher did not hesitate to give a positive answer. She mentioned that the AR and AI technology merge reality and virtual together and give students new learning experience which bring them closer to the knowledge. The teacher said, "this kind of 3-dimension and interactive design can lead the teaching method to a more realistic level with lower cost compared to going out for a visit or using Virtual Reality devices." Indeed, our handwriting recognition AR application need only normal mobile device instead of some professional equipment like VR headset. And the application can better support the learning process for students which allow them to share their findings by using the tablet together instead of only operate them individually. This feature can also enhance the cooperation among the students.

When we asking about the effect of handwriting recognition AR in classroom, the keyword that the teacher mentioned is "interest". The teacher claimed that the students showed strong interest in the parts which based on the application and finished their tasks more concentratedly. "I find that students pay more attention to not only the instruction I've gave but also the tasks they were asked to achieve. Great interest lead them make better performance in the class, both tasks completing quality and enthusiasm. The application also help them to overcoming fear and trying to speak out when accomplishing tasks in their group."

Finally, about the technology we used, the teacher think that the AI well widen the application scenario. In the traditional AR applications, specially printed card are needed. But because of the AI text recognition technology, it's more convenient for teacher to prepare the word cards for they can even write them by hand. About the technology, the teacher added: "Students are much more proficient when operating the tablet and using the application than I expected. In this information age, schools should make more use of electronic equipment and cutting edge technical resources to help students to learn more efficiently and happily."

4.3.2 Interview with the Students

In this part, four students who have taken part in the class were interviewed.

The main purpose of the interview is to learn about students' attitudes toward the technology and the lesson with AI and AR. Moreover, we would like to know if they have the willingness to use the application to learn English in further learning.

In this interview, the most frequently mentioned words are "interesting" and "fresh". When being asked "Do you like the application in today's class?", all the students said "yes" without hesitation. "Today's class is far more interesting than the traditional ones." the students said, "I like this new way of learning very much." Also, the students showed their strong willing to continue using the handwriting recognition AR application in future's classes. They said that this application developed their interests in learning English.

The last question is aiming to check the differences between the traditional teaching tools and our application from student's perspective. The students said that the application is more vivid and intuitive than the traditional teaching tools(PowerPoint, videos etc.) and they are more willing to participate in learning activities. In addition, they mentioned that using the handwriting recognition AR application, they did more cooperation and communication during the class.

To sum up, the student's attitude towards the handwriting recognition AR application is mostly positive. Both the learning effect and learning enthusiasm were improved by this new type of learning tool.

5. CONCLUSION

In this study, an interactive application based on AI and AR is designed for an ESL lesson. The application is designed and implemented to assistant and guide students in the learning activities in English class.

The experiment result suggests that the handwriting recognition AR application can improve primary school students' English performance on corresponding context. Comparing the test scores of the experimental group and the control group, we conclude that controlling other unobserved variables, students gained more knowledge with the handwriting recognition AR learning tool. And through the paired sample t test between the scores of the experimental group, we come to the conclusion that the handwriting recognition AR application is statistically significant useful in improving the learning performance of primary school students.

Not only the research indicates that through handwriting recognition AR learning tool, students' academic performance is enhanced, but also great acceptance and potential of it have been verified through questionnaire. The application can kindle the students' interest and enthusiasm of English learning greatly. Additionally, the effect of this application is evaluated by the students and teacher of the class. The handwriting recognition AR application created a vivid and realistic learning environment which can attract the students' attention and make them more concentrate on class. In terms of learning effects, the instant feedback(self-checking etc.) in this application allows students to complete class tasks better and faster. In terms of learning attitude, this software makes students more motivated in class and better participate in group cooperation and communication.

Moreover, the Artificial Intelligence text recognition function made it more convenient for teacher to prepare the class materials. Good recognition accuracy ensure the students' task completing process and make it possible for students to write words on their own and scan it by the tablet to get information they needed.

For students, by analyzing the data we collected, we find that both better learning performance and more positive attitude are demonstrated.

Reflecting our study, we also find that there are still some further work and improvement to be done to make the research result more reliable. Further studies could design more strict experiment study with a larger sample which is representative and adopt some quantitative research methods to strengthen the study. There are some extra possible factors, like different individual characters of students(self-efficacy and cognitive style, learning status etc.), could be considered in the research. How the handwriting recognition AR application helps students in the learning process and ow to better integrate them with teaching is worth studying as well.

ACKNOWLEDGEMENT

Our work is supported by the National Natural Science Foundation of China (61602043) and 2018 Comprehensive Discipline Construction Fund of Faculty of Education, Beijing Normal University.

REFERENCES

Akçayır, M., & Akçayır, G. (2017). Advantages and challenges associated with augmented reality for education: A systematic review of the literature. *Educational research review., 20*, 1-11.

Azuma, R., Baillot, Y., Behringer, R., Feiner, S., Julier, S., & MacIntyre, B. (2001). Recent advances in augmented reality. *IEEE Computer Graphics and Applications, 21*(6), 34-47.

Azuma, R. T. (1997). A survey of augmented reality. *Presence teleoperators and virtual environments., 6*(4), 355-385.

Cai, S., Chiang, F.-K., Sun, Y., Lin, C., & Lee, J. J. (2017). Applications of augmented reality-based natural interactive learning in magnetic field instruction. *Interactive learning environments., 25*(6), 778-791.

Cheng, K.-H., & Tsai, C.-C. (2013). Affordances of augmented reality in science learning: Suggestions for future research. *Journal of science education and technology., 22*(4), 449-462.

Chiang, T. H.-C., Yang, S. J., & Hwang, G.-J. (2014). An augmented reality-based mobile learning system to improve students' learning achievements and motivations in natural science inquiry activities. *Interactive learning environments., 17*(4), 352-365.

Crandall, P. G., Engler III, R. K., Beck, D. E., Killian, S. A., O'Bryan, C. A., Jarvis, N., & Clausen, E. (2015). Development of an augmented reality game to teach abstract concepts in food chemistry. *Journal of Food Science Education, 14*(1), 18-23.

Cumming, G. J. (1998). Artificial intelligence in education: an exploration. *Journal of computer assisted learning, 14*(4), 251-259.

Han, J., Jo, M., Hyun, E., & So, H.-j. (2015). Examining young children's perception toward augmented reality-infused dramatic play. *Educational technology research and development ETR & D., 63*(3), 455-474.

Lu, S.-J., & Liu, Y.-C. (2015). Integrating augmented reality technology to enhance children's learning in marine education. *Environmental Education Research, 21*(4), 525-541.

Poersch, J. M. (2005). A new paradigm for learning language: Connectionist artificial intelligence. *Linguagem ensino, 8*(1), 161-183.

Richardson, D. (2016). Exploring the potential of a location based augmented reality game for language learning. *International Journal of Game-Based Learning, 6*(3), 34-49.

Safar, A. H., Al-Jafar, A. A., & Al-Yousefi, Z. H. (2017). The Effectiveness of Using Augmented Reality Apps in Teaching the English Alphabet to Kindergarten Children: A Case Study in the State of Kuwait. *EURASIA Journal of Mathematics, Science and Technology Education, 13*(2).

Troussas, C., Chrysafiadi, K., & Virvou, M. (2019). An intelligent adaptive fuzzy-based inference system for computer-assisted language learning. *Expert Systems with Applications.*

Yang, S., & Mei, B. (2018). Understanding learners' use of augmented reality in language learning: insights from a case study. *Journal of Education for Teaching, 44*(4), 511-513.

Yang, S.-h. (2007). Artificial intelligence for integrating English oral practice and writing skills. *Sino-US English Teaching, 4*(4), 1-6.

E-LEARNING AND STUDENTS' PERFORMANCE: GENDER PERSPECTIVE

Maryam Murad[1], Anjum Razzaque[2], Allam Hamdan[2] and Anji Benhamed[2]
[1]*Ministry of Education, Manama, Bahrain*
[2]*Ahlia University, Manama, Bahrain*

ABSTRACT

The present research paper has been focused on one of the most critical issues in the field of education in the most recent times which is the impact of educational technology on students' performance. Our paper aim to identify if there is a significant difference between respondents' attitudes towards the impact of educational technology in Ahlia University on students' performance attributed to gender (boys' schools & Girls' schools). Exploiting technology in the education sector is not a recent issue. The real start for integrating technology in education is actually known to be two decades ago when the internet started to be part and parcel of people's lives. Government of countries that have a vision and plans to develop their economies recognized that improving education and integrating the latest technologies is a key means for achieving their strategic plans and economic visions. education development was given due attention. The sample was selected randomly with the electronic sample calculator showing that the minimum number is 380 individuals. The questionnaire was circulated electronically via school administration in the four governorates. The received responses were 342 indicating that the return rate is 90%. Finally, it was concluded that there is a significant difference for gender (boys' schools & Girls' schools) was on the respondents' attitudes towards the impact of educational technology in Ahlia University on students' performance. The implications of the findings of the research showed that the findings of the study can be used as a basis for future research about the relationship e-learning and effective educational outcomes. Also, the findings of the study can be used by MOE to enhance educational technology experiences.

KEYWORDS

Educational Technology, Students' Performance, Gender, Bahrain

1. INTRODUCTION

Writings about incorporating technology in education assure that technology do actually represent a powerful instrument through which learning is transformed. Through education-based technology relationships between educators and students are affirm and advanced. In addition, it contributes to shrinking long-standing equity and accessibility gaps. Moreover, learning experiences become more and more compliant to satisfy all the learners' requirements (King, 2017). Due to the explosive growth of computers in academia in the second half of the twentieth century; the increasing individual use in early 1980s; the introduction of the internet in mainstream education in 1990s, incorporating technology in education turned to be something a habit and an influential thing that has positive impacts on students' learning process. There are diverse views about the implementation of technology in the educational processes. While there is a worldwide agreement on the merits gained from applying and exploiting the fruits human research in the teaching and learning process, there are opposers who disagree on this. Each team has numerous reasons for the why they accept or reject the implementation of technology in educational processes. For one thing, those who are not for educational technology supposes that the increased dependence on technology in this field does actually implant forgetfulness in the souls of the students. They are expected to practice any memory exercises since they become too much dependent on what is written for them by the symbols. Also, students will seem to know a lot of things while they actually know nothing (Salavati, 2016). On the other hand, this impact has favored teaching, because numerous innovative educational projects have been created based on studies to improve student learning. This type of technological innovation enriches the teaching-learning process, and also makes modern and digital teaching possible. From Kindergarten, students have to be introduced to the technological world so that they gradually acquire the necessary skills in computer management. In this way, technology is part of the children from the beginning of their educational process.

Bahrain is no exception from the entire world's attitude to make technology an outstanding feature in the education sector. The kingdom 2030 economic vision assures that education is the major pillar upon which development and other economic objectives are fulfilled. Various policies are adopted in order to make the education sector in the kingdom head towards more and more exploitation of the available technologies in facilitating the teaching and learning processes. This is attributed to the leadership recognition that judicious use of technology in the classroom, and e-learning generally, has the potential to raise standards. For such a purpose the kingdom's government has been working in partnership with some of the biggest names in the IT sector.

Various initiatives have been adopted in order to equip the Ahlia University with the latest technologies in the pedagogical sector first Education. These initiatives include the partnership between the Bahraini MOE and Microsoft in 2004 which was under the title of "Transformation Agreement" that was aimed at creating a central e-learning portal as well as training teachers on the usage. Another initiative was as late as the year 2015 when the Bahraini MOE got in another partnership with Microsoft for the period of five years (2015-2020). Three programs are planned to take place where schools are to be equipped with the most state of the art resources for technology education (Yung, 2016).

1.1 Research Significance and Aims

Significance of this research stems from the significance of the topic under research. Implementing technology for education purposes has become a significant issue that is paid due care by government. This is actually attributed to the fact that technology is now part and parcel of people's everyday life practices. Making use of computers. Tablets, mobile phones; the internet; smart boards; and many other facilities is considered as a must for individual and organizational success. So, using these devices at schools integrates education and life practices. Further to that, casting light on students' performance is another significant issue. This is understood in light of understanding what performance means for learners and educators. In addition, the research is significant for the ministry of education and secondary schools in particular. Since the research investigates and provides empirical evidence for the relationship between educational technology and students performance. This is also significant for the entire Bahraini society since it shows the extent to which students' academic performance gets improved in light of applying the state of art technologies brought to the students by the MOE. Moreover, the research is significant for future researcher where the findings of this research can represent a basis for their future research.

This paper aim to identify if there is a significant difference between respondents' attitudes towards the impact of technology-based education in secondary schools on students' performance attributed to gender (boys' schools & Girls' schools). From the key aim above the following questions are derived:

1. What is the impact of implementing educational technology in Ahlia University in the kingdom of Bahrain in terms of ease of use and users' perceived usefulness?
2. What is the impact of students' performance in Ahlia University in the kingdom of Bahrain?
3. How can implementing educational technology in Ahlia University impact students' performance in the kingdom of Bahrain?

The rest of the paper is organized as the following: the second part is concerned with the literature review and hypothesis development. The third part is concerned with the study sample and methodology. The fourth part presents a descriptive study. The fifth part discusses the empirical results. The final part is concerned with conclusions, implications and future studies.

2. EDUCATION AND TECHNOLOGY

It is argued that one of the most promising opportunities for improving school learning is to improve teaching materials and include the means, given their obvious relationship with teaching materials. In this theory, the means become more important in that they facilitate meaningful learning (Sung, et al., 2016).

2.1 The Influence of New Technologies

The influence of new technologies, primarily the computer and the internet, is increasing at the present time in all areas of our lives. Education of course is not exempt from this influence, so it could be said that new technologies have come to revolutionize many fundamental aspects of this. It is mentioned that the new technologies open the possibility of greater student participation in the construction and development of the curriculum (Higgins, 2012). The convergence of these two technologies requires understanding the impact and the transformation they cause in education. This provides researchers and teachers to take the best advantage of these technologies in order to achieve a greater and better teaching-learning process. They grow also more likely to address the challenges and problems that the merger causes. And this requires researchers and teachers to propose creative solutions for use in the educational process (Flanagan , 2008). Today, there is a great diversity of literature about new technologies that can be used for educational purposes. The importance of adopting the changes and technological advances in the education system is fundamental to facilitate a better understanding of the modern world where technology occupies a fundamental place in the productive system and in everyday life in general. For such a reason, this highlights the importance of always being at the forefront. Educational technology has been defined as a set of "teaching aids", such as language laboratories, projectors, fixed view, TV, radio and 16mm film. That is, it has been identified as a set of physical means of material equipment that can be used by the teacher in the teaching process (Jhurree, 2005).

2.2 Transformation of Education-based Technology

Nowadays, the use of computers and the internet in education has transformed the relationship between the elements in the teaching-learning process. They encourage the construction of new concepts and interpretations of the conception of educational work, school organization in consideration of the conditions, which these two technologies impose. They also strongly influence the presentation of new proposals enriching the educational process and the design of new products that revolve around them, such as the interactive whiteboard (Lister, 2015).

This way of conceiving the educational technology can be characterized as an "approach of hardware", since it is defined only in terms of physical means. People who conceive of it thus criticize the traditional way of teaching that consists in the mere dictation of classes by the teacher, which would lead to verbalism and academic memories in which the student does not perceive the concrete meaning of the utterances made by the Instructor. In order to overcome these barriers, they recommend the use of machines or audiovisual media as a teaching aid (Wajszczyk, 2014).

2.3 Educational Technology in Bahrain

All the government schools in the kingdom of Bahrain are now connected to the internet and have at least one IT setup. The government is easing the expansion of an e-learning environment in local schools via the King Hamad Schools of the Future Project. The project, which began in 2003, originally consists of five schools, 11,000 pupils and over 1000 teaching faculty, and included the expansion of a centralized portal for online teaching materials and training. By the year 2010 the project proved to be very fruitful as it was extended to contain every school in the Kingdom.

2.4 Students' Performance

It is assured that one of the concepts that are too much ambiguous and can be difficultly defined is the concept of "performance". This is attributed to the nature of the concept itself. Reviewers did not agree on one definition for it especially when it is related to students. Performance can be understood as "The accomplishment of a given task measured against preset known standards of accuracy, completeness, cost, and speed" (Buisness Dictionary, 2017). Nevertheless, one of the most widely accepted definitions is the one referring to students' performance as "how well the student has prepared for and performed in class and how well the student has mastered the material presented" (Al–Ammary, 2012). There are particular standards upon which students' performance can be measured. These standards are classified into three categories: class performance, essays and papers, oral presentations. To measure students' class performance, there are particular issues that are observed about the student. For one thing, his/her preparation which refers to the readiness of the student to participate in the classroom activities. Participation here is meant to show the extent to which the student contributes to the course and the quality of his/her efforts. Another thing is the student's mastery of the subject which shows his/her understanding of the presented material. Also, his/her attitude to interact within the group. Group interaction is an indicator that reflects the student's interest and enthusiasm and his/her cooperation in working within a group. Concerning students' written performance (essays and papers), the most significant issues that show the extent which the student perform well include the content presented by him/her. This is always measured in terms of clarity in thought and expression; logic and persuasiveness; and organization and flow of the ideas. In addition to the student's ability to compose the piece of writing. This is understood in terms of his/her usage of correct grammar, spelling, and punctuation in standard written English. Finally, students' oral representation constitutes a critical pillar upon which performance is assessed. This oral representation is assessed in terms of the student's content which depends on his/her organization, persuasiveness, and clarity in the presentation of ideas topics/issues. Also, delivery of the material does matter in terms of the student's style of speaking while audio visual aids are available (Haahr , 2005).

Hypothesis 1. *There is a significant difference between respondents' attitudes towards the impact of educational technology in Ahlia University on students' performance attributed to gender (boys' & Girls').*

3. STUDY SAMPLE

The population of the present research includes all the students of the in the four governorates of the kingdom of Bahrain. In accordance to the statistics of the ministry of education in Bahrain, the calculated sample size was 380 according to Roasoft electronic sample size calculator. Thus, 380 students were targeted in the secondary stage schools in the four governorates (Manama, Muharraq, the Southern, and the Northern). The questionnaires were sent to the students by what's app on their mobile phones by the school's administrations. The returned questionnaire responses to the researcher's Google account were 342. This means that the rate of the returned questionnaires is 90%. The following table 1 shows more details about the population of the research

Table 1. Statistics about University schools in Bahrain

Gender	Number of students
Boys	15279
Girls'	16240
Total	31519

4. EMPIRICAL STUDY

4.1 Demographic Characteristics

In light of the data collected about the gender of the respondents, it is found out that more than three quarters of the respondents (78.7%) are female while less than one quarter (21.3%) are male respondents. In light of the data collected about the age areas of the respondents, it is identified that those who are more than 19 represent 42.70 %. Those who are from 16-17 represent 32.50%. The lowest percentage 24.90% is for those work is in between 18-19. In terms of the nationality of respondents, who do participate in this research, it is elicited that 71.10% of them are Bahraini people. Those who are non-Bahraini respondents constitute 28.90% of the entire sample size. In terms of the respondents' governorate, it is found out that those who live in Muharraq represent one third of the sample 33.30%. The respondents who live the Norther governorate represent 20.20%. Those who live in Manama represent 19% of the entire sample size. Regarding the type of the school in which the questionnaire forms were circulated, it is identified that respondents in girls' schools are two times more than those who are in boys' schools. The Respondents in girls' schools are 78.7% while the respondents in Boys' schools are 21.30%. (see table 2).

Table 2. Demographic characteristics

Demographic characteristics		Frequency	Percent
Gender	Male	73	21.3
	Female	269	78.7
	Total	*342*	*100*
Age	16-17	111	32.5
	18-19	85	24.9
	More than 19	146	42.7
	Total	*342*	*100*
Nationality	Bahraini	243	71.1
	Non-Bahraini	99	28.9
	Total	*342*	*100*
Governorate	Manama	65	19
	Muharraq	114	33.3
	Southern	69	20.2
	Northern	94	27.5
	Total	*342*	*100*
School type	Boys' Schools	73	21.3
	Girls' Schools	269	78.7
	Total	*342*	*100*

4.2 Impact of Technology-Based Education

In accordance to the table 3 that shows the overall results for the 24 items making up the section of status of technology-based education, the research finds out that the respondents feel neutral about this status. This means that technology-based education does exist and the students of the secondary stage schools feel there is a perceived ease of use by 61.6%. There is also perceived usefulness for educational based technology by 72.4%. The respondents refer to the status of educational-based technology in their secondary schools' stage by 67%.

Table 3. Status of technology-based education in terms of ease of use

Technology-based education in terms of.	Number of items	Mean score	Standard deviation	Relative weight
Perceived ease of use	12	3.08	1.3	61.6%
Perceived usefulness	12	3.62	1.07	72.4%
Total	24	3.35	1.185	67%

4.3 Impact of Students' Performance

In accordance to the table 4 that shows the overall results for the 17 items making up the section of status of students' performance, the researcher finds out that the respondents agree that their performance level is good as the average mean score for the 17 items is 3.47 (69.5%).

Table 4. Impact of Students' performance

Technology-based education in terms of:	Number of items	Mean score	Standard deviation	Relative weight
Participation	7	3.17	1.21	63.4%
Oral representation	6	3.57	1.19	71.4%
Written work	4	3.69	1.19	73.8
Total	17	3.47	1.19	69.5%

4.4 One-Way ANOVA

The one-way ANOVA (table 5) is employed herein to investigate whether or gander (Boy and Girls') generates a significant impact on the respondents' attitude towards the relationship between technology-based education and students' performance in secondary schools in the kingdom of Bahrain.

Table 5. One-Way ANOVA

		Sum of Squares	df	Mean Square	F	Sig.
Perceived ease of use	Between Groups	2.428	1	2.428	2.297	.131
	Within Groups	359.383	340	1.057		
	Total	361.812	341			
Perceived usefulness	Between Groups	.709	1	.709	2.032	.155
	Within Groups	118.685	340	.349		
	Total	119.394	341			

In accordance of the outcomes of the one-way ANOVA, the researcher concludes gander (Boys' and Girls') does not create any significant difference for respondents' attitude towards the impact of perceived ease of use on students' performance in the Ahlia University in Bahrain as the sig value is 0.131 which is above 0.01 and 0.05. Likewise, type of school (Boys' and Girls') does not create any significant difference for respondents' attitude towards the impact of perceived usefulness on students' performance in the secondary school's stage in Bahrain as the sig value is 0.155 which is above 0.01 and 0.05. Gander (boys'& Girls') was found to generate no significant difference between respondents' attitudes towards the impact of technology-based education in secondary schools on students' performance. In spite of the conclusion that the demographic variables were proved to make no significant difference in the respondents' recognition of the relationship between the two variables, they are still significant for the research as demographic variables do provide data regarding research participants. Demographic variables are also necessary for the determination of whether the individuals in this particular study constitute a representative sample of the target population for generalization purposes. It is acknowledged that demographics or research participant characteristics are reported in the methods section of the research report and serve as independent variables in the research design (AlNoaimi, 2018).

5. CONCLUSION

Technology-based education has become a pivotal issue in Ahlia University in the kingdom of Bahrain. The ministry grants all University the required devices and Instructors and students are equipped with the necessary applications and programs through which teaching and learning and made easier. Classes are now equipped with overhead projectors, smartboards. There is at least one IT class in each University. More and more fund is specified for the process of bringing technology into Ahlia University. Instructors are trained to make the best use of these technologies and facilitating such usage to the students. Teaching and learning is becoming more and more electronic while traditional means are vanishing gradually. Students are no more negative followers for what is presented within the class context since they become a positive part of the technological endeavor. They are motivated to prepare and share funny videos that are likely to add more excitement and enthusiasm to them while they are learning. More interaction is created by students and teachers within class and at home since instructors provide homework, project requirements, grades, notices, etc. MOE grow more and more interested on linking instructors, students, parents, and the ministry itself online for better educational outcomes. Secondary schools' students in Bahrain suppose that there is a good level of ease of use of technology in education in Bahrain. Implementing technology in the processes of learning and teaching in the Ahlia University in Bahrain is found to be of perceived usefulness. It contributes to enhancing students' innovativeness' specially on employing technological facilities. Students' physical attendance at University is becoming a less required issue since virtual learning is increasing gradually. Student are given more and more opportunities to employ critical thinking that they can identify creative solutions especially when there are electronic lessons. The teaching and learning process are now more exciting while traditional lessons are not as many as before. The process of assessment can now be carried out through the using internet applications including Kahoot, Flickers and Socrative where the students are provided with instant feedback about their understanding of the taught material. Being assessed online is a fantasy for the student where they feel more confident, enthusiastic and challenged. Gamification is one of the most recent issues that contribute to increasing success of the learning process since students' attention and enthusiasm grows more and more. Its numerous positive impacts on the processes of teaching and learning. There is a significant difference for gander (boys' & Girls') was on the respondents' attitudes towards the impact of technology-based education in Ahlia University on students' performance.

REFERENCES

Al–Ammary, J., 2012. Educational Technology: A Way to Enhance Student Achievement at The University Of Bahrain. The Online Journal of New Horizons in Education, 3(3), pp. 45-54.

AlNoaimi, H., 2018. The Impact of Person-Organization Fit on Employee Retention: The Case of Ministry of Education in Bahrain A dissertation in partial fulfilment of the requirements for the degree of master of business administration, , Manama: cAhlia University, college of business and finance.

Buisness Dictionary, 2017. Definition of Performance. [Online] Available at: http://www.businessdictionary.com/definition/performance.html [Accessed 1 September 2018].

Flanagan, A., 2008. Technology: The Positive and Negative Effects on Student Achievement, New York: The College at Brockport: State University of New York.

Haahr, J., 2005. Explaining Student Performance Evidence from the international PISA, TIMSS and PIRLS surveys., s.l.: Danish Technological Institute.

Higgins, S. & Xiao, Z., 2013. The Impact of Digital Technology on Learning: A Summary for the Education Endowment Foundation. Journal of King Saud University - Languages and Translation, s.l.: School of Education.

Jhurree, V., 2005. Technology integration in education in developing countries: Guidelines to policy makers. International Education Journal, 6(4), pp. 467-483.

King, J., 2017. Reimagining the Role of TEchnology in Eduaction: 2017 NAtional Education technology Plan, Washington, DC: US Department of Education.

Lister, M., 2015. Gamification: The effect on student motivation and performance at the post-secondary level. Issues and Trends in Educational Technology, 3(2), pp. 1-22.

Salavati , S., 2016. Use of Digital Technologies in Education:The Complexity of Teachers' Everyday Practice. Doctoral dissertation, Department of Informatics, Sweden: Växjö: Linnaeus University Dissertations.

Sung, Y.-T., Chang , K.-E. & Liu, T.-C., 2016. The effects of integrating mobile devices with teaching and learning on students' learning performance: A meta-analysis and research synthesis. Computers & Education, Volume 94, p. 252–275.

Wajszczyk, R., 2014. A study of the impact of technology in early education., s.l.: Uppsala University.

Yung, L., 2016. Bahrain 2016, s.l.: Oxfor Business Group.

LIASCRIPT: A DOMAIN-SPECIFIC-LANGUAGE FOR INTERACTIVE ONLINE COURSES

André Dietrich
Otto-von-Guericke-Universität, Magdeburg / Germany

ABSTRACT

LiaScript is an attempt to enable everyone to create free and interactive online courses, without the need of being an experienced programmer. Instead, it aims to bring both parties, software- and course-developers, closer together by introducing Open-Source techniques into the Open-courSe development process. LiaScript was designed to be compatible to Common-Markdown, but it introduces lots of language extensions that deal with quizzes, surveys, ASCII-art, text2speech, animations, online programming, the integration of JavaScript, etc. as well as its own macro-system that simplifies tedious and repetitive tasks. It comes along with its own just-in-time compiler that runs in the browser and therefor does not require additional tooling.

KEYWORDS

Markdown, DSL, eLearning, Online-Course, OER

1. INTRODUCTION[1]

LiaScript was initially developed within the *"Industrial eLab-Project[2]"*, which aims to make university hardware and laboratories accessible via the Internet. But, I soon realized that only by giving remote access to these resources via a fancy website I will run into problems. The mobile Arduino-Bots could be used to teach programming, sensing, navigation, dive into operating systems or even to apply artificial intelligence. Thus, the real problem was to develop an extendable and adaptable system for creating courses (instead of a single Web-App) with different objectives and for students with different backgrounds.

Surely, creating an online-course from scratch requires a lot of expertise in different web technologies at front-end (e.g., HTML, JavaScript, CSS, testing), back-end (e.g., webservers, databases), and different communication standards to connect both sides (e.g., CRUD, websockets, AJAX). Hence, it is nearly impossible for a non-programmer to understand all of these issues, before starting to develop his or her own online course. Screen- or podcasts are not a real alternative, since they are expensive and time-consuming in production, not easy to change or translate, and require additional skills in movie cutting. That is why platforms such as Udacity or Coursea invest a lot of effort and money in high-quality course productions, which is comparable to movie productions, including screenplays, actors, different sets and locations.

Fortunately, there also exist so called Learning Management Systems that try to ease the course development (Dobre, 2015). But how is such a kind of "simplicity" achieved? Mostly, by offering integrated configuration-systems, editors and authoring-tools, that shall enable the user to create a course with a lot of buttons and menus, sub-sub-menus, and masks, whose only purpose is to hide the non-intuitive syntax and semantics of a language that can be easily interpreted machines, not by humans.

We should instead start to create languages that can be easy understood and applied by humans, in order to describe their intentions, and let the machine rack its CPU in order to find an appropriate translation.

---

1 See the LiaScript version at: https://liascript.github.io/course/?https://raw.githubusercontent.com/andre-dietrich/e-Learning-2019/master/README.md#1

2 Project-site: http://www.elab.ovgu.de

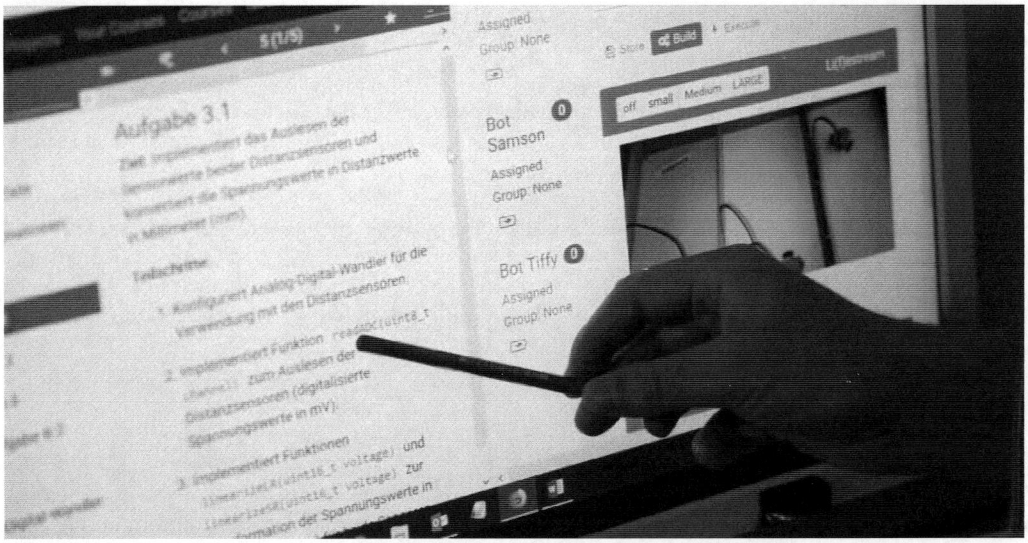

Figure 1. Picture of the eLab website with LiaScript and remote robots

2. ADAPTING OPEN-SOURCE DEVELOPMENT

More or less, all currently used systems have drawbacks in some of the following points:
Requirements from an Open-Source perspective

1. No support for larger course developer-teams, including those who develop additional functionality and those who provide content
2. No versioning, in contrast to Wikipedia as a single source of truth, content shall be provided in different "styles" for heterogeneous groups of students
3. No re-usability, parts of one course cannot simply be applied of copied into another project
4. No support for internationalization/localization (i18n), thus a course cannot simply be translated into another language
5. No variance in representation
6. Difficulties in adopting and integrating new web technologies

Pin-points 1 and 2 can be easily solved by applying a purely text-based approach for the course development and version control systems[3] (Zhou et al. 2018). All required resources, including images, videos, data-sheets, JavaScript and CSS, and everything else can be easily uploaded and made available via the internet.

2.1 Why Markdown?

Markdown (Wikipedia, 2019) is a simple meta-markup language used to structure and annotate simple text documents. Its goal is to keep the source text easy to read and write, that is why it has become more or less the standard documentation-format for Open-Source projects. Originally, it was developed to write HTML content efficiently, without having to use a WYSIWYG[4] editor. Directly writing a markup language such as HTML is considered too error prone and annoying for the writing process. Of course, I am not the first who applies Markdown to ship educational contents, earlier examples are:

3 E.g. Git (https://git-scm.com) and its web-based hosting services https://github.com or https://gitlab.com.
4 Stands for: *What You See Is What You Get*

- GitBook/Pandoc: free Markdown parser that have been widely applied in OER generation (Ovadia, 2019)
- elearn-js: converter for Markdown documents into responsive OER websites, which allows integrating quizzes, interactive images, videos, etc. (Heinecke, 2016)
- Iodide: Jupyter Notebooks brought to the internet, next to OER it can be interpreted as an example of literate programming

And of course there are other approaches that have to be mentioned (McKiernan, 2017), but the commonality of all system is that it's about creating static documents, which, although it is translated into a more beautiful format, still have to be read. To my knowledge, this approach is the only one that deals with the creation of interactive presentations, which are still generated from simple and static Markdown documents.

2.2 What is LiaScript

In contrast to other Markdown compilers that generate static HTML, LiaScript is an interpreter that downloads and renders the original Markdown document directly within the browser. That means, if the Markdown document is updated, the resulting representation will be updated too. Thus, there is no need for additional tooling, compiling steps, or server-side support. LiaScript was implemented from scratch with Elm[5] for efficiency and speed, which includes its own parser and run-time environment.

- Online interpreter, that runs directly within the browser
- Written in Elm
- Support for different representation styles (see Sec. 2.3.5)
- New Markdown language features: *Quizzes*, *Coding*, *Animations*, *Multimedia*, *ASCII-art*, …

One of the design goals was to support different rendering modes, which cover the traditional textbook mode, next to presentations with animations and spoken text. Furthermore, language itself was extended with various features, that should transform Markdown from a traditionally static markup approach into something new, suitable for interactive online courses and more.

2.3 Extensions to Markdown

Why does Markdown only support static content?

We came a long way from written scrolls to printed books to electronic books, which can still be printed out or copied by hand! But, actually it is the same old format that has been brought to a new device. Although a computer and the Internet give us much more opportunities for visualization, interaction, and story telling ...

2.3.1 Multimedia

Markdown supports 2 types of links (onto internal and external resources), which can be either direct or formatted:

```
* Direct reference: https://LiaScript.github.io
* Formatted reference: [Link to LiaScript](https://LiaScript.github.io)
```

Images can be included via formatted references that start with an exclamation mark:

```
![School in the year 2000](https://...France_in_XXI_Century._School.jpg)<!--width="100%"-->
```

In contrast to this, it is still complicated to include multimedia content. Based on the previous notation, it is possible in LiaScript to mark a link as an audio-file by adding a starting question-mark, which can be interpreted as an ear.

```
?[Joy to the world](http://www.orangefreesounds.com/...18/11/Joy-to-the-world-song.mp3?_=1)
```

---

5 Elm is a functional programming language that compiles to JavaScript, see the project-website: https://elm-lang.org

Due to the combination of images and sound, it is possible to insert videos. One of the benefits that lays in this notation is that every common Markdown-viewer will still generate a fully working link to these resources.

```
!?[The eLab-Project on YouTube](https://www.youtube.com/embed/bICfKRyKTwE)<!--
  width="560px" height="315px" -->
```

You might probably have noticed, that some examples contain HTML-comments with additional annotations. This is a cheap way of formatting any kind of elements, such as text, images, tables, videos, etc. A starting comment defines the format of the entire block, whereby a trailing comment changes the format of its predecessor only.

```
<!--style="color: red"-->
This whole paragraph will be colored in red ;-)<!--
class="animated infinite bounce" style="animation-delay: 3s;" -->,
but only this smiley is going to start jumping after 3 seconds.
```

This way it is even possible to define complex animation-sequences, while the content remains readable with another Markdown-viewer, since they tend to ignore comments.

2.3.2 ASCII-Art 1

From my experience, I know that a lot of produced images represent simple diagrams that represent functions, signal waves, trends, etc. These have to be generated with Excel, Gnuplot, Matlab or other tools, and to be exported, which makes it also difficult to change them or to translate labels. LiaScript offers the opportunity to draw diagrams directly within the document. Such diagrams can be easily updated and it is not necessary to switch to other "tools". The example below is turned into a nicely rendered diagram, wherein the color and the size of dots is defined by the original characters.

```
              Title and axes are optional
1.9 |    DotS
    |                 ***
  y |               *     *
  - | r r r r r r r*r r r r*r r r r r r r
  a |             *         *
  x |            *           *
  i | B B B B B * B B B B B B * B B B B B
  s |         *                 *
    | *  * *                       * *  *
    +------------------------------------
    0              x-axis               1
```

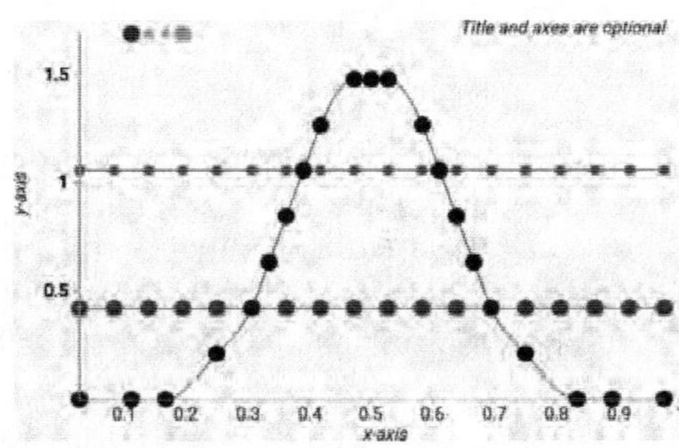

2.3.3 ASCII-Art 2

If necessary, it is also possible to depict complex issues, such as graphs, UML-diagrams, or even pictures with the help of simple characters. Additionally, it is also possible to use any kind of Unicode-character. Thus, LiaScript has support for Chinese, Greek, Arabic, or any other kind of characters and symbols.

```
                                .---->  F
A        B      C    D         /
*--------*-------*-----*------*------>  E
          \                  ^ \
           v                /   '---->  G
            B ------> C ---'
```

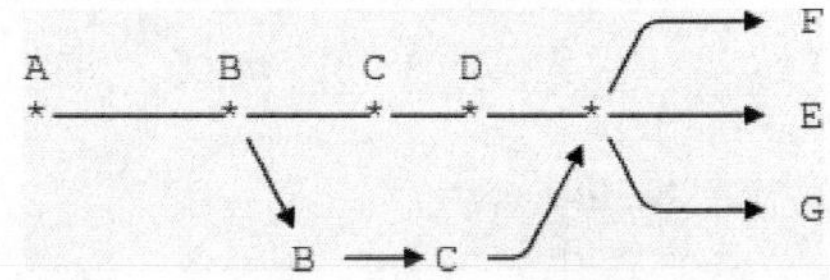

2.3.4 Quizzes

One of the language feature I wanted the most, was an easy way to integrate quizzes in different flavors and thus, to give learners the possibility to check their knowledge. Quizzes are always associated with double brackets, such that to add a text quiz, you only have to enter the solution in double braces and the input field, check-, and resolve-buttons are generated automatically.

```
.What did the **fish** say when he hit a
**concrete wall**?

    [[dam]]
```

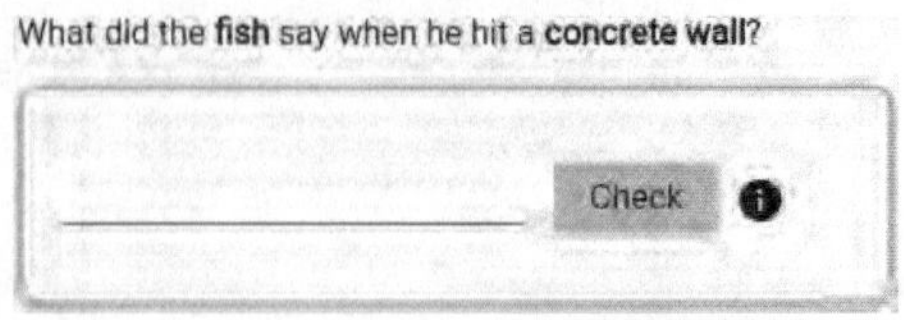

Some might adapt the question to handle the ambiguity in this case. But let us try out what LiaScript has to offer. It is either possible to add hints, by adding question-marks in double brackets and let the user decide if he needs help, by clicking onto the associated button in the rendered course. The optional `script`-tag allows to check the input, in this case to trim it and to transform it to lower-case and finally to compare it with different possible solution. Therefor the `@input`-macro gets replaced by the current user input. The trailing Markdown-blocks surrounded by two lines of stars show a more detailed explanation, which appears either if the user input was correct or if the user clicked onto the resolve button.

```
[[dam]]
_[[?]]   Do not take this question serious.
[[?]]   Do not take this question serious.
[[?]]   ...
<script>
  let input = "@input".trim().toLowerCase();
  input == "damn" || input == "dam";
</script>
**********************************************
A __dam__ is a barrier obstructing flowing
water and __damn__ usually refers to
damnation, a condemnation, usually by a god.

$$
   \sum_{i=1}^\infty\frac{1}{n^2}
        =\frac{\pi^2}{6}
$$
**********************************************
```

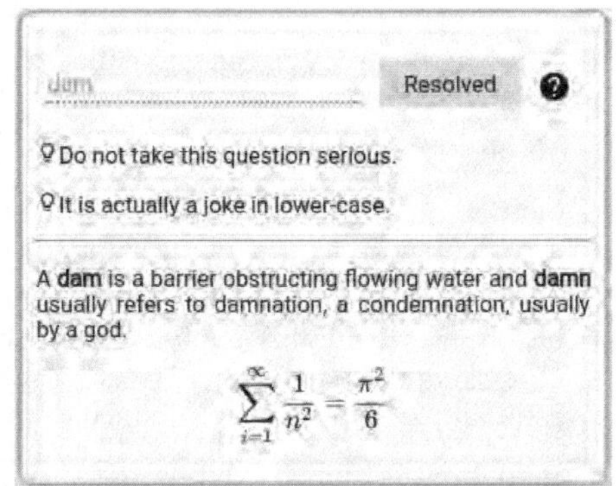

How would you encode a multiple-choice quiz with a typewriter, probably similarly to the example below. It looks like a list of simple check-buttons that define the solution. You can add as much rows/options and of course add also hints, scripts, or an explanation. A single-choice quiz is defined by stylized radio buttons, where the `X` marks the right solution and only one line is allowed to contain the `X` contain. Extensions with hints, solutions, or JavaScript checks can also be applied.

```
**Just add as many points as you wish:**
[[X]] Only the **X** marks the correct point.
[[ ]] Empty ones are wrong.
[[X]] ...
```

```
[( )] Option 1
[( )] Option 2
[(X)] Option 3
[( )] Option 4
```

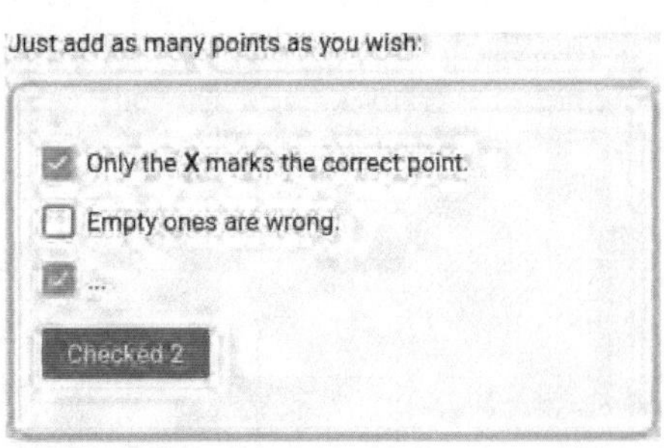

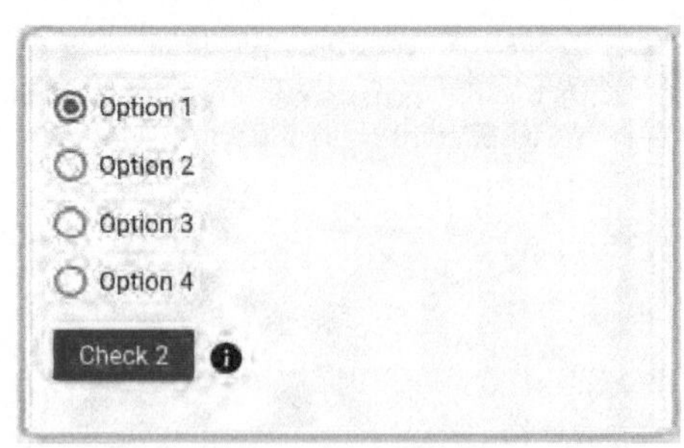

A generic quiz can be defined with the help of an exclamation-mark in double brackets and a script-tag. In this case a random-number is used to generate the outcome. Additional HTML-elements might be required to define different input possibilities.

```
[[!]]
<script> Math.random() < 0.2; </script>
```

2.3.5 Output Modes

The following two parts are intended to explain, how a section can be divided into several fragments and how speech output can be generated. If you are using the online rendered version of this course at LiaScript website, then you will probably have noticed that there is a button in the upper right corner. It allows switching between three different display modes. The user can decide, if he or she rather wants to listen to the explanatory text as in a presentation or to read it like a book.

1. Presentation (with voice output)
2. Slides (with notes ...)
3. Textbook (without fragmentation and voice output)

Fragmentation

Defining fragments and revealing them step by step is quite simple, only a number in double braces has to be put in front of a Markdown-block. Fragments with only one number will sustain until the end of a slide. A point of disappearance can be defined by putting a minus and a second number into double braces. Inline fragments can be defined by putting the fragment number and the elements to appear into successive braces. And it is also possible to attach different blocks to the same fragment number, either by attaching a number to every block or by putting them into a body of stars, as it was done with the solution in Sec. 2.3.4.

```
                 {{1}}
This text will appear at {3}{__inline is also possible__}first.

{{2-4}} This block will appear afterwards and
disappear at step number 4.

I am here to the end of slide ...

{{4}} I come at last.
```

Voice Output

Voice output is implemented with the help of ResponsiveVoice[6]. Within an initial `comment`-tag at the beginning of the document, it is possible to define the default voice for a course. This voice can be changed at every section as well as within every voice comment itself. Such comments are treated as extended fragments, which are used explain certain fragments in more detail. Therefore, they are defined similar to block-fragments surrounded by minuses, whereby only paragraphs are allowed to follow. Depending on the presentation mode, these texts are either displayed within the slide or read out loud. This way it is also possible to implement dialogs between different persons.

```
<!--
narrator: US English Female
-->

--{{1}}-- This text is spoken by a female.

     --{{2 UK English Male}}--
I should speak with a UK like accent.

--{{3 Russian Female}}-- Я говорю по-русски с женским голосом.
```

2.4 Extending LiaScript

In the previous sections syntactic extensions to Markdown have been presented. But the Internet is full libraries and possibilities that a might be necessary for a particular course or topic. In contrast to many other Markdown-interpreters LiaScript allows integrating JavaScript, HTML, and CSS directly within the document. Additionally, it has support for a macro-notation that enables automating and thus simplifies repetitive and tedious tasks.

6 http://responsivevoice.org

2.4.1 ... with JavaScript and HTML

It is possible use HTML everywhere and if you want to make use of a certain JavaScript library or CSS-file, their URLs have to be included in the main comment-tag at first. Using the keyword script followed by a colon and a URL or multiple URLs, JavaScript can be integrated and similarly by using the keyword link style-sheets can be loaded. Afterwards it is possible everywhere to access the new functionality. The following example depicts, how the JavaScript library Chartist[7] is used to plot a certain graph.

```
<!--
script: https://ajax.goog...3/jquery.min.js
        https://cdn.jsdel...chartist.min.js

link:   https://cdn.jsde...chartist.min.css
-->
...
<div class="ct-chart" id="chart">
</div>
<script>
  let chart = new Chartist.Line('#chart', {
    labels: [1, 2, 3, 4],
    series: [[100, 120, 180, 200]]
  });
</script>
```

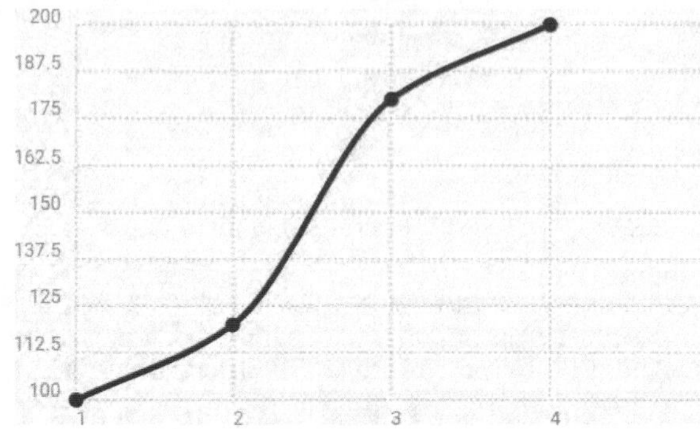

2.4.2 ... with Macros

In Sec. 2.3.4, the `@input` macro has already been used to mark the replacement for the user input. A macro always starts with an `@` symbol and can be defined in the "main" comment of a document. Macros describe simple rules for text replacement. For the one-line `@red` macro, everything following the colon defines the replacement text. Parameter substitutions are defined by a `@` symbol followed by a number. These extensions can then be used arbitrarily in the document, as shown in the following example.

```
<!--@red: <b style="color: red"> @0</b>
-->
> This is a block-citation contains
> a @red(very important) example...
```

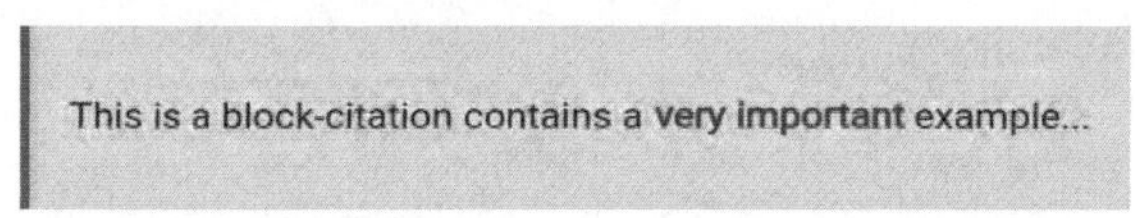

A macro can also call other macros, and more complex macros can be defined as a block consisting of multiple HTML, Markdown, or JavaScript elements. In this example the use of Chartist should be simplified by changing the ID for the `div` element and the content to be drawn is passed as the second parameter. This macro can also be called via a "function-like" notation. Since commas are used as separators for the parameters, back-ticks must be used here to pass the second parameter as an entire string. Admittedly, for very long entries, this can quickly become unreadable.

```
<!--
@Chartist
<div class="ct-chart ct-golden-section" id="chart@0">
</div>
<script>
  let chart = new Chartist.Line('#chart@0', {@1});
</script>
@end
-->
@Chartist(id1,`labels: [1,2,3], series: [[1,3,1]]`)
```

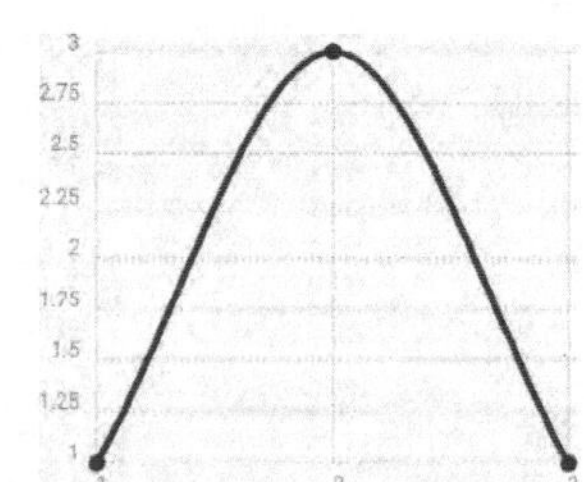

For this reason, macros can also be called within a code-block, therefor only the respective macro must be called in the head of the block. The body of the block is then passed as a single parameter. This makes it easier to define complex macros and additionally, all popular Markdown-viewers should at least display this kind of inputs in a nicely rendered code-block with syntax highlighting, which enables the interpretation of data.

7 A responsive charting library built with SVG: https://gionkunz.github.io/chartist-js/

```json @Chartist(id2)
labels: [1, 2, 3, 4, 5, 6, 7],
series: [
  [100, 120, 180, 200,  0, 12,   -1],
  [10,   20,  30,  40, 50, 90, -100]]
```

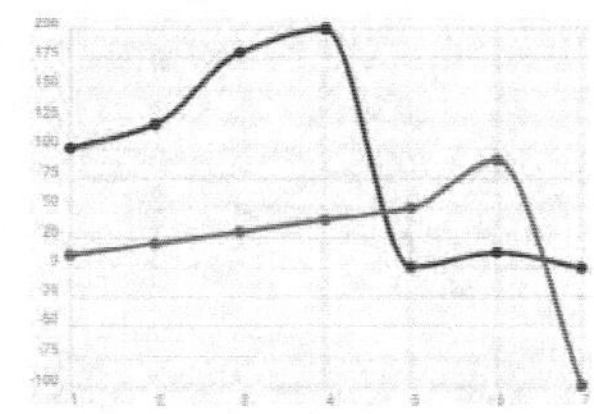

2.5 Executable Code

The following syntax can be used to combine several Markdown code-blocks into one project. To the different files, titles can be associated, and they can be opened and closed. The additional `script`-tag at the end identifies these blocks as executable code and defines how the content of each block is handled. In this case the `@input` macro is called with a parameter that defines which code-block gets substituted at this position. See the LiaScript interpretation of these blocks, all files are editable and a linear version management system is used to track changes.

````
``` js      -EvalScript.js
  let who = data.first_name+" "+
            data.last_name;
  if(data.online) who+" is online";
  else            who+" is NOT online";
```
``` json     +Data.json
  {
    "first_name"  :  "Sammy",
    "last_name"   :  "Shark",
    "online"      :  true
  }
```
<script>
  let data = @input(1); // insert the JSON dataset into a local variable
  eval(`@input(0)`);    // eval the script that uses the dataset
</script>
````

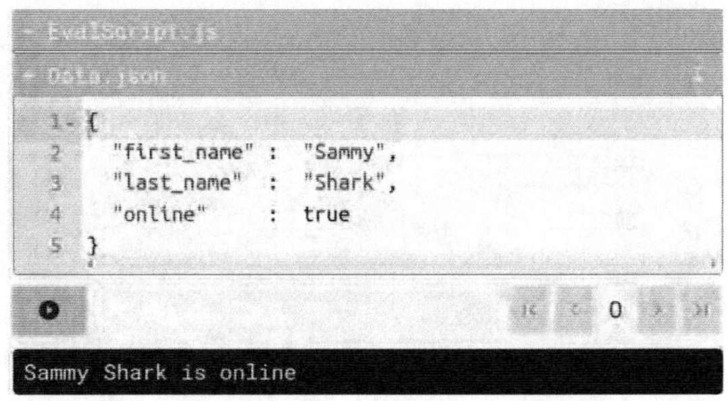

As shown in Sec. 2.3, it is also possible to integrate different JavaScript functionalities and libraries, so that also different programming languages can be supported. The example in Fig. 2 shows a simple *C* program that can be compiled and executed using the rextester-API[8]. The more complex definition of the associated `script`-tag was provided using the `@Rextester.eval` macro. Only by attaching such a macro, any code block can be turned into an executable one. The combination with other languages and visualizations (using HTML and JavaScript) is also possible, see the example for the programming language *Processing*. For such JavaScript libraries and also for the use of other functionalities, templates are offered that have been implemented with the help of the macro system[9]. These can be used freely and furthermore it also minimizes the breaks when reading the original Markdown document.

3. CONCLUSION

Looking back onto Sec. 2, points 3 to 6 have not been discussed so far. LiaScript was build around the idea of course-development as Open-Source projects. Thus, anything from one course can be used in another course, either by linking directly onto a slide or by simply copy and pasting the required parts (*req 3*). Furthermore, a growing number of templates is offered, which is founded on the internal macro-system, that ease the usage and integration of new and complex web technologies (*req 6*).

- (3.) Re-usability → anything can simply be copied into any course
- (6.) Integrating new web technologies → via a macro-system and templates
- (5.) Variance in representation → three different modes
- (4.) Internationalization/localization (i18n) → supported by specific header tags

8 An online-compile service for more than 45 different languages: https://rextester.com/main
9 List of LiaScript templates: https://github.com/liaScript/templates

LiaScript currently supports three different styles of rendering modes (see Sec. 2.3.5), allowing every user to choose his/her preferred type (req 5). Concerning the preferred course language, translating a single text-document is much easier than translating a whole software-project or a YouTube-video or podcast and LiaScript offers some options that allow to host different language versions of one course at the same project (req 4).

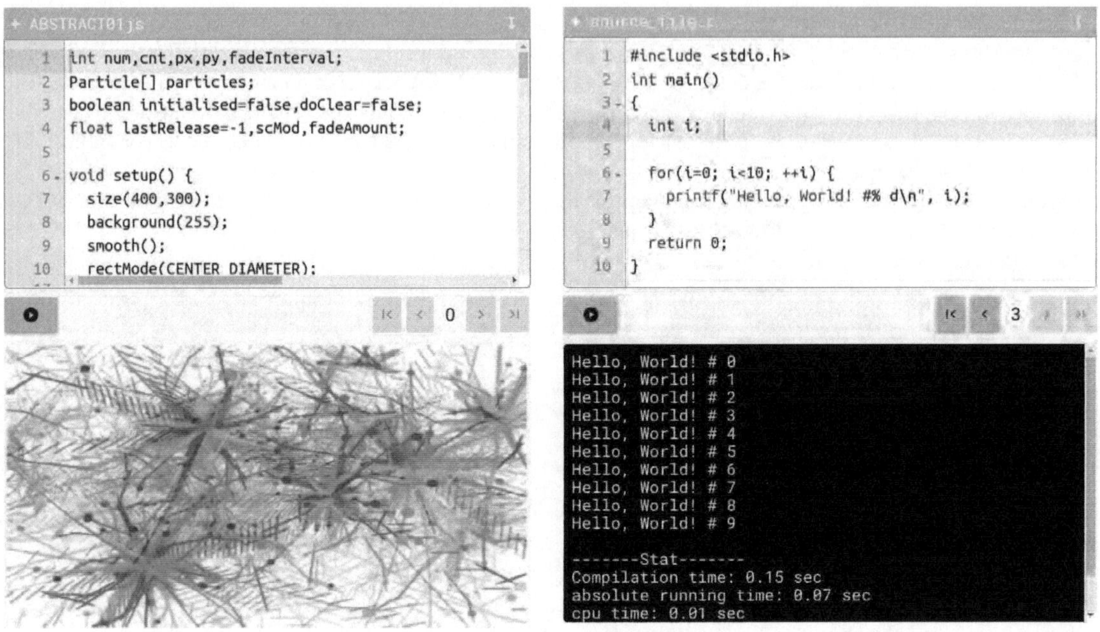

Figure 2. Programming C with rextester (left) and Processing with Prossessing.js (right)

ACKNOWLEDGMENT

This work was partially supported by the German Federal Ministry of Education and Research (BMBF, Funding number: 16DHL1033).

REFERENCES

Dobre, Iuliana. (2015). *Learning Management Systems for higher education-an overview of available options for Higher Education Organizations*. In: Procedia-Social and Behavioral Sciences 180, pp. 313-320.

Heinecke, Michael. (2016). *Production digitaler Skripte*. [online] Available at: http://www.sumo.uni-hamburg.de/DigitaleSkripte/ URL [Accessed Date 26 Mar. 2019].

McKiernan, Erin C. (2017). *Imagining the "open" university: Sharing scholarship to improve research and education*. In: PLoS biology, 15.10.

Ovadia, Steven. (2019). *Addressing the Technical Challenges of Open Educational Resources*. In: Portal - Libraries and the Academy, 19.1, pp. 79-93.

Wikipedia contributors. (2019). *Markdown*. [online] Available at: https://en.wikipedia.org/wiki/Markdown URL [Accessed Date 26 Mar. 2019].

Zhou, Qingguo, et al. (2018). *A collaborative and open solution for large-scale online learning*. In: Computer Applications in Engineering Education, 26.6, pp. 2266-2281.

INSTRUCTIONAL DESIGN TO "TRAIN THE TRAINERS": THE START@UNITO PROJECT AT THE UNIVERSITY OF TURIN

Marina Marchisio[1], Matteo Sacchet[2] and Daniela Salusso[3]
[1]*Dipartimento di Biotecnologie Molecolari e Scienze per la salute, Università degli studi di Torino, Via Nizza, 52, 10126 Torino TO, Italy*
[2]*Dipartimento di Matematica "G. Peano", Università degli studi di Torino, Via Carlo Alberto, 10, 10123 Torino TO, Italy*
[3]*Dipartimento di Lingue e letterature straniere e culture moderne, Università degli studi di Torino Via Giuseppe Verdi, 10, 10124 Torino TO, Italy*

ABSTRACT

Online learning has become essential in higher education. In order to follow the best practices in education and innovation and provide quality of online courses, careful and thorough instructional design is necessary. In this research we analyze the instructional design methods employed and focus on the training of the professors and grant holders who created and developed the 50 open online courses in a variety of disciplines developed in the start@unito project, a recent enterprise of the University of Turin with the aim of bridging the gap between secondary and higher education and provide open online courses that can be accessed anytime anywhere. The data gathered from the questionnaires given to the grant holders before and after the training show encouraging results as far as the effectiveness of our instructional method is concerned. At the same time, though, they reveal a lack and a disparity of technical, pedagogical and linguistic competences, which in turn require tailored and individualized support. In light of the feedback received, we conclude by envisaging possible improvements and further research, in order to understand what can be done to perfect the instructional design of an ever-expanding project.

KEYWORDS

Digital Education, Educational Technology, e-Learning, Instructional Design, Open Online Courses, Teacher Training

1. INTRODUCTION

It is an undeniable fact that online learning has become essential in higher education, not only as a way to showcase the university's programmes and departments, but also and especially to contribute knowledge to the world, enhance teaching and learning, promote internationalization, facilitate working students and ease the transition from high school to university, following the best practices in education and innovation.

The University of Turin has recently embarked upon the start@unito project (Bruschi et al., 2018; Marchisio et al., 2019), financed by Compagnia di San Paolo and aimed at using the Moodle LMS to create and provide open online courses targeted at both university students and high-school students in their last year. Before start@unito, the University of Turin had already had experience in developing high-quality online teaching programs, such as PPS Problem posing and solving (2012) (Brancaccio et al., 2015; Barana et al., 2019), aimed at high-school teachers of STEM disciplines, the Scuola dei compiti project (2013) (Barana et al., 2017c) as a support for high-school students, and the university guidance modules Orient@mente (2014) (Barana et al., 2017a; Barana, et al., 2016; Barana, et al., 2017b). In addition, it is worth mentioning the Foundation Programme (2018), aimed at foreign students who wish to learn Italian and earn the credits required to study at the University of Turin. So far, the university offers 20 online courses across a wide range of subjects, and 30 additional courses will be available.

In the first phase of the project start@unito (academic year 2017-2018), 20 online courses were created, developed and implemented. The disciplines covered belong to the scientific (e.g. Physics, Mathematics, Informatics, Zoology, etc.), the legal (e.g. Political Science, Law and Justice, European institutions and rights, etc.), the economic (Economics and firms) and the humanistic (e.g. Philosophy, Contemporary History, etc.) area. The second phase of the project is currently undergoing. This year 30 additional online courses are being prepared and will be available soon. In addition to the areas covered the previous year, some linguistic disciplines have been added (e.g. English Language and Linguistics, German Language, Swahili Literature), as well as many courses taught completely in English.

Throughout these experiences in designing and helping others design online courses, we came across a major difficulty, namely the resistance towards changing one's didactic approach. Especially when dealing with established University Professors, who have been perfecting their materials and their teaching methods for a long time, it is often challenging to adopt the more student-centered, modular, multimodal and interactive approach that the online context demands. The technical, pedagogical and methodological skills required cannot be learned overnight, therefore our team decided to offer a course to "train the trainers". The course was composed of 12 in-person meetings, in which the main topics of e-learning were presented and discussed by experts (University professors and technical staff): how to design an online course, how to communicate effectively with videos, how to use the online platform, the Automated Assessment System (AAS) and some software for creating digital contents. Somme issues about copyright, accessibility and HTML language were presented to make professors more aware of the context of Digital Education. The training was supported by an online course where all the materials presented were available, together with additional resources.

The professors were supported by postgraduate grant holders, each experienced in the subject of study and with some background experience in using learning management systems, video making, and online teaching. Ideally, the training programme was conceived for both professors and grant holders, but in practice, given the numerous academic commitments, the grant holders' participation was much higher. For this reason, we will focus on the analysis of their training. Our aim is precisely to evaluate and interpret the data gathered from the questionnaires given to grant holders in order to self-reflect on our instructional design choices. We will briefly review the relevant literature on instructional design and present the theoretical framework within which we operated. After that, the methodology, the model and the data will be discussed. The results show that our instructional design model proved indeed to be effective in facilitating the transition between classroom and online teaching. However, it also emerged that the initial low and very uneven technical and linguistic competences would require a more practical approach, personalized support and differentiated training, especially among different subjects. Personalized guidance also seems to be beneficial in understanding how to put together the pedagogy and the technology.

2. BRIEF LITERATURE REVIEW

As the demand for online distance courses gradually increases in the academic world, so does the need for a professional figure that can help professors throughout transition from face-to-face courses to online ones. An analysis of the topic "instructional design and technologies" reveals that lately it has become one of the most popular among scholars (Hsu, 2012; West, 2017) as well as teacher education and training (West, 2014; West 2017). Although many authors have suggested a constructivist approach to distance education (Crotty, 1994; Garrison, 1993), very few have proposed clear, specific strategies to put it into practice. The majority of experts, nevertheless, agree on one point: the need to replace the usual teacher-centered paradigm in favor of a more student-centered one, which employs the technologies available in order to create a learning environment that supports the knowledge construction process (Barr and Tagg, 1995; Taylor, 2000). This model has often been referred to as constructive alignment. The concept of constructive alignment dates back sixty years (Tyler, 1949) but it has recently been applied to the higher education online context (Biggs, 2014). Biggs contends that in the transition between a teacher-centered design of courses to a more student- and outcome-based one, constructive alignment needs to be embedded in a supportive culture in order to work properly at the departmental, institutional and even national levels. As for a model that would allow a smoother transition, Biggs and Tang (Biggs, and Tang, 2011) describe a "training the trainers" model.

The discipline concerned with training the trainers is instructional design, whose aim is to create a stimulating learning environment where learners can actively interact with contents and knowledge transmitted via a teacher or interactive material, thus supporting learning as an active process of constructing (Duffy and Cunningham, 1996). Instructional design aims at training the trainers on how to design those materials and how to use the technologies available to match their educational purposes, assisting teachers and tutors by providing them with a set of principles and concept models (Wilson, 1996). Instructional designers in higher education "use a wide variety of tools for a wide variety of purposes ranging from course design to supporting faculty in delivering online courses to facilitating meaningful workshops for faculty" (Kumar and Ritzhaupt, 2017). Furthermore, instructional design has been defined as the sector that operates at the international level to identify the didactic criteria and models applicable in the different contexts, in such a way that learning has the highest possible probability to be effective, efficient, and interesting (Calvani and Menichetti, 2015). Despite the popularity of online courses such as MOOCs, however, very little study has been carried out consistently on the quality of instructional design in those courses (Margaryan, Bianco, and Littlejohn, 2015), whereas we believe it to be a key component and an essential prerequisite of the potential for effective learning but also for effective teaching. Many scholars, among whom Speck (Speck, 2000), noted that, these changes in higher education often disregard academics' pedagogical expertise. Online teaching is a relatively new field for most university professors, and without careful training that also includes the pedagogical aspects, they may end up perceiving "greater intrinsic and extrinsic barriers" when approaching it (Lloyd et al., 2012). Therefore, we have designed a training course that takes into account all of these factors; in the following chapter we will outline the basic principles of our own instructional design method.

3. THEORETICAL FRAMEWORK AND RESEARCH QUESTIONS

Our main goal was to find a set of clear principles on which to base our training course, following a method that puts together the pedagogy and the technical aspects.

After the first tentative year of start@unito, in which the basic theoretical principles were laid out, a more in-depth analysis followed, and a more structured program was implemented. According to this program, the instructional designers' task is to structure a training course based on the following theoretical grounds:

- Course structure: modular structure of courses (Rogerson-Revell, 2007) with a grid format and each section corresponding to an ECTS, organized in learning objects that comply with the LTSC standards; mindful engagement of students in tasks and in the interaction with the learning-objects (Bruschi and Perissinotto, 2003). The design process took an important role prior to any implementation: professors and grant holders had to clearly outline the structure, specifying which concept to be explained and how. Comparison between different courses must be encouraged, in order to make the quantity of materials homogeneous.
- Use of technology: principles of multimedia learning (Mayer, 2005; 2014) that support integration between text, image and voice in order to adapt the cognitive load (Plass et al., 2010) of the contents to learn. Materials organized according to the principles of segmentation, sequencing, and pacing. Prior experience on the use of technology for learning at the University of Turin was taken into account, especially in the choice of the online platform in which the courses are hosted.
- Learning outcomes: constructive alignment of learning outcomes. Instructional design must adapt the cognitive load by diminishing the external one and optimizing the intrinsic one according to the attainment target (Landriscina, 2015).
- Assessment: formative assessment and feedback to enhance teaching and learning and provide self-regulation (Barana et al., 2018; Bloom, 1971) paired with automated assessment and adaptive methodologies (Barana et al., 2015; Hattie and Timperley, 2007) especially for scientific subjects.
- A variation of the ADDIE model of instructional design based on a five-phase project: Analyze, Design, Develop, Implement, and Evaluate.

Once the theoretical principles were outlined, we designed our training programs, whose aim was to prepare grant holders and professors to create online courses based on such principles. For the purpose of the present paper, we decided to focus on grant holders because, not being burdened by academic commitments, they were the ones who actually participated in the whole training. Secondly, the professors have more expertise in terms of contents and didactics, but fewer in terms of technical skills. In light of the feedback received, our research question is how effective the training actually was in proposing a coherent instructional design method and what may be done to improve it.

4. METHODOLOGY

The methodology we adopted for this research relies on three modalities of data collection:

1) The specific issues that emerged and were discussed during the training course. The subjects covered in the training, during traditional lessons and/or laboratories, ranged from online pedagogy and assessment techniques, to basics of videomaking and practical use of the Moodle platform, from editing, automatic assessment and advanced computing environment software, to copyright and website accessibility. All the lessons were held by experts in their field.
2) The questionnaires administered both before and after the training course: all the 29 grant holders with whom we worked this year replied. We chose to distribute the questionnaires online and we opted for a non-anonymous survey, as we were interested in understanding the points of view of each individual and be able to relate the criticalities encountered to their subject of study. The pre-training and the post-training questionnaires were structured in the same way; the questions – a mix of multiple selection, Likert Scale, and open questions – were repeated to maximise the potential for comparison. Furthermore, the post-training questionnaire also contained a set of questions about the self-study materials (lesson recordings, tutorials, manuals, templates, etc.) that we provided.
3) The individual and group support we offered throughout the creation of the courses, aiming at solving problems and finding solutions together, as well as promoting dialogue between grant holders, professors, the technical staff and the scientific committee. We offered support in the form of official monthly group meetings where grant holders presented their materials and discussed their effectiveness with us. These meetings were attended by the technical staff too, who offered advice whenever needed; on-request one to one meetings in our office and or on-site for both professors and grant holders who wished to be counselled or supported on specific issues; daily support via e-mail and phone to solve the most pressing problems.

5. DATA AND REFLECTIONS

After examining the answers to the questionnaire given to the grant holders at the beginning and at the end of the experience, two main trends can be noticed.

First of all, a general lack of technical competence before the training and only a passive knowledge and understanding of the e-learning environment emerge. 57,14% of grant holders had already had some experience of e-learning as students: many grant holders studied at the University of Turin, where many departments have been adopting e-learning strategies since 2004. Nevertheless, only 24,14% had had the same experience as tutors and as provider of education through an online platform. In addition, 51,72% were already familiar with the concept of Virtual Learning Environment (VLE), whereas only 27,59% were aware of what an Automated Assessment System (AAS) is and how it works. This shows that even if some people used an online tool for learning, they may not have been aware of all its potentialities. The lessons belonging to the technical area were also the ones considered the most useful. Some of the open answers also confirm the same trend; the question "what are your expectations of this training course?" generated such answers as "understanding the e-learning world, learning how to improve my technical skills, learning how to use the Moodle platform, an introduction to the VLE, learning about the software available to design online courses." Some grant holders expected more examples of online learning materials, especially for specific humanistic disciplines. About this, after an introductory meeting to show the start@unito project with its objectives and its outcomes, we let grant holders freely navigate the web to clear their mind about how their subjects is presented in online materials. Two questions were about personal experience on three different areas: technical, organizational and didactic areas, before and after the training. As we can see in Table 1 below, the medium level of competence in the technical area was rather low before the training, while the median for the level of competence in the organizational and didactic areas was average. Less than 50% of the answers were "average" or above in the technical area, while around 40% of the answers were "Good" or "Very good" in the organizational and didactics areas.

Table 1. Level of competence in the three areas of expertise before the training

Level of competence	Technical area	Organizational area	Didactic area
No competence	17,24%	6,90%	10,34%
Low	37,93%	13,79%	24,14%
Average	31,03%	37,93%	24,14%
Good	13,79%	34,48%	37,93%
Very good	0,00%	6,90%	3,45%

Secondly, the instructional design training had a positive impact: when asked how ready they felt to create and develop and online course, 48.3 % of grant holders reported feeling almost ready to start designing it before the formative lessons. After the training, though, only 20,7% of grant holders reported feeling almost ready, while 55,2% reported feeling ready enough and 24,1% very ready. Nobody reported not feeling ready. The training also proved to be effective to improve the perceived competence of the grant holders in the three main areas of expertise required. The technical area, in particular, in which more than a half of grant holders were lacking, reported a consistent improvement, because the median is Good. It must be noticed that the median improved in all three areas to Good, more than 60% of the answers attested Good or Very good and, luckily, no grant holders selected No competence. Detailed results are shown in Table 2.

Table 2. Level of competence in the three areas of expertise after the training

Level of competence	Technical area	Organizational area	Didactic area
No competence	0,00%	0,00%	0,00%
Low	10,34%	13,79%	17,24%
Average	17,24%	24,14%	17,24%
Good	41,38%	48,28%	44,83%
Very good	31,03%	13,79%	20,69%

It is worthwhile to mention that grant holders participated in an average of 9.27 in-person meetings over 12. Grant holders were asked about the usefulness of each meeting via a 5-point Likert scale (1 = Not useful, 5 = Very useful). The average score was 4, quite useful, again with higher points on technical meetings. After the in-person training, all grant holders expressed an improvement in their skills (median 4 out of a 5-point Likert scale) and reported feeling ready to prepare an online course with their professors (median 4 out of a 5-point Likert scale with 100% of the data with score 3 or above), thus the formative lessons had a big influence on the way they prepared their materials and 17,2% reported being highly influenced. The online support materials that were particularly appreciated are tutorials, manuals, templates and sample materials. Nevertheless, the open question regarding which aspects of the training course may be improved highlighted the widespread necessity for a more practical, hands-on approach, focusing on specific issues, promoting learning-by-doing strategies and providing more examples of how to create quality contents and a good course structure. Furthermore, many grant holders expressed the need for targeted and tailored interventions, concentrating on the critical areas of each subject rather than attending group lessons or laboratories. This conclusion is in line with our observations throughout the academic year, since we also offered one-to-one meetings and personalized technical, didactic and linguistic support. According to the data gathered from the questionnaire and our considerations, the main areas in which grant holders needed individualized and differentiated training were:

- the technical area: as mentioned before, there was a general low level of technical competences in the required sub-categories: video-making, using Maple TA automated assessment, managing and making the most of the tools offered by the VLE Moodle, creation of multimedia contents such as screencasts and interactive pdfs, using an Advanced Computing Environment (ACE) and rudiments of HTML. However, it must be pointed out that those grant holders who already had a technical-scientific background, especially in Mathematics, were accustomed to using most of the tools proposed or simply more inclined to learning the basics easily. On the contrary, those whose subjects belonged to the humanistic, linguistic or legal areas found it difficult to cope with the specificity of the training and to reflect on how some of the tools proposed may be effectively used in a non-scientific context. One example is adaptive feedback, made possible when designing tests with Maple TA. Some grant holders and professors of linguistic subjects, for example, saw the potential of the adaptive features in an asynchronous context where the language student does not have the opportunity for interacting either with a tutor or with peers, but only few of them used it because they lacked the time to learn how to use the tool effectively. Similarly, 69% of grant holders revealed that they had no need to use an ACE to build their interactive materials, and their follow-up answer on the reason why they did not need it made it clear that it was not due to a lack of interest or skills, but the subject did not require the ACE.
- The pedagogical area: many professors and grant holders struggled with shifting the teaching paradigm to a more student-centered one, and found it challenging to rethink contents and materials. In particular, some of the open answers in the post-training questionnaire revealed that the pedagogical differences between designing an online course for the bachelor's and one for the master's degree had not been accounted for enough.
- The linguistic area: most grant holders and professors who worked on courses held entirely in English required systematic linguistic support. The professors had already received EMI training for their traditional classroom courses held in English, but the online context generated further complications, such as the necessity to create materials from scratch because of copyright issues, and the need to speak in front of the camera in one's second language.

Finally, the last part of the post-training questionnaire focused on the online support materials we provided. One of our aims, in fact, is to perfect a self-study online programme based on the same instructional design principles of the traditional training, which can accompany and guide professors and grant holders in their journey. We asked our participants if they would recommend the use of the online materials only to prepare for the creation of an online course, and 41,4% of grant holders said yes. The remaining 58.6% explained their position in the comments: they said that despite finding the self-study materials very useful, the face-to-face time to exchange ideas, discuss problems and find solutions both with their peers and with us was invaluable.

However, many of them agreed that most of the materials provided were a good alternative to attending the lesson, as long as the element of interaction is always present, either as an online tutoring format or as individual meetings after the general training course has been completed.

6. CONCLUSION

Thanks to the feedback received, the observations made, and the results obtained, we can learn from our experience and reflect on how a self-study training course should be organized in order to achieve the ultimate goals of the instructional design model presented.

First, training courses may consist in a general, common part that, following the instructional design Addie Model, may correspond to the "analysis" phase. After this first phase, though, before starting the actual "design" phase, some room for individual and tailored support must be available. In fact, early prediction and identification of problem areas may avoid an imbalance between course content and course design, as well as the technology used and their effectiveness, bearing in mind the learning outcomes. To partially solve this problem, we provided some common general training modules, both in person and online. Then, the trainer can choose between different paths, according to whether the online course is held in Italian or in English, whether it is aimed at students of the bachelor's or the master's degree, and whether the subject in question is scientific, linguistic, legal, economic, humanistic or other. Another way to give individual support consists in providing users with content models, ready to be shared, cloned and adapted to the instructional need. By providing personalized guidance in the early stages of the course design, we expect the development of materials to be easier and smoother, and as a consequence, teachers' and grant holders' confidence to improve. We will continue to investigate the results after the implementation and the evaluation phases take place. So far, our experience reveals that in order to "train the trainers" in higher education in order to facilitate the transition between traditional classroom teaching and online teaching, we need the flexibility to rethink content creation, teaching methods, and assessment techniques, maintaining the same quality yet at the same time accounting for the fact that we are working in a different environment.

REFERENCES

Barana, A., Bogino, A., Fioravera, M., Floris, F., Marchisio, M., Operti, L., Rabellino, S.2017a. Self-paced approach in synergistic model for supporting and testing students: The transition from Secondary School to University. Proceedings of 2017 IEEE 41st Annual Computer Software and Applications Conference (COMPSAC), pp. 404-409.

Barana, A., Bogino, A., Fioravera, M., Marchisio, M., Rabellino, S., 2016. Digital Support for University Guidance and Improvement of Study Results. Proceedings – Social and Behavioral Sciences 228, pp. 547-552.

Barana, A., Bogino, A., Fioravera, M., Marchisio, M., Rabellino, S., 2017b. Open platform of self-paced MOOCs for the continual improvement of academic guidance and knowledge strengthening in tertiary education. Journal of e-Learning and Knowledge Society, 13(3), 109-119.

Barana, A., Brancaccio, A., Conte, A., Fissore, C., Floris, F. Marchisio, M. Pardini, C., 2019. The Role of an Advanced Computing Environment in Teaching and Learning Mathematics through Problem Posing and Solving. Proceedings of the 15th International Scientific Conference eLearning and Software Education (ELSE 2019), Bucarest, vol. 2, pp. 11-18.

Barana, A., Fioravera, M., Marchisio, M., Rabellino, S., 2017c. Adaptive teaching supported by ICTs to reduce the school failure in the Project "Scuola dei Compiti", Proceedings of 2017 IEEE 41st Annual Computer Software and Applications Conference (COMPSAC), pp. 432-437.

Barana, A., Conte, A., Fioravera, M., Marchisio, M., Rabellino, S., 2018. A Model of Formative Automatic Assessment and Interactive Feedback for STEM. Proceedings of 2018 IEEE 42nd Annual Computer Software and Applications Conference (COMPSAC), Tokyo, Japan, pp. 1016–1025.

Barana, A., Marchisio, M., Rabellino, S., 2015. Automated Assessment in Mathematics. Proceedings of 2015 IEEE 39th Annual Computer Software and Applications Conference, Taichung, Taiwan: IEEE, pp. 670–671.

Barr, R. B., and J. Tagg, 1995. From teaching to learning – A new paradigm for undergraduate education. *Change*, pp. 13–25.

Biggs, J., 2014. Constructive alignment in university teaching. *HERDSA Review of Higher Education Vol. 1*, Hammondville, Australia, pp. 5-22

Biggs, J., and Tang, K., 2011. *Teaching for quality learning at University*. 4th ed. Maidenhead: Oxford University Press.

Bloom, B., Madaus, G. F., and Hastings, J. T., 1971. *Handbook on Formative and Summative Evaluation of Student Learning*. New York: McGraw-Hill.

Brancaccio, A., Marchisio, M., Palumbo, C., Pardini, C., Patrucco, A., Zich, R., 2015. Problem Posing and Solving: Strategic Italian Key Action to Enhance Teaching and Learning Mathematics and Informatics in the High School. In: Proceedings of 2015 IEEE 39th Annual Computer Software and Applications Conference (COMPSAC), IEEE, Taichung, Taiwan, pp. 845–850.

Bruschi, B., Cantino, V., Cavallo Perin, R., Culasso, F., Giors, B., Marchisio, M., Marello, C., Milani, M., Operti, L., Parola, A., Rabellino, S., Sacchet, M., Scomparin, L., 2018. Start@unito: a Supporting Model for High School Students Enrolling to University. IADIS International Conference Cognition and Exploratory Learning in Digital Age 2018, pp. 307–312.

Bruschi, B., and Perissinotto, A., 2003. *Come creare corsi on line.* Carocci, Roma.

Calvani, A., and Menichetti, L., 2015. *Come fare un progetto didattico*. Carocci, Roma.

Crotty, T., 1994. Integrating distance learning activities to enhance teacher education toward the constructivist paradigm of teaching and learning. *Distance Learning Research Conference Proceedings, 3,* pp. 1-37. College Station, TX: Department of Education and Human Resource Development, Texas A & M University.

Duffy, T. M., and Cunningham, D. J., 1996. Constructivism: Implications for the Design and Delivery of Instruction. *Handbook of Research for Educational Communications and Technology*. Macmillan Library Reference, New York, USA.

Hattie, J., and Timperley, H., 2007. The Power of Feedback. *Review of Educational Research*, Vol. 77(1), pp. 81–112.

Garrison, R., 1993. Quality and access in distance education: Theoretical considerations. *Theoretical Principles of Distance Education,* pp. 9-2 1, Routledge, New York.

Hsu, Y.-C., Ho, H. N. J., Tsai, C.-C., Hwang, G.-J., Chu, H.-C., Wang, C.-Y., and Chen, N.-S., 2012. Research trends in technology-based learning from 2000 to 2009: A content analysis of publications in selected journals. *Educational Technology & Society*, Vol. 15(2), pp. 354–370.

Kumar, S & Ritzhaupt, Albert., 2017. What do instructional designers in higher education really do?. *International Journal on E-Learning: Corporate, Government, Healthcare, and Higher Education*. 16. 371-393.

Landriscina, F., 2015. Instructional Design e progettazione curricolare. Un binomio possibile per la scuola italiana. *Form@re. Open Journal per la formazione in rete*, Vol 15, N° 3.

Lloyd, S. A., Byrne, M. M., & McCoy, T. S., 2012. Faculty-perceived barriers of online education. *Journal of Online Learning and Teaching*, 8(1), 1-12.

Margaryan, A., Bianco, M., and Littlejohn, A., 2015. Instructional quality of Massive Open Online Courses (MOOCs). *Computers & Education* 80, pp. 77–83.

Marchisio, M., Operti, L., Rabellino, S., Sacchet, M., 2019. Start@unito: Open Online Courses for Improving Access and for Enhancing Success in Higher Education. Proceedings of the 11th International Conference on Computer Supported Education (CSEDU 2019), Heraklion, Crete, Greece, pp. 639-646.

Mayer, R. E., 2005. Cognitive Theory of Multimedia Learning. *The Cambridge handbook of multimedia* learning. New Cambridge University Press, York, NY, US pp. 31-48.

Mayer R. E., Lee H. and Peebles A., 2014. Multimedia Learning in a Second Language: A Cognitive Load Perspective, *Applied Cognitive Psychology 28*, pp. 653–660

Plass, J. L., Moreno, R., and Brünken, R. (Eds.), 2010. *Cognitive load theory*. Cambridge University Press, New York.

Rogerson-Revell, P., 2007. Directions in e-learning tools and technologies and their relevance to online distance language education. *Open Learning 22(1),* pp. 57–74.

Speck, B. W., 2000. The academy, online classes, and the breach in ethics: Principles of effective teaching in the online classroom. *New Directions for Teaching and Learning*, 84(Winter), 73-81.

Taylor, P. G., 2000. Changing Expectations: Preparing students for Flexible Learning. *The International Journal of Academic Development 5(2),* pp. 107–115.

Tyler, R. W., 1949. *Basic principles of curriculum and instruction*. University of Chicago Press, Chicago.

West, R.E., Thomas, R. A., Bodily, R., Wright, C., and Borup, J., 2017. An analysis of instructional design and technology departments. *Education Tech Research Dev 65: 869.*

West, R. E., and Borup, J., 2014. An analysis of a decade of research in 10 instructional design and technology journals. *British Journal of Educational Technology 45(4),* pp. 545–556.

Wilson, B. G., 1996. Constructivist Learning Environments: Case Studies in Instructional design. *Educational technology Publications*. Englewood Cliffs NJ

DEVELOPMENT OF AN ONLINE TOOL BASED ON CFD AND OBJECT-ORIENTED PROGRAMMING TO SUPPORT TEACHING FLUID MECHANICS

Concepción Paz, Eduardo Suárez, Adrián Cabarcos and Christian Gil
School of Industrial Engineering, University of Vigo
Campus Universitario Lagoas-Marcosende, 36310, Vigo, Spain.

ABSTRACT

Fluid Mechanics is one of the most complex branches of science to learn. Traditionally, it has been taught from a positivism point of view. However, the latest technologies have led to the creation of new educational tools based on a constructivism approach as a complement to conventional teaching. This paper addresses the development of a course to spread knowledge related to Fluid Mechanics. It combines theoretical explanations with interactive applications to allow the student to assimilate the information easier. Computational Fluid Dynamic simulations have been performed to create the educational content shown in the applications. Users will be able to select from different boundary conditions, and the program will display the corresponding simulation results. Therefore, motivation is generated through gamification, retention is generated based on the Multimedia Learning Theory and transfer is generated by inductive teaching. A preliminary version of this course has been launched to a group of users with previous knowledge in Fluid Mechanics. The results indicate how users support the inclusion of multimedia and interactive tools in conventional teaching, because they help them to assimilate complex concepts. Furthermore, the created tool has been endorsed by the users in terms of organization and quality. The adaptation of current resources, such as CFD, to teaching Fluid Mechanics is an evident need that enriches both the student and the teacher. Thus, the educational goals of motivation and knowledge transfer are promoted under the auspices of a constructivism approach.

KEYWORDS

Fluid Mechanics, Educational Software, Distance Learning, Simulation

1. INTRODUCTION

It is a fact that education is one of the most important pillars on which modern society is based (Galor, 2011), and technology is one of the most powerful driving forces for change (McClure, 1991). Consequently, computers become more powerful, manufacturing machines become more advanced and metrology instruments become more accurate; therefore, the adaptation of the current education to the newest technologies is a clear necessity (Hernández, 2008). Future professionals and workers should be educated in accordance with new technological paradigms as well as social paradigms, such as globalization, and the digitalization of information should be considered (Cheng, 2005).

Fluid Mechanics is the branch of science that addresses the study of fluids, either in motion or at rest (White, 2008); it is a subject with a greater mathematical basis in any scientific degree. Furthermore, Fluid Mechanics is one of the most difficult subjects to understand. However, the primary objective of those teaching Fluid Mechanics is typically focused on students' understanding beyond extensive but necessary numerical developments. Nevertheless, this educational goal based on understanding, which was previously a considerable challenge for teachers, must take advantage of the synergies of these new social and technological paradigms to simplify and improve the educational experience of students studying Fluid Mechanics.

Furthermore, as a primary result of computing and the current trend towards globalization, digitalization and universal access to education, an early educational model known as MOOC was recently developed. This model, whose acronym corresponds to Massive Open Online Courses, is characterized by web development, i.e., making use of the facilities allowed by this type of approach, such as multimedia, encouraging user interaction or flexible timetables (Ruiz, 2015). Therefore, its onset presents a new framework in relation to the development of educational actions to improve the understanding and spread of Fluid Mechanics. Additionally, they are designed for massive distribution, thus providing free access to all their content in spite of the fact that semi-commercial platforms, such as edX or Coursera, have existed since 2011. These platforms provide additional services, such as verified certificates or online meetings, in exchange for a fee, thus leaving authors wondering if this funding model is legal (Daniel et al, 2015).

In 2012, an article titled "The year of MOOC" was published by The New York Times. The Massachusetts Institute of Technology (MIT) announced that the MOOC model was the most important educational innovation over the last 200 years (Regalado, 2012). Additionally, engineering students can benefit from these types of initiatives. Hence, the "Circuits and electronics (6002x)" course, which was developed by MIT in 2012 (for 155,000 students initially enrolled), has been one of the most important and analysed MOOCs in history (Breslow et al. 2013). This course has been a turning point when considering the volume of users. It was taken by students from 194 countries, who were encouraged by the knowledge they could obtain. However, this course was only completed by 5 percent of the users, and decreasing the dropout rates is one of the largest challenges that needed to be overcome by the MOOC model to ensure global and universal access (Brahimi & Sarirete, 2015). The current trend holds important demographic imbalances caused by the detriment of developing countries (Hone & El Said, 2016). However, there have been projects that have considered the education of people who are at risk of social exclusion.

Furthermore, engineering courses such as "Circuits and electronics (6002x)" typically add a few features to encourage learning support, e.g., virtual laboratories, where students will be able to assemble electronic and electrical circuits for testing, as well as other branches of science, such as medicine, which also includes numerical simulations of complex biological processes with an educational goal (Christ & Thews, 2016). Moreover, Computational Fluids Dynamics (CFD) is one of the most powerful tools used for the study of Fluid Mechanics (White, 2008), which consist of a set of numerical methods whose final objective is to obtain a numerical approach (Jiyuan et al, 2008). As well as circuit simulation programs are essential to electronic education innovation, CFD can be an important tool for learning Fluid Mechanics remotely.

In fact, the purpose of this paper is to provide a description of the development of an online course as a tool to support learning Fluid Mechanics using CFD and object-oriented programing to allow users to understand the main effects and principles of this branch of science easily.

2. DESCRIPTION

The solution to the proposed problem involves the integration of three different action lines, as depicted in Figure 1, because the development of a course structure is needed to add the educational content that will guide the user through the Fluid Mechanics topics. eXeLearning, which is an open software used for educational web content development, will be used for this purpose. Although this tool traces its origins to 2007 in New Zealand, the Spanish educative authorities took charge of project management in 2010 and has enabled HTML5 content format development since 2013 (Aznar, 2016). Furthermore, the course must be distributed online; thus, as a complement to eXeLearning, a file hosting service will be used as a cloud hosting server by sharing the public link of an "Index.html" file of the course, which will allow the home page to be viewed.

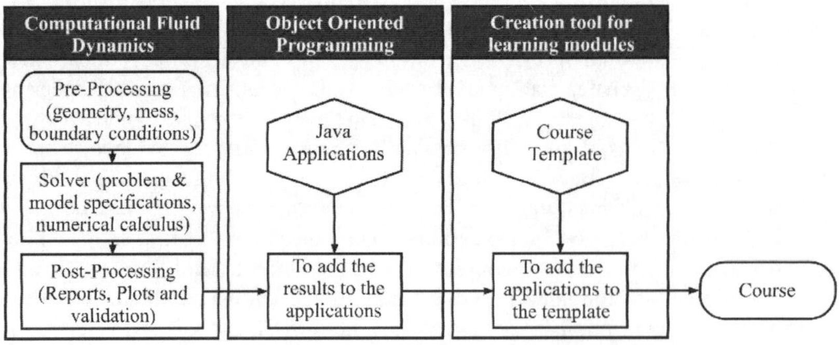

Figure 1. Action lines

Conversely, it is necessary to encourage autonomous learning and provide tools to ensure the interaction between the student and the system. Thereby, CFD will be used with a different goal in regards to the primary two objectives that have sustained its development. Instead of being used to solve industrial fluid flows or for research purposes, CFD will be used for an educational goal, thus allowing the development of realistic simulations to represent the primary effects and principles of Fluid Mechanics to students. It should be noted that unlike other initiatives, such as the CFD Educational Interface described by Stern et al. (2006), this tool does not inform the student regarding the preparation or launch of these type of simulations; it instead uses its results as a learning vehicle.

Additionally, CFD allows avoiding one of the largest problems in teaching Fluid Mechanics. It is necessary to teach a branch of science supported by such a powerful mathematical basis to the general public, without allowing a lack of advanced mathematical knowledge to keep students from completing the course. Non-engineer users interested in science and knowledge must be able to learn the primary topics right from the start whereas engineer users may use this course as complementary to their conventional teaching.

The user must be able to confidently handle a large volume of graphical results, such as contour maps and streamlines. At this stage, the object-oriented programing will be used as the third action line to create graphical interfaces allowing the selection between predefined boundary conditions; thus, the student can observe the influences of the primary variables on the desired effect or principle based on a comparison between the simulations shown.

3. METHODOLOGY

As previously stated, eXeLearning enables the creation of the web pages that will constitute the course. These pages will be related to each other in the order mark by an index whereas the program will independently create the hyperlinks between these items, thus allowing the user to move from one page to another by a simple click of the mouse. Each of these pages represents the HTML file that would be shown using a web browser. Furthermore, if the created contents are saved as a self-container folder, which is one of the exportation actions allowed by the software, it is possible to guarantee online access to the course by hosting those files on a cloud file service and sharing the URL of the "Index.html" file. Thus, it is possible to launch a preliminary version by minimizing the cost required in comparison to acquire a proprietary domain.

3.1 Course Topics

The first topic is based on previous Fluid Mechanics ideas: viscosity and density properties, surface tension and types of flow. Using aeronautic principles, the flow over simple geometric shapes has been considered. Different object sizes and flow velocities have been analysed to visualize the trail type relative to the Reynolds number. Values ranging between (48-180) require special attention because that is where the Von Karman effect occurs (Rajani et al, 2009). These phenomena are an expression of the drag force; however, this force is not the only one. Lift force, which is responsible for the flight of an airplane or the deflection of a rotating sphere from its main flight path, is also taught in this topic. Jet propulsion will be considered in an additional module, which is the high speed ejection of a gas from a combustion chamber at high pressure.

Furthermore, there are two modules that address Bernoulli's principle. The first one is Torricelli's law, which describes the flow of a fluid in a tank discharge. The second one is the Venturi effect, in which a fluid through a lower section in a pipe increases its dynamic pressure while simultaneously decreasing its static pressure. Both of these phenomena are a consequence of the same equation, the Bernoulli's principle. This principle emphasizes that the energy per unit volume must remain constant along a streamline.

3.2 CFD Simulations

CFD simulations were performed using the ANSYS Fluent solver (ANSYS, 2013). The first few cases, based on the supersonic propulsion phenomena though a Laval nozzle, are steady simulations, where a density-based algorithm has been used to solve the fluid flow. A tank discharging process has been simulated with a multiphase model named the "Volume of Fluid" (VOF). This model solves a set of momentum equations and tracks the volume fraction of each of the fluid phases over the entire domain (ANSYS, 2013). Additionally, this model has been used for an open and ideal tank, for Mariotte's flask simulation.

The Magnus effect, which is the phenomenon in which lift is generated by a rotational body, has been simulated by the creation of a sliding mesh, thus enabling the mesh motion option for the region containing the domain. Furthermore, drag over a cylinder (Mallick & Kumar, 2014, and Gautier et al, 2013) and airflow over 0012, 2424 and 2408 NACA profiles cases have been introduced. The primary characteristic of the second of those groups of simulations has been the use of the same 3 domains for all of the simulations, thus attributing the velocity due to its components whereas the pressure contours and domain are rotated in the post-process stage to visually transform these velocity components using an attack angle.

Additionally, the Venturi effect has been simulated. This effect describes how a fluid through a lower section in a pipe increases its dynamic pressure while its static pressure decreases (White, 2008, and Çengel et al, 2006). It should be noted that Fluent provides two different wall conditions: a specific shear condition or a no-slip option (ANSYS, 2013). The no-slip option has been selected because it is the most realistic alternative, and the null velocity at the contact surface between the solid and the fluid based on the Boundary Layer Theory must be considered.

Lastly, other isolated simulations have been introduced to complete the educational content, such as a rotating naval and aircraft propeller as a supplement to the propulsion explanation, animation of a wave propagation using the "BC Open Channel" condition at the velocity inlet and the "Open Channel Flow" at the pressure outlet of a square domain. Numerical beach treatment has been considered to smooth the influence of the wave diffraction (Black & Rosenberg, 1992).

Lastly, internal flow through a pipe, and external flow through a torpedo completes the simulations launched.

3.3 Object-oriented Programming

Object-oriented programming is the link between the structure of the course and the CFD results. Instead of handling a large amount of images and videos in a gallery, mechanisms are needed for organizing data. Thereby, users have access to a computer tool for each main topic so that they can set boundary conditions, among several options, to display the corresponding simulation.

The first step involves identifying which programs will be created. eXeLearning allows the integration of Applets to create the educational content. These type of Java programs are characterized because they do not have a main class, instead an HTML tag calls the full content (Schildt, 2000). They are designed for a network transmission, which would be a suitable choice to address the proposed problem, and they have already been used to manage similar projects (Graham & Trick, 1998). However, once the first prototypes were created and tested on a local Tomcat server, Google Chrome compatibility problems were detected. Based on the aid support, the technology required for displaying Applets is no longer supported after the 4.1.1 version. Therefore, to ensure access to the material regardless of the browser used to open the course, common applications have been used instead of Applets, and the final programs are thus attached instead of embedded. These applications are similar to those that can be developed using other languages, such as C or C++; however, the operating principles of Java are completely different (Deitel, 2004). In fact, its creation responds to an interpreted language instead of one that is purely complied.

Java applications have been designed as Graphical User Interfaces (GUI) using Swing and Abstract Window Toolkit (AWT) packages from the Java Foundation Classes (JFC). In all cases, a JFrame has been used as the primary container, and JTabbedPanes have been created to host theoretical explanations and simulations tabs. Contour maps and streamlines have been added to the "src" folder of the project as "png" files, and they are displayed as icons of a JLabel object inside those simulations tabs. The initialization of these labels was performed with a constructor method using the School of Industrial Engineering logo.

When considering videos and animations, instructions to call a user's web browser have been used to display these types of multimedia data. Additionally, it should be noted that a video player has been created using the classes provided by the external package to the Java Development Kit, known as the Java Media Framework (Xiong & Jia, 2012); however, the supported codecs are extremely limited. The videos played in this method must be converted to unusual formats, thus losing quality, and it is necessary to take appropriate measures to protect the intellectual property according to the current Spanish law. Therefore, private videos can be uploaded to a cloud storage service using a "Creative Commons-BY" labeling (Aliprandi, 2011), which is a better idea with respect to the intellectual property, quality and number of code lines.

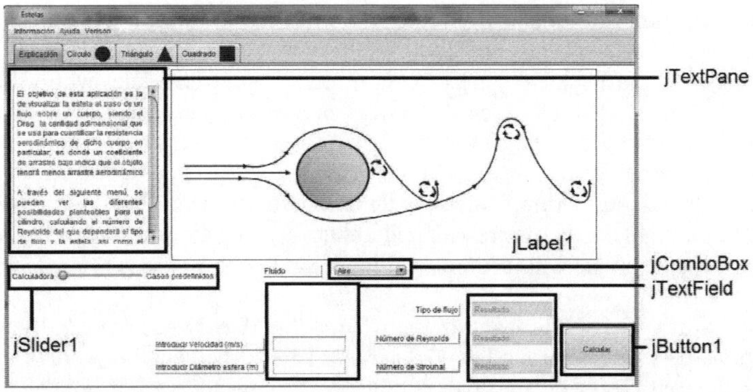

Figure 2. Sample simulation tabs for air flow around a cylinder.

In any case, as indicated in Figure 2, the interfaces also contain JComboBox and JSlider objects to enable the boundary condition selection. Based on the selected condition, internal program variables take a particular value so that the selected picture is displayed while the chosen URI is loaded in the web browser through "if" and "switch" loops.

3.4 e-Learning Criterions

According to Cabero (2006), it should not be forgotten that the network is used as a way to distribute information, which provides an e-learning aspect to the tool. Furthermore, although a significant fraction of users are Fluid Mechanics students at Vigo University, it should be noted that the tool does not fit into the b-learning profile of combining on-line and face-to-face instruction. As previously stated, this is a tool created to improve the educational experience for both the student and teacher. Additionally, it has been promoted to combine conventional teaching with more innovative methodologies that make use of current technologies but with different curricula and a clear boundary. One of the primary causes of error in these types of e-learning initiatives, which rarely occurs in conventional teaching, is the technocentrism (Vasquez, 2007). This concept refers to the fallacy of referring all knowledge acquisition to the technology used, without considering organization and clarity (Papert, 1990). Therefore, in spite of the fact that there is a powerful technological exercise behind the CFD and object-oriented programming, one of the goals set when developing requirements has been that the average user does not spend more than five minutes to understand the operating principle of the applications and the creation of a friendly interface without lengthy technological demonstrations. Any user can go from any menu to another with a single click and enter the web page right from the start without cumbersome registration steps, which typically result in a noticeable decrease in the number of participants. Auto-evaluation tasks consist of mark, relate or select from various items without ever losing sight of the content. Users are given the appropriate hyperlink to quickly and directly install or update their Java version to the correct one. Thus, the user does not have to evaluate incompatibility problems on his own. Furthermore, applications have been converted from jar files, which may not be familiar to users without programming knowledge, to Windows-, Mac- and GNU/Linux-based (tested in the latest versions of Debian and Ubuntu) operating systems' native executables. Users must only click on the hyperlink corresponding to their operating system. According to Pfeffer & Sutton, (2000), there is a gap between knowledge and know-how, thus the entire course has a clear connection with the real world, i.e., how Fluid Mechanics phenomena are manifested in everyday life, such as sports or transportation (Heather et al, 2016), hence attempting to avoid technocentrism and infocentrism, which are two of the greatest causes of failure for e-learning initiatives.

4. RESULTS

Once the course has been completed by the addition of CFD results to the applications and those applications have been uploaded to the eXeLearning structure as attached files to be downloaded by the user, a zero-beta version is launched via email to a group of more than 200 users with prior knowledge of Fluid Mechanics (members were students or ex-students from the Industrial Engineering School), and an anonymous satisfaction survey has been distributed for feedback, (Evans, 2004).

Out of the users who participated in the survey, 71.42 percent were males while 28.58 percent were females. Moreover, it should also be emphasized that 14.28 percent of the users could be current Fluid Mechanics students with an engineering degree, and it should be noted that users can distort information despite the fact that they have been warned of the absence of subject qualification retaliation and confidential data treatment according to Spanish law. Furthermore, the selected group for the zero-beta release were mostly students. Thus, the study reveals that most of the users worried about teaching innovation were student repeaters, industry professionals or students about to finish their engineering degree whereas Fluid Mechanics students appeared less motivated.

Additionally, most survey participants acknowledge that they have interacted with other online courses in similar proportions between both genders (75 percent and 70 percent for women and men, respectively). It should be noted that the average mark given by the users to the course as feedback remains unchanged by the user experience. Students with experience in distance learning marked the course at an 8.75/10 whereas novice students marked it at an 8.80/10. In fact, the same marks resulted when distinguished by gender. The average mark for males was an 8.7/10, and females set a 9/10 as a general quantitative mark.

The statistically average mark was an 8.71/10 with a mode of 9 points. Moreover, the lowest mark was a 6, indicating that the course was approved by all of the survey participants.

It must be emphasized that all participants consider that the use of interactive tools facilitate learning, and 93.8 percent of them would incorporate a similar tool into conventional classroom teaching. Furthermore, 100 percent of the participants consider the use of videos and animations beneficial to assimilating concepts.

Additionally, Figure 3 presents the responses recorded on the structural and functional issues of the course, where it can be seen that, except for isolated cases, users gave high marks to the clarity of the explanations, quality and organization. Moreover, it should be emphasized that the lowest marks refer to organization whereas the worst score over among all of the categories results from the same fraction of users. It should be noted that the beta-testers have not been advised of a massive distribution of the course. Therefore, as it can be seen by the general comments given by the survey, the remarks suggest to follow the teaching guide of the subject. However, this type of approach is impossible to achieve due to the consideration that any user is a final "customer". Because the goal of the course is to provide an online course that allows users with no advanced mathematical knowledge to understand the main effects and phenomena of Fluid Mechanics while an engineer profile can use this tool to strengthen their knowledge of this branch of science, a specified educational content management is required.

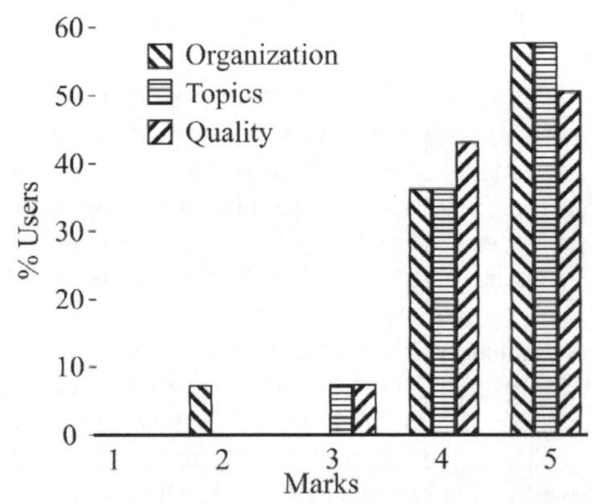

Figure 3. Organization, topics and quality validations

Furthermore, the goal is not to create a tool that replaces conventional teaching, and although these types of remarks are reasonable, they are inconsistent regarding the primary objective. Based on the user's remarks beyond the discussion on whether a deductive model is better than a inductive model or other pedagogical discussions, in terms of encouraging user motivation, analysing the users' observations can be seen as a simple fact of proposing a change or an adaptation in the educational model to the new technological paradigms, which is perceived as a motivating factor for the users, and the student, when perceiving a clear and true interest on the part of the teachers in their training instead of believing their education is a simple task to complete, corresponds that interest with a greater motivation to learn.

Based on Java applications, one of the objectives set as a non-functional requirement of the software engineering process was its simplicity, thus using the estimated learning time needed by users to understand the operation principle of applications as an indirect measure for quantifying this property.

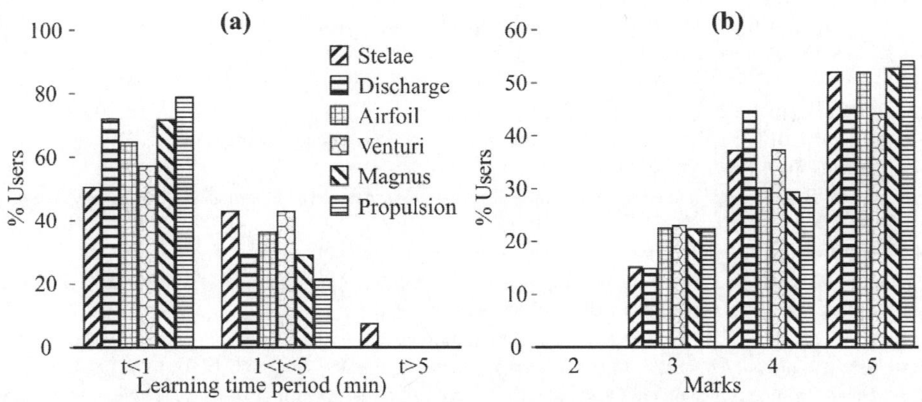

Figure 4. Learning time period and marks given by users.

Figure 4-a illustrates the responses recorded regarding this criterion, where it can be seen that there is only one application where 8 percent of the users estimated that they needed more than 5 minutes to understand how the program worked. This software requirement is verified through Figure 4-a. For example, applications on "deposits discharging" and "stelae", which are complex because they have more code lines than the rest are perceived by students as the most difficult to understand whereas applications referring to the "Venturi effect" and "propulsion", which are chronologically accessed last by the user, are perceived as easier applications to understand.

As indicated in Figure 4-b, users had a positive view on all of the applications, and all of them gave the highest mark as the mode score in each case. It should be noted that significant differences between genders were not detected by the survey.

5. CONCLUSION

In this paper, the solution adopted for the course development has been explained, and a free access online learning application for Fluid Mechanics has been developed. To achieve this goal, eXeLearning has been successfully used as an educational tool while Java has been used to optimize the organization of the information in the course. Furthermore, applications to improve user experience through videos and images have been created. Conversely, the integration of CFD tools for educational use has been achieved, and the main principles of Fluid Mechanics have been typified computationally. In fact, CFD is one of the most important features of the course, and its use has allowed the development of a more user-friendly course simplifying the understanding of Fluid Mechanics for the student. Additionally, the integration of technologies in learning Fluid Mechanics is based on a powerful pedagogical and psychological basis, which is justified from constructivist and inductive perspective contributions to motivation, retention and transfer of knowledge.

In short, this project fulfils the primary objective of sharing knowledge on Fluid Mechanics. However, it is a fact that the final assessment cannot been given by the course developers; the responsibility for assessing the course depends on its users. Against this background, a zero-beta was launched to a group of people with previous knowledge of Fluid Mechanics as a beta-tester. All of them claimed to repeat a similar course, and more than 95 percent of them would add it as a supplement to conventional teaching.

REFERENCES

Aliprandi, S., 2011. *Creative commons: A user guide*. Ledizioni.

ANSYS Fluent User´s Guide., 2013. Release 15.0. ANSYS, Inc.

Aznar, S., 2016. *Generación de recursos educativos digitales en formato estándar con eXe Learning*. Conselleria de Educación de la Comunidad Valenciana.

Black, K.P. and Rosenberg, M.A., 1992. Semi-empirical treatment of wave transformation outside and inside the breaker line. *Coastal Engineering*, Vol. 16, pp 313–345.

Brahimi, T. and Sarirete, A., 2015. Learning outside the classroom through MOOCs. *Computers in Human Behavior*, Vol. 51, Part B, pp 604–609.

Breslow, L. et al, 2013. Studying learning in the worldwide classroom research into edX's first MOOC. *Research & Practice in Assessment*, Vol. 8, pp 13–25.

Cabero, J., 2006. Bases pedagógicas del e-learning. *Revista de Universidad y Sociedad del Conocimiento*, Vol. 3, No. 1, pp 1–10.

Çengel Y. and Cimbala, J., 2006. *Fluid mechanics: fundamentals and applications*. Editorial McGraw-Hill.

Cheng, C., 2005. *New paradigm for re-engineering education: Globalization, localization and Individualization*. Asia-Pacific educational research association, Springer.

Christ, A. and Thews, O., 2016. Using numeric simulation in an online e-Learning environment to teach functional physiological contexts. *Computer Methods and Programs in Biomedicine*, Vol. 127(C), pp 15–23.

Daniel, J. et al, 2015. The future of MOOCs: Adaptive learning or business model?. *Revista de Universidad y Sociedad del Conocimiento*, Vol. 12, No. 1, pp 64–74.

Deitel, P., 2004. *Cómo programar en Java*. Editorial P. Educacion.

Evans, M.J., 2004. *Probabilidad y estadística*. Editorial Reverté.

Galor, O. 2011. *Inequality, human capital formation and the process of development*. Rhode Island: Brown University.

Gautier, R. et al, 2013. A reference solution of the flow over a circular cylinder at Re = 40. *Computers & Fluids*, Vol. 75, pp 103–111.

Graham, C.R., and Trick, T.N. 1998. Java applets enhance learning in a freshman ECE course. *Journal of Engineering Education*, Vol. 87, No. 4, pp 391–397.

Heather, D. et al, 2016. Use of image based sports case studies for teaching mechanics. *Procedia Engineering*, Vol. 147, pp 884–889.

Hernández, S. 2008. El modelo constructivista con las nuevas tecnologías: aplicado en el proceso de aprendizaje. *Revista de Universidad y Sociedad del conocimiento*, Vol. 5, No. 2, pp 26–35.

Hone, K.S. and El Said, G.R., 2016. Exploring the factors affecting MOOC retention. *Computers & Education*, Vol. 98(C), pp 157–168.

Jiyuan, Tu. et al, 2008. *Computational Fluid Dynamics: A Practical Approach*. Editorial McGraw-Hill.

Mallick, M. and Kumar, A., 2014. Study on drag coefficient for the flow past a cylinder. *International Journal of Civil Engineering Research*, Vol. 5, No. 4, pp 301–306.

McClure, M.L., 1991. Technology-A driving force for change, *Journal of Professional Nursing*, Vol. 7, No. 3, pp 144.

Papert, S. 1990. *A critique of technocentrism in thinking about the school of future*. M.T.I. Media Lab Epistemology and Learning Memo, No 2. Editorial Cambridge.

Pfeffer, J. and Sutton, R.I., 2000. *The Knowing Doing Gap*. Harvard Business School Press.

Rajani, B.N. et al, 2009. numerical simulation of laminar flow past a circular cylinder. *applied mathematical modelling*, vol. 33, no. 3, pp 1228–1247.

Regalado, A., 2012. the most important education technology in 200 Years. *MTI Technology Review*.

Ruiz, C., 2015. El MOOC: ¿un modelo alternativo para la educación universitaria?. *Apertura. Revista de innovación educativa*, Vol. 7, No. 2, pp 86–100.

Schildt, H. 2000. *Java: The complete reference*. Editorial Mcgraw-Hill.

Stern, F. et al, 2006. Hands-On CFD educational interface for engineering courses and laboratories. *Journal of Engineering Education*, Vol. 95, No. 1, pp 63–83.

Vasquez, S. 2007. Beyond technocentrism and infocentrism: Designing effective e-learning courses for professional education. *International Journal of Continuing Engineering Education and Life-Long Learning*, Vol. 17, No. 6, pp 41–46.

White, F., 2008. *Fluid Mechanics*. Editorial McGraw-Hill.

Xiong, F. and Jia, Z. 2012. Design and implementation of telemedicine based on Java media framework. *Physics Procedia*, Vol. 25, pp 1850–1856.

A CASE STUDY EXAMINING THE COST MEASUREMENTS IN PRODUCTION AND DELIVERY OF A MASSIVE OPEN ONLINE COURSE (MOOC) FOR TEACHING THE RELATIONSHIP BETWEEN HUMAN HEALTH AND CLIMATE CHANGE

Edward Meinert[1,2], Abrar Alturkistani[2], Kris A Murray[3], Philippe Sabatier[4] and Josip Car[2]
[1]*University of Oxford, Healthcare Translation Research Group, Department of Paediatrics, Oxford OX3 9DU, United Kingdom*
[2]*Imperial College London, Global Digital Health Unit, Department of Primary Care and Public Health, School of Public Health, London W6 8RP, United Kingdom*
[3]*Imperial College London, MRC Centre for Global Infectious Disease Analysis, School of Public Health, London W6 8RP, United Kingdom*
[4]*Université Grenoble Alpes, 621 avenue Centrale 38400 Saint-Martin-d'Hères, France*

ABSTRACT

A Massive Open Online Course (MOOC) is a form of online education that makes available learning to a large number of individuals at no charge. The impact of climate change on public health has been introduced in MOOCs in various forms, for example, examining the impact of natural disasters, the increase in temperature on work productivity, and the monitoring and evaluation of health adaptation to climate change and its implications for policy. However, despite this work completed to advance understanding in both online and postgraduate education, more effort is required to provide the tools and capabilities to analyse evidence and present findings that demonstrate its impact on specific outcomes, including health and wellbeing. Although these courses are made publicly available, understanding the costs associated with their production and delivery will provide evidence to develop sustainable models for deployment of this form of citizen engagement education.

KEYWORDS

Education (MeSH), Education, Distance (MeSH), Education, Professional (MeSH), Online Education, Online Learning, Costs and Cost Analysis (MeSH), Economics (MeSH)

1. INTRODUCTION

Climate change is already having a negative impact on human health through direct and indirect effects and is considered one of the most significant public health challenges for the 21st century (Watts et al., 2018, pp. 2479-2514; Wuebbles et al., 2017, p. 669). While the 21st Conference of the Parties (COP21) and the subsequent Paris Agreement represent critical international progress towards tackling this global threat, the world remains off target in terms of reducing emissions to the extent required to limit warming to 'well below 2C' and implement adaptation plans to help meet the challenge of present and future impacts. There is thus a continuing and growing need for active citizen engagement and education on to help facilitate the technological and social transitions required across sectors if global targets to limit warming and manage impacts are to be achieved (Glanz, Rimer, & Viswanath, 2008).

A Massive Open Online Course (MOOC) is a form of online education that makes available learning to a large number of individuals at no charge (Veletsianos & Shepherdson, 2016). The impact of climate change on public health has been introduced in MOOCs in various forms, for example, examining the impact of natural disasters, the increase in temperature on work productivity, and the monitoring and evaluation of health adaptation to climate change and its implications for policy (Milligan, Littlejohn, & Margaryan, 2013). However, despite this work completed to advance understanding in both online and postgraduate education, more effort is required to provide the tools and capabilities to analyse evidence and present findings that demonstrate climate change's impact on target outcomes, including health and wellbeing.

A principal aim of an MOOC focused on the relationship between climate change and public health is to allow citizens to have a critical awareness of the key issues and to possibly inspire a new generation of actors who can help address the challenges, such as climate scientists who will develop skills in integrating both public health and data science or health professionals able to catalyse the incorporation of climate change impacts into public health policies. Although these courses are made publicly available, understanding the costs associated with their production and delivery will provide evidence to develop sustainable models for deployment of this form of citizen engagement education (Joshi & Perin, 2012).

The purpose of this study was to determine how the total costs for the production and delivery of an MOOC are calculated and the factors that influence the production and development of an open-access course.

1.1 Objectives

1. Identification of the components or 'ingredients' for the production and delivery of an MOOC to form a comprehensive project budget
2. Use of a variance calculation of the ingredients for the cost of production and delivery of an MOOC
3. Explore the factors that have an impact on the planning of costs for eLearning delivery.

2. STUDY OVERVIEW

The MOOC instructional design was focused on connectivist learning theory, where networking and skill acquisition will be enhanced through the development of sustainable peer learning and engagement in a peer-to-peer concept (Milligan et al., 2013). Through enhancement of information flow and exchange, the MOOC instructional design was centred on building online social networks promoting collaborations and discussion between learners and various stakeholders. Consequently, stakeholders were engaged in the learning process whilst developing digital skills. By virtue of challenge-based learning, learners were informed on national and regional health-climate-related issues. Through an increase in awareness and participation of local communities, the educational platform was designed to empower citizens with informed decision-making skills thereby leading to, *inter alia*, European economic prosperity. In addition to expanding the proportion of people aware of the MOOC through use of social media, the establishment of networks was designed to enable a deeper understanding of the target population. Additionally, a post-course collaboration between stakeholders was to be promoted, thereby improving sustainability and positive impacts of the course and maintaining citizen engagement.

The course was developed from July through October 2017 and delivered to participants from November to December 2017. The course was produced as a consortium including Imperial College London, University Grenoble Alpes, and the European Institute of Innovation and Technology – Climate Knowledge Innovation Community Video Production Team.

2.1 Methods

2.1.1 Study Design

The study focused on analysing the variance of the cost of production of a massive open online course. The study design employed a case study design for production course observation of financial decision making and cost analysis to understand variances in production costs to budgeted costs. The study made modifications to a study protocol executed by the research team in the previous year, to gather further evidence concerning production cost variance in online learning (Meinert, Eerens, Banks, & Car, 2019). While that study was focused on a Small Private Online Course (SPOC), this course would focus on the broader learner engagement management of an open-access course. Ethical approval for the study was obtained through the Imperial College Education Ethics Research Committee (EERP1617-030).

2.1.2 Methodological Framework

A case study research design was selected because the study would not introduce changes to the way in which the course was designed and therefore strictly focus on the financial actions taken in the production and development of the course.

This investigation was structured via a six-stage process for case study investigations (Yin, 2017) to identify the implementation and delivery costs associated with the production of an MOOC.

Stage 1: Plan

This was the second study to investigate cost analysis in the production of eLearning (Meinert et al., 2019). On consideration of study design, we focused on a case method because the study was focused on eLearning implementation which would not undergo experimentation on influencing actions of the course designers; the principal objective was to analyse what happened and determine the reasons for impact on the course implementation. A governing proposition established and reinforced from previous research (Meinert et al., 2019) was that there would be significant variance in the actual costs to the budgeted cost of the course; the critical variance in this implementation context, however, would be the way in which designing for an MOOC varied from a targeted Small Private Online Course implementation.

The study question centred on capturing the cost elements for the creation, design, and deployment of the online course. The literature suggests a good understanding of costs and their associated impact on production and delivery in online learning (Al-Shorbaji, Atun, Car, Majeed, & Wheeler, 2015), so the research question was focused on providing evidence to understand this relationship better.

Stage 2: Design

The research design was structured to investigate how the total costs for the production and delivery of the MOOC were calculated. In line with previous findings and evidence from the literature on the insufficient nature of budgets as means of determining that the total cost of education delivery (Levin, McEwan, Belfield, Bowden, & Shand, 2017; Meinert, Reeves, Eerens, Banks, Maloney, Rivers, Ilic, Walsh, Majeed, Car, 2019), the core proposition of the investigation was focused on measuring an expected variance between cost of delivery from budget in course production, influenced by the nature of iterative development of eLearning and potential underreporting of costs. To test this principle, the 'ingredients method' (Levin et al., 2017) was used to capture all the components of the cost of production.

Table 1. Case study research design (Yin, 2017)

Study question	Proposition	The case (definition)	Logic linking data to the proposition	Criteria for interpreting findings
How are the total costs for the production and delivery of a massive open online course calculated?	Actual costs and budgeted costs will vary due to the iterative nature of eLearning and underreporting of staff costs	Determination and measurement costs	Cost analysis of project costs, actual cost, and underreported costs	Variance calculation of the project budget

Three tests (Yin, 2017) were used to ensure and validate the quality of the study research design.

Test 1: Construct validity

The purpose of a construct validity test is to show that data sources are triangulated and validated from multiple sources (Yin, 2017).

Test 2: External validity

The purpose of an external validity test is to demonstrate how principal findings can find applicability in other use cases (Yin, 2017).

Test 3: Reliability

The purpose of the reliability test is to show how the activities of the study are repeatable (Yin, 2017).

Stage 3: Prepare
A study protocol modified from the previous cost investigation was used to manage the study process. Levin et al's (2017) model for cost measurement was used to analyse budget vs. actual spending. This model implements an activity-based costing standard accountancy approach, which assigns costs as they are consumed per implementation area (Kaplan, 1994, 104; Mak & Roush, 1994, 93; Mak & Roush, 1996, 141).

Stage 4: Collect
Data collection
The data collection strategy was executed from a *realist* perspective to capture the financial decision making of the course designers in order to avoid interference in the course delivery. In order to control selectivity and reporting bias, data was triangulated following construct validity tests. A traceability log was maintained linking the study questions to the relevant data sources and the study findings.

Stage 5: Analyse
Data analysis centred on three cost categories in the design of the pre-production budget submitted to the funder.

Category A: Concept and measurement of costs
The pre-production budget was analysed for the following ingredient categories: 1) personnel, 2) estate charges, 3) equipment and materials, 4) indirect costs, and 5) stakeholder costs.

Category B: Placing values on ingredients
With the full cost of production defined, values were associated with each ingredient sub-category to reflect the chargeable cost.

Category C: Analysing costs
The course was analysed for the one-time cost of the project because it was designed as a one-year project (initially); therefore, the variance from implementation costs was the critical variable under consideration. Variance calculation of the budget to the incurred costs was reviewed on a fortnightly basis for tracking and completed as a summary report at project completion.

Variance = Actual spending – Budgeted spending

Stage 6: Share

The findings of the variance calculation and analysis of reasons leading to variation were presented in a draft case report to the course design team. The key findings for this report were prepared for publication for a peer-review journal (this manuscript).

2.2 Results

2.2.1 Course Production Costs

Category A: Concept and measurement of costs

Table 2. Ingredient categories

Ingredient categories	Cost components
Personnel	University staff
Estate charges	IT services charges
Equipment and materials	Course production equipment, application development costs for the creation of software to support the MOOC
Indirect costs	University overheads
Stakeholder costs	Staff for third-party subject matter consultancy

Category B: Placing values on ingredients

Upon completion of the analysis of the ingredients of the course production, the initial budget was created and submitted to the funder.

Table 3. Ingredient Costs of the Climate Change and Public Health MOOC

	Cost in 2017
Personnel	£43,646
Estate charges	£2,345
Equipment and materials	£3,255
Indirect costs	£11,725
Stakeholder costs	£25,999
	£86,970

Category C: Analysing costs

Budget variance calculation

The actual spending had a negative variance from budgeted spending in Personnel, Equipment and materials and Stakeholder costs, with the total cost of production being 113% the budgeted amount. The most significant negative variance was in stakeholder costs, where the total time for external lecturers and subject matter experts (as sub-contracted third parties) to deliver cost work was significantly underbudgeted, by 190%. The reason for this underestimate was that videos had to be reshot twice and the amount of time allocated to retrieve stakeholders and complete associated course updates had a dramatic impact on the budget. The second-largest negative variance was in personnel; the cost variance was directly related to the additional production time required for the video reshoots, in addition to the iteration of the development of the platform. During the course delivery, there was change in facts relating to course content, also requiring a reshoot; due to the nature of this course, this material will require constant updating to keep it timely and relevant. Additionally, the course implementation online learning provider also switched through in the project from edX to FutureLearn (edX and FutureLearn are MOOC learning management systems), requiring a rework of previously completed tasks. Finally, equipment and materials were also underestimated with a 133% overage, having to do with additional software required for video editing and additional workstations gathered to deal with additional editing required in the course development.

Table 4. Ingredient Costs variance calculation

	Budget	Actual	Variance	Var %
Personnel	£43,646	£88,456	£44,810	103%
Estate charges	£2,345	£2,345	£0	0%
Equipment and materials	£3,255	£7,599	£4,344	133%
Indirect costs	£11,725	£11,725	£0	0%
Stakeholder costs	£25,999	£75,332	£49,333	190%
	£86,970	£185,457	£98,487	113%

The construction of the cost ingredients and subsequent cost analysis underwent three validation tests:

A. Construct validity test: Multiple sources of cost data and reporting data were used to validate the accuracy of data sources as a record of what occurred: 1) the project budget created at the project commencement, 2) the actual cost report submitted at the completion of the project, 3) the timesheet log of hours captured by each team resource, 4) a third-party work-log for course production and monitor of billable hours recorded charged to the program, 5) external audit reports on the course construction, and 6) review of notes from monthly reviews of budget spending. The final case report was reviewed, and feedback gathered from the course designers (BS, MT); feedback was provided and reviewed by the research team to ensure implementation accuracy.
B. External validity test: The repetition of a model used in prior research (Meinert et al., 2019), application of Levin's ingredients method for education intervention analysis and use of standard costing and a variance calculation (horizontal budget analysis) demonstrated a common analytic framework which is transportable to other studies.
C. Reliability test: To achieve this test, a study protocol was used and formed the governing basis for the study.

2.2.2 Participant Information

Nine-hundred and sixty-eight learners participated in the MOOC from November to December 2017. Of the 968 learners, 17% completed the course. The course completion ratio was in-line with completion rates for MOOCs (Li & Wan, 2016, pp. 503-505), where despite a high uptake of initial learners, completion of course activity ranges from 8% to 15%.

3. CONCLUSION

3.1 Principal Findings

While the course was delivered and reported to the funder on the original budget, the actual cost of delivery had a 113% overrun. Despite developing an extremely rigorous project management methodology to avoid time and cost overruns, the production team were faced with several challenges that led them to expend far more effort than they were compensated for and than was planned. The project benefited from in-kind work by university staff with permanent positions. The team was not able to slip timelines to allow for reduction of effort over a more extended period, resulting in an additional effort towards the end of each delivery of the project plan. The negative variance in the project budget demonstrates critical lessons in the implementation of this eLearning type. In reviewing these case results, four principal findings were derived influencing the production budget and adherence to plan:

1. Resource task estimation and management

While the project employed a rigorous project management approach, this activity was based on overall milestones and not linking sub-activities to the time estimate required per task. Because there was not tracking to this level, it was difficult for the project manager to know when tasks were going significantly over budget and then how to alter subsequent tasks to compensate for these changes. A key lesson learned from the implementation in retrospective task analysis was the importance of tracking tasks at this level to allow for better adherence to the overall schedule.

2. Contingency planning

Three project events had a significant impact on the planned delivery schedule: the change in learning platform from edX to FutureLearn, the need to redo a series of video shoots due to issues with the lighting of one of the cameras, and the loss of principal staff member in the development of the course production. The original budget did not account for any contingency scenarios in the course planning, which meant that when these events occurred, it created automatic overages in the amount of time allocated for the course delivery that has an ultimate impact on the anticipated effort for the delivery of the project.

3. Third-party resource management

The project made use of several sub-contractors in order to speed up delivery of the course. These projects were billed on a time and materials basis and when the project overran, the associated costs of the delivery of the project had an impact on the project budget. An alternative model for the third-party development could be fixed-price outcome-based projects, such that the core project does not need to incur overruns for delivery in the execution of tasks. Of course, this shifts the basis of charge from the project to the third party, but different commercial management of these resource costs will control spending in the primary project.

4. Need for an update of course materials

The public health content and environmental content within the course indicated a need for continuing updates of the course content. While the costs for the production of the course did not capture these incremental changes, this costing would be necessary to capture the total costs of this deployment type.

3.2 Strengths and Limitations

The strengths of this study are that it provided a rigorous examination of the implementation of eLearning via a Massive Open Online Course. The use of MOOCs for disseminating information to encourage behavioural change to address a global issue like climate change has broad applicability and reuse. The study leveraged previous investigations into eLearning cost variance calculation by the core research team (Meinert et al., 2019) and implemented management accountancy methods which have been purpose-built for cost evaluation of learning (Levin et al., 2017). The study design was reinforced through a detailed review of real-time project decisions and activities through regular checkpoints of financial data with the core stakeholders, leading to additional data sources to reference in a cost review of data analysed in the project implementation.

We noted two primary limitations with the study. The first is that we did not use a further qualitative investigation of decisions by survey or interview of the course designers in order to conclude course impact. Incorporating such data could have provided further insight as to decision making. Due to the time constraints of the execution and delivery of this study, it was not possible to incorporate such an examination into the study design; however, such additional data points would have made for more detailed data into issues and considerations of this course type. The second limitation is that there was not costing completed on the required updates to implement the course; this multi-year costing would be essential to capture the total costs of the delivery necessary in eLearning of rapidly changing health content.

3.3 Summary Perspectives

eLearning in the form of MOOCs provides an opportunity to engage a large audience to disseminate information, which could be critical in promoting awareness of crucial topics. The ability to reach vast audiences and create engagement on course content provides the capability to leverage the efficiencies in the delivery of content. The key challenges in the development of this learning involve the associated planning required and the ability to deal with issues in the delivery of the course content. Such issues that can have an impact on the project can have a dramatic impact on the course implementation, thus altering the planned budget in course delivery. Factors accounting for the project management and associated cost tracking of the delivery of the development of this type of eLearning are necessary to capture the costs associated with this learning content accurately.

ACKNOWLEDGEMENT

Boris Serafimov and Mel Toumazos provided detailed data contributing to the study in their design, development, and deployment of the online course. This project was supported by the European Institute of Innovation and Technology – EIT Health Knowledge and Innovation Community.

REFERENCES

Al-Shorbaji, N., Atun, R. A., Car, J., Majeed, A., & Wheeler, D. E. (Eds.). (2015). *eLearning for undergraduate health professional education: a systematic review informing a radical transformation of health workforce development*. World Health Organization.

Glanz, K., Rimer, B. K., & Viswanath, K. (Eds.). (2008). *Health behavior and health education: Theory, research, and practice*. John Wiley & Sons.

Joshi A, & Perin D. M. P. (2012). Gaps in the existing public health informatics training programs: A challenge to the development of a skilled global workforce. *Perspect Health Inf Manag* 2012;9:1-13

Kaplan, R. S. (1994). Flexible budgeting in an activity-based costing framework. *Accounting Horizons*, 8(2), 104.

Levin, H. M., McEwan, P. J., Belfield, C., Bowden, A. B., & Shand, R. (2017). *Economic evaluation in education: Cost-effectiveness and benefit-cost analysis*. SAGE publications.

Li, Q., & Wan, F. (2016, July). A Case Study of the Characteristics of MOOCs Completers: Taking an Online Professional Training MOOC for Example. In 2016 IEEE 16th International Conference on Advanced Learning Technologies (ICALT) (pp. 503-505). IEEE.

Mak, Y. T., & Roush, M. L. (1994). Flexible budgeting and variance analysis in an activity-based costing environment. *Accounting Horizons*, 8(2), 93.

Mak, Y. T., & Roush, M. L. (1996). Managing activity costs with flexible budgeting and variance analysis. *Accounting Horizons*, 10(3), 141.

Meinert E, Eerens J, Banks C., Car J. (2019). *A case study examining the cost measurements in production and delivery of a Small Private Online Course (SPOC) for teaching administrative staff to engage with young patients*. (In review).

Meinert E, Reeves S, Eerens J, Banks C, Maloney S, Rivers G, Ilic D, Walsh K, Majeed A, Car J (2019). Exploring the cost of eLearning within the field of health professions education: key findings from a Systematic Scoping Review. *JMIR Preprints*. 11/02/2019:13681 (In review)

Milligan, C., Littlejohn, A., & Margaryan, A. (2013). Patterns of engagement in connectivist MOOCs. *MERLOT Journal of Online Learning and Teaching*, 9(2).

Veletsianos, G., & Shepherdson, P. (2016). A systematic analysis and synthesis of the empirical MOOC literature published in 2013–2015. *The International Review of Research in Open and Distributed Learning*, 17(2).

Watts, N., Amann, M., Arnell, N., Ayeb-Karlsson, S., Belesova, K., Berry, H., et al. (2018). The 2018 report of the Lancet Countdown on health and climate change: shaping the health of nations for centuries to come. *The Lancet*, 392(10163), 2479-2514.

Wuebbles, D. J., Fahey, D. W., Hibbard, K. A., DeAngelo, B., Doherty, S., Hayhoe, K., et al. (2017). Climate Science Special Report: A Sustained Assessment Activity of the US Global Change Research Program. US Global Change Research Program: Washington, DC, USA, 669.

Yin, R. K. (2017). *Case study research and applications: Design and methods*. Sage publications.

INCLUSIVE DIGITAL LEARNING THROUGH SERIOUS GAMES: A CLIPPING FOR INCLUSION

Paula Escudeiro[1], Dirceu Teixeira[2], Bruno Galasso[2], Nuno Neto[1] and Flávio Costa[1]
[1]*GILT/ISEP, R. Dr. Bernardino de Almeida, Nº 431, 4249-015 Porto, Portugal*
[2]*INES, R.das Laranjeiras, Nº232, Rio de Janeiro 22240-003, Brazill*

ABSTRACT

Serious games have a great potential to help people developing new skills or improving previously existing ones. Deaf and blind community face considerable challenges and difficulties regarding to the acquisition of skills in literacy. The design of serious games to meet the needs of the target groups where the deaf and blind people are struggling to master literacy would therefore seem to offer a very considerable contribution. With this project, not only we are promoting the knowledge for this restricted community, but we are also encouraging other people to learn and become able to better understand this communities. Therefore, this article aims to discuss the use of serious games for deaf and blind people, as well as illustrate the development methodology of inclusive serious games by presenting specific concepts for each target audience. We have used the cognitive model proposed by Mayer (2005) to describe some fundamental principles behind multimedia learning, defined from his theory and based on the evidences that are essential for the elaboration of serious games for deaf and blind people. We hope that the games developed, and guidelines provided will help game designers to achieve successful implementation in inclusive games.

KEYWORDS

Serious Games, Inclusive Games, Accessibility, Design Model for Inclusive Games, Development Methodologies for Inclusive Games, Assistive Technology

1. INTRODUCTION

The popularity of digital games has skyrocketed in a last couple of decades – the Entertainment Software Association reports that 60% of Americans play digital games daily and 70% of parents believe video games have a positive influence on their children's lives (Entertainment Software Association, 2018).

Game as a concept can be labeled as an activity where components such as temporal limitations, an area defined to play or rules to keep participants rights and duties intact, while providing a competitive environment different than usual (Huizinga, 1970). According to Avedon and Sutton-Smith (1971), "games are an exercise of voluntary control systems, in which there is a contest between powers, confined by rules in order to produce a disequilibrial outcome".

A game represents a subjective and oversimplified emotional reality. It is not objectively an exact representation of reality, in fact is mainly represented enough to fulfil a player expectation. A player's fantasy is the key to make a game psychologically real (Crawford, 1984). When it comes to interaction, which not only is associated with game representation, there's ways to make it dynamic and to change it accordingly through interactions. A player can't distort reality by making simple choices and see the unfolding of those events. There can be physical threats towards the player, however, a game allows the player to experience psychological conflicts without having any physical alteration, resulting in an action / consequence dissonance. Crawford (1984) refers that even though it may not threat the player in real life, it can have a negative impact in the game by missing a reward for instance.

Michael Zyda (2005) pointed that the primary objective is to create daily simulations to offer training for professionals, enterprise critical situations or raise awareness in a diverse age bracket to topics such as education. Serious games combine digital games with entities to fulfil a theoretical practical education. Learning is the guiding force and includes educational games, business games, simulation games, among others, and they cross a whole range of topics, contexts and target groups (Sørensen & Meyer, 2007).

Serious games have a great potential to help the population develop new skills or improve previously existing ones. However, part of the population does not have the means to play these games. Some may be unable to experience all the elements that are present in these games. Besides, larger companies usually do not develop games for these audiences considering their reduced size (Cardoso *et al.*, 2016). That is why inclusive games were created, "games proactively designed to optimally fit and adapt to individual gamer characteristics and to be concurrently played among people with diverse abilities, without requiring particular adjustments or modifications" (Grammenos *et al.*, 2009).

This article aims to discuss the use of serious games for deaf and blind people, as well as show the development of serious games inclusive, presenting specific concepts for each target audience.

2. DESIGN MODEL OF INCLUSIVE GAMES

During the process of designing inclusive games, Mayer's principles on Multimedia Learning (Mayer, 2005) were applied as a form of quality validation. All the examples provided in this section follow these principles, alongside a quality evaluation model.

2.1 Game Development Methodologies for Deaf People

Considering the way in which deaf people organize thought and language, as well as the potential of the students' development in the visual field, the project of serious games needs to be designed through a visual-spatial perspective. Therefore, we develop serious games following the "deaf way", that is, "a way of formulating ideas based on imagery representations capable of being translated in the Sign Language itself and in visual aspects" (Rodrigues & Quadros, 2015).

Such an understanding does not deny the presence of the oral Portuguese language to listeners, who are also part of the audience of the game proposed here. The idea here, as suggested above, is that there are advantages in adopting different languages, Portuguese and Libras. In addition, if the visual-spatial perspective – whether being that through Libras or imagery texts – is essential for deaf people, for the non-deaf it is extremely enriching. Within this context, the use of serious games reveals great potential in the field of educational sciences, because in this modality "thought is mapped by domains of distinct concepts, structured by image schemes" (Galasso, 2014).

Currently, there are several research projects exploring multimedia instruction and learning focusing on hearing students; however, studies focusing on deaf students or students with some kind of hearing impairment are rare. When developing serious games for deaf people, we also take into account some principles based on knowledge about how the brain processes information during learning. According to Mayer (1997), one of the most important areas of Cognitive Psychology is the understanding of technology as a tool to promote efficient learning. Through the main theories of cognition, concrete and effective learning occurs following a few steps or stages. In Figure 1, we provide how information processing occurs according to Mayer's Cognitive Theory of Multimedia Learning (2005), adapted to the perspective of the deaf student.

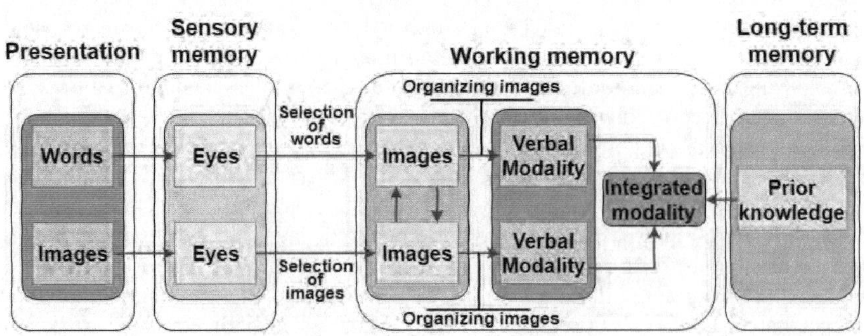

Figure 1. Mayer's (2005) information processing model adapted to the perspective of a deaf person

The processing of information starts from the moment the deaf student assimilates images and words from a multimedia presentation, which can be, for example, a game in Sign Language. To capture this presentation, written words and images enter through the eyes of the deaf student and are briefly represented in the sensory memory. Then, in the working memory, the deaf student selects the main words and images and organizes them, categorizing written words in a verbal model, and images in a pictorial model. From this organization an integrated model of information is structured. This integrated model is directly linked to the long-term memory, where the student can activate pre-existing knowledge to be integrated with verbal and pictorial models in the working memory, storing the resulting knowledge in the long-term memory.

2.1.1 Evidence-based Principles in Serious Games for Deaf People

The cognitive model proposed by Mayer (2005) describes some fundamental principles behind multimedia learning, defined from his theory and based on the evidences that are essential for the elaboration of serious games for deaf people:

1. *The Multimedia Principle – Words and images are better than words alone*

This principle proposes the combined use of images and words, as it allows the brain to process more information in the working memory (Paas & Sweller, 2014). Thus, people learn better with words and images than words alone. In this context, words include written and spoken text, and images include videos, animations, and static graphics. In the education of deaf people, which uses Sign Language as a means of communication, images are essential for understanding academic concepts and, when words are used as well, they help students in the learning process. Due to the visual-gestural characteristic, Sign Language can be presented along with the Portuguese Language, respecting the phrasal structure of each one of these languages, composing two informational processing channels necessary for bilingual education. Similarly, in the serious games developed, we present simultaneity between the presentation of Sign Language and characters. This simultaneity enables deaf students to have a variety of integrated learning styles, broadening their understanding of the content worked. The interaction between image and caption constitutes student-oriented meaning, proposing the textual interpretation of the video and its occurrences.

When we use serious games, we strengthen the compatibility of the readings, establishing singular dynamics in the learning process. The application of the concept in the development of bilingual teaching materials also privileges the hearing, since the signaling in Sign Language appears to the students synchronized with the caption and speech in Portuguese Language within the scope of the statement, respecting the syntactic and grammatical structures of each language.

Figure 2. Representation of the Multimedia Principle. In this example, a game designed for deaf and hearing-impaired people that consists of multiple-choice questions about Education

2. *Principle of Spatial Contiguity – Words should appear close to images*

This principle includes spatiality as a didactic element to the learning of deaf students. Animation, as a figuration of reality, ratifies the meaning that the text should convey. From the point of view of bilingual education, the use of images close to words composes a mechanism of interface between the two languages (Sign Language/Portuguese Language), as they are part of the linguistic daily life of the deaf and the hearing. Considering the spatiality of Sign Language, written words should be part of the discourse of the deaf presenter, since there is spatial interference between the written register of the Portuguese Language and the movements of the Sign Language. Thus, a truly bilingual learning object is structured with the integration of the two languages into the same statement.

3. *Segmentation Principle – Contents must be presented by parts*

This principle states that people learn best when a multimedia lesson is presented in segments of the user's rhythm instead of a continuous unit. In this context, games are developed at various levels of theoretical depth, so that the student may learn through videos with segmented content.

2.2 Serious and Inclusive Games for Blind and Deaf People

Regarding blind people, the project of serious games needs to be designed with audio-based gameplay. Using this architecture during development allows the user to enjoy the game without the need of a graphical user interface either to interact or understand the application context (Beksa *et al.*, 2015). Even though its target audience is a niche market, these games are often omitted from general population due to its accessibility standards.

Audio games focus group are blind and visually impaired people because they are developed with audio only in mind. With the growth of text-to-speech software and major improvements related to digital assistant voices such as Cortana, Alexa or Siri, serious games targeted to blind people became a must, because "this type of video game has been growing and its use has spread to several areas of education" (Salvador-Ullauri *et al.*, 2017). These tools follow two very important principles in multimedia learning, introduced by Mayer - the Personalization Principle and the Voice Principle. The former states that people learn better when words are in conversational style rather than formal style and the latter promotes learning through hearing a friendly human voice rather than a machine voice (Mayer, 2005). Voice assistants have gradually become more human-like and less formal, trying to make their users feel more comfortable.

These games' narrative is created mainly through sound sources, typically with the help of pre-recorded sounds or text-to-speech limited to the languages implemented by the developers. Moreover, audio games have a tactile or haptic feedback (e.g vibration and/or sound) which can result in an immersive video game atmosphere to blind people (Csapó *et al.*, 2015).

2.2.1 An Example of a Game for Blind People

The Field Trip is a single-player digital game being developed for desktop computers and mobile systems, set in a real-world forest, that develops the player's spatial awareness and orientation, by creating an environment where the player is guided exclusively by sound. It is being developed in Unity3D, using C#. It revolves around the use of 3D audio sources – objects in the world that emit sound depending on the position of the player. This means that if the player is to the right of the audio source, he/she will hear the sound coming from the left, and if the player is to the left of it, the sound will be coming from the right. Moreover, the sound from an audio source only becomes hearable when the player steps into its range, and it becomes louder as the player approaches the center of the source. These audio sources are being developed in accordance to Mayer's multimedia learning principles mentioned in section 2, in order to provide a good player experience.

The game is separated in several layers, each with its own responsibilities, displayed in Figure 3. The user only interacts with the interface layer, which handles the player's inputs and the sounds that the player hears. This layer then interacts with two layers – the game engine and the business layers. The game engine layer is responsible for executing the game, in this case represented by Unity. The business layer manages the logic behind the game, the rules and mechanics that will be described in this section. Lastly, these two layers communicate with the hardware layer, which is the device that is used to play the game.

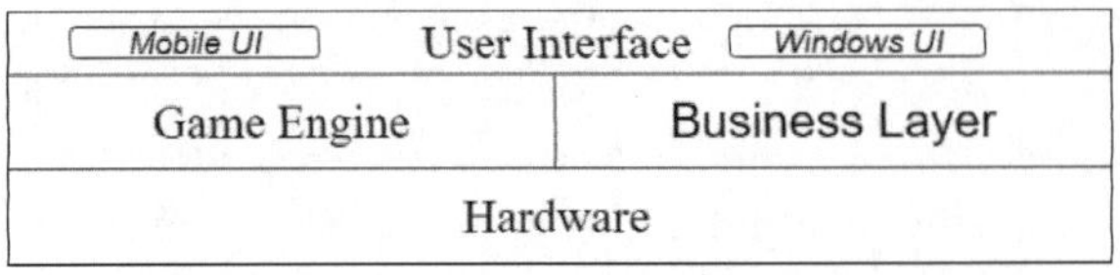

Figure 3. *The Field Trip*'s application architecture

As the player traverses through the world and collects items, he/she learns about the forest they are in, as well as the fauna and flora that is being collected. This allows the player to enhance abilities that are useful not only in the context of this game, but also in real-life scenarios where a person must be guided by sound.

In this game the player has been separated from his/her field trip group and must move through the forest in order to find them, going from the starting (spawn) point to the ending area. To do this the player must rely on his/her senses to figure out where he/she is in the map, given audio cues such as the sound that is made when walking through a certain type of terrain or when stepping on tree branches.

To make the movement through the map more challenging, obstacles block the path that the player is trying to take. Elements such as trees or knocked down logs, big rocks or shrubbery that isn't traversable force the player to make slight detours so that he/she can avoid these barriers. By memorizing which the obstacles and terrain in each area, the player can build a mental map of the forest he/she is in, making movement more effective. The second goal of the game is to collect items that are spread out on the map. These range from animals that the player must interact with, to plants that the player can pick up or water from a waterfall that must be collected. When interacting with these items, voice lines give a short description of the item that is picked up.

When the player reaches the end of the level, his/her score is calculated. Each item has an associated score. Items that are harder to get have a higher score than those that are in the natural path the player walks through. At the end of the level, the final score is the sum of all items collected and a previously determined level completion bonus, minus the time the player took to go from the spawn point to the ending area and the number of times the player died.

Lastly, the player would have the objective of surviving threats that would be placed in the environment. These threats are described in Table 1.

Table 1. Action table for the *The Field Trip* game

Player Event	Player Response	Effect
Hears bear sound	Moves	Player loses a life and enemy disappears
Hears bear sound	Does not move	Enemy disappears
Hears snake sound or turbulenc in water	Does not press the spacebar	Player loses a life and enemy disappears
Hears snake sound or turbulenc in water	Presses the spacebar	Enemy disappears
Hears bees sound	Stays in range for longer than 3 seconds	Player loses a life
Hears bees sound	Leaves range before 3 seconds have passed	No effect
Is near item	Presses the spacebar	Player gets points, item disappears, and voice line describes item
Loses a life when no lives left		Player respawns in last checkpoint or start of the level
Reaches the end of the level		Player receives level completion points, advances to next level, and voice lines informs player of points
Walks on terrain		Specific terrain sound is played
Walks into map edge		Informative sound is played

Figure 4 displays some of the elements that exist in the game, such as items (represented as small spheres), enemies (the larger sphere acts as a swarm of bees and the cube represents a bear) and different types of terrain (the larger one serves as grass and the smaller one acts as water).

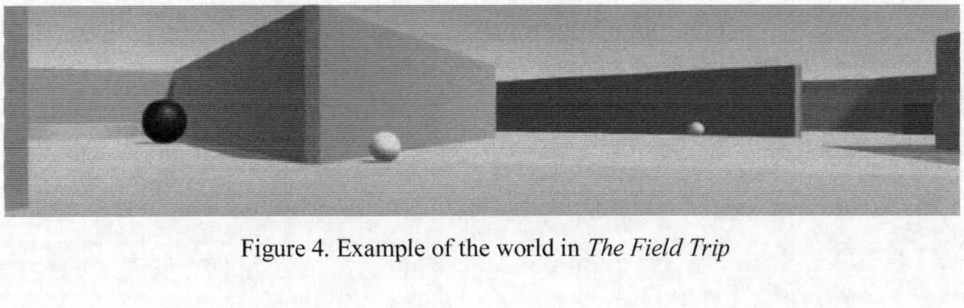

Figure 4. Example of the world in *The Field Trip*

2.2.2 An Example of a Game for Deaf and Blind People

Morseline is a multiplayer serious game in development for computer and mobile systems in order to help users learn Morse code. To that end same tools are integrated to achieve proper support for both blind and deaf people. To assist blind users, a text-to-speech and speech-to-text functionalities are integrated by using Microsoft's Cortana digital assistant Portuguese voice package, while on Android, Google's own text to speech voice packages. In order to support deaf people, GILT's (Graphics Interaction Learning Technologies) own sign language avatar is used to translate all text in-game to Portuguese Sign Language.

The serious game is not only capable to help on learning Morse code, but also lets users test their knowledge against each other. To this end, three game modes were developed. A one-on-one matchup where both users must finish a course that consists in hearing Morse code being transmitted by three telegraphs, and when in close range they will be presented with two options, one being the correct answer and the other one a decoy. The player who decodes more Morse messages by the end of the match wins. A cooperative mode where both users try to get correct answers in order to achieve success. Using implemented chat system, both players can communicate and share their opinion on what the correct answer is by either using voice or text which is adapted on the other player's end following accessibility needs as defined in Section 2. Last but not least, a four-player mode which consists on the same rules as one-on-one mode, but with the purpose to lay foundations for a massive multiplayer online serious game. To this end, an action table was planned to understand game flow since the game start until the game has ended.

Table 2. Action table for Morseline game

Type of Game Mode	Trigger	Object	Action	Result
All types	Check if players have joined game lobby	Player	Load proper game scenario	Game starts
All types	Move to checkpoint	Player	Listen to Morse code on telegraph	Player chooses correct answer
All types	Choose letter that matches listened Morse code	Letter	Reply sent to server	Server waits for all players answers and then proceed them to next checkpoint
All types	Last checkpoint	Lobby	Players reached final checkpoint	Triggers game as finished
1v1 and 1v1v1v1	Check results	Lobby	Calculates new player ratings	Updates player ratings on the server and marks lobby as finished
Cooperative	Check checkpoints progress	Lobby	Players met the necessary criteria	Quest is marked as successful or failed
All types	Game has ended	Server	Verifies if all preceding criteria is verified	Removes players from lobby and sends them back to main menu

After a user picks his desired game mode, he's placed in a queue where he will meet users that are in his range of skill level. With the help of a DDA (Dynamic Difficulty Adjustment), the user will never matchup with someone of much higher or lower skill, but instead with someone of similar competitive level.

When the server meets the necessary players to start a game and allocates them to a game lobby, a message is broadcasted using sockets meaning that an opponent is found and therefore the game will start. Afterwards, when both users connect to the lobby, they are shown a different scenario, and while blind users have audio support given by the implemented voice assistant, deaf users will have their accessibility needs fulfilled by the Portuguese Sign language avatar. Moving towards to the first checkpoint, both players will have Morse cues (either by sound or image) and they have unlimited time to pick the correct answer. Next, a reply is sent to the server where user's answers will be processed and saved while the game is running. It was mentioned before that a DDA is used, and when playing the game, difficulty is adjusted using both user's correct answer streak.

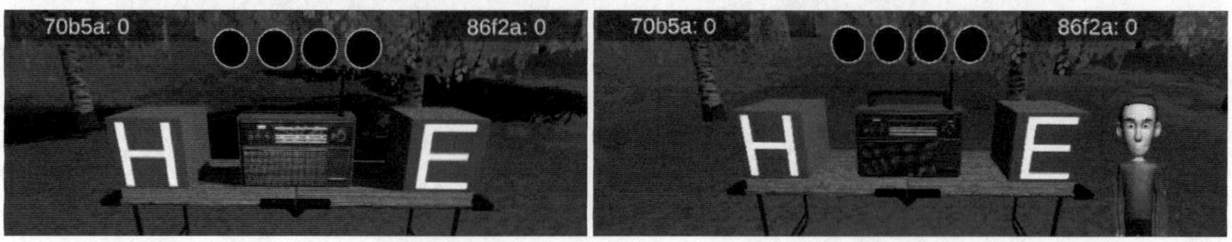

Figure 5. Checkpoint example in a matchup between a deaf user (left) and blind user (right) accessibility point of view

Since it is a multiplayer game, real time difficulty adjustment must be fair for both users so that one won't have a significant advantage against the other. Reaching the final checkpoint and answering the last Morse code message, judging by the answers given, server will then calculate the final score and present it via audio or image to all users inside the game lobby. While one-on-one and four users' modes have a competitive rating, cooperative mode doesn't have that, since its purpose is to let users help with each other along the way.

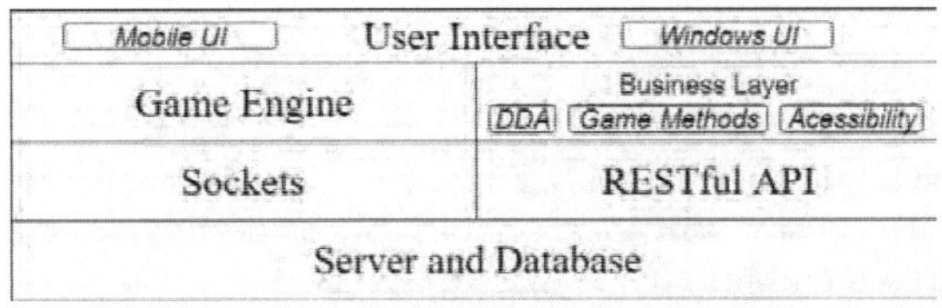

Figure 6. Morseline application architecture

The game is divided into four layers. At the top level there is the user interface. All game functionalities can be accessed through this layer by the user on his preferred device. Actions transmitted by the user go through the following layers. The second layer is where all client-side code is developed, with business layer component containing the DDA, game and accessibility scripts which linked with Unity offer an accessible front-end for its users. The next level which contains sockets and a RESTful API, help pass through information sent and received on users end between the game and server. The fourth layer represents the game back-end, where persistent data is stored with the help of an online hosted database hosted.

3. EVALUATION

We normally use three steps of the Social Networking Learning (Krouska *et al*, 2019) model to evaluate our learning objects:

1) Pedagogical module
- Teaching strategies: The principles and methods that are used for instruction.
- Learning outcome: The system analyses the achievement of the students' learning outcome during the tutoring process.

2) Personalization
- Adaptive interface: It includes adaptive presentation and adaptive navigation. Adaptive presentation is to display certain information based on user's characteristics. For instance, the system will provide more detailed information and capabilities to a user with advanced knowledge level. Adaptive navigator intends to assist users in achieving their learning goals through the presentation of the appropriate options, such as enabling/disabling topics' links.
- Advice generator: It is a component that responds to user when an error is occurred, about the cause of the error, in order to help him or her.
- Error diagnosis: It is a module that can identify the category of assessment's mistakes based on associated misconceptions with the use of algorithmic approaches.

3) Usability
- User interface friendliness: The system is easy to be learned and used

4. CONCLUSION

This work presented guidelines for the design of serious games for deaf and blind people. The process of building digital games, which is based on a diverse set of tasks, requires the structuring of a multidisciplinary team capable of developing pedagogical, linguistic and techniques. We hope that the guidelines provided alongside with system architectures designed for specific accessibility needs, help game designers and game developers to achieve successful implementation in inclusive games, so that players can have an enjoyable learning experience.

In this way, we conclude that the references of multimedia learning combined with the guiding principles of the education of the deaf and blind create a line of development possible, with innovation and interdisciplinary methods, to a deepening of knowledge capable of contributing to the qualitative expansion in the production of inclusive serious games.

ACKNOWLEDGEMENT

This work was supported by FCT/ COMPETE2020 – project ACE ref: PTDC/IVC-COM/5869/2014, POCI-01-0145-FEDER-016584), by ISEP (Instituto Superior de Engenharia do Porto), and GILT (Games, Interaction and Learning Technologies).

REFERENCES

Avedon, E.M. & Sutton-Smith, B. (1971) *The Study of Games*. J. Wiley New York.

Beksa, J. et al. (2015) Audio Games: Investigation of the Potential Through Prototype Development. In: Pradipta Biswas et al. (eds.). *A Multimodal End-2-End Approach to Accessible Computing*. Human–Computer Interaction Series. [Online]. London, Springer London. pp. 211–224. Available from: doi:10.1007/978-1-4471-6708-2_11 [Accessed: 27 May 2019].

Cardoso, T. et al. (2016) Games' "Social Tech Booster". In: Carlos Vaz de Carvalho et al. (eds.). *Serious Games, Interaction, and Simulation*. Lecture Notes of the Institute for Computer Sciences, Social Informatics and Telecommunications Engineering. 2016 Springer International Publishing. pp. 119–126.

Crawford, C. (1984) *The Art of Computer Game Design*. New York, NY, USA, McGraw-Hill, Inc.

Csapó, Á. et al. (2015) A survey of assistive technologies and applications for blind users on mobile platforms: a review and foundation for research. *Journal on Multimodal User Interfaces*. [Online] 9 (4), 275–286. Available from: doi:10.1007/s12193-015-0182-7.

Galasso, B.J.B. & Souza, D.T.R. de (2014) Educação online colaborativa: implicações teórico-metodológicas de uma nova modalidade de ensino e aprendizagem. *Revista História Hoje*. [Online] 3 (5), 43–60. Available from: doi:10.20949/rhhj.v3i5.125.

Grammenos, D. et al. (2009) Designing Universally Accessible Games. *Comput. Entertain.* [Online] 7 (1), 8:1–8:29. Available from: doi:10.1145/1486508.1486516.

Huizinga, J. (1970) *Homo Ludens: a study of the play element in culture.* London, Maurice Temple Smith Ltd.

Krouska, M. et al. (2019). A literature review of Social Networking-based Learning Systems using a novel ISO-based framework. *Intelligent Decision Technologies*, 13 (1), 23-39.

Mayer, R.E. (1997) *Multimedia learning: Are we asking the right questions? Educational Psychologist, , 1.* In: [Online]. 1997 p. Available from: doi:10.1207/s15326985ep3201_1.

Mayer, R.E. (2005) *The Cambridge handbook of multimedia learning*. The Cambridge handbook of multimedia learning. [Online]. New York, NY, US, Cambridge University Press. Available from: doi:10.1017/CBO9780511816819.

Paas, F. & Sweller, J. (2014) Implications of cognitive load theory for multimedia learning. *The Cambridge handbook of multimedia learning, 2nd ed.* [Online] 27–42. Available from: doi:10.1017/CBO9781139547369.004.

Rodrigues, C.H. & Quadros, R.M. de (2015) Diferenças e linguagens: a visibilidade dos ganhos surdos na atualidade. *Revista Teias*. 16 (40), 72–88.

Salvador-Ullauri, L. et al. (2017) *A Serious Game Accessible to People with Visual Impairments*. [Online]. Available from: doi:10.1145/3175536.3175576.

Sørensen, B.H. & Meyer, B. (2007) *Serious Games in language learning and teaching - A theoretical perspective*.

Sweller, J. (2005) Implications of Cognitive Load Theory for Multimedia Learning. In: *The Cambridge handbook of multimedia learning*. [Online]. New York, NY, US, Cambridge University Press. pp. 19–30. Available from: doi:10.1017/CBO9780511816819.003.

The Entertainment Software Association. *Essential Facts About The Computer and Video Game Industry 2018*. [Online]. Available from: http://www.theesa.com/article/essential-facts-computer-video-game-industry-2018/ [Accessed: 27 May 2019].

Zyda, M. (2005) From visual simulation to virtual reality to games. *Computer*. [Online] 38 (9), 25–32. Available from: doi:10.1109/MC.2005.297.

GAMIFICATION OF IN-CLASSROOM DIAGRAM DESIGN FOR SCIENCE STUDENTS

Andreas Mallas and Michalis Xenos
Computer Engineering and Informatics Dep., University of Patras
Rio Campus, University Building B, Patras, Greece

ABSTRACT

Merging the content of learning with the motivation of games can be a successful combination, if done properly and supported by the appropriate tool. Towards this goal, we developed Diagram•-∘atic an environment used to gamify the in-classroom activity of designing diagrams during a lecture. Using Diagram•-∘atic the professor, instead of lecturing about diagrams or showing examples of such diagrams, can design short games where the students could play by competing during the lecture. Diagram•-∘atic is a complete environment offering to the professor a design application to create games and a management application. The management application is used for monitoring the games while students play, as well as to present the results to the students after the end of each game, or to evaluate these results after classroom time. The students may use the mobile application on their mobiles to practice by designing diagrams outside of the classroom, as well as to play a game during classroom time, but only after the professor starts this game. The environment handles the communication from students' mobiles to the professor's applications and vice versa, while the students submit their diagrams or receive the correct ones, so to proceed to follow up games. The current version of Diagram•-∘atic is tailored for designing flow graphs used for path testing into a higher education software engineering course, but the environment can be used in any similar case requiring the design of diagrams (e.g. math, physics, chemistry).

KEYWORDS

Gamification, Blended Learning, Mobile Learning, Diagrams, in-Classroom Game

1. INTRODUCTION

Research in learning shows that deep learning is an active and constructive process (Council, 2000) and it can be more effective when it comes through real-world learning styles; problem-based, cooperative, activity-led learning, etc., can boost student's critical thinking skills. A typical problem in higher engineering education is when the professor explains something complex in the whiteboard (e.g. a complex diagram) while students are trying to understand it, most time unsuccessfully. In some extreme cases the students might even start focusing on their mobiles, since they have lost connection with the lecture. This was the motivation for our work: what if all the students could use their mobile devices to work on this diagram in a fun and engaging manner?

The use of mobile technologies helped educators to facilitate learning after classroom in places where learning occurs naturally (Huang et al., 2010), but there also is a great potential in using mobile devices into classroom to support learning. A success story of such usage is "Kahoot!"[1] which has been proven valuable in classroom, since it adds positive energy, support concept exploration, and adds fun to the classroom (Plump and LaRosa, 2017). On the other hand, "Kahoot!" has the limitation of not supporting complex responses which are common in engineering (such as in our case is the design of diagrams).

Towards this, we have designed and implemented Diagram•-∘atic, which is a learning environment that gamifies the process of designing and working with diagrams inside the classroom. In the current version, using Diagram•-∘atic, the professor presents a problem to the students, the students must design and submit the proper diagram to represent the problem, receive feedback and the correct diagram and then they must identify paths on the correct diagram. To work on the diagrams the students use their mobiles, while the professor shows the problem using a projector and monitors the results from the professor's application (app). The current version

[1] https://kahoot.com/

of Diagram•-○atic is tailored for designing flow graphs used for path testing into a higher education software engineering course, where the focus is on software quality and in particular on software metrics (Xenos and Christodoulakis, 1995), users perceptions of quality (Stavrinoudis et al., 2005) and structured testing (Watson et al., 1996). Of course, Diagram•-○atic can be used in any similar case requiring the design of diagrams, such as mathematics, physics, chemistry and in all levels of education. The only requirement for the students is to use a mobile phone and a motivated professor to design one or more short games to be played during classroom time.

The rest of paper is structured as follows. In the following section, we discuss related works about serious games and using mobile devices for learning in classroom. Section 3 presents the technologies used to develop Diagram•-○atic, the environment technical characteristics and the user interfaces of the environment applications, while conclusions and limitations of this work and future goals are discussed at section 4.

2. RELATED WORKS

Gamification is the use of game design elements in non-game contexts. Whereas "serious game" describes the design of full-fledged games for non-entertainment purposes, "gamified" applications merely incorporate elements of games (Deterding et al., 2011). Gamification as an academic topic of study is relatively young, and there are few well-established theoretical frameworks or unified discourses (Hamari et al., 2014). In the field of education, the use of games has a rapid growth (De Gloria et al., 2014), since a lot of the content that needs to be learned by the students is not directly motivating to them, therefore, merging the content of learning with the motivation of games can be a successful combination (Prensky, 2003). Most studies agree that gamification, if used properly, has the potential to increase student's intrinsic motivation (Forde et al., 2015).

In higher education and in the computer engineering field, related works have showed that even non-context related games can aid into developing graduate skills (Barr, 2017). Examples of recent works using games in computer engineering include games allowing students to collaborate and experience simulated events related to software project management (Maratou et al., 2016), to work on data structures and algorithms (Hakulinen, 2011), to learn a programming language such as C (Ibanez et al., 2014), to be informed about software engineering ethics (Xenos and Velli, 2018), to learn about version control and compete by committing frequently changes in code (Singer and Schneider, 2012) and many more (Losup and Epema, 2014). All these games are played during the course duration, but not inside the classroom, as in the Diagram•-○atic case.

Mobile phone usage is on the rise with 5 billion mobile subscribers worldwide in 2017 and projected 5.9 billion subscribers by 2025 of which 57% and 77% of connections are smartphone users, respectively (GSM, 2018). Smartphone penetration is even higher in developed countries, in the U.S specifically, 2018 show 69% of high school graduates and 91% of college graduates owning a smartphone[2]. Due to the popularity of mobile phones, they present a wide-reaching platform for educational purposes. Having the students use their mobiles into the classroom could be associated with positive student perceptions of collaborative learning but with increased disengagement by students (Heflin et al., 2017). Most works in the field focus on the use of mobile technology for informal learning (Khaddage et al., 2016), while other works emphasize on the positive examples of using tablets in the classroom (Rossing et al., 2012). There is great potential in using mobile devices to transform how students learn by changing the traditional classroom to one that is more interactive and engaging (Zydney and Warner, 2016, Sha et al., 2012, Shen et al., 2008). With that in mind, Diagram•-○atic was developed targeting mobile devices such as smartphones and tablets alike, which are used by the students inside the classroom.

Applications (apps) for mobile devices (Android and iOS) are usually implemented with a development technique usually referred to as Native (Smutny, 2012). Developing a Native app for different devices and operating systems requires knowledge of the development environment as well as the programming language of each operating system. Due to the complexity of Native app development different development techniques have been introduced that are usually referred to as cross-platform development (Rieger and Majchrzak, 2018). Therefore, the ultimate goal of cross-platform mobile app development is to achieve Native app performance and run on as many platforms as possible (Xanthopoulos and Xinogalos, 2013). Following these concepts Diagram•-○atic developed as a cross-platform environment to gamify the learning process of designing diagrams into the classroom.

---

[2] Source: http://www.pewinternet.org/fact-sheet/mobile/

3. THE DIAGRAM•⊸ATIC ENVIRONMENT

Diagram•⊸atic was developed using Xamarin.Forms[3] a cross-platform framework that uses the C# programming language. Xamarin.Forms tools enable developers to create Android, iOS, and Windows applications with native user interfaces and to share code across multiple platforms, including Windows. The Diagram•⊸atic learning environment consists of three applications: a) the student's app, which students use on the mobile devices to play the game in the classroom, b) the professor's design app, where the professor designs a new game, c) the professor's games management app, where the professor manages the games and views students' answers and the server-side web application programming interface (API) where the exercises and student responses are stored. Currently, student's and professor's design apps are developed for Android devices, while the professor's games management app for Windows (Universal Windows Platform). As a result of using a cross-platform framework, builds for the other supported platforms can be introduced without substantial development effort.

Before the lecture, to prepare one or more in-classroom games using Diagram•⊸atic, the professor uses the professor's design app and creates the games that students will play during the classroom time. These games are locked with a code that is required to enable playing. Then, the professor adds into the typical slideshow lecture presentation the additional information required for the games (e.g., the game code, the questions that will lead into the graph design, and the correct answers that will be presented to the students after the game). Finally, the professor installs the professor's games management app on their laptop, to be able to monitor the games during classroom.

Students preparation requires only to download the student's app on their mobile devices. Since this is something that takes just a few minutes, it can be done during the classroom break before starting the games, but ideally the students could spend some time playing with the mobile app to be better prepared for the classroom games. Upon opening the student's app, students are greeted with two options: the first option is to practice designing a diagram and the second option is to enter a code in order to start the in-classroom interactive play. Therefore, students willing to familiarize themselves with the app before class can access the first option that enables them to practice designing a diagram and familiarize themselves with the application user interface and features.

In order to start the game, during the classroom, the professor must give a code verbally or through the presentation for the students to enter in their mobile app. This is a security measure that ensures that access to the games is possible only during the classroom. After successfully entering the code the student identification number must also be submitted. Consequently, a list of available games will be displayed. When the first game is selected, the professor shows on the presentation, a piece of programming code. By examining the programming code, the student must design the corresponding diagram and submit it. This way, like "Kahoot!", students are not only focusing on their mobile phones but also direct their attention to the presentation which increases participation in the classroom. While students are designing the diagrams, the professor can monitor the number of players using the app, the number of answers submitted, and preview the answers that are already submitted. When the professor decides to finish the first part of the game (diagram submission), the second part of the game is initiated by the professor, or there is the option that the second part will start individually for each student that finished the first part. The student app now will display the correct diagram –the one that should have been created in the first part– in which the student must find the correct paths and submit them. The submission concludes the first game and the student's answers are available in the professor's games management app for the professor to evaluate or share with the students using the projector. When all students' answers are submitted the professor may proceed to explain the correct answers in the presentation, discuss common mistakes (by presenting anonymously diagrams with errors) and show examples of successful designs.

3.1 Student's Application

Student's app comprises of two main user interfaces (UI) which are presented on Figure 1. In this tailored version, Diagram•⊸atic was used for the design of graphs as part of structured testing (Watson et al., 1996). Students are asked to design a control flow graph with respect to this methodology which is based on the

[3] https://docs.microsoft.com/en-us/xamarin/xamarin-forms/

cyclomatic complexity metric (McCabe, 1976). A control flow graph depicts a program as a graph which consists of nodes that represent processing tasks and edges that represent control flow between the nodes. Cyclomatic complexity (*CC*) is a software metric used to measure the complexity of a program. For a single program, *CC* is defined as $CC = e - n + 2$, where e equals the number of edges and n equals the number of nodes of the graph.

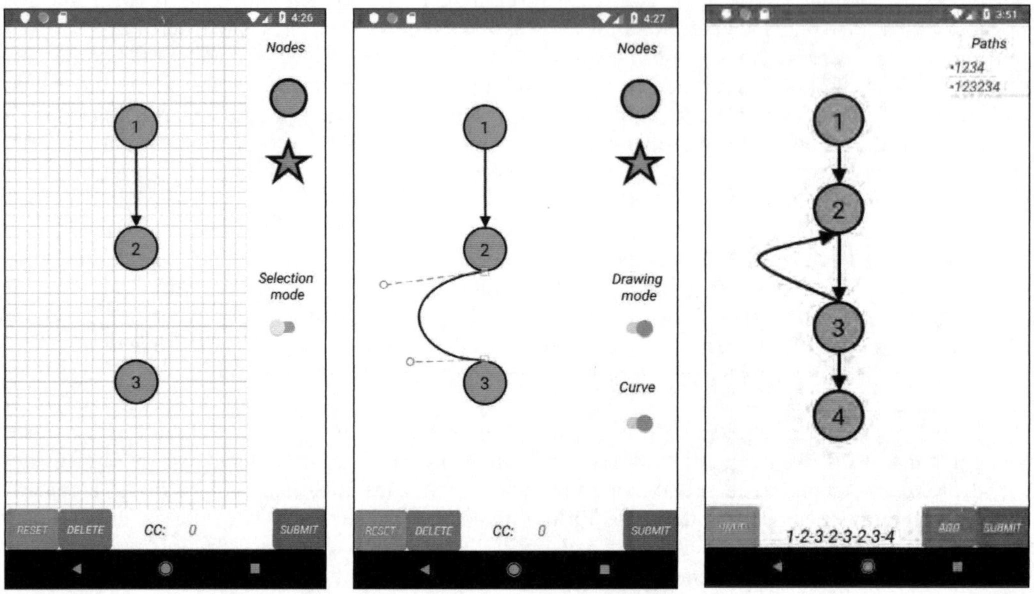

Figure 1. The UI for designing the requested diagram on the left and middle (selection and drawing mode respectively) and the UI for finding the correct paths on the right

The UI for designing the requested diagram (on the left side of Figure 1) has a canvas with a grid in which the diagrams are created. The grid design was adopted because it affords the necessary alignment of nodes and lines. Designing diagrams on the canvas involves using the right-side panel which consists of two parts. The upper part titled Nodes is where the user selects the type of node that they wish to insert by drag and dropping it into the canvas. Nodes in the shape of a star are not part of the graph but are inserted into the diagram to define a region as Figure 2 shows. The number of regions contained in the graph equals the cyclomatic complexity. Inserting a circle node into the canvas automatically assigns the node with a number based on the number of nodes already residing inside the diagram. For instance, in the diagram shown on the left side of Figure 1, that already contains three nodes inserting an additional node will assign the number 4 to it. If a node is deleted, the next node that will be inserted will receive the number the node that was last removed had. In any case, the algorithm that assigns numbers to the nodes ensures that a diagram which contains n nodes, these nodes will be numbered from 1 through n with no duplicates. The lower part of the right-side panel contains a switch for changing from selection to drawing mode. During both modes, students can use pinch-to-zoom gesture to zoom in and out of the diagram by simply placing two fingers on the screen and move them toward each other to zoom out or away from each other to zoom in. Pinch-to-zoom is a natural gesture that is used in browsers, photo apps, etc. that almost all mobile phone users are familiar with. It enables precise interaction with the diagram on circumstances that the student wants to zoom in and with refined movements micromanage a diagram item, as well as having an overall view of the diagram by zooming out. The "Selection mode" is the default mode that enables the student to select items from the diagram and manipulate them (e.g. move them around, resize them, etc.). Additionally, by placing a finger on an empty space of the canvas students can move the whole canvas across its horizontal or vertical axis by simply moving their finger in the opposite direction, analogous to how scrolling in a mobile web browser is performed.

The "Drawing mode" (illustrated on the middle of Figure 1) is only used to connect nodes with a line and, in contrast to selection mode, users cannot select an item and manipulate it. The straight line is the default one, but the user can choose the curve line if it's required. Designing a straight line is straightforward by sliding a finger from one node to another. The curved line requires additional user input; students may select the curved line switch and draw a line with their finger between the two nodes that they want to connect, similarly to the straight line. At this point an almost straight line is designed with one difference, it contains 2 vector points that control the curvature of the line. Selecting the vector points and moving them around defines the required curvature. This is shown in the drawing in the middle of Figure 1. The inclusion of a curved line allows the design of more complex diagrams. As an indication to the student that drawing mode is enabled the grid lines of the main area disappear transforming the canvas into a piece of drawing paper.

Lastly, the bottom part comprises of buttons and a number indicator. Reset clears the canvas as to begin the design of the diagram from the start. Delete, removes the currently selected item from the diagram. Submit, sends the diagram as the student's final answer to the server. CC corresponds to the cyclomatic complexity number, as the user populates the diagram adding star nodes the CC number indicator informs the student about the current cyclomatic complexity number which depends on the number of star nodes contained in the diagram. For example, in the more complex diagram illustrated in Figure 2, the CC is measured as 3 since the student has inserted three nodes with the star symbol.

The task of finding the correct paths is implemented by the UI shown on the right side of Figure 1. Students must identify independent paths by examining the source code on the professor's presentation while also taking in their consideration the graph that the student's app is displaying. The work that was done in the previous part of the game is helpful because the number of independent paths equals the number of cyclomatic complexity, therefore students already know the number of paths they must identify. Same to the diagram design UI, there are also three parts in this UI. The main one is where the given diagram resides. Pinch-to-zoom gesture is also available to accommodate the use of different screen sizes. Students naturally zoom in or out of the diagram to fit the screen size of their device. The bottom part contains three buttons (undo, add and submit) and an entry. Selecting a node registers the node's number to the bottom entry; the student repeats this procedure until the desired path is created (e.g. 1-2-3-2-3-2-3-4 as shown in the example of Figure 1). When the path is complete selecting the add button inserts it into the list of paths positioned on the right-side panel titled Paths. Selecting a path from the list triggers a notification to remove it from the list. Upon completing the list of paths, the student submits their answer by selecting the submit button. This sends the current list of paths as the student's final answer to the server. Only after each submission, the professor can see the paths submitted, using the professor's app.

3.2 Professor's Game Design Application

Professor's design app is quite like the student's app, since they both share the same UI. The primary difference is that this application only implements the diagram design, as shown on the left side of Figure 1. Its functionality is the creation of a new game by the professor that, after locked using a password, gets uploaded to the server creating a pool of games. These games, then, are available to the students to play in the classroom, only when the professor reveals the password.

3.3 Professor's Games Management Application

The purpose of the professor's games management app is to present the student's answers and simultaneously enable the professor to evaluate and manage them. A student answer consists of two parts, the diagram they designed and the paths they created. In order to increase the professor's productivity, both parts are displayed simultaneously as shown in Figure 2. Specifically, the professor's games management app UI is divided into three sections. On the left side of the screen (labeled "Answers"), is the list of the student answers from an actual in-classroom experiment. Each item on the list contains a student identification number (AM), the date and time the game was played, as well as the game number. Selecting an answer populates the other two sections of the screen, while right-clicking it, triggers a notification to permanently delete it from the list. Once an answer is selected, the middle section of the UI displays the diagram designed by the student, while the section on the left (labeled "Paths") shows the paths the student entered as an answer.

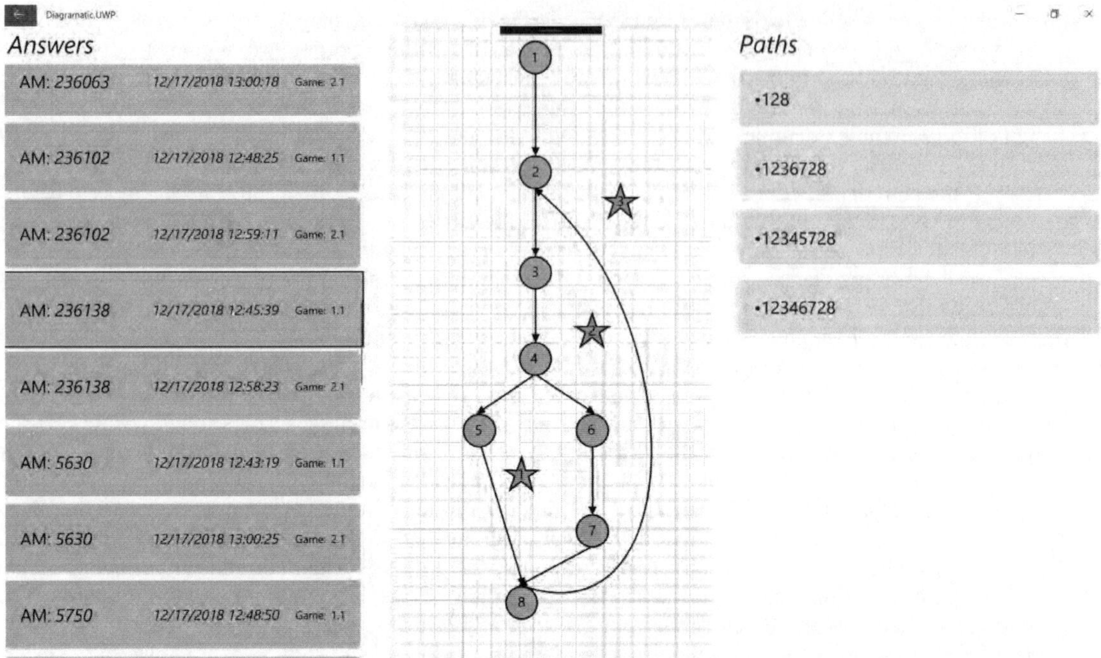

Figure 2. The professor's management application with results from an actual in-classroom game

Figure 2 illustrates an example of the professor's games management app which took place in a small in-classroom experiment. On the left, the student with the identifier (AM): 236138 is selected, while on the center is displayed the diagram the student designed. In this case, the diagram contains eight nodes and nine edges which translates in a cyclomatic complexity equal to 3. This number corresponds to the number of the correctly positioned stars which means that the submitted diagram is correct. On the right, is the list of paths that the student identified, in this case, the number of paths is 4 while the *CC* is 3 which means that the student answer is incorrect. The maximum number of paths is equal to *CC* number, while in some cases (after reviewing the code) the number of paths could be lower to *CC* number. Examining the paths this student submitted the professor would notice that, the first one is 1-2-8 which is incorrect because there is an edge from node 1 to node 2 but there is no edge from node 2 to node 8 (in fact there is an edge from node 8 to node 2). Likewise, the following paths are also incorrect.

4. CONCLUSION AND FUTURE WORK

Diagram•-○atic is an environment used to gamify the in-classroom activity of designing diagrams during a lecture. Using Diagram•-○atic the professor, instead of lecturing about diagrams or showing examples, can design short games where the students can play by competing during the lecture using their mobile phones. Diagram•-○atic is a complete environment offering the professor a design application to design games and a management application for these games and the corresponding results.

As any continuous research work, Diagram•-○atic is not without limitations. A limitation lies in the nature of the diagrams; designing too complex diagrams present a time-consuming endeavor, transforming the gamification of this process in a less enjoyable experience. Furthermore, diagrams with a high number of nodes are challenging to design in a mobile device due to the device's narrow screen size. Therefore, in most games we used graphs with 10 nodes or less, which are more than adequate for short in-classroom games. Finally, in the current version the mobile student's app and professor's design app are available only for the android platform, while the professor's games management app is available only for the windows platform.

Future work includes builds for all supported platforms, thus making the environment truly cross-platform. Also, a unification of the professor's design app and games management app will remove the inconvenience of using two different apps and will allow the professor to design or evaluate games outside the classroom transforming the process into a truly mobile experience. Further improvements that could be introduced in the gamification process *per se*, include automated mechanism for students winning points after a game, sound effects and student rankings. Implementing these features requires an automatic evaluation of the students' answers by the application, which also is a challenging future work.

REFERENCES

Barr, M. 2017. Video Games can Develop Graduate Skills in Higher Education Students: A Randomised Trial. *Computers & Education,* 113, 86-97.

Council, N. R. 2000. *How People Learn: Brain, Mind, Experience, and School: Expanded Edition*, National Academies Press.

De Gloria, A., Bellotti, F. & Berta, R. 2014. Serious Games for Education and Training. *International Journal of Serious Games,* 1.

Deterding, S., Dixon, D., Khaled, R. & Nacke, L. From Game Design Elements to Gamefulness: Defining Gamification. Proceedings of the 15th International Academic Mindtrek Conference: Envisioning Future Media Environments, 2011. ACM, 9-15.

Forde, S. F., Mekler, E. D. & Opwis, K. 2015. Informational vs. Controlling Gamification: A Study Design. *Proceedings of the 2015 Annual Symposium on Computer-Human Interaction in Play.* London, United Kingdom: ACM.

GSM 2018. *The Mobile Economy 2018,* London, UK.

Hakulinen, L. 2011. Using Serious Games in Computer Science Education. *Proceedings of the 11th Koli Calling International Conference on Computing Education Research.* Koli, Finland: ACM.

Hamari, J., Koivisto, J. & Sarsa, H. Does Gamification Work?--A Literature Review of Empirical Studies on Gamification. 2014 47th Hawaii International Conference on System Sciences (HICSS), 2014. IEEE, 3025-3034.

Heflin, H., Shewmaker, J. & Nguyen, J. 2017. Impact of Mobile Technology on Student Attitudes, Engagement, and Learning. *Computers & Education,* 107, 91-99.

Huang, Y.-M., Lin, Y.-T. & Cheng, S.-C. 2010. Effectiveness of a Mobile Plant Learning System in a Science Curriculum in Taiwanese Elementary Education. *Computers & Education,* 54, 47-58.

Ibanez, M., A, D.-S. & Delgado-Kloos, C. 2014. Gamification for Engaging Computer Science Students in Learning Activities: A Case Study. *IEEE Transactions on Learning Technologies,* 7, 291-301.

Khaddage, F., Muller, W. & Flintoff, K. 2016. Advancing Mobile Learning in Formal and Informal Settings via Mobile App Technology: Where to from Here, and how? *Journal of Educational Technology & Society,* 19.

Losup, A. & Epema, D. An Experience Report on Using Gamification in Technical Higher Education. Proceedings of the 45th ACM Technical Symposium on Computer Science Education, 2014. ACM, 27-32.

Maratou, V., Chatzidaki, E. & Xenos, M. 2016. Enhance Learning on Software Project Management Through a Role-Play Game in a Virtual World. *Interactive Learning Environments,* 24, 897-915.

McCabe, T. J. 1976. A Complexity Measure. *IEEE Transactions on Software Engineering,* SE-2, 308-320.

Plump, C. M. & Larosa, J. 2017. Using Kahoot! in the Classroom to Create Engagement and Active Learning: A Game-Based Technology Solution for Elearning Novices. *Management Teaching Review,* 2, 151-158.

Prensky, M. 2003. Digital Game-Based Learning. *Computers in Entertainment (CIE),* 1, 21-21.

Rieger, C. & Majchrzak, T. A. A Taxonomy for App-Enabled Devices: Mastering the Mobile Device Jungle. 2018 Cham. Springer International Publishing, 202-220.

Rossing, J. P., Miller, W., Cecil, A. K. & Stamper, S. E. 2012. ilearning: The Future of Higher Education? Student Perceptions on Learning with Mobile Tablets.

Sha, L., Looi, C.-K., Chen, W., Seow, P. & Wong, L.-H. 2012. Recognizing and Measuring Self-Regulated Learning in a Mobile Learning Environment. *Computers in Human Behavior,* 28, 718-728.

Shen, R., Wang, M. & Pan, X. 2008. Increasing Interactivity in Blended Classrooms Through a Cutting-Edge Mobile Learning System. *British Journal of Educational Technology,* 39, 1073-1086.

Singer, L. & Schneider, K. It was a bit of a Race: Gamification of Version Control. 2012 Second International Workshop on Games and Software Engineering: Realizing User Engagement with Game Engineering Techniques (GAS), 9-9 June 2012 2012. 5-8.

Smutny, P. Mobile Development Tools and Cross-Platform Solutions. Proceedings of the 13th International Carpathian Control Conference (ICCC), 28-31 May 2012 2012. 653-656.

Stavrinoudis, D., Xenos, M., Peppas, P. & Christodoulakis, D. 2005. Early Estimation of Users' Perception of Software Quality. *Software Quality Journal,* 13, 155-175.

Watson, A. H., Wallace, D. R. & Mccabe, T. J. 1996. *Structured Testing: A Testing Methodology Using the Cyclomatic Complexity Metric*, US Department of Commerce, Technology Administration, National Institute of Standards And Technology.

Xanthopoulos, S. & Xinogalos, S. A Comparative Analysis of Cross-Platform Development Approaches for Mobile Applications. Proceedings of the 6th Balkan Conference in Informatics, 2013. ACM, 213-220.

Xenos, M. & Christodoulakis, D. 1995. Software Quality: The User's Point of View. *In:* Lee, M., Barta, B.-Z. & Juliff, P. (eds.) *Software Quality and Productivity: Theory, Practice, Education and Training.* Boston, MA: Springer US.

Xenos, M. & Velli, V. 2018. A Serious Game for Introducing Software Engineering Ethics to University Students. *21st International Conference on Interactive Collaborative Learning, ICL2018.* Kos, Greece: Springer-Verlag Berlin Heidelberg 2011.

Zydney, J. M. & Warner, Z. 2016. Mobile Apps for Science Learning: Review of Research. *Computers & Education,* 94, 1-17.

"GAMING IN EDUCATION AND E-LEARNING: MOCK-TRIALS, MOCK-ELECTIONS AND CRISIS-SIMULATIONS FOR POLITICAL SCIENCES AND COMMUNICATIONS COURSES"

Marco Rimanelli[1] and Krzysztof Gurba[2]
[1]*Ph.D. Saint Leo University, USA*
[2]*Ph.D. Pedagogical University Kraków, Poland*

ABSTRACT

Among recent e-Learning Pedagogical Strategies, gaming and crisis-simulation games are increasingly used in recent years in university-learning and Blended-courses as an out-of-context effective tool for role-playing and education, especially in Law Schools and Business Schools. Gaming covers several sub-fields (war-games; Law School Mock-Trials; Tailor-made educational games in Business; playing commercials-off-the-shelf games; programming and code-learning; games to promote social inclusion of marginalized groups; Model U.N. and crisis-simulations) and are recently enhanced by the impact of using multi-modality and on-line education to apply several concurrent modes of presentation/communications, which are now being applied also in Political Sciences and Communications courses. In recent years, the much-touted future role of the *Net-Generation* of children and youth who grew-up with computer games should find a natural educational outlet in gaming, but this has been limited to the entertainment field, rather than university education, or in computer coding and programming, where gaming (both on-line and face-to-face) has only marginal effects, due to students' inability to grasp theoretical concepts, poor preparation or poor motivation. Thus, despite already existing methods of gamification in education, its promise as a didactic method in schools and universities is still at its beginnings. This paper analyzes as case-studies the emerging impact of gaming simulations in Political Sciences Blended-courses at Saint Leo University, USA and in Communications courses at the Pedagogical University of Kraków, Poland.

KEYWORDS

Gamification, Gaming, e-Learning Pedagogical Strategies, Blended-Courses, Political Sciences, Communications, Mock-U.S. Presidential Elections, crisis-simulations, International Relations, Model U.N., Mock-Trials, War-games

1. ON-LINE E-LEARNING AND GAMING IN UNIVERSITY EDUCATION

Since the 1990s, universities and schools in the West and increasingly world-wide have benefitted from the rapid growth of on-line e-Learning education, which has been spurred by the parallel impact of the Internet-driven technological revolution and the overwhelming public use of professional and public computer networks at cyclically lowering costs. This technological revolution in education has expanded the academic reach to both traditional (by increasing the availability of on-line courses alongside with traditional campus classes) and non-traditional student-populations (by providing cheaper on-line e-Learning alternatives to traditional campus brick-and-mortar academic programs). However, the overall percentage of tenure-track faculty which has steadily increased until the 1970s, has declined since, being first replaced by the ubiquitous rise of Adjunct-faculty on-campus, followed by exponential growth on non-tenured faculty in on-line academic institutions.

Thus, Western universities in the U.S. and Europe were the first to enjoy massive growth rates after World War II by expanding their earlier traditional brick-and-mortar academic reach from the male-dominant upper- and middle-class students to new inflows of veterans, women and lower-class youths, which was enhanced across-the-board demographically by the post-war long "Baby Boom" of 1946-60 to reach 8.6 million university students by 1970. However, by the 1970s, higher inflation in the operations-costs of higher education institutions provoked in-turn continuous rises in tuitions and student-debt, as well as a freeze in new tenure-track hires compared to the growth in Ph.D. programs creating highly-specialized student-mills. Then, by the 1990s, U.S. and European universities experienced a twin unexpected gradual decline of traditional university enrollments and state contributions to public universities. This forced all academic institutions to match cyclical rises in tuitions with across-the-board cost-savings in infrastructures, while halving permanent, tenure-track faculty by stalling new replacement tenure-track hires, despite widespread generational retirements, who were replaced by a rising sub-class of cheaper massive amounts of part-time Adjunct-faculty (skyrocketing from 105,000 in 1970 to 755,000 in 2019), composed of ABDs ("All-But-Dissertation" Doctoral students), graduated Ph.D.s unable to land permanent jobs, and professionals teaching on-the-side.

These latter dual trends continued at the onset of the Twenty-First Century, despite the nation-wide positive rise in universities' student enrollments to 20 million during the 2000-2015 "Baby Boomlet" years, with consequent higher retentions and revenue-streams, because all university institutions have remained saddled with fast growth in institutional operation costs, rising tuitions, declining state contributions to public institutions and smaller endowments (especially private colleges). Thus, as the Adjunct-faculty underclass has continued to rise, many Western universities have set aside initial skepticism to embrace the fast rise of Internet-based e-Learning academic revolution as a major cost-saving educational tool to expand enrollments among traditionally under-served student populations, while overcoming local constraints (remote areas, military bases, abroad).

With new distance-learning delivery-systems and wide-range academic courses for credit coming first from "for-profit" business-academic providers (like Phoenix, Argosy, DeVry, Keiser, Cappella), also many traditional universities have joined e-Learning by accepting many credits-transfers from accredited on-line distance-learning providers, while slowly developing their own "non-profit" academic blended classrooms and e-courses. By the 2000s, traditional universities also accepted credits-transfers from any accredited on-line distance-learning academic provider, while many also offer their own on-line classes in conjunction with traditional campus ones. This has spurred in Western higher education systems (North America, Japan, East Asia, Europe) competition between public, private and "for-profit" business-academic education providers to control these new educational markets and reach working professionals, working class, military (bases and abroad) and low-income social groups (stay-at-home parents, urban poor, rural poor and immigrants).

E-Learning digital modes of education-delivery are seen as "easier" to grasp, more "democratic" and inclusive for non-traditional students, not usually part of the dominant traditional education system, while also providing needed "critical-thinking" skills, rather than traditional regurgitation of knowledge. The high growth-rate and popular use of on-line education programs stimulated the acceptance of both on-line and blended courses in both virtual "for-profit" universities and more innovative campus-based traditional academic institutions. Yet, e-Learning has expanded the existing pool of non-traditional students with new on-line course-offerings at cheaper costs than traditional campus education, rather than systematically reduce rising operational-costs and tuition costs, or increase new tenure-track Faculty hires.

Within this technological and e-Learning revolution, in recent years the rise of the *Net-Generation* of children and youth who have grown-up with computer games since age-2 is now seen as a natural educational outlet through gaming. But in Western university education and computer coding or programming, gaming (both on-line and face-to-face) has had only marginal effects, due to the students' inability to grasp theoretical concepts, poor preparation or poor motivation. Thus, despite already existing methods of gamification in education, so called gamification as a promising didactic method in schools and universities is still at its beginnings. Instead, gaming has evolved especially in Law Schools and Business Schools as an effective role-playing educational tool for Mock-Trials and case-studies. Gaming covers several sub-fields (war-games; Law School Mock-Trials; Tailor-made educational games in Business; playing commercials-off-the-shelf games; programming and code-learning; games to promote social inclusion of marginalized groups) and are recently enhanced by the impact of using multi-modality and on-line education.

2. GAMING IN POLITICAL SCIENCES AT SAINT LEO UNIVERSITY

This paper analyzes as limited case-studies the emerging impact of gaming simulations in Political Sciences Blended-courses at the private "non-profit" Catholic Saint Leo University in the United States and in different universities in Poland for Education and Communications courses. Saint Leo University under the visionary leadership of its 8th President Arthur F. Kirk Jr. (1997-2015) has pursued innovative technological strategic goals to enhance the institution's teaching excellence and national reputation as Florida's modern, tech-savvy Catholic University. In three cycles (1998-2005, 2005-2015 and 2015-2020) Saint Leo University applied new technologies to enhance teaching excellence and standardization at both traditional campus and far-flung non-traditional Distance Centers for its 8-weeks On-line and Blended courses, while applying audio-visual technologies, standardized Master-Syllabi and rigorous assessments to campus and on-line classes.

By 2005, Saint Leo University switched to a university-owned on-line platform (Learning Studio leased from Peterson), standardized both on-line and campus teaching with 8-weeks Master Syllabi and Internet resources for campus and Blended-courses, while redeveloping university-owned on-line courses-content (PIE, outcomes, assessments). Since 2015, on-line teaching shifted to a new university-owned on-line platform D2L and redeveloped courses, while imposing D2L also on-campus as multi-use skeleton platform for grades, assessments, permanent content-loading and Blended-courses, which allows also the inclusion of gaming.

In the Political Sciences discipline, games and role-playing have developed in Graduate schools since the 1980s-90s out of earlier military war-games, which in the past few years have been revitalized in academia through educational game case-studies. Indeed, currently the use of gamification is becoming very relevant as a promising didactic method in universities, beyond traditional Law and Business Schools. In this context, Saint Leo University's Political Sciences faculty (Professor Marco Rimanelli and Director of Polling Institute Frank Orlando) have striven with limited resources to reapply to their classes the academic use of international crises-simulation, Model United Nations, U.S. Presidential elections and mock-trials.

First, Political Sciences students were exposed since 2010 to education gaming based on free-standing Model U.N. at local and regional competitions (Florida Southern College and University of Pennsylvania) by training motivated student-members of local ΠΣΑ (Pi-Sigma-Alpha) Honors Society for Political Sciences and International Affairs. Then, with the ability to rely on the more flexible D2L computer platform, this was followed in 2014-2017 by the creation of specialized Political Sciences courses where Director Frank Orlando applied gaming through the university-wide "Alternate Reality Learning Experience" (ARLE) concept to teach both U.S. Presidential Elections and Mock-Trials for the two new Minors of "Campaigns and Elections" and "Legal Studies". Faculty participation university-wide was encouraged under the 9th President Bill Lennox Jr. (2015-18) and Dr. Jeff Borden, Chief Innovation Officer at Saint Leo University, with his Teaching and Learning Innovation Department funding the ARLE experiential learning.

While many Political Sciences programs take part in some form of experiential learning or simulation based on political phenomena, there are a variety of factors that made ARLE a unique experience for the students involved. The vast majority of simulations in Political Sciences are contained within the confines of a single course, but at Saint Leo University, the ARLE experiential-learning combined many classes, departments and schools. In 2015 Director Orlando's new upper-level "Presidency" class first applied the ARLE experiential learning project and repeated it in 2016-2020 with the 2016 and 2020 U.S. Presidential Election in his newly-developed "Campaigns and Elections" class through learning-objectives and assignments. Director Orlando's courses provided the chief players, with other courses pooled in planning and execution of campus-wide multi-disciplinary simulations with 100 students.

Saint Leo University's Social Sciences Department faculty have promoted more creative opportunities for students to engage in experiential learning and the 2015 "U.S. Presidential Election ARLE" simulation was the first one related to applying gaming to e-Learning. It involved not only the "Presidency" students, but also a "Communications" class that aided the campaigns in honing their message, a "Psychology" class that ran analyzed the effectiveness of the rival campaign strategies, two "Communications" classes on "Social Media" that helped to handle the *Twitter, Facebook* and *Instagra*m pages for the rival candidates, a "Multi-media Management" class that filmed campaign commercials and filmed the climactic debate event, an "Education" class (at a Center campus hours away from University Campus) that acted as an education interest group, and an on-line "Criminal Justice" class that provided a security plan for the event. There was such interest in the event that the only negative feedback was from faculty members disappointed that their classes were not invited to participate, except as external resources for policy experts to help create party-platforms.

In planning the event, involved faculty met weekly from March through Fall 2015, while facilitating cooperation between students in each class was of utmost concern, especially because most courses met at different times (and some at remote campuses or in different learning environments), while natural rivalry emerged between students of different disciplines. Even though several classes were taking part in the 2015 "U.S. Presidential Election ARLE", "Presidency" students were the focal point of the experience: students from that class provided the rival Presidential candidates, Vice-Presidential candidates, Party Leaders, Campaign Managers, Communication Directors and key policy experts. All students were allowed to apply for any positions and party teams (Republicans vs. Democrats), but final "casting" decisions were coordinated by Instructors. The Presidential candidates were the centerpieces of the experience and needed to act in ready-made commercials, conduct interviews and participate in several debates. Vice-Presidential candidates had similar duties and participated in their own Vice-Presidential debate. Party Leaders were responsible for compiling their respective party platforms and shaping general policy. Campaign Managers were tasked with coordinating strategy. Communications Directors were in charge of media requests and messaging. Policy experts focused on specific issues and wrote reports that comprised their party's platform and researched topics that were useful in debate preparations.

It is important to note that these students were not just imitating real life politicians, and there was no requirement that the ARLE Simulation's political platforms needed to align completely with their counterpart in reality. In order to protect the students involved and separate their personal life from the ARLE Simulation, the Presidential and Vice-Presidential candidates were given fake-names and background-stories provided by the Instructor who approved any student "tweaking" their fake-biographies to personalize their candidacies.

The ARLE "U.S. Presidential Elections" simulation ran for almost the entire 2015 Fall Semester. During that time the campaigns were afforded a great deal of autonomy to pursue the strategies that they best believed would lead to victory. Along the way, both campaigns performed in debates, filmed commercials, produces flyers and buttons, engaged in voter outreach and wooed interest groups for their support. The culminating event was a Mock Presidential Debate, moderated by top students from other classes. The debate was modeled on the 2016 Presidential debates, but the questions were original and created by Instructor Orlando with input from students in other disciplines. Neither campaign had access to the debate questions beforehand, but in addition to agreements on format, their rival campaigns were able to mutually decide what issues would be focused on during the 90-minute debate. This led to a situation where students spent a great deal of time preparing for the event, because the prize was around the corner. At the conclusion of the debate, audience members watching on a live *YouTube* stream were allowed to vote for the Mock U.S. President.

The 2015 ARLE Simulation became the all-encompassing focus for the students in the "Presidency" class. While some of their "colleagues" in other classes treated it as just another assignment, the goal for the "Presidency" students was to be all in. In order to facilitate this, the course assessments changed, but not the desired learning outcomes: readings were assigned and lectures presented on Presidential campaign strategy, but the total number of tests and quizzes was decreased. Instead, students were directed to focus their energies on carrying-out the simulation by applying what they had learned. They were graded not only on the effort and success of their performance as judged by the Instructor, but also on the evaluation of their final work by their teammates (with many team meetings taking place away from the classroom). Finally, students provided their personal assessment of the experience at the end of the semester.

The results of such experiential gaming were overwhelmingly positive. The event was attended by over 200 students, faculty and staff, with Saint Leo University President William Lennox Jr. providing opening remarks. Local media covered the events of the campaign, and students in the "Presidency" class were featured in radio interviews throughout the Tampa Bay area. Hundreds of people watched the final event on-line live on *YouTube* and cast their ballots. Students in this experience extolled the virtues of this type of experiential learning in their class exit-survey, with many declaring it to be the best course that they could apply towards their future careers. In fact, during the 2016 U.S. Presidential Elections of Donald Trump (R) vs. Hillary Clinton (D), one Senior was able to parlay their performance in the ARLE simulation into a job position with the Florida Democratic Party (despite portraying the Republican Vice-President candidate in class!). A final assessment in class showed how students learned from this game and interiorized the U.S. Presidential Elections.

The successful 2015 performance was repeated in 2016 with a completely new group of students. Students were made aware of the ARLE university exercise in advance of their registration to the courses, and this increased overall course enrollments to the maximum number capped by the University. The onus was on faculty to improve communication between classes, and to streamline the ARLE process. Because of the success of these type of events, ARLE exercises planned mock-elections every even year in Fall to capitalize on the excitement of campaign season and to maximize the educational element for students involved.

In odd Fall 2017, Political Sciences students in several multi-disciplinary classes ("Presidency", "International Relations", "Comparative Politics" and two classes in Criminology), were also integrated in a mock-trial called: "The Trial of the Century: Oswald". This was another ARLE organized by Saint Leo's TALI department that involved classes from across the university, including Criminal Justice and Multimedia Management. Again, planning began since the previous term to find a case not tried before and reflected back to the "real world". As Saint Leo's School of Arts & Sciences was commemoration the 1960s decade in a year-long celebration, the ARLE game focused o one of the most famous events from that era was the live-TV assassination of U.S. President John F. Kennedy in 1963 by Lee Harvey Oswald.

On account of the later dramatic subsequent assassination by the infamous Jack Ruby of Oswald on live-TV, while in Police custody, Oswald never stood trial for his unprecedented political crime and so took to the grave all secrets surrounding the assassination decision, which in turn syphoned out decades of conspiracies. This mock-Trial scenario offered an illusory experience where the truth could finally come out in a trial setting: instead of creating an "alternate universe" to conduct the trial of a "living, wounded" Oswald in 1964, ARLE focused on the facts of the trial and legal process. Since Oswald had been killed, this mock-criminal trial innovatively used a plausible fictitious scenario showing the Oswald's family seeking to cash in on a life insurance policy. But the policy would not pay out if the holder committed a felony. Thus, the Oswald family challenged the insurance company's decision to withhold benefits to his descendants through a civil trial to litigate the domestic aspect of the Oswald Case in our game: "Trial of the Century: Oswald!"

While students from Criminal Justice classes were arguing the case on strictly legalistic terms, Political Sciences students were involved as background experts: students in the "International Relations" and "Comparative Politics" classes acted as country and leadership experts on different governments and organizations that were interacting with the United States at the time of the assassination, such as the Soviet Union, European countries and NATO. Students in the "Presidency" class served as experts on a variety of domestic conspiracy theories (on who Oswald worked for) that have circulated over the past 50 years, including FBI, CIA, Mafia and/or foreign conspirators. Students learned a great deal about their subject area in the context of the larger class. This experience took place as a graded class project. Support was provided to both the plaintiff and defendant throughout the process until the trial at the end of the semester.

The ARLE faculty coordination team met regularly during the Summer 2017 to plan and develop the learning exercise, and then actual ARLE mock-trial took place over two-days in November 2017. The ARLE team was able to secure a respected former judge to preside over the trial in order to add another layer of verisimilitude to the proceedings. As with the mock-election the years before, local media covered the case as a learning exercise open to the public to attend. The jury was comprised of volunteers, and because of the high visibility of the experience, there was no shortage of students willing to join in. The mock-Trial staffed two juries, one that served as the actual jury, and the other that consisted of jurors that were eliminated after *voir dire.* Neither of the juries knew which of their groups was the actual jury whose decision was accepted by an actual retired Judge as guest.

In addition to the jury, dozens of students, faculty members, school administrators and members of the local community attended the trial. Within the University's blended-courses and technologies, this event was live-streamed across the world so family members and others curious about the outcome could enjoy the hard work of the participants, and other students from Saint Leo Centers in different locations. Most students in Political Sciences courses were called to the stand as expert witnesses in their respective fields, and successfully withstood examination and cross-examination, while sticking to their well-rehearsed researched version of events. In the end, the main jury found Oswald guilty and allowed the insurance company not to pay benefits to the Oswald family. Instead, the alternate jury (comprising dismissed members) found the opposite! In future mock-Trials, cameras will be in the deliberation room to record the jury's decisions as another post-fact learning tool.

This process was successful for all classes involved, including Political Sciences. All students were able to learn a great deal about an important period in political history from a variety of different perspectives (legal, domestic, international, communications, and conspiracies), but perhaps more importantly, they were forced to work on their individual critical communication skills and team-efforts, while faculty strove to coordinate multi-disciplinary assignments and the mock-trial between all classes. Preparing witnesses involves a lot of research, but answering hostile questioning in front of hundreds of people in a courtroom setting was a raw experience for many students and helped build their self-confidence in public speaking. By observing in this mock-trial context the interaction of the different elements of the legal system (judges, prosecutors, defense, jury, experts, witnesses, security), the ARLE game has emerged as both a solid blended learning tool and a recruiting ground for future careers-preparation, or Law School as professional goals.

Today, Saint Leo University's 10th President Jeffrey Senese (2018-current) continues innovative strategic goals ("Renaissance 2021", while cutting costs through infrequent annual ARLE multi-disciplinary mock-trials and mock-Presidential Elections, blending only Political Sciences and Criminologist students. Essential is to continue faculty supervision as a group, with both types of students and classes assembled together for briefings, because the negative element that emerged out of the intense preparation for ARLE mock-trials was the deep-seated rivalry and unwillingness to cooperate between students in Criminal Justice and Political Sciences, when the former classes, once in-charge of the trial, did discount the latter's expertise and recommendations, even refusing to use them as pre-trial experts because the Political Scientists' international and diplomatic policy-papers and knowledge challenged the pre-ordained ways Criminologists approached Prosecution and Defense as a purely domestic legal proceedings with only minor international input. This enraged the Political Sciences students who strenuously insisted that all legal challenges (from either Prosecution or Defense) meant to prove that Oswald had, or had not, acted as a "foreign agent", and related conspiracies tied to this or that enemy countries (USSR, Cuba, Red China) or government agencies (CIA, FBI) or non-state actors (*Batistas* Cuban exiles, or the Mafia), did require detailed expert-witnesses (Political Sciences students) who were the only experts qualified to recount the geo-strategic role of the Cold War and positions of each major enemy countries to provide proof or debunking most conspiracy theories. Only in this way could the Insurance company legally debunk Oswald's family claim by proving his actions as part or not of a global conspiracy based on the Cold War. This clash of visions among students shows the danger of "tunnel-vision" in rigidly applying only institutional positions learned in class.

Finally, concerning applying games to International Relations (IR), security and international organizations, Statecraft Simulation offers 5 automated on-line commercial war-games for classes with scoring. Instead, Professor Marco Rimanelli experimented on a compressed ARLE model as a 2-days live war-game simulation on an important current international political crisis: "Crimea and Eastern Ukraine Secessionism: Russia vs. Ukraine/E.U./NATO/U.S./U.N., 2013-19". This could become at a graded Cap-Stone experiential assessment for both first-time students in introductory courses ("International Relations"; "Democracy") and more advanced classes ("Comparative Governments", "Diplomatic History/Foreign Policy", "International Law & Organizations"), by using the global crisis-simulation he previously launched in 2014 at John Cabot University in Rome, Italy, during his 2013-14 U.S. Fulbright-Schuman Chair Award. This IR crisis-simulation (Maidan Revolution, Crimea, Ukraine) has students from different Political Sciences classes re-enacting in person the current Russo-Ukrainian international clash (U.S./NATO/E.U./U.N. backing Ukraine with international sanctions against Russia for its sponsoring of pro-Russian Ukrainian secessionists (Crimea and East Ukraine).

This latest Saint Leo faculty-led gaming exercise mirrors traditional war-games (used at the Pentagon, U.S. State Department and CIA) in which the student-players are led through the crisis' timeline, key stages and actors to then develop a plausible future conflict-resolution scenario. This faculty-led war-game exercise provided student-players with background information on the timeline of the 2013-19 Ukrainian crisis and conflicting political interests pursued by the major Powers (Russia, Ukraine, U.S.A., Germany, Great Britain, France, China), international organizations (North Atlantic Treaty Organization/NATO, European Union/E.U., United Nations/U.N.) and non-state actors (pro-Russian ex-Ukrainian President in exile, pro-Russian Ukrainian secessionists in Crimea and Eastern Ukraine, international media, demonstrators, terrorists). As all students become familiar during class-time with the basic issues at play, and each parties' claims and counter-claims, they also become able to re-enact the 2013-19 time-line of events and diplomatic duels in the first part of the gaming exercise during an initial two-days weekend war-game. Then they can re-enact with realistic confidence their chosen roles and take over specific *personae* out of the official players roles, often with most students re-enacting 2-3 different roles in multiple policy settings (based on numbers of roles vs. numbers of student volunteers).

Student-players rehearse the following IR actors and enact multiple policy roles: *U.S.A.* (U.S. Presidents Barack Obama to Donald Trump, Vice-Presidents, National Security Advisors, Secretary of State, Secretary of Defense, Joint Chiefs of Staff, Secretary of Homeland Security/C.I.A.); *Russia* (President Vladimir Putin, Prime Minister Dmitry Medvedev, Foreign Affairs Minister Sergey Lavrov, Defense Minister, FSU Intelligence Chief); *NATO* (Secretary-General, Supreme Allied Commander-Europe/SACEUR, North Atlantic Council/N.A.C.); *E.U.* (President, Foreign Affairs Secretary, Security Chief, EuroParliament); *U.N.* (Secretary-General, Security Council 5 Veto permanent Powers—U.S.A./Russia/Great Britain/France/China—General Assembly; International Court of Justice); *pro-West Ukraine* (Ukrainian President Petro Poroshenko, Foreign Affairs Minister, Defense Minister, Intelligence Chief); *pro-Russian non-state actors* (pro-Russian ex-Ukrainian President Viktor Yanukovych in-exile after the 2013-14 Maidan Revolution, pro-Russian secessionists in Crimea in 2014 and East Ukraine in 2014-19, pro-Russian demonstrators); and *non-state actors* (Media).

The key sites for policy-decisions to be debated and announced are: U.S.' White House NSC; Russia's Kremlin; NATO's NAC; E.U.'s Secretariat; U.N.'s Security Council and General Assembly; Ukraine's Kiev government; and pro-Russian secessionist hide-away. As a blended campus war-game all these policy players have to meet in different classrooms, relabeled by their flags, to develop decision-making positions and resolutions, and then announce them to both other international diplomatic counterparts in their own rooms ahead of their own decision-making proceedings, as well as public press-releases to the international media. On-line students at Saint Leo University Centers and military bases can also participate in this blended exercise through instantaneous video-conferencing, experts and policy contributions and mini-videos on smart-phones via Discussion Board postings displayed on scroll-down screens, plus live-feeds.

In the second part of the gaming exercise during a follow-up two-days weekend war-game all student-players were able to re-apply their policy roles and national interests rehearsed previously along the 2013-19 timeline to a new rational possible alternative policy future for 2019 to bring this international crisis-simulation to a successful conclusion or an explosive surprise end. Thus, student-players were forced to pursue both free-wheeling (students-initiated from their respective policy roles) and controlled policy interactions (by faculty's hidden involvement to stir-up the diplomatic waters through secret initiatives or surprise events) with related responses and changes in their respective policy positions until they could arrive to an agreed conclusion spinning the same lessons-learned of the original crisis' timeline in whichever way the student-players saw it fit and logical as end-result of their polities and crisis-simulation.

In this context, the faculty made gaming more uncertain for the players by adding surprise interventions from hostile non-state actors: demonstrators; pro-Russian terrorists against Ukraine and secretly controlled by the Kremlin; or Islamic terrorists attacking a "soft" key international gathering as target of opportunity (U.N. or E.U. compared to "hardened" ones, like NATO or the U.S.A.) to provoke uncontrolled Western reactions and chaos. Thus, students-players rationalize each actor's current and desired policy positions vs. collective push-&-pull from the interactions of the others in a live, unscripted and uncontrolled IR war-game, promoting either some diplomatic conflict-resolution or an uncontrollable explosive escalation of the crisis into a wider war.

3. COMPUTER-BASED GAMIFICATION IN POLAND

In Poland the development of computer-based gamification has been on-going for about 20 years and its educational use is not much younger. This has been the result of the rapidly developing commercial market of computer games, with the simultaneous high level of competence of Polish computer programmers, which produced a boom in the creation of various types of native computer games in Poland. One of the elements of this trend is the computer design and production of games for education. Although it must be admitted that this is not a large segment of the national market for the production of computer games.

The most frequently used method of learning using gamification is reliance on so-called "serious games". In contrast to pure gamification, "serious games" do not rely on the use of game mechanisms in educational scenarios, but the use of games in learning. While games remain autonomous and can serve as entertainment, they also play an educational function. In "serious games", the educational effect is an intended side-effect. Applications with the use of simulation games are also common at leading Polish technical and military universities, as well as in Education and Communications courses at the Pedagogical University of Kraków.

In higher education programs and educational scenarios developed in Poland for about 10 years now, more and more often elements of gamification and application of "serious games" are applied to schools. This is due to projects aimed at improving the competences of academic and school teaching staff, financed by the Ministry of Education and the National Centre for Research and Development.

4. PEDAGOGY AND CONCLUSION

All these successful experiential-learning blended exercises in both countries have as educational goal to bring together both campus and on-line/Center students in contemporary IR war-games, mock-trials, mock-U.S. Presidential Elections and also traditional Model U.N. remote exercises. However, a good pedagogical criteria to systematically evaluate all these games in Political Sciences, Criminology and International Security is not really available, although these various games satisfy similar requirements, but are still works in-progress. The Saint Leo University faculty applied 6 pedagogical goals, by mixing written exams, learning-guides, videos of electoral candidates as mock-publicity spots or mock-Trials, rubric assessments and collective voting to select winners.

- The first pedagogic lessons-learned is that through planning and faculty control of all related learning materials and gaming exercise proceedings, the students will become exposed to the complexity of contemporary international diplomatic interactions or domestic political elections or legal scenarios (first pedagogic goal), giving them the ability and self-confidence through role-playing to arouse the interest and understanding of the public (in the game this refers to all participants and judges, as well as through remote VTT sensing and video-recording all future viewers) in the different stages of the game-exercise (second pedagogic goal), while bring the student-players to live through their actions each policy-decision and consequences to the best of their academic abilities (third pedagogic goal).

- Thus, as much of the first pedagogic goal of the gaming is based on preparation before the actual game, both learning and assessments must initially rely on the traditional preparatory learning conducted within a structured university class along its scholarly discipline points to be reviewed and assessed through two written exams on traditional and interactive course materials (each 20% of course grade).
- The second pedagogic lessons-learned (second and third pedagogic goals) are attained through students prepping and oral application of their class studies and discipline-related previous knowledge to the related theme of the game-exercise (in this there is similarities between Political Sciences, International Studies and Criminology). Thus, students will form group-studies that prepare each members' stated positions (political postures and campaign elections, or international diplomatico-security postures, or Trial Prosecution vs. Defense arguments) and each team's respective roles, position-papers, communiqués and strategies (second pedagogical goal). Student-teams will morph into live action during a 2-days gaming-exercise as trained teams (be them countries and diplomatico-military teams running a war-game; or rival political parties and platforms vying for elections; or clashing arguments by Prosecution and Defense teams towards Judges and Jury/Audience), with each student taking on few different roles as leaders, experts or audience (third pedagogical goal).
- The third pedagogic lessons-learned (fourth and fifth pedagogic goals each at 10% of course grade) focuses on how the gaming-exercise eventually leads to a specific outcome for the winning team completing the third pedagogical goal through a voting selection, although the after-game debriefing with the faculty, staff and student-teams will attain a clearer understanding if the actual victory of one specific team was due to superior academic preparation, or sheer charisma by the winners in swaying opinions of participants, or a slow-slog among mediocre teams with the slightly better one edging victory out of the errors of the others (fourth pedagogic goal). This last point is very important in highlighting the lessons-learned for faculty to apply in future games, and for students to learn singly or collectively in teams to evaluate their own performance and their ability to evaluate others (fifth pedagogic goal).
- Assessments of the game-exercise's first 3 pedagogic goals (1-2-3 each at 10% of course grade) require the use of a single custom-designed rubric filled by the faculty at the conclusion of each goal by comparing visual and exercise-based observations of the each student's role-playing and activities.
- A second rubric can be added to evaluate as a technical pedagogic goal 4 (at 10% of course grade) the clarity of scope and result of each candidates' video spots or campaign forums for candidates in mock-elections (Political Sciences), or longer videos on teams performance in mock-trials (Criminology), or longer videos for the concluding moments of a war-game (International Studies).
- Assessments of the game-exercise's last 2 pedagogic goals (5-6 each at 10% of course grade) requires that the faculty use visual assessments and note-taking of the students' own ability as an audience to reward at the end of the game-exercise one team with victory through a collective secret vote (Political Sciences mock-elections or Criminology mock-Trials) or a collective assessment by a panel of judges (faculty and students team-leaders) on how clean or messy is perceived to be the end of a war-game to declare a presumptive winner (International Studies) as fifth pedagogic goal.
- The faculty then combines in a third rubric the students' own votes and an oral interview of all students and teams in a post-action oral analysis to draw a third rubric on gaming performance as individuals and teams, with extra-points for the winning team (as sixth pedagogic at 10% of course grade).
- All assessments for coursework exams (1-2) and gaming-exercise (3-4-5-6) in 3 rubrics are added to reach a max. score of 100 points as identified in the course's on-line electronic grading portfolio.

Finally, the costs of staging such experiential-learning blended exercises remains limited for multi-disciplinary or single-discipline classes coordination (regardless of cuts), while the game proceedings are filmed and posted on *YouTube* and the University's website as visual record to advertise academic activities and inside for future training of a new generation of student-players in similar annual scenarios.

REFERENCES

"ARLE Vice-Presidential Debate [Fall 2016 Saint Leo University]" video in *YouTube* (2015), 58 min.: https://www.youtube.com/watch?v=2kFUTqMsncQ

Christine Bocchino & Tom Buckley, "Reflecting on the Past and Looking into the Future (Interview with President Kirk)" in *Lions' Pride*, vol. LII, n.26 (Saint Leo University, 17 April 2015): p.1 & 3.

Peter Calvocoressi, *World Politics, 1945-2000* (New York: Longman, 2001).

Herb Childress, *The Adjunct Underclass* (Chicago: University of Chicago Press, 2019).

Democrat Commercial-Saint Leo University Mock Presidential Debate" video in *YouTube* (2016), 0.60 min.: https://www.youtube.com/watch?v=v2AVUEhy6Rg

Democrat Commercial-Saint Leo University "Mock-Republican Presidential Debate" video *YouTube* (2016), 0.60 min.: https://www.youtube.com/watch?v=r8bAxB-Fl98

Education Commercial 1-Saint Leo University "Mock-Presidential Debate" video in *YouTube* (2016), 0.51 min.: https://www.youtube.com/watch?v=7CBcm4Yz2tc

Education Commercial 2-Saint Leo University "Mock-Presidential Debate" video in *YouTube* (2016), 0.59 min.: https://www.youtube.com/watch?v=0I2wLOqx8jY

Thomas Friedman, *The World is Flat* (New York: Farrar, Straus & Giroux, 2005).

John Hall, "The Way Forward: Renaissance 2021" in *Lions' Pride*, v. LVIII, n.14 (Saint Leo University, 30 November 2018): p.1-3.

James Horgan, *Pioneer College* (Saint Leo University: Wadsworth Publ., 1989).

B.H. Khan, *A Framework for Web-based Learning* (Englewood Cliffs, N.J.: Educational Technology Publ., 2001).

Arthur F. Kirk Jr., "Saint Leo University: a Leading Catholic Teaching University of International Consequence for the Twenty-First Century" (Saint Leo University: Office of President, August 2007): slides 1-56.

Marie Olsson & Peter Mozelius, "Game-Based Learning and Game Construction as E-Learning Strategy in Programming Education" in *Digital Universities: International Best Practices & Applications* (Rome: GUIDE, November 2016): p.43-54.

B.-A. Lundvall & S. Borras, *The Globalising Learning Economy: Implications for Innovation Policy* (Brussel: 1999).

A. Marengo & V. Marengo, "Measuring the Economic Benefits of E-Learning: a Proposal for a New Index for Academic Environments" in *Journal of Information Technology Education*, v.4 (2005): p.329-346.

Marco Rimanelli, "Modern Saint Leo University, 1989-2014" in Saint Leo University, "Conference on Florida's First Catholic College's 125th Anniversary of International Consequence" (SLU: UTS Video, 13 November 2014).

Marco Rimanelli, *NATO and Other International Security Organizations: Historical Dictionary* (Lanham, MD: Scarecrow/ Rowman & Littlefield, 2009), p.980 & 2nd Edition (forthcoming Fall 2019).

Marco Rimanelli & Frank Orlando, "Saint Leo University's Renaissance & Mixing On-line, Blended Courses & Gaming to Teach American & International Politics" in *Proceedings XII International GUIDE Conference-Orlando On-line Learning in 21st Century, 15-17 February 2017*, v.4, n.3 (Rome: Universitá Marconi/GUIDE, November 2017): p.99-130.

"Saint Leo University ARLE Presidency Interviews—Bill Bunkley Show" video in YouTube (2016), 41 min.: https://www.youtube.com/watch?v=MzEr6SU1fgw

Saint Leo University, *Chronicles: 125 Years* (Saint Leo University: Public Relations Office, 2014): p.1-12.

"Saint Leo University by Drone-4K" video in *YouTube* (2015), 1.55 min.: https://www.youtube.com/watch?v=56N8rRJS9Qw

Saint Leo University, *Leading Change: Kirk Years, 1997-2015* (Saint Leo University: University Communications, April 2015): p.0-25.

"Saint Leo University–Overview" video in YouTube (2015), 7,48 min.: https://www.youtube.com/watch?v=cfg7O2haxSc

"Saint Leo University Mock Presidential Debate—Democrat Commercial" video in YouTube (2015), 0.30 min.: https://www.youtube.com/watch?v=VSlgXkm7kXU

"Saint Leo University Mock-Trial" video in *YouTube* (2016), 6,33 min.: https://www.youtube.com/watch?v=XlvTs5OQ0h0

Saint Leo University, *Now and Then: a Look at Saint Leo through the Years, 1881-2004* (SLU: 2005).

Saint Leo University, *President's Report 2014: Transformation and Trends* (Saint Leo University: President Office, 2014): p.1-26.

Saint Leo University, *Vision 2017: a Strategic Narrative* (Saint Leo University: Office of President, 2012), p.1-10 also at: http://www.saintleo.edu/about/office-of-the-president/vision-2017.aspx

Statecraft Simulations, "American Government, IR, Security, U.S. Foreign Policy", see: https://www.statecraftsims.com/international-relations-simulation/

Marcy Stern, "Opinion: Adjunct-Professors Struggle as Colleges Prosper" in *Wall Street Journal* (8 May 2019).

Barton Swain, "Teachable Moments" in *Wall Street Journal* (1 May 2019).

"Trial of Century [Saint Leo University Innovation]" video in *YouTube* (2017), 3,55 min.: https://www.youtube.com/watch?v=tyqHMGmQdZk

"2015 Presidential Debate Presented by Saint Leo University" video in *YouTube* (2015), 1.55 min.: https://www.youtube.com/watch?v=w0seprhD0JE

Short Papers

RESEARCH ON CHANGE AND GROWTH OF STUDENTS AND TEACHERS EXPERIENCED PROBLEM BASED LEARNING

Kyungwon Chang and Seonyoung Jang
Kyonggi University, Mokpo National Maritime University, South Korea

ABSTRACT

The purpose of this study is to identify change and growth of students and teachers experienced PBL. For this purpose, this study used both quantitative and qualitative approach to examine the impact of PBL and the change and growth of students and teachers. 2,970 students and 172 teachers participated in this study. The results of the students' change and growth based on students' answer to a survey and interview are as follow; first, the satisfaction of PBL class has statistically increased at the end of term than the beginning of the term. Second, PBL have the effects on improving students' self-efficacy. Third, based-on students' interview, it was identified that a good class and a PBL have common points in communication, cooperation and cooperation among learners, knowledge acquisition and understanding of contents. Forth, students experienced PBL had enhanced their skills in five areas; solving problem, cooperation, communication, academic motivation, and human relations. The results of the teachers' change and growth are as follows; first, teachers realized the importance of PBL higher than before, and had the volition to do the PBL consistently. Second, the teachers' efficacy has improved at a significant level. Third, teachers recognized that the characteristics of PBL classes were full of energy, not boring, and students are able to lead the class, understand learning contents, and focus on the class and a good class was similar to PBL. Forth, teachers experienced PBL have acquired the knowledge (property of PBL/property of students), behavior (confidence of PBL class), and techniques (designing PBL class, PBL tutoring) at a level 1(level of PBL implementation). In addition, they have figured out the necessary of extension of PBL (school organization, teacher community; researching) at a level 2.

KEYWORDS

Problem-Based Learning, Growth of Students and Teachers, Quantitative and Qualitative Approach

1. THE PURPOSE OF THIS STUDY

Problem-based learning (PBL) is a teaching and learning method in which students learned learning contents and skills during solving authentic problem (Barrows & Myers, 1993). Many studies reported that students improved their skills of problem solving, communication, interpersonal relationship, and learning deepen knowledges by PBL. Also, the teachers' efficiency on teaching also enhanced through PBL. However, those researches have the limits of presenting their specific stories. The purpose of this study is to identify that how students and teachers who experienced PBL are changed and grown.

2. THEORETICAL BACKGROUND

PBL is the teaching-learning method of suggesting the learning experience to the students with the authentic problems (Barrows & Myers, 1993). The main features of PBL are as follows. First, the learning starts from the problem. In PBL, the learning experience starts from the activities for solving the suggested problem. Therefore, solving problems in PBL is comprehensive activities including the learning issues. Authentic, ill-structured problems are used to recognize the appropriateness of the learning which can experience in real world (Dunlap, 2005). Second is the learning environment focused on learners. PBL is held with the activities by learners, not through teacher-led lecture (Barrows, 1996). Thus, learners have the responsibility to their learning by themselves. Third, PBL learning is based on the group activities. Problem solving process in PBL is held by group activities. Furthermore, personal learning is held during the group activities. Fourth, learners study the new knowledges through self-directed learning. Thus, PBL requires not only group activities, but also self-directed learning.

The effectiveness of PBL suggested by precedent researches is focused on the aspects of learners' content knowledge, academic motivation, problem-solving ability, cooperative ability and communication skills (Barron et al., 1998; Grant, 2011; Krajcik et al., 1994). Moreover, some studies suggested the effectiveness of PBL on teachers who held PBL classes. Following are the details.

First is the effects on the aspect of students. To check the effectiveness of PBL, other major techniques are teamwork, cooperation, problem solving skills, motivation, communication skills (speaking and writing), content knowledge, collecting information, expert knowledge and techniques, data analysis, critical thinking, project management, self-efficacy, and time management. To synthesize, learners got the content knowledge (Barron et al., 1998; Geier et al., 2008; Mergendoller et al., 2007; Walker & Leary, 2009), academic motivation (Belland et al., 2006; Brush and Save, 2008), and learning capability for 21st century (Krajcik et al., 1994; Markham et al., 2003: Belland et al., 2006; Blumenfeld et al., 1991; Grant, 2011; Mergendoller et al., 2006) through the experience of PBL.

Second is the effectiveness in the aspect of teacher. PBL class requires considerable preparation and different running strategies compared to previous classes to teachers. Therefore, it will bring the noticeable change not only to students, but also to teachers. However, most studies are focused on the change of students who experienced PBL classes, so it is difficult to find the researches about the effectiveness on teachers of the PBL. Nevertheless, through the several researches introduced, PBL has increased the level of knowledge of teachers about the teaching materials, capability related to PBL; problem development, running capability, and self-efficacy (Finkelstein et al., 2010; Goodnough & Hung, 2009; Tawfik, Trueman, & Lorz, 2013).

3. RESEARCH METHODS

This study was conducted on five middle school students and teachers designated as PBL research schools in Daegu, South Korea. Daegu City has designated schools for PBL practice as part of its project to implement and expand PBL. Five schools in 2017 were designated PBL research schools. Students and teachers of five designated middle schools in 2017 were participated in this study.

Specific research procedures are as follows. First, the researchers have conducted the workshop and consulting for teachers to understand PBL and design PBL class. The PBL classes were implemented from September to December on 2017 in five middle schools. During this period, both quantitative and qualitative studies were conducted to identify student and teacher growth and change through PBL experience.

Quantitative research was conducted as follows. We surveyed at the beginning and the end of the semester to identify changes in students and teachers. A questionnaire for students' self-efficacy developed by Kim and Kim (2004) was adopted in this study. This questionnaire is consisted of demographic variables (sex, age, school, and grade), PBL satisfaction, and self-efficacy. 2,970 students responded to the questionnaire. Questionnaire for teachers developed by Kim and Park (2001) was adopted in this study. The questionnaire was consisted of demographic variables (gender, age, school, career experience, charge subject, grade in charge) and teachers' efficacy. 172 teachers responded to the questionnaire. The results of students and teachers' responses were analyzed using SPSS 24.

Qualitative research was done as follows. We interviewed students and teachers to understand their change and growth. In the interview, 43 students were asked about the characteristics of good class, the perception of PBL, the experience of PBL team activities, problem solving process, outcomes of PBL, and the role of teachers in PBL. Interviews were conducted at 5 schools, and 3-4 students were interviewed at each grade level. We also conducted interviews with teachers. 30 teachers were asked about the characteristics of good classroom teachers, perception of PBL, experience of PBL design and implement, and teachers' role. Interviews with students and teachers were recorded and cross-analyzed by researchers.

4. RESULTS

4.1 The Change and Growth of Students

The quantitative and qualitative data collected from students is shown as follows. First, the satisfaction of PBL class has statistically increased at the end of term than the beginning of the term (Table 1). In detail, the satisfaction of team activities in PBL class showed the highest rate of change and the satisfaction of PBL facilitation skill and attitude showed relatively lower rate of change.

Table 1. Comparison in satisfaction of students before and after PBL classes

item	Pre-test		Post-test		difference		t-value
	M	SD	M	SD	M	SD	
Problems in PBL	3.67	.981	3.84	.975	-.176	1.341	-5.271^{***}
Teacher's facilitation skill and attitude	3.81	.916	3.94	.929	-.128	1.271	-4.026^{***}
Team activities in PBL	3.60	1.032	3.81	.992	-.214	1.401	-6.112^{***}
Evaluation in PBL	3.70	.964	3.87	.954	-.171	1.338	-5.132^{***}

$^{*}P<.05$, $^{**}P<.01$, $^{***}P<.001$

Second, PBL have the effects on improving students' self-efficacy (p<.05) (Table2). In particularly, comparison in before and after PBL experience, the factor of task difficulty preferences has increased from 3.54 to 3.25 (p<.001), self-regulated efficacy statistically decreased from 3.58 to 3.51 (p<.05).

Table 2. Comparison in self-efficacy of students

Variable		Pre-test		Post-test		Difference		**t-value**
		M	SD	M	SD	M	SD	
Self-efficacy		3.42	.567	3.46	.585	-.042	.804	-2.098^{*}
Sub-Variable	Task difficulty preferences	3.17	.681	3.25	.681	-.080	.951	-3.357^{**}
	Self-regulation efficacy	3.54	.664	3.64	.723	-.093	.985	-3.762^{***}
	Confidence	3.58	.850	3.51	.939	.068	1.260	2.157^{*}

$^{*}P<.05$, $^{**}P<.01$, $^{***}P<.001$

Third, students reported a good class is consisted with the factors such as students' communications, interactions, developments, achievements, interests and attentions. Also, they answered that the significant characteristics of PBL are learner-centered, authentic problems and assignments based, progress of learning, growth and achievements of learning. Based-on students' interview, it was identified that a good class and a PBL have a common point in communication, cooperation and cooperation among learners, knowledge acquisition and understanding of contents.

Fourth, the learners experienced PBL had enhanced their skills in five areas; solving problem, cooperation, communication, academic motivation and human relations. The parts of learners' growth are classified based on cognitive-affective domain and learning-relationship domain. The cognitive domain and the affective domain are the main factor of consisting the human-ability and itis the taxonomy in generic term of mental ability related to gaining and using knowledge. The cognitive domain contains the thinking abilities such as understanding, application, analytical skills, synthesizing, problem-solving, logical thinking, critical thinking, creativity, and evaluation. The affective domain is about human's interests, attitude, admiring, value, emotion and belief. Complex factors as like focusing on some situation and internal coherent personality and conscience are included in the affective domain. It also contains the attention, reaction, acceptance of values, conviction and systematization, internalization, personification of value. Learning is continuous transition of attitude by the results of practice and experiences, and generally, ideal and progressive change is regarded as learning. Relation is the idea of pairing and thinking of the two objects and the relations learners have in school is included the relations with other learners and tutors. According to those criteria, students had made growth through PBL in the aspects of problem solving, communicating, academic motivation, human relations and cooperation because PBL is held with individual and team learning activities.

4.2 The Change and Growth of Teachers

The change and growth of teachers are shown as follows. First, teachers who experienced PBL realized the importance of PBL higher and had the volition to do the PBL consistently as they implement the PBL and checking the results of students (Table 3.).

Table 3. Comparison in teachers' perspective and volition before and after PBL

items	Pre-test		Post-test		Difference			t-value
	M	SD	M	SD	M	SD		
PBL is a teaching method to improve higher order thinking ability	3.88	.947	4.07	1.012	-.188	1.282		-1.727
I will implement PBL classes in the future	3.64	1.086	3.99	1.124	-.348	1.392		-2.936**
Extension of PBL is necessary	3.72	1.025	3.96	1.100	-.239	1.343		-2.092*

$^{*}P<.05$, $^{**}P<.01$, $^{***}P<.001$

Second, with implementing the class, the teachers' efficacy for the overall school education has improved ($p<.05$) (Table 4.). From this point of view, teachers' efficacy is an important psychological mechanism to figure out the teachers' improvement in applying new teaching methods such as PBL.

Table 4. Comparison in self-efficacy of teachers

Variable	Pre-test		Post-test		Difference		t-value
	M	SD	M	SD	M	SD	
Teacher efficacy	3.65	.405	3.79	.423	-.139	.628	-2.589*

$^{*}P<.05$, $^{**}P<.01$, $^{***}P<.001$

Third, teachers suggested a good class is that students can do self-directed learning, feel enjoyment, and be interest in the class. In addition, they mentioned PBL is full of energy, not boring, and students are able to lead the class, understand learning contents, and focus on the class. In addition, teachers reported that PBL is a class where students' cooperation, various outcomes, participation and communication are occurred and thinking ability is enhanced

Fourth, teachers experienced PBL have acquired the knowledge (property of PBL/property of students), behavior (confidence of PBL class), and techniques (designing PBL class, PBL tutoring) at a Level 1 (PBL implementation). In addition, they have figured out the necessary of extension of PBL (school organization, teacher community; researching) at a level 2 (PBL extension). Teacher change and growth has a unique character that includes not only the implementation of PBL at the individual teacher level but also the recognition of the need to expand the PBL to other teachers and schools. Two third of all teachers' answer were about implementing PBL, one third of overall were about PBL extension in school and other teachers. These results suggests that in order to expand PBL classes, it is important not to stay in training and education for teachers but to increase the number of teachers who actually have experience in designing and implementing PBL classes.

5. CONCLUSION

According to results of this study, PBL is helpful to make change and growth to both students and teachers. Considering the educational situation in South Korea where in instructor-led class is a lot, the strategies of PBL implement are needed as follows.

First, the specific outcomes and feedbacks of PBL must be shared to students and school parents. Students and school parents would feel hard to be sure about the effects of PBL because the education in South Korea is competitive and focused on students' grade. Therefore, beyond just explaining the PBL and why it is necessary to the students and school parents, it is necessary for school parents and students to bring out the empathy of PBL necessity and participation in PBL by sharing the change and growth of students and teachers have been made.

Second, the training for implementing PBL are required to the teachers according to the degree of PBL experience. In details, the PBL training need to be separated into three courses; beginner's course, intermediate course, and advanced course. In the beginner course, it is necessary to provide workshops on the main characteristics of the PBL, the development of the problem, and the role of the teacher. In the intermediate course, it needs to be provided a workshop on reflection and consulting after PBL operation. Advanced courses require the PBL case sharing and workshops to improve the competences of PBL instructional consultant. Even if teachers work in the same school, it is desirable to conduct training by experience because PBL implement experience is different.

Third, efforts should be made to secure excellent teachers in PBL field. For this purpose, collaboration between the pre-service teacher training institutes and the offices of education should be the premise. Furthermore, the training content and method should be improved so that the new teacher training program does not simply introduce PBLs and that new teachers have full experience of PBLs.

REFERENCES

Anderson, L. W. (1976). An empirical investigation of individual differences in time to learn. *Journal of educational psychology*, *68*(2), 226.

Barron, B. J. S., Schwartz, D. L., Vye, N. J., Moore, A., Petrosino, A., Zech, L., Bransford, J.D. & The Cognition and Technology Group at Vanderbilt (1998). Doing with understanding: lessons from research on problem- and project-based learning. *The Journal of the Learning Sciences, 7*(3), pp. 271-311.

Barrows, H. S. (1996). Problem-based learning in medicine and beyond: A brief overview. *New directions for teaching and learning, 68,* 3-12.

Barrows, H. S., & Myers, A. C. (1993). Problem-Based Learning in Secondary Schools. Unpublished monograph. Springfield, IL: *Problem-Based Learning Institute*, Lanphier High School and Southern Illinois University Medical School.

Belland, B. R., Ertmer, P. A., & Simons, K. D. (2006). Perceptions of the value of problem-based learning among students with special needs and their teachers. *The Interdisciplinary Journal of Problem-based Learning, 1*(2), 1-18.

Blumenfeld, P. C., Soloway, E., Marx, R. W., Krajcik, J. S., Guzdial, M., & Palincsar, A. (1991). Motivating project-based learning: Sustaining the doing, supporting the learning. *Educational psychologist, 26*(3-4), 369-398.

Brush, T. & Saye, J. (2008). The effects of multimedia-supported problem-based inquiry on student engagement, empathy, and assumptions about history. *The Interdisciplinary Journal of Problem-based Learning, 2*(2), 21-56.

Dunlap, J. C. (2005). Problem-based learning and self-efficacy: How a capstone course prepares students for a profession. *Educational Technology Research and Development*, *53*(1), 65-85.

Finkelstein, N., Hanson, T., Kevin (Chun-Wei) Huang, Klarin, B., & Huang, M. (2010). *Effects of Problem-Based economics on high school economics instruction.* US Department of Education.

Geier, R., Blumenfeld, P. C., Mark, R. W., Krajcik, J. S., Fishman, B., Soloway, E. & Clay-Chambers, J. (2008). Standardized test outcomes for students engaged in inquiry-based science curricula in the context of urban reform. *Journal of Research Science Teaching, 45*(8), 922-939.

Goddard, R. D., Hoy, W. K., & Hoy, A. W. (2000). Collective teacher efficacy: Its meaning, measure, and impact on student achievement. *American Educational Research Journal*, *37*(2), 479-507.

Goodnough, K., & Hung, W. (2009). Enhancing pedagogical content knowledge in elementary science. *Teaching Education*, *20*(3), 229-242.

Grant, M. M. (2011). Learning, beliefs, and products: students' perspectives with project-based learning. *The Interdisciplinary Journal of Problem-based Learning, 5*(2), pp. 37-69.

Kim, A., & Kim, M. (2004). Validation of Teacher-Efficacy Scale, *The Korean Journal of Educational Psychology, 18*(1), p.37-58.

Kim, A., Park, I. (2001). Construction and Validation of Academic Self-Efficacy Scale, *The (Korean) Journal of Educational Research, 39*(1), 95-123.

Krajcik, J. S., Blumenfeld, P. C., Marx, R. W., & Soloway, E. (1994). A collaborative model for helping middle-grade science teachers learn project-based instruction. *The Elementary School Journal, 94*, 483-497.

Markham, T., Larmer, J., & Ravitz, J. (2003). *Project-based learning handbook: a guide to standards-focused Project-Based learning for middle and high school teacher* (2nd ed.). CA: Buck Institute for Education.

Mergendoller, J. R., Markham, T., Ravitz, J. & Larmer, J. (2006). Pervasive management of project-based learning: teachers as guides and facilitators in Evertson, C. M. & Weinstein, C.S. (Eds), *Handbook of Classroom Management: Research, Practice, and Contemporary Issues (*pp. 583-615). Mahwah, NJ: Lawrence Erlbaum Associates.

Tawfik, A. A., Trueman, R. J., & Lorz, M. M. (2013). Designing a PBL environment using the 3C3R method. *International Journal of Designs for Learning*, *4*(1).11-24.

Walker, A., & Leary, H. (2009). A Problem-Based learning meta analysis: differences across problem types, implementation types, disciplines, and assessment levels. *The Interdisciplinary Journal of Problem-based Learning, 3*(1), pp. 12-43.

TWENTY-FIRST CENTURY INTERVIEWING FOR TWENTY-FIRST CENTURY JOBS. ARE WE PREPARING OUR STUDENTS FOR TODAY'S JOB MARKET?

John R. Lax and Ioannis Pantzalis

Saint Leo University, P.O. Box 6665; Saint Leo, FL 33574, USA

ABSTRACT

One of the challenges that many undergraduate students face when they start their lives after college is that there is no clear career path. The nature of each job in today's fast-changing economic and technological environment is fluid, and students should be prepared to reinvent themselves and adjust their career paths more than once during their working years. Based on these observations, we present a framework to help students market themselves during their interviews, and we explain how these interviewing skills can be included and practiced not only in a traditional classroom but also in an online teaching environment. Particular attention is devoted to the introduction of virtual avatar technology under development at Saint Leo University.

KEYWORDS

Interviewing, Avatars, Experiential, Student Job Preparation

1. INTRODUCTION

While the greater issue of how to develop pedagogies and curriculum content to address the need for soft skill development in undergraduates remains a topic of considerable interest to academia, this article examines how those skills are manifested in the final stages of business education. Specifically, how do we train students to demonstrate these skills in the recruitment and interview process? Our position is that not only are soft skills fundamental to entry-level job success and thus deserve a central role in business education, but that business schools need to teach soon to be graduates how to conduct interviews that demonstrate those skills. Rather than a "shotgun" approach addressing broad curriculum issues, we discuss a specific initiative at Saint Leo University in Florida employing high-level interview simulations utilizing intelligent avatars.

This paper first provides a brief discussion of the state of the business environment in the context of preparing students for job interviews and transition into the workforce. This is followed by a short literature review of the relationship between avatars and experiential learning. We then provide a discussion of the avatar project at our university. We conclude with closing thoughts and the implications for faculty and administrators at business schools.

2. THE STATE OF STUDENT INTERVIEWS

The world of business has changed a lot during the last quarter century. It provides unprecedented opportunities, as well as challenges both to businesses and individuals. In this paper we look at the driving forces that shape employment preferences in the 21st century, and we provide some key tips on how business students should prepare for their interviews if they want to succeed.

In the early 1990s two things changed the practice of business globally. The first one was geopolitical. The collapse of the Soviet Union and China's opening to the global economy turbocharged globalization and created a global network of supply chains that spanned the globe.

The second thing was technology. The integration of the global marketplace opened up opportunities for businesses too. Although competition became tougher, it also allowed easier access to markets far away, and opportunities to expand the customer base. Essentially the environment for businesses became more lucrative if they planned and executed well, but less forgiving when they slacked off or made mistakes.

By now these effects are being magnified even more with the use of big data analytics, expert systems based on artificial intelligence, and faster global logistics networks. It is hard to hide mistakes, and the reaction of customers, financial markets, government regulators, and other stakeholders put pressure on companies to be vigilant, fast, and proactive.

In this environment, where everyone has access to similar technology the key question is: What are the key traits that employers are looking for, and what should the students do during interviews to position themselves as having these traits? The latest research identifies the following key attitudes and traits (Selingo, 2017; Borzt 2018):

(1) Communication skills, both verbal and written. Communication is critical because in today's technological environment just about all business employees are the company's ambassadors every time they interact with any stakeholder. Being able to communicate effectively with stakeholders is essential. One has to deal with diverse audiences with different habits of communication, different cultural norms and traditions, and different agendas. Today one must be able to go beyond basic communication skills and be able to adjust the content, style, and code of the message as well as the timing and type of medium to send it, in order to adapt to each different audience.

(2) Teamwork. Business is a team sport. Employees must work well in teams, being able to present their ideas, be open to ideas of other team members, avoid groupthink, avoid unnecessary and personal conflict, stay professional regardless of how enjoyable the task is (or is not) or if one likes or dislikes the other team members.

(3) Creativity, critical thinking and originality. In a fast-changing environment, clinging to the past can be a major obstacle to adaptation. Many companies come up with a winning formula, but then stick with it for too long, way past its expiration date. The history of business is full of examples like Kodak that became the victims of their previous successes. Over time management becomes conservative, they succumb to the status quo and endowment biases, and become oblivious to new opportunities. One of the reasons companies want creative new employees is to bring in people with new ideas and people who will be willing to challenge the existing business paradigm.

(4) Ability to learn new skills quickly and with minimum help. Companies need employees with initiative and drive, people who will try to stay up-to-date with new technologies and developments regardless of the formal support of the company. The more an employee can learn on his or her own, and the faster he or she can acquire new skills, the more valuable this person is. This is part of general leadership skills, where you become the leader and driving force in your own education. It also fits in with having a strong work ethic, which is another trait employers are looking for. Learning on an ongoing basis has become a necessity for people who want to have successful careers (Weber 2019).

The key to getting, and keeping, a job is to demonstrate high competence in the above criteria. At Saint Leo University we try to prepare our students to be successful on the job in many ways, and helping them with improving on the four criteria is an integral aspect of the training. Since we both teach marketing majors, we will focus on how we train them, but the ideas and approach can be adjusted to any business major.

Active learning, involving group projects with hands-on applications, both in the classroom as well as online are the foundations of our teaching. In addition, all marketing majors have to design a personal website to promote their careers. The website will be about their professional brand – it includes their CV, a short video of them explaining their business and marketing philosophy, as well as their career goals, pictures and links to stories and activities that highlight their skills and attitudes, and a section where they have a portfolio of accomplishments and projects.

Such a website, when done properly sends powerful signals about all four key criteria. By itself it is a tool of communication, and the different ways it presents the information demonstrates the student's proficiency in them. The portfolio of accomplishments includes team projects and thus shows how the student has worked in teams in the past and accomplished significant results. The creativity aspect is the design of the website and the way the information is presented. Finally, the website design, style, and innovative graphics show that the student is comfortable with technology and is willing to learn it on his or her own.

The website and portfolio we use to prepare our students have proven to provide them an advantage in competing for entry-level jobs. However, we discovered we were still missing a piece of the job preparation "puzzle" which brings us to a new emerging technology – avatars.

2.1 Literature Review

Experiential education has been perceived through a number of lenses, both theoretical and applied. While there is considerable consensus in both domains of the value of experiential learning in business curriculums, there is far less agreement on how best to implement and apply the many tools and pedagogies technology has made available to contemporary business programs. Mandel and Noyes (2014), in their survey of entrepreneurial-focused experiential programs note that while the effectiveness of such education is "practically beyond debate" (p. 164) the extant literature is far less revealing regarding what constitutes an academic best practice.

While the use of avatars in the classroom is in its infancy, especially in business and job preparation, we can draw on similar works in higher education to assess the potential impact on our students. The technology employed in this article was originally developed for use in elementary education and research in that domain suggests undergraduates benefit from the pedagogy. Results, both in the classroom and in research, suggests that the use of avatars has contributed to not only learning theory but also to improved student outcomes. (Chini, Straub & Thomas, 2016; Dawson & Lignugaris, 2017).

Consistent with the emphasis on soft skill development which is the theme of this article, DeSimone and Buzza (2013) examined the value of critical thinking and abstract decision making in business school curriculums. Not surprisingly they found that not only were these skills important in developing successful students, but that experiential learning can be a key component in curriculums focused on those outcomes. Eckhaus, Klein and Kantor (2017) reached similar conclusions finding that although business schools tended to under-utilize experiential tools in the curriculum, students that participated in a cost accounting board game demonstrated a higher mastery of the skills important to their success. While both empirical research on the efficacy of avatars and the application of the pedagogy in experiential education remain largely unexplored, our work with the technology suggests considerable promise for enhancing the soft skills students require for successful interviews and transition to their new positions in the workforce

2.2 The Role of Avatars

Projects external to the classroom offer what is arguably the pinnacle of experiential education, allowing students to interact with practitioners and gain first-hand real-world experience. For example, at Saint Leo University our students offer consulting services to both small businesses on a fee for service model and pro-bono to local non-profits, emulating what they might experience with a progressive, community-minded firm. Inside the classroom, a recent marketing class provided area non-profits with projects to promote fundraisers for meal backpacks for elementary school children and efforts to combat rural homelessness while another worked with the local city government to develop a cooperative project between the university and city to serve local children.

While these projects provide students with an exceptional hands-on experience we found two shortcomings. First, like many schools, we were constrained by both budget and the time available to faculty to sponsor the programs, thus limiting the number of students that could participate. Second, we needed a vehicle for students to practice sharing with a potential employer what they had learned from the experiential learning and "closing the sale" on securing a post-graduation position. While the extant research in experiential education provides considerable guidance to course developers and teaching faculty (Mandel & Noyes, 2016) we discovered that the literature was virtually silent with regards to meaningful equivalents in experiential interview preparation. However, once again, many of these techniques require considerable time, money and resources which may in short supply in today's academic environment. We needed an interactive solution for teaching the soft skills, and by extension interviewing skills, we believed to the missing component to our students securing the best opportunities.

Prior to selecting the avatar technology to address this need, we attempted to use some of the training and interviewing techniques that are common to many campuses. Two of the more common are peer to peer role-playing and mock interviews conducted by staff members in our career development office. While helpful, both lacked the dynamic real-life experience we believed we needed to produce a superior student. Very similar constraints applied to teaching sales and customer service, which were the genesis for the interview pilot. The mock interviews, peer to peer selling or interviewing worked just fine, provided that the student only interviewed with faculty members or peers in a controlled, predictable and friendly environment. However, the practice transferred poorly to the real world, which is far less predictable and friendly. Avatars proved to address these shortcomings.

Avatars provided the bridge between classroom training and the students' first internship or practicum. Unlike the limited avatars used in other games or online simulations, such as Second Life, our avatars are driven by behind-the-scenes actors that allow the characters to not only move and physically react to our students, but also allows their verbal responses to be real-time and adapt instantly to what the college students do, or fail to do. Our student will not be forewarned going into the classroom exercise, but the avatar hiring manager is about to challenge the student's ability to think on their feet, much like what might be experienced by a student in a real interview. This allows the student training for a top tier position to be tested much as they would in a real interview.

Chine, Straub & Thomas (2016) who conducted some of the early work with the avatar technology liken it to the flight simulators used by student pilots. Rather than fly the aircraft for the first time in a real meeting room with a real hiring manager, the avatar simulators allow the student to get the aircraft safely on the ground with no risk to the "passengers". In the business school we enabled the avatar managers to exhibit many of the same traits as business-to-business customers in a sales environment or interviewers in a hiring situation. Both were unpredictable and the environment in which they operated was dynamic and required real-time and real-world unstructured responses.

How Avatars Work: Many readers will be familiar with avatars from their experiences with Second Life, online shopping or advanced video games. The medical community has employed avatars for clinic and surgery training, reducing the need for cadavers ((Fowler, Phillips, Patel, Ruggiero, Ragucci, Kern & Stuart, 2018). Manufacturing and heavy industry have employed avatars for simulated training in engineering, plant operations and in reducing expensive hands-on education. (Wu, Wu, Liang, Ching-Mei & Shih-Chung, 2017). Shopping aficionados may have encountered online avatars that allow retailers to enhance the buying experience and promote customer engagement (Peng & Ke, 2015). While all of these applications of avatar technology serve the purposes for which they were designed, none met the requirements we need for sales, service and interview training.

The primary distinction between the avatars described above and those used for our projects, is the use of real actors that drive the interactivity between the student and the avatar. Unlike most, our avatars operate in real time and provide dynamic responses to the students. A far more accurate analogy than the avatars used in retailing or most online simulations, would be those portrayed in the hit film, Avatar. In the movie, the avatar that interacted with the locals was an extension of the character Jake Scully, played by actor Sam Worthington. Rather than rely on computerized scripting or limited artificial intelligence, the Scully avatar interacted in real-time with the planet's natives. Our avatars operate in a similar fashion.

While the computer provides the visual images of the interviewers or customers, the actual voices and conversations are provided by a Scully-like actor who never speaks to the students out of character. The faculty developer provides the actor, known as a Simulation Specialist, a written scenario and the outline of a script. The student is provided with a modified version of the scenario. Thus, each sales, service or interview training session is individualized for the type of training and each adapts to the student's responses, mistakes, and successes. In a typical training scenario, the faculty designer might create the Nice Marketing Lady, the Raging Nut Case CEO and the Mellow Millennial as these are the very characters a student might meet in any given interview. The scenario might be a high-tech firm hiring a new graduate for an entry-level management program or selecting a student for their first international assignment. Each of the characters is described by the faculty developer and shared with the Simulation Specialist. The faculty developer rehearses with the Specialist (this is the fun part) to refine the characters and scenario.

As the Simulation Specialist reacts and adapts in real time, each student's experience is unique to them. These meetings may be individual or in small teams. The latter allows the students to debrief and critique one another, as well as receiving feedback from the instructor and from the Specialist in the guise of their character. The Specialist might be coached to suggest that the student advance to the next round of interviews or chastise them for being unprepared and wasting the CEO's time. Once the student has completed the sales pitch or interview, the avatar disappears to Avatar Neverland and a new set of avatars and characters take their place. Much like the interviews in the real world, each experience is new and different. As the Specialist is physically isolated from the student, the experience in an online course is very similar and efficacious. This resolves the on-going issue of bringing experiential training to online students preparing for the job market.

3. CONCLUSION

As some readers may note, parts of this paper are somewhat less formal than the traditional academic article. This was by intent and in keeping with one of the more valuable traits we discovered in transitioning into the experiential world of avatars in the university setting. Unlike traditional role-playing and simulations, and much more similar to real-life, the avatar experience can be unpredictable, informal and at times, amusing. We are reminded of the pitch from one student that discovered the avatar had a scripted fondness for cats. She told the interviewer of her experience in volunteering at a shelter and how it allowed her to develop her interpersonal communication skills when chatting with prospective pet parents. The avatar hired her. We share this story as it is emblematic of the potential the avatar technology offers not only for interviewing, but also for sales and customer training, human resources and other interactive business skills. We have only begun to explore the avatar universe. As the technology crosses language and cultural boundaries, we look forward to readers across disciplines and oceans to contribute to this stream of research both academically and to the practical applications of training our students to enter a global employment market.

At Saint Leo University, our next steps are to develop a library of scenarios and characters that can be applied to multiple student outcomes, disciplines and cultures. Additional empirical research is warranted to compare student and employer perceptions as well as longitudinal studies of the efficacy of avatar-based training. We hope to see other faculty join us in developing this largely unexplored stream of research and experiential application.

REFERENCES

Bortz, D, 2018. Skills Employers Look for In College Graduates, *Monster.com*, retrieved on 2/28/2019 from https://www.monster.com/career-advice/article/5-skills-employers-want-in-new-grads-and-arent-finding

Chini, J. et al., 2016. Learning From Avatars: Learning Assistants Practice Physics Pedagogy in a Classroom Simulator. *Physical Review Physics Education Research,*. Vol *12*, No. 010117

Dawson, M.R. and Lignugaris/Kraft, B., 2017. Meaningful Practice: Generalizing Foundation Teaching Skills from TLE TeachLivE™ to the Classroom. *Teacher Education and Special Education.* Vol. 4, No. 1., pp 26–50

DeSimone, F. and Buzza, J., 2013. Experiential Learning: Improving the Efficacy of an Undergraduate Business Degree. *American Journal of Business Education*, Vol. 6, No. 1, pp 7-24.

Eckhaus, E. et al., 2017. Experiential Learning in Management Education. *Business, Management and Education,* Vol. 15, No. 1, pp 42-56.

Fowler, T. et al. (2018). Virtual Interprofessional Learning. *Journal of Nursing Education*, Vol. 57, No. 11, pp. 668-674.

Mandel, R., and Noyes, E. 2016. Survey of Experiential Entrepreneurship Education Offerings Among Top Undergraduate Entrepreneurship Programs. *Education & Training*

Mercer, T. G., et al., 2017. The Use of Educational Game Design and Play in Higher Education to Influence Sustainable Behaviour. *International Journal of Sustainability in Higher Education,* Vol. 18, No. 3, pp. 359-384

Peng, Y. and Ke, D., 2015. Consumer Trust in 3D Virtual Worlds and its Impact on Real World Purchase Intention. *Nankai Business Review International,* Vol. 6, No. 4, pp. 381-400. Retrieved from https://saintleo.idm.oclc.org/login?url=https:// search-proquestcom.saintleo.idm.oclc.org/docview/1722914646?accountid=4870

Selingo, J.J., 2017. The Future of Work: How Colleges Can Prepare Students for the Jobs Ahead. *The Chronicle of Higher Education.* Vol. April 14, 2017.

Triberti, et al., 2017. Changing Avatars, Changing Selves? The influence of Social and Contextual Expectations on Digital Rendition of Identity. *Cyberpsychology, Behavior and Social Networking.* Volk. 20, No. 8, pp. 501-507

Weber, L. (2019). Workers Find Learning Is a Lifelong Job. *Wall Street Journal, 2/28/2019*, p. B5

Wu, T. et al. (2017). A Virtual Reality Tool for Training in Global Engineering Collaboration. *Universal Access in the Information Society*. pp. 1-13.

ONLINE GRADUATE DEGREES: PERCEPTIONS OF MOROCCAN UNIVERSITY STUDENTS

Karima Slamti[1] and Layla Ajrouh[2]
[1]*Faculty of Arts and Humanities, Cadi Ayyad University, Marrakech, Morocco*
[2]*Faculty of Arts and Humanities, Moulay Ismail University, Meknes, Morocco*

ABSTRACT

Online education is one of the new approaches emerging around the world, and particularly this adopted approach targets to build students' future career. This study aims at identifying the university students' perceptions of online education and the extent to which online degrees are credible for their academic and professional life. Online degrees are now implemented in higher education worldwide; however, this type of education is new and rarely operational in Moroccan universities. Qualitative data were collected and analyzed through a semi-structured interview in which 53 university students participated, from9 Moroccan higher education institutions. This exploratory study seeks to examine the students' perceptions about theuse and enrollment in online programs specifically those offered by their institutions and that yield to e-degrees. The results of this current study indicate that most students use only free online programs for their personal development as complementary to their studies. Interviewees expressed their worry towards the acceptability and credibility that the holders of online degrees may encounter in the Moroccan job market. They also revealed that the Moroccan higher education still lacks solid, developed and useful online platforms, such as MOOCs, to use beyond the educational environment entities. Thus, the present research urges further studies with Moroccan employers to probe their perceptions towards hiring students with online degrees.

KEYWORDS

Online Education, Online Degrees, Personal Development, University Students, Academic and Professional Life, Future Career

1. INTRODUCTION

Nowadays, the way of doing studies, getting knowledge and learning is under a constant change. New technology is now allowing everyone to learn in a flexible way in terms of money, time and place. Many studies in the field of education confirmed that the emergence of internet technology is being very helpful to access online higher education degrees for university students around the world (Fan-Wei Kung, 2017, p. 42). Most students around the world want to enroll in online graduate programs, as they offer a flexible knowledge. Kaupins, Wanek, and Coco (2014) affirmed that "online degrees have increasingly gained employer acceptance" (p.222). Besides, in colleges and universities nation-wide more students are enrolling in online classes in order to successfully manage the demands of their daily lives while still achieving their academic and career goals (Simlicio, 2019).

E-learning, distance learning, online learning and a myriad of other labels are now used to sell and promote alternatives to face-to-face classrooms as systems and changing social and communication norms (Ragusa, & Crampton, 2017, p.1210). Multiple indicators suggest that we are in the "golden age" of e-learning (Isaac, & Bernstein, 2018, p.1617) to be promoted in universities. However, still e-learning approach is struggling to take its right value within higher education and the job market in Morocco.

The present study is conducted to explore the presence of online education and the Moroccan university students' perceptions of online degrees. The students' viewpoints are very significant because they are the future employees. This research raises two main questions to be answered in the part of results:

1- How far university students are dealing with online education in their studies?
2- To what extent are online degrees present in the Moroccan higher education?

2. METHODS

This exploratory study uses a qualitative approach to investigate the students' perceptions about online degrees. Out of 65 students who were approached, 53 students expressed their will to participate. They were briefed via email about the purpose of the study. The research instrument was a semi-structured interview in which questions were about what students know in relation to online education, its usage and its benefit in their lives and what they think about enrolling in Moroccan or international online programs that offer degrees or certificates. The pattern of the study (n=53) was representative since all of the students are Moroccans, enrolled in different (9) Moroccan universities and in different academic levels (1st, 2nd& 3rd year, Masters). The representation was important also because the interviewees belong to different disciplines and departments including humanities, engineering, computer science, economics, in addition to, Arabic, French and English studies…etc

3. RESULTS

All the interviews results were satisfactory, since they gave a valuable addition and more insights to the subject. The interviews were interpreted and analyzed in two emerging themes, which are related to the research questions.

3.1 Theme 1: Positive Attitude towards Online Education

The majority of the interviewees reported, that online education is of a great benefit to them, it enhances their level in the field of their study or other subjects of their interest. For them, this type of learning is more appealing and motivating than the face to face one. Another participant declared that the major advantage of using technology is the numerous interactive activities, which allow more sharing of knowledge and more understanding of the courses. Most of the interviewees stated that the Moroccan universities have MOOCs (Massive Open Online Courses) platforms but are not up dated; most of them are still under try and only few courses are free of access, open and available. Some MOOCs need invitations and others need personal accounts with passwords.

Moreover, all participants declared that they face difficulties when using the universities' online learning platforms since they are just in a trial phase. They affirmed that their professors advise them to use any available external MOOCs and electronic information for more knowledge enrichment. Furthermore, students reported that collaborations between universities had been settled to improve online platforms; however, most of such projects still need promotion and more enhancements at different levels. Some interviewees confirmed that few universities are developing MOOCs for some foundation courses and credit bearing courses to help students enlarge their academic background.

Interviewees agreed that the adoption of online education will foster, in addition to their academic knowledge, other skills related to students' personalities; such as being responsible, independent and creative. Students expressed that they appreciate the increase use of blended learning classrooms, as a balance and complementary style. Besides, an interviewee affirmed that e-learning now is occupying a great part in students' life as they benefit from online lectures, courses, conferences...In addition to that, building connections with learning communities and responsive instructors.

3.2 Theme 2: Absence of Online Degrees and the Worry about their Credibility

One of the interviewees declared: "we are in a globalized world… e-degrees should have its place within our educational system". Besides, participants expressed their vital need for more ICT courses to excel in online learning. Some of the interviewees pointed that the "mobile learning", has facilitated their learning process, and that of their professors, as it is accessible at any time and place. Most interviewees agreed on the fact that the presence of online degrees in Morocco is nearly absent, which makes them worry about their integration in the job market, and that might elevate the percentage of unemployment within this category. They also highlighted that Moroccan employers give more chance to applicants with classical degrees.

An interviewee stated that employers should ensure competent e-degree holders a job, and encourage this new method of online learning; which is suitable for some students' life constraints. One added "a student may have a dangerous health problem that urges him/her to take a distance course". Another participant stressed that distance learning is a precious chance for working students. Most interviewees insisted on the need of having well-structured online learning programs that fit their levels and life situations.

More than 50% of the interviewees agreed that the absence of online degrees is unacceptable, since this digital generation impose the use of technology and favours the e-learning process. Participants affirmed that the Moroccan higher education ought to cope with this digitalized world and adapt, simultaneously, the traditional education with the challenges of the online one. Finally, an interviewee added that with the support and help of the decision makers it would be easy to form an e- learning environment because students are usually using e-devices and are already familiar with them.

4. DISCUSSION

Online education is fastly becoming the most popular alternative to traditional face-to-face education (Bejerano, 2008, p. 408). Students expressed their willingness and interest in using online education as a part or whole of their study program. The most important is that the program, be it online or face to face, should bring real and relevant knowledge. For example, students gain knowledge from blended learning environments (Bojoviæ, M. D. 2017). interviewees revealed that the ultimate thing for them is the easy access to education, and distance learning/education is the easiest. It should only be well implemented.

Interviews show the urgent need to adopt and adapt online programs within the Moroccan higher institutions, as it is a requirement for this digital generation. As "twenty-first century learners find themselves involved in online learning" (Lumbreras & Rupley, 2017, p. 381). Online education is present in the Moroccan universities, in a way that students are using online courses independently for their personal benefit, without the intention of earning any e-degree. Interviews showed that professors advise students for online autonomous work, as to use the existing MOOCs even if they are in their premature functional stages.

Students are ready to be engaged in the online education experience if they get any reassuring viewpoints from employers about online degrees credibility. Vukelic, and Pogarcic (2011) agreed that "numerous employers refuse to employ a person with an online degree because they cannot estimate their level of knowledge and skills based on this degree" (p.1471). Employers will have to build their refusal or acceptance (Kaupins, Wanek, & Coco, 2014) of online degrees on tangible evidence and reasons because online education is highly increasing. The results of this research are not conclusive; however, a concern about online degrees for Moroccan students, like elsewhere, in terms of credibility and career is raised.

5. CONCLUSION

This exploratory study has shown a clear viewpoint of university students about online education as a positive approach for their learning process. However, online degrees are far away to be implemented in the Moroccan higher education, due to the lack of its credibility in the Moroccan job market. That is why students expressed their big worry about their future if they choose to sign up to complete their studies through this option of getting e-degrees. The research participants insisted on the need of an effective online education at different levels to be promoted among the students' community. The present study contributes to the field of higher education's development in a way of implementing developed online education for university graduate students.

6. RECOMMENDATIONS

It is recommended that university management explore more online education for university students to get the needed awareness of the field and be able to implement credible online programs. Moroccan universities should go forward on a daily basis in the use of technology; they should also ensure that their students can successfully navigate the online platforms. The best way for universities to improve online education could be working on internal and external partnerships, i.e. public/private, Moroccan/international and offering online degrees for the students' benefits. It is also recommended to work within conventions or consortiums for more credibility in terms of knowledge, expertise and certification. Thus, the present paper may open the door for other studies to promote and value online degrees for university students and also to rethink the human resources' processes in hiring newly graduate students with online degrees from different disciplines.

REFERENCES

Bejerano, A. (2008). *The Genesis and Evolution of Online Degree Programs: Who Are They for and What Have We Lost Along the Way?* Communication Education, 57(3), 408–414.

Bojović, M. D. (2017). *Blended Learning as a Foreign Language Learning Environment*. TEME: Casopis Za Društvene Nauke, 41(4), 1017–1036.

Isaac, C., & Bernstein, A. (2018). *On(line) Being Relational: A Case Study*. Qualitative Report, *23*(7), 1617–1630.

Kaupins, G. E., Wanek, J. E., & Coco, M. P. (2014). The Relationship of HR Professionals' Online Experiences with Perceptions of Organizational Hiring and Promotion of Online Graduates. *Journal of Education for Business*, *89*(5), 222–229.

Kung, F.-W. (2017). *Perceptions and career prospects of the distance doctor of education degree: voices from the mid-career ELT tertiary practitioners.* Innovations in Education & Teaching International, 54(1), 42–52.

Lumbreras, R., & Rupley, W. H. (2017). ¡Si, se puede! *Achieving academic excellence online. Distance Education*, 38(3), 381–393.

Ragusa, A. T., &Crampton, A. (2017). Online learning: Cheap degrees or educational pluralization? *British Journal of Educational Technology*, *48*(6), 1208–1216.

Simplicio, J. S. C. (2019). *Strategies to Improve Online Student Academic Success and Increase University Persistence Rates*. Education, 139(3), 173–177.

Vukelic, B., & Pogarcic, I. (2011). Employers' Evaluation of Online Education. *Annals of DAAAM & Proceedings*, 1471–1472.

DEVELOPMENT OF AN ONLINE LABORATORY: APPLICATION FOR THE CHARACTERIZATION OF NTC TEMPERATURE SENSOR

Ameur Ikhlef, Boubekeur Boukhezzar and Nora Mansouri
Laboratoire d'Automatique et de Robotique, Université Frères Mentouri, Constantine, Algérie
Route Ain ElBey, Université Frères Mentouri, Constantine 25000, Algérie

ABSTRACT

This paper presents the development of practical experiences and their implementation on a remote Lab. Among the implemented experiences, we describe here the one that concerns the characterization of the NTC temperature sensor. For this experience, students collect data by varying gradually the temperature of a closed space and verify the effect of the variation of the temperature on the resistance of the sensor through a graphical interface. The measurement results are then saved automatically for further analysis. The remote control system was implemented using the LabVIEW environment whereas the platform that manages these i-Labs is based on the Interactive Shared Architecture ISA.

KEYWORDS

Remote Laboratories, Online Learning, Virtual Instrumentation, Sensors Characterization

1. INTRODUCTION

The development of Information and Communication Technologies (ICT), specially the internet, has widely contributed to introduce changes in many activities. Beyond the changes in the technical aspect, the different uses of these technologies have induced the emergence of and various efficient services. Today, ICT are present almost in all sectors including education and training. In many countries, the use of ICTs in education is well advanced and students are trained to use different forms of work offered by digital tools. In higher education, more and more universities propose to their students, in addition to traditional classroom teaching, remote activities. On the other hand, a growing number of universities suggest distance learning programs to people who wish to learn throughout their lives. The majority of these programs are based mainly on distance-learning courses and tutorials.

The development of distance laboratory works is a very active and attractive research topic, particularly in the scientific and technical fields where practice represents a very important part of the training (Aktan, Bohus, Crowl, & Shor, 1996) (Leva & Donida, 2008) (Wu & Kuo, 2008) (Delong, et al., 2010) (Mujkanovic, Zutin, Schellander, Oberlercher, & Vormaier, 2015).

Teaching laboratory works in classical way places the teacher in front with the following problems and constraints:

1. **Massification:** The increasing number of students does not allow to ensure laboratory works in suitable conditions. To do this, more equipment, more space, more time and more teachers are needed.
2. **Equipment:** Laboratory works require equipment that is often very expensive and bulky. It cannot be purchased in multiple copies for budget or space reasons.
3. **Time:** Time slots are often limited. That implies rotations and therefore restricts the number of laboratory works. It also implies that some students will have to do a laboratory work before addressing the topic in course

Therefore, remote laboratories are an interesting alternative to overcome all these problems while providing new features. New technologies bring onboard tools that facilitate access to machines that can be controlled, piloted and manipulated remotely. They allow the development of i-labs that offer to students and teachers new perspectives as well from a spatial and temporal point of view. I-labs experiments can be accessed remotely without having to move, saving time and reducing laboratory days of inactivity. Students can also redo the manipulations at suitable times. They just need to reserve their place beforehand.

The main advantage of these remote laboratories is therefore this possibility of being able to share the same experimental equipment between many users distributed in different geographical areas. Several educational teams around the world have already taken advantage of these technological advances to implement digital laboratories for distance learning.

In Frères Mentouri University of Constantine (UFMC), the development of physical remote laboratories (i-labs), is very active, particularly in the automatic control, electronics and electrical engineering areas. In this paper, we present the development of practical experiences and their implementation on the UFMC i-lab. For that, we organize it as follow: The architecture of UFMC i-Lab, the hardware and the software part are reported in section II. In section III, the objectives, technical content and procedure of the remote experiment are presented. In this section we present also the tests results of the remote experiment from remote-student side. Finally, conclusions and some perspectives are given.

2. PRESENTATION OF THE UFMC I-LAB

I-Labs are remote laboratories accessible through an Intranet or Internet network. They use web platforms to provide the users an interactive interface. This interface allows them to control hardware or drive real-time experiences via a simple web browser. To a remote access of these laboratories, the user needs to set up a platform that manages authentication problems, users flow, access to experiments, measurements visualization and recording and so on.

The UFMC i-lab platform was set up as a part of the Tempus E-science project: *Maghreb network of distance laboratories (2012 - 2015)*. One of the project objectives is the setting up of three i-labs platforms in the Maghreb, including the UFMC i-Lab. At the end of the project, the UFMC i-Lab was in place with some e-Experiments developed by the UFMC team in the electronic and automatic fields (Hobar & Semra, 2014) (Rebiai, Touidjen, & Mouissat, 2014) (Latreche, Ziari, & Mouissat, 2015) (Ikhlef, Kihel, Boukhezzar, Guerroudj, & mansouri, 2015) (Ikhlef, Kihel, Boukhezzar, Mansouri, & Hobar, 2016). These e-Experiments have been tested and evaluated by the different project partners.

2.1 UFMC i-Lab Architecture

The UFMC i-Lab is based on the ISA architecture that supports interactive labs (Harward, et al., 2008). This architecture allows the user to change the settings during the experiment. For the interactive labs, the simultaneous access of students to the same experience is impossible.

The UFMC i-Lab architecture is represented by the figure 1. As shown, the platform has a measurement server that manages experiments and a Web server that manages user access. Real-time remote visualization and control is performed using the LabVIEW Environment Web Server. In this case, the developed VI (Virtual Instrument) is available on the LAN or Internet through web browsers with an installed appropriate plug-in (JRE for applets based interfaces, runtime engine for a LabVIEW based remote experiments). The remote user only regains control of the experience after requesting and receiving acceptance from the server. As described above, this interactive interface gives students the opportunity to start and stop the experiment at their convenience. They can change the parameters of the experiment at any time from any terminal connected to the Intranet or Internet network. Moreover, it is also possible to store all data from experimental results. The UFMC i-Lab consists in 3 parts that complement each other: software, hardware and an experiments part:

2.1.1 Software Part

The UFMC i-Lab laboratory is based on the ISA architecture. This platform allows experiences deployment and sharing with different users. The platform is accessible through the university portal at *http://ilab.umc.edu.dz/ilabservicebroker* . The user logs to the platform via a username and a password. After the authentication phase, the user can communicate directly with the measurement server without having to go through the Web server each time. The first pass through the web server is required only to establish the connection with the experiment.

2.1.2 Hardware Part

The hardware used in this experiment is represented by the figure 2. The temperature chamber has a light heating resistor and three fans for cooling. The fan and resistor control boards have been designed for PWM control. In this case the cyclic ratio of the PWM signal will determine the rotation speed of the fans and the heating power of the resistor. The temperature inside the chamber is measured by an LM35 analog temperature sensor. To automate the temperature regulation, we have implemented two PID controllers; one for the fans and another for the heating resistor. The parameters of the controllers are previously identified by the Ziegler-Nichols method. It is also possible to implement self-tuning PID controllers.

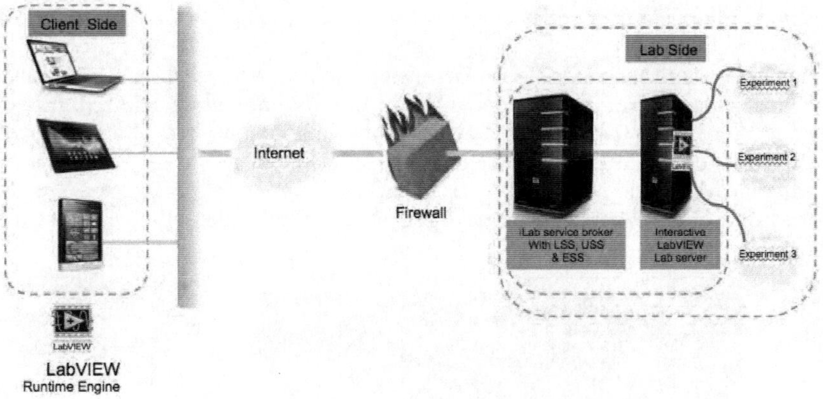

Figure 1. UFMC1 i-Lab architecture

The acquisition card is used to send the command signals to the heating resistor and the fans, and to retrieve the measurements delivered by the sensors.

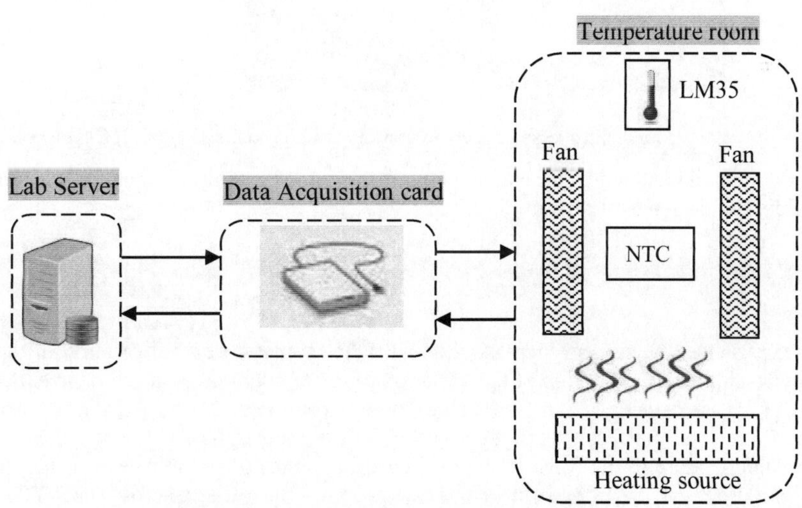

Figure 2. Hardware used in the NTC experiment

3. NTC SENSOR CHARACTERIZATION EXPERIMENT

Sensors are the basic elements of data acquisition systems. They are widely used in industrial systems, automated systems, and electronic instruments. A variation of the studied or measured physical phenomenon causes a variation on the physical and dimensional properties of the sensor. This variation is often expressed by a variation of voltage, current or impedance. In order to characterize the correspondence between the sensor output variation and the physical quantity to be measured, it is essential to establish a table or a calibration curve that represents the output of the sensor as a function of the physical quantity.

In this paper, the characterization of a temperature sensor (NTC thermistor) is considered. A thermistor is a temperature sensing element composed of a semiconductor material that exhibits a significant variation in resistance, proportional to a small change in temperature. Typically, a thermistor has negative temperature coefficients (NTC). It means that the resistance of the thermistor decreases as the temperature increases. The characterization of this thermistor consists in measuring the variation of the resistance value as a function of the temperature. In the classical method (hands on experiment), a NTC is placed in contact with a heating resistor powered by a voltage *V*. An Ohmmeter is connected to the terminals of the NTC and a thermometer is placed in contact with the heating resistor. The voltage *V* is then slightly varied and the value of the NTC is recorded for each temperature.

For a remote characterization of the NTC thermistor, it is necessary to initially set up an automated system to control the manipulation. For this, a temperature control system is firstly realized. It is equipped with heat sources and a cooling device (fans) to stabilize the temperature to a desired value. Temperature regulation is provided by two PID controllers: one for the heat source and the other for the fans. This system can be used for other e-experiments such as regulation for example.

So, for the needs of the experience, we have executed the realization of the automated temperature room shown in Figure 3.

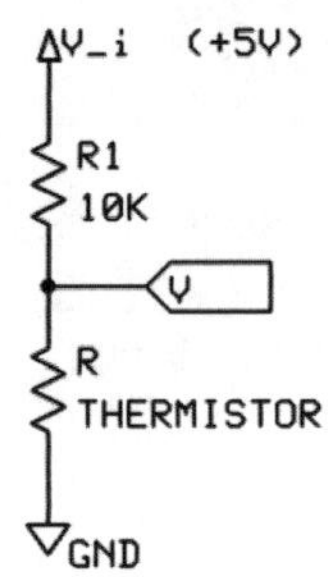

Figure 3. Temperature regulation room and the connection of NTC Sensor

The NTC is putted inside the temperature room and in order to simplify the sensor operation, It is placed in a voltage divider bridge as shown in Figure 3.

The resistor value is then given by:

$$R = \frac{R_1.V}{(V_i - V)} \tag{1}$$

For the experience, the student increase gradually the temperature, the variation of the resistance is then continuously visualized as a function of the variation of the temperature. To drive the experiment, a graphical user interface (GUI) is developed using the LabVIEW environment. The graphical user interface is represented in Figure 4. From this interface, the student can choose a temperature value and the system automatically stabilizes the temperature of the room to the desired value. Once the system reaches the desired temperature, the student can use the *Take Measurement* button to capture the voltage across the NTC. The values will be automatically saved in a table. The *heating-cooling* button is used to select the heating or cooling cycle. The pull-down graphs display respectively the desired temperature steps and the voltage across the NTC. All measurement results are saved for later analysis.

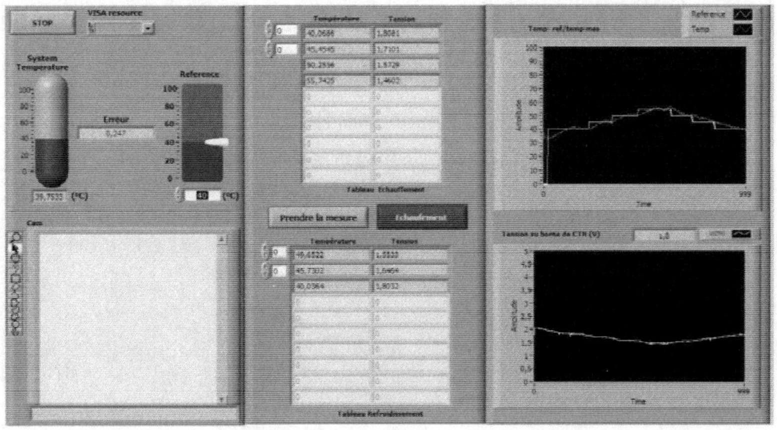

Figure 4. Graphical user interface

4. CONCLUSION

The NTC sensor characterization experiment exploits the UFMC web-based platform to give an interactive interface to the users. Thanks to the i-Lab, the experiment is available for all the subscribed students every day, 24 hours per day.

This learning method leads to save time and reduce inactivity days. For this remote experiment we noticed that the time allotted to the experiment decreased considerably compared to the classical method. So, it is possible now to share the experiment with the students of other specialties. Therefore, the use of these new technologies in the design of remote labs has given very satisfactory results whether in terms of pedagogy or logistics. As a perspective, it is also possible to use the same system to characterize other sensor types.

REFERENCES

Aktan, B., Bohus, C., Crowl, L., & Shor, M. (1996). Distance learning applied to control engineering laboratories. IEEE Transactions on Education, 39(3), 320-326. doi:10.1109/13.538754

Delong, K., Harward, V. J., Bailey, P., Hardison, J., Kohse, G., & Ostrocsky, Y. (2010). Three online neutron beam experiments based on the iLab Shared Architecture. IEEE EDUCON 2010 Conference. doi:10.1109/educon.2010.5492587

Harward, V., Alamo, J. D., Lerman, S., Bailey, P., Carpenter, J., Delong, K., . . . Zych, D. (2008). The iLab Shared Architecture: A Web Services Infrastructure to Build Communities of Internet Accessible Laboratories. Proceedings of the IEEE, 96(6), 931-950. doi:10.1109/jproc.2008.921607

Hobar, F., & Semra, L. (2014). Development and implementation of an e-course and a remote laboratory for analog electronics study. 2014 International Conference on Interactive Mobile Communication Technologies and Learning (IMCL2014). doi:10.1109/imctl.2014.7011109

Ikhlef, A., Kihel, M., Boukhezzar, B., Mansouri, N., & Hobar, F. (2016). Online PID control of tank level system. 2016 IEEE Global Engineering Education Conference (EDUCON). doi:10.1109/educon.2016.7474566

Ikhlef, A., Kihel, M., Boukhezzar, B., Guerroudj, A., & Mansouri, N. (2015). Online Temperature Control System. International Journal of Interactive Mobile Technologies, 9(2), 22-25. doi:10.3991/ijim.v9i2.4382

Latreche, S., Ziari, Z., & Mouissat, S. (2015). UC1 Oscillator Remote Lab for Distant Electronics Education. International Journal of Interactive Mobile Technologies (iJIM), 9(2), 9. doi:10.3991/ijim.v9i2.4375

Leva, A., & Donida, F. (2008). A remote laboratory on PID autotuning. IFAC Proceedings Volumes, 41(2), 8147-8152. doi:10.3182/20080706-5-kr-1001.01376

Mujkanovic, A., Zutin, D. G., Schellander, M., Oberlercher, G., & Vormaier, M. (2015). Impact of students preferences on the design of online laboratories. 2015 IEEE Global Engineering Education Conference (EDUCON). doi:10.1109/educon.2015.7096067

Rebiai, S., Touidjen, N. E., & Mouissat, S. (2014). Implementation of online optoelectronic devices course and remote experiments in UC1 iLab. 2014 International Conference on Interactive Mobile Communication Technologies and Learning (IMCL2014). doi:10.1109/imctl.2014.7011117

Wu, P., & Kuo, C. (2008). The Design and Implementation of a Remote Automatic Control Laboratory: Using PID Control as an Example. Tamkang Journal of Science and Engineering, 11(2), 219-228.

DIGITAL COMPETENCE IN THE INITIAL TRAINING OF THE TELESECUNDARIA TEACHER. CASE STUDY

Anna Luz Acosta Aguilera[1], Rubén Edel Navarro[1] and Yadira Navarro Rangel[2]
[1]*Universidad Veracruzana., Av. Jesús Reyes Heroles s/n Zona Universitaria, Fracc. Costa Verde, CP 94294, Boca del Río, Ver., Mexico*
[2]*Benemérita Universidad. Autónoma de Puebla,* Calle 4 Sur #104; Col. Centro C.P. 72000; *Puebla de Zaragoza, Puebla, México*

ABSTRACT

The development of digital competence is undoubtedly an issue that has been subject of numerous research and development proposals at the institutional level in recent years (Punie and Breco, 2014, Pech and Prieto, 2017, Adell, 2010, Silva Mirada, Gisbert, Morales and Onetto, 2016), knowing its meaning and the relationship of this with the initial teacher training is essential because it allows to know the way in which teacher training schools face the challenge of forming competent citizens for life in the knowledge society (Lion, 2012). A quantitative research is presented, through an exploratory factorial analysis, whose objective is to identify the level of digital competence of the student and the factors associated with its development. A survey was applied to 248 students who are studying the Bachelor in Teaching and Learning in Telesecundaria. The results allow to identify different levels of competence. However, digital evidence shows a positive perception from students in the three dimensions established to measure their digital competence. Therefore it would be advisable to design an evaluation instrument that allows to contrast what students say they know how to do, with what they really do, as well as to observe the type of activities that are developed within a normal school in orden to obtain information regarding the educational policy implemented at the institutional level.

KEYWORDS

Digital Competence, Initial Teacher Training, Telesecundaria, Basic Education

1. INTRODUCTION

The development of digital competence has become a priority for governments and international organizations around the world (Punie and Breco, 2014, Adell, 2010, UNESCO, 2008, ISTE, 2016). The above has its origins in the Definition and Selection of Competences Project (DeSeCo) developed by the Organization for Economic Cooperation and Development (OECD), whose main objective is to determine the competences that are considered necessary for the 21st century citizen. Although this project began in 1997, it was not until 2003 that a relevant framework was created together with the final report that led to a series of transformations in the educational systems of various parts of the world.

That is why in 2006 the European Commission proposes eight key competences for lifelong learning, where digital competence is included, defining it as:

> the safe and critical use of information technologies for work, leisure and communication. It is based on the basic ICT competences: the use of computers to obtain, evaluate, store, produce, present and exchange information and communicate and participate in collaboration networks through the Internet (Lion, 2012, p.17).

When carrying out an analysis of the investigations that have been made around the subject of digital competence, it is clear that there is not a unique definition because it is defined, according to the purposes established in each investigation. However the aforementioned by the European Commission shows that being digitally competent not only involves the use of technological devices and tools but also requires the development of computer and information skills.

In this regard Adell (2010) defines digital competence in terms of 5 basic elements: 1) informational competence, 2) technological or computer skills, 3) multiple literacy's, 4) generic cognitive competence and 5) digital citizenship.

Unfortunately in Mexico there is no clarity regarding the way in which the educational system strengthens the development of digital competence in students, and considering that teachers play a determining role in the creation of learning environments that propitiate the pedagogical use of ICT in its daily performance, it has been considered opportune to analyze the way in which teacher training schools face the challenge of forming competent citizens for life in the knowledge society (Lion, 2012).

That is why a questionnaire was designed to measure the digital competence of the future teacher of Telesecundaria with the purpose of identifying strengths and weaknesses that highlight the possible relationship between the type of activities proposed by teachers and the development of digital competence of student. It is important to note that these results are part of a broader research called "The pedagogical usability of ICT and its relationship with digital competence, in the initial teacher training of Telesecundaria".

2. METHOD

The research is proposed from a quantitative approach, through a case study, to identify the digital competence of teacher-training students.

2.1 Development of the Instrument

The questionnaire was prepared after carrying out a systematic search for the identification of instruments that have been applied by other researchers at a national and international level. Exact questions of the instruments reviewed were not transcribed but were considered as an important basis. The works from Zúñiga (2016), Pech (2016) and Esteve (2015) were analyzed in greater depth, which developed their research in higher education contexts related to the educational field; This is how the three dimensions and the fourteen indicators that make up the variable of "digital competence" that was intended to be measured with this instrument were chosen.

The survey consists of 48 items or questions, whose answers are presented on a scale Likert type, which includes the options "Incapable, A bit capable, Quite capable and Very capable". The application of the instrument was self-administered online through the LimeSurvey application , which is a free software for the development and application of surveys very simple and easy to use.

2.2 Subjects / Population

It was applied to 320 students representing the population of students enrolled in the Bachelor of Teaching and Learning in Telesecunaria, offered by the Benemérita Escuela Normal Veracruzana "Enrique C. Rébsamen" in the city of Xalapa, Veracruz, Mexico.

2.3 Validity

The validity of contents was determined through the review of experts, which were selected given their outstanding trajectory and knowledge in the field of digital competence in initial teacher training; Although there were some comments related to the structure of the indicators, in general, the judges considered the items designed in each dimension to be appropriate and relevant.

As far as the construct validity is concerned, according to Castro and Galindo (2000), the Kaiser Meyer-Olkin test (KMO) and the Bartlett sphericity test help to verify if the sample is acceptable for the factoring of the variables.

Table 1.

KMO and Bartlett test

Sampling adequacy measurement Kaiser-Meyer-Olkin		.765
Bartlett's sphericity test	Aprox. Chi-square	2560.611
	gl	990
	Sig.	.000

From the results it is concluded that the sample is acceptable for the factorization of the variables, reaching a KMO index of 0.765 (very close to 0.8, which is normally required), while the correlation matrix was spherical ($p < 0.01$), and, consequently, analyzable from the factorial point of view.

Likewise, for the reliability analysis, the Cronbach's Alpha coefficient was used, resulting in a value of 0.976, as a result the tool is considered reliable to measure what is intended to be measured.

Table 2.

Cronbach's Alfa tool

Reliability statistics		
Cronbach's Alfa	Cronbach's Alfa based on standardized elements	N of elements
.976	.976	45

3. RESULTS

The digital competence of the student was measured by three dimensions: 1) field of learning, 2) field of information and communication and 3) field of digital culture, in a general way, the results obtained in each dimension will be presented below.

The questionnaire was answered by students whose ages ranged between 18 and 24 years, of which 64% are women and 36% men, which could be justified by virtue of the fact that in Mexico the teachers' association that works in basic education is formed mostly by females.

In dimension 1 Scope of learning, the results show a positive perception on the part of the students (Graph 1).

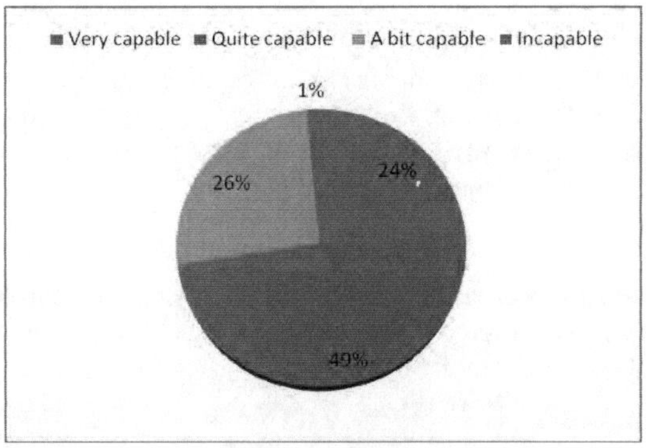

Graph 1. Concentrate dimension 1. Source: Own elaboration

49% of the participants consider themselves capable enough to identify software that supports their academic activities, use ICT as an instrument that strengthens reflective and critical thinking, use technology to improve the quality of their products or evidence of learning (tasks, investigations, essays, writings, presentations, etc.) as well as to obtain the maximum benefit of the technology for personal and professional purposes.

In dimension 2 Scope of information and communication, the situation is not very different, since 44% of students consider themselves quite capable of using Internet browsers, doing some work or project, consulting texts, documentary videos, recordings, podcasts , images, among others, communicate effectively in digital environments, perform teamwork and distance through the use of ICT, in addition to collaborating in communities and/or learning networks about their area of study and/or interest.

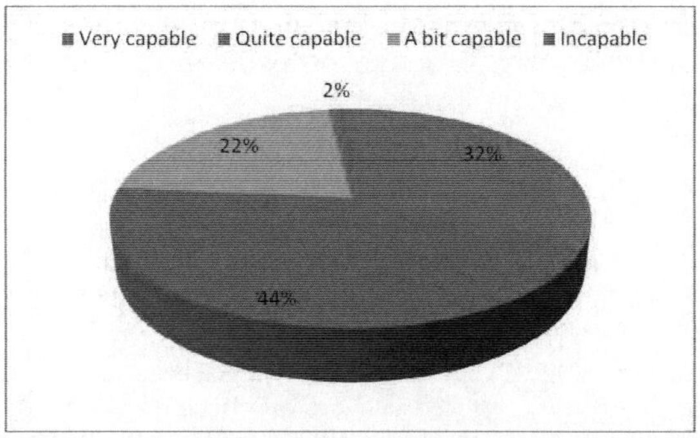

Graph 2. Concentrate dimension 2. Source: Own elaboration

However, the graph of dimension 2 shows that there is a high percentage of students who say they feel very capable of performing activities related to the search, generation and dissemination of content, which makes a lot of sense because at curricular level the current curriculum (SEP, 2019) promotes the use of ICT mainly for information purposes.

On the other hand, in dimension 3 Scope of digital culture, students' perception is even more positive, since among the 50% who consider themselves to be quite capable and the 32% who consider themselves to be very capable, more than 80% of the students have considered to have the ability to stay informed through digital media and participate actively in decision making, act responsibly and civically in the digital environment, know and respect intellectual property rights, consider the ethical and legal aspects of they share on the internet, as well as conduct themselves with respect and ethics within the digital environment.

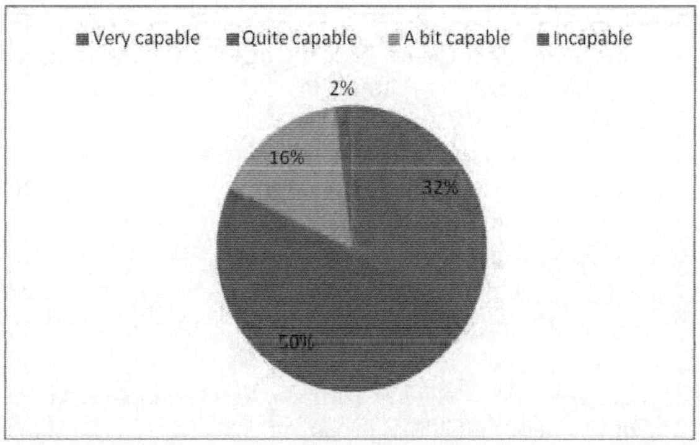

Graph 3. Concentrate dimension 3. Source: Own elaboration

In general, and considering all the answers provided by the students, dimension 2 is the one in which the students obtained the best results, which can be the result of the multiple activities that they carry out inside and outside the classroom that have to do with information search, use of social networks and other recreational activities they perform.

4. CONCLUSION

Although the results allow us to have a general panorama regarding the perception of teacher-training students in relation to their digital competence, it is opportune to contrast this information with the comments made by the teachers who are training them, in order to identify if they are being trained since the beginning of their studies with strategies, methodologies and activities to develop their digital competence.

It is also essential to observe the type of activities that are developed within the teacher-training collage, in relation to the strengthening of digital competence, on the part of students, teachers and educational authorities which can provide us information regarding the educational policy implemented at the institutional level.

In a future work, it would be convenient to design an assessment tool that allows us to contrast what the students say they know how to do, with what they really do, that is, an evaluation test that highlights their level of digital competence.

REFERENCES

Adell, A (2010) ¿Qué es la competencia digital? http://carraud.blogspot.mx/2010/10/jordi-adell-que-es-la-competencia.html

Banco Interamericano de Desarrollo (2012) Desarrollo de Competencias Digitales para portales de la Región. Red Latinoamericana de Portales Educativos. Buenos Aires, Argentina. En red: http://www.uruguayeduca.edu.uy/sites/default/files/2018-02/09-Desarrollo-de-Competencias-Digitales-para-Portales-de-la-Regi%C3%B3n%20%281%29%20%281%29%281%29.pdf

Castro, J., Galindo, M. (2000) Estadística Multivariable: análisis de correlaciones, Amarú: Ediciones, Salamanca: España. ISBN 848196137.

Colorado, B. y Edel, R. (2012). La usabilidad de TIC en la práctica educativa. En red: http://www.um.es/ead/red/30/edel.pdf

Diario Oficial de la Unión Europea (2006) Recomendación del Parlamento Europeo y del Consejo de 18 de diciembre de 2006 sobre las competencias clave para el aprendizaje permanente. En red: http://eurlex.europa.eu/LexUriServ/LexUriServ.do?uri=OJ:L:2006:394:0010:0018:ES:PDF

Esteve, F (2015) La competencia digital docente Análisis de la autopercepción y evaluación del desempeño de los estudiantes universitarios de educación por medio de un entorno 3D. Departamento de Pedagogía, Universitat Rovira i Virgili. Tarragona. España. http://francescesteve.es/tesis/

ISTE (2016). Estándares ISTE para estudiantes. En Red https://www.iste.org/docs/Standards-Resources/iste-standards_one-sheets-students_bilingual.pdf

Lion, C (2012). Desarrollo de competencias digitales para portales de la región. Banco Interamericano de Desarrollo y Red Latinoamericana de Portales Educativos. https://documentop.com/queue/desarrollo-de-competencias-digitales-para-portales-de-la-region-relpe_5a0d2f6a1723dd99282eedfb.html

OCDE (2005) La Definición y Selección de Competencias Clave. Resumen ejecutivo. Organización para la Cooperación y el Desarrollo Económico (OCDE). En red: http://www.deseco.admin.ch/bfs/deseco/en/index/03/02.parsys.78532.downloadLi st.94248.DownloadFile.tmp/2005.dscexecutivesummary.sp.pdf

Pech, S. (2016) Competencia digital docente. Cuestionario en línea. Ciudad Real: España. https://docs.google.com/forms/d/e/1FAIpQLSeoPt3bZlU_mUlhaUCq4GjGt0AYAI5XpmcM7niSogPg3uxI1Q/viewf orm

Punie, Y, Brecko, B (2014) DIGCOM: Marco Europeo de competencias digitales. European Commission. http://jakintza.eus/wp-content/uploads/DIGCOMP_Donostia_ES-Rev.pdf

SEP (2018) Plan de estudios de la Licenciatura en Enseñanza y Aprendizaje en Telesecundaria. Centro Virtual de Innovación Educativa (CEVIE). En red: https://www.cevie-dgespe.com/index.php/planes-de-estudios-2018/10-planes-de-estudios-2018/67-telesecundaria-a?tmpl=component&print=1

Silva. J, Miranda, P, Gisbert, M, Morales, J, Onetto, A (2016) Indicadores para evaluar la competencia digital docente en la formación inicial en el contexto Chileno-Uruguayo. Revista Latinoamericana de Tecnología Educativa RELATEC. Vol. 15, No. 3 ISSN: 1695-288X. https://relatec.unex.es/article/view/2807/1982

UNESCO (2008) Estándares de competencias en TIC para docentes. Londres: UNESCO. Recuperado el 18 de noviembre de 2014 de http://www.eduteka.org/EstandaresDocentesUnesco.php

Unión Europea (2013). DIGCOM: A Framework for Developing and Understanding Digital Competence in Europe. En Red: http://blog.guadalinfo.es/wp-content/uploads/2014/03/digcomp.pdf

Zúñiga, J (2016) Las competencias digitales en el perfil universitario: el caso de la Facultad de Pedagogía de la Universidad Veracruzana. Veracruz, México. Universidad Veracruzana; Facultad de Pedagogía. https://cdigital.uv.mx/bitstream/123456789/41455/1/Zuniga.pdf

LEARNING STRATEGIES THAT CONTRIBUTE TO ACADEMIC EFFICIENCY IN RELATION TO THE BUSINESS SCHOOL STUDENT'S LEARNING STYLES

María de Jesús Araiza Vázquez[1], Mayra Elizabeth Brosig Rodríguez[1]
and Claudia Ivonne Niño Rodríguez[2]
[1]PhD, [2]MAE
Universidad Autónoma de Nuevo León
Ave. Universidad S/N Cd. Universitaria, San Nicolás de los Garza, N.L., Spain

ABSTRACT

In the XXI century one of the main challenges facing the education system at the superior level, is to promote education through the creation of flexible teaching environments, which allow raising the level of autonomous learning in students, that is why, in this research, the study of learning styles and their correlation with academic performance is proposed, demonstrating that if it is taught based on the strategies of each learning style, the flow in the teaching-learning process channel is accelerated, which will favor the development of skills and abilities that build meaningful knowledge.
The results reveal that among the styles of reflexive, active and pragmatic learning there is a correlation between the variables analyzed, while in the students with emphasis on theoretical styles no significant correlation was found. This information shows the importance of establishing strategies for learning style that contribute to improving academic performance.

KEYWORDS

Learning Styles, Academic Performance, Meaningful Learning

1. INTRODUCTION

Education has been one of the main axes, in which the government has paid special attention, in its search to achieve development and economic growth in the country.

Due to the nature of this study we will define learning style as, the diversity of ways in which an individual, reveals their abilities to think, understand, and observe the facts or situations. Given that, under the new educational schemes, where students must develop autonomous learning.

The purpose of this study was to propose strategies related to each learning style for the 2nd year students who were studying the learning unit cost elements in a business school in Northeast Mexico in relation to his academic performance. As a delimitation of this study, academic performance is considered the final note or grade of the course obtained by the student, codified in the results of achievement obtained by the students in the integral system for the administration of educational services.

There are studies that show information about learning styles and learning strategies: (Valencia, 2014; García, Gutiérrez, Jiménez & Sánchez 2012; Cantú Hinojosa, 2004). These investigations reflect results in which learning styles are associated with variables such as effective learning, perceived effectiveness, academic performance, among other factors that underpin deep or meaningful learning.

1.1 Justification

The study presented here is justified in the understanding that educational institutions and their teachers are always looking for improvement in their daily work, the purpose is to find better discrepancies in the teaching-learning process, in order to lead to progress of them looking for the improvement of the system actors.

From the point of view of the researchers this work, should contribute to the student in discovering the way in which it is feasible to learn, at the same time, it will allow the construction of a significant autonomous knowledge, and developing the capacity to take decisions to the challenges that the society of the knowledge demands..

1.2 Overall objective

Propose strategies related to each learning style by the students of 4th semester of a business school in the COURSE cost elements in relation to their academic performance.

1.3 Hypothesis

H1 Students who do not apply their learning style properly need learn a strategy to pretend optimal academic performance.
H2. Students who apply their learning styles obtain an optimal academic advantage

2. THEORETICAL FRAMEWORK

Throughout this research, it has been proven that among the protagonists of education, -student, teacher and educational institutions- there are different ways of learning, and teaching, however nowadays these are subject to the regulations of the new educational models, which allow us to be at the forefront of technological advances, using tools and strategies in journeys to achieve significant student learning, converting the teacher from an active protagonist to a guide, facilitator and mediator of education, there the importance of identifying and directing the strategies that go according to each learning style and thus achieve effective interaction, directed to the teaching-learning process, which contribute to the construction of autonomous knowledge, directing it in the search of an effective academic performance.

2.1 Academic Performance

Based on the above considerations, we could appreciate that there is a diversity of studies related to academic performance, usually focusing on two primary aspects: those measured in the teachers and their work in teaching. For this paper, the work and theoretical support projected by Pizarro (1985) was considered as support, and its consideration of the academic performance as "a measure of the respondent or indicative capacities that it shows, in an estimated way, [what a student] has learned as a consequence of a process of instruction or training ".

2.2 Learning Strategies

Strategies are techniques that are used as a means to make the learning process effective; There is a large diversity of authors that conceptualize this term, for example (Nisbet and Shucksmith, 1986) "learning strategies are the integrated sequences of procedures or activities that are chosen with the purpose of facilitating the acquisition, storage and / or use of information or knowledge. " And that according to; (Díaz and Hernández 2010 cited in García, et al., 2012) mention "seven learning strategies widely used in educational psychology and pedagogy, directing them according to their learning style: active, reflective, theoretical, pragmatic.

For Cantú-Hinojosa, (2004) "A learning style implies preferences, tendencies and disposition, as well as behavioral patterns that distinguish a subject from the others in the form that acquires and processes the information" (p.73). In the same sense, are the cognitive, effective and physiological features that serve as relatively stable indicators of how students perceive, interact and respond to their learning environments. (Keefe, 1988; cited by Gallegos & Martínez, 2003, p.4). It is therefore appropriate to emphasize the various ways in which an individual manifest his thinking abilities in order to understand, discern concepts, observations and facts.

Therefore, it is important that each person identifies their learning style, this being a competence that allows them to interact in their social and professional environment. (Acevedo, 2012).

For Pizarro (1985); "Academic performance is an indicator of the learning that a student presents in terms of skills and abilities, as a result of the participation of an educational situation." In the field of higher education, this issue has gained strength as an indicator of the quality of institutions. (Isaza 2012).

3. DESCRIPTION OF THE METHOD

This research is quantitative descriptive and longitudinal applied to a sample of 103 students currently in the fourth semester of January-June 2018 of public accountant in a business school in Northeast Mexico. The sample consisted of 49 men (48%) and 54 women (52%). The course considered in the study was cost elements, which is taken in the 2nd year of the degree.

Using as a measuring instrument the Honey-Alonso Learning Styles questionnaire with a reliability of .80 of Cronbach's alpha, consists of 80 short and structured questions in four groups of 20 questions corresponding to the 4 styles of learning. The instrument was piloted to check that the vocabulary was related to the context of Mexican culture.

4. RESULTS

This research work was carried out by running the data with correlation analysis, frequency distribution and percentages, as well as measures of central tendency. Table 1 shows that the average achievement of the study population is within the accreditation index which is 70 points; with a standard deviation of 15.12 showing a high variance between results, which is considerable; 25 points being the grade with the highest degree of deficiency, while 100 points reflects a high performance rating.

Table 1. Average of achievement of the 103 students in the course

Variable	N	Mean	Desv. Standard	Rank	Minimum	Maximum
	103	70.9708738	15.1211652	75	25	100

Source: Own elaboration with study data.

Table 2 shows that the theoretical style shows a standard deviation of 10.48; which indicates that the students' achievement of this learning style is very attached to academic performance, accepted by the institution under study (according to quality indicators > 85).

The Pragmatic style obtained a standard deviation of 19.98, and the Active reflected a standard deviation with a course of 16.93, both with similar standard deviation.

In the expected of the rates, the Pragmatic and Active return to similar: Pragmatic with a score average of 67 and the Asset with an average of 65.36.

On the other hand, the reflective learning style shows a mid-range style in measure, with a significant standard deviation between its data with a of 14.75, being the learning style with the best academic performance with respect to its mean with a value determined of 74.19 points.

Table 2. Average and Standard deviation by style of Learning in course Cost Elements

Learning styles	Average	
	Rates	Desv. Standard
Active	65.36	16.93
Reflexive	74.19	14.75
Theoretical	73.78	10.48
Pragmatic	67.00	19.98

Source: Own elaboration with data collected

Table 3. Academic performance <84, > 85 in the course Cost Elements for learning styles

Learning styles	Rates Percentage		Rates Subjects	
	<84	> 85	<84	> 85
Active	91%	9%	twenty	two
Reflexive	67%	33%	18	9
Theoretical	81%	19%	30	7
Pragmatic	82%	18%	14	3

Source: Own elaboration based on the data obtained

In Table 3 we can see in the Active style, 91% of the students who developed this style obtained an average grade of < 84, thus being the learning style with the largest number of subjects, with a lower academic performance. Only 9% of the students of this learning style obtained an average grade > 85.

In the Reflective style, 67% of the students who developed this style obtained an average of < 84, while the students who obtained an average > 85 were 33%. Being the style that shows the highest index of subjects in the variable > 85.

The Theoretical Style reflects in the variable < 84 an 81% leaving 19% in the variable > 85; finally, the Pragmatic learning style which obtained 82% in the variable < 84 and an 18 in the variable > 85

In figure. The Reflective style shows a non-significant positive correlation derived from its academic performance demonstrated by its R^2 (0.1112) and its ascending slope (0.0448) which indicates that these students with respect to the learning style will obtain a good result in the learning unit Cost Elements.

In Figure 2. The Pragmatic learning style shows a positive relationship (0.2073) however its negative slope (-0.0267) clarifies an offspring due to the few students that show a good academic level.

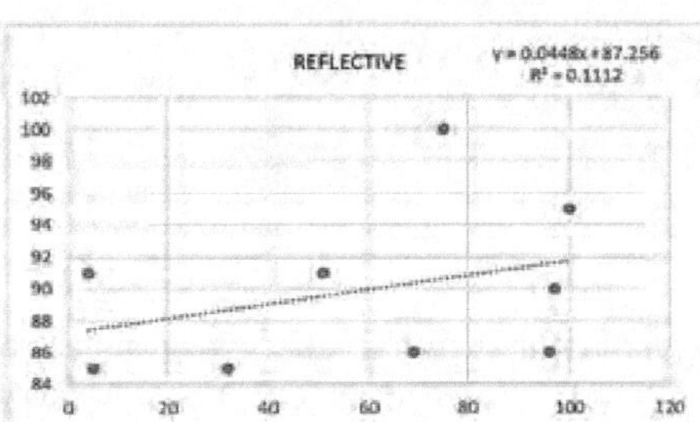

Figure 1. Correlation coefficients and Reflective significance vs. performance academic
Source: Elaborated by the authors

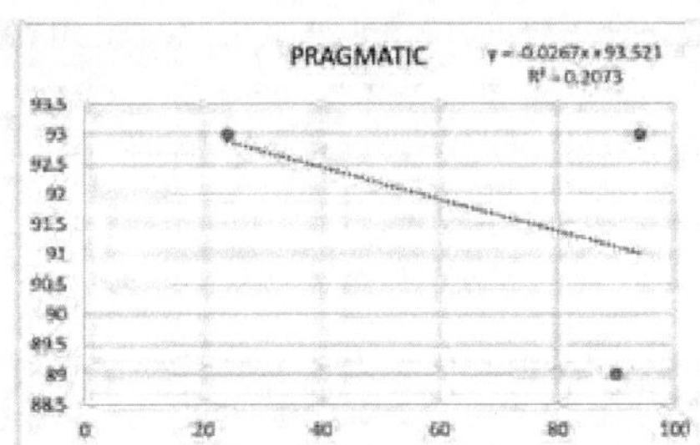

Figure 2. Correlation coefficients and significance of the pragmatics vs. the academic performance
Source: Elaborated by the authors

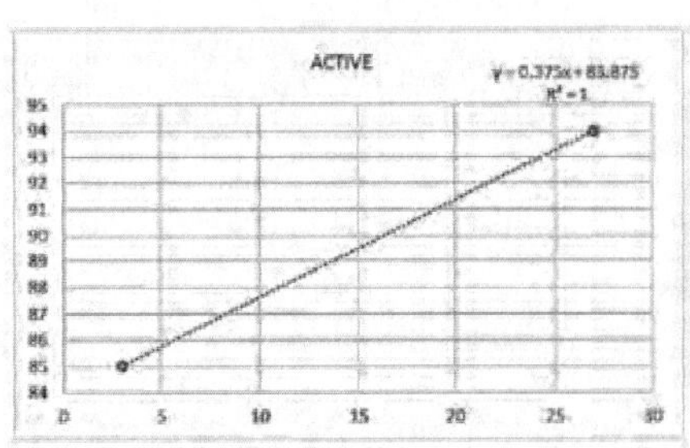

Figure 3. Correlation coefficients and significance of the asset vs. the performance academic
Source: Elaborated by the authors

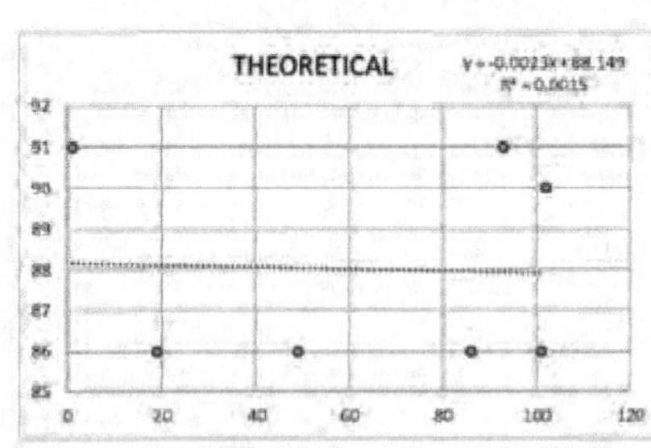

Figure 4. Correlation coefficients and significance of Theoretical vs. academic performance
Source: Elaborated by the authors

In Figure 3. The Active learning style shows the highest correlation with the academic level shown by the school (85 points) indicating its R^2(1) and its ascending slope (0.375) which reflects that the academic performance of the students who scored 85 points or above 85 points is acceptable and will look ascending.

Figure 4 shows the correlation between academic performance and the theoretical learning style, which has a of 0.0015; with a slightly downward slope of -0.0023. These indicate that the students who develop this learning style did not increase their academic performance, but on the contrary, which reduces the use in the course of the cost elements.

5. CONCLUSION

This study is of great importance due to the new educational scenarios in the area of quality in Higher Education and changes that bring with it paradigmatic ruptures in the student's teaching-learning process, which hides the search for autonomous learning, hence the importance of the conducive in identifying the strategies directed to each style of learning of the student, this link is directed towards the pretension of an optimal academic performance; That is why the empty contribution that this study throws through the following hypotheses.
This research work aims to identify the learning styles and their correlation with academic performance in course "Cost Elements", in students of the public accountant career of a Business School of the Northeast of Mexico; demonstrated by its slope and R^2, by proposing learning strategies; for this purpose, the two alternative hypotheses are approved.

H1: Students who do not apply their learning style well, occupy developing a learning strategy to pretend an optimal academic performance.

Table 3 shows the percentages of students who obtained established scores to measure academic performance, according to the quality standards issued by the institution under study; the learning styles are the following: Active (91%), Theoretical (81%) and Pragmatic (82%) obtained a higher percentage in the average $\leq$ 84 of the grade, emphasizing the Active style due to the small number of subjects therefore showing a higher percentage in the variable already mentioned (<84).

In Figure 4, the correlation between academic performance and the "Theoretical" type style is shown, with an $R^2 = 0.0015$ and its negative descending slope -0.0023. These indicate that the students who develop this learning style did not increase their academic performance, but on the contrary, that the use of cost elements decreased in the unit of learning. *The H1 is approved*

While Figure 2 indicates that the Pragmatic learning style shows a positive correlation 0.2073; however, its slope is negative -0.0267 because the students in this learning style, require a facilitator to claim optimal academic performance. *The H1 is approved*

The *H2: Students who apply their learning style obtain an optimal academic advantage. This hypothesis is approved* with Figure 3, which shows that the "Active" learning style with an $R^2 = 1$ and its ascending slope is 0.375, and with Figure 1, where the "Reflective" style is observed with an $R^2 = 0.1112$ and its ascending slope 0.0448. Both learning styles reflect a significant correlation and an ascending slope, which indicates that students are autonomous in their learning. Table 3 shows 33% of the students who developed the Reflective learning style, with an average grade $\geq$85. Because this (Reflective) style has a better academic performance, *the approval of this hypothesis is confirmed (H2).*

6. RECOMMENDATIONS

It is suggested that the teacher at the beginning of each school year apply a questionnaire of Learning Styles to identify and address based on the learning style the teacher; and in this way to link the teaching strategies with the learning styles in communion to the learning unit, being these some of the factors that help the learner in an agile and skillful way to process information that is used in the teaching-learning process by detonating in the development of competences, attitudes and abilities for the construction of an autonomous learning where it probably has repercussions towards the search of an optimal academic performance.

Based on the results obtained from this research and in compliance with the objective, the following learning proposals are presented. With the descriptions that distinguish each learning style, according to the Kolb theory model, we propose the following learning strategies as viable, according to the styles that apply to the students in the LU Cost Elements. a) *Analysis and interpretation of real commercial situations, for the reasonable determination of the accounting record of a transaction.* Which is suggested to the students with *Reflective* and *Theoretical* style by facilitating the critical analysis and possessing the ability to carefully observe each of the transactions to make the decision in a well-founded manner, as well as to carry out the process of the information where they use logic by detonating the reasoning in the accounting record of the transactions of an entity. The learner with *Active style* like the previous ones fits into this same strategy. By developing the ability to solve practical cases based on real situations when considering it as a novel learning experience and attractive in its understanding. The *pragmatic style* shows an interest in the practical problems of real cases, hence its spontaneous decision-making. b) *Solution of online cases (business simulators) to respond to a problem or situation.* We recommend for students in the LU Elements of Cost, familiarization with the use of technology and remote applications, which will help them develop and implement other styles, acquiring new skills, attitudes and competencies in the search for problem solving that appear in their environment. c) *Determination of flows of information systems based on the application of accounting logic.* Consider the *theoretical style* since it can develop the ability to easily understand the sequence and logic of the processes that are applied in the LU cost elements. On the other hand, *Reflective style* for its agile ability to observe complex situations and allows them to perform the analysis under a skillful scheme, to establish a detailed conclusion of each situation raised.

REFERENCES

Acevedo, C, & Rocha, F. (2011). Estilos de aprendizaje, género y rendimiento académico. *Revista Estilos de Aprendizaje, Vol.8, No. 8* octubre; Universidad de Concepción, Concepción, Chile Extraído https://www2.uned.es/revistaestilosdeaprendizaje/numero_8/articulos/lsr_8_articulo_5.pdf

Cantú Hinojosa, I.L. (2004). El Estilo de Aprendizaje y la relación con el desempeño académico de los estudiantes de arquitectura de la UANL.*Ciencia UANL. Vol. VII* No.1 Enero-Marzo 2004.

Gallego Rodríguez, A., & Martínez Caro, E. (2003). Estilos de aprendizaje y e-learning. Hacia un mayor rendimiento académico. *RED. Revista de Educación a Distancia, (7)* p.4.

García, Sánchez, Jiménez y Gutiérrez. (2012). Estilos de Aprendizaje y Estrategias de Aprendizaje: un estudio en discentes de posgrado. *Revista de estilos de aprendizaje, Vol.10, No.. 10*. Pp.8-9

Isaza Valencia, L. (2014). Estilos de Aprendizaje: una apuesta por el desempeño académico de los estudiantes en la Educación Superior. *Revista Encuentros, 12(2),* pp.25-34.

Nisbet, J.; Shucksmith, J. (1986). Learning Strategies. Routiedge & Kegan Paul, Londres. Trad. cast.de Bermejo, A. (1987): *Estrategias de aprendizaje*. Santillana/Aula XXI, Madrid.

Pizarro, R. (1985). Rasgos y actitudes del profesor efectivo (Tesis de Maestría). Pontificia Universidad Católica de Chile.Mariscal.

SOCIAL LEARNING NETWORKING DIGITAL AFFORDANCE DESIGN

Ben Chang and Rotua Zendrato
Institute of Learning and Instruction, National Central University, Taiwan
No. 300, Zhongda Rd., Zhongli District, Taoyuan City 32001, Taiwan (R.O.C.)

ABSTRACT

Social networking platforms, such as Facebook, WeChat, and Line, are affecting and reshaping on how we think and what we communicate. This phenomenon reveals that the use of social networking platforms might not only be in private daily life but also in learning as well as teaching. For learning purpose on social networking platforms, we will argue that a learning activity needs a deliberate program and clear design principles. Based on the argument, in this article, we elaborate an idea named digital affordance and propose a digital affordance model following three types' practical activities.

KEYWORDS

Social Networking Platform, Learning Activity Design, Digital Affordance

1. INTRODUCTION

Tremendous students use social networking platforms for communicating and sharing thoughts every day. The phenomenon is inspiring researchers to consider how to apply social networking platforms to support learners' teaching and learning. Although traditional classrooms have many advantages including face-to-face lecturing, in-class small group discussions and so on, social networking platforms taking the advantages of multimedia, dynamic, instant, and ubiquitous computing can further provide traditional classrooms with pre-class, in-class and after-class learning activities for learners to exchange thoughts and ideas seamlessly. However, on social networking platforms for the learning purpose, teachers and students need well-designed learning activities since learning has its pedagogical and unique approaches. Obviously, it is worth to explore how to design a good instructional and learning approach on social networking platforms (Hung & Yuen, 2010) so that the social networking platforms can be applied for learning purpose.

Affordance proposed by Gibson (1979) has been using over the decades in many disciplines (Blewett & Hugo, 2016; You & Chen, 2007; Hartson, 2003), which well explains how a learner is affected in an environment whatever it is in a natural environment or a manipulated environment. Social networking platforms reveal various new opportunities to traditional affordance settings, which inspire researchers considering the possibility of extending traditional affordance to digital affordance. To sum above, having learning activities on social networking platforms need well design and the aim of this paper is to explore a digital affordance model and its' possibility of digital affordance design in a social networking environment.

2. DIGITAL AFFORDANCE

As mentioned above, Gibson's affordance theory (1979) is well accepted, and now the technology evolution makes the traditional affordance settings can be digitalized. Compared with the traditional affordance, digital affordance has many advantages, such as dynamic, multimedia, anytime, anywhere and so on. Below, the attributes of digital affordance are elaborated from several perspectives.

2.1 Traditional Affordance vs. Digital Affordance

Digital affordance compared to traditional affordance idea has many advantages. Figure 1 elaborates the advantages from the environment, affordance type, participant role, and participant location perspectives.

The differences between traditional and digital affordances are discussed below:

- Environment: The affordance settings in a traditional environment are used to be physical, fixed, and hard to change. However, the settings of a digital affordance on an online social networking platform can be very dynamic and easy to be re-arranged.
- Affordance Type: The traditional affordance due to physical constraint is usually practiced face-to-face, but the digital affordance can be either face-to-face or non-face-to-face.
- Participant Role: The participants in the traditional affordance environment should be real persons. However, in the digital affordance environment, the participants can be real users, remote users, or even non-real users, such as avatars and non-player characters created and manipulated by the computer.
- Participant Location: The participants' location in the traditional environment should be in the same place, but on a social networking platform, the affordance activities can occur in many different places simultaneously.

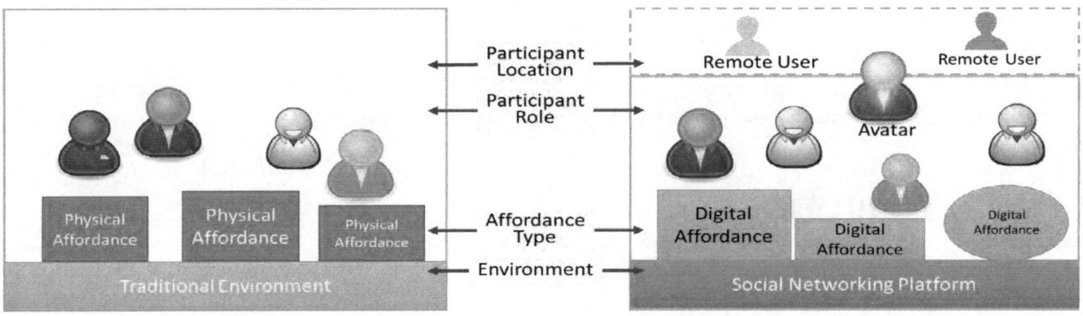

Figure 1. Affordance design in a traditional environment and social networking environment

2.2 Digital Affordance Role in Social Learning Networking

To illustrate how a digital affordance is applied in a social learning networking environment, a model with four layers including social networking platforms, basic tools, digital affordances, and learning activities is proposed. As shown in Figure 2, the first layer of the model is the social networking platforms layer. Various social networking platforms, such as Facebook, Line, and Twitter, are available for users to have interactive activities in this layer. Beyond the social networking platforms, as the second layer of the model, various basic tools with functions such as file uploading, photo taking, video exchanging, chatting, etc. support the activities occurred on the social networking platforms. Based on the basic tools layer, many designed digital affordances are available, and beyond the digital affordances, many learning activities are provided.

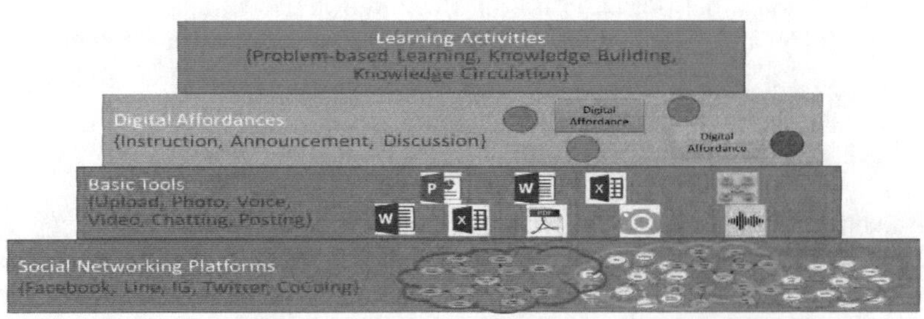

Figure 2. Social learning networking combining with digital affordance model

As a digital affordance, there are several attributes illustrated below:

- The first attribute of a digital affordance is its GOAL SETTING or AGENDA SETTING. Goal setting or agenda setting attribute lets the teachers and the students can have a shared vision.
- The second attribute of digital affordance is TIME SEQUENCE. The time sequence can be pre-class, in-class or after-class.
- The third attribute of digital affordance is ASYNCHRONOUS or SYNCHRONOUS, which means that digital affordance can be designed as an asynchronous or synchronous activity.
- The fourth attribute of digital affordance is an INSTANT MESSAGE or NON-INSTANT MESSAGE. This means that the interaction among the users can be instant messages activity or non-instant messages activity.

Currently, only four digital affordance attributes are proposed. However, more attributes might be found in further exploration.

2.3 Digital Affordance Examples

To illustrate what is a digital affordance and how it operates, three examples are proposed below. These digital affordances design can be applied for social learning networking platforms to conduct learning activities.

2.3.1 Type I: Idea Generation, Discussion, and Integration Activity

As shown in Figure 3, type I example illustrates how a digital affordance is applied to support idea generation, discussion, and integration learning activity.

<u>Pre-class activity</u>

In this case, at the pre-class stage, the teachers or students need to set the learning goal or learning agenda. All the students at this stage generate as many ideas as possible non-face-to-face asynchronously on the social networking platform.

<u>In-class activity</u>

In the class, the students are assigned to their groups according to their pre-class discussion to discuss and to settles down their ideas. Each of the group students illustrates their idea at the end of the class. Instant message software can be applied in the in-class activity to support the students to incorporate their discussions of a topic.

<u>After-class activity</u>

After the class, all the students need to have some reflections on their social learning networking to extend the learning effect. The asynchronous discussion board can be applied at this stage.

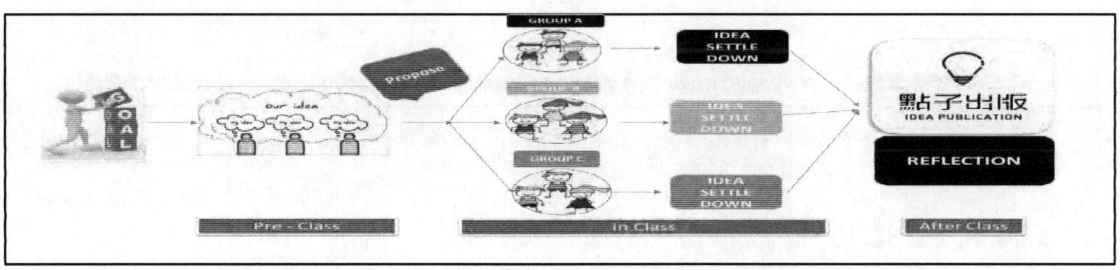

Figure 3. Type I: Idea generation, discussion, and integration activity

2.3.2 Type II: Topic-oriented Discussion, Idea Settle Down, Meta-Analysis, and Reflection

As shown in Figure 4, type II example illustrates how a digital affordance is applied in a topic-oriented discussion, settling down idea, meta-analysis, and reflection.

<u>Pre-class activity</u>

In the pre-class stage, the students are grouped, and they have their own topic to study in their group. Before the class, the students with their team members need to settle down their idea. Synchronous software like video conferencing or asynchronous software like discussion board can be applied in this stage.

In-class activity

In the class, all the students elaborate their subject discussed in the group to others and try to integrate their subject into a complete one. Once they finish their topic discussion, they all have the meta-analysis activity on the complete topic together.

After-class activity

They all have the topic reflection in the after-class activity. Asynchronous software can support reflection.

Figure 4. Type II: Topic-oriented discussion, idea settle down, meta-analysis, and reflection

2.3.3 Type III: Topic Study following with Exercise, and Peer Review

As shown in Figure 5, type III example illustrates how a digital affordance can support topic study, exercise, and peer review activity.

Pre-class activity

At the pre-class stage, the students acquire their domain knowledge by themselves. Through the self-learning activity, the students consolidate their background knowledge.

In-class activity

In the class, all the students study the topic and do the exercise together. The synchronous tool can be applied to have the coordinate activity.

After-class activity

After the class, the students reflect their topic discussion and exercise results.

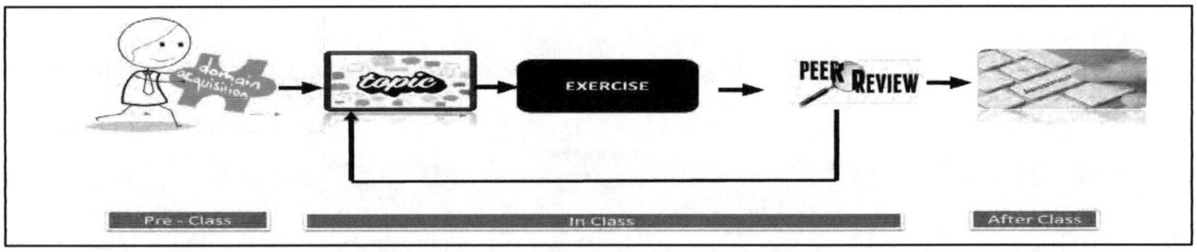

Figure 5. Type III: Topic study following with exercise, and peer review

3. CONCLUSION

Social networking platforms have become ubiquitous in our daily life, and have demonstrated their potential to assist with learning. However, applying social networking platforms for education and learning purposes need deliberate designs. In this study, the authors extend the traditional affordance concept to digital affordance. On the digital affordance concept, four attributes including goal/agenda setting, time sequence, asynchronous/synchronous, and instant/non-instant messages are discussed. Meanwhile, three digital affordance types are illustrated. Currently, the study focuses on digital affordance idea elaboration. In the future, these digital affordances need to be explored on social learning networking platforms and study their effects.

REFERENCES

Blewett, C., & Hugo, W. (2016). Actant affordances: A brief history of affordance theory and a Latourian extension for education technology research. *Critical Studies in Teaching and Learning, 4*(1), 55-76.

Gibson, J. J. (1979). *The ecological approach to visual perception*. New York: Houghton Mifflin.

Hartson, R. (2003). Cognitive, physical, sensory, and functional affordances in interaction design. *Behaviour & Information Technology, 22*(5), 315-338.

You, H. C., & Chen, K. (2007). Applications of affordance and semantics in product design. *Design Studies, 28*(1), 23-38.

SECURITY VULNERABILITIES IN MODERN LMS

Alexei Scerbakov, Frank Kappe and Nikolai Scerbakov
Graz University of Technology, Graz (Austria)

ABSTRACT

An effective learning management system (LMS) is a vital component of an E-Learning infrastructure in universities nowadays. Learning Management System can be seen as a structured repository of courseware materials provided with additional communication facilities such as discussion forum, annotations, chats, etc. LMS can be also seen as a communication area where students upload their assignments and get feedback from the teachers. From the technical perspective, LMS is an Internet-Based Information system serving a big number of remote users. In this paper, we present a list of security issues that we experienced during the years of practical LMS usage on the university level. We especially investigate security issues that are specific for the modern LMS that are constructed in accordance with the so-called AJAX architecture. The practical value of this paper is defined by possible reproduction of the security preconditions that are also described in the paper.

KEYWORDS

E-Learning, Learning Management System, Software Architecture, Cloud Service, Security

1. INTRODUCTION

Learning Management System is a vital component of the educational infrastructure in schools and universities. From the technical perspective, LMS is an Internet-Based Information system serving a big number of remote users (Cochran, 2015; Ramani, 2017; Uzunboylu, Bicen & Cavus, 2011). Common LMS functionality includes libraries of educational materials, course announcements, file repositories, curriculum descriptions, file exchange, discussion forums, chats, email exchange, online quizzes, opinion polls, document annotation, evaluation facilities (Ramani, 2017; Uzunboylu et al., 2011; Dobre, 2015), etc. Modern LMS are often built using comparatively new architectural solutions known as Asynchronous Java and XML (AJAX) (Khanna & Mistry, 2012). Two aspects make LMS a frequent target for security attacks. LMS is a huge repository of sensitive data and the system functionality is highly important for the university as such. Hence, the LMS must be provided with a relevant level of security. Graz University of Technology has been using LMS for 20 years. During such a long period of actual application of the system for serving dozens of thousand students simultaneously, a number of basic security threats were identified and the attacks were successfully prevented.

In this paper, we mainly concentrate on security vulnerabilities that are related to the specific functionality of LMS and to special properties of AJAX architecture. It is demonstrated that LMS vendors need to take these kinds of threats seriously.

2. COMMON LMS SECURITY THREATS

LMS must support a certain functionality by definition (A. Scerbakov, Ebner & N. Scerbakov, 2015; N. Scerbakov, 2018; Kappe & N. Scerbakov, 2017). Thus, there must be facilities for

- uploading students' training assignments and other materials to the server;
- commenting on the materials on the server;
- participation in the topic or course-oriented discussion forums;
- checking the students' knowledge online, etc.

All such LMS specific actions create reasonable security threats that are discussed below.

2.1 Sharing User Accounts

Assessing learner progress is an important phase of e-learning programs (N. Scerbakov, Kappe & Pak, 2018). To grade the students' progress with the educational materials, teachers need to carry out certain evaluations and assessments. Potentially electronic exams is a highly effective tool for testing learner knowledge.

An important component of the electronic examination is correct identifying the student that performs the e-learning tasks. Simply stated, the credentials issued for the particular student must be used

- by this particular student;
- exclusively by this student;
- by the student without assistance from other students.

We address a possible violation of the rules above as "Sharing User Accounts". There are potentially three methods for assuring fair play during the online examinations:

The first method is rather obvious, the online examination is carried out from an especially allocated room equipped with a sufficient number of computers. In this case, the examination is monitored by the teacher or an assistant who is responsible for checking the user IDs, and their behavior during the examination.

Another method is based on the usage of video conferencing software. In this case, all the students must login into the video session first. The teacher may check the students' IDs and behavior during the examination by means of the video conferencing tool.

Finally, the LMS may be equipped with the special software component that can:

- Randomly make snap shots of the user in front of computers;
- Recognize the faces to prove that the students with the particular credentials, are indeed seating in front of computers.
- Recognize the scene in front of the computer to prove that the student works alone and is not assisted by someone else seating along.

2.2 Deny of Services via Uploading

Any LMS provides facilities for gathering (uploading) students' assignments, commenting and evaluating the assignments by teachers (N. Scerbakov & Kappe, 2018). Normally, this functionality is provided by the combination of two components: HTML form on the client that allows selecting the local file for uploading and a server-side component that get the HTTP request from the form and physically creates the new file on the server.

There are two aspects that make this situation potentially dangerous:

- HTML 4.0 does not allow to check size and extension of the file selected by the user before physical uploading this file on the server.
- The HTML form contains all the information on the server application (URL + parameters) as plain text.

As a result, users may potentially select files of a rather big size and send them for uploading. For example, we monitored attempts to upload whole distributions of operating systems, huge movie files, etc.

More dangerous would be a usage of Internet bots that send requests to the uploading URL automatically with the correct set of parameters. Such bots can easily initiate uploading of hundreds of files in a second. This may cause "deny of service" for other users.

LMS can be easily protected from this kind of malicious activity. Recent extension (HTML 5.0) provide a special file object that allows reading size and extension of local files before uploading. Thus, the LMS may be easily prevented from uploading oversized files of the wrong type. Uploading bots can be prevented from the functionality by using special tokens giving permission for uploading as parameters of the HTML forms (see below).

2.3 Injection of Malicious Code

The malicious code can be injected for two reasons (A. Scerbakov, Kappe & N. Scerbakov, 2018). The first and most common situation is an attempt to post the executable code or fragment of such code to the server where it can be executed to retrieve some sensitive data or disrupt the server functionality.

Obviously, the files containing the executable code can be uploaded as student assignments (see above). Such HTML 5.0 extension as the new "file" objects allows verification of the files on the client site before uploading. Unfortunately, such verification of files on the client is not fully sufficient. As it was mentioned above, the file uploading transactions to the server can be easily mocked up. Hence, special preconditions like temporary tokens are needed. Moreover, all the files uploaded by the students must be verified on the server immediately after uploading.

Another type of thread is based on code snippets embedded into textual messages to be interpreted on the user clients. The simplest way for this kind of attacks is embedding references to external JavaScript files or the JavaScript snippets directly into texts of messages or comments. The messages and comments are visualized on the client as components of the dynamically generated HTML files, and, thus, will be automatically interpreted on the clients.

Many people think that injection JavaScript fragments is not dangerous and can be seen as a kind of kidding. In reality, such fragments can be used to carry out serious attacks on the clients and the server.

Thus, for example, JavaScript code may access the cookies on the client computer, the cookies normally contain the session ID. The "xmlhttp" JavaScript object may potentially send the session ID to another server. If the session ID is used as the special token for the verification of the HTTP requests, the server security can be essentially compromised. Client security can be also very seriously compromised. For example, if the generated HTML document contains references to other files as for example for downloading the files from the trusted server, the references can be easily scanned and replaced with references to other malicious executable files. The files then will be downloaded by users as training materials and potentially executed locally. Hence, the LMS must automatically scan all the incoming messages and remove any executable fragments and/or JavaScript references to other servers.

3. AJAX SECURITY THREATS

Many LMS are implemented nowadays as so-called AJAX applications. AJAX is a technique for accessing Web services from the client by means of special XMLHTTP JavaScript objects. AJAX-based LMS can be seen as a combination of two main components: server-side WEB services (Back-End Application) and an especially developed client (Front-End application). Front-End is developed using concepts of HTML objects and JavaScript programming. This combination of HTML and JavaScript is called Dynamic HTML (DHTML).

DHTML documents can be downloaded from the server and visualized on the browser screen. The documents are dynamic in the sense that the documents change their appearance directly on the client without re-loading the documents from the server. Such DHTML documents can access the WEB services and request data from the server. The client sends the HTTP request to the server by means of the special JavaScript object. The WEB service processes the request on the server site and sends the response back to the client. The client gets the response and processes data on the client side. Normally, Front-End and Back-End components use Extensible Markup Language (XML) and/or JavaScript Object Notation (JSON) as a communication protocol.

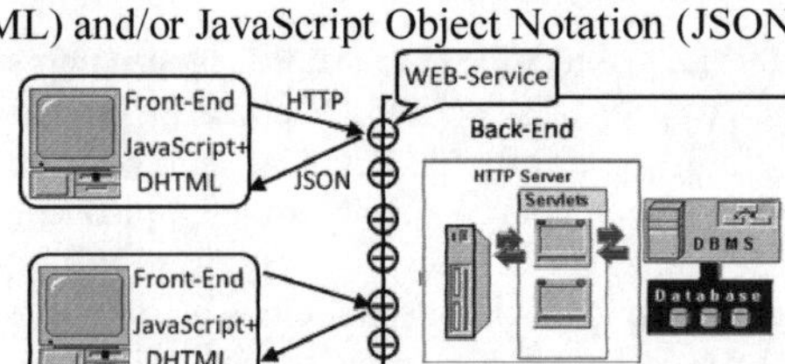

Figure 1. AJAX Architecture

AJAX architecture has a number of well-known advantages:

- Such systems demonstrate very good performance and comfortable response time because the user actions do not require re-loading HTML pages from the server;
- The workload on the server site is greatly decreased since the server just implements a number of WEB services for accessing/modifying database, and all the data processing is carried out on the client side.

Thus, such applications facilitate user satisfaction with the system functionality and performance especially in the situations where hundreds or even thousands of students work simultaneously in the condition of time restrictions, for example, online examination, approaching deadlines, etc. Moreover, the actual configuration of the production server for the LMS back-end does not require powerful hardware and/or special software solutions like server clusters, load balancers, reverse proxy, etc.

Another important aspect of this architectural solution is a possibility to use multiple front-ends for communicating with one and the same Back-End (Cloud). In other words, there may be different user-clients that can be used in different circumstances (desktop client, tablet, smartphone, etc.) working with the same WEB Services. Even mobile applications that are distributed via vendor-oriented software repositories (application shops) can be developed as such clients for the AJAX applications.

Moreover, the architecture provides new possibilities for implementing User Interface in LMS. Traditionally, User Interface is implemented as a combination of „Jump" actions when users click on active HTML fragments - so-called "Anchors", to download and visualize another document. AJAX architecture allows using such modern User Interface solutions as - document event model, dynamic prompts, floating windows and virtual pop-ups. The AJAX architecture allows embedding so-called local sensors into the communication between users and the system as well. Thus, video camera, information on the current location, sound, etc. can be used as the interface elements.

AJAX architecture itself creates a certain security threat. Recollect that we see the AJAX based system as two components – Front-End and Back-End that communicate by means of the HTTP protocol. The Front-End generates HTTP requests by means of JavaScript objects. The Back-End process the requests, potentially retrieve and/or modify data and generate the response to the server. The security of such AJAX LMS can be compromised by means of two types of attacks discussed below.

3.1 Mocking the Client-Server Communication

The functionality of the AJAX LMS is distributed over two different components – Front-End and Back-End. Back-End is normally responsible for retrieving the data from the database and modifying the data in the database. Front-End implements GUI and certain data processing logic. Thus, the Back-End component expects HTTP requests that come from the relevant Front-End. The requests invoke WEB Services that retrieve and/or modify the data in accordance with the logic of the data processing implemented by the client. The WEB services potentially can be invoked by any Internet client that can mock the request format (see Figure 2).

In this case, the WEB services are invoked without the proper Front-End context and potentially can illegally retrieve the data, or even do the illegal modifications of the database. This problem can be efficiently solved by dynamically generated tokens that identify authorized clients. The tokens can be applied using the following schema: as a particular client is authorized, the system generates a token that is kept on the server as a session variable and on a client as a JavaScript variable. Any further requests are additionally authorized with this token that is checked on the server before fulfilling the request.

This method is not secure enough since the token value is kept on the client as a JavaScript variable, and the token value is valid for a number of requests. Thus, after performing the first request, the value may be read and used to generate a further set of requests.

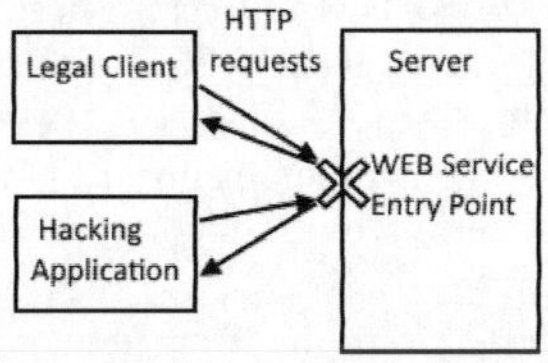

Figure 2. Mocking the client-server communication

In cases that require a higher level of security, tokens are generated for each request.

3.2 Changing JavaScript on the Client Site

The second type of security leak is explained by the main AJAX principle where software (JavaScript functions) are fetched from the server and evaluated on the client side. Using a simple tool like FireBug, anyone can change JavaScript code and parameters on the client side. If anyone takes time and studies LMS for a while, they can learn how to change JavaScript code resulting in hacking LMS.

Actually, the problem of manipulation with client-side scripts does not have an ultimate solution in AJAX. The only possible remedy is double checking the most sensitive transactions on the server site. For example, if a WEB service that returns info on a particular student by ID is invoked, the WEB service may check whether the client has really got rights to do so by checking user-name and privileges on the server session. Generally speaking, when any JavaScript function calls the WEB service, the server side needs to check if this client is authorized to do this action. Building additional server-side permissions mechanism to prevent unwanted actions takes a lot of time and almost double the LMS development expenses. To implement such a mechanism, for every action the LMS must validate it on the server, and can only do this by fetching the needed data from DB.

Of course, some security preconditions can be done on the client site as well. Obvious things could be decreasing readability of the JavaScript. JavaScript files can be compressed and all the function/variable names replaced with plain numeric notation. The JavaScript fragments can look, for example, as:

```
var v000234=false;var v000237='';var v000238='';var v000244='/wbtmaster/room_icn/';function
v000315(v000656){var v000234=v000656;var v000237=v000656.indexOf(';'+v000713+':');
if(v000612==-1) ...
```

The other method is based on checking the flow of control between the JavaScript functions. The function may identify a so-called "caller", i.e. another function that calls this one. The list of all legal callers can be predefined, and if the function is called from a not-legal caller, the function may send an alert to the server.

REFERENCES

Cochran, K. (2015). Report - LMS Trends 2015: Is it Time for Something Different? Retrieved from https://www.docebo.com/blog/report-lms-trends-2015-brandon-hall/

Dobre, I. (2015). Learning Management Systems for Higher Education - An Overview of Available Options for Higher Education Organizations. Procedia - Social and Behavioral Sciences, 180, 313-320. doi:10.1016/j.sbspro.2015.02.122

Kappe, F., & Scerbakov, N. (2017). File Uploading Scenarios in a Modern Learning Management System. In L.G. Chova, A.L. Martínez & I.C. Torres (Eds.), Proceedings of EDULEARN17, 9th International Conference on Education and New Learning Technologies (pp. 4904-4909), Barcelona, Spain: IATED Academy. doi:10.21125/edulearn.2017.2100

Khanna, S.V.O., & Mistry M. (2012). Impact of Ajax in Web Applications. International Journal of Advanced Engineering Technology, 3(1), 144-145. e-ISSN: 0976-3945

Ramani, R. (2017). 2017 Preview: 11 Learning Management System Technology Trends by the Industry's Top Analysts. Retrieved from https://elearningindustry.com/11-learning-management-system-technology-trends-top-analysts-2017-preview

Scerbakov, A, Kappe, F. & Scerbakov N. (2018). Block-Chain Based Grading Students Assignments. In L.G. Chova, A.L. Martínez & I.C. Torres (Eds.), Proceedings of ICERI2018, 11th International Conference on Educational Data Mining (pp. 8773-8778), Seville, Spain: IATED Academy. doi:10.21125/iceri.2018.0615

Scerbakov, A., Ebner, M., Scerbakov, N. (2015). Using Cloud Services in a Modern Learning Management System. Journal of Computing and Information Technology, 23(1), 75-86. doi:10.2498/cit.1002517

Scerbakov, N. & Kappe, F. (2018). WBT-Master - Modern Learning Management System. In R. Damaševičius, G. Vasiljevienė (Eds.), Proceedings of the 24th International Conference on Information and Software Technologies, ICIST 2018, Vilnius Lithuania, Communications in Computer and Information Science, 920, 461-475. doi:0.1007/978-3-319-99972-2_38

Scerbakov, N. (2018). TU Graz WBT-Master. Retrieved from http://coronet.iicm.tugraz.at/wbtmaster/welcome.html

Scerbakov, N., Kappe, F. & Pak, V. (2018). Collaborative Document Authoring as an E-Learning Component. In T. Bastiaens, J. Van Braak, M. Brown, L. Cantoni, M. Castro, R. Christensen, G. Davidson-Shivers, K. DePryck, M. Ebner, M. Fominykh, C. Fulford, S. Hatzipanagos, G. Knezek, K. Kreijns, G. Marks, E. Sointu, E. Korsgaard Sorensen, J. Viteli, J. Voogt, P. Weber, E. Weippl & O. Zawacki-Richter (Eds.), Proceedings of EdMedia, World Conference on Educational Media and Technology (pp. 101-107), Amsterdam, Netherlands: Association for the Advancement of Computing in Education (AACE).

Uzunboylu, H., Bicen, H., & Cavus, N. (2011). The Efficient Virtual Learning Environment: A Case Study of Web 2.0 Tools and Windows Live Spaces. Computers & Education, 56(3), 720-726. doi:10.1016/j.compedu.2010.10.014

EFFECTS OF EPISTEMIC PREPARATIVE ACTIVITIES ON STUDENTS' UNDERSTANDING IN A FLIPPED CLASSROOM

Wakako Fushikida[1], Hiroki Oura[2] and Ryo Yoshikawa[3]
[1]*University Education Center, Tokyo Metropolitan University, Japan*
[2]*Center for Innovative Teaching and Learning, Tokyo Institute of Technology, Japan*
[3]*Faculty of Information and Media Studies, Nagoya Bunri University, Japan*

ABSTRACT

This study aims to evaluate cognitive learning outcomes using a comprehension test in a flipped classroom designed to integrate both acquisition and utilization of new knowledge. In this study, as *epistemic preparative activities* (EPA), we proposed authentic adventure games that are relevant to the learning contents of lecture videos and face-to-face activities, which can encourage students to understand and apply knowledge. Furthermore, we compared students' scores in the comprehension tests between an *individual EPA group* and a *collaborative EPA group,* in order to determine which EPA style has a greater advantage in a flipped classroom model. These findings indicate that the *collaborative EPA group* tended to perceive greater understanding of the material. We assumed that collaborative EPA effectively encourages students in knowledge acquisition and construction.

KEYWORDS

Flipped Classroom, Epistemic Cognition, Statistical Education

1. INTRODUCTION

1.1 Review of Previous Studies

The flipped classroom model was invented in the United States around the year 2000, and spread to primary and secondary education as a part of teachers' grassroots efforts within the country. It was rapidly introduced in Japan in the 2010s as a new effective teaching method. Flipped classroom is an instructional approach that employs lecture videos and quizzes as homework assignments before class. Students engage in advanced tasks with individual tutoring or interactive and collaborative activities during class. According to Bergmann and Sams (2014), the shift in direct instruction from traditional lectures to teacher-created videos produces richer and more meaningful experiences for students in face-to-face learning.

Even though flipped classroom is considered an extremely innovative approach, there is a history that has been practically improved through trial and error by the teachers in charge. In the process of development, some previous studies emphasized the necessity to connect the flipped classroom's online learning with face-to-face activities to facilitate leaner knowledge construction and application in higher-order thinking (Strayer, 2012, Kim *et al.*, 2014). However, there are few studies that explore design principles and look objectively at the evaluation of learning outcomes (Bishop & Verleger, 2013).

1.2 Perception of the Present Study

This study aims to evaluate cognitive learning outcomes using a comprehension test in a flipped classroom designed to integrate both acquisition and utilization of new knowledge. Some earlier studies suggested the effectiveness of *preparation for future learning* (PFL), that engages students in some exploratory activities before conducting lectures and explanation of learning content (Schwartz & Martin, 2004, Schneider & Blikstein 2015, Oura *et al.* 2018). Based on these findings, we incorporated problem-solving activities using an adventure game into PFL before students watched lecture videos as online learning. The following research questions were explored: (1) What changes have occurred in students' understanding? (2) What kind of PFL activities are effective for achieving learning outcomes?

Recently, *epistemic cognition* (EC), which is related to acquisition, understanding, judgement, and application of knowledge, has drawn attention in the context of complicated modern societies. EC involves thoughts about people's behaviors that are concerned with what and how people perceive knowledge, and activation of EC is helpful for effective learning (Greene *et al.*, 2016). In this study, as *epistemic preparative activities* (EPA), we proposed authentic adventure games that are relevant to the learning contents of lecture videos and face-to-face activities, which can encourage students to understand and apply knowledge. Furthermore, we compared students' scores in the comprehension tests between two EPA groups in order to determine which EPA style has an advantage in a flipped classroom.

2. METHODS

We conducted a flipped classroom experiment in an introductory course "X" of statistical and data analysis during the winter semester of 2018 at Y University in Tokyo. Fig 1. shows the schedule of this practical experiment. First, students played statistical adventure games for about 30-45 minutes, individually or collaboratively, in class as EPA. They read a story which assumes a population with a certain probability distribution, and solved scenario-based problems (such as "Which store has the longest waiting time?") that involved the collection of sample data by choosing a sample size (N=10, 100, or 1000) and interpreting histograms, boxplots, and descriptive statistics (Figure 2).

Prior to the next class, they were required to watch lecture videos uploaded on the dedicated webpage using a personalized login ID and password. The five online videos (of about four and a half minutes each) dealt with basic statistical concepts such as "parameter estimation," "normal distribution," and "histogram." Finally, in class, they collaboratively solved practical statistical problems in smalls group (of about four students each). All students were allowed access to the lecture videos and computation tools, and instructed to share their thinking process with each other during problem solving.

Seventeen undergraduate students participated in the course, including one overseas student, and agreed to our request of experimental cooperation. They included 11 males (68.8%) and 5 females (31.3%), 14 first-year students (87.5%) and 2 students of other grades (12.5%), and 4 students of humanities (25.0%) and 12 students of science (75.0%). We divided the 17 students into two groups: 6 students in the *individual EPA group*, and 11 students in the *collaborative EPA group,* which included three sub-groups. There were differences between the two groups in terms of activity style; the former engaged in EPA individually, while the latter played the statistical adventure games collaboratively.

We administered pre- (before EPA), middle- (after EPA and watching lecture videos), and post- (after face-to-face collaborative inquiry activities) comprehension tests in order to evaluate students' understanding. A total of sixteen valid responses were obtained, excluding one absentee. The three tests were identical and were designed with regard to the following: "population and sample," "frequency distribution table and histogram," "parameter estimation," and "normal distribution and representative value." They included multiple choice questions, written components, and computational problems, with no use of calculators or spreadsheet software. Each question was scored as 0, 0.5, or 1 by the first author of this paper. The average scores were 10.25 (*S.D.*=1.68) in the pre-test, 12.05 (*S.D.*=2.20) in the middle-test, and 12.48 (*S.D.*=1.74) in the post-test on a scale of 1 to 16.

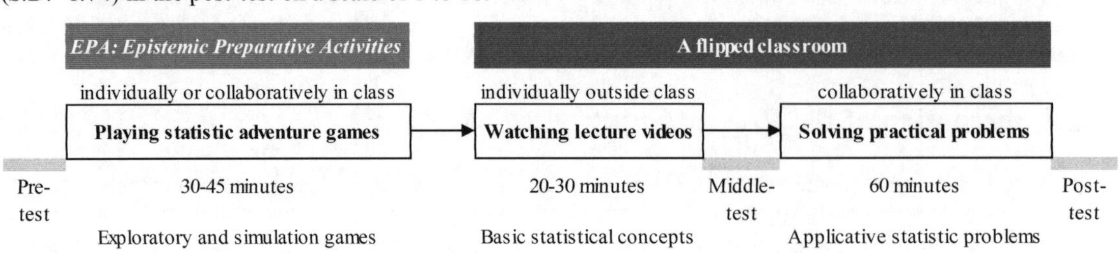

Figure 1. The schedule of the practical experiment

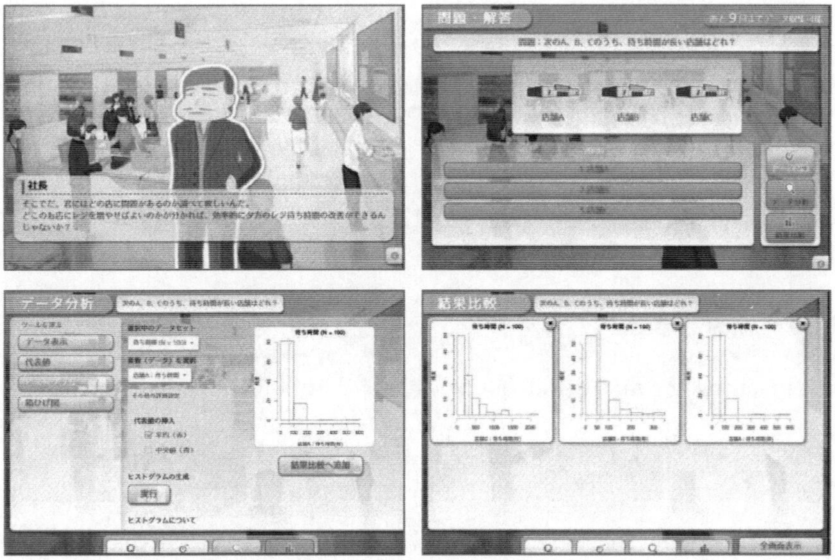

Figure 2. Screenshots of the statistical adventure games
(top left: a story of problem contexts; top right: a scenario-based problem; bottom left: analyzing data tools such as histograms and descriptive statistics; and bottom right: comparing results for answering the problem)

3. RESULTS AND DISCUSSION

We analyzed the comprehension test scores using a mixed-design analysis of variance model (also known as a split-plot ANOVA) to reveal the effects of a flipped classroom with EPA on students' understanding. The results in Figure 3 show that there were significant differences between test scores (F (2, 28) = 39.22, p = .00, η^2 = .74). According to a Holm's sequentially rejective Bonferroni test, in the *individual EPA group*, the post-score was significantly higher than the pre-score (d = 1.35, 95%CI = .15～2.56), and in the *collaborative EPA group*, the middle-score (d = .86, 95%CI = .00～1.72) and post-score (d = 1.10, 95%CI = .19～2.01) were significant higher than the pre-score. These findings indicate that the *collaborative EPA group* tended to perceive greater understanding of the material.

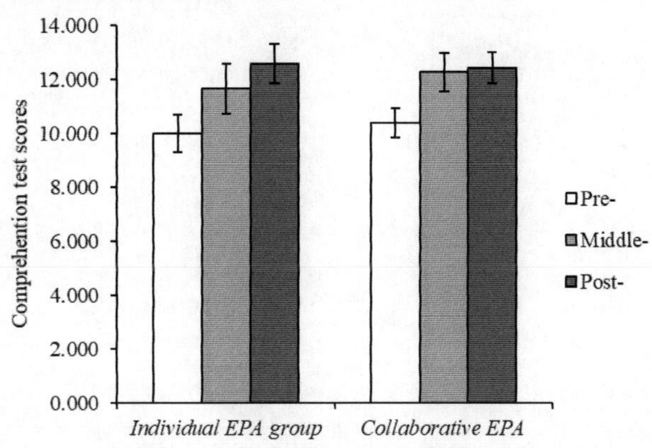

Figure 3. The result of ANOVA
(Error bars indicate standard error)

4. CONCLUSION

The present results suggested that a flipped classroom with EPA of statistical adventure games gradually improves students' understanding. Furthermore, we assumed that collaborative EPA effectively encourage students in knowledge acquisition and construction while watching lecture videos. However, in this study, the reason for which collaborative EPA have a greater effect than individual EPA remains to be identified. We would like to analyze log data of lecture videos and short reflection reports about EPA to consider the ways in which collaborative EPA motivate students to learn statistics.

ACKNOWLEDGEMENT

This work was supported by *JSPS KAKENHI Grant Numbers 18K02815.*

REFERENCES

Bergmann, J., & Sams, A. (2014). *Flipped Learning: Gateway to Student Engagement*. Eugene. OR: International Society for Technology in Education.

Bishop, L. J., & Verleger, A. M. (2013). The flipped classroom: a survey of the research. *120th ASEE Annual Conference & Exposition. American Society for Engineering Education*, Atlanta.

Greene, A. J., Sandoval, A. M., & Bråten, I. (2016) *Handbook of Epistemic Cognition*, Routledge: NY

Kim, K. M., Kim, M. S., Khera, O., & Getman, J. (2014). The experiences of three flipped classrooms in an urban university: an exploration of design principles. *Internet and Higher Education*, 22, 37-50.

Oura, H., Ikejiri, R., Nakaya, K., Yamamoto, R., & Yamauchi, Y. (2018). Preparing Students for Learning Statistics with Adventure Game: Learning Cycle Model of Gaming, Watching, and Practicing. In Kay, J. and Luckin, R. (Eds.) Rethinking Learning in the Digital Age: Making the Learning Sciences Count, *13th International Conference of the Learning Sciences (ICLS) 2018*, Volume 3. London, UK: International Society of the Learning Sciences.

Schneider, B. & Blikstein, P. (2015) Flipping the flipped classroom: a study of the effectiveness of video lectures versus constructivist exploration using tangible user interfaces. *IEEE Transactions on Learning Technologies*, 9(1): 5-17

Schwartz, D. L. & Martin, T. (2004). Inventing to prepare for future learning: The hidden efficiency of encouraging original student production in statistics instruction. *Cognition and Instruction*, 22(2): 129-184

Strayer, F. J. (2012). How learning in an inverted classroom influences cooperation, innovation and task orientation. *Learning Environments Research*, 15 (2), 171-193.

DEVELOPMENT OF PROJECT-BASED LEARNING (PBL) IN BLENDED LEARNING MODE FOR THE ACQUISITION OF DIGITAL COMPETENCE

Olga Arranz-García and Vidal Alonso Secades
Faculty of Education, Universidad Pontificia de Salamanca, Salamanca, Spain

ABSTRACT

The objective of this research is to know the perception of future teachers of Elementary and Early Childhood Education in Blended Learning mode of the Faculty of Education at the Pontifical University of Salamanca on the use of an innovative methodology as is the Project Based Learning (PBL) for the acquisition of digital competence. In order to do this, we are here presenting a didactic proposal using Project Based Learning (PBL) as a methodological approach, which is framed in the subject of Information and Communication Technologies (ICT) in the field of education.
A quantitative methodology has been carried out using the technique of the questionnaire for data collection. For the assessment, the Questionnaire of Effectiveness of the use of methodologies for Active Participation (CEMPA) has been used. This has been divided into 4 dimensions: Specific Skills, General Skills, Systemic and Interpersonal Skills (Carrasco, Donoso, Duarte-Atoche, Hernandez & Lopez, 2015). The outcomes are highly positive. These results are supported by other results obtained in former investigations which underwent similar research. Likewise, it is shown that the use of this methodology facilitates the acquisition of digital competence, as well as the development of different skills that are addressed with the use of this type of methodology.
In conclusion, it can be established that the PBL has helped students of the Blended Learning mode to obtain a significant learning both, in the Specific skills as in the General and Systemic ones. On the contrary, no significant learning in Interpersonal skills has been obtained. This may be due to the fact that students under the Blended Learning mode have little interaction with the rest of their peers since it takes place mainly through digital channels.

KEYWORDS

Project-Based Learning (PBL), Blended Learning, Information and Communication Technologies (ICTS), Digital Competence

1. INTRODUCTION

Today's teaching-learning process, stands out for the huge breakthrough caused by Information and Communication Technologies (ICTS) in the classroom. Likewise, the current educational legislation is determined to creating scenarios that are required for a didactic transformation that will place the student as an active subject in the teaching-learning process (Organic Law 8/2013).

Therefore, the impact of ICT in education requires teachers not only to be trained in the use of technological tools, but also the acquisition of new methodologies by applying innovative pedagogical strategies that promote optimal results, placing the student as a central axis of learning as well as fostering their multiple intelligences.

After reviewing several studies on the use of ICT in education (Area, 2008; Cabero, 2015; Cabero & Roman, 2006; Marquès, 2012; Salinas, 2008; Bustos & Gómez, 2018), many are the experts who state that technology itself, doesn't generate changes or improvements in education. An important factor is to analyze the methodology to be applied and the role that the teacher will perform in this teaching-learning process in order to obtain a successful result. The educator becomes a designer of learning spaces, and technology plays a mediating role in the construction of knowledge and social interaction(Cabero, 2015).

In this sense, the educational law also states that one of the basic skills that students must acquire is the Digital Competence (RD 126/2014), but before this really occurs, teachers need to accomplish this objective as well.

As indicated by García-Valcárcel & Basilotta (2017), students' motivation for learning through the implementation of projects in a collaborative way using technological tools goes hand in hand with a very positive self-perception of learning achieved.

Therefore, this paper establishes as its main aim the implementation of innovative active methodology of Project-Based Learning (PBL) for the acquisition of digital competence in their five areas of competence: information, communication, content creation, digital security and problem resolution.

Besides the acquisition of digital competence, other skills related to Project Based Learning (PBL) collaborative methodology are developed:

- Systemic skills: drawing conclusions, problem resolution and management.
- Interpersonal skills: which will develop healthy social interactions with others.

2. METHOD

2.1 Participants

The present study is framed in the subject of Information and Communication Technologies in Education (ICT) within the syllabus in the Degree of Primary Education and also in the Degree of Early Childhood Education, at the Pontifical University of Salamanca. This study has been conducted in 28 students studying exclusively under the Blended Learning mode. The average age is 33.93. This is high because students who access this modality of learning are mainly students who already have a university degree.

2.2 Instrument

As for the instrument the Questionnaire of Effectiveness of the use of methodologies for Active Participation (CEMPA) has been used (Carrasco et al., 2015). This questionnaire has been validated in Spanish and consists of 25 items, with a Likert scale type with five levels of responses (1: little, 2: low, 3: moderate, 4: fairly and 5: much). The items are grouped into four different dimensions:

1. Development of Specific Skills (Items 1-5). This dimension values the abilities related to their own Degree. In our case, the acquisition of digital competence in their five areas of competence within the subject of ICT in education has been assessed.
2. Development of General Skills (items 6-13). In this dimension the skills needed for employment and life as a citizen have been assessed, which are of paramount importance for all students regardless of the Degree chosen. In addition, within this dimension, it is important to establish a close link with the development of the Specific Skills, that is to say, with the acquisition of digital competence in its five areas of competences, since items such as problem resolution, the use computers, database management (search for information), verbal and written communication which are framed within the 5 areas mentioned above.
3. Systemic Skills (Items 14-18). These are related to the overall vision and the ability to properly manage the totality of the question posed.
4. Interpersonal Skills (Items 19-25). In this last dimension, the capabilities that allow you to maintain good social relationships with others are assessed.

2.3 Process

The didactic proposal presented here is titled "The Saddlebags Digital Competence". The purpose for using the methodology of Project-Based Learning (PBL) is the creation of a personal learning environment (PLE) containing the main ICT resources to be used in the classroom in Early Childhood and Primary Education according to the major selected (Foreign Language, Music, Physical Education, Special Needs Education and Speech Therapist).

The abilities and capabilities targeted in this didactic proposal are:

- ✓ To promote experiences of initiation to information and communication technologies.
- ✓ To know, use and incorporate ICT in teaching-learning activities.

✓ To develop a professional approach to facilitate decision-making on the use, design and evaluation of educational materials in computer support.

✓ To raise awareness in the need for continuous professional development promoted by the daily evolution of ICT.

"The Saddlebags Digital Competence" takes place in three different phases:

1. Phase 1. The stages in this phase are:
   - Specify the theme of work. In our case, the search for ICT resources to be used in the classrooms of Early Childhood and Primary Education.
   - Teams building. The teams are organized in groups of 4 students per computer and the roles within the teams are assigned.
   - To clarify the final outcome for each of the teams.
2. Phase 2. In the 2nd phase the following elements are defined:
   - Planning: A work agenda is established as well as all the members' contributions.
   - Research: consist of searching, selecting and dealing with existing ICT resources in the web with the use of different technological programs of content curators (Pinterest, Pocket, Digital Whiteboard).
   - Analysis and Synthesis: consist of analyzing the information obtained and withdraw it wisely, critically and ethically in order to display it and share it.
3. Finally, in phase 3 the final product is originated:
   - Creation of the final content collecting all groups' contributions using the different ICT tools (Symbaloo).
   - Exposure of the content elaborated using digital resources (Mindomo).
   - Raising a debate among the projects developed by the different groups.

3. DATA ANALYSIS

Once this proposal for teaching was applied, the students completed the Questionnaire of Effectiveness of the use of methodologies for Active Participation (CEMPA). In order to analyze the data, the statistical package SPSS 24 was used.

3.1 Results

According to the data obtain in the different items, the average of the 4 dimensions established in the questionnaire, has been examined in the first place, as it is shown in Figure 1:

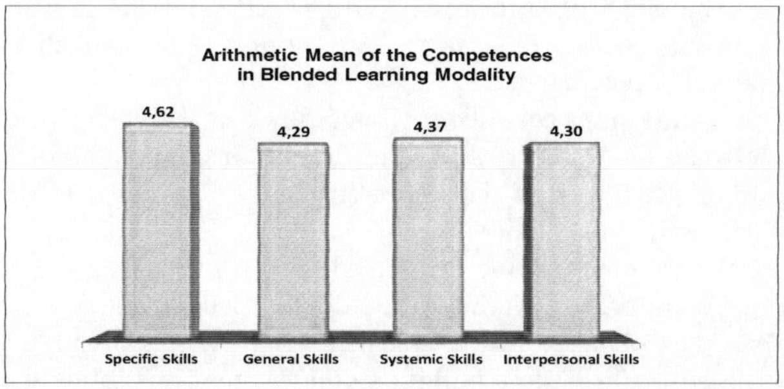

Figure 1. Arithmetic mean of the four dimensions of the questionnaire

As can be observed from the average values obtained in the 4 dimensions that encompasses the questionnaire, students in Blended Learning modality believe they have acquired the different competences in a very significant level, that is to say, they believe that the use of the innovative methodology of PBL is very appropriate for the acquisition of the digital competence. As for the learning of Specific Skills (M = 4.62), these prevail over the rest of the competences which have a very similar arithmetic mean.

Once the arithmetic averages were observed, a statistical analysis Chi-square to the data obtained in the sampling was carried out. Values resulting from the asymptotic significance level by linking the different competences described in the questionnaire CEMPA are reflected below in Table 1. The values in the table are symmetrical, therefore only values represented in the middle of the table are shown.

Table 1. Representation of the values of the asymptotic significance using Chi-square test for the relationship between the different skills

	Specific Skills	General Skills	Systemic Skills	Interpersonal skills
Specific Skills		0.018	0.000	**0.063**
General Skills			0.045	**0.119**
Systemic Skills				**0.476**
Interpersonal Skills				

Since the 95% in the confidence coefficient was used, the significance level obtained is 5% (0.05). Therefore, taking into account the values of the asymptotic significance represented in Table 1, it can be considered that:

- ✓ The asymptotic significance (bilateral) of the Specific skills with the General skills, is 0.018 <0.05, and with the Systemic skills is 0.000 < 0.05, therefore, in both cases, we do consider that there is a relationship between these competences. However, the asymptotic significance (bilateral) of the Specific skills with the Interpersonal is not significant (0.063> 0.05) therefore, it cannot be stated that there is relationship between the two skills.
- ✓ The asymptotic significance (bilateral) of the General skills with the Systemic skills is 0.045 <0.05, therefore, it can be ratified that there is a relationship between these competences. However, as in the case mentioned above, there is no significant relationship with Interpersonal skills (0.119> 0.05).
- ✓ As for the Systemic skills, we haven't found any variation with the Interpersonal skills (0.476> 0.005). In this way, it cannot be said that there is any relationship.
- ✓ Finally, the Interpersonal skills don't have relationship with any of the rest of the competences. Its asymptotic significance is greater than 0.05, in all the values.

4. CONCLUSION

After applying this didactic proposal, students in the Blended Learning modality believe they have acquired a very high level in the different skills described in this study. The Specific skills stand out the rest of skills. With an almost identical value but with a lower score, the General skills as well as the Systemic skills emerge. Interpersonal skills, though showing a fairly high rating, are the ones that get the lowest values if we compare them with the rest of competences.

Statistically significant relationships between the Specific skills and the General skills ($p < 0.05$) have been found, as well as between the Specific skills and the Systemic ($p < 0.05$), as happens between the General and the Systemic ($p < 0.05$). However, no statistically significant relationship has been found between the Interpersonal skills and the other skills.

In conclusion, it can be established that the PBL has helped students of the Blended Learning mode to obtain a significant learning both, in the Specific skills as in the General and Systemic skills. Nevertheless, no significant learning has been obtained in the Interpersonal skills, as Prendes, Castañeda & Gutiérrez (2010), and Fernandez-Cabezas (2017) show in their studies, where it is stated that the greatest students' shortcomings are those related to collaboration, leadership and management of the information in teamwork. As stated by Hernandez (2016) there are other studies where it is confirmed that this type of methodologies requires an effort in planning and monitoring in order to guarantee the communication or collaboration among students.

Following Thomas (2000), the results obtained show, not only the importance of students' motivation for accomplishing significant learning, but also for the need of a good planning and organization of the tasks in the projects. Therefore, it is very important within this methodological context, to find a solution in order to obtain greater Interpersonal skills for the students in the Blended Learning modality where group interactions occur primarily through digital channels.

REFERENCES

Area, M. (2008). ICT pedagogical innovation and development of information and digital competencies. Journal of Research in school, 64, 5-17.

Bustos, H.G., & Gómez, M.G. (2018). Digital competence in teaching high school as a means of Innovation Educative. Journal of Educational Research, 26, 66-86.

Cabero, J., & Román, P. (2006). E-activities: a basic reference for Internet training. Editorial MAD. ISBN: 84-665-4768-1, 11-22. Retrieved from https://dialnet.unirioja.es/servlet/libro?codigo=10840

Cabero, J. (2015). Reflexiones educativas sobre las tecnologías de la Información y la Comunicación (TIC). Technology, Science and Education. Revista de carácter científico multidisciplinar, 1, 19-27.

Carrasco, A., Donoso, J.A., Duarte-Atoche, T., Hernandez, J.J., & Lopez, R. (2015). Design and validation of a questionnaire that measures the perceived effectiveness of using methodologies of active participation (Cempa). The case of project-based learning (ABPrj) in the teaching of accounting. Innovating, 25 (58), 143-158.

Fernandez-Cabezas, M. (2017). Project-based learning at university level: an experience of methodological innovation in education. International Journal of Developmental and Educational Psychology, Monograph, 1, Nº. 1, 269-278.

García-Varcálcel, A. & Basilotta, V. (2017). Project-based learning (PBL): assessment from the perspective of primary school students. Journal of Educational Research, 35 (1), 113-131.

Hernandez, M. (2016). Evaluating Project-Based Learning. Recovered, http://www.edutopia.org/blog/evaluating-pbl-michael-hernandez

Organic Law 8/2013, of 9 December, for improving educational quality. Official Gazette, December 10, 2013, nº. 295

Marquès, P. (2012). Impact of ICT in Education: Functions and Limitations. Journal 3ciencias, 4, 1-15. Retrieved from https://www.3ciencias.com/wp-content/uploads/2013/01/impacto-de-las-tic.pdf

Prendes, M.P., Castañeda, L. & Gutiérrez, I. (2010). Skills for using ICT future teachers. Communicating Journal, V. XVIII, Nº. 35, 175-182.

Royal Decree 126/2014 of 28 February, the core curriculum of primary education is established. Official Gazette, March 1, 2014, nº. 52

Salinas, J. (2008). educational innovation and ICT use. (UI of Andalusia, Ed.). Seville. ISBN: 978-84-7993-055-4. Retrieved from https://dspace.unia.es/bitstream/handle/10334/2524/innovacioneduc2008.pdf?sequence=1

Thomas, J. (2000). A review of research on project-based learning. Recovered from http://www.bobpearlman.org/BestPractices/PBL_Research.pdf

PROFUTURO, A SOCIAL INITIATIVE TO IMPROVE EDUCATION WITH E-LEARNING ANALYTICAL TOOLS

Vidal Alonso Secades, Olga Arranz-García and Alfonso Jose López Rivero
Universidad Pontificia de Salamanca
C/Compañía, 5, 37002, Salamanca, Spain

ABSTRACT

One of the main factors that governments and enterprises have to bridge the digital gap in society is Education. Profuturo is a foundation that develops a proposal on digital education in order to reduce that gap in vulnerable areas working with e-learning programs. These e-learning activities bring them a large data set that can be analyzed with learning analytics tools, such as big data or artificial intelligence technology. The use of these technologies has the aim to improve the learning process in those vulnerable areas and to act in a personal way such as the students have been demanded. This short paper shows how the data analysis obtained from mathematics and linguistic data can be used in order to identify talented students in those areas.

KEYWORDS

e-Learning, Online Education, Profuturo Foundation, Artificial Intelligence, Big Data

1. INTRODUCTION

The development of a society has in education one of the main factors of wellbeing and progress in order to satisfy their citizens. This makes that most of the leaders and business entities have always education as an area for improvement, in order to provide a quality educational training to look to the future with hope. (U.S. Department of Education, 2012).

UNESCO, as the Organization of the United Nations responsible for the education, has focused, on two of its last working papers, in the reorientation of the use made of the stored data in information systems to a more equitable and inclusive process that promotes a quality education (UNESCO, 2018) and to the use of artificial intelligence as an item of information processing that allows for a more sustainable educational development (UNESCO, 2019).

This short paper aims to show, in this context, the initiative implemented by Profuturo Foundation to improve education in vulnerable areas, (Guatemala, Peru, Angola, Philippines, Colombia, Belize, Brazil,...), through e-learning processes. The initiative is in a continuous improvement process fed by a data analysis with technological tools based on Big data analytics or artificial intelligence, that is currently being executed in collaboration with the Computer Science Faculty of the Pontifical University of Salamanca. So, the paper makes a brief introduction to the project of the Profuturo Foundation, addresses the relationship between technology and the analytical e-learning processes and displays a case study analyzed from the data collected.

2. PROFUTURO FOUNDATION

Profuturo is a digital educational proposal launched by Telefonica Foundation and "La Caixa" Foundation, whose mission is to reduce the educational gap, providing a quality digital education to boys and girls who are in vulnerable environments in Africa, Latin America and Asia. This proposal involves the main educational agents such as school principals, teachers, students and families, and seeks to promote agreements with governments and relevant educational institutions of each country, to work in conjunction with the official plans. (Profuturo, 2019)

Its objective is to prevent that the digital gap in education joined with the existing gap of the socioeconomic environment of these areas and offer an inclusive, equitable and quality digital education, to achieve equal opportunities. To achieve this goal it uses the digital technology as a way of affordable and effective access to quality education, where geographical barriers are removed and the scalability will be favored. Through this digital technology is facing three educational challenges:

1) New learning models: Going from a student-centered learning in a model of project based learning.
2) New skills: Creativity, critical spirit, innovation or learning to learn.
3) New teacher role: Proactive, guide, coach.

The pedagogical model is a blended learning model, customized, modular, flexible and coordinated with the local entities. This model can be deployed to any vulnerable environment, with or without connectivity, as it adapts to the circumstances of each area or country, even in schools without equipment or connectivity. The model focuses on the skills development linked with linguistics and the STEAM (Science, Technology, Arts and Mathematics) area, as well as it develops common digital skills, communication skills, teamwork, creativity, problem solving, or decision-making process.

The key to the program is the teacher training. ProFuturo train them in the use of digital tools to develop personalized learning resources, helps them to improve their digital competence and encourages collaborative work for creating a large international network of education centers that teach, learn and share knowledge, fostering the creation of their own content.

In order to assess the effectiveness of this method and its subsequent adaptation and replication in other educational centers, Profuturo sets a set of analytical processes to measure and evaluate the impacts of continuous improvement. These analytical processes are being implemented with learning analytics tools based on algorithms and big data for assessing the results and the impact of the quality and transformation of education. We must highlight, as an example, the application "Teacher Assistant" that through e-learning analytics allows you to detect, daily, if a child is falling behind and put measures in their recovery, as well as offer more challenges to the more advanced students.

3. ELEARNING & TECHNOLOGICAL TOOLS

The data collection and the data storage obtained from the different activities of e-learning, engaged in a learning management platform, enables subsequent treatment through technological tools. Big data, learning analytics, artificial intelligence, are some of the current trends that are extracting new knowledge in education area and are being used to improve student's education. (Hamoud et al., 2018) (Leading Countries of the World, 2018)

The application of Big Data to the education area has allowed a greater customization of the teaching methods and has brought a greater feedback to students (Daniel, 2014; Avella et al., 2016). This feedback increases the student´s motivation with respect to the current teaching-learning process, as they work with new teaching and learning methods through mobile apps or the combined learning process.

Regarding the term of Learning Analytics, Ferguson et al. (2016) defines it as "the measure, data collection, analysis and reporting on students and their contexts, in order to understand and optimize learning and the environments in which takes place". This definition allows us to extrapolate the importance that techniques and processing procedures used in learning analytics can reach, for the educational area, when it comes to understand and optimize the learning processes (Lee et al., 2019). This optimization should be developed in a process of four phases for success:

1. Set goals and metrics: It is important to establish, at the beginning of the process, which is the goal to be achieved and the metrics that will be used in order to verify the achievement of the goal.
2. Data Collection: The main source of analysis will be the data collected and cleaned from the activities developed by the students in the e-learning platform.
3. Analyze and visualize information: The analysis with technological tools, adapted to the established objectives, allow us to view the new knowledge obtained.
4. Act: The application of this knowledge will modify the activities of the e-learning process in order to improve student´s marks.

Also, the artificial intelligence is emerging as the technology of the future to predict or discover knowledge in educational data sets. Processes such as Machine learning or Deep learning processes can discover patterns of behavior, based on the student´s actions, in order to improve the e-learning process (Tuomi, 2018). This trend was reaffirmed in the Mobile Learning Week (2019) where it was agreed, at the European Union and the UNESCO member countries, to establish policies to encourage the development of educational data analytics with artificial intelligence techniques, and, also, to train teachers in an education oriented to artificial intelligence. (UNESCO, 2019).

4. A STUDY CASE

This paper displays a study case which is interested in the identification of talented students in the respective vulnerable areas where the program is implemented. In order to verify the achievement of this aim, the study case will collect, as a metric of success, the percentiles of each student in the courses they have been completed. We shall estimate that a percentile greater than or equal to 90 will be considered as a successful event.

4.1 Data Collection & Data Cleansing

The data collection process starts with the recollection and storage of data from the vulnerable areas, using the platform e-learning activities. The number of participants varies from one area to another, but at least we collect more than 5000 records from each area. In order to obtain some useful information, we shall consider a data collection just for 2 subjects: Linguistics and Mathematics. For the linguistic subject we shall take data from activities that affect vowels, verbs, nouns, prayers, gender and adjectives, while for the mathematics subject we shall discuss activities that encompass volumes, measurement, addition, subtraction, geometry and numbering systems.

These data should be treated using technological tools of filtering, removing and cleaning, which allow us to retrieve data in a format that can be applied to the relevant analysis. In this study case, as a filter activity and to provide students with a meaningful activity, we shall only be regarded as students who have completed more than 10 activities. In the same way, and as a removing activity, we shall remove the inconsistent data detected.

Finally, data cleansing will be transforming the raw data in tidy data. For example, the cleaning process transforms all the characters in lower case, or updates the data noise, such as, those activities that have a mark bigger than 100 points.

4.2 Data Analysis & Data Visualization

Once you have preprocessed the data collected, you will continue the study case with a quality data set. So, it is time to start the learning analytics process, directing this analysis to the achievement of the goal set, i.e. the identification of talent.

In this analysis, it is used, both for the treatment of data as well as for exploratory analysis, the language R, where through the tool RStudio is implementing the corresponding code that allows you to analyze the undertaken platform activities and their results.

The analysis is made by the combination of several factors, such as the activity identifier, the identification of the student, the date of implementation, the type of activity, the number of students per course, the zone identifier, the materials used or the teachers involved.

The data visualization phase has been implemented with TIBCO Spotfire, which is a tool that builds graphics to display the results of the processed data, obtaining curious results. For example, Figure 1 represents data visualization for the linguistics subject, where the horizontal axis represents the students registered and the vertical one represents the mark obtained. It is possible to extrapolate from the Figure 1, that the fewer students to attend the course (between 10 and 15), worst are the results of the learning process. This association allows us to interpret a possible association between students' motivation regarding contents and the number of students that are enrolled in each course.

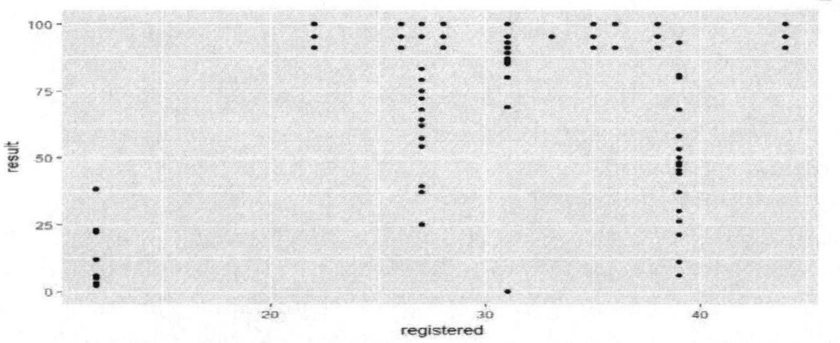

Figure 1. Marks / Enrolled Students

Considering this extrapolation we shall act, in the future, to enroll between 20 and 35 students in each course in order to improve student´s marks and their motivation.

Furthermore, we also obtained, in the Table 1 below, the data analytics relating to the results achieved in the e-learning activities of linguistics and mathematics. We used this table to observe the objective of the study case, and, so, we proceed to their classification with reference to the percentiles.

Table 1. Results of the analysis of activities of linguistics and mathematics

Percentiles	Linguistics Percent	Mathematics Percent
Greater than or equal to 90	**79,3 %**	**84,0 %**
Between 1 and 89	**16,1 %**	**8,3 %**
Equal to 0	**4,6 %**	**7,7 %**

The analysis of this table allows us to observe the presence of a greater talent in the field of mathematics (84%) than in the field of linguistics (79,3%), and a total failure lower in linguistic activities (4,6%) than in mathematics (7,7%). So, we will have more opportunities to find more talent in the students who have completed mathematics than in the students who have completed linguistics.

5. CONCLUSION

As we have observed, the commitment of Profuturo Foundation with evolution educative in vulnerable environments is a confirmed fact. This compromise encompasses not only the physical layout of equipment and connection, but also the analysis of e-learning activities carried out by students, in order to enhance the teaching/learning process.

This analysis, carried out with the latest technological trends, such as Big Data and Artificial Intelligence tools, feed the learning process to establish new and innovative activities that increase student motivation with respect to the training subject.

This optimization would be improved with the automation of the tedious work of data cleansing, as well as the thinning of the algorithms that are used in the e-learning analytical activities, implemented with artificial intelligence techniques or with big data technology.

As we have seen in the case study, it is possible to collect records from the student´s activities in the e-learning platform and process them with the analytical tools in order to identify who are the students with more talent, and what are the factors (number of students) that could improve e-learning education activities.

There is still too much work to realize in these vulnerable areas, but this proposal could be the first step to bring education closer to children and offer a better future.

REFERENCES

Avella, J., et al., 2016. Learning Analytics Methods, Benefits, and Challenges in Higher Education: A Systematic Literature Review. *In Online Learning*, Vol. 20, No. 2, pp 13-29

Daniel, B., 2014. Big Data and analytics in higher education: Opportunities and challenges. *In British Journal of Educational Technology*, doi: 10.1111/bjet.12230

Ferguson, R., et al, 2016. *Research Evidence on the Use of Learning Analytics - Implications for Education Policy*. Joint Research Centre Science for Policy Report; EUR 28294 EN; doi: 10.2791/955210

Hamoud, A., et al., 2018. Predicting Student Performance in Higher Education Institutions Using Decision Tree Analysis. *In International Journal of Interactive and artificial intelligence*, Vol. 5, No. 2, pp 26-31.

Leading Countries of the World, 2018. *Lessons from Using Advanced Learning Analysis in Education Sector.* Available at:https://www.leadingcountries.com/wp-content/uploads/2018/08/19498_MSEdu_LearningAnalytics12ppBrochure_V2.pdf

Lee, J., et al., 2019. Exploring Factors and Indicators for Measuring Students´Sustainable Engagement in e-Learning. *In Sustainability*, Vol. 11, No. 4, https://doi.org/10.3390/su11040985

Mobile Learning Week, 2019. https://en.unesco.org/mlw

Profuturo, 2019. https://www.fundaciontelefonica.com/educacion_innovacion/profuturo/

Tuomi,I., 2018 *The Impact of Artificial Intelligence on Learning, Teaching, and Education. Policies for the future*, Eds. Cabrera, M., Vooraki, R. & Punie, Y., EUR 29442 EN, Publications Office of the European Union, Luxembourg, doi: 10.2760/12297, JCR113226

UNESCO, 2018. Re-orienting Education Management Information Systems towards Inclusive and Equitable Quality Education and Lifelong Learning. *UNESCO Working Papers on Education*, No. 5.

UNESCO, 2019. Artificial Intelligence in Education: Challenges and Opportunities for Sustainable Development. *UNESCO Working Papers on Education*, No. 7.

U.S. Department of Education, Office of Educational Technology, 2012. *Enhancing Teaching and Learning Through Educational Data Mining and Learning Analytics: An Issue Brief.* Washington, D.C

DESIGN OF A NEW SCALE TO MEASURE THE LEARNER EXPERIENCE IN E-LEARNING SYSTEMS

Yassine Safsouf[1,3], Khalifa Mansouri[2] and Franck Poirier[1]
[1]Lab-STICC, University Bretagne Sud, France
[2]Laboratory SSDIA, ENSET of Mohammedia, University Hassan II of Casablanca, Morocco
[3]LIMIE Laboratory, ISGA Group, Centre Marrakech, Morocco

ABSTRACT

Nowadays, the user experience (UX) has become an essential concept of human-computer interaction (HCI) and occupies an increasingly important place in companies interested in this field. Designing a system or product with a good user experience is one of the main objectives of any digital project. E-learning systems must adapt because, beyond the benefits associated with good usability, creating a learning system with a better user experience (learner's experience) is a key competitive factor in the marketplace. This paper describes a new measurement tool based on a theoretical model presented in previous research that distinguishes the success factors of learners in an e-learning system. This tool for evaluating the learner experience is based on the AttrakDiff user experience measurement tool and uses the same subscale, namely the pragmatic and hedonic qualities of interactive systems. The proposed learning experience (LX) scale allow to know if a e-learning system is perceived by learners as interactive, effective, clear, reliable, challenging, or effortless.

KEYWORDS

Learner Experience, Learner Satisfaction, Learner Success, Usability, User Experience, AttrakDiff

1. INTRODUCTION

Today, information and communication technologies (ICTs) are of fundamental importance in society and must therefore be considered as a strategic sector that contributes significantly to economic and social development. These technologies are evolving at an accelerated rate. Their rapid obsolescence requires a constant updating of knowledge and know-how. Accordingly, the teaching and learning in universities are adapted to keep up with the changes in ICTs for the development of quality education.

The web-based technologies have been used as a powerful tool to increase the accessibility to education for people around the world. They provide now to the learners, the opportunity to access the information they need at the right time, and also online educational approaches to conduct distance teaching and learning. Nevertheless, it is not obvious how to measure the improvement of the learning process, for example are they related to learner characteristics, instructor, technology, course contents or social interactions?

Although the learner's experience (LX) has been the subject of several previous studies (Sudhakar A., 2015), it has been limited to certain concerns, such as student perceptions or friendliness. We have discussed and classified in previous articles models and factors for evaluating LX in a distance learning system (Safsouf, Mansouri and Poirier, 2017) (Safsouf, Mansouri and Poirier, 2018), such as learner characteristics, instructor characteristics, system characteristics, course characteristics and social aspects.

In this regard, this paper is an attempt to propose a new scale for measuring the learning experience in an e-learning system. The rest of this paper is organised as follows: section II discusses the concepts of usability and user experience with its roots and defines the term "learner experience"; section III provides a tool to evaluate learners' experience in an e-learning system and section IV concludes the paper.

2. RELATED WORK

The usability of a system refers in a broad meaning to its ease of learning and efficiency. This concept has become much more popular with the emergence of computer or interactive systems for a wider audience, but also because of increased competition between companies. Improving the usability of a system reduces user frustration and makes it easier and faster to complete the task. Shackel and Richardson (Shackel, B., Richardson, 1991) was among the first authors to focus on usability, for them the precise definition of system usability is the ability, in terms of human functionality, to be used easily and effectively by several users, with a certain level of training and support, to accomplish a specific range of tasks, within a specific series of scenarios. It can be seen that usability is therefore related to ease and efficiency of use. However, the most frequently cited definition is probably that of both standards ISO 9241-210 and ISO 9241-220 (ISO CD 9241-220, 2015) These standards specify that usability is the degree to which a service, product or system can be used by users to achieve specific goals with effectiveness, efficiency, and satisfaction in a specific use context. We see that this definition strongly mentions user satisfaction, but even with these definitions, usability is not a sufficiently encompassing concept to describe the experience with the product. Limiting user frustration is essential, but some products can also bring pleasure to users and make them feel different emotions. The concept of the user experience (UX) is dedicated to encompassing these aspects.

From the mid-1990s, the term UX appeared at Apple through Donald Norman (Norman, Miller and Henderson, 1995). In fact, the former explains that he proposed this term in order to encompass all the elements related to the experience with a product, including, among others, factors related to emotional and hedonic aspects. In the literature, one of the most frequently cited definitions is that of the two researchers Hassenzahl and Tractinsky (Hassenzahl and Tractinsky, 2011). These authors specify that UX is a consequence of characteristics of the designed system (e.g. usability, functionality, complexity, purpose, etc.), user's internal state (predispositions, motivation, needs, expectations, mood, etc.) and the context (or the environment) inside of which the interaction occurs (e.g. organizational/social setting, meaningfulness of the activity, voluntariness of use, etc.). They also point out that UX is strongly based on the idea of designing systems to please users rather than just to limit their frustrations.

In the field of e-learning, the literature indicates that the LX is designed to a large extent, such as the e-learner behaviour and satisfaction, or self-regulation and effort in learning, or even e-learner's knowledge (Ngamkamollert and Ruangkanjanases, 2015). In our previous research, we focused on the factors that evaluate LX in e-learning systems (Safsouf, Mansouri and Poirier, 2018). we proposed models to better understand the factors involved in measuring learner satisfaction, their intention to continue using the system, their self-regulation, their attitudes towards the same system and their success in online training.

3. EVALUATION OF THE LEARNER'S EXPERIENCE

To improve the user experience towards a system or simply to ensure that the final system has a good UX value, it is necessary to know how to evaluate it in a valid and reliable way. Self-assessment questionnaires are among the most commonly used instruments for evaluating UX. With UX scales, you will quickly know if your system is perceived by users as attractive, efficient, clear, reliable, challenging, or innovative.

UX evaluation scales are measurement tools used to collect user feedback and experience. They are in the form of questionnaires where users answer themselves, in order to evaluate users' perceptions of the system. They are currently used in all fields (Lallemand *et al.*, 2015): video games, professional applications, health-related systems, virtual worlds and e-learning platforms. The AttrakDiff questionnaire is one of the most widely used user experience assessment tools at the academic level. This tool is based on the theoretical model proposed by Hassenzahl to explain the perceived quality of an interactive system. It includes 28 items divided into 4 subscales (pragmatic quality, hedonic quality-stimulation, hedonic quality-identity, overall attractiveness). The 28 items of the questionnaire are presented as semantic differentiators (pairs of antonymous words) in a 7point scale (from -3 to +3). These scales are not graduated verbatim. The order in which the items are handed over is standardized.

In the field of e-learning, little research has been done on the experience of learners. Our contribution in this article is to propose a measurement instrument based on a theoretical model proposed in our previous studies in e-learning systems. We called it FASER LX for "Formation, Apprenant, Système, Enseignant,

Relation Learner eXperience" (Course, Learner, System, Teacher, Relationship). Like the AttrakDiff, the FASER LX scale is self-administered, which means that users complete the questionnaire themselves. It consists of a total of 30 items presented as pairs of contrasting words, divided into 5 sub-scales:

- **Pragmatic quality (PQ)**: with 9 items which describe the usability of the system and how it enables users to achieve their objectives;
- **Hedonic-stimulation quality (HQ-ST)**: with 5 items which indicate the extent to which the system can support the need for stimulation;
- **Hedonic-satisfaction quality (HQ-SA)**: with 4 items which indicate the extent to which the system allows the user to be satisfied;
- **Effort quality (EQ)**: with 6 items which indicate the extent to which the system allows users to measure the effort deployed when using the system;
- **Social quality (SQ)**: with 6 items which measure the appearance and social interactions of a user with the actors of the system (instructor and learners).

In FASER LX scale, each subscale has items where each represents a factor from our research and theoretical models. These factors have been previously classified by dimensions which are: learner characteristics, instructor characteristics, system characteristics, course characteristics and social aspects. In the following table we present the FASER LX scale, with the assignment items by dimensions and subscales.

Table 1. The items of the FASER LX scale to evaluate the learner experience in an e-learning system

Dimensions	Subscales	Success model factors	Antonym pairs	
Learner characteristics	PQ1	Computer self-efficiency	Autonomous -	Non-autonomous
	HQ-SA1	Self-enjoyment	Unpleasant -	Pleasant
	HQ-ST1	Perceived usefulness	Boring -	Captivating
	EQ1	Self-effort	Undemanding -	Demanding
	PQ2	Self-regulation	Free use -	Compulsory use
	HQ-SA2	Self-security	Confident -	Distrustful
	EQ2	Perceived anxiety	Calming -	Stressing
Instructor characteristics	SQ1	Communication ability	Easy communication -	Difficult communication
	HQ-ST2	Responsiveness	High reactivity -	Low reactivity
	EQ3	Informativeness	Not comprehensible -	Comprehensible
	SQ2	Fairness	Unfair -	Highly fair
System characteristics	PQ3	Connection access quality	Slow -	Fast
	EQ4	Device and context independence	Device dependent -	Device independent
	PQ4	Efficiency	Tedious -	Efficient
	PQ5	Security	Unreliable -	Very reliable
	PQ6	Perceived Ease-of-use	Difficult learning -	Easy learning
	PQ7	Availability	Not available -	Very available
	HQ-ST3	Interactivity	Not interactive -	Very interactive
	PQ8	Personalization	Customizable -	Not customizable
Course characteristics	EQ5	Course Quality	Confused -	Clear
	HQ-ST4	Content diversity	Not diversified -	Very divided
	EQ6	Course Flexibility	Rigid -	Flexible
	HQ-SA3	Design and system quality	Pleasant -	Unpleasant
	HQ-ST5	Up-to-dateness	Static -	Dynamic
	PQ9	Diversity in assessments	Diversified assessment -	Not diversified assessment
Social aspects	SQ3	Subjective norm	Recommendable -	Not recommendable
	HQ-SA4	Self-image	Valuable -	Non-valuable
	SQ4	Learner-learner interaction	Gets closer to learners -	Separates me from learners
	SQ5	Learner-instructor interaction	Get closer to teachers -	Separate me from teachers
	SQ6	Instructor-instructor interaction	Bring teachers together -	Separate teachers

The questionnaire is available for free online (www.safsouf.net/faserlx). However, only the French version is currently available. As well as for the AttrakDiff, to calculate a global score in the FASER LX scale, we must first reverse some items, that means, replace the score obtained by its opposite. Because sometimes the word on the left is negative and sometimes it is positive. The next step is to calculate the averages for each of the five sub-scales as well as the five dimensions. Finally, present the results as two graphs in radar form (see next figure).

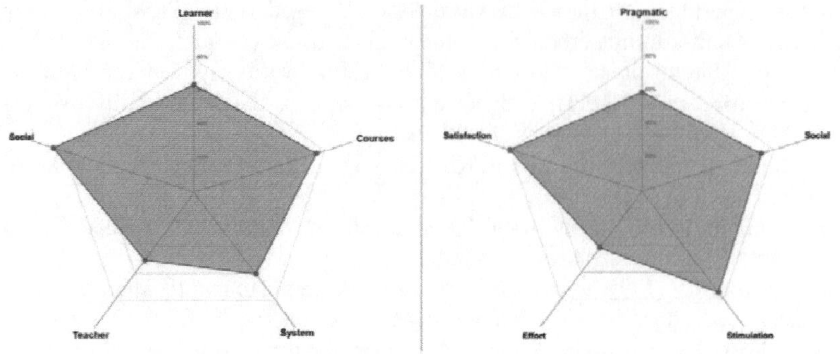

Figure 2. Presentation of the results of the FASER LX scale in graphical format

This graph shows the average percentage values for each pair of words. The items are grouped by dimensions in the left graph and by subscales in the right graph. This visualization makes it possible to quickly distinguish which aspects are perceived as critical and call for improvement actions or not.

4. CONCLUSION

In this work, we have attempted to present a new scale for measuring the learner experience in an online learning environment. Based on our previous research on success factors in understanding satisfaction, the intention to continue using the system, self-regulation and learner success in an online learning system and inspired by the AttrakDiff measurement scale, this scale is, according to our investigation, the first in the field of e-learning.

In our future work, we plan to validate this new scale of measurement in the context of higher education in Morocco.

REFERENCES

Hassenzahl, M. and Tractinsky, N. (2011) 'Behaviour & Information Technology User experience-a research agenda User experience-a research agenda'. doi: 10.1080/01449290500330331.

ISO CD 9241-220 (2015) 'Ergonomics of human-system interaction - Part 220: Processes for enabling, executing and assessing human-centred design within organizations'.

Lallemand, C. *et al.* (2015) 'Création et validation d'une version française du questionnaire AttrakDiff pour l'évaluation de l'expérience utilisateur des systèmes interactifs', *Revue Europeenne de Psychologie Appliquee*. Elsevier Masson SAS, 65(5), pp. 239–252. doi: 10.1016/j.erap.2015.08.002.

Ngamkamollert, T. and Ruangkanjanases, A. (2015) 'Factors Influencing Foreign Students' Satisfaction toward International Program in Thai Universities', *International Journal of Information and Education Technology*, 5(3), pp. 170–178. doi: 10.7763/IJIET.2015.V5.497.

Norman, D., Miller, J. and Henderson, A. (1995) *CHI '95 MOSAIC OF CREATIVITY s Organization Overviews 1 What You See, Some of What's in the Future, And How We Go About Doing It: HI at Apple Computer.*

Safsouf, Y., Mansouri, K. and Poirier, F. (2017) 'Towards a Multidimensional Model to Study a Critical Success Factors Affecting Continuity and Success in E-Learning Systems', *Proceedings - International Conference on Developments in eSystems Engineering, DeSE*, pp. 129–134. doi: 10.1109/DeSE.2017.26.

Safsouf, Y., Mansouri, K. and Poirier, F. (2018) 'A New Model of Learner Experience in Online Learning Environments', *Information Systems and Technologies to Support Learning*. Springer International Publishing, 111(Lx), pp. 29–38. doi: 10.1007/978-3-030-03577-8.

Shackel, B., Richardson, S. (1991) 'Usability—context, framework, design and evaluation', *Human Factors for Informatics Usability. Cambridge University Press, Cambridge*, pp. 21–38.

Sudhakar A., T. J. and W. J. (2015) 'Enhancing Student Experience and Performance through Peer-assisted Learning', *Issues in Accounting Education Journal*, 31(3), pp. 321–336. doi: 10.2308/iace-51249.

APPLICATION OF ALPHA AND BETA BRAINWAVES ON E-LEARNING PROJECTS IN TERMS OF EXPANDING CRITICAL AND COGNITIVE SKILLS: AN EXPERIMENTAL APPROACH

Miltiadis Staboulis[1] and Irene Lazaridou[2]
[1]*Assistant Professor, Department of Educational and Social Policy, University of Macedonia, 156 Egnatia str., GR-54636, Thessaloniki, Greece*
[2]*Ph.D. Candidate, M.Ed.-M.Sc.-B.Sc.(Math), Department of Educational and Social Policy, University of Macedonia*

ABSTRACT

The present paper wishes to discuss some basic concepts of Brain-Based Learning and its relation to optimizing learning procedures through physical and on line educational practices. In particular it examines the combinational use of alpha and beta brain waves, embedded in teaching activities as a way of enhancing knowledge information flow, advancing cognitive and critical skills, while supporting a relaxing, calming, creative, actively thinking and problem solving environment in a balanced state of mind. The research that took place with 40 young adults has shown a strong positive correlation between alpha, beta waves and overall educational progress and skills enhancement.

KEYWORDS

ELearning, Skills, Education, Brain, Brainwaves, Educational Practices

1. INTRODUCTION

The numerous studies of the human brain have involved throughout the years, not only medical doctors but also other fields like education, psychology, pharmacology, mathematical modeling, molecular biology, anatomy, etc. finally creating the wide branch of neuroscience as the scientific study of the nervous system mainly in relation to behavior and learning. According to Eric Kandel (Nobel Prize 2000 for discoveries concerning signal transduction in the nervous system) the basics of learning, memory, behavior, perception and consciousness is the ultimate challenge of science. Due to its significance many sub branches have evolved like computational neuroscience (Schwartz, 1990) that mainly deals with neural modeling, brain theories and neural networks. Computational modeling of higher cognitive functions has recently begun, hoping to create the bases for modeling the brain's electrical activity (Robinson, et al, 2005). The results might be replicated in improving intelligent systems in the near future. In addition, the emerging field of neuroeducation is estimated to shape the learning practices, providing new opportunities for training and development professionals. Cognitive neuroscience is the study of mental brain processes and neural systems, including thinking and behavior, investigating biological ways involved in becoming literate, numerate in addition to exploring learning, cognitive control, flexibility and motivation together with social and emotional experiences (Dam, 2013).

Presently brain theories focus on a holistic view of the brain. Based on recent neurological research (Bonomo, 2017 & Jensen, 2005) there are three relevant and essential features of the human brain: adaptability (the constantly changing brain), integration (the structures of the brain that compete and cooperate) and sophistication (the complexity of the brain).

The human brain is an amazing and complex living organ weighting about 1,1-1,4 kg that enables humans to talk, to think and to sense. A basic idea in its functionality is the fact that neurons' activity is both electrical and chemical. A neuron is a cell that communicates with other cells through synapses. A typical neuron consists of the cell body, the dendrites and the axon. The dendrites receive, the cell body integrates and the axon transmits and this is called polarization, because of the directional flow of information in the central nervous system as it is shown in Figure 1. The establishment and maintenance of neuronal polarization is crucial for correct development and function (Takano et al, 2015).

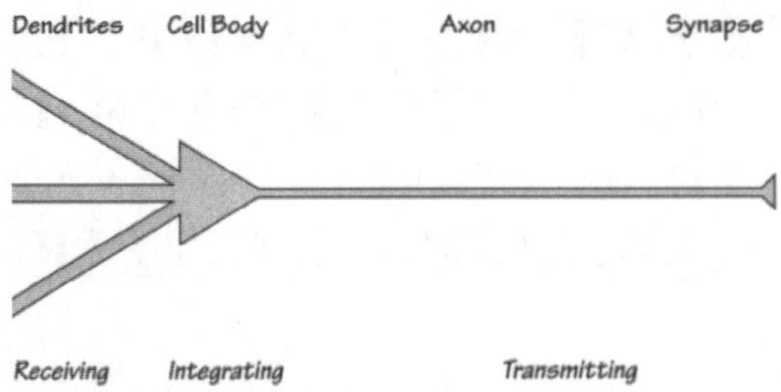

Figure 1. The basic concepts of a neuron
(Source: British Neuroscience Association)

These different parts of a neuron are in constant motion. The dendrites can change shape, sprout new connections or even withdraw from others and the axons grow new endings as the neuron struggles to communicate with other neurons. So, a neuron is like a miniature calculator constantly adding and subtracting messages from other neurons. These signals constitute the basis of sensation, thought and movement depending on the network the neurons are embedded (British Neuroscience Association, 2019). This dynamic and flexible ability of the brain leads to the fact that the brain is shaped by experiences and proper environmental enrichment, as the axonal circuits change, modify and redevelop even in older ages, providing an amazing plasticity throughout life (Jensen, 2000). So the brain changes as a result of experience and this happens much quicker than originally thought. The environment in which the brain operates determines, to a large degree, the functional ability of the brain (Roberts, 2002). As a result, learning is a physical process in which new knowledge is represented by new brain cell connections. The strength and formation of these connections are facilitated by chemicals in the brain called growth factors. Thus the creation of neural networks and synapses are what constitutes learning (Fishback, 1999). Consequently the term brain-based learning has evolved, studying the design of enriching appropriate experiences for learners while ensuring ways to increase the extraction of meaning of the received knowledge (Caine & Caine, 1991). Due to brain's neuroplasticity, some general ideas are now widely accepted, such as the brain is able to perform several tasks at once, the same information can be stored in multiple areas of the brain and learning functions can be affected by several reasons (exercise, diet, stress, emotional state, etc.).

As a result, schools, teachers, educators and educational programs have been recently trying to create certain conditions that facilitate learning activities. It is obvious that if some certain new model or way appears that significantly helps in advancing common learning procedures, then a whole new educational era could be on the way Yet as educational neuroscience is a relatively new field, the methods, strategies and development of cognitive science are still under progress, debate and testing.

Due to the fact that the brain is an electrochemical organ, the synchronized electrical pulses from neurons communicating with each other produce brain waves. Hans Berger (1873–1941), a German psychiatrist invented electroencephalography (EEG) for the recording of brain waves in 1924, by measuring electrical activity in the brains of hospital patients with skull damage. He documented alpha waves along with beta waves activity. He found out that when alpha waves decrease and beta activity becomes dominant, a person is fully awake. Today brainwaves are detected by using sensors placed on the scalp. One may think of brainwaves as musical notes of different frequencies that are able to change according to what we do or feel. Brainwaves accompany many mental stages and they occur in different locations of the brain. In fact, nowadays, many mobile applications offer real time feedback on brain activity in order to promote relaxation, alertness, mindfulness, etc. They work as EEG devices that passively sense brain's activity, promoting human centered technology.

Brainwaves are measured in Hertz (cycles per second) and they can be slow, moderate or fast, according to certain activities as shown in Figure 2.

Brain Waves	Brain State	Frequency (Hz)
Delta	Sleep	1 – 3
Theta	Alert	4 – 7
Low Alpha	Relaxed	8 – 9
High Alpha	Relaxed	10 – 12
Low Beta	Focused	13 – 17
High Beta	Focused	18 – 30
Low Gamma	Multi-Processing	31 – 40
High Gamma	Multi-Processing	41 – 50

Figure 2. The brainwaves, states and frequencies
(Source: https://www.researchgate.net/figure/List-of-brainwaves-with-state-and-their-frequencies_tbl1_305681552)

At the moment brainwaves are already connected to areas such as self-development, emotional balance, stress and anxiety, sleep and fatigue and are even connected to more specific issues such as trauma, PTSD, autism, dyslexia, etc.(https://brainworksneurotherapy.com). According to Jacobs (2018), waves are widespread in the human cortex (the part of the brain of higher cognitive functions) and they become more organized depending on how well the brain is performing a task. As a result, more consistent waves correspond to better task performance. These findings appear to support the concept that brainwaves are relevant to behavior, contributing to memory, perception, attention and even consciousness (Makin, 2018).

Based on the above facts, the present paper examines the consecutive use of alpha and beta waves by incorporating these waves in common traditional and on line teaching procedures, examining any possible progress in knowledge information flow, metacognition, expansion of cognitive and critical skills and thus optimization in the overall learning procedures, under certain predefined criteria. The reason of the combinational use of alpha and beta waves relies to the fact that alpha waves initially promote a calm, relaxing and creative state of mind while beta waves promote an engaged, alert and well-focused mind.

2. RESEARCH

The present research involves a sample of N = 40 young adult math graduates (23-28 years old, both male (24) and female (16)), with the intention of becoming intermediate level math teachers. Their university degree mark ranged from 5-6.2 (top mark is 10) so their overall performance as math students might be considered average. For this reason they choose a three month self-financing educational program of 300 hours about recent math teaching methods and techniques and latest mathematical software for calculations and graphical representations. According to the program's structure they joined a blended course that provided 100 hours of traditional teaching and 200 hours of on line learning

During the first meeting, they were notified about the contents of the program, the goals and the ways of evaluation and were asked for permission in using a combination of brain waves during the lessons as part of an experimental possible enhancement in learning procedures. They all agreed and gave in their written permission. Afterwards the sample was randomly divided into two equal groups of 20 namely group A (A1,..,A20) and group B (B1,..,B20). From that day on, group A (receivers) was always in contact with alpha and beta brain waves (both in physical teaching and with embedded sounds during on line learning), while group B (non receivers) received none. The combination of brain waves used ranged from 10-15 minutes of alpha waves (in order to relax and calm the brain) and 30-35 minutes of beta waves (in order to promote active thinking and problem solving skills).

In addition to the use of these waves, the educational material was structured in detail with very clear and segmented goals, so as to establish easy and accurate evaluation criteria during each month of the course. The evaluation criteria, during each month of the course, were divided into 3 parts (written evaluation, oral presentations and teaching simulations) as a repeated procedure at the end of every month. The marking scale was set from 1-10 (10 being the top mark). From the three different evaluations for every student, the average was calculated and kept for further comparisons. As this average mark for every single student, derives from a triple way of evaluation, it might be safe to conclude that it is an accurate and representative mark for each and every one of them. Obviously, each mark was entered in an Access data base for further processing. The first month appeared to be a period of adaptation that rapidly changed during the following two months. During the first month they became adapted to the requirements of the program while the evaluations at the end of the 1st month, appeared to be pretty similar (group A held an average mark of 5.8 while group B received 5.9). If the particular research had stopped at the end of the first month, no one could have guessed the upcoming changes. At the end of 2nd month, the average evaluation mark shows in tables 1 and 2 for both groups precisely.

Table 1. Evaluation in Group A (receivers)

(Group A) Evaluation at the end of the 2nd month																			
A1	A2	A3	A4	A5	A6	A7	A8	A9	A10	A11	A12	A13	A14	A15	A16	A17	A18	A19	A20
7	7	8	9	6	7	6	7	7	9	9	8	7	7	9	8	6	8	7	8

The average performance of group A (receivers) at the end of the 2nd month was $X_{A(2)} = 7.5$

Table 2. Evaluation in Group B (non receivers)

(Group B) Evaluation at the end of the 2nd month																			
B1	B2	B3	B4	B5	B6	B7	B8	B9	B10	B11	B12	B13	B14	B15	B16	B17	B18	B19	B20
7	7	6	6	6	5	6	6	5	7	7	6	7	5	5	7	7	8	8	9

The average performance of group B (non receivers) at the end of the 2nd month was $X_{B(2)} = 6.5$

Similarly, at the end of 3rd month, the average evaluation appears in tables 3 and 4.

Table 3. Evaluation in Group A (receivers)

(Group A) Evaluation at the end of the 3rd month																			
A1	A2	A3	A4	A5	A6	A7	A8	A9	A10	A11	A12	A13	A14	A15	A16	A17	A18	A19	A20
9	8	9	9	7	8	8	7	8	9	9	8	8	8	9	8	7	8	8	9

The average performance of group A (receivers) at the end of the 3rd month was $X_{A(3)} = 8.2$

Table 4. Evaluation in Group B (non receivers)

(Group B) Evaluation at the end of the 3rd month																			
B1	B2	B3	B4	B5	B6	B7	B8	B9	B10	B11	B12	B13	B14	B15	B16	B17	B18	B19	B20
7	7	6	7	6	6	6	7	6	7	7	6	7	6	5	8	7	8	8	9

The average performance of group B (non receivers) at the end of the 3rd month was $X_{B(3)} = 6.8$

From the above, it derives that the course in general had an overall positive effect on every participant as there is a clear rising. Obviously the group A (receivers) holds an amazing overall improvement starting with the average of 5.8 and reaching 8.2 out of 10. Figure 3, below, shows the comparison between the evaluation average marks among the two groups, throughout the entire three month program.

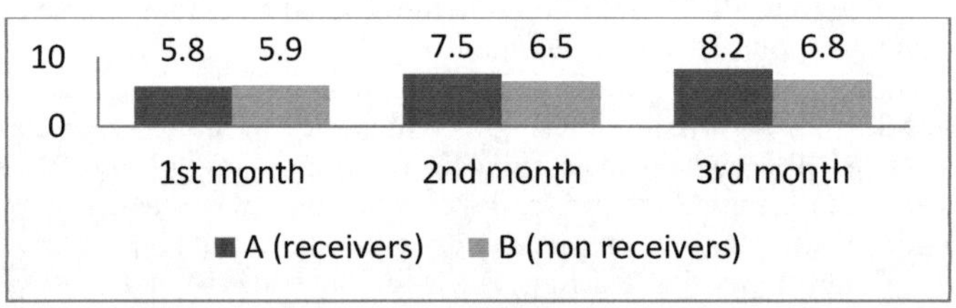

Figure 3. Comparison of evaluation average mark in both groups A and B during the entire 3-month course

The statistical analysis (t-test) of the results of the 3rd month for both groups A and B, show the following:

- P value and statistical significance: The two-tailed P value is less than 0.0001. By conventional criteria, this difference is considered to be extremely statistically significant.
- Confidence interval: The mean of Group A minus Group B equals 1.40. 95% confidence interval of this difference: From 0.87 to 1.93.
- Intermediate values used in calculations: t = 5, 3115, df = 38, standard error of difference = 0.264.

There are many questions unanswered, like why there was no rising during the first month, what would be the progress of group A if the program held longer, what would happen with group B performance given more time while turning them into receivers, what elements enriched group A self-motivation during the 2nd and 3rd month, was the quality of the educational material of the same significance with the use of brain waves, what other parameters hold a basic role, would the results be the same if we repeat the research using another sample of bigger scale and may another educational program, can we assume or prove that if repeated it would lead to the same results, etc. Of course, despite the fact that there is an obvious positive correlation between alpha, beta brainwaves and learning enhancement in the present research, there are still many restrictions such as the relatively small sample of 40 participants and the short period of the research itself. Another limitation could be related to the nature of the sample as it is formed from young average smart adults hoping for a better working position, knowing that to achieve this, they must do their best. So it might be said that the particular sample was already in the appropriate mood for effective learning.

3. CONCLUSION

From the above it derives that learning mechanisms are closely related to the brain's general state and that the calculated combination of alpha and beta brainwaves appears to have a positive role in overall learning optimizations. It also seems that alpha and beta waves may hold a significant part in eLearning courses where usually self motivation, responsibility and independence are in great demand compared to traditional courses, simply because the common student to teacher interaction is relatively limited. In the present research, the outcomes seem pretty astonishing and further investigation is needed in order to bring more light into the matter. As effective learning always involve alternation of several states of arousal (Caine & Caine, 1991), it appears that the alpha and beta waves contribute to this idea, possibly by helping the human brain to stay interconnected, calm, alert and focused. It is well known that emotions are critical to patterning and patterning is one of the ways that human brain learns. If the outcomes of this research are further verified, the results could open a whole new door to new learning theories, practices, strategies and curriculum programs. They could be applied in vocational education and training programs as well as in all levels of typical education and even in business environments using effective strategies, empowering reflection and metacognition progresses in order to finally create persons and citizens with deeper knowledge and enriched skills that could be used to achieve a happier and more fulfilled daily life.

ACKNOWLEDGEMENT

We would like to thank Dr.Taskos Nikolaos, Professor of Neurology, Department of Medicine (Aristotle University of Thessaloniki, Greece) for his useful collaboration to the present paper and the research itself.

REFERENCES

Bonomo V., 2017. Brain-Based Learning Theory. *Journal of Education and Human Development*, Vol.6, No.1, pp 27-43.

British Neuroscience Association (BNA), 2019. *Neuroscience: Science of the brain – An introduction for young students*. Liverpool, BNA.

Caine, G., Nummela-Caine, R. (1991). *Making Connections: Teaching and the Human Brain*. Menlo Park, CA.: Addison-Wesley Longman, Incorporated.

Dam N., 2013. Inside the learning brain. *Association for talent development*. www.td.org (30-03-2019)

Fishback, S. J., (1999). Learning and the brain. *Adult learning*, 10 (2), pp 18-23.

Jensen, E., 2005. *Teaching with the brain in mind*. Alexandria, VA: ASCD.

Jensen, E., 2000. *Brain based learning*. San Diego, CA: The Brain Store.

Makin, S., 2018. *Travelling brainwaves maybe critical for cognition*. Scientific American, https://www.scientificamerican.com/article/traveling-brain-waves-may-be-critical-for-cognition/

Robinson PA. et al, 2005. Multiscale brain modeling. *Philosophical Transactions of the Royal Society B*. 360 (1457), pp 1043-1050.

Roberts, J. W., 2002. Beyond learning by doing: The brain compatible approach. *The Journal of Experiential Education*. 25 (2), pp 281-285.

Schwartz, E., 1990. *Computational neuroscience*. Cambridge, Mass: MIT Press.

Takano T. et al, 2015. Neuronal polarization. *National Center of Biotechnology Information (NCBI)*. 142 (12), pp 2088-93.

Reflection Papers

THE UAV SIMULATION COMPLEX FOR OPERATOR TRAINING

Oleksandr Volkov, Mykola Komar, Kateryna Synytsya and Dmytro Volosheniuk
International Research and Training Center for Information Technologies and Systems
40, Glushkova ave. Kyiv 03187, Ukraine

ABSTRACT

UAV operators training programs vary depending on the category of the UAV, mission types, requirements to the certification and available platform. The essential part of the UAV operator training is the use of the simulations to facilitate mastering of the piloting skills and operation of the vehicle equipment. Due to the complexity of the simulations, it is desirable to use respective hardware and software complex for a range of training programs. Common topics have been identified based on the analysis of typical training programs, UAV missions and operator functions. The paper outlines the structure of the simulation complex and the framework of the program including simulation-based training and theoretical part which could be supported in a blended mode.

KEYWORDS

Unmanned Aerial Vehicle, Operator Training, UAV Pilot, Flight Simulation

1. INTRODUCTION

The term *unmanned aerial vehicle* (UAV) denotes a wide class of the platforms which either function in an autonomous mode or are remotely operated by a person or a ground team. The UAVs are successfully used in various situations and for various purposes, including civilian and military applications. The primary use of the UAVs was related to missions considered as "dirty, dull, or dangerous" (Elias, B., 2012), such as those related to a hostile environment, situations in which the human health is put on risk, or requiring long-term monitoring which does not require immediate actions. These missions include among others homeland and border security, disaster response, hurricane monitoring, traffic monitoring, application of pesticides. Recent civilian applications extended this list significantly by suggesting research data collection, geospatial imaging, wildlife or natural resources inspection and a variety of trial applications for learning purposes (Shakhatreh, H.et. al, 2018; Crutsinger, G., 2016.). Due to the wide range of potential applications it is important to ensure proper training of UAV operators providing them with the necessary knowledge and skills for the dynamically evolving area.

In Ukraine, UAV services are provided by some specialized organizations only. So far, the UAV operator training has been addressed mostly in security context due to the high cost of the related equipment and lack of the established training requirements. However, due to keen interest in AI, robotics and software engineering advances in the country, the need for efficient training of UAV operators is expected to be growing. The idea behind this research is that basic training could be organized using as a core a flight simulation complex initially developed for academic research of control algorithms. Thus, the purpose of this study is to investigate whether and how this simulation complex could be adapted for training, considering existing requirements and approaches to UAV pilot and operator training.

2. UAV OPERATOR TRAINING PROGRAMS

Expansion of civil and military applications of UAV has led to the appearance of various training programs. These programs are not standardized (Bennett, W., et al, 2016), they are different in volume and objectives and thus difficult to compare. There are several reasons for this variety. First, there are different requirements to the pilot qualification depending on the category of the UAV. Second, many training programs are linked to the specific platform producer, thus focusing on specific hardware, interfaces, and protocols. Third, the programs depend on the potential class of missions, as well as specific team organization ranging from a short course to a special training for pilot license holders (Szabolcsi, R., 2016).

As we intended creating a training environment appropriate for both military and civilian operator training, the next step was to determine respective UAV categories, most typical missions, and operator functions to start with. It has been anticipated that operator training could be similar for certain mission types that share many common operator functions.

In the absence of generally accepted classification of the UAV, several approaches have been studied, starting with (Korchenko, A., 2013) which considers 16 features describing construction, components, and behavior of the vehicle, as well as its category, size, and typical missions. In a more targeted description (Qi, C., 2018), six categories of the UAV are proposed based on the following characteristics: maximum take-off weight, altitude, radius of operation, endurance, i.e. maximum flight time, and typical use. For current modeling purposes, we follow the NASA classification which is limited to three categories based on UAV weight and speed as most representative characteristics. Although the computer modeling has been done for all three types, e.g. High Altitude Long Endurance (HALE), Medium Range (MR), and Mini plane types UAVs that have different aerodynamic characteristics and are used for different missions, the training program development is focused on MR and Mini UAVs.

Our analysis of the UAV missions and operator function taxonomies (Nehme, 2007; Pavlas, 2009) resulted in the selection of the missions related to intelligence, reconnaissance, and surveillance as those applicable in both civilian and military context. Common operator functions for all of them are monitoring the status of the UAV, resource allocation and scheduling, path planning, position or target tracking, monitoring sensors and analyzing sensor data. The last one is specific for mission and sensors. Skills for operators that actually pilot the small UAV also include take-off and landing, cruise, navigation, technical inspection, and reporting.

Most UAV pilot and operator training programs offer some volume of general learning content that explains the basics of aerodynamics, meteorology, electronics and other disciplines. This content is not specific to the vehicle or mission and provides necessary background for operation of the flying vehicle. Another important component of the training program is related to safety issues and regulations, local/global legislation for flying vehicles, risk factors and operation in abnormal situations. Table 1 illustrates how certain topics could be addressed by using the simulation complex, classroom training with access to the real samples of UAV and devices, and distance learning content and tests offered via the LMS Moodle.

Table 1. A general structure of the operator training program

Module	Example of the topic	Learning Environment
General knowledge	Meteorology, navigation	Classroom, Moodle
UAV	Components	Hands-on, Moodle
Safety & Regulations	Safety procedures	Moodle
Equipment	Sensors	Hands-on, Moodle
Reporting	Data analysis	Moodle
Piloting	Take-off and landing	Simulation complex
Mission simulation	Traffic control	Simulation complex

3. UAV SIMULATION COMPLEX

Initially, the UAV simulation complex has been created to support research and development of control algorithms for UAV, in particular, in cases when non-linear model cannot be easily approximated by a linear one. Currently, it contains a collection of plane-type models and software enabling simulation of the UAV behavior in an auto-pilot mode and as a reaction to the manual control. Besides watching the computer simulation of the UAV behavior, the user can observe the behavior of the movable parts, control elements, and engine workload of the real sample of the UAV which is connected to the simulation complex.

The core of the UAV simulation complex contains the main computer with UAV manual flight control device and three displays intended for visualizing the behavior of the UAV, its control dashboard and other simulation-related information (fig.1). The computational environment consists of five main modules implementing dynamic behavior of the UAV, databases management, processing of the simulation parameters, mission and flight information, processing of the on-board control, and visualization of the UAV flight.

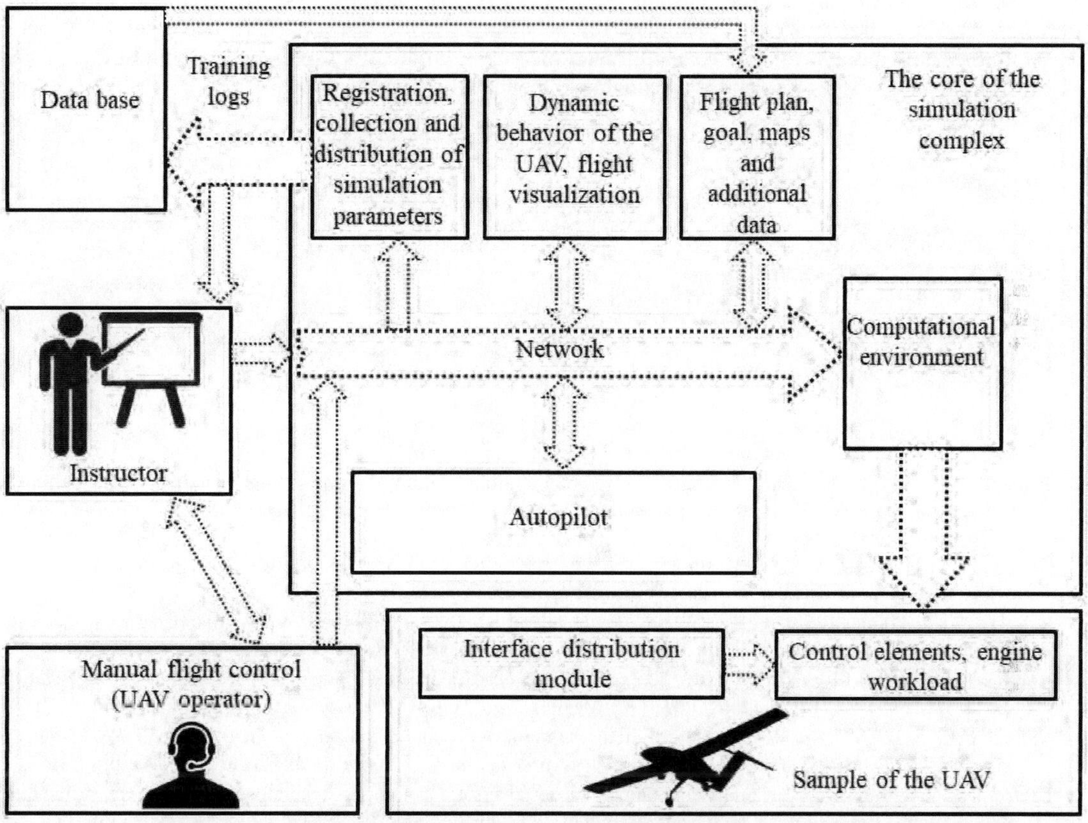

Figure 1. A general scheme of the UAV simulation complex

There are several options to implement training using the simulation complex. First, a student can be given a mission case to accomplish individually using a manual control of the UAV. The parameters of his/her performance are registered and thus the behavior can be reproduced by the simulator for trainer's evaluation and group discussion. For an immediate feedback, a trainer may observe the student's behavior and information available for him, such as dashboard indicators, maps, sensors (not only in the lab but also remotely) and intercept the UAV control or communicate with the student to correct his mistake. There is also an option to specify thresholds for students' deviation from the behavior simulated for a particular case so that they will be warned that remediation is necessary.

To support training of the piloting skills for the Mini UAV located in the lab, a set of tasks (mission cases and maps) has been prepared. Related theoretical part will contain the modules related to the UAV-specific knowledge, such as UAV components (airframe, engine, navigation and control system, on-board payload, launch and landing systems), ground control systems (control panels, communication equipment, and sensors), systems and procedures for UAV pre-flight preparation, take-off and landing, maintenance and repair.

4. CONCLUSION

The proposed approach illustrates the benefits of the existing simulation complex use for the UAV operator training. A common core of skills and knowledge of the UAV revealed in the study allows for suggesting a structure of the blended training program as a combination of simulations, classroom lessons and learning content deliverable via the LMS used by the organization. The proposed modular training program advancing from the basic skills and knowledge related to the UAV operation and arranged around the existing simulation complex may be adapted and extended to address the specific needs. The construction of the simulation complex allows for extensions (equipment, sensors, and models). At the moment, an additional workstation may be connected to simulate the behavior of a foe UAV (target) or partner UAV operating within the same mission. Therefore, the UAV simulation complex may support UAV pilot training for both military and civilian missions and is extendable to the team training.

ACKNOWLEDGEMENT

This research was partly supported by the grant of the National academy of sciences of Ukraine for young researchers groups and laboratories.

REFERENCES

Al-Tahir, R., 2015. Integrating UAV into geomatics curriculum. *The International Archives of Photogrammetry, Remote Sensing and Spatial Information Sciences*, Vol. 40, No.1, pp.387-390.

Bennett, W., et al, 2016. Training issues for remotely piloted aircraft systems from a human systems integration perspective. In Cooke, N., et al (eds.) *Remotely Piloted Aircraft Systems: A Human Systems Inte gration Perspective*, pp.163-176. John Wiley & Sons, Ltd.

Crutsinger, G.M., et al, 2016. The future of UAVs in ecology: an insider perspective from the Silicon Valley drone industry. *Journal of Unmanned Aerial Systems,* Vol. 4, pp. 161-168.

Elias, B., 2012. Pilotless drones: Background and considerations for Congress regarding unmanned aircraft operations in the national airspace system. CRS Report to Congress. Congressional Research Service.

Korchenko A. G. and Illyash O. S., 2013. The generalized classification of Unmanned Air Vehicles, *Proceedings of the 2nd IEEE Conference on Actual Problems of Unmanned Air Vehicles Developments (APUAVD)*, Kiev, pp. 28-34.

Nehme, C.E., et al, 2007, June. An operator function taxonomy for unmanned aerial vehicle missions. *Proceedings of the 12th International Command and Control Research and Technology Symposium*. Washington, DC, pp. 1-9.

Pavlas, D. Et al., 2009, October. Enhancing unmanned aerial system training: A taxonomy of knowledge, skills, attitudes, and methods. *Proceedings o f the Human Fa ctors and Ergonomics Soci ety A nnual Me eting*, Vol. 53, No. 26, pp. 1903-1907. Sage CA: Los Angeles, CA: SAGE Publications.

Qi, S., et al, 2018. Unmanned Aircraft System Pilot/Operator Qualification Requirements and Training Study. *Proceedings of the M ATEC Web of Co nferences.* Wuhan, China. Vol. 179, 03006. EDP Sciences. DOI: 10.1051/matecconf/201817903006.

Shakhatreh, H.et. al, 2018. Unmanned aerial vehicles: A survey on civil applications and key research challenges. IEEE Access. Vol.7. DOI: 7.10.1109/ACCESS.2019.2909530.

Szabolcsi, R., 2016, June. Beyond Training Minimums – A New Concept of the UAV Operator Training Program. *Proceedings of the International con ference K nowledge-Based Organization* . Sibiu, Romania. Vol. 22, No. 3, pp. 560-566. De Gruyter Open.

E-LEARNING ASSISTED DRAMATIZATION FOR COMMUNICATIVE LANGUAGE ABILITY AND COLLABORATIVE LEARNING

Young Mee Kim
Korea Science Academy of KAIST, Baekyang Kwanmoon-ro 105-47, Jin-gu, Busan, S. Korea

ABSTRACT

This study explores the possibilities of developing English communicative ability and fostering collaborative learning through a web-assisted dramatization project. The study aims to present hands-on class management approaches for the dramatization project including class strategies and teaching materials. The action research is based on the context of secondary school learners who use English as a foreign language. The study involves the process of the project model that covers from planning to producing dramas, using a web-assisted Learning Management System. The follow-up surveys indicate that using the dramatization project in English learning facilitates effective and collaborative learning environment as well as improving communicative abilities. The study discusses the benefits and potentials of using dramatization as a team-based project in language education.

KEYWORDS

Learning Management System, Collaborative Learning, Communicative Ability, Project-Based Learning

1. INTRODUCTION

Language learning within a communicative curriculum is, therefore, most appropriately seen as communicative interaction involving all the participants in the learning and including the various materials resources. Breen and Candlin (1980) state that language learning may be seen as a process which grows out of the interaction between learners, teachers, texts and activities. The pedagogic rationale for project-based learning rests on the claim that they will help to develop learners' communicative skills and their linguistic development. Communication tasks are important for both fluency and accuracy (Brumfit 1984). They aid fluency by enabling learners to activate their linguistic knowledge for use and contribute to accuracy by enabling learners to discover new linguistic forms and also by increasing their control over already-acquired forms (Nobuyosh and Ellis 1993:203). Long and Crooks (1992) adopt tasks and projects as the unit of analysis, support a focus on form and aim to help students systematize and extend their knowledge of particular grammatical or lexical features.

2. AIM

The dramatization project with the support of web-based Learning Management System intends to achieve the following aims:

1) To develop English communicative ability through project-based learning

2) To enhance integrated language learning through combination of productive and receptive language skills

3) To cultivate collaborative learning environment through team work.

The project is designed to explore the possibilities of developing English communicative ability and fostering collaborative learning through conducting dramatization project. In addition, the study aims to present hands-on class management approaches for the dramatization project including class strategies and teaching materials.

2.1 Process

The action research is based on the context of secondary school learners who use English as a foreign language. The study involves the process of the project model that covers from planning to producing dramas, using a web-based Learning Management System. Project guidelines and evaluation information were given to 116 students along with previous project samples. Twelve to sixteen students in 8 classes were grouped into four. Sixteen groups of three or four students conducted 15-minute dramatization group project together. Students started brainstorming together, exchanging ideas and opinions to write an outline after selecting chapters and roles of each member. Each group needed to submit a final script and perform acting in class for 15 minutes. Evaluation processes were followed at the end for feedback. The whole process continued and was completed for two weeks in the form of the round-tour method to maximize members' involvement and collaboration. The figure 1 shows the overview of the dramatization project in real classroom context. The figure 2 presents the whole process of the dramatization project. The process runs in parallel at the web-based Learning Management System as well as in the classroom.

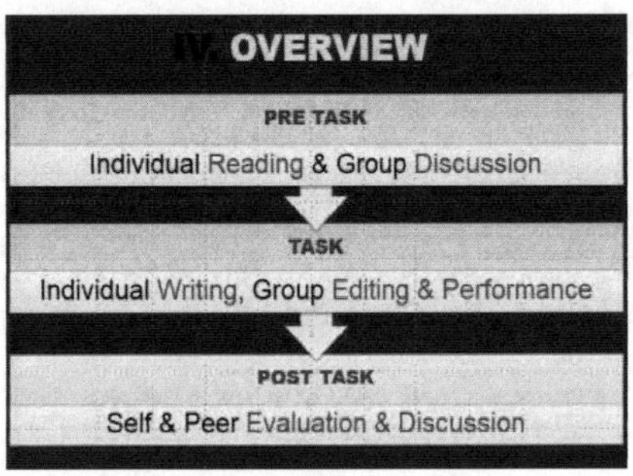

Figure 1. Overview of Project

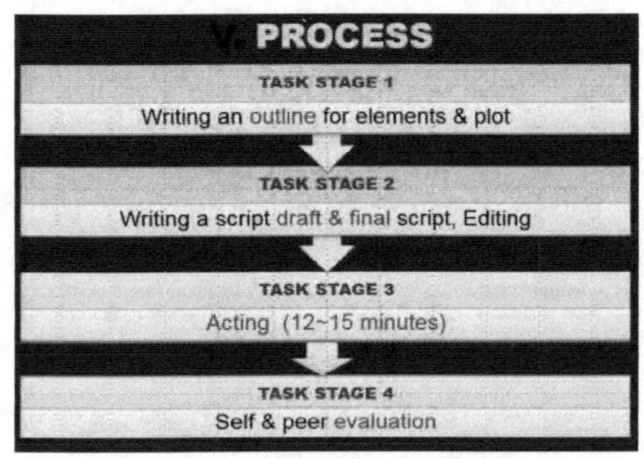

Figure 2. Process of Project

2.2 Content and Materials

Four parts of the main task stage are the core content of the dramatization project. The first part is to write an outline, including key elements and a plot for the project. After Students are introduced to the details of the project with specified guidelines, they are provided with two types of outline formats, descriptive and guided. One of students' main activities is to write a script for fifteen-minute acting. Students go through sessions of discussion and role taking and interact with a teacher to complete their final scripts in the form of draft script editing. The other main activity is the performance of fifteen-minute acting in class. During the performance other students conduct peer evaluation in the forms provided by a teacher. Right after the performance students evaluate themselves with a self-evaluation form. The figure 3 is the outline for students to fill out beforehand. The figure 4 is one of the various students' outcome of the outline.

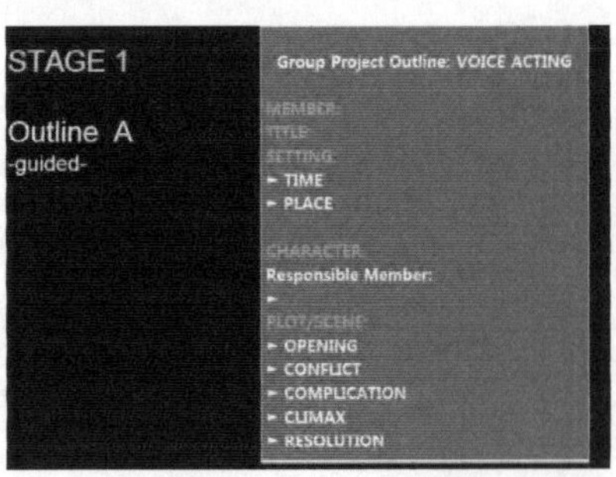

Figure 3. Outline of Project

Figure 4. Outcome of Outline

2.3 Evaluation and Outcome

At each part of the task stage, students are provided with relevant materials and appropriate outcome is expected to be produced. In the task stage one, documented specific guidelines for the whole project are given and students sign up for random grouping. In this stage, students' outcome is checked by the form of project outlines. For the stage of writing a script, teachers introduce script templates with samples of previous students' outlines and scripts. In the main performance and followed evaluation stage, teachers use formatted documents of peer evaluation and self-evaluation with the explanation of rationale of evaluation processes. Teachers provide each group with detailed feedback in the form of documented evaluation. The figure 5 and 6 are the teacher evaluation form and the outcome of peer evaluation. The figure 7 is the form of self-evaluation of the project and the figure 8 is the outcome of self-evaluation.

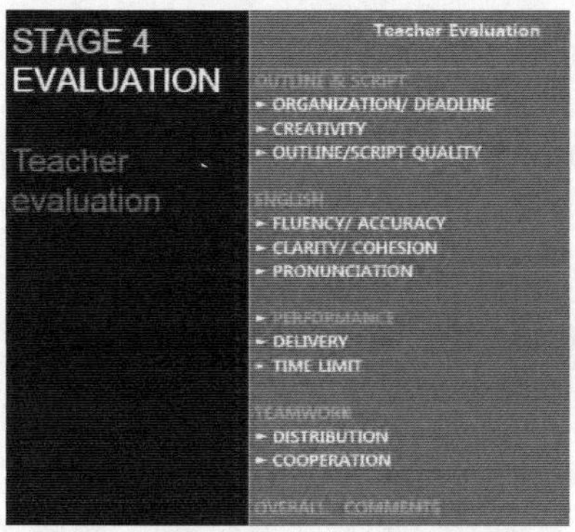

Figure 5. Teacher Evaluation of Project

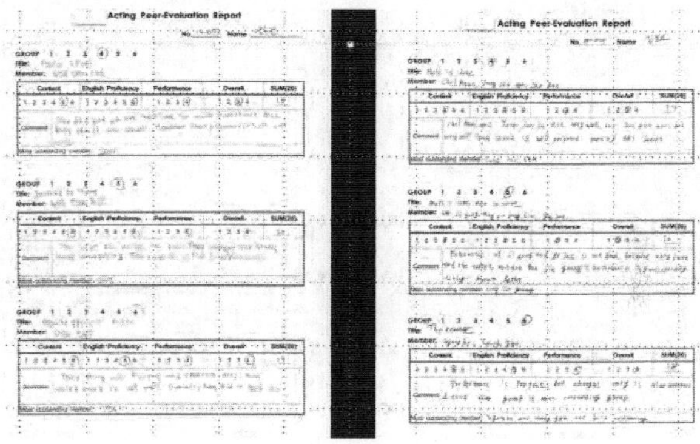

Figure 6. Outcome of Peer Evaluation

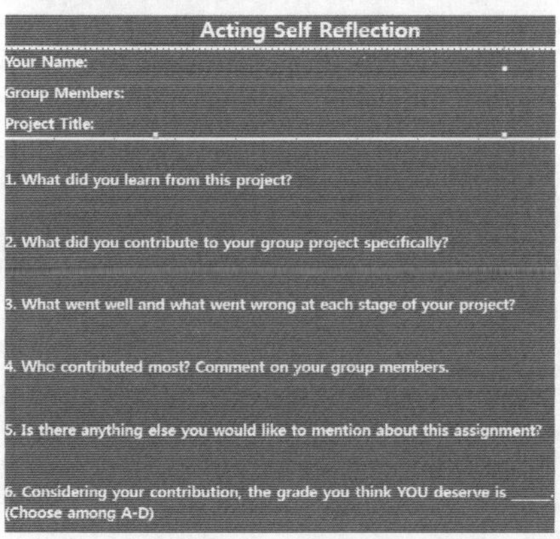

Figure 7. Self-evaluation of Project

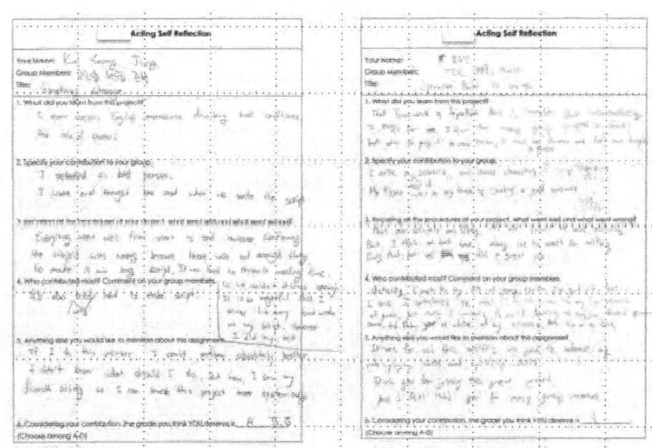

Figure 8. Outcome of Self-evaluation

3. CONCLUSION

The process of the dramatization project is focused on integrated language learning, covering speaking, listening, reading and writing. Collaborative learning environment is an additional merit for the project. The project is found to be useful for English communicative abilities with the main impetus of speaking ability. The purposely designed project materials and processes have positive influence on collaborative learning. The whole processes give an insight to educators for their decisions for communicative language learning and teaching strategies. The study discusses the benefits and potentials of using dramatization as a team-based project in language education for encouraging collaborative learning along with developing communicative skills.

ACKNOWLEDGEMENT

This work was funded by the Ministry of Science and ICT.

REFERENCES

Brumfit, C. J. 1984. *Communicative Methodology in Language Teaching*. Cambridge: CUP.

Breen, M. Candlin, C. 1980. The essentials of a communicative curriculum in language teaching. *Applied Linguistics* 1(2), 89-110.

Nobuyosh, J. and Ellis, R. 1993. Focused communicative tasks and second language acquisition, *ELT Journal* 47(1), 203-10.

Long, M. H. and Crookes, G. 1992. Three approaches to task-based syllabus design, *TESOL Quarterly* 26(1), 27-55.

GENERATING GRAPHS IN VIRTUAL REALITY

Simon So
The Education University of Hong Kong
10 Lo Ping Road, Tai Po, N.T., Hong Kong

ABSTRACT

Recent advances in Head-mounted Display (HMD) for Virtual Reality have been phenomenal. The quality of the latest HMDs such as Oculus Rift, HTC Vive and Sony PlayStation VR is high. These highly immersive devices create educational opportunities as well as challenges. Specifically, we can create or view graphs in a virtual environment. This innovative technology of generating graphs opens up a new horizon. We can plot 3D graphs so that the user can view the graphs from any angles and examine the graphs virtually. Furthermore, dynamic data can be summarized into diagrams and graphs. If such data are fed into the virtual system, we can view the change of the graphs virtually. In this paper, we will demonstrate the presentation of graphs using HMDs in Virtual Reality. We will illustrate hand-drawings and system-generated graphs in virtual spaces. Students' views on creating graphs in Virtual Reality will be examined. An overview of VR devices and software to produce graphs will also be discussed.

KEYWORDS

Virtual Reality, Head-mounted Display, Graphing, Virtual Data Visualization

1. INTRODUCTION

With the proliferation of consumer-level head-mounted displays and motion tracking devices, virtual reality experience has been phenomenal in recent years. Recently, the releases of Oculus Rift (2019), HTC Vive (2019) and Sony PlayStation VR (2019) have changed the consumer market of virtual reality significantly. We can now play highly immersive VR games with these devices. To educators, VR devices are becoming more affordable and accessible. VR applications are being released constantly. The education sector, the entertainment industry, the business sector and many other fields can be benefited from many of these applications.

In this paper, we will explore how VR can be used in creating virtual 3D graphs. We are interested to generating graphs virtually by either sketching or generating graphs in virtual space. Sketching graphs can promote learning (Fiorella & Mayer, 2016) and this is an important pedagogical approach for teachers. We will explore hand-drawing graphs in virtual space. This experience is unique and the approach may be useful for teachers.

Graphs and figures can be generated by machines. For example, a virtual reality system may take instructions from upstream systems to generate virtual models of molecular figures in Organic Chemistry (Stull, Barrett & Hegarty, 2012). Their findings suggest a benefit of using virtual models over concrete models. In this paper, we are more interested on graphs; system-generated graphs. These graphs are being generated in a virtual space by static data files or pre-processed data from dynamic sources. For example, stock market information can be accessed through Virtual Reality (Sá & Dähne, 2016). Many immersive and intuitive ways to interact with graphs can be found. This opens up a range of innovations and challenges to draw graphs.

In Section 2, we will discuss hand-drawing and system-generated graphs. Some of the possibilities are outlined in this section. The students' views on using VR for educational purposes and creating virtual reality graphs are revealed in Section 3. Section 4 will provide a summary discussion.

2. GRAPHING IN VIRTUAL REALITY

2.1 Hand-Drawing Graphs

Painting in 3D space with virtual reality has been made popular by Google Tilt Brush (2019). Tilt Brush allows the creator to completely immerse in virtual reality for 3D painting using paddles like HTC Vive's controllers or Oculus Touch controllers with their respective head-mounted displays. The creative potential of this technology is not restricted to artists, cartoonist, painters, designers, illustrators and other creators (TIME, 2019). Educators can make use of this tool for drawing, painting and sculpting. The tool allows educators to extend learning virtually. In our case, drawing graphs in virtual space are both creative and fascinating. Students can learn from graphs created by teachers in 3D space. They can walk 360° around the graphs. Viewing from different orientations can provide different perspectives to learners. For example, if 3D vectors were drawn on a 3D graph, students can observe the vectors' projection on a 2D plane by walking to the perpendicular position of a principle axis. Figure 1 illustrates an example and the vectors' projection is shown in Figure 2. Furthermore, sketching graphs in a virtual space are both fun and challenging.

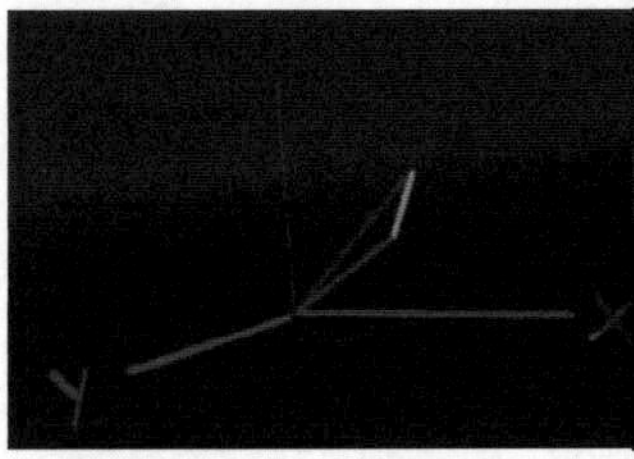

Figure 1. 3D vectors sketched on a virtual space

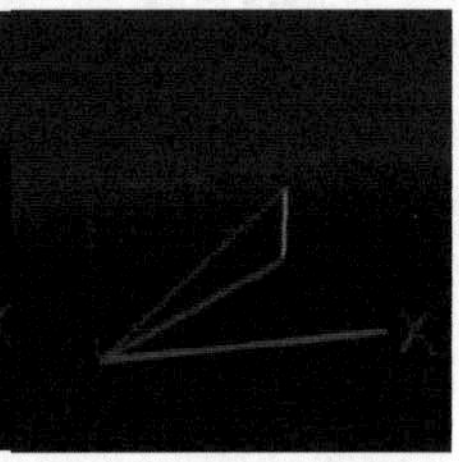

Figure 2. The vectors projected onto X-Z plane

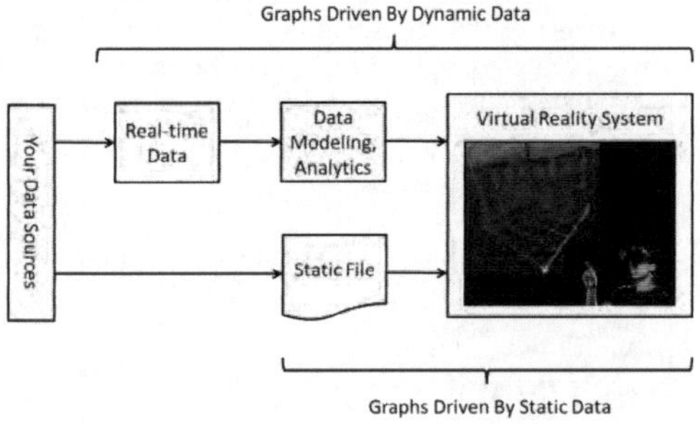

Figure 3. The concept of static and dynamic data driven graphs

Figure 4. The plot of the tallest buildings in the world

Figure 5. Point to the tallest building

Figure 6. The plot of a double helix

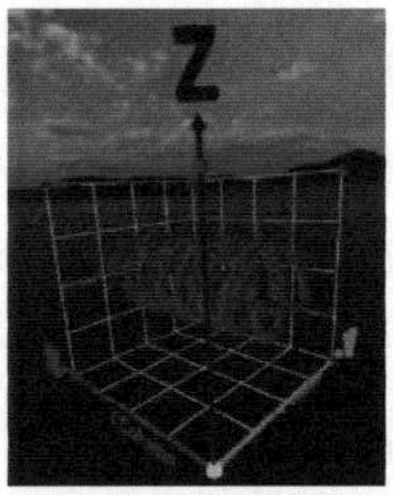

Figure 7. Swap the axes to see the helix differently

2.2 System-generated Graphs

Generating graphs in virtual reality can be carried out statically or dynamically. Data can be read from static files to generate graphs in a virtual space. Alternatively, data can be fed into the virtual reality system from dynamic sources (Sá & Dähne, 2016). Figure 3 illustrates the concept. Depending on the sophistication of the underlying software, the viewer can decide the required types of graphs, manipulate the presentation, examine the individual data points, and view the graphs from different positions (DatavizVR, 2018; Virtualitics, 2019; LookVR, 2019). The virtual reality system can be programmed generically to visualize standardized data or specifically coded to handle incoming data and present the specific graphs interactively.

This approach offers educators a whole new manner for students to learn graphs. Students can interact with graphs driven by the data in a virtual space. For examples, students can select any data point in the graphs to examine the values. Figure 4 illustrates the examination of a data point by a student on the data set of the tallest buildings in the world in the 3D graph using the paddles in DatavizVR (2018). In this VR system, users can configure the X, Y, Z-coordinates for 3D graphs. They can point and choose the data point to examine and view the data from all angles as shown in Figure 5. The examination of a double helix is shown in Figure 6 and 7. The color and size of each data point can be used to represent the fourth and fifth dimensions.

Dynamic data can be pre-processed and fed into a virtual reality system. To gain insights from the dynamic data sets, the data can be transformed by certain data modeling techniques or certain analytic tools as illustrated in Figure 3. These tools process and provide visualization and interaction of dynamic data in virtual space (Nagel, Granum, & Musaeus, 2001; Olshannikova, et. al., 2015). Figure 8 shows the processed data of Olympic medalists from LookVR (2019). Artificial intelligence and machine learning are some of the common processing tools as shown in Figure 9 from Virtualitics (2019). Data from finance, healthcare, transportation, security and many other disciplines can be huge. These data are commonly referred as big data. If these big data are processed and fed into the virtual reality system (Moran, et. al., 2015; Marks, Estevez, & Connor, 2014; Donalek, et. al., 2014), the viewers can immerse themselves in the processed data and inspect the dynamic nature of the data in a more natural and intuitive way. This revolutionizes the visualization of big data.

Figure 8. 3D bar charts of Olympic medalists

Figure 9. Visualizing data after processing techniques in AI and machine learning

3. STUDENTS' VIEWS ON CREATING GRAPHS IN VIRTUAL REALITY

Three students were asked to explore the applications of sketching and interacting with graphs in virtual reality. The lab has HTC Vive, Sony PlayStation VR, Oculus Rift and a number of handheld VR devices. The experiment was conducted mainly with HTC Vive. The other devices such as Sony PlayStation VR are mainly for VR games. The students worked with some of the above software. Interviews were conducted afterward. The following responses come from one of the students:

Question:	Response:
1. What is your general experience in VR?	It was fun and interesting.
2. Do you believe VR technologies can provide a highly immersive environment for learners?	Yes, indeed. This is a whole new experience to me and I am sure this is the same for other people like me.
3. Do you feel VR should be used in classroom?	Yes, but the equipment can be expensive and only one person can use it in the classroom if only one set is available.
4. Do you agree that VR allows the learners to proceed at their own pace?	I agree. In my case, I can undo the sketching steps that I don't like.
5. Do you agree that VR motivates students and encourage active participation rather than passivity?	It depends on the quality of imageries and the level of interaction.
6. Do you agree that VR provides new forms and methods of visualization?	I totally agree. With the graphs, having a close-up examination, observing from a distance and selecting a data point were allowed. This is a highly immersive experience on visualization.
7. In sketching graphs, how do you feel?	It is fun. I can freely express myself in the 3D canvas. To draw in 3D space, I am not used to it and the spatial orientation is a bit odd to me.
8. Do you encounter any problem in sketching diagrams?	Yes, sometime I thought two lines are touching but they don't. You need to walk around to see these.
9. In generating graphs from the data sets, how do you feel?	This is fascinating. I can walk around to see the plot at different positions. I can examine different data points in 3D.
10. Do you encounter any problem in plotting graphs?	Not really. The interaction in choosing items in the menu and data are new to me.

4. DISCUSSION

Sketching in Virtual Reality has never been so exciting before Google Tilt Brush (2019). The tool is not only good for artists (Tilt Brush AiR, 2019). You can also import objects into the virtual space which is a great feature for designers. The rich features in Tilt Brush allow educators to extend their teaching to Virtual Reality. In this experiment, we explored the use of this tool to sketch or draw graphs. Inside the virtual space, the users can freely express themselves. The analogy would be that students can use pencils or drawing tools to create graphs onto physical papers. They found some possibilities that the physical world does not have or cannot be easily achieved. The sketching process is intuitive. This is certainly an educational tool for sketching graphs in a virtual environment.

In system-generated graphs, we are interested in generating graphs from static and dynamic data. In the experiment, users can manipulate a range of features and examine data from any angle in the virtual space. The only limitation is from the software itself. Although these applications are still new to the market, we expect more universal applications will be launched in the coming years so that we can connect a range of structured and semi-structured data to the virtual systems. Visualization of small or big data can be more efficient, immersive and intuitive.

In Virtual Reality, it is possible to allow users from different locations to "teleport" to the virtual environment and work or learn collaboratively as a group. Each user is a fully featured avatar in the virtual environment. This feature can be useful and interesting for many tasks in education such as generating 3D graphs and in business. With the ever increasing power of hardware, the feature is around the corner.

Overall, students like the experience in Virtual Reality. They felt VR technologies can be useful for teaching and learning. They enjoy making graphs with the tools. They could proceed at their own pace.

REFERENCES

DatavizVR (2018). Dataviz VR. Retrieved on 15 April 2018, from http://www.datavizvr.com/

Donalek, C., Djorgovski, S. G., Cioc, A., Wang, A., Zhang, J., Lawler, E., & Davidoff, S. (2014). Immersive and collaborative data visualization using virtual reality platforms. *2014 IEEE International Conference on Big Data*. pp. 609-614. IEEE Press (2014, October)

Fiorella, L., & Mayer, R. E. (2016). Effects of observing the instructor draw diagrams on learning from multimedia messages. *Journal of Educational Psychology*, *108*(4), 528.

Google Tilt Brush (2019). Google Tilt Brush. Retrieved on 30 April 2019, from http://www.tiltbrush.com/

HTC Vive (2019). HTC Vive. Retrieved on 30 April 2019, from http://www.vive.com/

LookVR (2019). LookVR. Retrieved on 30 April 2019, from http://looker.com/vr/

Marks, S., Estevez, J., & Connor, A. (2014). Towards the Holodeck: fully immersive virtual reality visualisation of scientific and engineering data. *Proceedings of the 29th International Conference on Image and Vision Computing*. New Zealand. ACM. pp. 42-47

Moran, A., Gadepally, V., Hubbell, M., & Kepner, J. (2015). Improving Big Data visual analytics with interactive virtual reality. *High Performance Extreme Computing Conference (HPEC)*, pp. 1-6. IEEE. (2015, September)

Nagel, H. R., Granum, E., & Musaeus, P. (2001). Methods for visual mining of data in virtual reality. *Proceedings of the International Workshop on Visual Data Mining*, pp. 13--27 (2001, September)

Oculus Rift (2019). Oculus Rift S. Retrieved on 30 April 2019, from http://www.oculus.com/rift

Olshannikova, E., Ometov, A., Koucheryavy, Y., & Olsson, T. (2015). Visualizing big data with augmented and virtual reality: challenges and research agenda. *Journal of Big Data*, 2:22.

Sá, V. J., & Dähne, P. (2016). Accessing Financial Data through Virtual Reality. *Atas da Conferência da Associação Portuguesa de Sistemas de Informação*. Vol. 3. No. 3.

Sony PlayStation VR (2019). Sony PS4 VR. Retrieved on 30 April 2019, from https://www.playstation.com/

Tilt Brush AiR (2019). Tilt Brush Artist in Residence. Retrieved on 30 April 2019, from http://www.tiltbrush.com/air/

Stull, A. S., Barrett, T. J., & Hegarty, M. (2012). Design of a virtual reality system for the study of diagram use in organic chemistry. *Proceedings of the workshop on technology-enhanced diagrams research*. pp.33-41.

TIME (2019). Virtual reality for artists. Retrieved on 30 April 2019, from http://time.com/vr-is-for-artists/

Virtualitics (2019). Virtualitics. Retrieved on 30 April 2019, from http://www.virtualitics.com/

HTC Vive (2019). HTC Vive. Retrieved on 30 April 2019, from http://www.vive.com/

EXPERIENTIAL LEARNING WITH SANSAR PLATFORM – A CONCEPT OF MILITARY TRAINING

Małgorzata Gawlik-Kobylińska and Paweł Maciejewski
War Studies University
ul. Chrusciela 103, 00-910 Warsaw, Poland

ABSTRACT

The aim of this paper is to introduce a concept of military training using a three-dimensional platform, known as Sansar. This is an extensive virtual world that users can access via accessories. We propose basic assumptions, instructional design approach, and a training concept design for consideration as an additional voice in discussions on reliable virtual military training solutions. We also stress that performing dangerous tasks with simulations and gamified activities provide opportunities for experiential learning, which takes place in a completely safe, virtual environment. The paper concluded that hypothetical situations in scenarios based on four dimensions of learning will be beneficial for learners, teachers, and institutions organizing such trainings.

KEYWORDS

Sansar, Experiential Learning, Security And Safety, CBRN+E training, Military Training

1. INTRODUCTION

The emergence and accessibility of state-of-the-art virtual platforms encourage teachers to use them in didactic processes (Liagkou, Stylios, 2019; Lawrence, Ahmed 2018; Melchor-Couto, 2019). This paper proposes a concept of military training that incorporates a three-dimensional (3D) virtual platform, Sansar, in a didactic process; it assumes that the application of this environment in virtual military exercises will bring huge benefits to learners, teachers and institutions organizing such trainings. Sansar, or Project Sansar, is a host for user-created virtual experiences developed by Linden Lab (Perry, 2015). It can be described as a screen-based simulation (Bastung et al., 2017) or a metaverse, a collective virtual shared space that users can access via virtual (VR) reality headsets, VR body trackers, PCs and mobile phones (Mc Adory, 2015; Baker, 2016; Sansar website, 2019). It must be mentioned that Sansar inherits the idea of "the world by residents" from Second Life, a free online virtual world platform, but due to its highly realistic computer-generated imagery, the possibility of entering it with VR accessories, Sansar, together with another similar platform, High Fidelity, exceed the affordances of Second Life (Kwon, Hudson-Smith, 2018. However, it was noted that exercises in full immersion may cause short-time side effects, such as motion sickness, disorientation, and nausea. Headsets with higher refresh rates, increased resolution and proper game designs are recommended to reduce the effects (Liagkou, Stylios, 2019).

Sansar offers the possibility of creating realistic locations or fantastic places. The designed content can be explored and published by its users. Other possibilities such as movements, voice chat, and facial animations allow for the designing of tasks based on experiencing hypothetical situations in real-life scenarios. The functionalities and application of accessories, create opportunities for experiential learning tasks, since people learn best through experience (Kolb, 2014). In military environments, experiential learning can apply to simulations (Miller et al. 2008) and games (Guillén-Nieto, Aleson-Carbonell, 2012) used to teach specific behaviours and procedures.

The introduced proposal views Sansar platform as a tool for performing specific didactic activities related to chemical, biological, nuclear, radiological, and explosive (CBRN+E) defence training. The increasing number of reports in literature on the ability to learn from one's own mistakes in a simulated environment underlies the concept of creating a virtual island for CBRN+E defence training (Nedic et al. 2003; Klein, 2009; Konak et al. 2014; Lowe & Faniglione, 2016). The paper contributes to the review of open-source virtual platforms to be used in training.

2. VIRTUAL ISLAND IN CBRN+E TRAINING

2.1 Basic Assumptions

We propose to create a multifunctional virtual island in a 3D environment (Sansar) for CBRN+E training. A wide range of Sansar platform functionalities can be used for designing game-based exercises and simulations relevant for first responders training. The motivation for designing and using such an island is connected with the need to create a safe environment for exercises that are usually performed in a contaminated environment (behaviours before and after CBRN+E incidents). Safe environment refers to the performance of tasks without the risk of death or serious injury. This 3D platform allows for the creation of specific sites depicting dangerous places. What is more, training conditions that are not possible to recreate in real life can be easily created in the virtual world.

Virtualization does not replace traditional training, but it is a complementary element (blended form of training). In essence, virtualization reduces to the minimum "auxiliary activities" related to the design of a virtual hostile field for training. Learners (those performing activities in a virtual island) would be familiarized with issues such as preparedness against any disaster, contamination avoidance, CBRN mitigation, knowledge on characteristics and effects of chemical and biological agents, radiological material, and nuclear weapons (Maciejewski, 2017). In most of these topics, the scenarios will involve things that can harm human health and life environmental factors. The applied games and simulations will provide opportunities to acquire competences that are significant for first responders from the field of CBRN+E defence. Learning from their own mistakes without real-life consequences underlies the training concept assumptions.

2.2 Instructional Design Approach

Since the design of educational activities in the virtual environment is challenging, a four-dimensional instructional design (4D ID) approach is proposed for military training (Gawlik-Kobylińska, 2016, 2018). In this approach, the cognitive, emotional, social and psychomotor dimensions of learning are taken in consideration. The cognitive dimension concerns the design that specifically facilitates memorizing and processing of information; the emotional dimension concentrates on arousing positive emotions, attitudes and motivations, while the social dimension involves interactions between individuals and their social environments (cf. Illeris, 2003). Lastly, the psychomotor dimension focuses on the design of kinesthetic activities (e.g. Kinect technology), which are important for memorizing military drills (muscular memory) and exercising procedures. Balancing all dimensions in the scenario design is aimed at achieving better learners' performance (Gawlik-Kobylińska, 2018).

2.3 Training Concept Design

The target group consists of soldiers and officers who serve as CBRN+E first responders. It should be noted that the activities they perform in a virtual environment will concern selected issues from the area of CBRN+E defence, specifically chemical and radiological (CR) incidents response as they are easier for realization in VR environment. The participants in the training will play the avatar. They will perform exercises individually and as a team, in a synchronous mode, under the supervision of an instructor. Due to the fact that this type of training is usually performed in small groups, transferring a part of learning activities to the virtual environment and managing it should not be burdensome for a teacher. Within gaming and simulation activities, single learning experiences can be of a great value as they can be used to assess the performance of an individual. A virtual performance could be recorded for further discussion in a small group. Recorded actions can also be reused in other activities (Thomas, Schneider, 2017, Sicilia, Sanchez-Alonso, n.d., Harwood, 2016).

All learning activities can be supported with additional tools, for instance e-learning platform, which will provide the opportunity for asynchronous learning (self-education): it could be a specialized forum, multimedia materials, tutorials, e-learning courses, etc. Apart from the basic training island, other facilities can be developed, e.g. a library, cinema - display of training videos, and a conference room for the purpose of instructions, briefings, and seminars. An immediate feedback from teachers and systemic messages on learning progress will increase the self-awareness and commitment of learners (Sharmanska & Quadrianto, 2016; Fardinpour et al., 2017).

Due to rapid development and easier access to new technologies, the concept of training could be based on the integration of a virtual platform (Sansar) with smart accessories such as VR goggles, instruments for sampling, contamination measurement, and specialist equipment handling.

3. CONCLUSION

Sansar platform, with its functionalities and the possibility of full immersion through the use of accessories, has prospects in military training, especially training tasks that are related to dangerous situations. Learning through experience is reinforced with the use of simulations and gaming activities involving a hazardous environment. The advantages of the concept encompass the perspectives of learners, teachers, and institutions.

For learners, the virtual military island on Sansar platform provides experiential learning in safe training conditions, which can be performed anytime and anywhere, regardless of the weather condition or distance. Additionally, the application of the 4D ID approach to the scenario design process is to maintain greater motivation and engagement in the tasks among learners.

For teachers, it provides the possibility of teaching multinational groups and tracing of learning progress by recording activities. Due to the rapid development of new technologies as well as the versatility and modifiability of the virtual environment, Sansar can be a universal platform for the implementation of a wide range of military training activities, ranging from tactics to experimental laboratories for investigations after CBRN+E incidents (rapid virtualization of a contaminated site with depiction of loss) and the possibility of implementing non-invasive chemical experiments.

The benefits for institutions are connected with lower costs of preparation of on-site incident, which is related to a significant reduction in the overall cost of training. Sansar, as an open source tool, can be used by groups of military learners from different locations, and such a course may benefit a greater number of individuals. This can lead to greater international cooperation in crisis response situation trainings. Also, if required, the training island can be available only to authorized users, with access zone control.

It should be noted that when the training program is used, it would be appropriate that soldiers and officers value the experience. At the same time, a feedback should be provided by teachers (didactic challenges, teaching preferences) and decision-makers (overall assessment, which includes, among others, cost of the training and its effectiveness).

The limitations of the concept primarily concerns the technical aspects, as in some developing countries, access to teleinformatics infrastructure could be a hindrance. Also, the software may not allow for depicting all elements and military equipment; moreover, not all experiments based on the laws of physics can be executed. Regarding psychological and social limitations of such training, it is necessary to mention the learners' preferences regarding the use of such tools. Learners and teachers also may encounter technical barriers that discourage them from using VR tools.

The increasing use of virtual reality in various aspects of human activity generates an increasing demand for research in the field of potential use of new technologies, especially for security and defence purposes. The concept will be highly useful in developing innovative trainings in the field of education for security and defence. It will also contribute to the analyses of the virtual world's didactic potential.

REFERENCES

Barker, V. E. 2016. Flow in virtual worlds: The interplay of community and site features as predictors of involvement. *Journal for Virtual Worlds Research*, *9*(3).

Bastug, E., Bennis, M., Médard, M., & Debbah, M. 2017. Toward interconnected virtual reality: Opportunities, challenges, and enablers. *IEEE Communications Magazine*, *55*(6), pp. 110-117.

Fardinpour, A., Reiners, T., & Wood, L. C. 2017. Action-based learning assessment in virtual training environments. Authentic Virtual World Education, pp. 79–94. doi:10.1007/978-981-10-6382-4_6

Gawlik-Kobylińska, M. 2018. The Four-Dimensional Instructional Design Approach in the Perspective of Human-Computer Interactions. In *Applications of Intelligent Systems: Proceedings of the 1st International APPIS Conference 2018* (Vol. 310, p. 146). IOS Press.

Gawlik-Kobylińska, M. 2016, Cztery wymiary uczenia się w projektowaniu scenariusza kursu e-learning owego, *Zeszyty Naukowe Akademii Obrony Narodowej*, 105(4), pp.39-52.

Guillén-Nieto, V., & Aleson-Carbonell, M. 2012. Serious games and learning effectiveness: The case of It's a Deal!. *Computers & Education*, *58*(1), pp. 435-448.

Harwood, T. 2016. Co-curated Digital Culture: Machinima. *Leonardo*. MIT Press Journal, Massachusetts, USA.

Illeris, K. 2003. Towards a contemporary and comprehensive theory of learning. *International Journal of Lifelong Education, 22*, pp. 396–406.

Klein, R. 2009. Learning from Others and Learning from Mistakes Reflections on Health Policy Making. *Comparative Studies and the Politics of Modern Medical Care*, pp. 305–318.

Kolb, D. A. 2014. *Experiential learning: Experience as the source of learning and development*. FT press, New Jersey, USA.

Konak, A., Clark, T. K., & Nasereddin, M. 2014. Using Kolb's Experiential Learning Cycle to improve student learning in virtual computer laboratories. *Computers & Education*, *72*, pp. 11-22.

Kwon, H; Hudson-Smith, AP. 2018. Redesigning Experience Consumption in Social VR Worlds: Decentralised Value Creation, Mobilisation, and Exchanges. In *Proceedings of the Academic Design Management Conference: Next Wave ADMC18*. (pp. 269-278). DMI: Ravensbourne University, London, UK

Lawrence, G., & Ahmed, F. 2018. Pedagogical Insights into Hyper-Immersive Virtual World Language Learning Environments. *International Journal of Computer-Assisted Language Learning and Teaching (IJCALLT)*, *8*(1), pp. 1-14.

Liagkou, V., & Stylios, C. 2019. A Case Study of a Virtual Training Environment. In *Advances in Manufacturing II*, pp. 352-367. Springer, Cham.

Lowe, G., & Faniglione, D. 2016. Virtual Training for the Development of Real World Skills. ICERI 2016 Proceedings.

Maciejewski, P. 2017. ICT tools in CBRN troops' education and training. *Zeszyty Naukowe/Wyższa Szkoła Oficerska Wojsk Lądowych im. gen. T. Kościuszki, 49*(4), pp. 121-137.

Melchor-Couto, S. 2019. Virtual worlds and language learning. *Journal of Gaming & Virtual Worlds*, *11*(1), pp. 29-43.

McAdory, P. 2015, August 20. Second Life developer invites first creators to next-gen made-forVR virtual world [blog post]. Retrieved from http://www.roadtovr.com/second-life-developerinvites-first-creators-to-next-gen-made-for-vr-virtual-world/

Miller, K. K., Riley, W., Davis, S., & Hansen, H. E. (2008). In situ simulation: a method of experiential learning to promote safety and team behavior. *The Journal of perinatal & neonatal nursing*, *22*(2), pp. 105-113.

Nedic, Z., Machotka, J., & Nafalski, A. 2003. Remote laboratories versus virtual and real laboratories. *IEEE.33rd Annual Frontiers in Education,* Vol. 1, pp. T3E-T3E).

Perry, T. S. 2015. Virtual reality goes social. *IEEE Spectrum*, *53*(1), pp. 56-57.

Sansar website. 2019, June 11.Sansar compatibility FAQ. Retrieved from https://help.sansar.com/hc/en-us/articles/360027483852-Sansar-compatibility-FAQ.

Sharmanska, V., & Quadrianto, N. 2016. Learning from the Mistakes of Others: Matching Errors in Cross-Dataset Learning. *2016 IEEE Conference on Computer Vision and Pattern Recognition (CVPR)*.

Sicilia, M.-A., & Sanchez-Alonso, E. n.d. Reusable Learning Resources for Virtual Learning Environments. *Encyclopedia of Virtual Communities and Technologies*.

Thomas, M. & Schneider, C. 2017. Language Learning with Machinima: Video Production in 3D Immersive Environments. In: Teaching English reflectively with technology. IATEFL, Canterbury, UK.

A CRITIQUE OF JACQUES ELLUL (FRENCH PHILOSOPHER) ON TECHNOLOGY

George A Lotter
Prof., North-West University, South Africa

ABSTRACT

In this paper it is investigated if the influential book published in 1990 by the French philosopher Jacques Ellul about *The Technological Bluff* was valid in its predictions about the development of technology. The main thesis of the book was that technology always begets more technology and he warned against the "absolutization of the scientific design". It will be shown how influential this book is today while Ellul's legacy is still kept alive. A critical discussion of Ellul's book will be given and the development of current technology, followed by some pointers in dealing with current technology, conclusion and a summary.

KEYWORDS

Ellul, Technology, French Philosopher

1. INTRODUCTION

The problem statement this paper will be focusing on, is whether what the French philosopher Jacques Ellul had written in *The Technological Bluff* is fictitious or relevant. A short overview on different positions regarding the influence of technology on human beings will be given, followed by a discussion on the views of Ellul and a critique of it to see if they are still applicable in the new millennium. Technology, the internet and cyberspace have developed and give an excellent opportunity to evaluate Ellul views and if it really happened what he had predicted in 1990. Following that, some suggested pointers will be proposed in dealing with "modern technology" (as typified by Ellul), a conclusion and a summary of the paper will be given.

2. ELLUL'S VIEW ON TECHNOLOGY

The French philosopher Jacques Ellul (1912-1994) is well-known for reflection and critique on technology and the influence it would have in the world. In searching the WWW one still finds many references to Ellul, in the Google site for instance, about 26 500 hits by March 1st 2019.

Ellul had altogether written 43 books in which four where he had specifically critiqued the overestimation of science's potential in technology. They are: *The Technological Society*; *Propaganda: The Formation of Men's Attitudes*; *Perspective on Our Age* and the last one: *The Technological Bluff.*

There is even an International Jacques Ellul Society (http://www.ellul.org/ijes.htm) which has it as their aim to preserve and make broadly available and support his legacy. In this paper only *The Technological Bluff* will be discussed as the *magnus opera* of Ellul.

The Technological Bluff is a comprehensive work of 412 pages (without the bibliography) divided into 22 chapters. It was first published in French with the title *Le bluff technologique* and translated by G W Bromiley in 1989 and published in 1990. The difficulty with the translation into English is explained by Bromiley himself:

> Established usage in English makes it difficult to retain the distinction that Ellul himself always makes and emphasizes between *la technique* (technique) and *la technologie* (technology). It should be remembered, however, that in the title Ellul has the stricter sense in view, is technology as discourse, study, or system.

For the purposes of this paper, technology will be focused on as an overarching term for all development in that area.

The book makes for difficult reading and is definitely not material for leisure and relaxation!

In all the books Ellul had written, he dealt in more or lesser terms with his view of technology as something which, when "...let out of the laboratory, cannot be turned off", and suggested that technology begets more technology. Ellul also predicted that when technology triggers unforeseen events (Ellul, 1990:82) and warned against the absolutization of the scientific design as well as its having a trait of "imperialism" and described the bluff of "consisting essentially of rearranging everything in terms of technical progress".

A limitation the English reader of the book experiences, is that Ellul often refers to other French authors which are not accessible and can therefore not be consulted independently.

Just by gleaning the chapter names and divisions, one gets the idea that Ellul is very much against many of the developments of technology: he uses words like *uncertainty, ambivalence, internal contradictions, unreason, philosophy of the absurd, waste, the bluff of productivity* and even *terrorism in the velvet glove of technology* (which may have a prophetic ring to it if one bears in mind how terrorists use technology today!).

Another observation is that Ellul coined (or used) **words which have strong emotional contents** to it like *technocrats* and *meritocracy* (Ellul, 1990:24), showing that the (then) contemporary rulers, the *aristoi*, are those who have the greatest technical competence (Ellul, 1990:25). He mentions that the America invented the *technopolis* (Ellul, 1990:27) and suggests that all powers pass through the hands of a group of *technocrats* in the *technopolis* (most probably a city run by and exist due to technology).

A fresh breeze is however detected in chapter V where he deals with **humanism** (Ellul, 1990:125 ff) and writes: "Human freedom supposedly increases with every new technical advance", and: "The development of technique is for humanity alone" (Ellul, 1990:127). This positive view is (again) qualified by a warning where he makes a connection between the use of technique to suppress people and the possibility which is pursued by for instance the military to use it against human beings (Ellul, 1990:131) being the very opposite to the humanistic discourse!

Ellul saw the power of the media as another example of technology exerting control over human destiny (cf also Ellul, 1990:347 ff) and manipulated by special interests, whether by the market, society or the state. The reference to Ellul then gives the connection:

Jacques Ellul has theorized that technologies available to modern societies, specifically the sciences of public opinion (e.g., polling and surveys) and sociology distinguishes modern propaganda from what he termed "primitive" propaganda.

3. CRITIQUE ON THE TECHNOLOGICAL BLUFF

It is difficult for any anyone to predict exactly what will be happening in the future regarding technology and although Ellul was a philosopher with a good grasp on his contemporary world, he still could not foresee what would happen in this fast-changing world. He admitted in the book itself that forecasting is virtually impossible (Ellul, 1990:87).

Many references show that he worked within older paradigms which were still rampant in 1990 like the discussion of the Industrial Revolution (Ellul, 1990:15) and the description of the "world of gadgets" (Ellul, 1990:257) – whereas humanity has now already entered the phase of the Fourth Industrial Revolution (cf Schwab, 2016).

In a discussion of the "human mastery over technique" Ellul takes a dim view of the result the advancement of technology may have for workers (Ellul, 1990:154), something which has developed into a complete different direction. In fact, some new work possibilities arose from this development, as Lotter (2004:3) indicates, ". . . there is a new world opening up for research in different fields of the Humanities regarding these issues and in which ways the *information society can be utilized to the fullest extend (*italics by author*)."*

4. RECENT RESEARCH ON THE INFLUENCE OF THE TECHNOLOGY ON HUMAN BEINGS

A magnitude of research and study with regards to the effect of technology on human beings have been produced at the end of the previous millennium and the beginning of the new millennium (cf inter alia Schuurman [1995]; Hearn [1997]; Katsikides [1998]; Lotter [2003]; Coteanu [2004]; Jutte [2005]; Klang & Murray [2005]; Scharff & Dusek [2014]). In these studies different positions towards technology are taken. A synoptic view should be maintained in this paper in order to show how the issues discussed by Ellul are still valid and worth researching in a highly technocratized society (Lotter, 2005:1).

Some criticism come from Matlack (2014:50 ff) regarding Ellul, which should also be taken into account but he ends his article:

> We ought instead to take Ellul's book, placed in the context of his larger work, as an appeal to walk a middle path between unrestrained *technophilia* and reactionary *technophobia*… (Matlack, 2014: 64).

More recently Scharff & Dusek (2014) published a standard work which also deals with these issues and in two chapters references are made to Ellul (cf pp 205 & 430).

Different aspects of the influence of technology (including the internet, WWW, and cyberspace) have been researched as well. They also have a living interactive relationship with the mass communication media (Rushkoff, 1996:31) and spend more time with the TV than their parents did (Beaudoin, 1998:5). Some warn that technocracy is perfected in *computerocracy* (Schuurman, 1995:20)! The danger also arises (connected to the above-mentioned) of *technomyopia* which is defined as a

> "…a strange phenomenon that causes us to overestimate the potential short-term impacts of new technology. And when the world fails to conform to our inflated expectations, we turn around and we underestimate the long-term implications" (Bucy, 2002:24).

The power and effects of the cyber world has been the area of research for Lotter (2006:7) who refers to at least five different areas where technology could have a detrimental effect on people: *cyberaddiction*, *cyberloneliness, cyberphilia, cybersex* and *cyberphobia*. It is without doubt a field of research which is growing daily, since the influence of the internet is growing every day and with speeded-up inventions and innovations in the technological world, it is virtually impossible to say what the next "tool" may be invented or in which way something unethical, criminal or illegal will be done.

5. POINTERS ON DEALING WITH TECHNOLOGY

In order to maintain a balanced view on technology and also put the issues addressed by Ellul in proper perspective, it is necessary to finally at the end of this paper suggest certain pointers which could be used as broad guidelines how to approach technology:

- Gratitude and acknowledgement for the wonderful possibilities opened up by technology. It should never be forgotten that technology was invented and still develops continually for the primary reason of "helping human beings".
- Technology should always be a tool and "slave" to human beings, not a "slave driver" or something people may become addicted to.
- A distinction between the "good" and "evil" uses of technology is important. It should be realized that *horrific things* are being done with the available technology on the other hand technology are saving lives and giving a better quality of life to many.
- Ethics should always be maintained when dealing with technology and issues like human rights and privacy should be considered.
- Ongoing research in different related disciplines like Sociology, Psychology, Practical Theology and Physiology of the effects technology may have on people, should be done.
- Debates on the crucial issues of the technology in society and the role it plays should be allowed and encouraged.

6. CONCLUSION

It is clear to any observer that Ellul had done a tremendous amount of research for this work, hence the interest still abounding nearly 30 years on. He was trying to explain most of the areas where technology will affect people's lives and what influence it may have. He addressed the French context, but also referred to the USA (see inter alia Ellul, 1990:28, 248, 298) which is an important factor since the most development of technology originated there. Ellul showed all the detrimental effects technological development can have and warned against different kinds of dangers emanating from technology (see *inter alia* Ellul, 1990:111, 203, 207, 228, 288, 350).

7. SUMMARY

In this paper it is argued that the book by Jacques Ellul in 1990 titled *The Technological Bluff* is still being read and highly influential and the philosophy regarding technology, is still valid. The main tenet of the book (keeping in mind the "datedness" of it) is discussed and critiqued and the paper ends by proposing certain pointers on how one should go about in dealing with technology in people's lives.

REFERENCES

Beaudoin, T. 1998. Virtual Faith: The Irreverent Spiritual Quest of Generation X. San Francisco: Jossey-Bass Publishers.

Coteanu, C. 2004. Cyber consumer law and unfair trading practices. Hants: Ashgate.

Ellul, J. 1990. *The Technological Bluff.* Grand Rapids, Mi.: Eerdmans.

Google. 2006. Jacques Ellul. [Online]. Available WWW: http://www.google.co.za/search?hl=af&q=ellul+technological+bluff&btnG=Google+soek&meta [Accessed May 31 2006]

Hearn, W.R. 1997. Being a Christian in science. Downers Grove, Ill.: InterVarsity Press.

Jutte, R. 2005. A history of the senses. From antiquity to cyberspace. Cambridge: Polity Press.

Katsikides, S.A. 1998. The societal impact of technology. Brookfield, Ve.: Ashgate Publishers.

Klang, M. & Murray, A. (ed). 2005. Human rights in the digital age. London: Cavendish Publishing.

Lotter, G.A. 2003. Privacy issues in counselling online. In: Proceedings of the 5th WWW Applications Conference, August 2003. Durban. [Online]. Available WWW: http://general.rau.ac.za/infosci/www2003/ [Accessed 31 May 2006].

Lotter, G.A. 2004. Information society: helping humans or dehumanizing them? In: Proceedings of the Second International Conference on New Directions in the Humanities, July 2004. Prato.

Lotter, G.A. 2005. Technologizing and technocratization: where does the human side fit in? In: Proceedings of the 7th WWW Conference, August 2005. Cape Town. [Online]. Available WWW: http://www.uj.ac.za/www2005/documents/Lotter,%20GA.pdf [Accessed 31 May 2006].

Lotter, G.A. 2006. Dehumanization by cyberfication. In: Proceedings of the IPSI conference, February 2006. Marbella.

Matlack, S. 2014. "Confronting the Technological Society," The New Atlantis, Number 43, Summer/Fall 2014, pp. 45–64.

Reed, C. 2004. Internet Law. Text and materials. Cambridge: Cambridge University Press.

Rushkoff, D. 1996. Playing the Future: How Kids' Culture Can Teach Us to Thrive in an Age of Chaos. New York: Harper Collins.

Scharff, R.C. & Dusek, V. 2014. Philosophy of Technology. The Technological condition. An Anthology (Second Edition). Chichester: Wiley Blackwell.

Schuurman, E. 1995. Perspectives on technology and culture. Potchefstroom : PU for CHE.

Schwab, K. 2016. The fourth industrial revolution: what it means, how to respond. *World Economic Forum,* 14 Jan. http://www.weforum.org/agenda/2016/01/the-fourth-industrial-revolution-what-it-means-and-how-to-respond Date of access: 16 Jan. 2018.

MAKING VIRTUAL CLASSROOMS OF GOOGLE PLATFORM MORE REAL USING TRANSPARENT INTERACTIVE SCREEN-BOARD (tiSb-Albania)

Romeo Teneqexhi[1] and Loreta Kuneshka[2]
[1]*Director of Distance Education Centre, Polytechnic University of Tirana , Albania, Sheshi "Nënë Tereza", No 4. Tirana, Albania*
[2]*Lecturer of Statistics, Medical University of Tirana, Albania, Rruga e Dibres, Tirana, Albania*

ABSTRACT

Virtual & Real Face to Face teaching (Teneqexhi, & Kuneshka, 2016) infrastructure, presented in 10Th international conference of e-learning organized by IADIS, Madeira 2016, is improved now very much. We have baptized this new infrastructure "transparent interactive Screen-board (tiSb-Albania). Transparent interactive Screen-board is now easy implementable in traditional classrooms. The new feature of ex Screen-board is the interactivity. The interaction is done by using e-beam edge tool which comes with very interesting software for organizing lecture materials. We use e-beam tool in a very special way making lessons much more interesting. The teacher never shows his back to the students because the transparent board is between him and the students. We can write on Screen-board with normal markers (and erase by eraser) or with electronic ones (and erase electronically). Using our system it is possible to add new notes on board images (written by normal markers) even if they are already erased with the eraser. Thanks to e-beam software[1] it is not necessary for the students to kip notes. Everything written by the teacher on the screen-board or showed in prepared slides are automatically saved in student's smart phone. So student can have forever "in his/her pocket" all the lectures in video form (stored in YouTube or somewhere else) and notes in slides form. The lessons organized with tiSb-Albania which are recorded can be transmitted live stream on the internet. So the number of students is not limited by the size of the classroom. Every student can follow live lessons being in the classroom or from home having the possibility to ask question and write on the screen-board if the teacher "gives" him the "chalk" to write on the screen-board. This is the idea of a "Mix Classroom". So mix classroom is a combination between traditional face to face teaching and e-learning. We have successfully experimented this kind of classroom teaching "Basic Circuit Theory" subject in Polytechnic University of Tirana. We also have experimented doing video based on real lecture's notices without using video camera. Every teacher can do it using nowadays smart phones. For the near future Polytechnic University of Tirana is planning to have common classes with Pristina University in Kosovo. In this way twin classes in different universities can have common lessons (even exams) in the same time with the same teacher. Virtual classroom of Google platform[2] is perfect for organizing mix classrooms. Among other teaching materials for students used during lectures, we upload all recorded lessons in Google platform and every student can see real recorded lessons whenever he wants.

KEYWORDS

Virtual and Real Face To Face (VRFF) Teaching, Transparent Interactive Screen-Board (tiSb), Mix Classroom, Twin Classes, Preliminary Exam At Home Without Limitation in Time

1. WHY RECORDING REAL LECTURES?

Nowadays it is a pity doing a 50 or 100 minutes lecture and "erasing" at the end everything what is written (and said) on the black board. Historically students use to take notes during lecture most of the time not 100% focused on what teacher says but not to lose or wrong copy anything from the blackboard. Nowadays a lot of students do by them self pictures of the blackboard or record audio using different audio recorders for future use at home during studding. I think it is teacher's duty to make students more focused on the lecture than the notes in their own notebooks. This is why we are working on recording real lectures in different ways.

[1] http://www.classroom.google.com - Google platform for virtual classrooms
[2] http://www.e-beam.com/education/ebeam-edge/overview.html

2. VIRTUAL & REAL FACE TO FACE AND "tiSb" INFRASTRUCTURE

Virtual & Real Face to Face teaching infrastructure, presented in 10^{Th} international conference of e-learning organized by IADIS, Madeira 2016, is improved now very much. In old infrastructure we needed: 1) two environments one for the teacher with a small number of students (Figure 1.a/b), and the big classroom for the rest of the students (Figure 2.a/b), 2) a sophisticated audio system for communication with most of the students in big classroom, 3) video system for the teacher to see and communicate with his students in the big classroom, 4) video switcher (blue box on desk Figure 1.a) used by the teacher, 5) a TV & mirror system (TV in front of a big mirror and the students between TV and mirror) for the students in teacher's room for image flipping purpose (Figure 1.a TV behind the students, Figure 1.b mirror in front of students), 6) post production process for including computer graphics in final video lecture. This relatively complicated infrastructure is impossible to be widely use, so we have simplify this infrastructure and improved the features of our system involving in a very spatial way the well known "e-beam edge" tool produced by Luida[2].

Figure 1 a/b. In teacher's office. Teacher's (a) and student's (b) point of wiev in old VRFF infrastructure

Figure 2 a/b. In big classroom. Student's point of wiev in old VRFF infrastructure

The most important features of our system are the interaction using e-beam tool and live mixing of images taken from web camera in front of transparent board and computer screen. The new system we are representing here excludes all elements mention above (point 1 to 6). No more need for post production processes. We have baptized this new infrastructure "transparent interactive Screen-board" (tiSb-Albania). Transparent interactive Screen-board is easy implementable in traditional classrooms (Figure 3 a/b). The teacher now is in the same classroom with the students. They can communicate without any problem like in every classroom. The only thing witch make the difference is the fact that students see the teacher, in a way virtually, via video projector (Figure 3b), of course bigger then normally. In fact the teacher is not virtually in the classroom. He is behind the white curtain at the corner of the classroom. The white curtain has two reasons to be there. First it creates a white background necessary for the teacher to see what he writes on the transparent board and second because for the student everything is written on the transparent board is left side right so it is unreadable in a way. In Figure 3a, on the left side of transparent board you see the e-beam tool incorporated in our system.

Figure 3 a/b. Teacher's (a) and (b) student's point of wiev in traditional classroom equipped with "tiSb"

3. PRODUCING VIDEO OF REAL LECTURE WITHOUT USING VIDEO CAMERA

We have successfully experimented another way for making video lectures without using any special infrastructure. In Figure 4a/b there are pictures of traditional black boards taken by the teacher using his smart phone. At the beginning of the lecture teacher starts audio recording of his voice using an audio recording application in his smart phone. During the lecture teacher keeps his phone in a pocket of his shirt to record audio in good quality. After the lecture, teacher uploads black board's pictures and corresponding audio files in Google Drive. So students can see and listen real material of real lecture whenever he / she wants. But in this case it is a little bit difficult to listen audio from real lecture and understand which part of the notices the teacher is (was) writing in this moment.

Figure 4 a/b. Notes of a real lecture with associated audio uploaded in Google Classroom

This handicap can be eliminated by producing a true video using audio with teacher voice and the picture taken from the black board or last frame of any existing video of a good teacher on You Tube or some were else. But this kind of video needs a post production process and video editing. In Figure 5 the area more lighted in the picture is part of black board already written up to the corresponding time code.

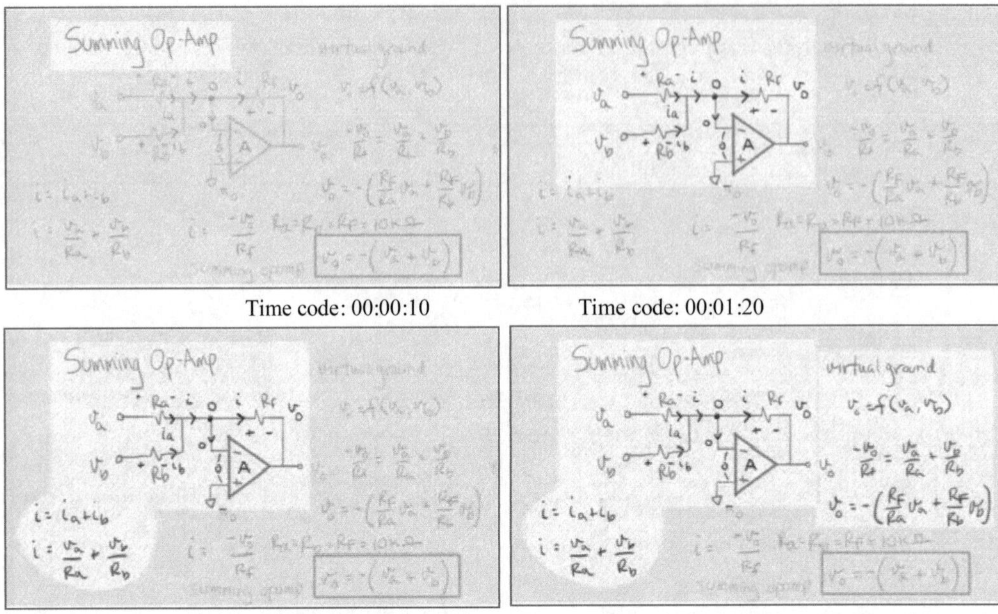

Time code: 00:00:10 Time code: 00:01:20

Time code: 00:05:11 Time code: 00:07:45

Figure 5. Video lecture generated using just a final frame of a video lecture taken from YouTube[3]

Using virtual Classroom of Google platform we organize some kind of preliminary exams at home (before final exam) without limitation in time "forcing" students to get all the points of the test trying as many time as they need to do that. A considerable number of questions in this test are pieces of my video lecture (some seconds). To get the points of questions students must see the entire lecture to find out the right answer.

4. FINAL DECLARATION

Students of the future will be students without notebooks but not a single lost notice on the black board during all the period of studying in university. I still feel nostalgia for my studding time in university when I find any old notebook. Pages of these notes are becoming more and more yellow during the time pass. Nowadays notices in the smart phone never get yellow. We are lucky generation.

REFERENCES

Teneqexhi, R. Kuneshka, L. (2016). Virtual & Real Face to Face Teaching. In MCCSIS 2016, 1-4 July, Madeira, Portugal ISBN: 978-989-8533-51-7, pp. 227-230.

http://www.classroom.google.com - Google platform for virtual classrooms

http://www.e-beam.com/education/ebeam-edge/overview.html

https://www.youtube.com/playlist?list=PLzUN9-WgjT3PcvDFD5cI9COE9E53CrcgA

[3] https://www.youtube.com/playlist?list=PLzUN9-WgjT3PcvDFD5cI9COE9E53CrcgA

FROM STYLES 0 TO STYLE E-0. COGNITIVE STYLES IN E-LEARNING

María Rosa Pinto Lobo
Faculty of Communication. Pontifical University of Salamanca
Salamanca, Spain.

ABSTRACT

The question posed by e-learning is that it does not always comply with any of the characteristics that define the process of interpersonal communication according to the classical paradigm, for example, sharing space and time and/or knowing the agents receiving the communicative process. The non-shared space-temporal variables imply a difficulty processing the information from the styles or cognitive styles of the last century for both the teacher and the student. We propose a new style of knowledge: the e-0 style. This style is developed in a virtual space. Its objective is to ensure that the transmission of information becomes knowledge with the same effectiveness as with face-to-face teaching-learning.

KEYWORDS

Styles 0, e-0 Style, Communication, Knowledge, e-Learning, Learning

1. INTRODUCTION

Learning e-learning is a communication process that does not always comply with all the characteristics that define interpersonal communication. If we stop at space and time dimensions we can observe that on many occasions they are not shared. This presents a difficulty in processing information from the cognitive styles of the sending agent and the receiving agent, whether teacher or student.

During the twentieth century, studies on cognitive styles, known as the styles of the zero years, were published because the research was published in 1950, 1960 and 1970. In 1950 the work on the authoritative cognitive style of Theodor Adorno appeared. (1950). In 1960, Milton Rokeach (1960) offers us his contributions to dogmatic style and open-minded style. Richard Christie and Florence Geis (1970) present the characteristics of the Machiavellian style in the seventies. All these cognitive styles allow us to study the processes of communication and learning, with an adaptation of the teacher to the students or vice versa.

2. FROM STYLES 0 TO STYLE E-0

The cognitive style is the way the subject has to respond to information that comes from outside. How do we respond to the avalanche of information that we receive every day through the multiple screens that populate our communicative universe? The response we give to the informative exposition depends on the style of knowledge we develop. In face-to-face learning processes, cognitive styles manifest themselves in a physical space and in a time-shared by communicative agents. The teacher can adjust and redefine his style to the knowledge styles of the students with whom he shares the classroom and the student can do it in the same way.

2.1 Styles 0

Cognitive styles are also known as styles 0 or styles of years zero. The publications of the results of the investigations were, as we have already indicated, in the 1950s, 1960s, 1970s. An exhaustive exposition of these styles can be found in the General Information Theory (Valbuena, 1997: 145-154).

Authoritarianism was studied by Adorno (1950) and his collaborators at the Frankfurt School. The authoritarian subject shows submission to the people who hold power. They do not make value judgments or criticisms of the authority. It moves in the context of conventional norms accepted by the group. Reject people who do not follow these rules. It does not accept subjectivity or opinions that are contrary to those established by the authority, which in many cases is considered a predestined person. He sees the world as threatening and with conspiracy subjects with destructive objectives. It only perceives the most negative of the human being.

Dogmatism or the closed-minded subject was studied by Milton Rokeach (1960). For this researcher, the response to external information that characterizes the authoritarian is not only limited to individuals of a certain ideology, fascism, as underlined by Adorno but can correspond to individuals of any ideology. Rokeach added the reverse side of the dogmatic or closed-minded subject and showed us the characteristics of the open-minded cognitive style.

The open-minded subject admits conflicting information from the outside. He is able to rectify because he does not mind questioning his own positions if circumstances have changed. It does not have rigid categories, which allows it to establish nuances and exceptions to the rules. Believe more in the strength of reasoning than the power of authority. The open-minded style emphasizes that respect is earned while authority prevails. It is not against authority because it is the authority. He respects it, but the open-minded subject knows how to be autonomous and decide for himself. It recognizes the authority for the information and experience it may have but does not need it to act. Has the ability to see the positive potential of people.

The researchers realized that a group of people did not respond to stimuli and external information according to the characteristics discussed so far. Richard Christie and Florence Geis (1970) exposed the characteristics of another cognitive style known as Machiavellian style or Machiavellianism. The name comes from the characteristics that we can find in works like The Speech and The Prince of Machiavelli.

The Machiavellian subject is a manipulative subject, who uses others to achieve their ends. Thus, the end justifies the means, although in these media is the immoral employment of people. The Machiavellian has no feelings towards others. It treats people as objects and does not identify with them so as not to lose their objective. It is not guided by moral criteria, but utilitarian. The Machiavellian subject is a great information processor and he uses this always in his benefit for the achievement of his ends. He is not an idealist, but a very practical and versatile subject, capable of adopting any ideology or none when circumstances require it. He knows how to move very well in situations of uncertainty and chaos. Do not be afraid of confusing situations.

In a traditional teaching-learning process in the classroom, in which space and time are shared, it is possible to identify each of the styles of knowledge and, therefore, perform an emission/reception of the information that allows the subject to adjust to the cognitive style of the other agents. What happens if the teacher and the student do not know each other? How are cognitive styles identified in virtual spaces? How do we get the e-learning teaching-learning process to be effective?

2.2 Methodology

The methodology used to propose the e-0 style has been a qualitative inductive methodology. The approach is exploratory, observational, prospective and comparative. It starts from consolidated concepts, exposed in section 2.1 Styles 0, and these concepts are related for describing the quality of a new construct, the cognitive style: e-0. In this way, we reduce the complexity of the teaching-learning process in a virtual environment to our object of study: teacher-student interaction with a style cognitive own e-learning. It is the virtual environment that modifies the conceptual relationship that occurs in face-to-face processes and generates the coherence of the proposal that requires scientific rigor.

The teaching experience of three decades makes it easier for us to use a constructivist paradigm and an interpretive paradigm. The first, the constructivist paradigm, with a hermeneutic and dialectical methodology, entails the result of the research and reflection presented here. This result is created by the same process and experienced by the observer. The results are reinforced from the interpretative-participant methodology. The interpretation is carried out from the experience in face-to-face and virtual teaching in the university environment.

2.3 Results. The Style e-0

The search for similarity and the difference between styles 0 in face-to-face teaching and virtual learning leads to results that imply the construction of a new style of knowledge for the teacher and for the student. We are before a qualitative study of action research, oriented to a change in the interpersonal relations of the agents that intervene in the process.

In face-to-face teaching, the cognitive style of the teacher can be adjusted to each of the student's knowledge styles and vice versa. However, we must know what cognitive style is the one that stimulates students to learn and acquire knowledge when teaching, for example, with Blackboard Collaborate to unknown students, and they follow the sessions on platforms such as Moodle at any time This is an interesting line of research that has been developing in recent years (Fatai, 2019, Merchán, 2018, Morado, 2018 and Valencia-Vallejo, 2018).

The case studied, therefore, is that of individual learning of students unknown to the teacher. The sessions are virtual with Blackboard Collaborate through the Moodle online platform. For the elaboration of these sessions, it is necessary that the interaction contemplate characteristics of all the styles 0. This allows identification of the student, whatever their style, with the teacher. This facilitates the acquisition of knowledge. For the issuer supposes to recompose the style that defines him according to the virtual context in which the classes are taught. The teacher and the student no longer have an interaction with any of the styles 0 described, but the interpersonal relationship is reached with the homogeneity of the e-0 style that is shared by all the agents.

The e-0 style is the synthesis of the features that characterize cognitive styles. The context and content that determines this virtual context are taken into account for the synthetic process, according to the dialectical method.

The thirteen characteristic features of the e-0 style are: admission of all types of information; ability to rectify and question different positions; primacy of reasoning; recognition of authority without submission; assessment of autonomy; interest in the nuances; originality versus conventionalism; understanding towards the different; multiple and plural view of the events versus the dichotomous vision; appreciation of subjectivity, creativity, aesthetics; assessment of the emotional aspect of interpersonal relationships; application of ethical judgments to dilemmas and decision making; commitment to moral values.

Each of the features of the e-0 style refers to the front or back of a style. All the features of the e-0 style allow, in a virtual environment, to move from mere information to knowledge. These features facilitate the teacher-student interaction and with it the intellectual and emotional action of the individual who wants to learn and acquire knowledge.

3. CONCLUSION

The e-0 style synthesizes the characteristics of the different styles of knowledge: authoritarian-dogmatic style, open-minded style and Machiavellian style.

The conjunction of features that characterize the e-0 style allows the information to be processed correctly in a virtual environment. In this virtual environment, all the characteristics that define interpersonal communication according to the classical paradigm are not always present.

The features of the e-0 style have to be shared by all agents of the teaching-learning process to achieve an effective teacher-student interaction in a virtual space.

The e-0 style proposal is the result of participatory and exploratory observation, with a prospective and comparative nature. This result, the reason for the reflection that has been presented here, requires future research that corroborates the need to apply this style to improve the educommunicative processes of the 21st century.

It continues, with this proposal, an interesting line of research that deals with and concerns all those involved in the communication process, whatever the medium in which the exchange of teaching and learning takes place.

ACKNOWLEDGEMENT

To Octavio Aguilera Perelló, journalist, teacher and, forever, friend. Porto, 2019.

REFERENCES

Adorno, T. et al, 1950. *The Authoritarian Personality.* Harper and Row. New York, USA.

Aguilera, O., 1998. *El proceso creativo.* Fragua, Madrid, España.

Christie, R. et al, 1970. *Studies in Machiavellianism.* Academic Press, New York, USA.

Fatai, S., 2019. An experimental study on an adaptive e-learning environment based on learner's personality and emotion. *Education and Information Technologies.* 17 pp. Available in: https://doi.org/10.1007/s10639-019-09868-5. [Viewed: 3-03-2019].

Merchán, C.A., 2018. Modelamiento pedagógico de Ambientes Virtuales de Aprendizaje (AVA). *Revista de la Facultad de Ciencia y Tecnología,* No. 44, pp 51-70.

Morado, F., 2018. Entornos virtuales de aprendizaje complejos e innovadores. *Revista Electrónica Educare,* Vol. 22, No. 1, pp 1-17.

Pastor, G., 1982. *Síndrome frío de personalidad sagaz.* Universidad Pontificia de Salamanca, Salamanca, España.

Pinto, M.R., 2018. Comunicación e inteligencia artificial. Propuesta del modelo de comunicación BS. *VI Congreso Internacional de la AE-IC. Comunicación y Conocimiento.* AE-IC. Salamanca, España, pp. 83-103.

Rheingold, H., 1994. *Realidad virtual: Los mundos artificiales generados por ordenador que modificarán nuestras vidas.* Gedisa, Barcelona, España.

Rokeach, M., 1960. *The Open and Closed Mind. Investigations into the Nature of Beliefs Systems and Personality Systems.* Basic Books Inc. Publishers, New York, USA.

Siddique, A., et. al, 2018. Developing Adaptive E-Learning Environment Using Cognitive and Noncognitive Parameters, Journal of Educational Computing Research. Available in: https://journals.sagepub.com/doi/full/10.1177/0735633118769433 [Viewed: 6-03- 2019].

Valbuena, F., 1997. *Teoría General de la Información.* Editorial Noesis, Madrid, España.

Valencia-Vallejo,N. et. al, 2018. Efect of Motivational Scaffolding on E-learning Evironments: Self-efficacy, Learning Achievment, and Cognitive Style. *Journal of Educators Online*, Vol. 15, No. n1, 14 pp.

CAN WE DESIGN AND TEACH TO IMPROVE STUDENT PERCEPTIONS OF "COHORT"?

Tom Whitford
Faculty of Business & Economics, The University of Melbourne
Department of Management, 198 Berkeley St, Parkville, 3010, Australia

ABSTRACT

The modern-day university is undergoing major transformations in teaching delivery and design to accommodate massive growth in scale of student enrolments, especially remote learners. Part of this requires a fundamental adjustment to the ways in which we consider the student experience, one of which is the act of dedicated online students participating in a collegial higher-education experience. This is prompted by consistent research highlighting a lack of online student satisfaction in levels of interaction with peers and educators, and an unfulfilling subject experience. This paper will present the ways in which interaction, community, and sociality has been discussed historically in the online learning literature. Finally, it will expand upon this traditional understanding as to how quality learning design(s) could improve cohort experience for the next generation of online learners and instructors alike.

KEYWORDS

Online Learning, Pedagogy, Community, Cohort Management, Distance Education

1. INTRODUCTION

Distance education (see also or online learning) continues to grow at a pace globally which affords higher-education institutions the ability to access education markets previously outside their reach (Norton, Cherastidtham 2018). By way of definition, it goes beyond simply a difference in the way content is delivered via instruction, but distinctly the cohort by which is targeted; with their own unique set of learning challenges which require a focus on student support (Webster, Hackley 1997). Due to such scalar growth, online cohorts are larger and student attention competes against various other personal and professional distractions. Indeed, the very idea of "student cohort" is under pressure due to a fragmentation of the student base; acknowledging varying degrees of delivery method in their past educational environments. This has importance for our learning design, which serves to support delivery and achieve comparable student experiences to face-to-face modes (Hannon, D'Netto 2007). Higher education institutions also have responsibilities towards access and equity of student experience, thus to ensure consistency and fairness in this approach to subject offering.

More recent research suggests a return to focusing on cohort experience in online environments (including MOOCs), and the links between performance, participation and attrition (De Freitas et al. 2015). Evidence suggests a positive correlation between peer engagement and improved learning achievement and satisfaction with an online subject (Arbaugh, Duray 2002). Students often indicate a lack of student satisfaction due to the nature of the online spaces designed, and teacher and peer disconnect (O'Shea et al. 2015). The emotional factors of online learning – as reported by student interviews – suggest that cohort's experience of online learning can be anxiously isolating, but ultimately this is resolved as the scheduling is preferable; as it can "fit" to their current lifestyle (Reilly et al. 2012). Most importantly, students have reported intellectual gains, skill mastery, and valid links to their professional practice, which serve to illustrate the promise of well-designed online environments.

This flexibility has been a hallmark of the student preference for learning online, however is not widely replicated in degrees of student motivation. For instructors and teachers alike, a consistent challenge has been how to best manage student cohorts towards a social learning community. Beyond teacher activity, instructional design strategies that involve peers with each other are shown to enhance prosocial communication and interaction (Jaggars, Xu 2016).

This reflection paper considers a literature review of the notion of "cohort" across the past three decades, and considers foundational learning theories alongside associated constructs such as *social presence, sociality, sociability* and *social space*. The paper also proposes some pedagogic strategies to best foster 'cohort', as well as future research directions to support a greater student community.

2. BODY OF PAPER

2.1 Foundational Theories to Assist in our Understanding of "Cohort"

To situate the literature historically, the corpus on distance education and its subsequent relationship with learning (and, instructional) design accumulates in the late 1990s to early 2000s. This is perhaps characteristic of the ways by which researchers initially conceptualized learners as remote; learning as mediated and isolated, and centered around the phenomena of self-directed or asynchronous instruction. This sense of "space" is further compounded by the rate of technological advancement, which was a prescient concern of Web 1.0 and 2.0 studies (Allen, Seaman 2013).

The late 1980's and early 1990s saw a resurgence in interest for social learning models to explain both offline and the increasing virtualization of education. The links to higher-order thinking were consistent across authors such as Ramsden (1988) and Lipman (1991) who sought to stress the importance on student meaning-creation through robust interaction. Communication and engagement with peers is seen as the epitome of a complete, rich educational experience, and this has been explored thoroughly in classical face-to-face learning settings in the early developmental and educational corpuses.

Bandura's social learning theory soon emerged, which responded to both the classic behaviorist theories (including conditioning) and the importance of the social context (1977). Didactic conversation, and the importance discussion plays in social learning was conceptualized not only between student-student, but also triangulated between content and teacher. This model became foundational for future studies in distance and remote education literatures, and subsequent theories of spatial and relative interaction behaviors, such as transactional distance (Moore 1993).

2.2 Why Social Learning Works: Defending a Desire for "Cohort" Experiences

The importance of collaboration emerges around this time as a discourse of its own in the early virtual learning corpus, or what Schrage (1995) describes as shared creation and discovery. In doing so, involving learners in a more active co-construction of knowledge, confirming meaning-making, while going beyond a classic (perhaps, static) view of the importance of student discussion. Gunawardena and Zittle continued the empirical focus on distance education and critical thinking processes (1997). More relevant to this paper, this model proposed a process of negotiation and co-creation of knowledge that included: sharing, dissonance, negotiation, co-construction, application and testing. Once again, the role of peer cooperation and interaction is emblematic of the strong links made between critical-thinking, inquiry-based learning, and social meaning making (between peers) (Wenger, 1998).

Related closely to past notions of collaborative interaction and student motivations to learn is the *Community of Inquiry* (CoI, henceforth). This now widely-cited model affords a comprehensive description of the ways in which students co-construct a sense of meaning, where shared solutions are sought alongside teachers in a learning environment (Garrison et al. 1999). The CoI offers a baseline to explore online experiences mediated between actors: explaining the social, pedagogic and cognitive interactions which combine towards sense-making and students' understanding for learning. What Garrison and Arbaugh call for is explanation of how social presence creates purposeful connections between peers, and how this evolves and shifts within a CoI (2007).

Table 1. Historical Taxonomy of Key Constructs in "Cohort" Conceptualisation: *Social Presence vs Sociality vs Sociability vs Social Space* (as adapted from Lowenthal, Snelson 2017)

Construct	Key Authors	Literature Domains	Construct Conceptualisations(s)
Social Presence	Short et al, 1976; Garrison, 2000; Picciano, 2002; Swan, Shi, 2005	Education, Online Learning, Computer-Mediated-Communication	**Salience of relationship**: "…the degree of salience of the other person in the interaction and the consequent salience of the interpersonal relationships…" (Short et al. 1976 p. 65), and **immediacy**: "a measure of the psychological distance which a communicator puts between himself and the object of his communication, his addressee or his communication" (ibid, p. 72). **Being there**: "the ability of participants in the Community of Inquiry to project their personal characteristics into the community, thereby presenting themselves to the other participants as "real people"" (Garrison 2000, p. 89). **Connecting**: 'The degree of feeling, perception, and reaction of being connected on CMC to another intellectual entity' (Swan, Shih 2005, p. 115) **Belonging**: "A student's sense of being in and belonging in a course and the ability to interact with other students and an instructor" (Picciano 2002, p. 22)
Sociality (mostly, offline conceptualisations)	Long, Moore (2013); Grabher (2004); Enfield, Levinson (2006);	Sociology, Geography, Cultural Anthropology, Linguistics, Behavioral Psychology	A **sense of place or provenance** (human conceptualisations), a sensory experience that shares the imaginings of a community (Long, Moore 2013) An **exchange of knowledge** that is narrational in the sense that it develops **interpersonal trust**. This could be based on shared experience, familiarity with one another (Grabher 2004) Shared goal of participants **to share a common ground**, an exchange and organization of relevant information (Enfield, Levinson 2006)
Sociability	Simmel (1949); Rheingold (1993); Kreijns et al. (2002)	Sociology, ICT, Education, Online Learning	The pleasure of **the company of others**, and the central ingredient in many social forms of recreation and play (Simmel 1949). Cyberspace as a constructed space to allow for the **development of community, informal discussion and commitment to one another** (Rheingold 1993) The sociability of an environment (online) is defined as the degree to which this fulfils not only the needs of the learner, but also t**he psychological needs of students,** rendering this socially complete. They enable socio-emotional processes such as **affiliation, trust, interpersonal connection and sense of community** (Kreijns et al. 2002)
Social Space	Kreijns, et al. (2004); Harasim (1993); Rourke (2000); Gunawardena (1995)	Education, Online Learning	Social Space acknowledges the **psychological health and wellbeing of a group**, such as the ability to **foster trust, making friends within a space that is cohesive** (Kreijins et al. 2004) The **climate or atmosphere of an environment,** whether or not this is **prosocial and supportive** by way of **conducive to social activity** by users (Harasim 1993; Rourke 2000, Gunawardena 1995)

2.3 Calls to Advance "Cohort" Theoretically: What Next?

Ebben and Murphy's meta-analyses suggests that with an increased focus and interest in online learning, pedagogy and student engagement, there is a distinct "phase" by which chronologically we can view the work, and how theories of "social" and "cohort" are both used to help inform the literature, and possibly, distract it (2014). Initially, the focus stems from connectivism and engagement, and how we can virtually develop and support inquiry. More recently, we are beginning to see seminal theories to explain cohort – such as social presence - being challenged and compared to other socially-regulated behavioral theories (Mykota 2018). Oztok and Kehrwald challenge the very definitional construct of social presence itself as being relevant to cotemporary online education studies (2017). The authors believe that the breadth of activities and attitudes covered under the umbrella term "social presence", do harm to the analytic ability to study and isolate the phenomena of sociality in virtual spaces.

2.4 Learning Design Strategies to Address Perceptions of Cohort

In the MOOC literature, practitioner guides suggest that cohorts can be further engaged with a combination of teaching strategies that include gamification, interactive content, immediacy of feedback, branched presentation of content (adaptive), and authentic assessment that encourages reflection (De Freitas et al. 2015). Beyond these explicit approaches to improve student involvement in content, teachers should foremost aim to design spaces that encourage knowledge-sharing between peers.

Suggestions here could include a greater emphasis on team-building activities, as well as relationship development tasks that could include projects that explicitly require collaboration (Tisdale et al. 2004). Jaggers and Xu note the impact of attaching assessment weightings to forums, showing greater student volume and frequency of engagement and a stronger commitment to perform (2016). More recent research confirms this relationship between immediacy and interactivity being reinforced by appropriate scaffolding, primarily through the use of novel and experimental assessment designs, including peer moderation to further cohort participation (Xia, Fielder, Siragusa 2013). When these deeper and more social approaches to learning are encouraged and supported enthusiastically by teachers and learning designers, a "...love of learning" can be inspired (O'Shea et al. 2015, p. 54).

Teaching delivery that evokes emotional responses, and encourages students relating to each other (personally), and the content to their own lives (perhaps professional), will have a significant determinant on how a sense of cohort is achieved. These emotional factors should be prioritized in our contemporary learning design philosophy; one which both considers student mood, states of mind, and perceptions of peer and teacher support (see Reilly et al. 2012).

Furthermore, a sense of student belonging could be fostered in the design of spaces that represent the physical location of their academic or scholarly communities. Boyer's influential work on campus life distilled the essence of these myriad benefits as "purposeful community" (1990), similar to previous conceptualizations of an academic, or college cohort. Moreover, in the case of online education, it also has been linked to improved retention rates (Hajrasouliha, Ewing 2016). Beyond this representation of the "campus", we should aim to design programs which have consistent groups of students moving through courses and subjects together. This will further encourage a sense of learning community, but also develop participatory behaviors (Engstrom et al. 2008). Here, students will have familiarity with one-another, and faculty staff, where reciprocal and support behaviors tend to follow.

3. CONCLUSION: FINAL COMMENTS AND FUTURE RESEARCH IMPLICATIONS

The teaching challenges presented by online and remote learners have been often addressed through intuitive, and often creative, management of our online learning systems. An emergent consideration for cohort understanding is presented by an increased demand for online learning. As this paper proposes, many of these challenges are inherently spatial, with attempts to remove a sense of distance. To be made more aware of the challenges this presents to learning design and teaching is to be aware of the history of the theoretical research on online communities and sociality.

The author calls for us to reflect upon the degree to which 'cohort' is addressed (if at all) in the planning of online education within higher education institutions. Furthermore, are instances of innovation, and pro-social and community-minded learning design and teaching strategies championed within faculties? Do knowledge sharing forums exist within academic departments to better understand "cohort"? These calls require further investigation and empirical support beyond 'best practice'; and should acknowledge the wealth of foundational theory to support positive correlations between social cohorts and quality of learning improvements.

REFERENCES

Allen, I.E. and Seaman, J., 2013. *Changing Course: Ten Years of Tracking Online Education in The United States*.

Arbaugh, J. B., & Duray, R., 2002. Technological and structural characteristics, student learning and satisfaction with Web-based courses: An exploratory study of two online MBA programs. Management Learning, 33(3), pp. 331–347.

Bandura, A., 1977. *Social Learning Theory*. Prentice-Hall Englewood Cliffs, NJ.

Boyer, E.L., 1990. "Campus Life: In Search of Community". *Carnegie Foundation for The Advancement of Teaching.*

De Freitas, S.I., Morgan, J., and Gibson, D., 2015. Will MOOCs Transform Learning and Teaching in Higher Education? Engagement and Course Retention in Online Learning Provision. *British Journal of Educational Technology*, 46(3), pp. 455-471.

Ebben, M. and Murphy, J.S., 2014. Unpacking MOOC Scholarly Discourse: A Review of Nascent MOOC Scholarship. *Learning, Media and Technology*, 39(3), pp. 328-345.

Enfield, N. J., & Levinson, S. C., 2006. Roots of human sociality. New York: Berg.

Engstrom, M. E., Santo, S. A., & Yost, R. M., 2008. Knowledge building in an online cohort. Quarterly Review of Distance Education, 9(2), pp. 151.

Garrison, D.R., Anderson, T. and Archer, W., 1999. Critical Inquiry in A Text-Based Environment: Computer Conferencing in Higher Education. *The Internet and Higher Education*, 2(2-3), pp. 87-105.

Garrison, D.R. and Arbaugh, J.B., 2007. Researching The Community of Inquiry Framework: Review, Issues, And Future Directions. *The Internet and Higher Education*, 10(3), pp. 157-172.

Grabher, G., 2004. Learning in projects, remembering in networks? Communality, sociality, and connectivity in project ecologies. European urban and regional studies, 11(2), pp. 103-123.

Gunawardena, C.N., 1995. Social Presence Theory and Implications for Interaction and Collaborative Learning in Computer Conferences. International Journal of Educational Telecommunications, 1(2/3), pp.147-166.

Gunawardena, C.N. and Zittle, F.J., 1997. Social Presence as A Predictor of Satisfaction Within a Computer-Mediated Conferencing Environment. *American Journal of Distance Education*, 11(3), pp. 8-26.

Hajrasouliha, A.H. and Ewing, R., 2016. Campus Does Matter: The Relationship of Student Retention and Degree Attainment to Campus Design. *Planning for Higher Education*, 44(3), pp.30.

Hannon, J. and D'Netto, B., 2007. Cultural Diversity Online: Student Engagement with Learning Technologies. *International Journal of Educational Management*, 21(5), pp. 418-432.

Harasim, L. M., 1993. Networlds: Networks as Social Space. In L.M. Harasim (Ed.) Global Networks: Computers and International Communication (pp. 15 – 34). Cambridge, MA: MIT Press.

Jaggars, S.S. and Xu, D., 2016. How Do Online Course Design Features Influence Student Performance? *Computers & Education*, 1(95), pp. 270-284.

Kreijns, K., Kirschner, P. A., & Jochems, W. 2002. The sociability of computer-supported collaborative learning environments. Journal of Education Technology & Society, 5(1), pp 8–22.

Kreijns, K., Kirschner, P. A., Jochems, W., & Van Buuren, H, 2004. Determining sociability, social space, and social presence in (a) synchronous collaborative groups. CyberPsychology & Behavior, 7(2), pp.155-172.

Lipman, M., 1991. *Thinking in Education*. Cambridge University Press, Cambridge.

Long, N. J., & Moore, H. L. (Eds.)., 2013. Sociality: new directions (Vol. 1). Berghahn Books.

Lowenthal, P. R., & Snelson, C. (2017). In search of a better understanding of social presence: An investigation into how researchers define social presence. Distance Education, 38(2), 141-159.

Moore, M.G., 1993. The Theory of Transactional Distance. *Theoretical Principles of Distance Education.* Routledge: London, pp. 84-103.

Mykota, D., 2018. The Effective Affect: A Scoping Review of Social Presence. *International Journal of e-Learning & Distance Education*, 33(2), pp.2.

Norton, A. and Cherastidtham, I., 2018. *Mapping Australian Higher Education 2018.* The Grattan Institute, Melbourne.

O'Shea, S., Stone, C. and Delahunty, J., 2015. "I 'Feel'like I Am at University Even Though I Am Online." Exploring How Students Narrate Their Engagement with Higher Education Institutions in an Online Learning Environment. *Distance Education*, 36(1), pp. 41-58.

Oztok, M. and Kehrwald, B.A., 2017. Social Presence Reconsidered: Moving Beyond, Going Back, Or Killing Social Presence. *Distance Education*, 38(2), pp. 259-266.

Picciano, A.G., 2002. Beyond student perceptions: Issues of interaction, presence, and performance in an online course. Journal of Asynchronous Learning, 6(1), pp. 21-40.

Ramsden, P., 1988. *Improving Learning: New Perspectives.* Nichols Pub Co.

Reilly, J.R., Gallagher-Lepak, S. and Killion, C., 2012. "Me and My Computer": Emotional Factors in Online Learning. *Nursing Education Perspectives*, 33(2), pp. 100-105.

Rheingold, H., 1993: The Virtual Community: Homesteading on the Electronic Frontier. Cambridge, MA: MIT Press.

Rourke, L., 2000. Exploring Social Communication in Computer Conferencing. Unpublished Master Thesis. Alberta, Edmonton Alberta.

Schrage, M., 1995. *No More Teams! Mastering The Dynamics of Creative Collaboration.* New York: Doubleday.

Short, J., Williams, E., Christie, B., 1976. The social psychology of telecommunications John Wiley & Sons, Ltd, Hoboken, NJ

Simmel, G., & Hughes, E. C., 1949. The sociology of sociability. American journal of sociology, 55(3), pp.254-261.

Swan, K., & Shih, L. F., 2005. On the nature and development of social presence in online course discussions. Journal of Asynchronous learning networks, 9(3), pp.115-136.

Tisdell, E. J., Strohschen, G. I., Carver, M. L., Corrigan, P., Nash, J., Nelson, M., & O'Connor, M., 2004. Cohort learning online in graduate higher education: Constructing knowledge in cyber community. Journal of educational technology & society, 7(1), pp.115-127.

Webster, J. and Hackley, P., 1997. Teaching Effectiveness in Technology-Mediated Distance Learning. *Academy of Management Journal*, 40(6), pp. 1282-1309.

Wenger, E., 1998. *Communities of Practice: Learning, Meaning, and Identity*. Cambridge University Press.

Xia, C., Fielder, J. And Siragusa, L., 2013. Achieving Better Peer Interaction in Online Discussion Forums: A Reflective Practitioner Case Study. *Issues in Educational Research*, 23(1), pp. 97-113.

Posters

MIXING EDUCATIONAL TECHNIQUES: E-LEARNING, FLIPPED CLASSROOM AND THE USE OF SOCIAL NETWORKS. AN EXPERIENCE IN A UNIVERSITY SETTING

Roberto Espejo Mohedano and Arturo Gallego Segador
Department of Statistics. University of Córdoba, Spain

ABSTRACT

This paper describes an experience, in a university setting corresponding to a degree in engineering, of mixing some of the trends in current distance education. It is a mixed learning methodology using the inverted classroom through the combination of learning management systems and social networks services in an introductory course on statistical methods applied to engineering. Finally, it shows the impact on the degree of success that the implantation of the experience has had in those students who have followed the established guidelines against those who have opted for a traditional method.

KEYWORDS

e-learning, Learning Management Systems, Modular Teaching Mini-Videos, Social Networks, Flipped Classroom

1. INTRODUCTION

Advances in information and communication technologies (ICT) play a key role in the development of the university education system: intelligent tutoring systems, multimedia educational platforms and virtual educational environments. These advances have led to the emergence, among others, of the concept of virtual education and Learning Management Systems (LMS). In addition, in recent times, ICTs have enabled the growth of new lines of research applied to technological development in the educational field, resulting in the acquisition of a wide variety of interactive teaching tools accessible through electronic devices such as the computer, mobile phone or tablet (García et al., 2014).

The use of this kind of tools in class favours the degree of interactivity, increases the collaboration between students in their educational process (Cavus and Ibrahim, 2007) and significantly improves the performance shown by the students, developing a sense of connectivity and community that increases the learning capacity of the students (Kok, 2008). This leads to a high motivation and interest in working with these kind of tools (Martín and Serrano, 2009). There is no doubt that these tools are a boost for the educational process and must be incorporated in class, not only as a tool for remote learning, but also to be combined with both face-to-face and non-face-to-face work by the student (Espejo et al., 2018). This kind of applications improve the performance of the educational process and the self-learning capacity of the student, facilitates the self-evaluation of their knowledge and validates the teaching/learning process (Sánchez et al., 2009).

On the other hand, in recent years, countless efforts have been made to improve the in-depth and quality learning, which have resulted in the emergence of various ways of approaching this learning. Among these, the inverted learning model should be noted as one of the most outstanding ones. The inverted classroom (flipped classroom) is a blended learning modality that fits perfectly with the use of LMS systems in class. This approach raises a pedagogical model that proposes the need to transfer part of the teaching and learning process out of the classroom in order to use class time for the development of more complex cognitive processes that favours self-learning.

Along with these virtual tools, it is necessary to provide the students with good material that allows them to prepare the subject. In this sense, the modular teaching mini-videos (MDM), (Letón et al., 2013), turn out to be a very useful teaching resource, characterized by specific elements in terms of duration, support, methodology, philosophy, format and interconnection (modularity). MDMs have proven to be useful and contribute to the improvement of the face-to-face (real or virtual) moment within distance, face-to-face and semi-face-to-face teaching. At the same time, Social Network services and technologies (SNS) have achieved impressive participation from both students and teachers. In addition, through their mobile applications, they have managed to become a daily habit inseparable from a large number of users. For this reason, more and more authors are proposing teaching methods that include SNS (Celik et al., 2015).

This paper presents the results of the implementation, in a University setting, of a learning methodology using the inverted classroom through the combination of LMS with social network services in an introductory course on statistical methods applied to engineering. The objective is to verify, as far as possible, the benefits that this mixture of teaching practices can have for learning.

2. METHODOLOGY

The proposed experience was carried out in a group of 76 students of the Statistical methods in Engineering subject corresponding to the first year of the Degree in Computer Engineering of the University of Córdoba (Spain). Volunteer students were asked to agree to participate in the experiment and the initial group was divided into two subgroups. A first subgroup consisting of 35 students who participated in the new experience (experimental group) and a second subgroup of 41 students who were given lessons through a classical methodology of Blackboard (control group). The theory and practical contents proposed in both subgroups were the same.

In both subgroups, the LMS platform used was Moodle, in which all the course materials were provided: theory transparencies in PowerPoint format, proposed exercises, additional readings, non-face-to-face self-evaluation activities and face-to-face evaluation activities. The difference between one group and another was the fact that the experimental group was provided membership in a SN group in Telegram and the teaching methodology of flipped classroom was used. In this methodology, each classroom session is preceded by the need of viewing one or several teaching mini-videos, dedicating the face-to-face class time to comment on the visualized material and resolve both questions about the content and questions raised by the teacher and discussed in group. In addition, comprehension tests are carried out in these classes, through the LMS survey module, where the difficulties offered by each theory content are detected, and again resolved in a group manner. The use of Telegram as a SN tool is oriented to the resolution of doubts at the time of the visualization of the MDM by the students, where they themselves are the ones who propose and resolve, in real time, the difficulties they may have.

3. RESULTS

Related to the degree of success of the methodology used in the experimental group (inverted class, MDM and Telegram), the information collected through a survey conducted at the end of the course shows that 92% of students are in favour of use of the MDM, basically because they can visualize the sessions as many times as they want and at the most appropriate time for them. Regarding the inverted class, none of the students had participated in a similar experience and indicate that at the beginning it has not been a simple task and that the time dedicated to the work done has exceeded their initial expectations. They also indicate that the use of the Telegram group has been very useful in the preparation of the sessions.

The descriptive values of the academic results are those presented in table 1. The scores obtained in the practical component are similar in both groups (experimental and control). Otherwise, and with respect to the theory, the means scores are different, detecting a difference of 0.767 in favor of the control group.

Table 1. Academic results

	Experimental group		Control group	
	Theory	Practical	Theory	Practical
Mean scores	6.279 ± 1.981	4.443 ± 2.245	7.046 ± 1.980	4.738 ± 2.751
% of passed	97.21	41.46	85.32	42.86
% not presented	14.3		21.9	

The percentage of passed students in the practical component it is similar, but in the theory it is quite superior in the experimental group with a difference of 11.89%. Finally, the percentage of not presented students is significantly lower in the experimental group.

4. CONCLUSIONS

As shown by the results presented, the implementation of the teaching experience is positive in terms of the degree of satisfaction expressed by the students who have participated.

On the other hand, the number of dropouts (students not submitted for exam) is lower in the experimental group, which may mean an advance on the problem of abandonment in higher engineering studies. Among the authors who treat the causes of the abandonment of this type of students can be cited, among others, the work of Marra et al. (2012).

To conclude, the personal work together with the collaboration in teamwork and participation in group discussions produces an additional workload that is compensated through a socialization of the knowledge acquired, and which results in greater uniformity of the educational levels reached.

REFERENCES

Celik, I. et al., 2015. A Model for Understanding Educational Facebook Use. *EURASIA Journal of Mathematics, Science and Technology Education*, vol. 11, no. 4, pp. 899- 907.

Cavus, N. and Ibrahim, D., 2007. Assessing the success rate of students using a LMS together with a collaborative tool in web-based teaching of programming languages. *Journal of educational computing research,* 36(3), 301-321.

Espejo R. et al. 2018. Some results on the application of different teaching techniques in the field of a STEM subject in computer engineering student. *10th Intern. Conference on Education and New Learning Technologies,* Mallorca. Spain.

García-Valcárcel et al., 2014. Las TIC en el aprendizaje colaborativo en el aula de Primaria y Secundaria. *Comunicar: Revista Científica de Comunicación y Educación*,21(42), 65-74.

Kok, A. 2008. An online social constructivist tool: a secondary school experience in the developing world. *Turkish online Journal of Distance Education,* 9(7), 87-98.

Letón, E. Et al., 2013. ¿Cómo diseñar un MOOC basado en mini-vídeos docentes modulares. *Actas del XVIII Congreso Internacional de Tecnologías para la Educación y el Conocimiento*, UNED, Madrid, Spain.

Marra, R. M. et al., 2012. Leaving engineering: A multi-year single institution study. *Journal of Engineering Education,* 101(1), 6-27.

Martín, T. and Serrano, A., 2009. The role of new technologies in the learning process: Moodle as a teaching tool in Physics. *Computers & Education,* 52(1), 35-44.

Sánchez, P. F. Et al., 2009. Active learning through self-assessment using a virtual laboratory. *Revista Iberoamericana de Tecnologías del Aprendizaje, 4*(1), 53-62.

USING REN'PY AS A DIGITAL STORYTELLING TOOL TO ENHANCE STUDENTS' LEARNING

Hsiu-Ling Chen and Yun-Chi Chuang
National Taiwan University of Science and Technology
No.43, Sec. 4, Keelung RD, Taipei 10607, Taiwan

ABSTRACT

The present study aims to explore students' learning experience with the use of Ren'py as a tool to approach digital storytelling in their collaborative design of digital stories. Digital storytelling is adopted by the present research as an approach for a total of 46 high school students to consider social issues with critical thinking and present the learning outcomes of their collaborative design through projects of digital stories. Students were divided in groups of three to four to engage in collaborative learning in all of the following three different aspects: critical thinking, game script design, and game production, all of which require students to collect or generate information and collaborate with one another toward successful design of digital stories. An in-depth interview was given to each student in the present study at the end of the course. Interview results indicate that students must pick up the programming language in order to control necessary elements in the production of their games and that learning simultaneously two sets of high level skills both in the programming language and in critical thinking might cause them to experience cognitive overload. Nonetheless, the proposed approach was still recognized among student participants, all of whom reported enhanced skills in communication, problem-solving, and media literacy.

KEYWORDS

Digital Storytelling, Ren'py, Critical Thinking

1. INTRODUCTION

Ren'py is a game engine dedicated to the production of visual novels. Its select menu offers an alternative to the linear mode of plot development commonly seen among conventional stories. Its non-linear and divergent structure of digital storytelling allows designers to develop content comprised of multiple branches. This also allows users to choose different plots and preferred endings at their will for any stories they intend to create. Users also benefit from enriched interaction and entertainment through the kind of digital storytelling supported both by a large collection of imagery as well as sound effect and by a wide selection of background designs, where various modes of conversation are also available for any characters involved. Ren'py is thus selected as a tool for digital storytelling in the present research.

Digital storytelling is an application of integrated multimedia. It alters its own artistic forms and techniques among different kinds of software to appeal to students in various learning activities (Hung, Hwang, & Huang, 2012). Malita and Martin (2010) think that the sharing of knowledge, wisdom, and values through digital storytelling not only enhances one's memory but helps him/her create links to former experience. In addition, scholars also think that digital storytelling increases students' ability in writing (Xu, Park, & Baek, 2011), critical thinking (Gaeta, Loia, Mangione, Orciuoli, Ritrovato, & Salerno, 2014), and problem-solving (Yang & Wu, 2012).

To sum, the present study aims to explore students' learning experience where they used Ren'py as a tool to approach digital storytelling in their collaborative design of digital stories.

2. METHODS

The present study includes a total of 46 (26 males and 20 females) high school students enrolled in Think Utopia, an elective course in civics education. Students are required to consider social issues with critical thinking and present the outcomes of their collaborative learning through the design of game stories. Three kinds of learning activities were featured in the course by the present study. The first one involves the learning of critical thinking. Students were presented with everyday situations that help them appreciate the importance of critical thinking and were taught to apply it in their daily activities. The second one features the design of game scripts, where students were divided in groups of three to four. A total of twelve groups were formed. Each group worked on one of the five themes in civics education. These themes were "fundamental human rights and the right to freedom," "fundamental human rights and the right to equality" "media literacy," "cultural diversity," and "sustainable development." The learning objective for students in this course was to incorporate the concepts they learned in critical thinking into the above themes and to use the result of such incorporation as the pivot of background design in their game stories. The third one focuses on the production of games. Upon the completion of their game scripts, students proceeded to a computer lab, where they used an abundance of sound effect, imagery, and animation techniques to add appeals to their games and to engage in the production process in collaboration with their peers. Each student in the present study was given with an in-depth interview at the end of the course.

3. RESULTS

The present study engaged every student participant in an in-depth and semi structured interview at the end of the semester. Student responses in the interviews were collected for an integrated analysis, where several inferences derived as follows:

Some stated that the need for topics of civics education to be integrated in the script of their games actually encouraged them to develop a data base and a mechanism where they may sort out various information for themselves and clear things up for their users. Furthermore, the technical need for cohesion and logic within game stories also drove student participants to consider matters such as causation and attributions in the scripts and hurdle questions for their game stories.

Others spoke positively of the need for them to recall some of the knowledge they had learned previously in a lecture and use it towards the design of hurdle questions. This process of inquiry had successfully liberated them from their previous positions as passive listeners and turned them into active learners where they were able to engage in comprehensive thinking related to their learning. In addition, the need for them to provide users with detailed illustrations of every single choice on the menu has also contributed to their understanding of how each skill in critical thinking may be applied.

Still others mentioned that they have benefitted from group discussions where they engaged in critical thinking and scrutinized, talked about, and took stances on what others had shared about a topic in question. This also allowed them to practice expressing themselves with organized thoughts and persuading others through one's original perspectives and words.

As for the concern about cognitive load among student participants, it was found that some students were confident in applying critical thinking to their daily lives while others did not think so. Such division is reflected among students in their interviews where some students approved the approach proposed by the present research for its strength in improving their skills in effective communication, problem solving, and media literacy while others did not find much appeal in the approach due to the reason of cognitive overload where they experienced difficulty in game design, timely completion of assignment and learning tasks both related to computer programming and critical thinking. Additional obstacles in learning were also pointed out by students regarding various confusions with the similarities and differences among the skills in critical thinking.

In general, it can be inferred from the result of the interview that a majority (38 out of 46) of student participants was supportive of and satisfied with the approach proposed by the present research. They think that the approach incorporated learning by doing and effectively increased their motivation in learning critical thinking through the design of hurdle questions and everything else ranging from game trials to a final production. They also described learning with the approach as one where the need for original designs in story plots and voluntary efforts in getting the basics of critical thinking amounted to some valid trainings for one's independent thinking.

4. CONCLUSION

Results from the qualitative interview on the integration of both the learning strategies and its content indicate that students must pick up the programming language in order to control necessary elements such as image configuration, sound effect, animation, and transition between scenes in the production of their games. However, the subsequent demand for high level thinking skills such as programming and critical thinking may result in cognitive overload among students who ran out of time to complete all of the tasks. Nonetheless, the proposed approach was still recognized among student participants, all of whom reported enhanced skills in communication, problem-solving, and media literacy.

ACKNOWLEDGEMENT

This research was supported by a Grant from the Ministry of Science and Technology, Taiwan (MOST 106-2511-S-011-002-MY2).

REFERENCES

Gaeta, M. et al, 2014. A methodology and an authoring tool for creating Complex Learning Objects to support interactive storytelling. *Computers in Human Behavior*, Vol. 31, pp 620-637.

Hung, C.-M.et al, 2012. A Project-based digital storytelling approach for improving students' learning motivation, problem-solving competence and learning achievement. *Educational Technology & Society*, Vol. 15, No. 4, pp 368-379.

Malita, L. and Martin, C., 2010. Digital Storytelling as web passport to success in the 21st century. P*rocedia Social and Behavioral Sciences*, Vol. 2, pp 3060-3064.

Xu, Y. et al, 2011. A new approach toward digital storytelling: An activity focused on writing self-efficacy in a virtual learning environment. *Educational Technology & Society*, Vol. 14, No. 4, pp 181-191.

Yang, T. C. and Wu, C. I., 2012. Digital storytelling for enhancing student academic achievement, critical thinking, and learning motivation: A year-long experimental study. *Computers & education*, Vol. 59, No. 2, pp 339-352.

USING AN ONLINE FORUM TO ENHANCE THE LEARNING OF SPANISH GRAMMAR AS A SECOND LANGUAGE

Jiyoung Yoon
University of North Texas, 1155 Union Circle #311127, Denton, Texas 76203, USA

ABSTRACT

This study presents e-learning methods for learning grammar that can provide more contextualization and meaning than explanations in traditional textbook, thus enhancing second language students' active and interactive learning of Spanish grammar. An online forum shared among students in a class is used to share interview reports with native speakers and to respond to the reports of the classmates using the target grammar -infinitival complements in Spanish- as a second language.

KEYWORDS

Second Language, Spanish, Grammar Learning, Online Forum, Infinitival Complement, Guided Induction Model

1. INTRODUCTION

To many instructors and students, learning grammar in a traditional second language classroom setting often means understanding the textbook explanations and memorizing the rules presented in them in order to produce grammatically correct sentences. Even with the incorporation of technology along with communicative approaches into the classroom, many instructors still rely heavily on the explanations of textbooks and the activities presented in them to teach grammar. Textbooks alone, however, often do not provide enough input and clear explanations about a second language (L2) grammar (Frantzen 2013; Yoon 2018). Students often feel that real communication ability in L2 can be acquired through authentic content-based input such as interaction with speakers who speak L2 as a native tongue in authentic cultural settings.

One part of Spanish grammar that often causes confusion among native speakers of English learning Spanish as L2 is infinitival complements (*María evita comer carne* 'Mary avoids eating meat'). Students often produce ungrammatical sentences such as **María evita comiendo carne* 'Mary avoids eating meat' in which a gerundial complement is used just like in English. The confusion mainly stems from the syntactic transfer from their own first language, but also textbooks are also to be blamed for the insufficient and sometimes unclear explanations of the grammatical concepts along with the lack of contextualized grammar activities. In order to help students to understand and correctly use this particular grammar structure, this pilot study created interactive activities via an online forum (available in Blackboard learning, for example) which incorporate interviews, guided writing, and written discussion. The grammatical concept of the infinitival complement was not explicitly explained, but it was presented through the gradual process of learning examples and using them in authentic cultural settings (See Cerezo et al. 2016 for the 'guided induction model'). A pilot study of college students participating in a study abroad program in Costa Rica will be presented to show how the e-learning methods can be used to teach grammar.

2. METHODS

A pilot study was conducted as part of the study abroad context in Costa Rica with college students from U.S. taking an advanced undergraduate Spanish conversation course. Fifteen students participated in this pilot study while taking this course for four weeks. The instruction of the infinitival complement construction in Spanish was not formally given to the students, but rather, this grammatical concept was introduced via various examples and models of sentences containing this construction in given activities. The purpose of this approach was to introduce the grammar topic through an inductive way rather than explicitly explaining the concepts. The activities include oral interviews with native speakers of Spanish, guided writing tasks summarizing the oral interviews which are shared through online forums with the classmates, reading classmates' online reports, and writing guided reactions to them (using the required infinitival complement forms). The purpose of these interactive activities was to promote the actual language use not only in authentic contexts but also within a virtual environment rather than just memorizing and applying the grammar rules presented in textbooks.

Phase 1: During the second week of their stay abroad, students were asked to interview native speakers (in particular, their host moms or dads) about their preferred activities and type of food they would like to have on their birthdays, as part of the lesson of the chapter they were learning. This task was completed outside the classroom. Then they were asked to write the interview responses using the infinitival complement construction in the shared online forum, so that other peer students could see what they have written. Students were required to use at least four of the infinitival complement constructions from the given list (*preferir* 'to prefer', *creer* 'to think', *decider* 'to decide', *odiar* 'to hate', *lamenter* 'to regret', *pensar* 'to plan', *necesitar* 'to need'), and a sample interview question was provided (e.g., *¿Qué tipo de comida prefiere comer en su cumpleaños?* 'What kind of food does she/he prefer to eat on her/his birthday?').

Phase 2: During the third week of their stay abroad, students had to write their reactions to two classmates' written survey responses of their choice, using the infinitival complement construction again. They were asked to write some similarities and differences they found between their host mom and their classmates' host moms regarding their food/activity preferences. Once again, students were offered an inductive guide about the infinitival complement in the instruction: they were required to use at least three of the infinitival complement-taking verbs from the list (*temer* 'to be afraid of', *odiar* 'to hate', *negar* 'to deny', *esperar* 'to hope', *lamenter* 'to regret', and *aceptar* 'to accept/admit'). The purpose of these activities was to enhance their communication skills through the exchange of the meaningful messages, but more importantly, to induce the target grammatical form and usage through interactions with native speakers and also with their classmates in a virtual space. The online forum, in this case, was vital to help them to incorporate authentic information gathered from native speakers of Spanish, and also to interact with their peers.

Towards the end of the program (around the fourth week), students were tested on their knowledge of this grammar by writing a mini-composition about health, including five sentences containing infinitival complements from the given list (*evitar* 'to avoid', *pensar* 'intend', *odiar* 'to hate', *preferir* 'to prefer', *lamentar* 'to regret). In addition, students took a pre-test and a post-test about the infinitival complements in which they had to choose the correct form of the complement type between an infinitive and a gerund (e.g., *No puedo imaginar [tener / teniendo] un novio tan talentoso como el tuyo* 'I can't imagine having such a talented boyfriend like yours').

3. RESULTS AND DISCUSSION

Students engaged themselves actively in writing the interview reports in the online discussion forum and they also reacted to their peers' reports online using the infinitival complement appropriately in most cases. Samples responses and reactions to the peers' reports are presented in (1) and (2):

(1) Interview report: *Mi mamá tica <u>prefiere comer</u> arroz con pollo en su cumpleaños, con queque de churchill. Ella dice que este queque es frío como el helado, y es muy delicioso. Ella <u>cree tener</u> invitados en su casa es mejor que ir a un restaurante. Generalmente ella invita a la familia y a cuatro amigas. Si mi mamá tica <u>decide ir</u> a un restaurante, iría a Antojitos, porque a ella le gusta su comida mexicana. Si hizo algo más especial para su cumpleaños, <u>piensa ir</u> a la playa con sus amigos para celebrar.*

(2) Reaction: *Hola! A mi mama tica también le encanta comer postre, ella <u>espera poder</u> comer mucho postre la noche de su cumpleaños. A tu mama tica le gustaría tener familia en casa pero mi mama tica <u>odia tener</u> que cocinar la noche su cumpleaños así que ella <u>prefiere salir</u> a un restaurante.* [...]

Towards the end of the program, students wrote a mini-composition about health using the required infinitival complements, and they overall performed well in this final production task and assessment. An example of paragraph is presented in (3) and the summary of the score is presented in Table 1:

(3) *Yo prefiero tomar agua normalmente, pero en Costa Rica, es más difícil encontrar.* [...] *Lamento decir que no he tomado mucho aquí. Odio pedir cosas que son inconvenientes a otras personas.* [...]

Table 1. Student score distributions of the five sentences with infinitival complements in a mini-composition

Scores (out of 5)	5	4	3	2	1
Number of students (N = 15)	7	6	2	-	-

In summary, the data show that students were learning the usage and the form through online discussion forums in an engaging manner and they were overall able to use the form appropriately and correctly in the final mini composition task as shown in Table 1. The form-focused tests, however, show that the actual learning of the form seemed to still be in progress without showing much difference between the pre-test and the post-test scores (Table 2).

Table 2. Comparison of the pre-test and post-test results for infinitival complement constructions

Pre-test average	Post-test average
7.0 (out of 10 points)	7.4 (out of 10 points)

The outcome of the quantitative comparison between the pre-test and the post-test does not clearly show the immediate significant improvement in terms of the test scores (pre-test score 7.0 vs. post-test score 7.4). The reason for about the same scores between the two tests may be due to the fact that the test format itself (that is, choosing between the infinitival complement vs. the gerundial complement) was focusing on the form without requiring students to understand the content or the context in which it was used. In addition, the period between the two tests was not long enough for the students to fully grasp the inductive meaning of the grammar exposed through the two activities facilitated online. There was clearly a limitation for the time and the amount of input the students were able to receive in order for them to perform better on the post-test, especially when the explicit grammar explanations were not given to them. Nonetheless, the communicative ability and the overall accuracy of the form observed in their final mini-compositions clearly showed that the incorporation of the interviews with native speakers into learning L2 via online discussion forums did indeed seem to help them develop the ability to use this particular grammar construction in a meaningful way.

4. CONCLUSION

This study has presented a pilot study applying e-learning activities in learning the infinitival complement constructions in Spanish as L2 and involving local native speakers through students' oral interviews. The virtually shared online space among students helped students enhance their comprehension and the appropriate use of the target grammar in an authentic setting, but knowing the long-term learning effect requires further investigation.

REFERENCES

Cerezo, L., Caras, A., and Leow, R. P. 2016. The effectiveness of guided induction versus deductive instruction on the development of complex Spanish *gustar* structures. *Studies in Second Language Acquisition*, 38, pp. 265-291.

Frantzen, D. 2013. Using literary texts to reveal problematic rules of usage. *Foreign Language Annals,* 46, pp. 628-645.

Yoon, J. 2018. Teaching infinitival complements in Spanish as a second language: Spanish textbook explanations. *International Journal of Languages' Education and Teaching*, 6(4), pp. 300-320.

Doctoral Consortia

ORGANISATION OF KNOWLEDGE FROM TRACES OF HUMAN LEARNING

Baba Mbaye

EFFET B company, France , Laboratory of ELLIADD, University of Franche-comtè, France

ABSTRACT

Faced with the diversity and the large number of learning resources available on e-learning platforms, learners often face problems of inadequacy between the training path to choose and the skills sought.

Indeed, many learning platforms with recommendation exist, but these do not often include information and different characteristics of learners. This problem can be mitigated by the semantisation of the content and the organization of the knowledge of the different actors involved on the learning platform.

In this paper, we make a modeling of the knowledge representation (thesauri and concept maps) of learning resources, based on information from learner's written records on a learning platform and knowledge modeling from expert interactions on resource and learner assessments.

These models make it possible to represent knowledge from written tracesthese written traces are metadata resulting from the interactions made on a learning platform by the learners and the experts (for example the expert in charge of the content of the trainings, the expert in charge of the evaluation of the trainings carried out).

KEYWORDS

E-Learning, Semantic Network, Knowledge Representation, Semantic Web, Written Records

1. INTRODUCTION

Knowledge is the activity by which man seeks to understand reality. The term "representation" will be examined here in the context of the theory of knowledge. In fact, knowledge representation is a set of tools and technologies. In our research, this set is used to represent on the one hand and on the other hand to organize human knowledge for the purpose of using it in an automated way and to share it (Luca Stefanutti et al, 2017).

The organization of knowledge consists of making a representation of a set of knowledge in a formalized and schematic way. It is an essential link in the process of managing knowledge and skills in an organization. Knowledge modeling is an activity at the center of many knowledge management occupations by positioning knowledge modeling at their center (Rappin, Baptiste, 2014).

2. CONTRIBUTION

The purpose of this research is to refine the content of the learning platform (CLP) and to facilitate the management of online CLP by opting for the relevance, accessibility of knowledge useful to learners. This knowledge is refined and adapted according to the learning pathways of the learners. The management of the CLP is facilitated by the reproduction of the actions of the experts on the learning platform in a automat.

3. CONCEPTS, PROCESSING AND MODELING

3.1 Information and Knowledge

It is important at first to present the difference between the concepts of information and knowledge. Information is the set of all data external to people, communicated orally or mediated in documents. Whereas knowledge is the result of any mental construct internationalized by an individual from information he obtains.

The interpretation of information by a person consists in transforming these into internal knowledge in his memory, which can also be called "learning". Knowledge representation is the reverse process by which a person produces information usable by other people, using a representation system, which can also be called "knowledge extraction" (Sanetake Nagayoshi et al, 2017).

The processing of information and knowledge, the acquisition, the construction of work processes require a system of representation external to our memory. The history of mankind is rich in such systems, starting with oral, written or pictorial languages that allow objects and ideas and ideas to be represented by words or symbols and to establish relations between these objects and these ideas.In the fields of mathematics and science, the geometric representations and Cartesian diagrams that we study in primary or secondary school are other examples of commonly usedrepresentation systems(Mostafa Al-Emran et al, 2018).

In the early sixties, the evolution of cognitive sciences and computer science led to the creation of knowledge representation systems such as concept maps, semantic networks, schemas or semantic frameworks, entity-relationship models, information flow models, object-oriented models, etc (Antonio Lieto et al, 2018).

The purpose of these systems is to propose a formal language, often graphic, to make a representation of the knowledge that "hide" in the information, what is called in English "knowledge level". For example, two texts, one in French and one in English, translation from one another, will be represented in the same way by a knowledge model that groups together the concepts that these texts deal with and the relationships between them. concepts. Similarly, an order describing a work process and a written text describing the same sequence of operations will be represented in a similar way in a knowledge representation system (Xing Tang et al, 2019) . This is called representation of the meaning of a document or semantic representation.A semantic representation is an image of the mental model of knowledge derived from the peculiarities of the format chosen to present the information (Zhenyong Wu et al, 2016).

3.2 Information Processing vs. Knowledge Processing

Information processing consists of circulating within the organization the information of the field in which the organization operates, as well as internal and external information on the goods and services produced by the organization and its working processes. Some of this information is retained and processed to constitute the memory of the organization in the form of banks of documents or database, which used to produce goods and services.

The processing of knowledge adds to this traditional process, the interpretation, ie the transformation of information into knowledge by staff through learning and the reverse process, ie the extraction and presentation of knowledge held by some members staff in the form of information that will be integrated into the organization's memory made available to all staff. In this sense, it can be said that the treatment of knowledge is characteristic of the "learning" organization (Nopparat Thepthepa et al, 2016).

The central component of a knowledge-processing system is the knowledge base, which is a standard representation of the knowledge of the domain the organization wants to deal with and which is used to make a representation of the content of the documents as well as the data found in the memory of the organization (Meenakshi Malhotra et al, 2016). The knowledge base is used to refer in an integrated way the documents and the information it contains, then to look for the information, to locate alternative, neighboring or complementary documents, or to identify the needs of the organization in terms of knowledge. not covered or covered incompletely (Layla Unger et al 2016).

The representation of knowledge is limited to the processing of documents. It is an approach that leads to unstructured and unrelated activities of creation, import, capture, research and use of knowledge. Knowledge components may exist in a large type of document format or in implicit knowledge held by individuals but still expressed in the organization's memory. In terms of information retrieval, documents are syntactically referenced by a ranking engine, instead of direct referencing to a knowledge model. Thus the problem is the follow-up of associations between concepts to identify related or complementary documents.

It is an association that allows IT agents to search and find documents by their semantics, their content, rather their syntax, their form.

The documents accessible by internet are associated with each other and the representation of knowledge of this association is at the bottom of the semantic web.

The process of knowledge processing has four main steps :

- The creation or import of information in the form of text, still and moving images, graphic templates, etc.
- The semantic referencing of information, doCcuments, information is indexed and described by their attribute, by metadata, by their position in classifications, e, using ontologies and generally in the framework of a system of knowledge representation.
- Research and access to information by first identifying knowledge elements in the knowledge base, rather than data in a database. The latter being referenced according to knowledge, it will be found using metadata as the basis of the research. We can also use the knowledge model or semantic referencing ontology for browsing information, doing research, getting access to web pages, documents, people.
- The use of information in the context of work processes by segmenting, aggregating, annotating and integrating information into new information resources or documents that will in turn be semantically referenced and integrated into the process of processing knowledge.

3.3 The Graphical Representation of the Knowledge Model

There are several techniques for representing knowledge. Each representation technique has characteristics that allow optimal adaptation to certain realities to be modeled. The characterization of objects, the study of processes, the construction of decisional or logical system, there is a technique of representation more adapted for the modeling of the system.Trees and semantic networks, flow charts, causal diagrams, decision trees, and object-oriented models are all ways of representing knowledge that is based on a graphical approach.

- **Semantic tree** is used a lot in pedagogy. The latter is used to highlight components of knowledge in the form of hierarchical structure starting from a general object and classification by specialization of classes into subclasses and class into individuals. There are no links between the branches of the hierarchy. This is a technique that is often used in website design.
- **Semantic Network** (conceptual map or relationship entity graph): a semantic network makes it possible to relate concepts and facts by the naming of links. This representation is widely used in computer science, especially for database design, thus linking tables that groups the concepts described by their attributes. In artificial intelligence a semantic network makes it possible to establish a base of facts that makes a characterization of a specific domain.
- **The flowchart** is used for the purpose of modeling the procedures so far the graphs represented concepts and their relationships. In a flowchart, objects are actions or decisions, and links represent the flow of information from one action or decision to another. The notion of sequence is thus introduced in this type of representation.

4. OUR APPROACH

We will use semantic networks for the graphical representation of our knowledge model. The semantic network simulates our representation of memory, it is a model that shows us how knowledge could be represented in memory and how we could access this knowledge. Indeed, the memory is an immense pool of raw data containing concepts, events, and written traces resulting from interaction. All these elements form an immense inter-relational network. A semantic network is composed of nodes whose interrelations are established by labeled pointers. These nodes represent the different types of knowledge in memory. These nodes can be associated with properties that apply to the networks.

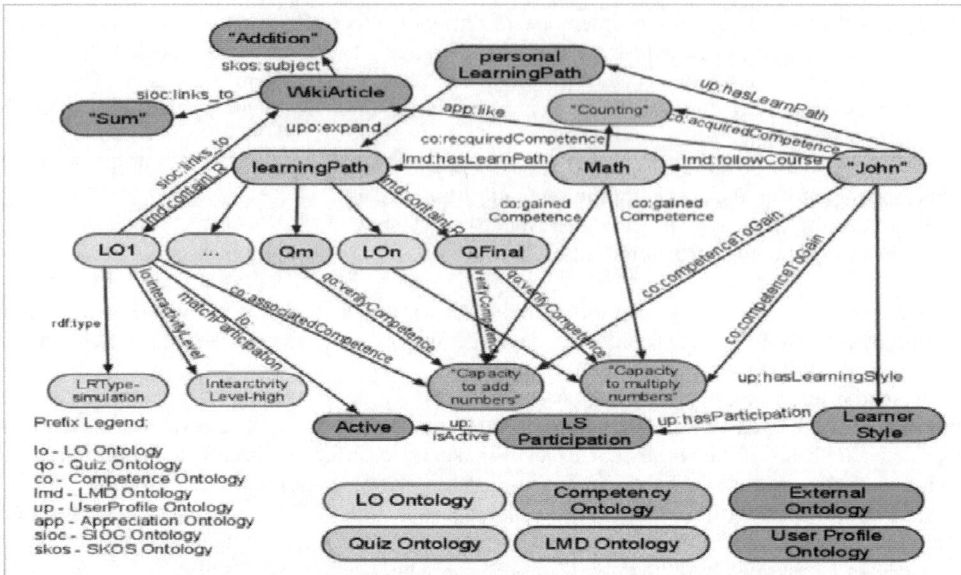

Figure 1. Example of semantic network (Ioan Szilagyi et al, 2011)

Our approach is based on reuse of the traces obtained from the interactions made by the different agents on the platform to generate a semantic network for each learner according to his profile and needs.The idea here is to set up an adaptive semantic network generator according to the needs and profile of the learner and his tutor. In our study, our traces of the various agents of the platform are stored in a LRS (learning record store) with Tin Can (TC) in Json format. The use of the traces will allow us to include the events which occurred during the execution of the trainings by the learners.

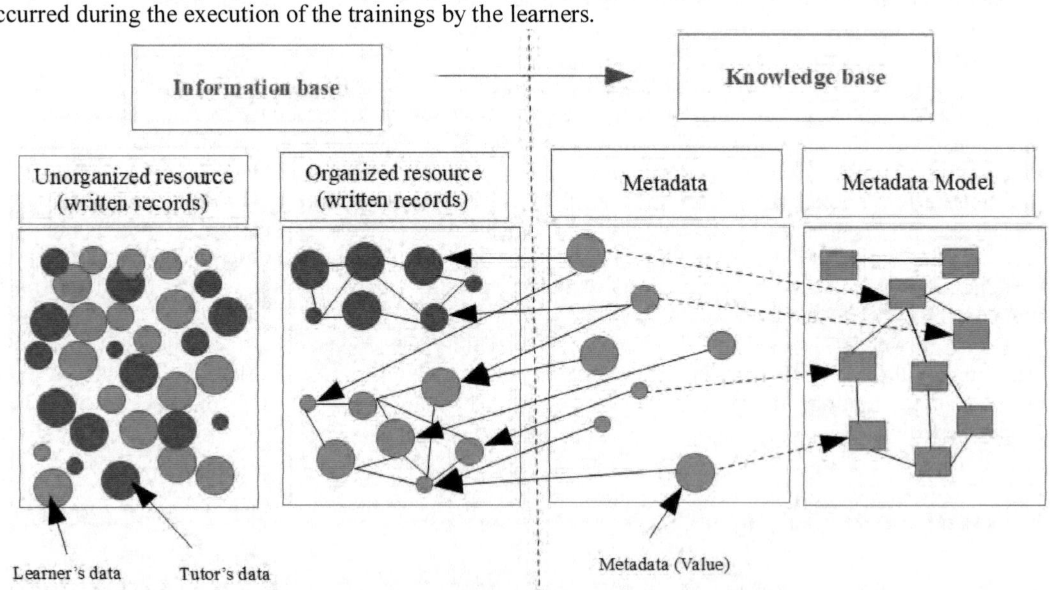

Figure 2. Written records knowledge organisation Model

5. CONCLUSION

In this paper, we present a representation model of knowledge from written traces made by the agents of an e-learning platform. This study allows us to show that the content management of an e-learning platform can be done automatically, efficiently and adapt to the profile of each learner.

REFERENCES

Antonio Lieto, Christian Lebiere, Alessandro Oltramari, The knowledge level in cognitive architectures: Current limitations and possible develoments, Cognitive Systems Research, Volume 48,2018, Pages 39-55,ISSN 1389-0417

Johanna Gast, Katherine Gundolf, Rainer Harms, Elvin Matos Collado, Knowledge management and coopetition: How do cooperating competitors balance the needs to share and protect their knowledge?,Industrial Marketing Management, 2019,.

Luca Stefanutti, Debora de Chiusole, On the assessment of learning in competence based knowledge space theory, Journal of Mathematical Psychology, Volume 80, 2017, Pages 22 32, ISSN 0022-2496, https://doi.org/10.1016/j.jmp.2017.08.003.

Layla Unger, Anna V. Fisher, Rebecca Nugent, Samuel L. Ventura, Christopher J. MacLellan, Developmental changes in semantic knowledge organization, Journal of Experimental Child Psychology, Volume 146, 2016, Pages 202-222, ISSN 0022-0965 https://doi.org/10.1016/j.jecp.2016.01.005.

Meenakshi Malhotra, T.R. Gopalakrishnan Nair, Knowledge network model with neurocognitive processing capabilities, Cognitive Systems Research, Volume 40, 2016, Pages 186-201, ISSN 1389-0417, https://doi.org/10.1016/j.cogsys.2015.11.002.

Mostafa Al-Emran, Vitaliy Mezhuyev, Adzhar Kamaludin, Khaled Shaalan, The impact of knowledge management processes on information systems: A systematic review, International Journal of Information Management,Volume 43,2018, Pages 173-187, ISSN 0268-4012, https://doi.org/10.1016/j.ijinfomgt.2018.08.001.

Nopparat Thepthepa, Toshioa Mitsufuji, Knowledge Process and Learning Organization Development in Science Museums, Procedia Computer Science, Volume 99, 2016, Pages 157-170, ISSN 1877-0509, https://doi.org/10.1016/j.procs.2016.09.108.

Sanetake Nagayoshi, Jun Nakamura, Accelerate Information Interpretation in the Organizational Failure Learning, Procedia Computer Science, Volume 112, 2017, Pages 971-979, ISSN 1877- 0509, https://doi.org/10.1016/j.procs.2017.08.139.

Szilagyi, I., Balog-Crisan, R., Roxin, A. and Roxin, I., 2011, July. Ontologies and Knowledge Aggregation in the Active Semantic Learning System. In *2011 IEEE 11th International Conference on Advanced Learning Technologies* (pp. 388-392). IEEE.

Xing Tang, Ling Chen, Jun Cui, Baogang Wei,Knowledge representation learning with entity descriptions, hierarchical types, and textual relations, Information Processing & Maagement,Volume 56, Issue 3, 2019, Pages 809-822, ISSN 0306-4573, https://doi.org/10.1016/j.ipm.2019.01.005.

Zhenyong Wu, Jihua Liao, Wenyan Song, Hanling Mao, Zhenfeng Huang, Xinxin Li, Hanying Mao, Semantic hyper-graph-based knowledge representation architecture for complex product development, Computers in Industry, Volume 100, 2018, Pages 43-56, ISSN 0166-3615, https://doi.org/10.1016/j.compind.2018.04.008

TECHNOLOGY-CONFIDENT TEACHERS ENABLING DEEP E-LEARNING PEDAGOGIES

Roy Rozario
Monash University, Australia

ABSTRACT

There are various types of successful teachers in the use of e-learning pedagogies when delivering curriculum in primary school context. That is, novice users, intermediate users and confident/expert users. But little is known about how confident teachers successfully integrate technologies in a dynamic and rapidly changing classroom context to enable quality pedagogies. This study conducted a baseline survey of 42 teachers to select three confident/expert teachers to undergo nine interviews and six classroom observations. An interpretivist and qualitative approach enabled deeper understandings from these teachers, while expansive learning framework facilitated capturing the various interactivities between m-devices, learners, teachers and curriculum content. A case study method using two levels of analysis, thematic and theoretical, helped unfold the key factors that constitute quality e-learning pedagogies. This paper presents two of its five findings, explorative learning and device affordances, that were critical to confident/expert teachers to enable deep learning with technologies using multiple pedagogic strategies.

KEYWORDS

Pedagogy, Classroom E-Learning, Expansive Learning, Interactivity

1. INTRODUCTION

E-learning offers a rich potential of deep learning, but the challenge lies with teachers on how they can explore this opportunity to transform their practice (Sharples et al, 2005). According to expansive learning (also called third generation activity theory), classroom learning activities pose the challenge of being unpredictable and uncertain (Engeström, 1987). With e-learning allowing for multiple interactivities between the device and those involved, classrooms have become even more dynamic, thereby posing further complexity in quality pedagogic practice (Wong, 2019).

Many pedagogical concepts/factors in classroom are the cause for learning uncertainties (Gonzalez & Gómez, 2014; Kumar & Chand, 2018). For instance, the technologies used, teaching-learning sequence, resources, learning goals, students' difficulties, pedagogy, professional development of the teacher, interactivity of device software and hardware, classroom management and teacher mind-sets, to name a few (Rozario & Ortlieb, 2015). To illustrate one of these factors, if we took the example of interactivity of the device software, such as an app. They can variously impact the users (teachers, students, teacher-colleagues, etc.) through its affordances on how they interact with the device content through its semiotic features. The ability of the various users to interact with the curriculum content to permit text, audio, video, pictures and spatiality to attain lesson objective can impact on their e-learning (Rozario et al., 2016). This body of knowledge is referred to as Human Computer Interactions (HCI) and allows for understanding e-learning interactions using activity theory (Bakke, 2015). Understanding the processes involved in dynamic e-learning classrooms, especially among technologically-confident teachers, on how they transform surface level teaching-learning practices to enable deep e-learning pedagogies is significant. Few studies focus on how technologically confident teachers can successfully integrate e-learning pedagogies using expansive learning principles.

This study focussed on the device's pedagogical affordances on the users, the context of use and the learning processes involved. Expansive learning provided a sound theoretical framework to capture the various dynamic pedagogical practices involved by technologically-confident teachers as and when they occurred (Mwanza & Engeström, 2005). Interviews were conducted immediately after classroom observations to capture the teaching-learning strategies adopted by teachers to overcome unpredictable and uncertain classroom challenges. The study's results showed five key pedagogical strategies used by technologically-confident teachers to enable deep learning using e-devices. This paper focuses on two strategies of best teacher practice to foster better e-learning pedagogies. Namely, device affordances and explorative learning, that confident teachers use to enable deep learning.

Teachers in this study during classroom sessions regularly used various features of the technologies which impact on their teaching-learning sequences. Because these new features in the technology were never previously been conducted, teachers were often learning on-the-go and skilfully orchestrating the class e-learning activities towards the lesson object. This process is referred to in this paper as explorative learning. This paper pays attention to how teachers orchestrated e-learning using explorative learning skills to successfully attain their end goal. Additionally, this paper also deals with how the affordances of the device impact on pedagogy to facilitate deep learning among students. The interactivity or interface of the device manifests itself through its affordances (Churchill et al., 2014). Therefore, it is no surprise that most definitions, classifications and instructional designs have included the element of device affordances as an integral part of quality pedagogies (Cochrane & Bateman, 2009). This paper goes beyond the superficial affordances of devices to demonstrate how teachers can orchestrate them into e-learning pedagogies that enable deep learning.

This paper was guided by the research question- What do m-learning device teachers consider as facilitating or inhibiting their pedagogical practices?

2. METHODOLOGY

The study used an interpretivists approach because it allowed for many interpretations of reality in primary school context (Ling & Ling, 2016; Valsiner et al., 2017). It helped collect deep data to inductively answer the research questions asked (Cowling, 2016). Case study as a method also complemented this approach because its methods of data collection, description and explanation, best suited qualitative research (Merriam, 2009). The theoretical lens that the study adopted required to be one that embraced the notion of adaptability and changing context; hence activity theory was most useful (Allen et al, 2011). It was particularly useful because it helped capturing the various interactions (teachers and students) with m-devices (Mwanza-Simwami, 2011).

Case study method allowed the researcher to seek cases that were specific to the need of the study, be present in classroom sessions as an observer, speak to the teachers, collect e-learning artefacts and make field notes relevant to the research questions. The data was collected in two phases. The first phase involved a survey to seek teachers who self-declared that they were confident users of technologies. A pilot-study was implemented to check for robustness of the survey questions after which 42 teachers from three Catholic Primary Schools participated in the survey. Three teacher participants were selected for the second phase of data collection. The second phase involved the researcher observing two classroom sessions per teacher. That is, six observations in total, one initial interview with the three teachers and one post interview after each of the classroom observations, a total of nine interviews.

Ethics clearance was sought at three levels and the Merriam's (2009) ethics checklist served as a guide in this process. The first level involved ethics clearance from the relevant university department, namely, Monash University Human Research Ethics Committee (MUHREC). The second level of ethics clearance was sought from the Catholic Education Offices of the Melbourne and Sale diocese. The third level of ethics clearance was sought from respective participating Catholic Primary Schools. As part of the ethics process the schools were requested to complete Consent and Explanatory forms by the principal, participant teachers, students and parents. During the various data collection stages, the study had no issues with ethics to report. The study addressed the feasibility and trustworthiness by adopting multiple strategies to validate findings, such as, cross case analysis, researcher reflexivity, triangulation and peer review (Merriam, 2009).

3. DATA ANALYSIS

The data-set (teacher interviews, classroom observations, informal interviews, post-classroom observations and e-learning artefacts) was analysed at two levels. The first level involved the 'framework' approach using the Ritchie and Spencer's (2002) model. In this phase the corpus of data was analysed using the five stages of analysis proposed by Ritchie and Spencer (2002). Namely, familiarization, identifying a thematic framework, indexing, charting, mapping and interpretation. The second level involved the theoretical approach using expansive learning theory. This approach allowed for deep analysis of the data-set using tools, such as *activity system, activity structure, expansive matrix* and *expansive cycle*, which assisted in analysing, scrutinising and interpreting data.

At the first level of analysis, namely 'framework' approach, the researcher first familiarised himself with the data by immersing into the various audio recordings of teacher interviews, video recordings of the classroom observations, researcher field notes, e-learning artefacts (sample e-activities completed by students), lesson plans and other relevant information provided to the researcher by the teacher. From the corpus of "unstructured and unwieldy" qualitative data, amounting to 80,000 words of interview transcripts, the researcher made notes of recurrent themes, key ideas, indexing, charting, mapping and finding patterns (Bernauer, 2015; Gough & Scott, 2000; Ritchie & Spencer, 2002, p.176). Five main themes were finalised. Verbatims and relevant concepts revealed links to overlapping themes that needed further decoding for deep analysis to be done at the theoretical level. Expansive learning concepts like activity structure (*operations, actions* and *activity*) and activity system (*actors, tools, rules, community, division of labour* and *object*) helped simplify and scrutinise e-learning classroom activities (Engeström; 1987).

4. FINDINGS

The study results found five key themes in the data analysis. They are, explorative learning, device affordances and pedagogies, inclusive pedagogies, collaborative and individualised learner centred interactions, and finally challenges as learning opportunity. These concepts emerged as surface level and deep level pedagogic activities. The surface level activities like classroom management, device features and device challenges were no less important, but rather key to enabling deep learning. Teacher participants of this study used surface level activities to convert them into deep level learning using their five pedagogical practices, like a tool-kit of instruments, to orchestrate classes. When these repertoires of pedagogical practices were used, it unintentionally led to quality pedagogies and deep level learning. Only two elements of these findings, that is explorative learning and device affordances, are presented for constraints in word limit and the need to thoroughly understand these concepts. These two themes overlapped during the coding and decoding process and hence are intermingled in their discussion below presented as sub-headings.

4.1 Explorative Learning

The study revealed teachers were constantly adapting and changing their classroom practices to accommodate deep learning using a repertoire of best practices they have gained over the years. Teachers only had an imaginary picture of the lesson activity to be conducted and skilfully worked to attain this object. E-learning classroom sessions were quite explorative in nature as many dynamic factors required the teacher to improvise and learn on-the-go making changes to teaching-learning sequences not previously planned. Some dynamic factors, such as, classroom management, cyber safety, device challenges, learner inclusivity, time management, content delivery and deep level learning needs, made teaching-learning complex and unpredictable. The contributing factors to these uncertain e-learning sessions often were consequent to new features of the technologies introduced through their professional learning, unexpected challenges encountered with software and hardware of the device, and e-coaches directly introducing new apps/software or their features.

Many pedagogical strategies were resorted to explore an alternate solution to these challenges. For instance, teachers resorted to their repertoire of skills (five themes of this study's findings) to help explore new ways to deal with these challenges. Participants of this study changed their teaching-learning sequences, included peer-mentorship, inclusive pedagogies, encouraged dialogic interactions, resorted to changed classroom management techniques and other practices that emerged as sub-themes. They used their expert knowledge and experience that they had gained over the years as methods/strategies to address new classroom challenges. Additionally, teachers were also mindful, reflective, open-minded, willing to take risks and flexible, even if it meant seeking help from students. They were transparent with their difficulties encountered and openly discussed them with their colleagues and students. They enabled collaborative learning spaces with their colleagues to share their challenges and successes to help same year-level colleagues in their forthcoming lesson activities on the same topic.

Of course, not always the unpredictable nature of e-learning sessions led to challenges but rather successes. Teachers were pleasantly surprised with how smooth and eloquent teaching-learning activities led to unintentional deep learning sessions. Participants in this study anticipated certain difficulties from students on account of device shortage or in trying to conduct a series of complex device interface tasks. However, these tasks were completed very differently as planned but with much ease providing learning results beyond teacher expectations. Kate, one of the teacher participants of this study, reveals her surprise of an unplanned e-learning activity that was not previously introduced-

"I was actually really surprised about how well it worked [use of i-pads]. I didn't expect it [e-learning] to go as smoothly as what it did, because it was really the first time and they did just really pick it up, really quickly".

4.2 Device Affordances and e-Learning Pedagogies

The factor of device affordance in enhancing e-learning pedagogies was so significant to this study that it had a spill-over effect to all other findings of this research. In the previous section we understood that teachers often introduced various device affordances during their classroom practice. Data analysis revealed that when these various device affordances were integrated into the curriculum delivery, teachers' pedagogies often enhanced. This was because the devices offered a context relevant, ubiquitous, collaborative, individualised learner-centred and multimodal learning opportunities. Many instances of quality pedagogies occurred during classroom observations. This was done through the ability of the device to deliver the curriculum in multiple ways using both physical and ubiquitous spaces for learners to submit their learning goal using semiotic methods that they were confident and comfortable with. For instance, students who had learning difficulties with writing/typing text used the audio voice recording, drawing, colouring and video features. Additionally, students were able to individually and collaboratively work with technologies to complete tasks. This resulted in a hybrid pedagogical approach that involved inclusive learning, collaborative learning (physical and virtual), user-friendly and individualised learning, new professional learning skills, enhanced interactivity and deep level learning. The benefits were both for students and teachers. As one teacher participant comments,

"...And that's what the great thing about the recording feature is on here, that you do get that [reference to audio recording enabling deep learning]. Whereas if I was to sit down and ask her a question- what do you do at seven O'clock? I probably wouldn't get the same response as when she can just sit there and happily talk to herself and record her message. So, I get a lot more of these videos [using iPads] than at times sitting there and asking them the question".

5. CONCLUSION

Classroom teaching-learning are complex activities and many factors accounted for their success (Gonzalez & Gómez, 2014). Of the many factors, this paper points that successful e-learning classrooms often avail many technological affordances pedagogically. These teachers pedagogically orchestrate teaching-learning sequences using explorative learning to enable deep learning. These pedagogies include one or more of the pedagogies simultaneously occurring. For instance, e-learning pedagogies, such as, individualised learning, collaborative learning, contextual learning and inclusive learning. Expansive learning framework provides a robust approach to unpack these complex classroom activities to understand how we may be able to use these tool-kit of pedagogical practices to enable deep learning (Mwanza-Simwami, 2011). The understanding of this tool-kit of expert/confident teacher pedagogical practices can serve as a guide to bridge the gap between current professional development, teacher standards and the new generational e-learning requirements.

ACKNOWLEDGEMENT

I am grateful to my supervisors Assoc. Prof. Joseph Seyram Agbenyega and Dr. Hilary Monk for their ongoing support during my PhD journey. I also acknowledge the time and commitment provided by research participants to make this project possible. I am thankful to my family for their continued encouragement and finally dedicate this paper to my sister Ruby Rozario who recently passed away.

REFERENCES

Abiteboul, S. et al, 2000. *Data on the Web: From Relations to Semistructured Data and XML*. Morgan Kaufmann Publishers, San Francisco, USA.

Allen, D., Karanasios, S. and Slavova, M., 2011. Working with activity theory: Context, technology, and information behavior. *Journal of the American Society for Information Science and Technology*, *62*(4), pp.776-788.

Bodorik P. et al, 1991. Deciding to Correct Distributed Query Processing. *In IEEE Transactions on Data and Knowledge Engineering*, Vol. 4, No. 3,pp 253-265.

Bernauer, J.A., 2015. Opening the ears that science closed: Transforming qualitative data using oral coding. *The Qualitative Report*, *20*(4), pp.406-415.

Bakke, S., 2015, August. An Activity Theory Approach to Intuitiveness: From Artefact to Process. In *International Conference on Human-Computer Interaction* (pp. 3-13). Springer, Cham.

Churchill, D., Lu, J. and Chiu, T.K., 2014. Integrating mobile technologies, social media and learning design.

Cochrane, T. and Bateman, R., 2009. Transforming pedagogy using mobile Web 2.0. *International Journal of Mobile and Blended Learning (IJMBL)*, *1*(4), pp.56-83.

Cowling, M. A. (2016). Navigating the Path Between Positivism and Interpretivism for the Technology Academic Completing Education Research. In *Constructing Methodology for Qualitative Research* (pp. 45-58): Springer.

Engeström, Y. (1987). *Learning by Expanding: an activity-theoretical approach to developmental research* (Helsinki, Orienta-Konsultit).

Gough, S. and Scott, W., 2000. Exploring the purposes of qualitative data coding in educational enquiry: Insights from recent research. *Educational Studies*, *26*(3), pp.339-354.

Gonzalez, M.J. and Gómez, P., 2014. Conceptualizing and describing teachers' learning of pedagogical concepts. *Australian Journal of Teacher Education (Online)*, *39*(12), p.13.

Kukulska-Hulme, A., Sharples, M., Milrad, M., Arnedillo-Sánchez, I. and Vavoula, G., 2009. Innovation in mobile learning: A European perspective. *International Journal of Mobile and Blended Learning (IJMBL)*, *1*(1), pp.13-35.

Kumar, B.A. and Chand, S.S., 2018. Mobile learning adoption: A systematic review. *Education and Information Technologies*, *24*(1), pp.471-487.

Ling, L. and Ling, P. eds., 2016. *Methods and paradigms in education research*. IGI Global.

Merriam, S.B., 2009. Qualitative research: A guide to design and implementation (Revised and expanded from qualitative research and case study application in education). Qualitative research science and education. San Francisco: Jossey-Bass

Mwanza, D. and Engeström, Y., 2005. Managing content in E-learning environments. *British Journal of Educational Technology*, *36*(3), pp.453-463.

Mwanza-Simwami, D., 2011. AODM as a framework and model for characterising learner experiences with technology. *Journal of e-Learning and Knowledge Society*, *7*(3), pp.75-85.

Ritchie, J. and Spencer, L., 2002. Qualitative data analysis for applied policy research. *The qualitative researcher's companion*, *573*(2002), pp.305-29.

Rozario, R. and Ortlieb, E., 2015. Using Expansive Learning as a Model for Video Reflection in Teacher Education. In *Video Research in Disciplinary Literacies* (pp. 287-305). Emerald Group Publishing Limited.

Rozario, R., Ortlieb, E. and Rennie, J., 2016. Interactivity and mobile technologies: An activity theory perspective. In *Mobile learning design* (pp. 63-82). Springer, Singapore.

Sharples, M., Taylor, J. and Vavoula, G., 2005, October. Towards a theory of mobile learning. In *Proceedings of mLearn* (Vol. 1, No. 1, pp. 1-9).

Valsiner, J., Chaudhary, N. and Benetka, G., 2017. *From methodology to methods in human psychology* (p. 115). New York: Springer.

Wong, L.H. and Looi, C.K., 2019. The Conceptual Niche of Seamless Learning: An Invitation to Dialogue. In *Seamless Learning* (pp. 3-27). Springer, Singapore.

AUTHOR INDEX

International Association for Development of the Information Society (IADIS)
Rua Sao Sebastiao Da Pedreira
No. 100, 30, 1050-209
Lisbon, Portugal

ISBN 978-1-5108-9240-8

CURRAN ASSOCIATES INC.
proceedings.com